KS3 Maths Progress θ TWO

Confidence • Fluency • Problem-solving • Progression

Series editors:
Dr Naomi Norman • Katherine Pate

PEARSON

ALWAYS LEARNING

Published by Pearson Education Limited, Edinburgh Gate, Harlow, Essex, CM20 2JE.

www.pearsonschoolsandfecolleges.co.uk

Typeset by Tech-Set Ltd, Gateshead

Cover illustration by Robert Samuel Hanson
Index by Martin Brooks

First published 2014

17 16 15 14
10 9 8 7 6 5 4 3 2 1

British Library Cataloguing in Publication Data
A catalogue record for this book is available from the British Library

ISBN 978 1 447 96234 2

Printed in Italy by Lego S.p.A

Acknowledgements
The publisher would like to thank the following for their kind permission to reproduce their photographs:
Alamy Images: Colin Underhill 25, Jeff Greenberg 114, Jon Arnold Images Ltd 167, Justin Kase zsixz 241, Thornton Cohen 170; **Corbis:** Ocean 35; **Fotolia.com:** Andrey Armyagov 189, Borys Shevchuk 6, NAN 54, pixel_dreams 57, Sharpshot 211, withGod 192; **Getty Images:** Digital Vision 93, Iconica / Cavan Images 173; **Pearson Education Ltd:** Coleman Yuen 91, Gareth Boden 135, 245; **Photos.com:** Andrey Armyagov 37, ITStock Free 32, Jupiterimages 220, Lev Kropotov 29, Olga Chernetskaya 27; **Rex Features:** Offside 119; **Science Photo Library Ltd:** Alexis Rosenfeld 197, Andrew Brookes, National Physical Laboratory 83, Chassenet / BSIP 63, Ian Hooton 107, TRL Ltd. 235; **Veer / Corbis:** Antikainen 146, Ben_Heys 194, chaoss 214, Corepics 164, Danicek 238, Darren Kemper 116, Dmitry Kutlayev 144, Harvepino 161, JRMurray76 187, Kzenon 109, leaf 1, Lisafx 8, Mechanik 10, Monkey Business Images 243, Moodboard Photography 138, pashabo 88, pattarastock 112, photobac 51, pixeldreams.eu 86, pixelsaway 80, Stocksnapper 3, urfin 141, Veer / _human 60; **www.imagesource.com:** Jon Feingersh Photography Inc. 217

All other images © Pearson Education

We are grateful to the following for permission to reproduce copyright material:
Graphs on p126 adapted from 'Internet Access - Households and Individuals, 2012 part 2', Office for National Statistics licensed under the Open Government Licence v.2.0; Population data on p137 from 'Population Estimates for UK, England and Wales, Scotland and Northern Ireland', Office for National Statistics licensed under the Open Government Licence v.2.0; Table on p64 adapted from data in 'OECD Family database', OECD; World record times for Rubik's cube on p73, Record Breakers' Club; Road traffic accident statistics on p77, RAC Foundation; Data on visitor numbers on p115, VisitEngland; Data on distance travelled using different types of transport (p115), number of UK airline passengers (p122), average distance travelled by car per person (p124), laptop ownership (p125), average temperature inside a centrally heated home (p133) from 'Energy Consumption in the UK', Department of Energy and Climate Change licensed under the Open Government Licence v.2.0.

Every effort has been made to trace the copyright holders and we apologise in advance for any unintentional omissions. We would be pleased to insert the appropriate acknowledgement in any subsequent printings.

CONTENTS

Course introduction vi

Welcome to KS3 Maths Progress student books viii

Unit 1 Number 1

1.1 Calculations 1
1.2 Calculating with negative integers 3
1.3 Powers and roots 6
1.4 Powers, roots and brackets 8
1.5 Multiples and factors 10
1 Check up 13
1 Strengthen 15
1 Extend 19
1 Unit test 23

Unit 2 Area and volume 25

2.1 Area of a triangle 25
2.2 Area of a parallelogram and trapezium 27
2.3 Volume of cubes and cuboids 29
2.4 3D shapes 32
2.5 Surface area of cubes and cuboids 35
2.6 Problems and measures 37
2 Check up 39
2 Strengthen 41
2 Extend 45
2 Unit test 49

Unit 3 Statistics, graphs and charts 51

3.1 Pie charts 51
3.2 Using tables 54
3.3 Stem and leaf diagrams 57
3.4 Comparing data 60
3.5 Scatter graphs 63
3.6 FINANCE: Misleading graphs 66
3 Check up 68
3 Strengthen 70
3 Extend 74
3 Unit test 78

Unit 4 Expressions and equations 80

4.1 Algebraic powers 80
4.2 Expressions and brackets 83
4.3 Factorising expressions 86
4.4 One-step equations 88
4.5 Two-step equations 91
4.6 The balancing method 93
4 Check up 95
4 Strengthen 97
4 Extend 101
4 Unit test 105

Unit 5 Real-life graphs 107

5.1 Conversion graphs 107
5.2 Distance–time graphs 109
5.3 Line graphs 112
5.4 Complex line graphs 114
5.5 STEM: Graphs of functions 116
5.6 More real-life graphs 119
5 Check up 122
5 Strengthen 124
5 Extend 129
5 Unit test 133

Unit 6 Decimals and ratio 135

6.1 Ordering decimals and rounding 135
6.2 Place-value calculations 138
6.3 Calculations with decimals 141
6.4 Ratio and proportion with decimals 144
6.5 STEM: Using ratios 146
6 Check up 149
6 Strengthen 151
6 Extend 155
6 Unit test 159

Unit 7 Lines and angles 161

7.1 Quadrilaterals 161
7.2 Alternate angles and proof 164
7.3 Geometrical problems 167
7.4 Exterior and interior angles 170
7.5 Solving geometric problems 173
7 Check up 175
7 Strengthen 177
7 Extend 181
7 Unit test 185

Unit 8 Calculating with fractions 187

8.1	Adding and subtracting fractions	187
8.2	Multiplying fractions	189
8.3	Fractions, decimals and reciprocals	192
8.4	Dividing fractions	194
8.5	Calculating with mixed numbers	197
8	Check up	199
8	Strengthen	201
8	Extend	205
8	Unit test	209

Unit 9 Straight-line graphs 211

9.1	Direct proportion on graphs	211
9.2	Gradients	214
9.3	Equations of straight lines	217
9.4	STEM: Direct proportion problems	220
9	Check up	222
9	Strengthen	224
9	Extend	229
9	Unit test	233

Unit 10 Percentages, decimals and fractions 235

10.1	Fractions and decimals	235
10.2	Equivalent proportions	238
10.3	Writing percentages	241
10.4	Percentages of amounts	243
10.5	FINANCE: Solving problems	245
10	Check up	247
10	Strengthen	249
10	Extend	253
10	Unit test	257

Index **259**

KS3 Maths Progress

Confidence • Fluency • Problem-solving • Progression

Pedagogy at the heart – This new course is built around a unique pedagogy that's been created by leading mathematics educational researchers and Key Stage 3 teachers. The result is an innovative learning structure based around 10 key principles designed to nurture confidence and raise achievement.

Pedagogy – our 10 key principles

- Fluency
- Mathematical Reasoning
- Multiplicative Reasoning
- Problem Solving
- Progression
- Concrete-Pictorial - Abstract (CPA)
- Relevance
- Modelling
- Reflection (metacognition)
- Linking

Progression to Key Stage 4 – In line with the 2014 National Curriculum, there is a strong focus on fluency, problem-solving and progression to help prepare your students' progress through their studies.

Stretch, challenge and support – Catering for students of all abilities, these Student Books are structured to deliver engaging and accessible content across three differentiated tiers, each offering a wealth of worked examples and questions, supported by key points, literacy and strategy hints, and clearly defined objectives.

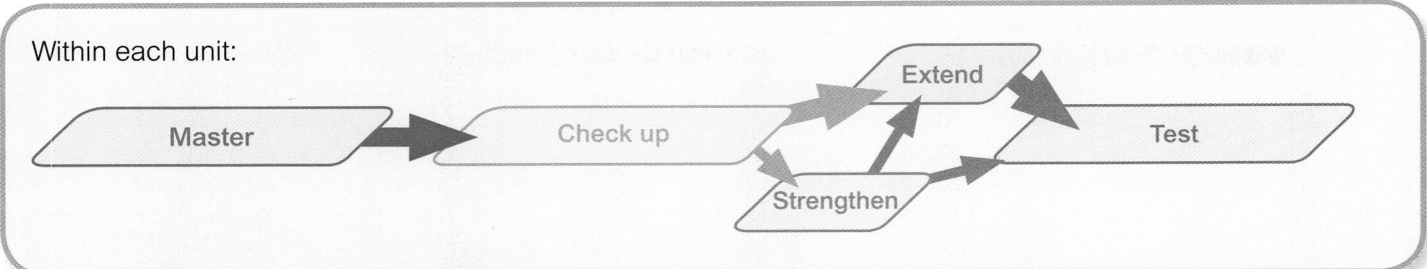

Differentiated for students of all abilities:

Alpha	Pi	Theta	Delta
Tier Access	Tier 1	Tier 2	Tier 3

Progress with confidence!

This innovative Key Stage 3 Maths course embeds a modern pedagogical approach around our trusted suite of digital and print resources, to create confident and numerate students ready to progress further.

Help at the front-of-class – **ActiveTeach Presentation** is our tried and tested service that makes all of the Student Books available for display on a whiteboard. The books are supplemented with a range of videos and animations that present mathematical concepts along a concrete - pictorial - abstract pathway, allowing your class to progress their conceptual understanding at the right speed.

Learning beyond the classroom – Focussing on online homework**, ActiveCourse** offers students unprecedented extra practice (with automarking) and a chance to reflect on their learning with the confidence-checker. Powerful reporting tools can be used to track student progression and confidence levels.

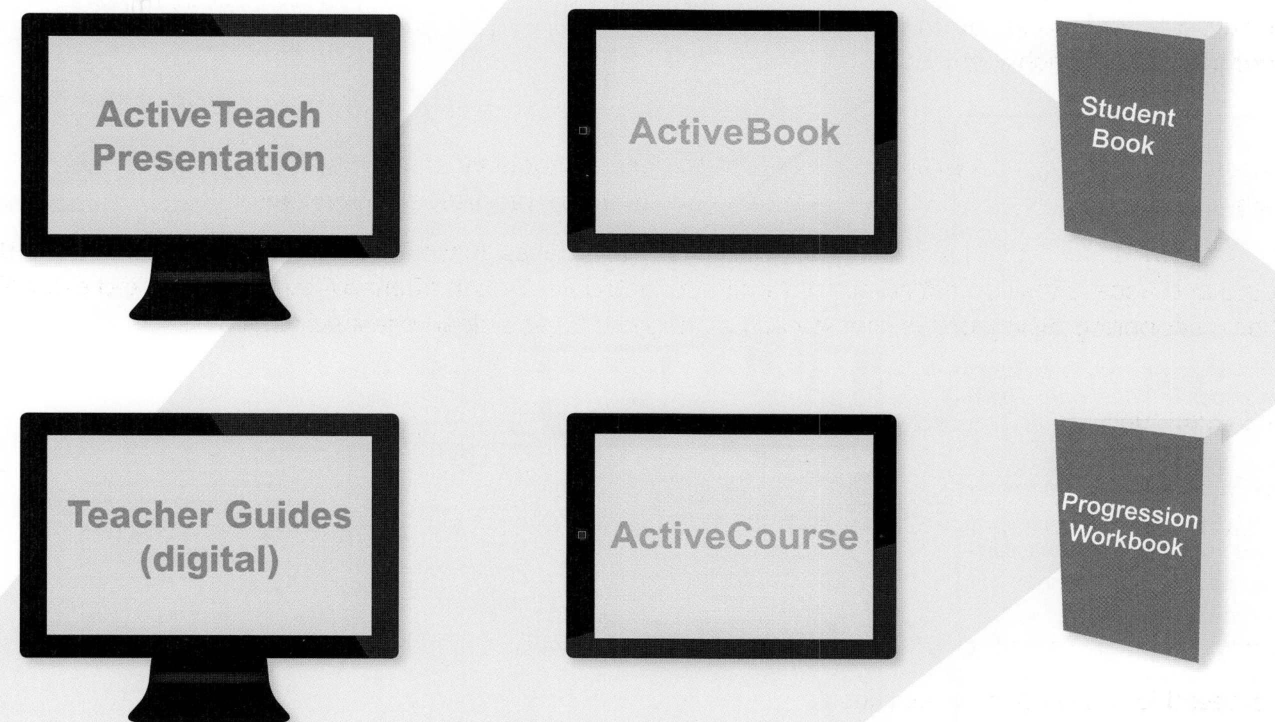

Easy to plan, teach and assess – Downloadable **Teacher Guides** provide assistance with planning through the Schemes of Work. Lesson plans link both front-of-class **ActiveTeach Presentation** and **ActiveCourse** and provide help with reporting, functionality and progression. Both **Teacher Guides** and **ActiveTeach Presentation** contain the **answers** to the Student Book exercises.

Teacher Guides include **Class Progression Charts** and **Student Progression Charts** to support formative and summative assessment through the course.

Practice to progress – KS3 Maths Progress has an extensive range of practice across a range of topics and abilities. From the **Student Books** to write-in **Progression Workbooks** through to **ActiveCourse**, there is plenty of practice available in a variety of formats whether for in the classroom or for learning at home independently.

For more information, visit www.pearsonschools.co.uk/ks3mathsprogress

Welcome to KS3 Maths Progress student books!

Confidence • Fluency • Problem-solving • Progression

Starting a new course is exciting! We believe you will have fun with maths, at the same time nurturing your confidence and raising your achievement.

Here's how:

Extend helps you to apply the maths you know to some different situations. *Strengthen* and *Extend* both include *Enrichment* or *Investigations*.

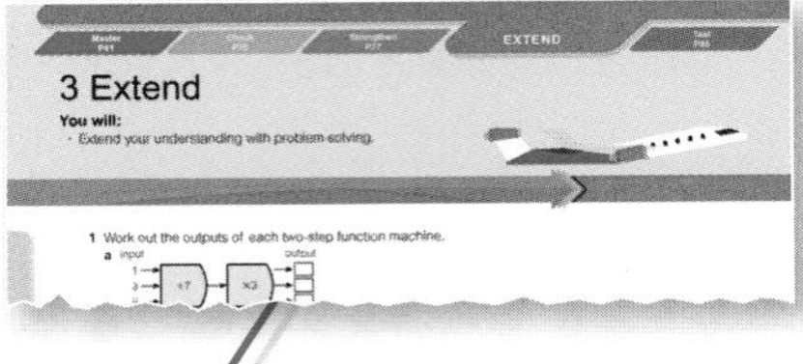

At the end of the *Master* lessons, take a *Check up* test to help you decide to *Strengthen*, or *Extend* your learning. You may be able to mark this test yourself.

Choose only the topics in *Strengthen* that you need a bit more practice with. You'll find more hints here to lead you through specific questions. Then move on to *Extend*.

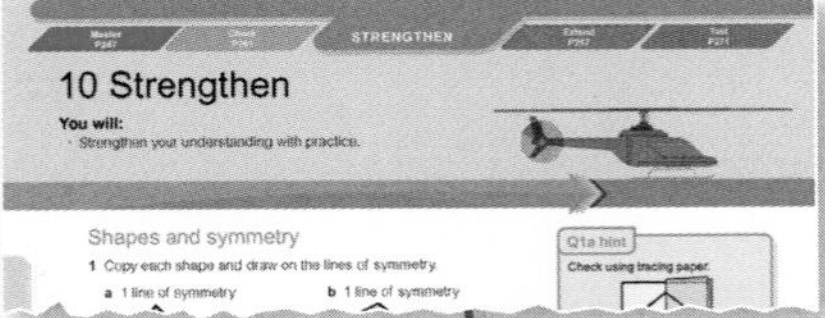

When you have finished the whole unit, a *Unit test* helps you see how much progress you are making.

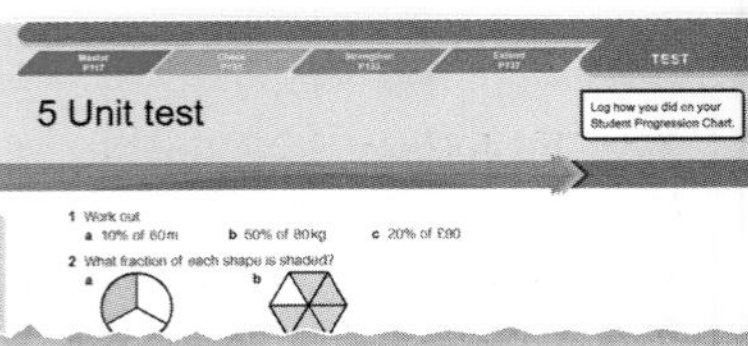

Clear *Objectives,* showing what you will cover in each lesson, are followed by a *Confidence* panel to boost your understanding and engage your interest.

Have a look at *Why Learn This?* This shows you how maths is useful in everyday life.

Improve your *Fluency* – practise answering questions using maths you already know.

The first questions are *Warm up*. Here you can show what you already know about this topic or related ones…

…before moving on to further questions, with *Worked examples* and *Hints* for help when you need it.

Your teacher has access to Answers in either ActiveTeach Presentation or the Teacher Guides.

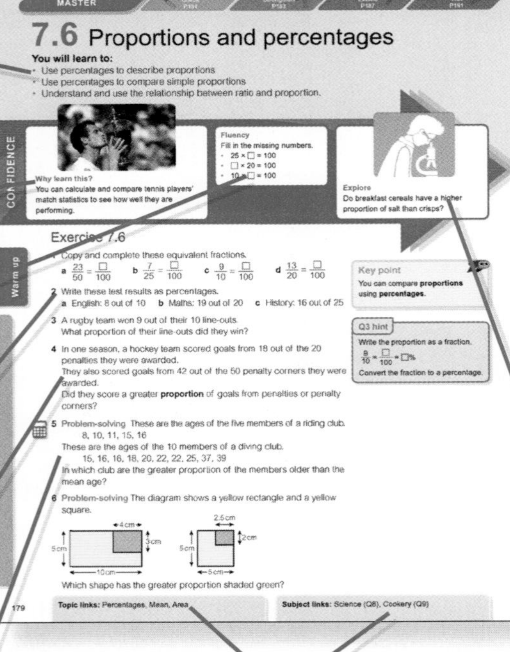

Topic links show you how the maths in a lesson is connected to other mathematical topics. Use the *Subject links* to find out where you might use the maths you have learned here in your other lessons, such as science, geography and computing .

Explore a real-life problem by discussing and having a go. By the end of the lesson you'll have gained the skills you need to start finding a solution to the question using maths.

At the end of each lesson, you get a chance to *Reflect* on how confident you feel about the topic.

STEM and Finance lessons

Context lessons expand on *Real, STEM* and *Finance* maths. Finance questions are related to money. STEM stands for Science, Technology, Engineering and Maths. You can find out how charities use maths in their fundraising, how engineers monitor water flow in rivers, and why diamonds sparkle (among other things!)

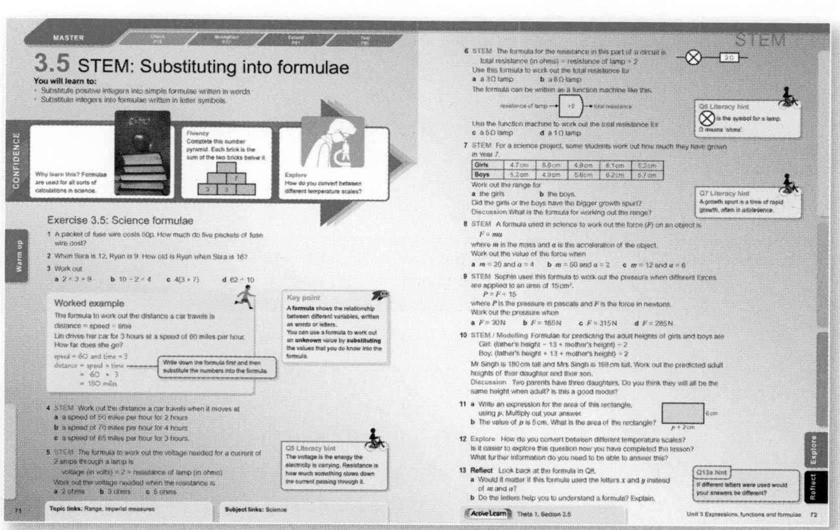

You can improve your ability to use maths in everyday situations by tackling *Modelling, Reasoning, Problem-solving* and *Real* questions. *Discussions* prompt you to explain your reasoning or explore new ideas with a partner.

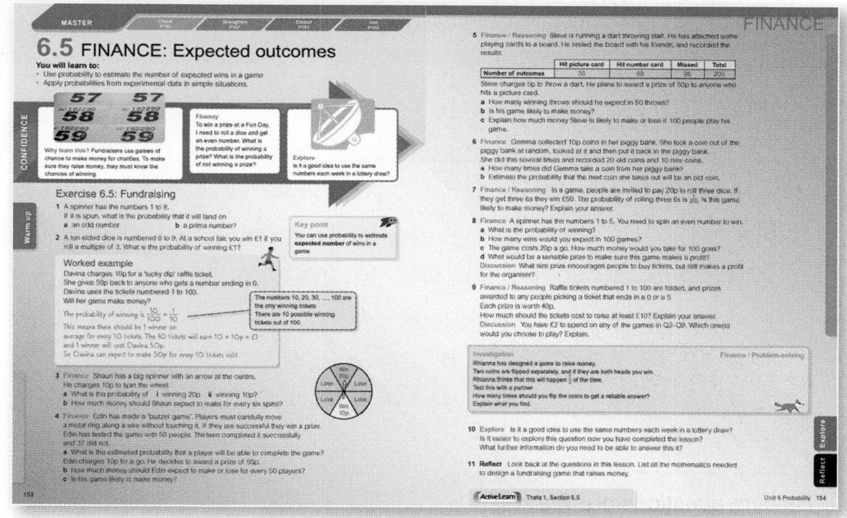

As well as hints that help you with specific questions, you'll find *Literacy hints* (to explain some unfamiliar terms) and *Strategy hints* (to help with working out).

Some questions are tagged as *Finance* or *STEM*. These questions show how the real world relies on maths. Follow these up with whole lessons that focus on how maths is used in the fields of finance, science and technology.

Your teacher may give you a Student Progression Chart to help you see your progression through the units.

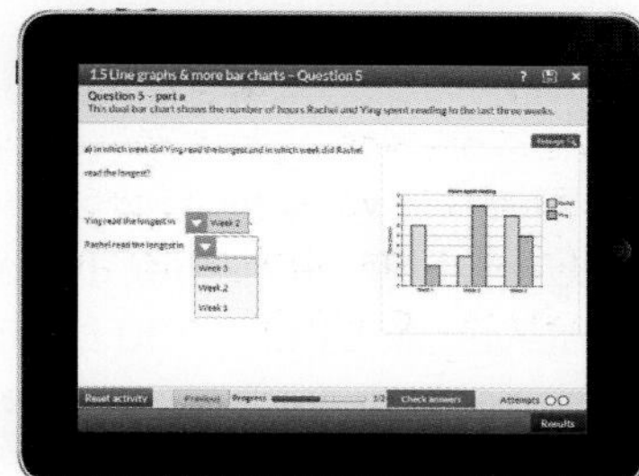

Further support

You can easily access extra resources that tie in to each lesson – look for the ActiveLearn icon on the lesson pages for ActiveCourse online homework links. These are clearly mapped to lessons and provide fun, interactive exercises linked to helpful worked examples and videos.

The Progression Workbooks, full of extra practice for key questions will help you reinforce your learning and track your own progress.

Enjoy!

1 Number

MASTER | Check P13 | Strengthen P15 | Extend P19 | Test P23

1.1 Calculations

You will learn to:
- Use written methods to add and subtract with decimals
- Use mental calculation
- Calculate with money
- Estimate answers to calculations.

CONFIDENCE

Why learn this?
Estimating the cost of your shopping helps you check that you have enough money to pay!

Fluency
- Work out: 15 × 2, 80 ÷ 2, 32 × 2, $\frac{38}{2}$, 2.5 × 2
- Round 197.8 to the nearest whole number, the nearest 10 and the nearest 100.

Explore
When you go out with a group of friends for a meal, how do you estimate the cost per person?

Exercise 1.1

Warm up

1 Use a written method to calculate these.
  a 772 + 89 + 1062 **b** 1352 − 270 − 95

2 **a** Round 24 so that it is easy to divide by 5.
  b Round 91 so that it is easy to divide by 3.

3 Estimate these by rounding.
  a 12.3 ÷ 3.8 **b** 8.72 × 20.05 **c** 22.4 + 17.77
  d 48 × 52 **e** 176 ÷ 58

4 Calculate these.
  a 64 × 5 **b** 32 × 10 **c** 64 × 10 ÷ 2
  What do you notice?

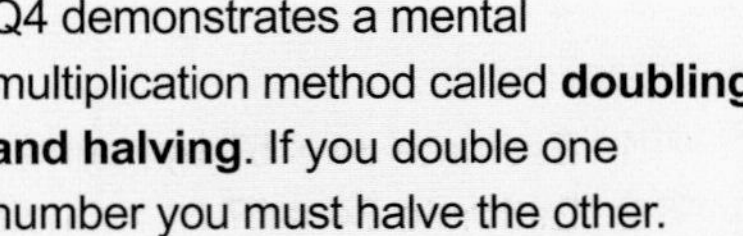

Key point
Q4 demonstrates a mental multiplication method called **doubling and halving**. If you double one number you must halve the other.

5 Use **doubling and halving** to calculate these.
  a 36 × 5 **b** 50 × 46 **c** 35 × 8

6 Use doubling and halving to calculate these.
  a 1.5 × 26 **b** 3.5 × 18 **c** 24 × 7.5
  Discussion How could you mentally multiply by 99? By 9.9?

Q6c hint
Double 7.5 twice.

7 Use a written method to calculate these. Estimate the answers first.
  a 1592 + 178 − 83
  b 3266 − 180 + 31
  c 68 000 + 3250 − 19 241

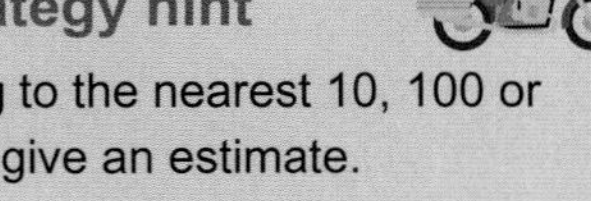

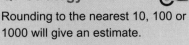

Q7 Strategy hint
Rounding to the nearest 10, 100 or 1000 will give an estimate.

Q7a hint
First, work out 1592 + 178.
Then subtract 83.

8 Heathrow Airport has 21 075 car parking spaces altogether. Terminal 4 has 890 short-term spaces, 1700 long-stay spaces and 330 business spaces. Work out the total number of spaces in the other terminals. Estimate the answer first.

Topic links: Priority of operations, Formulae

9 Use a written method to calculate these. Estimate the answers first.
a 23.7 + 1.06 + 0.88 **b** 96 + 8.3 − 0.47 **c** 9.7 − 2.58 − 0.810

Q9a hint
Keep the decimal points in line.
Write 0s in the empty columns.
```
  23.70
   1.06
+  0.88
 ______
```

10 Lars cut two pieces, of length 2.7 m and 1.93 m, from a 5 m length of skirting board. How much was left?

Worked example

Work out £28.20 ÷ 12

```
      2 . 3 5
12)2 8 . 2 0
   2 4          2 × 12 = 24
     4 2
     3 6        3 × 12 = 36
         6 0
         6 0    5 × 12 = 60
           0
```

£28.20 ÷ 12 = £2.35

11 Use a written method to work out these.
a £261.80 ÷ 11 **b** £5808 ÷ 15 **c** £8.50 ÷ 25

12 Hanna saved 15 weeks of pocket money to make a total of £62.25
a Estimate the pocket money she received each week.
b Work out the exact amount she received each week.

13 Substitute the values into each formula and estimate the answers.
a $v = u + at$ when $u = 49$, $a = 6.1$ and $t = 24$
b $x = (a + b + c) \div 3$ when $a = 347$, $b = 255$ and $c = 1233$
c $A = \frac{1}{2} \times (a + b) \times h$ when $a = 7.1$, $b = 8.8$ and $h = 1.9$
Discussion Do you need to round all of the numbers when estimating a calculation?

Q13 hint
Use priority of operations.

Q13a hint
at means $a \times t$

14 **Real / Problem-solving / Finance** Maurice bought a car costing £8248. He paid a deposit of £1975 and 6 monthly instalments of £511. Estimate the amount Maurice still owes.

Investigation — **Problem-solving**

1. Estimate 34 × 57 by rounding both numbers up. This will give you an **overestimate**.
2. Estimate 34 × 57 by rounding both numbers down. This will give you an **underestimate**.
3. Estimate 34 × 57 by rounding one number up and one number down.
4. Repeat part 3 rounding the numbers the opposite way.
5. Which estimate do you think is closest to the exact answer? Check to see if you are right.

Repeat parts **1** to **5** using two different 2-digit numbers. Write a rule for making the closest estimate.

15 **Explore** When you go out with a group of friends for a meal, how do you estimate the cost per person?
Is it easier to explore this question now you have completed the lesson?
What further information do you need to be able to answer this?

16 **Reflect** In this lesson, you were asked to estimate.
Write down a definition for the word ‘estimate’ in your own words.
How did estimating help you with calculations in this lesson?
How might estimating help you in other subjects and in everyday life?

1.2 Calculating with negative integers

You will learn to:
- Add, subtract, multiply and divide positive and negative numbers.

CONFIDENCE

Why learn this? Calculating with negative numbers is a crucial skill for anyone working in finance.

Fluency
- What is the difference between 3 and 12?
- The temperature is −5 °C and rises by 8 °C. What is the new temperature?
- What is the fall in temperature from −7 °C to −13 °C?

Explore
What is the difference in the surface temperature of the Moon between midday and midnight?

Exercise 1.2

Warm up

1 Use a number line to work out these.
- **a** subtract 10 from 6
- **b** subtract 4 from −2
- **c** add 3 to −9
- **d** add 20 to −5

2 Work out these.
- **a** 11 − 5
- **b** 4 − 7
- **c** −2 + 5
- **d** −2 − 3
- **e** 0 − 7
- **f** −12 + 3

3 **a** Copy the tables and work out the answers to the blue calculations.

Calculation	Answer
3 + 3	6
3 + 2	
3 + 1	
3 + 0	
3 + −1	
3 + −2	
3 + −3	
3 + −4	
3 + −5	

Calculation	Answer
3 − 3	
3 − 2	
3 − 1	
3 − 0	
3 − −1	
3 − −2	
3 − −3	
3 − −4	
3 − −5	

b Continue the sequences to work out the rest of the answers.

c Fill in the missing signs.
- **i** 3 + −5 is the same as 3 □ 5
- **ii** 3 − −5 is the same as 3 □ 5

d Complete these rules.

+ − is the same as □   − − is the same as □

4 Work out these.
- **a** 12 + −4
- **b** 8 − −3
- **c** 3 − 5
- **d** −5 + 1
- **e** −2 − 3
- **f** −4 − −2
- **g** −10 + −1
- **h** −3 − −8

Topic links: Priority of operations, Averages and range, Formulae

Subject links: Science (Q6, Q15), Design and technology (Q12)

5 Work out the **difference** between these.

a 8 and 15 b −3 and 6 c −2 and 8
d −4 and −10 e 7 and −7 f −2 and −12

Key point

To find the **difference** between two numbers, subtract the lower number from the higher one.

Q5b hint

6 − −3 = □

6 **STEM** When hydrogen gas is cooled, it becomes a liquid at −253 °C and freezes solid at −259 °C.

a Hydrogen at −160 °C is cooled by 100 °C.
After cooling, is it a gas, liquid or solid?

b In a science lab, hydrogen is at 20 °C.
By how many degrees do you need to cool it for it to become liquid?

7 **Real / Finance / Problem-solving** The table shows Mrs Prestwick's **bank balance** each time she made a **deposit** (+) or **withdrawal** (−) in May.

Date in May	1	2	13	19	20	25	31
Deposit/Withdrawal (£)		+20	−37	+200	−12	+55	−25
Balance (£)	−128						

a Copy and complete the table.

b Work out the difference in her bank balance between 1 May and 31 May.

Q7 Literacy hint

A **bank balance** is the amount of money in a bank account. A **negative bank balance** (or **overdraft**) is an amount owed to the bank.
When you put money into a bank account, this is a **deposit**. When you take money out, this is a **withdrawal**.

8 a Copy the tables and continue the patterns of answers to complete them.

Calculation	Answer
3 × 4	12
3 × 3	9
3 × 2	
3 × 1	
3 × 0	
3 × −1	
3 × −2	
3 × −3	

−3

Calculation	Answer
4 × −3	
3 × −3	
2 × −3	
1 × −3	
0 × −3	
−1 × −3	
−2 × −3	
−3 × −3	

b Copy and complete the rules.

positive × positive = positive positive × negative = ________
negative × positive = ________ negative × negative = ________

Discussion What is an easy way to remember these rules?

9 Work out these.

a −2 × −4 b 8 × −3 c −6 × 6 d 5 × (−9)
e (−3) × (−3) f −20 × 6 g −4 × (−9) h (−12) × 5
i −10 × 0.5 j 100 × (−0.1) k −2 × −3 × −4 l 2 × −4 × 5

Q9d hint

(−9) is another way of writing the negative number −9.

10 a Fill in the missing number facts. The first one has been done for you.

i 2 × −3 = −6, so −6 ÷ 2 = −3 and −6 ÷ −3 = 2
ii −3 × −4 = 12, so 12 ÷ −3 = □ and 12 ÷ −4 = □
iii −2 × 5 = −10, so −10 ÷ −2 = □ and −10 ÷ 5 = □

b Look at the signs of the division facts in part **a**.
Copy and complete the rules.

positive ÷ positive = positive positive ÷ negative = ________
negative ÷ positive = ________ negative ÷ negative = ________

11 Work out these.

a $-8 \div -2$ **b** $15 \div -3$ **c** $-18 \div 6$ **d** $(-20) \div 5$

e $40 \div (-8)$ **f** $(-6) \div (-6)$ **g** $-1000 \div (-10)$ **h** $132 \div -11$

i $200 \div -25$ **j** $0.8 \div -2$ **k** $-12.4 \div 2$ **l** $16 \div (-2) \div 2$

12 **STEM / Real** A house has solar panels to generate electricity.
When it doesn't generate enough it uses electricity from the national grid.
When it generates too much it sends electricity back to the national grid.
The table shows the electricity sent to the national grid every 10 minutes for one hour.

Time	14 00	14 10	14 20	14 30	14 40	14 50
Electricity (power, W)	−130	220	−1395	640	−1565	−290

Discussion Why is the power negative sometimes?

Work out:

a the median **b** the range **c** the mean.

13 Substitute the values into each formula and work out the answers.

a $m = 2n - 1$ when $n = -7$

b $v = u + at$ when $u = -8$, $a = -10$ and $t = 6$

c $A = 3a - 4b$ when $a = -2$ and $b = -5$

d $T = k(e - f)$ when $k = -3$, $e = 4$ and $f = -2$

e $L = a - (2b + c)$ when $a = -10$, $b = -8$ and $c = 4$

Q13a hint

Use priority of operations.

14 Expand the brackets to calculate these.
Check your answers using priority of operations.

a $6 \times (-2 - 1)$ **b** $3 \times (-1 + 4) - 13$ **c** $-2(-3 + 5)$

d $-3(-4 - 1)$ **e** $-5(3 - 4)$ **f** $-4(-3 + 5) - 2$

Q14a hint

$6 \times (-2 - 1) = 6 \times -2 + 6 \times -1 = \square$

Check: $6 \times (-2 - 1) = 6 \times -3 = \square$

Investigation **Problem-solving**

1 **a** Work out -2×-3.

b Use your answer to work out $-2 \times -3 \times -4$.

c When you multiply three negative numbers together, is the answer positive or negative?

2 Is the answer positive or negative when you multiply these? Write some calculations for each

a positive × negative × negative

b positive × positive × negative

Explore

15 **Explore** What is the difference in the surface temperature of the Moon between midday and midnight?
Is it easier to explore this question now you have completed the lesson?
What further information do you need to be able to answer this?

Reflect

16 **Reflect** Look back at what you have learned in this lesson about negative numbers. What is different and what is the same about positive and negative numbers?
Copy this table and list all the things you can about positive and negative numbers.

Same for positive and negative numbers	Different for positive and negative numbers
When you multiply two negative numbers, or two positive numbers, you always get a positive answer.	As you move away from zero, negative numbers get lower, but positive numbers get higher.

1.3 Powers and roots

You will learn to:
- Calculate using squares, square roots, cubes and cube roots
- Give whole numbers that a square root lies between.

CONFIDENCE

Why learn this?
Powers and roots appear in all kinds of science formulae.

Fluency
- What is the square of 8?
- What is the **square root** of 36?
- Work out 2 × 2 × 2, 5 + 3 × 2

Explore
How could you write a formula for the perfect toy?

Exercise 1.3

Warm up

1 Work out these.
a 9^2 b $\sqrt{49}$ c $1 + 3^2$ d $\sqrt{100} - 9$

2 Match each square root to its value.

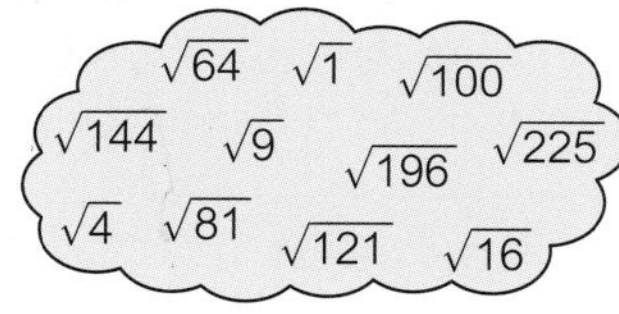

3 Work out these squares.
a $11^2 = 11 \times 11 =$ b 12^2 c 13^2
d 14^2 e 15^2 f 20^2 g 100^2

4 Work out these calculations. Use the priority of operations.
a 2×3^2 b 3×2^2 c 2×4^2 d $1 + 2 \times 5^2$
e $\sqrt{36} \times 5$ f $4 \times \sqrt{16} + 9$ g $9 - \sqrt{9}$ h $\sqrt{169} - 2^2$

Q4a hint
Work out squares before multiplying: $2 \times 3^2 = 2 \times 9$

Q4e hint
Work out the square root before multiplying.

Worked example
Which two whole numbers does $\sqrt{20}$ lie between?

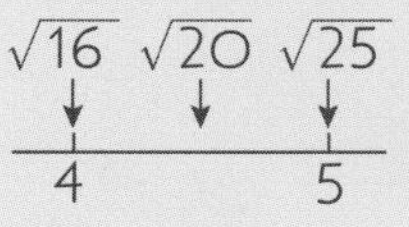

20 lies between the square numbers 16 and 25. So $\sqrt{20}$ lies between $\sqrt{16}$ and $\sqrt{25}$.

$4^2 = 16$ $5^2 = 25$

$\sqrt{20}$ lies between 4 and 5.

5 Which two whole numbers does each square root lie between?
a $\sqrt{6}$ b $\sqrt{40}$ c $\sqrt{92}$ d $\sqrt{175}$

6 Problem-solving 10 square tiles have a total area of $600\,cm^2$.

a Estimate the side length of a tile.

b Use a calculator to work out the side length to a suitable degree of accuracy.

Q6a hint
Find two whole numbers the side length lies between.

7 Work out these **cube numbers**. The first one has been done for you.

a $1^3 = 1 \times 1 \times 1 = 1$ b $2^3 = 2 \times 2 \times 2 =$

c 3^3 d 4^3 e 5^3 f 10^3

Key point
$2^3 = 2 \times 2 \times 2$
2^3 is '2 **cubed**' or '2 to the power 3'

8 Work out the missing numbers.

a $\sqrt[3]{125} = \square$ b $\sqrt[3]{\square} = 10$ c $\sqrt[3]{64} = \square$

d $\sqrt[3]{\square} = 3$ e $\sqrt[3]{1} = \square$ f $\sqrt[3]{\square} = 5$

Key point
Finding the **cube root** is the **inverse** of finding the cube of a number.
3 cubed is 27, so the cube root of 27 is 3.
The cube root of 27 is written $\sqrt[3]{27}$.

9 Use the **inverse** operation to decide whether each statement is true or not true.

a $\sqrt{528} = 23$ b $\sqrt{961} = 31$ c $\sqrt[3]{512} = 8$ d $\sqrt[3]{1441} = 11$

10 Use the x^2, x^3, $\sqrt{\ }$ and $\sqrt[3]{\ }$ keys of your calculator to work out these.

a $\sqrt[3]{729}$ b 16^3 c $\sqrt{289}$

d $\sqrt{40}$ e 250^2 f $\sqrt[3]{30}$

Discussion Is the cube root of a whole number always a whole number?

11 Work out these. Use the priority of operations.

a $4^2 - 2^3$ b 2×2^3 c $\sqrt{81} + \sqrt[3]{64}$

d $3^3 - \sqrt{225}$ e $\sqrt[3]{1000} - \sqrt{100}$ f $64 - \sqrt{64} - \sqrt[3]{64}$

12 Work out these.

a $(-2)^2 = -2 \times -2 =$ b $(-7)^2$ c $(-4)^2$

Discussion What do you notice about the answers?

13 Write the **positive** and **negative square roots** of these numbers.

a 25 b 81 c 1 d 144

Key point
$3^2 = 9$ and $(-3)^2 = 9$
The **positive square root** of 9 is 3.
The **negative square root** of 9 is −3.
You can write $\sqrt{9} = \pm 3$

14 Work out these.

a $(-2)^3 = -2 \times -2 \times -2$ b $(-3)^3$ c $(-4)^3$

Discussion What can you say about the cube of a negative number?

Investigation — Problem-solving

Give reasons or counter examples for your answers to these questions.

- Is the sum of two square numbers always a square number?
- Is the product of two square numbers always a square number?
- Is the cube of a square number always a square number?

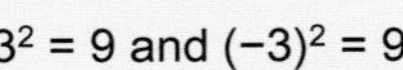

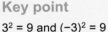

Literacy hint
A **counter example** is an example which proves that the statement is wrong.

Explore

15 Explore How could you write a formula for the perfect toy?
Is it easier to explore this question now you have completed the lesson?
What further information do you need to be able to answer this?

Reflect

16 Reflect The $\sqrt{\ }$ part of the root symbol began as an old-fashioned letter r in the 16th Century. You could remember r for root!
List all the mathematics notation used in this lesson, and ways you might remember it.
Make sure you know what all the notation in this lesson means.

Q16 hint
'Notation' means symbols.

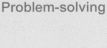

1.4 Powers, roots and brackets

You will learn to:
- Use mental methods to calculate combinations of powers, roots and brackets
- Substitute numbers into formulae involving powers, roots and brackets.

CONFIDENCE

Why learn this?
Surveyors, engineers and architects use square roots to find unknown lengths.

Fluency
- Work out 2^3, $\sqrt[3]{1000}$
- Work out $3 \times (9 - 2)$, $5 + 3^2$, $\sqrt{9} + 2$

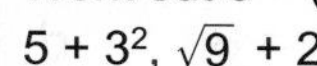

Explore
What size of square wall can be covered using a roll of wallpaper?

Exercise 1.4

Warm up

1 Work out these calculations. Use the priority of operations.
   a $3^3 - 3^2$ b $\sqrt{100} - \sqrt[3]{125}$ c $2 \times (5^2 + 8)$ d $(11 - 3)^2 \div 4$

2 Work out these.
   a 100^2 b 1000^2 c 100^3

3 **Reasoning** a Work out i $(2 \times 3)^2$ ii $2^2 \times 3^2$
   b What do you notice about your answers in part **a**?
   c Work out each calculation in two different ways.
      i $(2 \times 5)^2$ ii $2^2 \times 2^2$ iii $(5 \times 3)^2$

4 Work out these.
   a 30^2 b 90^2 c 200^2
   d 500^2 e 1200^2 f 8000^2
   Discussion Which of these are square numbers: 490 000, 49 000, 4900, 490, 49?

Q4a hint
$30 = 3 \times 10$, so $30^2 = (3 \times 10)^2$

5 **Problem-solving** At an exhibition, an image of a 14 cm square tile was projected onto a wall so that its sides were 100 times the original length. Work out the area of the image.

6 Work out these. Use the priority of operations.
   Check your answers using a calculator.
   a $4 \times (\sqrt{121} - 4)$ b $9^2 - (\sqrt{16} + 16)$ c $(3^2 + \sqrt{4})^2$
   d $(20 - 5 \times 3)^3$ e $(3^2 + 3^3) \div 6$ f $5^3 - (7 - 5)^3$

7 **Reasoning** a Work out i $\sqrt{4} \times \sqrt{9}$ ii $\sqrt{4 \times 9}$
   b What do you notice about your answers in part **a**?
   c Write a rule for finding the square root of a product.
   d Given that $16 \times 36 = 576$, work out $\sqrt{576}$.
   e Given that $81 \times 121 = 9801$, work out $\sqrt{9801}$.

Q7d hint
Work out $\sqrt{16 \times 36}$

8 Work out these. Check your answers using a calculator.

a $\frac{12 + 20}{12 - 8}$ **b** $\frac{4^2 + 9}{5}$ **c** $\frac{70 - 7}{2^2 + 5}$ **d** $\frac{60}{8^2 - 7^2}$

e $\frac{\sqrt{121} + 9}{10}$ **f** $\frac{4^2 + 4}{\sqrt{16}}$ **g** $\frac{6 + \sqrt[3]{1000}}{4}$ **h** $\frac{2^3 + 2}{\sqrt[3]{27} - 1}$

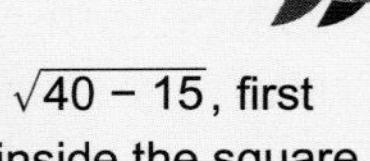

Key point

In a calculation like $\frac{12 + 20}{12 - 8}$ work out the top and the bottom before you divide.

9 Work out these. Check your answers using a calculator.

a $\sqrt{40 - 15}$ **b** $\sqrt{10 + 41 + 70}$ **c** $\sqrt{40 + 3^2}$ **d** $\sqrt{4^2 - 7}$

e $\sqrt[3]{35 - 8}$ **f** $\sqrt[3]{100 - 36}$ **g** $\sqrt{3^3 + 9}$ **h** $\sqrt{5^2 + 12^2}$

Key point

In a calculation like $\sqrt{40 - 15}$, first work out the value inside the square root.

10 Substitute the given values into each formula.
Work out the answers mentally.

a $V = a^3$ when $a = 5$

b $T = \sqrt{m} + \sqrt{n}$ when $m = 144$ and $n = 81$

c $d = y + \sqrt[3]{y}$ when $y = 8$

d $A = (c + 2)^2$ when $c = 2$

11 **Real / STEM** $h = 5t^2$, where h is height in metres and t is time in seconds.
A ball takes 2 seconds to fall from the roof of a block of flats to the ground. Use the formula to work out the height of the block of flats.

12 Substitute the given values into each formula.
Use your calculator to find the answers.
Round your answers to two decimal places where necessary.

a $V = L^3$ when $L = 2.6$

b $w = 10\sqrt{s}$ when $s = 5$

c $V = \frac{1}{2} b^2 h$ when $b = 2.5$ and $h = 12$

d $Z = \frac{m + n}{m - n}$ when $m = 340$ and $n = 122$

e $P = \frac{t^3}{\sqrt[3]{u} + 10}$ when $t = 3.8$ and $u = 20$

Investigation Reasoning

1 **a** Find $\sqrt{5}$ using your calculator.
b Square the answer. What do you notice?
c Complete this sentence: If you square the square root of a number, ____________________.

2 **a** Clear your calculator display. Find $\sqrt{5}$ again. Give the answer to two decimal places.
b Type in your answer on your calculator. Square this number.
c What do you notice? Explain why this happens.

3 Repeat part **2** using **i** five decimal places **ii** the entire calculator display.

4 Does your calculator give the exact value of $\sqrt{5}$? Explain your answer.

Explore

13 **Explore** What size of square wall can be covered using a roll of wallpaper?
Is it easier to explore this question now you have completed the lesson?
What further information do you need to be able to answer this?

Reflect

14 **Reflect** Look back at Q8h. Write down all the steps you took to work out the answer.
You may begin with, 'Step 1: I worked out 2^3.'
Now look back at each step. How did you decide what to do first, second, third ...?
Compare your decisions with others in your class.

Topic links: Formulae

1.5 Multiples and factors

You will learn to:
- Use index notation
- Write a number as the product of its prime factors
- Use prime factor decomposition to find the highest common factor (HCF) and lowest common multiple (LCM).

CONFIDENCE

Why learn this?
The lowest common multiple helps us predict when orbiting satellites will line up.

Fluency
- Write the factors of 24.
- Write the first 10 multiples of 7.
- Write the first 10 prime numbers.

Explore
How often will the Sun, Earth and Venus be in alignment?

Exercise 1.5

Warm up

1 **a** What is the highest common factor of 12 and 30?
b Work out the highest common factor of each pair of numbers.
i 16 and 36 **ii** 14 and 42 **iii** 27 and 60 **iv** 45 and 75

2 **a** Write the first 10 multiples of 6 and 8 in two lists.
b Circle the common multiples.
c What is the lowest common multiple of 6 and 8?
d Work out the lowest common multiple of each pair of numbers.
i 9 and 12 **ii** 7 and 8 **iii** 12 and 16 **iv** 6 and 21

3 Complete the Venn diagram to show the factors of 24 and 32.
Circle their highest common factor.

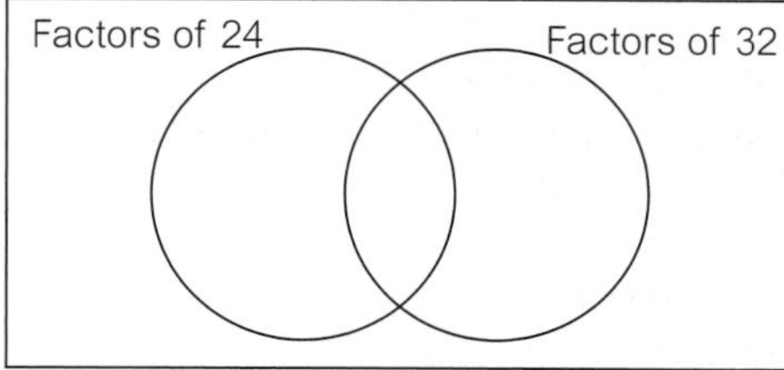

Key point
$2^4 = 2 \times 2 \times 2 \times 2$
2^4 is '2 to the power 4'.
$2^5 = 2 \times 2 \times 2 \times 2 \times 2$
2^5 is '2 to the power 5'.
The small number is called the **index** or **power** and tells you how many 2s to multiply together.

4 **a** Work out these.
i 2^4 **ii** 10^6 **iii** 3^5 **iv** 4^7
b Use the y^x key on your calculator to check your answers.

5 Write each product using powers.
a $2 \times 2 \times 2 \times 2 \times 2 \times 2$ **b** $10 \times 10 \times 10 \times 10$
c $3 \times 3 \times 4 \times 4 \times 4$ **d** $10 \times 10 \times 10 \times 2 \times 2 \times 2 \times 2 \times 2$
e $2 \times 3 \times 3 \times 3 \times 3$ **f** $2 \times 5 \times 2 \times 5 \times 2 \times 5 \times 2$

Q5 Literacy hint
The result of multiplying numbers or letters together is called their **product**. For example, the product of 3 and 10 is $3 \times 10 = 30$.

Q5c hint
$3 \times 3 \times 4 \times 4 \times 4 = 3^2 \times 4 \times 4 \times 4 =$

6 **Real** An allotment has three square vegetable-growing areas of side length 6 m and one square fruit-growing area of side length 8 m.

a Write a calculation for the total area using powers.

b Calculate the total area.

7 Write the **prime factors** of each number.

a 12	**b** 14	**c** 18	**d** 32
e 13	**f** 46	**g** 84	**h** 99

Key point

Prime factors are factors that are prime numbers.
The factors of 36 are 1, 2, 3, 4, 6, 9, 12, 18 and 36.
The prime factors are 2 and 3.

Worked example

Write 300 as the product of its prime factors.

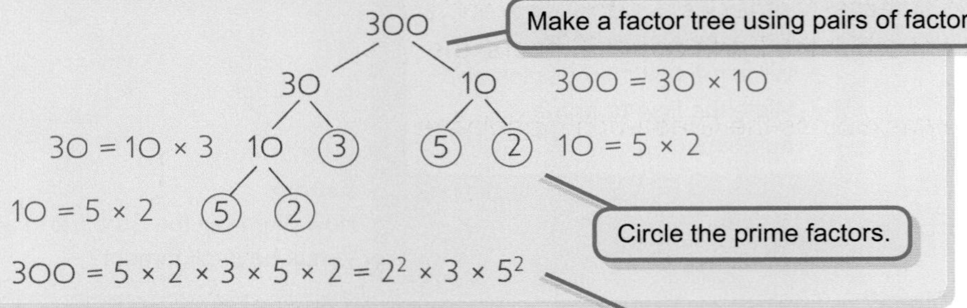

$300 = 5 \times 2 \times 3 \times 5 \times 2 = 2^2 \times 3 \times 5^2$

Write their product using index notation (powers). Write the factors in size order. Put the smallest first.

Key point

All numbers can be written as a product of prime factors.
This is called **prime factor decomposition**.

8 a Complete these factor trees for 18.

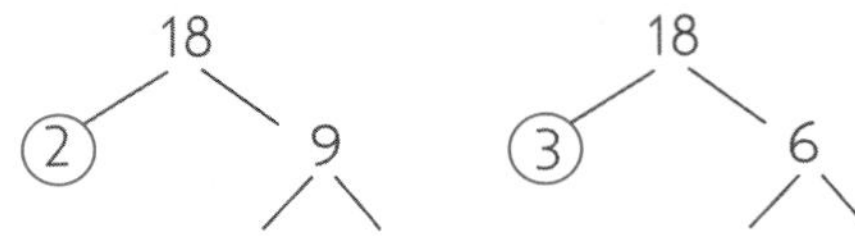

b Write 18 as a product of its prime factors.

Discussion Does it matter which two factors you choose first?

9 Write each number as the product of its prime factors.

a 32	**b** 50	**c** 84	**d** 120
e 200	**f** 900	**g** 338	**h** 576

Q9 hint

Use index notation.

Worked example

Find the highest common factor of 36 and 60.

$36 = 2 \times 2 \times 3 \times 3$

$60 = 2 \times 2 \times 3 \times 5$

HCF = $2 \times 2 \times 3 = 12$

The common prime factors are 2, 2 and 3.

Key point

You can use **prime factor decomposition** to find the highest common factor (HCF) of two or more numbers.

10 Use **prime factor decomposition** to find the highest common factor of each pair of numbers.

a 12 and 30	**b** 32 and 48	**c** 28 and 70	**d** 90 and 100

11 **Problem-solving** Cassandra won seven identical vouchers for a department store.
She used some vouchers to pay for a coat costing £96. She used some more vouchers to pay for a suit costing £72. She received no change for either purchase. How much was each voucher worth?

Subject links: Science (Q13, Q15)

Worked example

Find the lowest common multiple of 36 and 80.

36 = ②×②×③×③
80 = 2 × 2 ×②×②×⑤
LCM = 2 × 2 × 2 × 2 × 3 × 3 × 5 = 720

Circle all the prime factors of the first number and any extra prime factors of the second number not yet included.

Key point

You can use **prime factor decomposition** to find the lowest common multiple of two or more numbers.

12 Use prime factor decomposition to find the lowest common multiple of each pair of numbers in Q10.

13 **Problem-solving / STEM** Two satellites cross the Greenwich meridian at 3 pm on Monday. One of them orbits the Earth every 18 hours, the other every 21 hours.

- **a** How many hours before they next cross the Greenwich meridian at the same time?
- **b** When will this happen?

14 **Problem-solving**

- **a** Write 540 as a product of its prime factors.
- **b** Write 36 as a product of its prime factors.
- **c** Does 36 divide exactly into 540? Explain your answer.
- **d** Use prime factor decomposition to test whether these divisions have whole number answers.
  - **i** 336 ÷ 28
  - **ii** 410 ÷ 15
  - **iii** 336 ÷ 28
  - **iv** 544 ÷ 17

Q14c hint

How many prime factors in the product for 36 are also in the product for 540?

Investigation

1 What are the highest common factor and the lowest common multiple of:

- **a** two consecutive numbers
- **b** two consecutive even numbers
- **c** two consecutive odd numbers
- **d** two consecutive multiples of 3
- **e** two consecutive square numbers?

2 What are the highest common factor and the lowest common multiple of two different powers of 10?

Literacy hint

Consecutive means 'following on'. 11 and 12 are consecutive numbers; 8 and 12 are consecutive multiples of 4.

15 **Explore** How often will the Sun, Earth and Venus be in alignment?
Is it easier to explore this question now you have completed the lesson?
What further information do you need to be able to answer this?

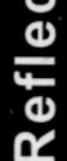

16 **Reflect** Write your own short definition for each of these mathematics words.

- prime
- factor
- decomposition

Now use your definitions to write (in your own words) the meaning of 'prime factor decomposition'.

Q16 hint

Compose means to make or create something. What do you think decompose means?

1 Check up

Log how you did on your Student Progression Chart.

Calculating with positive and negative numbers

1 Problem-solving / Finance Samuel buys a gaming laptop for £1385 and a designer case for £67. He pays a deposit of £177.

a How much does he have left to pay?

b Samuel pays the remainder in 12 equal monthly instalments. How much is each instalment?

2 Work out these.

a $23.9 + 0.54$ **b** $5.35 + 13 + 6.6$ **c** $20.1 - 8.88 + 19$

3 Work out these.

a 25×16 **b** 12×7.5 **c** 8×4.5

4 Estimate the answer to each of these.

a $1.87 + 4.04 - 2.99$ **b** $48 \div 9.8$

c $2.9 \times (7.4 - 1.6)$ **d** $55.5 \div 7.8$

5 Work out these.

a $6 - -2$ **b** $-5 - 3$ **c** $-8 + 12$ **d** $-3 + 2 - 5$

e 4×-2 **f** $15 \div -5$ **g** $12 \div -4 - 8$ **h** $-5 \times (4 - 7)$

Powers and roots

6 Work out these.

a 4^3 **b** 3×4^2 **c** $2^3 \times 5$

d $(-4)^2$ **e** $\sqrt[3]{8}$ **f** $\sqrt[3]{125}$

7 Use your calculator to work out $2.3^2 - (4.5 - \sqrt{5.29})$

8 Write the two whole numbers that $\sqrt{19}$ lies between.

9 $P = \frac{1}{4}(a^2 + b)$

Work out the value of P when $a = 9$ and $b = 19$.

10 Work out these.

a $\sqrt[3]{27} - \sqrt{4}$ **b** $\sqrt{60 + 61}$ **c** $(4 + 2^3) \div 4$

d 60^2 **e** $\dfrac{36}{1 + \sqrt{64}}$ **f** $(\sqrt[3]{1000} - \sqrt{49})^2$

11 Given that $9 \times 36 = 324$, work out $\sqrt{324}$.

12 Write the two square roots of 64.

Factors and multiples

13 Write 24 as the product of its prime factors using index notation.

14 Write the prime factor decomposition of 45.

15 a Work out the highest common factor of 48 and 100.
b Work out the lowest common multiple of 35 and 55.

16 Problem-solving Gavin and Birdi bought some identical books of stamps.
Gavin bought 24 stamps and Birdi bought 40 stamps.
What is the largest possible number of stamps in a book?

17 **How sure are you of your answers? Were you mostly**
Just guessing **Feeling doubtful** **Confident**
What next? Use your results to decide whether to strengthen or extend your learning.

Reflect

Challenge

18 STEM / Problem-solving / Modelling Helena did an experiment to investigate how salt affects the freezing point of water.
She mixed different amounts of salt in a litre of water and recorded when the water started to freeze.

Salt (g)	30	60	90	120
Temperature (°C)	−1.8	−3.6	−5.4	−7.2

a How does adding 30 g of salt affect the freezing point?
b When six scoops of 30 g of salt are added to a litre of water, what is the freezing point?
c Why do we spray salt on the roads in winter? Explain your answer.

19 This flow chart can help you find the highest common factor of two numbers.

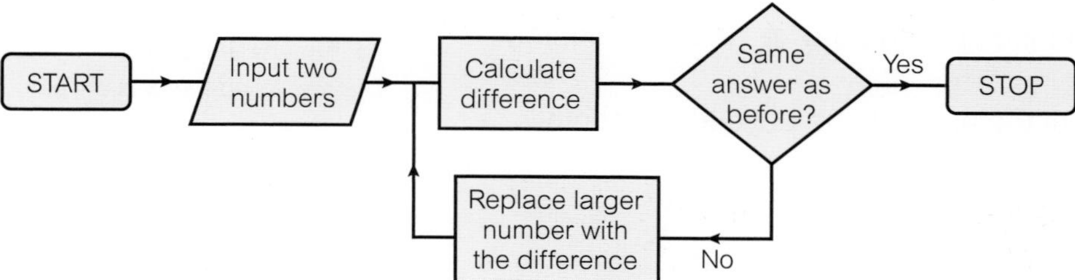

Here's what happens if you input the numbers 9 and 21:
Difference = 21 − 9 = **12**
Replace 21 with 12 and start again.
Difference = 12 − 9 = **3**
Replace 12 with 3 and start again.
Difference = 9 − 3 = **6**
Replace 9 with 6 and start again.
Difference = 6 − 3 = **3**
STOP because you have the same answer as before, 3.
Highest common factor of 9 and 21 is 3.

a i Work out the highest common factor of 8 and 20 in the usual way.
ii Now try the flow chart. Does it work?
b Test the flow chart using other pairs of numbers. Find the highest common factor in the usual way first so that you can check if the flow chart works.
c Which pairs of numbers less than 100 take the longest time? Could you modify the flow chart to speed it up for these pairs of numbers?

1 Strengthen

You will:

- Strengthen your understanding with practice.

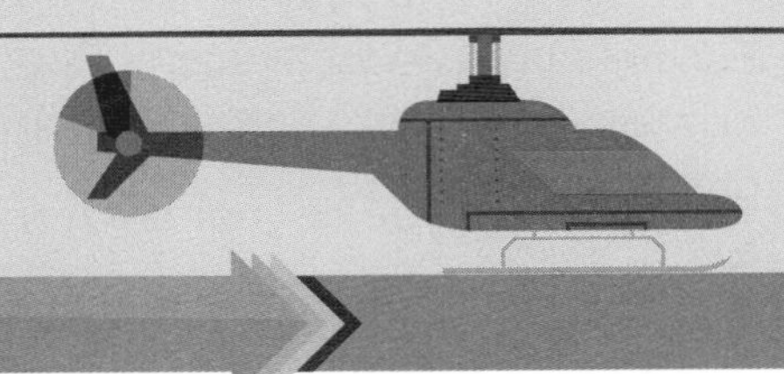

Calculating with positive and negative numbers

1 Use the column method to calculate these.

a 3828 + 187 **b** 3828 – 187

2 Work out these.

a 466 – 172 – 35 **b** 778 + 54 – 77

c 7625 – 84 + 555 **d** £12 004 + £804 – £9963

3 **Problem-solving / Finance** In 2013, Tariq earned £18 222 plus a bonus of £839.
His employer deducted £4722 for tax, insurance and pension.
How much did Tariq receive?

4 Use the column method to calculate these.

a 17.7 + 0.73 **b** 28.9 + 7.83 **c** 37.94 – 1.3

d 48.3 – 5.14 **e** 5.4 + 33.7 – 0.85 **f** 45.2 – 7.8 – 0.84

5 **Finance**

a Nicki pays for a saxophone costing £327 in 12 equal monthly instalments.
Use division to work out the amount she pays each month.

b Mike received £3589.96 for 11 weeks of work.
Use division to work out his weekly wage.

6 **a** **i** Double 5. **ii** Halve 48.

iii Use doubling and halving to work out 5 × 48.

b Use doubling and halving to work out these.

i 5 × 32 **ii** 26 × 5 **iii** 4.5 × 6

iv 2.5 × 16 **v** 24 × 3.5 **vi** 12.5 × 28

7 Work out these.

a 6 × 30 **b** 4 × 90 **c** 9 × 50 **d** 60 × 5

8 **a** **i** Double 7.5, then double the answer.

ii Halve 32, then halve the answer.

iii Use your answers to work out 7.5 × 32.

b Use doubling and halving to work out these.

i 2.5 × 48 **ii** 25 × 88 **iii** 24 × 25

9 **Real** Daniela filled her 4.5 litre watering can 16 times in a week.
Work out the amount of water she used.

10 Estimate the answer to each calculation.

a 37 + 52 (round each number to the nearest 10)

b 195 + 403 (round each number to the nearest 100)

Q1 hint

Line up the Units, Tens, Hundreds and Thousands.

Q2a hint

Work from left to right. Work out 466 − 172 first. Then subtract 35.

Q4d hint

```
  4 8 . 2̶3 10
−   5 . 1 4
  ________
```

Fill in any empty decimal places with zeros. Keep the decimal points in line.

Q6b iii hint

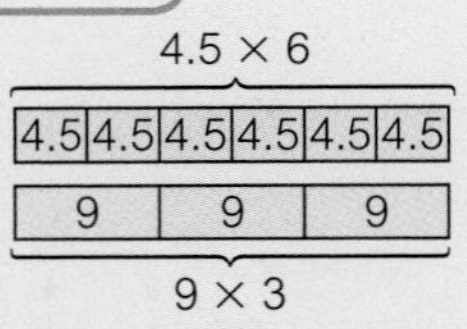

Multiplying by a whole number is easier than multiplying by a decimal.

Q7a hint

6 × 30 = 6 × 3 × 10 = 18 × 10 = □

Q8a iii hint

Multiplying by 30 is easier than multiplying by 7.5 or 15.

c 5.6 + 11.8 (round each number to the nearest whole number)
d 5.6 + 11.8 + 19.7   **e** 18.4 − 10.5
f 18.4 − 10.5 + 15.1   **g** 12.5 + 6.8 − 9.2

> **Q10f hint**
> Work from left to right.

11 Estimate the answer to each calculation. Use the priority of operations. Only round the numbers you need to. Use a calculator to check your estimates.
a $152 \div 48 + 11$ **b** $99 - 28 \times 2.8$
c $(29 + 29) \div 6$ **d** $4.8^2 + 3.5$

> **Q11d hint**
> Estimate 4.8×4.8.

12 **Real** A rectangular vegetable patch measures 2.9 m by 4.2 m. The vegetable patch is in a square garden of side length 9.8 m. Estimate the area of:
a the vegetable patch   **b** the garden
c the garden area excluding the vegetable patch.

> **Q12 Strategy hint**
> Draw a diagram and label the lengths.

13 Work out these.
a $10 + -5$ **b** $8 - -4$ **c** $-2 - -8$ **d** $-5 + -2$

> **Q13 hint**
> Replace different signs with a minus (−).
> Replace same signs with a plus (+).

14 Work out these.
a $-12 \div -2$ **b** -8×-3 **c** -4×3
d $3 \times -2 \times 4$ **e** $-2 \times 5 \times -7$ **f** $-3 \times -4 \div -2$

> **Q14 hint**
> For multiplying and dividing:
> same signs give positive answer;
> different signs give negative answer.

15 Work out these calculations. Use the priority of operations. Check your answers using a calculator.
a $5 - 2 \times 7$ **b** $5 \times -3 - 2$ **c** $-10 \div 2 + 3$
d $4 - 3 \times -2$ **e** $4 \times (3 - 6)$ **f** $-15 \div (5 - 8)$

Powers and roots

1 Copy and complete these calculations.
a $2^3 = 2 \times \square \times \square =$ **b** $\square^{\square} = 5 \times 5 \times 5 = \square$
c $\square^{\square} = 10 \times \square \times \square = \square$ **d** $\square^{\square} = \square \times \square \times \square = 27$
Discussion Is 2^3 the same as 2×3?

> **Q1 hint**
> 6^3 ← This number tells you how many 6s are multiplied together.
> $6^3 = 6 \times 6 \times 6$

2 a Copy and complete the diagram of square roots. Make your diagram as wide as possible. Label each square root on your diagram.

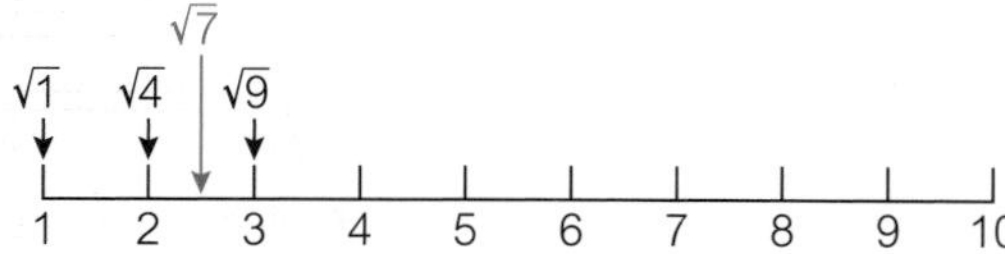

b Which two whole numbers does each of these roots lie between? The first one has been done for you.
i $\sqrt{7}$ $\sqrt{7}$ lies between $\sqrt{4}$ and $\sqrt{9}$. So $\sqrt{7}$ lies between 2 and 3.
ii $\sqrt{60}$ **iii** $\sqrt{20}$ **iv** $\sqrt{99}$ **v** $\sqrt{32}$

3 a Copy and complete these calculations.
i $\sqrt[3]{8} = 2$ because $2^3 = 2 \times 2 \times 2 = \square$
ii $\sqrt[3]{1000} = \square$ because $10^3 = \square \times \square \times \square = 1000$
iii $\sqrt[3]{\square} = 5$ because $5^3 = \square$
iv The cube root of 27 is $\square$

> **Q3a iii hint**
> Work out 5^3 first.

b Write the value of each root without using a calculator.
i $\sqrt[3]{64}$ **ii** $\sqrt{36}$ **iii** $\sqrt[3]{1}$ **iv** $\sqrt{121}$

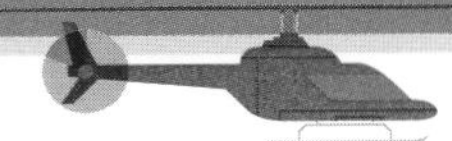

4 **a** Work out **i** 3^2 **ii** $(-3)^2$

b What do you notice about your answers to part **a**?

c Copy and complete the sentence:
The two square roots of 9 are □ and □.

d Write the two square roots of each number.

i 16 **ii** 100 **iii** 169

Q4a ii hint

The negative number −3 inside the brackets is being squared, so work out −3 × −3.

5 **a** Work out **i** $4^2 \times 10^2$ **ii** $(4 \times 10)^2$

b What do you notice about your answers to part **a**?

c Work out these.

i 50^2 **ii** 90^2 **iii** 120^2

iv 300^2 **v** 400^2 **vi** 800^2

6 Write each calculation using brackets.
Work them out using the priority of operations.
Check your answers using the fraction key of your calculator.
The first one has been done for you.

a $\frac{16 + 4}{9 - 4}$

$\frac{16 + 4}{9 - 4} = \frac{20}{5} = 20 \div 5 = 4$

b $\frac{9 \times 4}{5 + 7}$ **c** $\frac{10^2}{13 + 7}$ **d** $\frac{\sqrt{81}}{10 - 7}$ **e** $\frac{30 + 20}{5^2}$

Q6 hint

Work out top and bottom first.
Write the fraction as a division.

7 Work out these. Use the priority of operations.
Then use a calculator to check your answers: input the calculation from left to right, then press the = key.

a $\sqrt{144} - 4^2$ **b** $5^2 - \sqrt[3]{125}$

c $\sqrt{100} - 3^3$ **d** $3 \times (1 + \sqrt{16})$

e $2 \times (6^2 - 20)$ **f** $5 \times (3 + \sqrt[3]{64})$

g $(9 + 7) \div \sqrt{4}$ **h** $18 \div (\sqrt{25} + 2^2)$

Q7 hint

Priority of operations: Brackets then powers and roots.

8 Work out these. Use the priority of operations.
Check your answers using a calculator.
The first one has been done for you.

a $\sqrt{12 + 20 \div 5} = \sqrt{12 + 4} = \sqrt{16} = 4$

b $\sqrt{4 \times 8 - 7}$ **c** $\sqrt{8^2 - 60}$ **d** $\sqrt[3]{7 + 4 \times 5}$

Q8 hint

Work out the calculation under the square root sign first.
Division before addition

Factors and multiples

1 Write each product as a power. The first one has been done for you.

a $4 \times 4 \times 4 \times 4 \times 4 = 4^5$ **b** $2 \times 2 \times 2 \times 2 \times 2 \times 2$

c $5 \times 5 \times 5 \times 5 \times 5$ **d** $3 \times 3 \times 3 \times 3$

Q1a hint

There are 5 lots of 4 multiplied together.

2 Write each product using index notation (powers).
The first one has been done for you.

a $3 \times 3 \times 3 \times 3 \times 5 \times 5 \times 7 = 3^4 \times 5^2 \times 7$

b $2 \times 2 \times 2 \times 5 \times 5 \times 5$

c $2 \times 3 \times 3 \times 5 \times 5 \times 5$

d $2 \times 2 \times 2 \times 2 \times 3 \times 11$

e $2 \times 3 \times 3 \times 3 \times 3 \times 3$

Q2a hint

There is only one 7. You don't need to write the power 1.

3 a Copy and complete the factor tree for the number 450 until you end up with just prime factors.
b Use index notation to write 450 as the product of its prime factors.
c Use index notation to write each number as the product of its prime factors.
i 350 ii 84 iii 98 iv 216 v 225

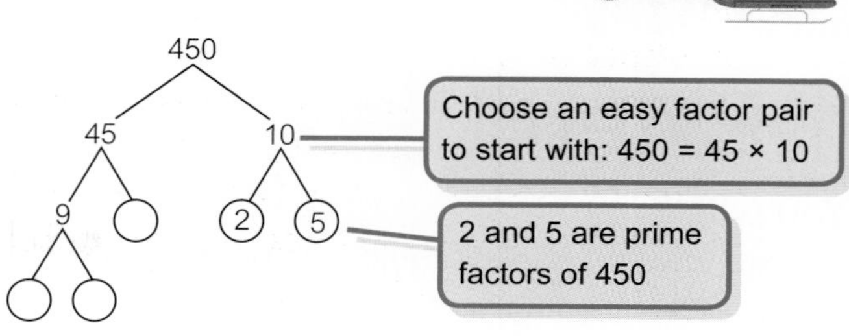

Worked example

a Write 18 and 30 as products of prime factors.
$18 = 2 \times 3 \times 3$ $30 = 2 \times 3 \times 5$

b Draw a Venn diagram of their prime factors. Use your diagram to find the highest common factor.

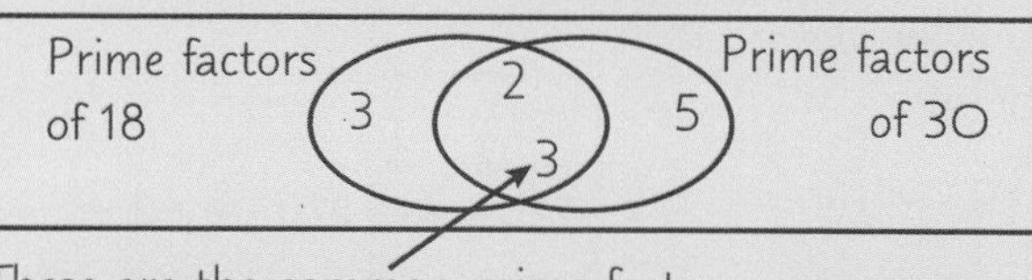

These are the common prime factors.
HCF = $2 \times 3 = 6$

To find the HCF, multiply the common prime factors.

c Find the lowest common multiple.
$3 \times 2 \times 3 \times 5 = 90$

To find the LCM, multiply all the prime factors.

4 For each pair of numbers below:
i Write each number as the product of its prime factors.
ii Draw a Venn diagram of their prime factors.
Use your diagram to find the highest common factor.
iii Find the lowest common multiple of the pair of numbers.
a 30 and 48 b 24 and 60 c 42 and 70

Q4 hint
Use the worked example to help you.

Enrichment

1 **Problem-solving / Reasoning**
a You are waiting for the best moment to escape from prison camp. A spotlight shines on your exit for 10 minutes then turns off for 2 minutes. A guard can see your exit for 7 minutes then is out of sight for 1 minute. At 8 pm the spotlight is turned on and the guard begins her patrol. Later in the evening, you look out of the exit and see that the spotlight is off and the guard is out of sight. It takes 1 minute for you to escape. When should you go?
b After your escape, the spotlight is turned on for 9 minutes and off for 1 minute. How long before the next inmate can escape?

Q1a Strategy hint
Draw timelines for the spotlight and guard using squared paper.

Q1b Strategy hint
Use the lowest common multiple.

2 **Problem-solving** Find a number between 200 and 300 whose product of primes has no repeated prime factors. For example, a suitable number between 100 and 200 is $105 = 3 \times 5 \times 7$.

3 **Reflect** Write five different ways you used your multiplication and division skills in these Strengthen lessons. Your first two might be:
1 When doubling, I multiplied by 2.
2 When dividing a negative number by a negative number, I divided the numbers and then wrote an answer which was positive.

Reflect

1 Extend

You will:

- Extend your understanding with problem-solving.

1 a Use doubling and halving to work out these.

i 5×0.16 ii 0.24×5 iii 50×0.32
iv 0.88×25 v 1.2×25 vi 25×3.6

b Use a mental method to work out these.

i $270 \div 18$ ii $180 \div 12$ iii $700 \div 14$ iv $360 \div 15$

> **Q1a hint**
> It is easier to multiply by 10 or 100 than by 5, 25 or 50.

> **Q1b hint**
> $270 \div 18 = 270 \div 9 \div 2$

2 a £1 buys \$1.60. How many dollars does £25 buy?

b 1 kg of tomatoes costs £2.40. How much does 12.5 kg cost?

3 Write the ratio $4^2 : 6^2$ in its simplest form.

4 Calculate these.

a 15×98 b 27×99 c 103×11 d 7×999
e 5.9×20 f 2.1×50 g 0.43×200 h 9.9×60

> **Q4a hint**
> $98 = 100 - 2$, so work out $15 \times 100 - 15 \times 2$

> **Q4e hint**
> $5.9 \times 10 \times 2$

5 Use estimation to find out which one of these calculations is incorrect.

A $3480 - 18 \times 122 = 2284$
B $(8.3 + 11.8) \times (15.8 - 10.9) = 98.49$
C $27 \times 48 \div 72 = 18$

6 Problem-solving A wire fence surrounds a square playground with area 115 m^2.
One side is replaced with a wooden fence. The removed piece of wire fence is used to enclose a square garden. Estimate the size of the garden.

> **Q6 Strategy hint**
> Draw diagrams.

7 Finance Lara owed £28 300 on her mortgage. She repaid £12 485 using her savings and a further £9100 from selling her sports car.

a How much did Lara still owe on her mortgage?

b She repaid the remaining mortgage in 12 equal monthly instalments. Work out her monthly instalment to the nearest penny.

8 Problem-solving Square A has sides of length 14 cm.
Square B has an area of 256 cm^2.
Square C has a perimeter of 60 cm.

a Which square has the greatest perimeter?

b Which square has the smallest area?

9 Problem-solving The table shows a pattern of calculations.

Pattern number	Calculation	Estimate
1	1980×198	
2	$1980 \times 198 \times 19.8$	
3	$1980 \times 198 \times 19.8 \times 1.98$	

a Copy and complete the table.

b Continue the pattern until the estimate is less than 1.

Topic links: Ratio, Algebra, Measures, Handling data

Subject links: Science (Q12, Q13, Q17, Investigation)

10 **Real** Gaerwyn recorded these outside temperatures at midnight on the first day of each month.

11.2 °C, −1.7 °C, 3 °C, 4.8 °C, −7.3 °C, −0.9 °C.

a Find the median temperature.

b Estimate the mean temperature.

c Work out the range.

11 **Real** The distance d km a train travels in t hours at a speed of s km/h is given by the formula $d = st$.
Estimate the distance the new L-Zero Japanese train travels in 2.55 hours at a speed of 310 km/h.

12 The formula $C = 0.56(F - 32)$ converts temperatures measured in Fahrenheit (F) to Celsius (C). Use an estimate to convert −11.8°F to Celsius. Check your estimate using a calculator.

13 **STEM** The approximate power intensity I watts/m^2 at a distance r metres from a radio transmitter of power P watts is estimated using the formula

$$I = \frac{P}{12r^2}$$

Use your calculator to find the power intensity I from

a a wireless router of power 0.5 watts at a distance of 2 metres

b a smart meter of power 2.5 watts at a distance of 5 metres.

14 The first term of a sequence is 4 and the term-to-term rule is 'multiply by −2'.

a Write the first five terms of the sequence.

b Work out the difference between the second and fourth terms.

c Write the fifth term using index notation.

15 Work out these.

a $11^2 - 12^2$

b $\sqrt[3]{-64} - \sqrt{64}$

c $30 \div \sqrt{25} - 9$

d $\sqrt[3]{1000} \times (-10)^3$

e $\sqrt{169} - (-4)^2$

f $\sqrt[3]{27} \times (-4)^2$

16 **a** Write the two square roots of 121.

b Here are three numbers.
13 824, 13 106, 12 544
Which one is

i a square number? **ii** a cube number?

17 **STEM / Modelling** The surface area S mm^2 of a spherical underwater air bubble of radius r mm is estimated using the formula $S = 12r^2$.

a When a bubble is 5000 m deep, its radius is 3 mm.
Work out its surface area.

b When the bubble has risen to a depth of 30 m, its radius is 5 times its size at 5000 m.
Work out the new surface area of the bubble.

Q17 Literacy hint

Radius = distance from centre of sphere to a point on the surface.

18 a Find the highest common factor of each set of numbers.
 i 48, 60 and 76 **ii** 28, 70 and 140

b Find the lowest common multiple of each set of numbers.
 i 9, 15 and 21 **ii** 6, 16 and 18

c Mary has written two numbers as products of their prime factors:
$2^3 \times 3^4$ and $2^2 \times 3^5$
Work out the highest common factor and the lowest common multiple of the two numbers.

Q18a hint
Write each number as the product of its prime factors.

19 The CN Tower in Toronto is 1815 ft tall.
Write its height as a product of its prime factors using index notation.

20 Real One of the ancient Mayan calendar cycles was called the 'calendar round'. The number of days in the 'calendar round' is the lowest common multiple (LCM) of two calendars of length 260 days and 365 days.

a Work out the number of days in a calendar round.

b How many years are there in a calendar round?

c The Mayans started their calendar at about 3114 BC. Some people recently thought it predicted the end of the world on 21 December 2012!
Roughly how many calendar rounds were completed up to 21 December 2012?

Q20c hint
Assume 365 days in a year. Ignore leap years.

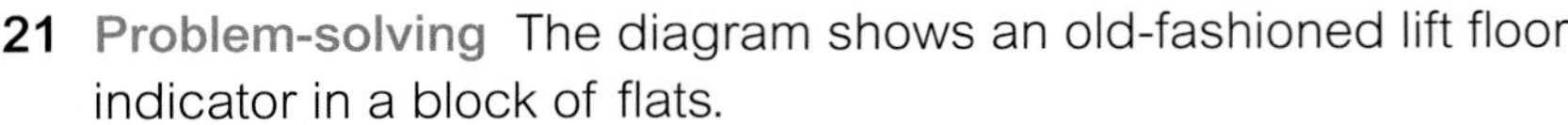

21 Problem-solving The diagram shows an old-fashioned lift floor indicator in a block of flats.
The lift has stopped at a floor. The arrow always points to a whole number of degrees.
What is the smallest number of floors the building could have?

22 Work out these.

a 1.2^4 **b** $\sqrt[3]{39\,304}$ **c** $(-5)^4$

23 Work out these.

a $\sqrt{1600}$ **b** $\sqrt{2500}$

c $\sqrt{12\,100}$ **d** $\sqrt{90\,000}$

e $\sqrt{4\,000\,000}$ **f** $\sqrt{36\,000}$

Q23a hint
1600 = 16 × 100

24 Work out these. Check your answers using a calculator.

a $\dfrac{5^2 - 1}{\sqrt{16} - 1}$ **b** $\sqrt[3]{100 - 36}$

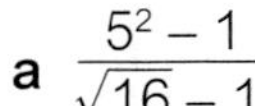

c $\sqrt{19 + 5^3}$ **d** $\sqrt[3]{11^2 + 2^2}$

e $\dfrac{20 + 50}{\sqrt[3]{20 \times 50}}$ **f** $\dfrac{11^2 - 1}{2^3 + 2}$

25 Work out $\sqrt{a^2 + b^2}$ where

a $a = 3$ and $b = 4$ **b** $a = 6$ and $b = 8$

Discussion Can you find any other values for a and b that give whole number answers?

26 Calculate $\dfrac{3^2 - \sqrt{3}}{3^3 - \sqrt[3]{3}}$ correct to two decimal places.

27 Use your calculator's memory function to subtract $107^3 + 203^3 - 550$ from each of these numbers.

a 50 000 000 **b** 319^3 **c** 4225×88^2

28 **Real / Problem-solving** One tin of decking sealant covers an area of 36 m². A square area of decking needs exactly nine tins of sealant.

a Write a calculation for the area of the square decking.

b Work out the length of one side of the decking.

29 **a** Given that $1728 = 27 \times 64$, work out $\sqrt[3]{1728}$.

b Given that $8000 = 64 \times 125$, work out $\sqrt[3]{8000}$.

Discussion Can you write 8000 as a product of two cubes in another way?

30 **Reasoning** Oliver planted some trees in a square plot of land with area 800 m².

a Estimate the length of the side of the plot.

b He worked out the length of a side of the plot and rounded the answer to the nearest metre. Oliver ordered four times this length of fencing to surround the plot.

i Should Oliver have ordered this length of fencing? Explain your answer.

ii Fencing is sold by the metre. How much fencing should Oliver have ordered?

Investigation **Problem-solving / STEM**

1 The time, t seconds, for a stone to hit the ground from a height of d m can be estimated using the formula $t = \sqrt{\frac{d}{5}}$.
Estimate the time it takes for the stone to hit the ground from a height of
a 20 m **b** 30 m **c** 60 m.

2 For a stone on the Moon, the formula is $t = \sqrt{\frac{6d}{5}}$.
Estimate the time it takes for the stone to hit the ground from a height of
a 20 m **b** 30 m **c** 60 m.

3 Does the stone fall faster on the Moon or on the Earth? Suggest why.

4 What height of drop on the Moon takes the same time as a 30 m drop on Earth?

5 For a stone on a planet where the acceleration due to gravity is g m/s², the formula is $t = \sqrt{\frac{2d}{g}}$.
For a planet where $g = 12$ m/s², estimate the time it takes from a height of
a 6 m **b** 96 m **c** 60 m.

6 Use the internet to find g for different planets. Estimate the time for a drop of 30 m on each planet.

31 **Reflect** Which of the questions in these Extend lessons made you think the hardest? Why?
What could you do so that questions like this don't make you think so hard in the future?

Q31 hint

You might look at the length of the question, how it was asked, whether you knew what to do first, or what maths skills and knowledge you had to use.

Reflect

1 Unit test

Log how you did on your Student Progression Chart.

1 The temperature in Moscow was −8 °C at 6 am and 2 °C at midday.
- **a** Work out the difference in temperature.
- **b** By midnight, the temperature had fallen by 14 °C compared to midday.
  - **i** What was the temperature at midnight?
  - **ii** What is the difference in temperature between 6 am and midnight?
- **c** Work out −4 − 6.

2
- **a** Estimate the answer to 4.1 × 8.9.
- **b** One calculator costs £5.95. How many can you buy for £43?

3 Work out these.

a $-4 \times 5 + 1$ **b** 9^2 **c** $\sqrt{25}$ **d** 5^3

e 2×5^2 **f** $13 + \sqrt{49}$ **g** $\sqrt{4 + 9 \times 5}$ **h** $\sqrt[3]{64}$

4 To make a tunnel, 17 220 tonnes of earth need removing.
In the first week 455 tonnes were removed, in the second week 8200 tonnes were removed.
Work out the amount of earth left to remove.

5 12 plates cost £30.60. How much does one plate cost?

6
- **a** Work out these.

  i 5 × 14 **ii** 8 × 99 **iii** 2.5 × 36 **iv** 64 × 12.5
- **b** Work out 240 ÷ 15.

7 Work out 9 + 83.8 – 0.07.

8 Which two whole numbers does $\sqrt{67}$ lie between?

9
- **a** Work out the highest common factor of 24 and 90.
- **b** Work out the lowest common multiple of 9 and 15.
- **c** A timer beeps every 12 seconds. Another timer beeps every 20 seconds.
  Dunstan hears the two timers beep at the same time.
  How long before they next beep at the same time?

10
- **a** Estimate the area of a square of side length 6.2 cm.
- **b** Estimate the answer to each of these.

  i $2.9 \times (178 - 99)$ **ii** $\frac{79 + 57}{7.1}$

11 Write the value of each of these.

a the two square roots of 36 **b** 70^2 **c** 2^4

12 Work out these.

a $5 - -8$ **b** -3×8 **c** $16 \div -8$ **d** $6 + 15 \div -3$

e $(-6)^2$ **f** $3^2 \times 2^3$ **g** $\sqrt[3]{1000} - \sqrt{121}$ **h** $-10 \times (7 - 12)$

13
- **a** **i** Work out the value of 2 × 2 × 2 × 3.
  - **ii** Write 2 × 2 × 2 × 3 using index notation.
- **b** Write 90 as the product of its prime factors, using index notation.

14 Work out these.

a $5^2 - (10 - \sqrt[3]{64})$ **b** $\sqrt[3]{6^2 - 3^2}$

15 The length of string S cm needed to tie a parcel is given by the formula $S = 6a + 2b$.
Find the length needed when $a = 8.2$ cm and $b = 36.5$ cm.

16 The length, L m, of a pendulum that swings back and forth in T seconds is estimated using the formula $L = 0.25T^2$.
Work out the length of a pendulum that takes 2.3 seconds to swing back and forth. Write your answer correct to the nearest mm.

17 Use your calculator to work out these.

a $1.5^2 \times (4^3 - \sqrt{64})$ **b** $\frac{20 \times 30}{5^3}$

18 **a** Given that $1296 = 16 \times 81$, work out $\sqrt{1296}$.

b Given that $3375 = 27 \times 125$, work out $\sqrt[3]{3375}$.

Challenge

19 The aim of this puzzle is to fill in the white squares on a 5×5 grid with as many integers as possible.
This diagram shows how you can move from one square to the next.
The example grid starts at the number 8.

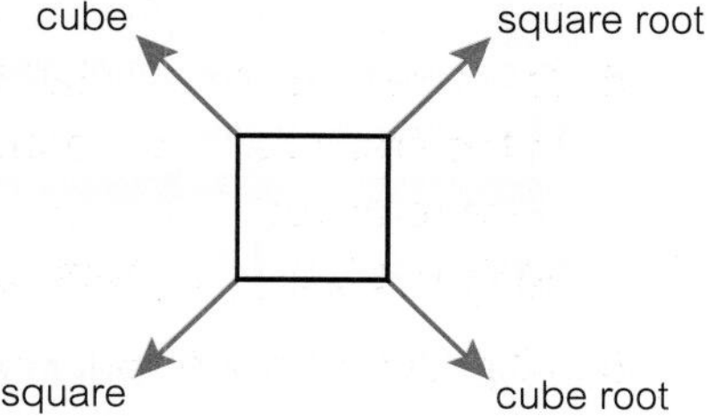

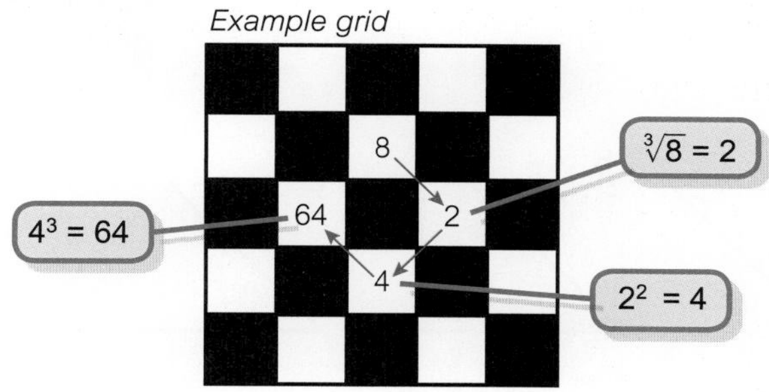

1. Draw your own copy of the grid.
2. Write any positive integer in a white square and circle it.
3. Start filling in the adjacent squares. Use arrows to show where you move to.
4. Continue until you cannot fill in any more squares.
5. Try again. Work out a strategy to fill in more squares this time.
6. Try again. This time start with a negative integer.
7. Try again. This time you can only use each operation twice.

20 **Reflect** In this unit you have done calculations involving
- decimals
- negative numbers
- powers
- roots
- factors.

Which type of calculation did you find easiest? What made it easy?
Which type of calculation did you find hardest? What made it hard?
Write a hint, in your own words, for the type of calculation you found hardest.

Q20 hint
Look back through the unit to remind yourself of each type of calculation.

Reflect

2 Area and volume

MASTER

Check P39 Strengthen P41 Extend P45 Test P49

2.1 Area of a triangle

You will learn to:

- Derive and use the formula for the area of a triangle
- Calculate the area of compound shapes made from rectangles and triangles.

CONFIDENCE

Why learn this?
Glass manufacturers work out the areas of triangles to calculate the amount of glass they need for some windows.

Fluency

- What is the perimeter and the area of these shapes?

- What does 'perpendicular' mean?

Explore
How much blue material is needed for a Union Jack?

Exercise 2.1

Warm up

1 These triangles are drawn on centimetre squared paper. Find the areas of the triangles by counting squares.

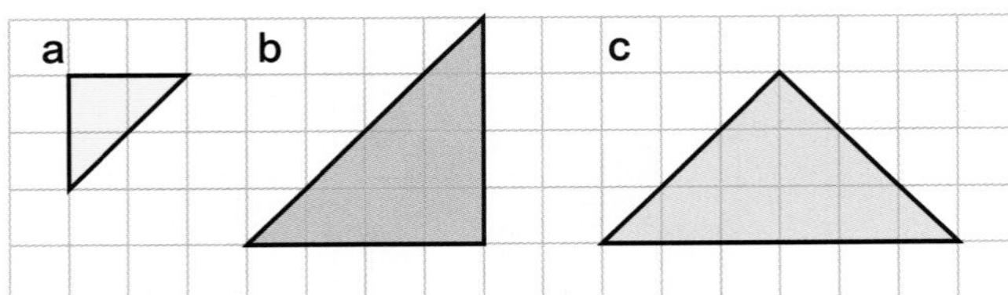

2 For this shape, work out
a the perimeter **b** the area.

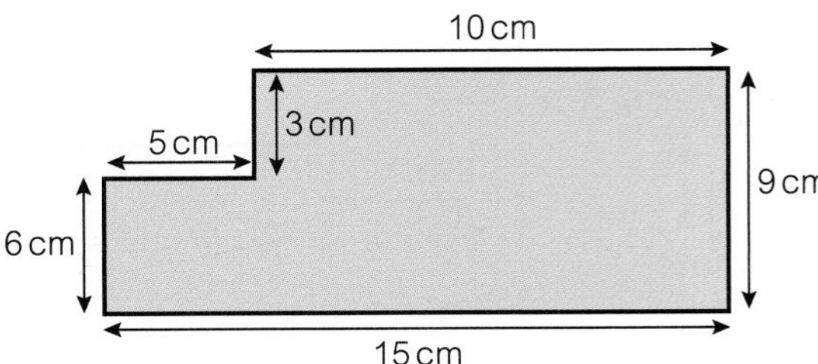

3 a Each diagram shows a triangle and a rectangle. For A and B:

i Work out the area of the rectangle.
ii How many triangles cover the same area as the rectangle?
iii What is the area of the triangle?

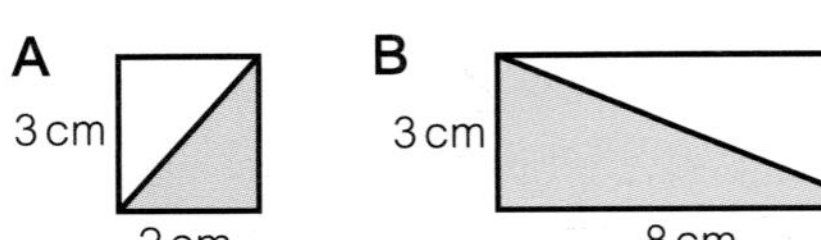

b This diagram shows A and B joined together to make another rectangle.

i Work out the area of the rectangle.
ii What fraction of the rectangle is the triangle?

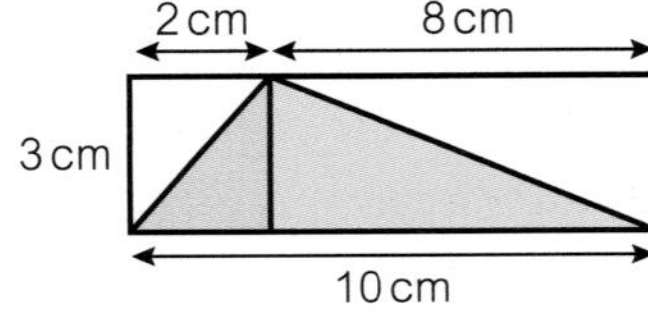

Topic links: Writing and using formulae

c Explain in words how to find the area of a triangle.

d Write a formula connecting the area of a triangle (A), its base length (b) and its height (h).

e Use your formula to check the areas of the triangles in parts **a** and **b**.

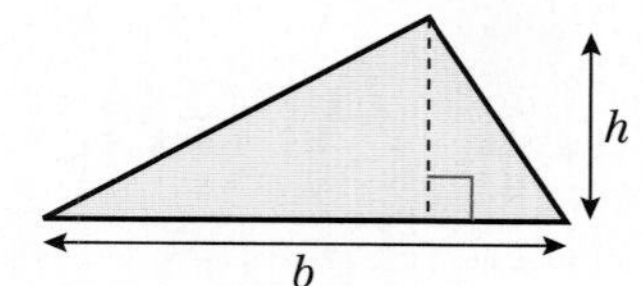

Worked example

Work out the area of this triangle.

$A = \frac{1}{2}bh$

$= \frac{1}{2} \times 12 \times 7$

$= 42\text{ cm}^2$

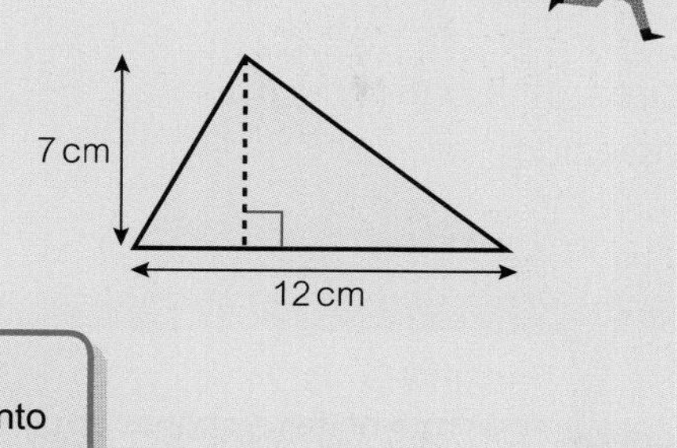

Write the formula, then substitute the numbers into the formula.

Key point

Area of a triangle = $\frac{1}{2}$ × **base** length × **perpendicular height** which can be written as $A = \frac{1}{2}bh$.

The height measurement must be perpendicular (at 90°) to the base.

4 Work out the area of each triangle.

a

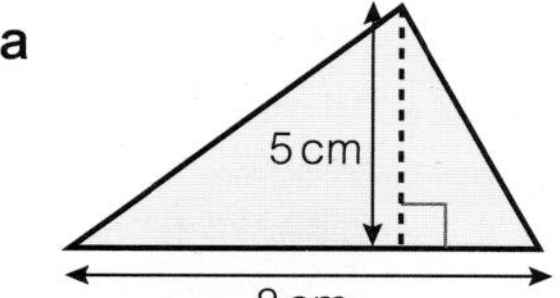

b

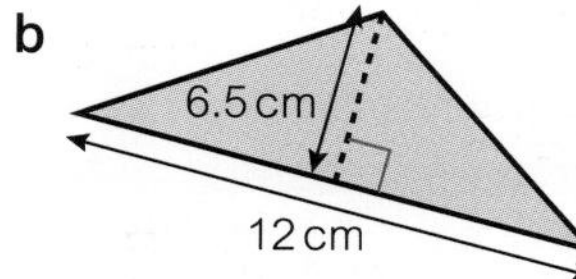

c

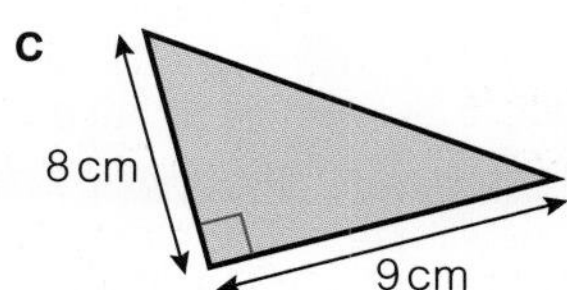

5 **Real / Problem-solving** Tariq makes red, white and blue flags for bunting.

Each length of bunting has 24 flags altogether, with equal numbers of red, white and blue flags.
Each flag is a triangle of height 45 cm and base 30 cm.
Tariq needs to make five lengths of bunting.
Work out the total area of each colour material that he needs.

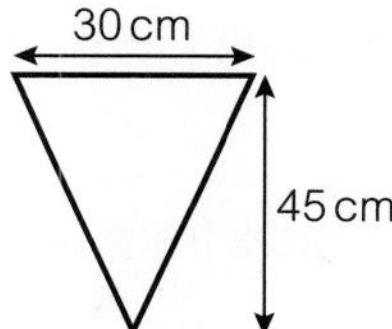

6 **Real** Sam makes stained glass windows like this.

a What is the area of the window?
Give your answer in square metres.

The stained glass costs £153 per square metre.

b What is the cost of the glass for this window?

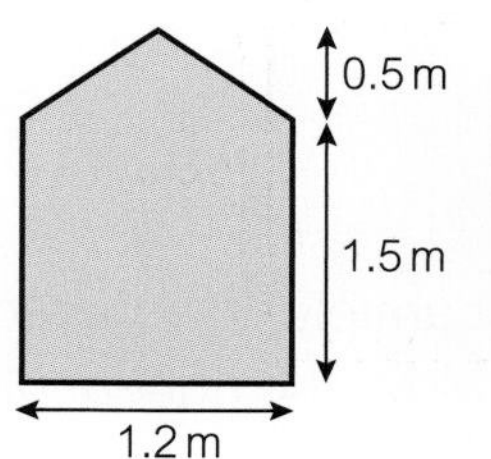

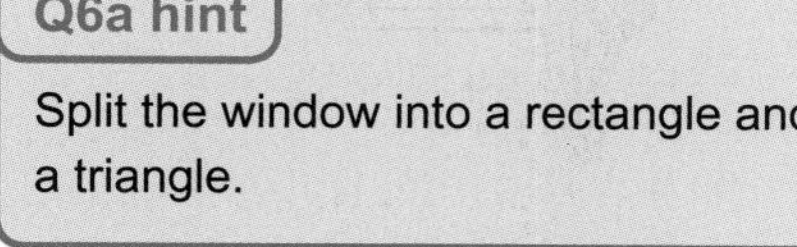

Q6a hint
Split the window into a rectangle and a triangle.

7 **Explore** How much blue material is needed for a Union Jack?
Is it easier to explore this question now you have completed the lesson?
What further information do you need to be able to answer this?

8 **Reflect** After this lesson George says, 'Area measures the size of a shape.'
Polly says, 'Area is the amount of space inside a shape.'
Hasid says, 'Area is the number of squares a space covers.'
Which definition do you like most? Why?
Use what George, Polly and Hasid say, and your own understanding of area, to write the best possible definition. Compare your definition with others in your class.

Explore

Reflect

2.2 Area of a parallelogram and trapezium

You will learn to:
- Derive and use the formula for the area of a parallelogram
- Use the formula for the area of a trapezium.

CONFIDENCE

Why learn this?
Designers use area to work out the amount of material they need to make their product.

Fluency
- Which of these shapes are parallelograms and which are trapezia?

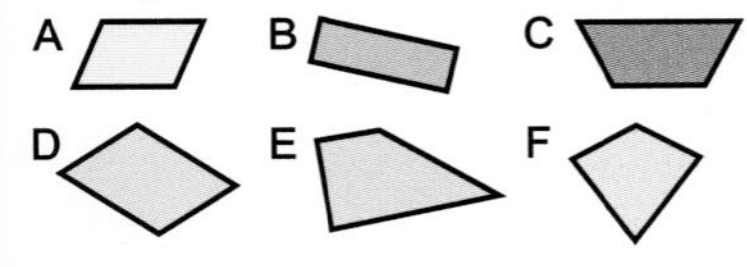

- What does 'congruent' mean?

Explore
The four sides of a waste-paper bin are congruent trapezia. What area of material would you need to make the bin?

Exercise 2.2

Warm up

1 Work out the area of each shape.

a

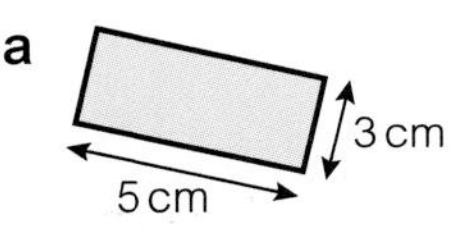

b

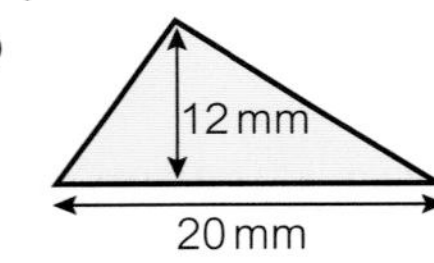

2 When $x = 5$ and $y = 9$, work out the value of

a $x + 2y$ **b** xy **c** $4(x + y)$ **d** $\frac{1}{2}(x + y)$

3 This parallelogram is made from two congruent triangles and a rectangle.
Work out the area of
a the rectangle
b one triangle
c the parallelogram.

3 cm, 5 cm, 4 cm, 3 cm

4 **a** Copy this parallelogram accurately on squared paper. Cut it out.
b Cut along the dashed line. Move the right-angled triangle to make a rectangle.
c Work out the area of the rectangle.
d Explain in words how to find the area of a parallelogram.
e Write a formula connecting the area (A), perpendicular height (h) and base length (b) of a parallelogram.

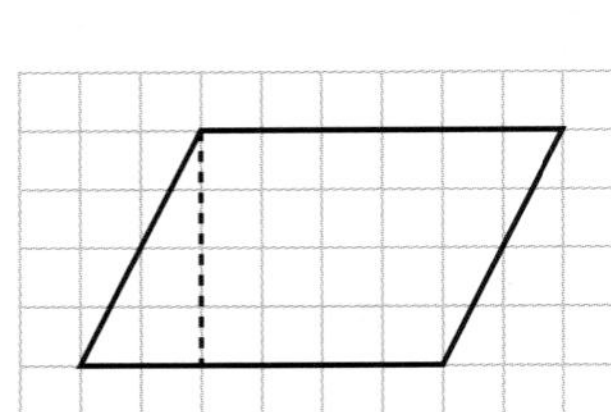

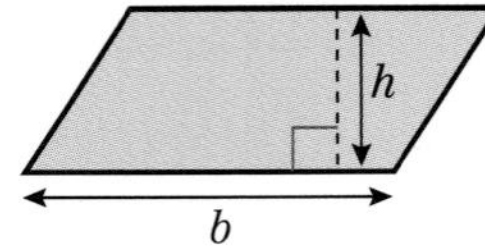

f Use your formula to check the area you found in part **c**.
g Use your formula to check the area you found in Q3.

Topic links: Writing and using formulae.

5 Work out the area of each parallelogram.

a
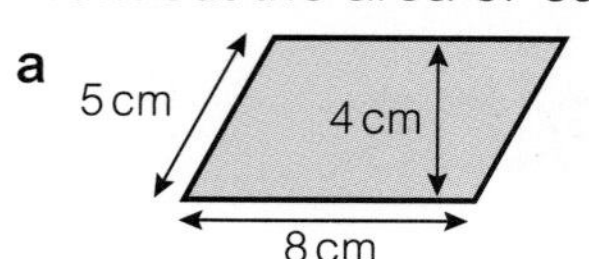

b
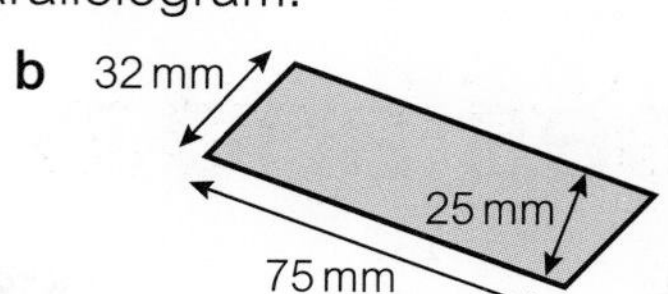

Discussion In Q5 parts **a** and **b**, which lengths didn't you use and why?

> **Key point**
> **area of a parallelogram** = base length × perpendicular height, which can be written as $A = bh$.

Worked example

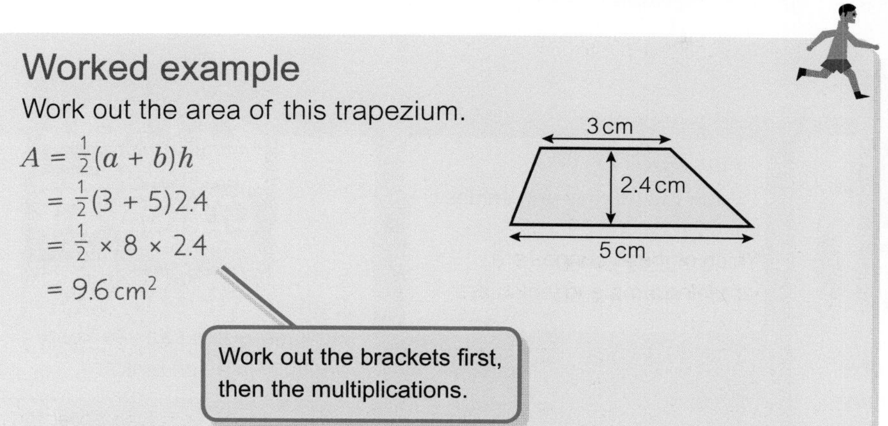

Work out the area of this trapezium.

$A = \frac{1}{2}(a + b)h$

$= \frac{1}{2}(3 + 5)2.4$

$= \frac{1}{2} \times 8 \times 2.4$

$= 9.6\text{ cm}^2$

Work out the brackets first, then the multiplications.

> **Key point**

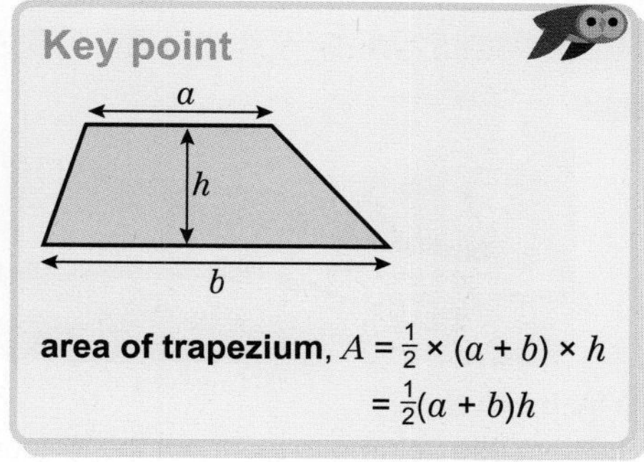

> **area of trapezium**, $A = \frac{1}{2} \times (a + b) \times h$
> $= \frac{1}{2}(a + b)h$

6 Work out the area of each trapezium.

a
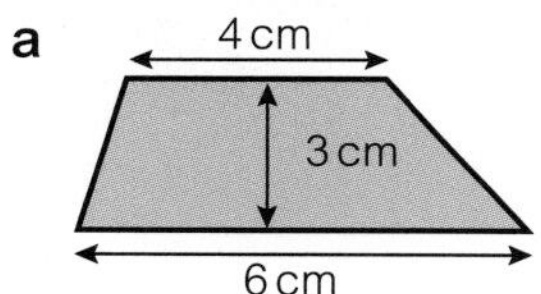

b
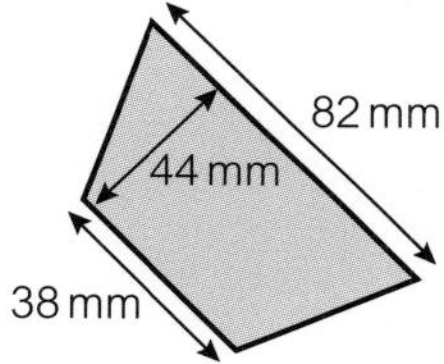

7 **Real / Modelling** The glass for a car windscreen costs £315 per square metre.
The shape of a car windscreen is modelled as a trapezium.

a Work out the cost of the glass for this car windscreen.

b Do you think that a trapezium is a good model to use for a car windscreen? Explain.

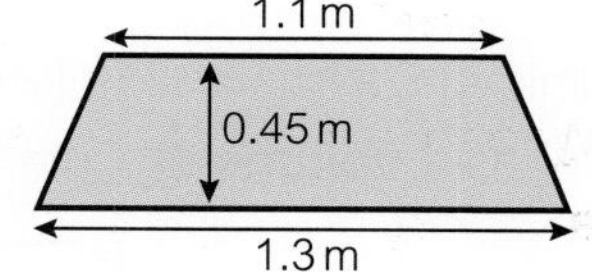

8 **a** Match each shape to its area.

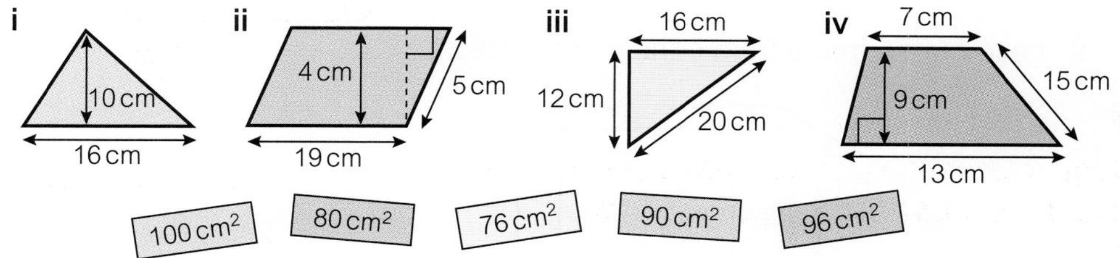

b Draw a shape to match the area that is left over.

9 **Explore** The four sides of a waste-paper bin are congruent trapezia.
What area of material would you need to make the bin?
What have you learned in this lesson to help you answer this question?
What other information do you need?

10 **Reflect** Q8b asked you to draw a shape with a particular area.
Which shape did you choose? Why?
Write all the steps you took to work out the lengths of the shape.
Choose another shape. Will the steps be the same or different? Explain.

Explore

Reflect

2.3 Volume of cubes and cuboids

You will learn to:
- Calculate the volume of cubes and cuboids
- Calculate the volume of shapes made from cuboids
- Solve volume problems.

CONFIDENCE

Why learn this?
Builders use volume to work out the amount of concrete they need for the foundations of a house.

Fluency
Work out the missing values.
- 3 × 2 × 5 = □
- 8 × 2 × □ = 80
- □ × 4 × 5 = 60

Explore
How many fish can you keep healthily in a fish tank?

Exercise 2.3

Warm up

1 a Write the first five cube numbers.
  b Write the value of 10^3.

2 When $a = 5$ and $b = 3$, work out
  a $a + b$ b $a \times b$ c a^2 d $b^3 - a$

3 This cube has a side length of 1 cm.
It has a **volume** of 1 cm³.

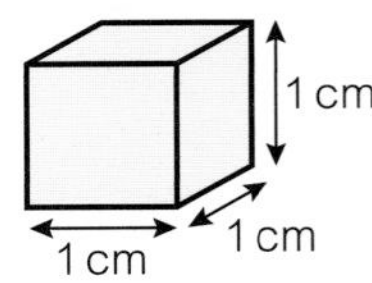

Work out the volume of these cubes made from centimetre cubes.

a
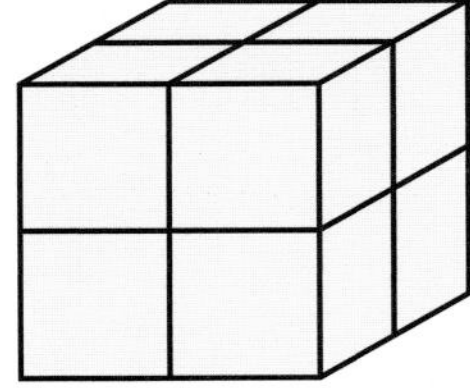

b
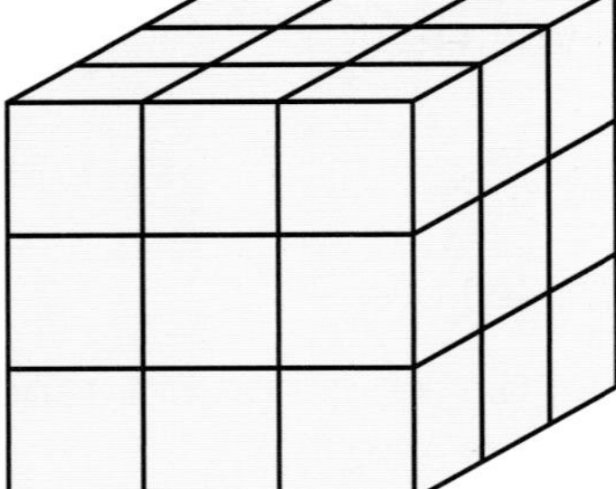

Key point
The **volume** of a solid shape is the amount of 3D space it takes up.
The units of volume are **cubic units** (e.g. mm³, cm³ or m³).

Key point
volume of a cube = (side length)³
which can be written as $V = l^3$

4 Work out the **volume of a cube** with these side lengths.
  a 5 cm b 4.2 cm
  c 12 mm d 3.5 m

Q4a hint
Use the x^3 or the y^x button on your calculator.

Topic links: Writing and using formulae, Using a calculator, Cube numbers

5 These cuboids are made from centimetre cubes.
Work out the volume of each cuboid.

a

b

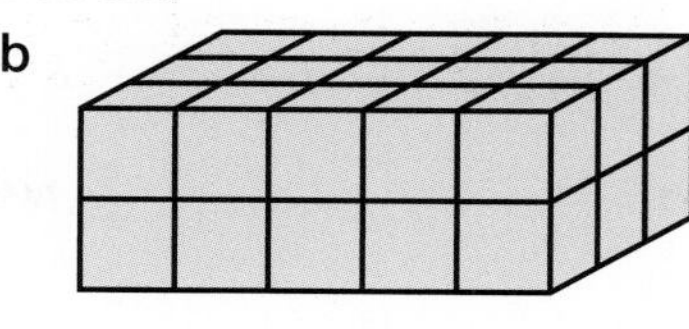

> **Q5a hint**
> Count the number of cubes on the top layer, then multiply by the number of layers.

6 This cuboid has length (l), width (w) and height (h).

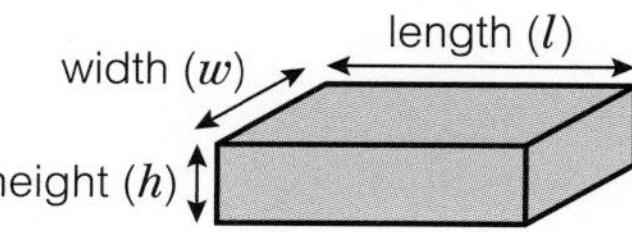

Complete these formulae.

a area of top = length × □

b volume = area of top × □ = length × □ × □

> **Key point**
> 
> **volume of a cuboid**
> = length × width × height
> which can be written as $V = lwh$

7 Find the volume of each cuboid.

a

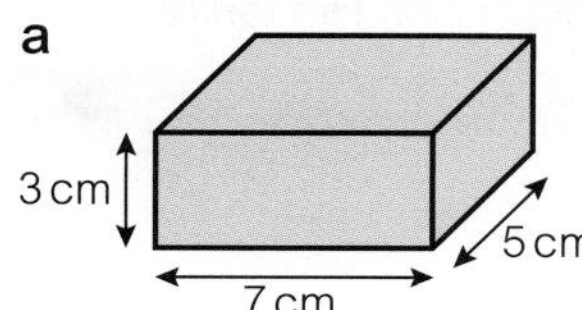

b

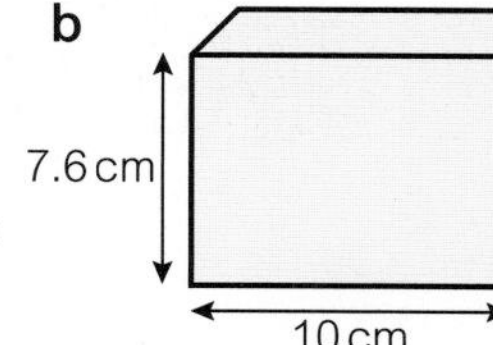

c

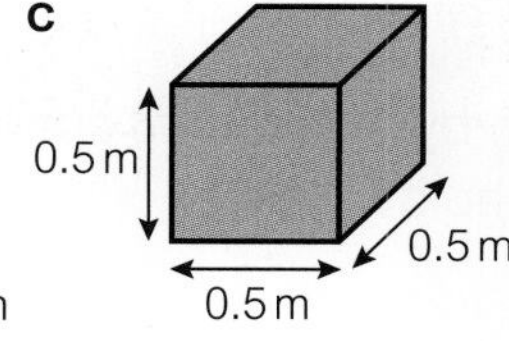

Discussion Is a cube a cuboid?

> **Q7a hint**
> 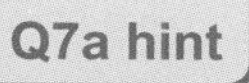
> $V = lwh$
> $= 7 \times 5 \times 3 = \square\ \text{cm}^3$

8 **Modelling** A lake is estimated to be about 1.5 km long, 200 m wide and 25 m deep.

a Work out an estimate of the volume of water in the lake, by modelling the lake as a cuboid.
Give your answer in cubic metres.

b Do you think a cuboid is a good model for a lake?
Explain your answer.

> **Q8 hint**
> Change 1.5 km to metres.

9 **a** Find the volume of cube A and cuboid B.

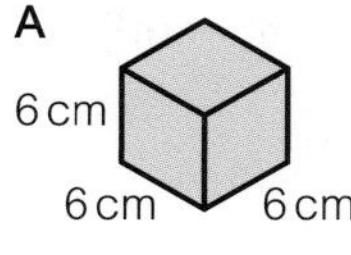

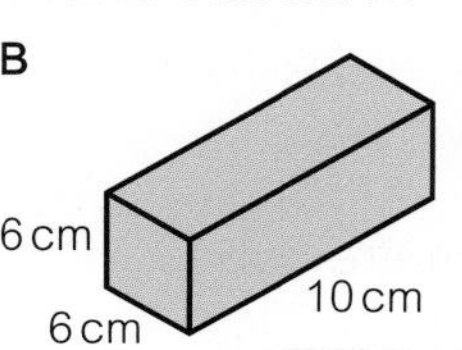

These composite shapes are made using A and B.

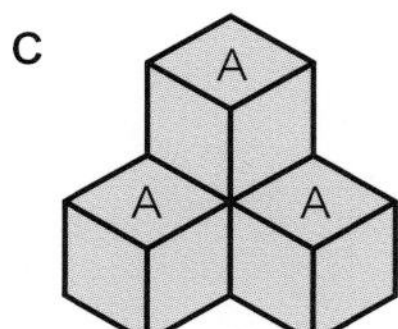

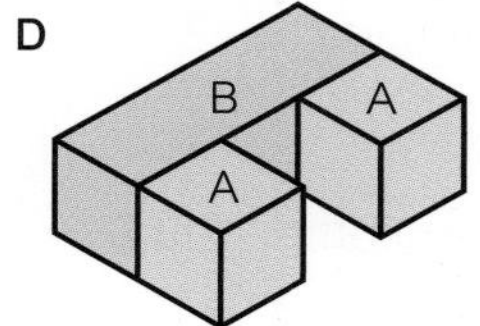

b Find the volume of each composite shape.

10 Find the volume of this shape.

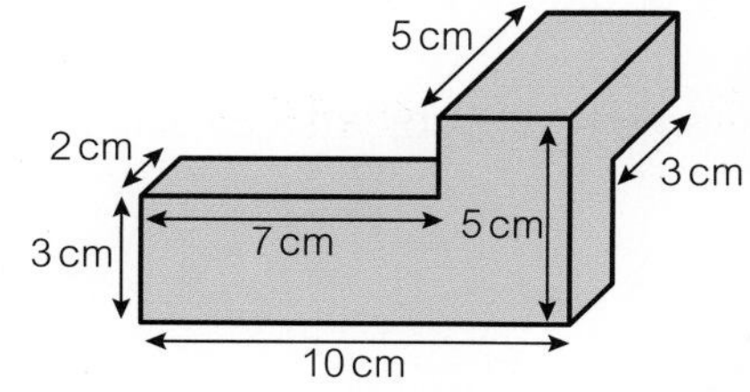

> **Q10 hint**
> Split the shape into two cuboids.

11 **Problem-solving** The diagram shows the dimensions of a water tank.

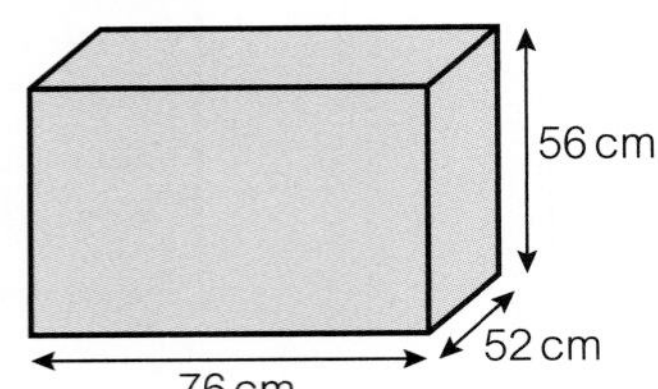

Alex puts water in the tank so that it is three quarters full.
What volume of water is in the tank?

Discussion In how many different ways can you work out the volume of a water tank that is three quarters full?

12 **Problem-solving** The diagram shows the dimensions of a dice.

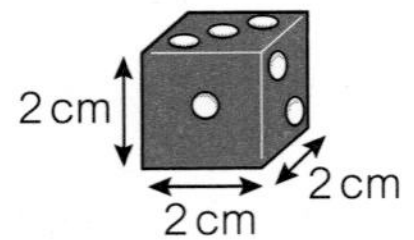

A box has dimensions 12 cm by 10 cm by 8 cm.
How many dice will the box hold?

Q12 hint

Start by working out how many dice will fit along the length of the box.

Investigation **Problem-solving**

Each box of Archie's Sweets contains 50 cm^3 of sweets, plus about 10% air.
Here are three designs for the box.

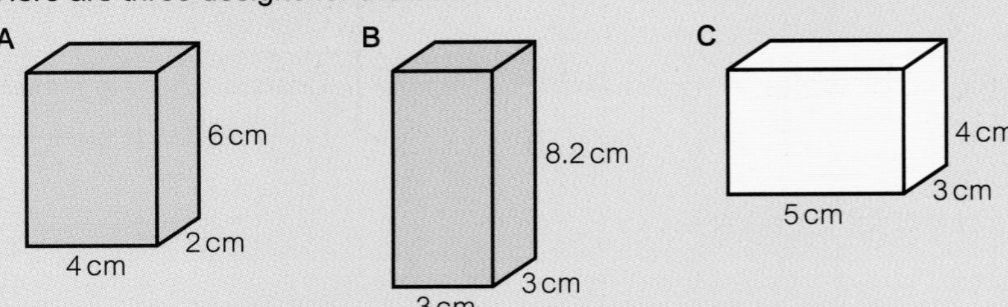

1 Which design is the most suitable? Why?
2 Work out the side length, to one decimal place, of a cube-shaped box that has the correct volume.
3 Work out the dimensions of two more boxes with the correct volume.

Explore

13 **Explore** How many fish can you keep healthily in a fish tank?
Is it easier to explore this question now you have completed the lesson?
What further information do you need to be able to answer this?

Reflect

14 **Reflect** Maths is not the only subject where you use volume. You use it in science too.
Describe when you have used volume in science.
In which ways is volume the same or different in science and in this maths lesson?
Do you think volume means the same in all subjects? Explain.

ActiveLearn Theta 2, Section 2.3

2.4 3D shapes

You will learn to:

- Sketch nets of 3D solids
- Use 2D representations of 3D solids.

Why learn this?
Packaging designers design nets to make up boxes to the shapes they want.

Fluency
Accurately draw these shapes.

- A square of side length 4 cm.
- A rectangle 7 cm by 3 cm.

Explore
Does every 3D shape have a net?

Exercise 2.4

1 Match the 3D shape to its correct name.

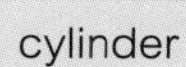

sphere | cuboid | triangular prism | triangle-based pyramid | cylinder | cube | square-based pyramid

A 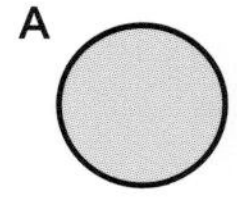 B 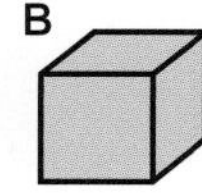 C 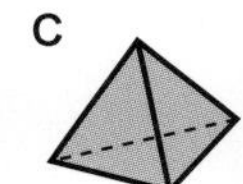 D 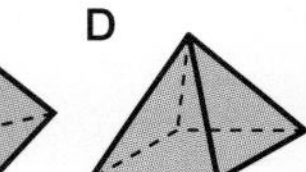 E 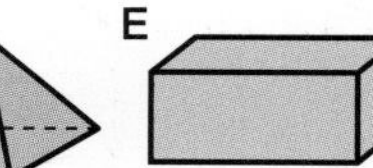 F 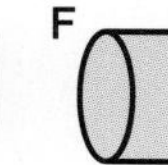 G 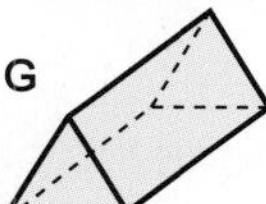

2 A cuboid has six faces that are rectangles. Describe the faces of these solids.

a 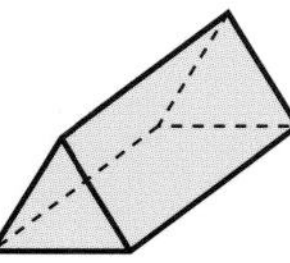

b 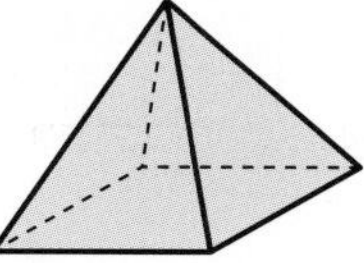

3 What 3D solid will each of these **nets** make?

a 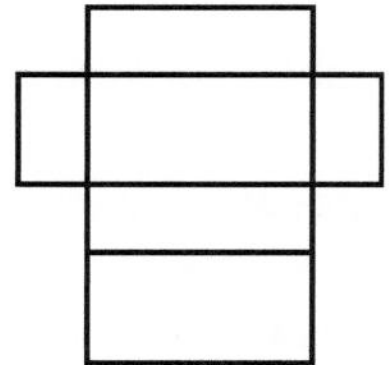

b 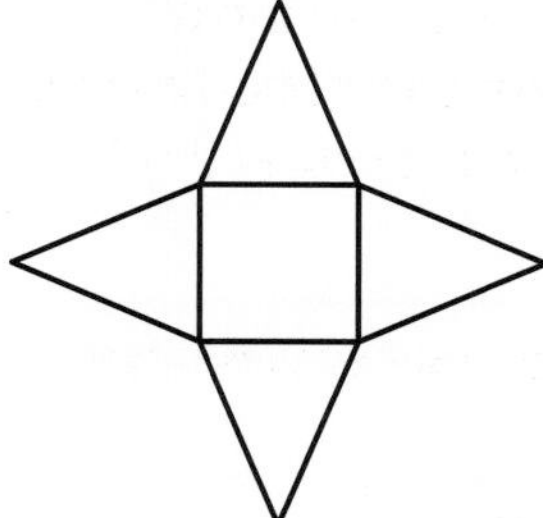

Key point
A **net** is a 2D shape that folds to make a 3D solid.

4 **Reasoning** Decide which of these are nets of a square-based pyramid. Give a reason for each of your answers.

A 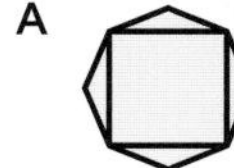 B 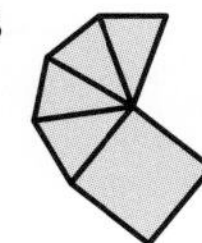 C 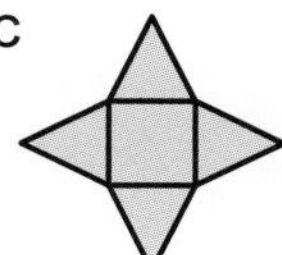 D  E 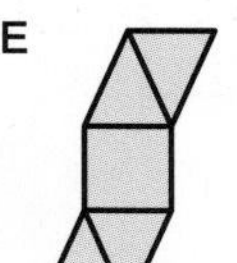 F 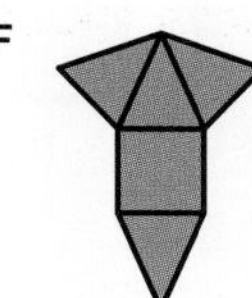

5 Sketch a net for each of these solids. Label the lengths.

a
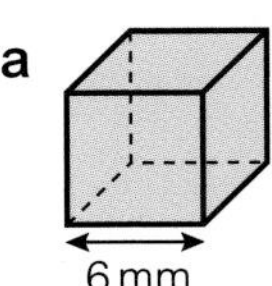

b
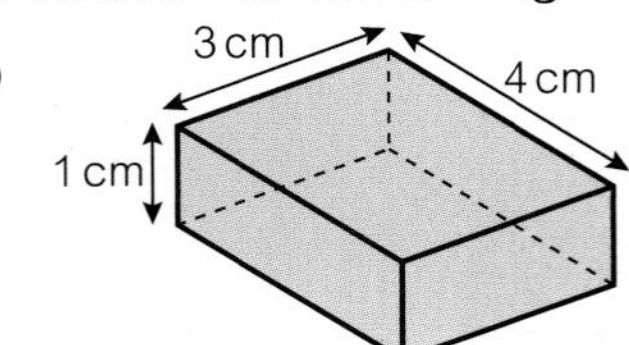

c
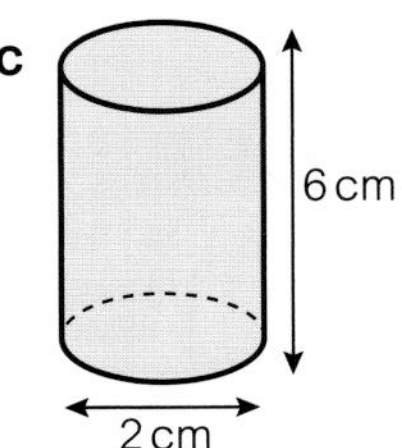

d
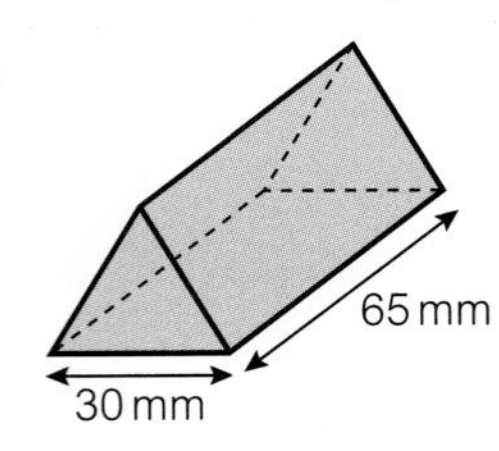

6 **Real / Problem-solving** Make a net for this dice.

Q6 hint

The numbers on opposite faces of a dice add up to 7.

7 Here are two views of the same cuboid.
The second is drawn on isometric paper.

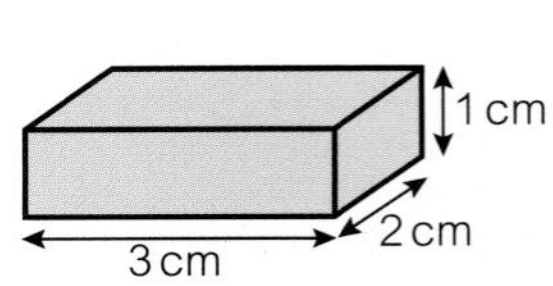

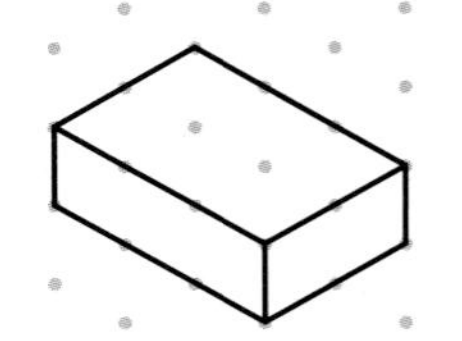

Q7 hint

The distance between two dots is 1 cm. Use a ruler.

Draw these shapes on isometric paper.

a
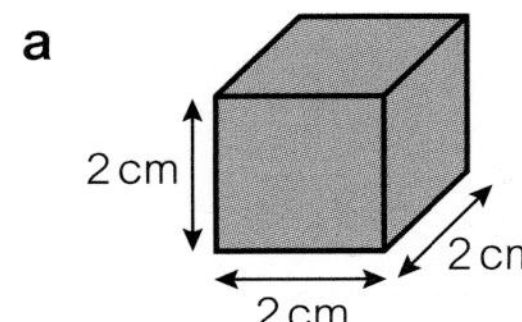

b
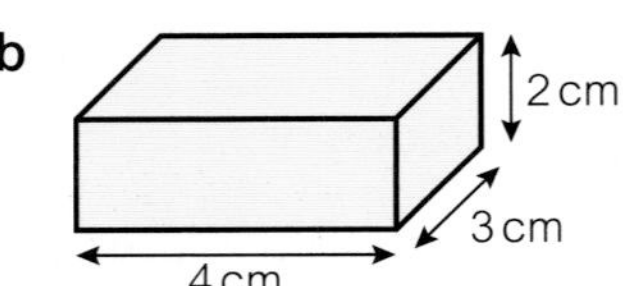

c
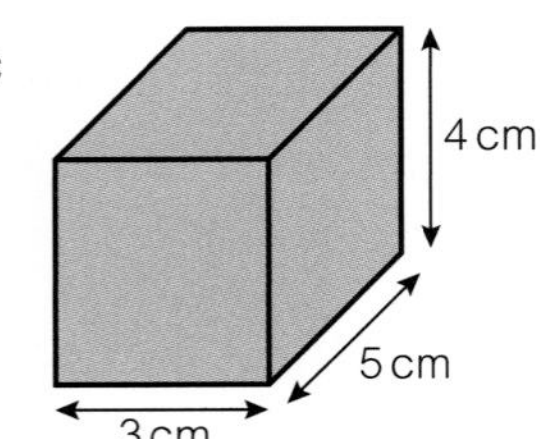

Worked example

Draw the **plan**, the **front elevation** and the **side elevation** of this cuboid on squared paper.

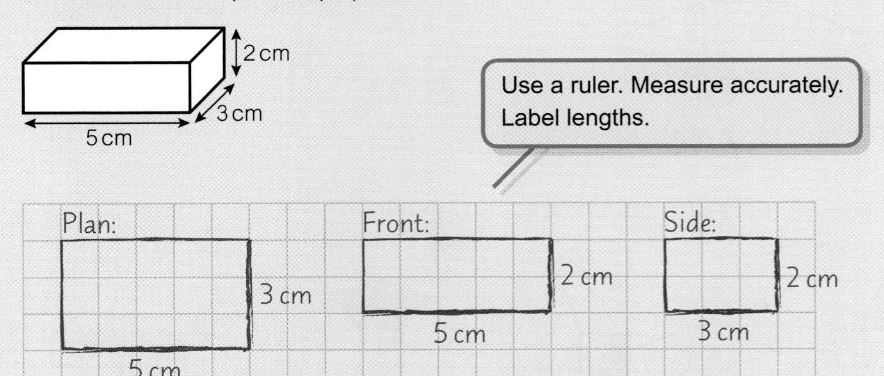

Key point

The **plan** is the view from above the object.
The **front elevation** is the view of the front of the object.
The **side elevation** is the view of the side of the object.

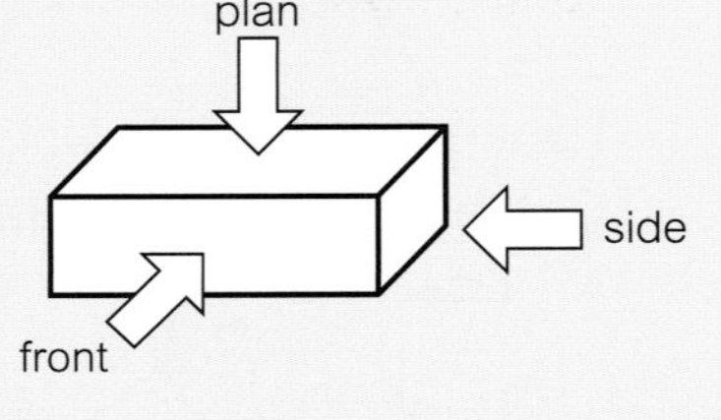

Topic links:

Subject links: Design and Technology (Q11)

8 Draw the plan, the front elevation and the side elevation of these cuboids on squared paper.

a

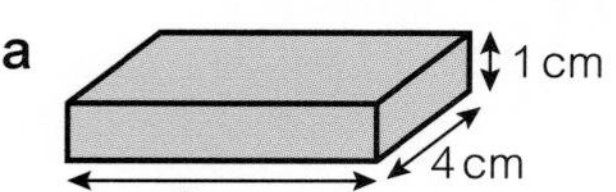

b

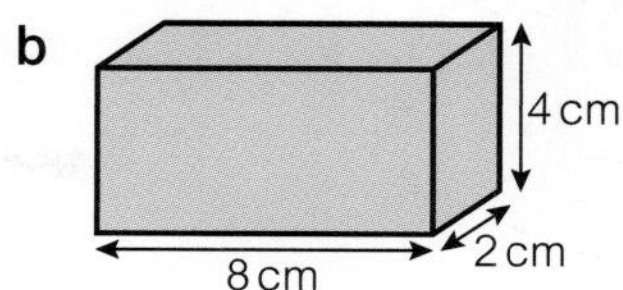

c

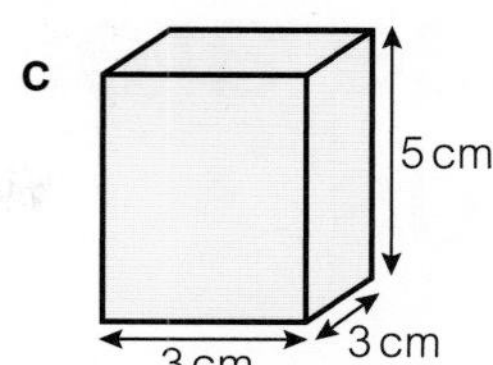

9 Here are the plan views of some solids.
What solid could each one be?

a

b

c

d

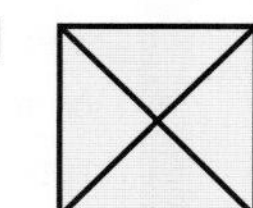

Investigation

Reasoning

1 Record the number of faces, vertices and edges for each 3D shape in the table.

Shape	Faces	Vertices	Edges
Cube			
Triangle-based pyramid			
Square-based pyramid			
Triangular prism			

2 Describe the link between the number of faces, vertices and edges of each shape.

3 Write a formula connecting the number of faces (F), vertices (V) and edges (E).

Part 2 hint

Add together the number of faces and vertices and compare with the number of edges.

4 Check that your formula works for a hexagonal prism.

5 Does your formula work for shapes with curved surfaces such as a cylinder and sphere? Explain your answer.

Part 4 hint

Draw a hexagonal prism. Count the number of faces, vertices and edges.

10 **Explore** Does every 3D shape have a net?
Look back at the maths you have learned in this lesson. How can you use it to answer this question?

11 **Reflect** In this lesson you have learned about nets.
Sketch all the nets that a tea bag manufacturer might use.
Beside each one, explain

a what the net is for

b the advantages and disadvantages of using this shape.

Explore

Reflect

2.5 Surface area of cubes and cuboids

You will learn to:
- Calculate the surface area of cubes and cuboids.

CONFIDENCE

Why learn this?
Bakers work out the surface area of their cakes to decide how much icing they need.

Fluency
Which of these nets will fold to make a closed cube?

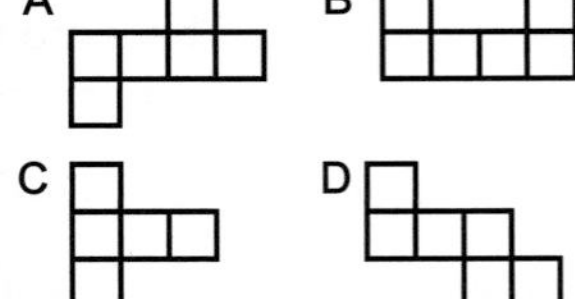

Explore
What size piece of card do you need to make a box for an Easter egg?

Exercise 2.5

Warm up

1 Work out the area of each shape.

a
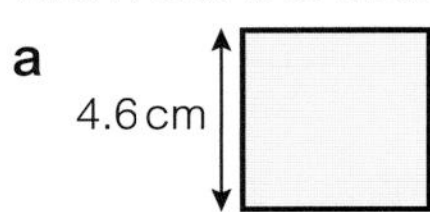

b
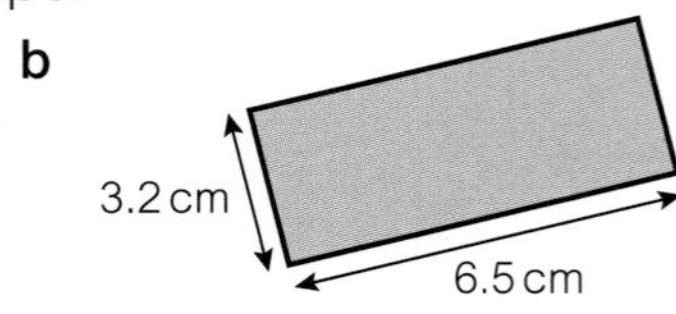

2 The diagram shows a cuboid with the edges labelled A to L.
Write down
- a two edges that meet at a vertex
- b a pair of parallel edges
- c two edges that do not meet and are perpendicular to each other
- d three edges that do not meet.

3 The diagram shows the net of a cube.
Work out
- a the area of one face of the cube
- b the **surface area** of the cube.

8 cm

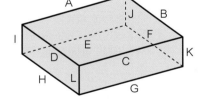

Key point
The **surface area** of a 3D shape is the total area of all its faces.
You can draw a net to help you find the surface area.

4 A cardboard box is in the shape of an open cube with sides of length 20 cm.
By sketching a net, work out the area of cardboard used in the box.

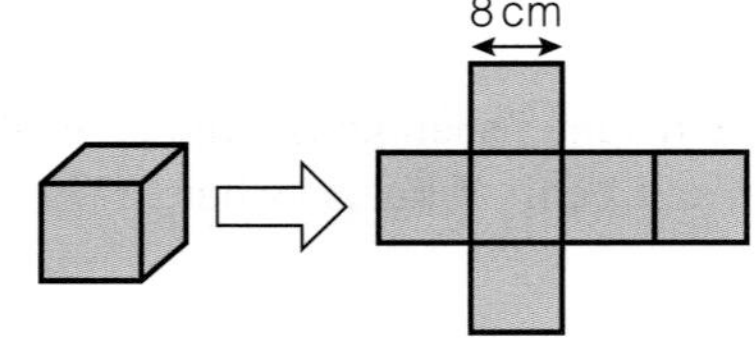

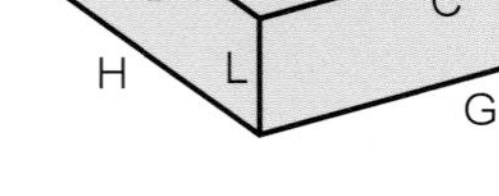

Q4 Literacy hint
An open cube does not have a top.

5 Here is a cuboid with length 5 cm, width 6 cm and height 3 cm.
- a Sketch a net of the cuboid.
- b Label each face with its area.
- c Find the surface area of the cuboid.

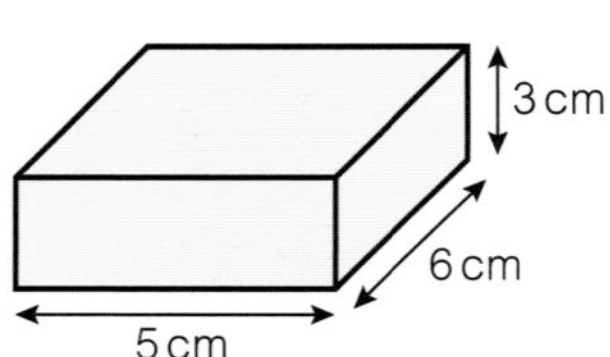

Q5c hint
Add together the areas of all the faces.

Topic links: Expressions and formulae, Estimation

Subject links: Design and Technology (Q8)

6 This cube has side length x.
Write an expression for

a the area of one face of the cube

b the surface area of the cube.

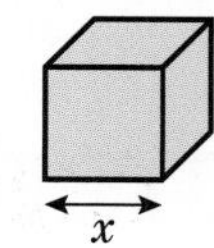

Discussion How can you change your answer to Q6 part **b** into a formula for the surface area of a cube?

Q6a hint
Write $x \times x$ in its simplest form.

Worked example

Calculate the surface area of this cuboid.

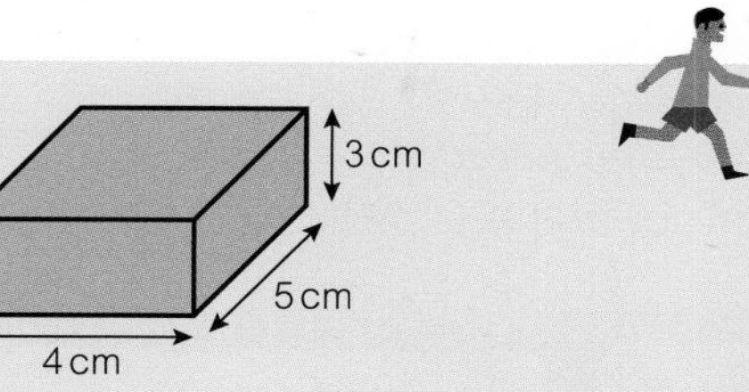

$$\begin{aligned}\text{surface area} &= 2(4 \times 5) + 2(4 \times 3) + 2(5 \times 3)\\ &= 2 \times 20 + 2 \times 12 + 2 \times 15\\ &= 40 + 24 + 30\\ &= 94\,\text{cm}^2\end{aligned}$$

There are two of each size face: top and bottom, front and back, left and right sides.

7 Calculate the surface area of each cuboid.

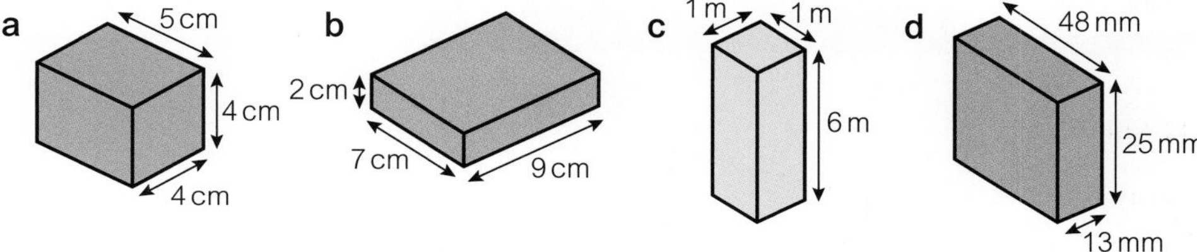

8 **STEM** A new building will be 65 m long, 40 m wide and 220 m high.
It will be covered in glass panels on all four sides, but not the roof.

a Work out the surface area of glass needed.

The glass panels cost £128 per square metre.

b Work out the cost of the glass panels for this building. Show how to check your answer using estimation.

9 **Problem-solving** A cuboid has a length of 3.6 m and a width of 2.5 m.
Its volume is 37.8 m³. Work out the surface area of the cuboid.

Q9 hint
Use the volume to work out the height of the cuboid first.

Investigation

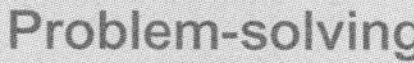

The width of a cuboid is twice its height. Its length is three times its height.
The surface area of the cuboid is 352 cm². What is its height?

10 **Explore** What size piece of card do you need to make a box for an Easter egg?
What have you learned in this lesson to help you answer this question?
What other information do you need?

11 **Reflect** This lesson showed you two methods for finding the surface area of a cube or cuboid.

Method 1: draw then add
Draw a net, write the area of each face on the net, add them together (Q5).

Method 2: visualise then calculate
Visualise pairs of opposite faces, calculate 2 × area of face for each pair, add them together (Q7).

Which method did you prefer? Why?

Q11 hint
What are the advantages and disadvantages of your method?

Explore

Reflect

2.6 Problems and measures

You will learn to:
- Solve problems in everyday contexts involving measures
- Convert between different measures for area, volume and capacity
- Use tonnes and hectares
- Correctly enter metric measures on a calculator
- Know rough metric equivalents of imperial measures.

CONFIDENCE

Why learn this
You can use volume calculations to find out how much water is needed to fill a swimming pool.

Fluency
Work out the area of a square with a side length of
- 1 m
- 100 cm
- 1 cm
- 10 mm

Explore
How many times will a water trough need to be refilled every day for a herd of cows?

Exercise 2.6

Warm up

1 Complete the missing values.
  a 1 m = □ cm **b** 1 km = □ m **c** 1 kg = □ g

2 Complete the missing values.
  a 650 cm = □ m **b** 4500 ml = □ l **c** 0.8 kg = □ g

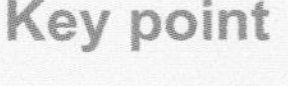
Key point

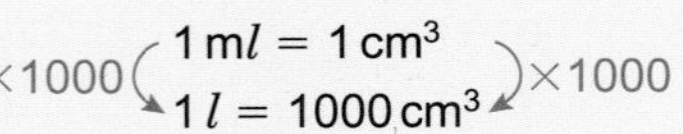

3 **Problem-solving** A medicine bottle says, 'Take two 5 ml spoonfuls four times a day.'
The bottle contains 0.15 litres. Sara has to take the medicine for 4 days.
Is there enough medicine in the bottle? Explain your answer.

4 Work out these conversions.
  a 2 litres = □ cm^3 **b** 3.5 litres = □ cm^3
  c 4200 cm^3 = □ litres **d** 750 cm^3 = □ litres

Q4a hint
×2 (1 l = 1000 cm^3 ; 2 l =) ×2

5 The mass of a new-born elephant is 4% of the mass of an adult female elephant.
The average mass of an adult female elephant is 3 **tonnes**.
What is the average mass in kilograms of a new-born elephant?

Key point
mass: 1 **tonne** (t) = 1000 kg

6 Joe is using his calculator to solve some problems. Which value, A, B or C, should he enter for each measure?

a 2 m 4 cm (in metres)	**A** 2.4	**B** 2.04	**C** 2.004
b 5 kg 250 g (in kilograms)	**A** 5.25	**B** 5.025	**C** 5.0025
c 950 ml (in litres)	**A** 9.5	**B** 0.95	**C** 0.095

7 An Olympic swimming pool has a length of 50 m, a width of 25 m and a depth of 2 m.
  a Write the dimensions of the pool in centimetres.
  b Work out the **capacity** of the pool in litres.

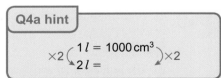

Q7b hint
$V = lbh$

8 **Reasoning** **a** A square measures 1 cm by 1 cm. What is its area?
b Another square measures 10 mm by 10 mm. What is its area?
c Look at your answers to parts **a** and **b**.
Complete this statement: $1\,cm^2 = \square\,mm^2$
d Complete this statement: $1\,m^2 = \square\,cm^2$

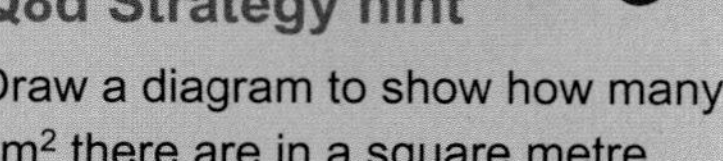

Q8d Strategy hint
Draw a diagram to show how many cm^2 there are in a square metre.

9 Complete these area conversions.
a $8\,cm^2 = 8 \times \square = \square\,mm^2$
b $9.5\,m^2 = 9.5 \times \square = \square\,cm^2$
c $700\,mm^2 = 700 \div \square = \square\,cm^2$
d $940\,mm^2 = 940 \div \square = \square\,cm^2$
e $30\,000\,cm^2 = \square \div \square = \square\,m^2$
f $420\,000\,cm^2 = \square \div \square = \square\,m^2$

Key point
$1\,cm^2 = 100\,mm^2$
$1\,m^2 = 10\,000\,cm^2$

10 **Reasoning** The diagram shows a plot of land.
a Work out the area of the plot in m^2.
Heidi works out that the area of the plot is 32.5 **hectares**.
b Is she correct? Explain your answer.

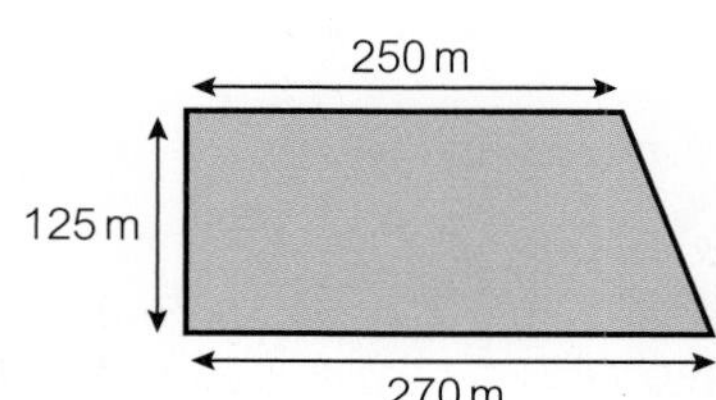

Key point
area: 1 **hectare** (ha) = $10\,000\,m^2$

11 Complete these metric/imperial conversions.
a 8 **gallons** = □ litres
b 7 **lbs** (**pounds**) = □ kg
c 4 litres = □ **pints**
d 15 litres = □ gallons
e 6 kg = □ lbs
f 8 pints = □ litres

Q11a hint
×8 (1 gallon = 4.5 litres) ×8
1 gallon = □ litres

Key point
You need to know these conversions between metric and imperial units.
1 **foot (ft)** ≈ 30 cm
1 **mile** ≈ 1.6 km
1 kg ≈ 2.2 **pounds (lb)**
1 litre ≈ 1.75 **pints**
1 **gallon** ≈ 4.5 litres

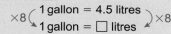

12 **Real** Visitors to a theme park must be taller than 1.4 m to go on a certain ride. Gemma is 5 **feet** tall.
Is she tall enough to go on the ride? Explain your answer.

13 **STEM** The distance from the Earth to the Sun is approximately 93 000 000 **miles**.
The distance from Mars to the Sun is approximately 227 000 000 km.
Which is closer to the Sun: Earth or Mars?

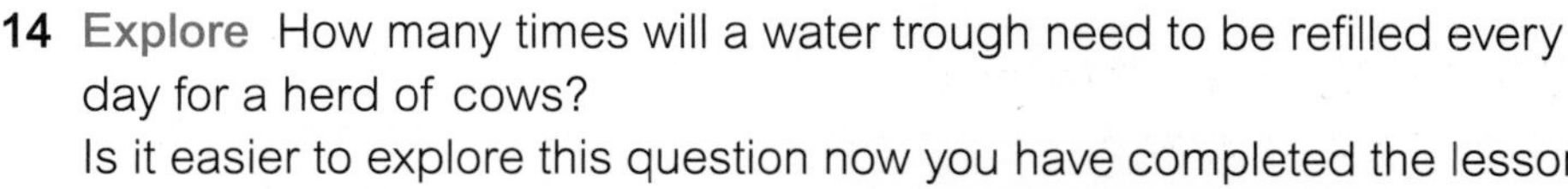

14 **Explore** How many times will a water trough need to be refilled every day for a herd of cows?
Is it easier to explore this question now you have completed the lesson?
What further information do you need to be able to answer this?

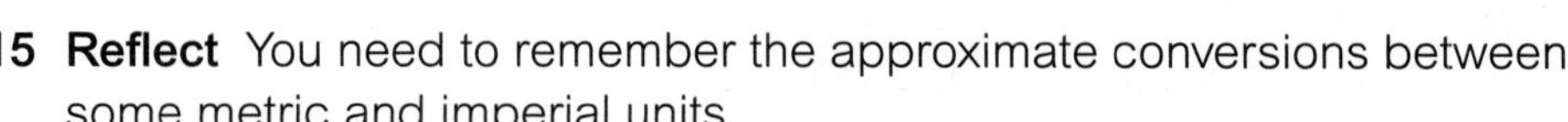

15 **Reflect** You need to remember the approximate conversions between some metric and imperial units.
Dee says, 'For feet, I remember that my ruler is 1 foot long and I know that is about 30 cm.'
Look at the other metric and imperial conversions in this lesson.
Write down a way to help you remember each of them.

Q15 hint
Use an object (like Dee), a rhyme, draw yourself a picture, make up a sentence or think of another way.

Explore

Reflect

2 Check up

Log how you did on your Student Progression Chart.

Areas of shapes

1 Work out the area of each triangle.

a

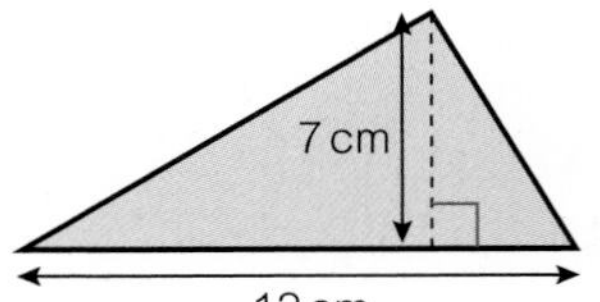

b

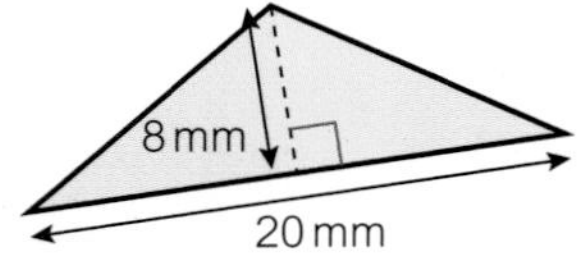

c

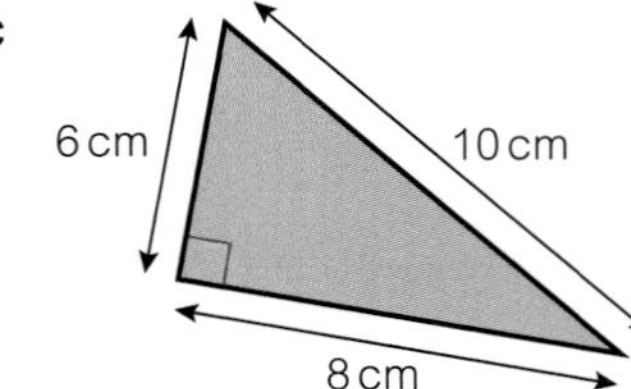

2 This triangle has a height of 4 cm and an area of 16 cm^2.
Ellen says, 'The base of the triangle is 4 cm because $4 \times 4 = 16$.'
Is she correct? Explain your answer.

3 The diagram shows the dimensions of a badge.
What is the total area of the badge?

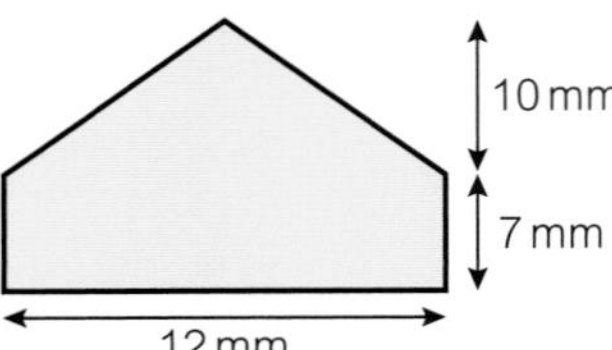

4 Work out the area of this parallelogram.

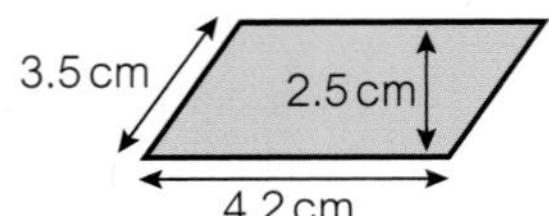

5 Use the formula $A = \frac{1}{2}(a + b)h$ to work out the area of this trapezium.

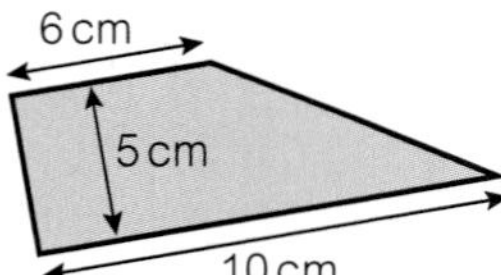

6 Ade works out the area of this trapezium.
This is what he writes.

area $= \frac{1}{2} \times 9 + 13 \times 8$
$= 4.5 + 104$
$= 108.5 \text{ m}^2$

13 m
8 m
9 m

a Explain the mistake that he has made.
b Work out the correct area.

Surface area and volume

7 Here is a cuboid with length 4 cm, width 8 cm and height 2 cm.
a Sketch a net of the cuboid.
b Write on it the area of each face.
c Find the surface area of the cuboid.

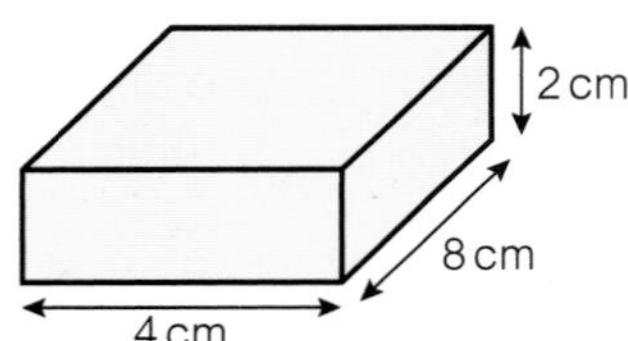

8 Work out the surface area of this cube.

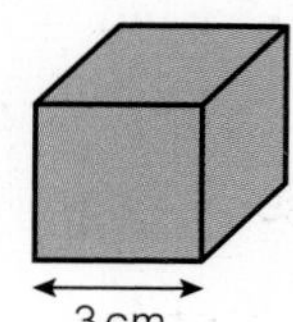

9 An open cardboard box has length 32 cm, width 12.5 cm and height 16.5 cm.
Work out the area of cardboard needed to make the open box.

10 Work out the volume of this cube.

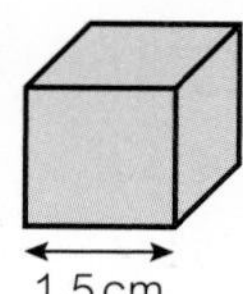

11 A biscuit tin is a cuboid of length 18 cm, width 9 cm and height 6 cm.
What is the volume of the tin?

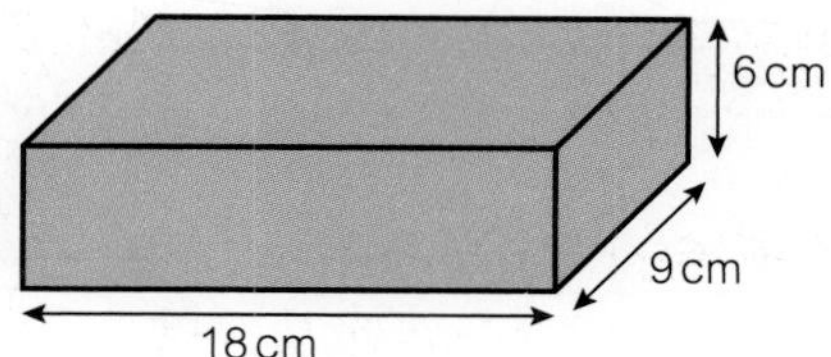

12 A cube has a side length of 15 cm.
How many cubes will fit into a box that measures 75 cm by 60 cm by 30 cm?

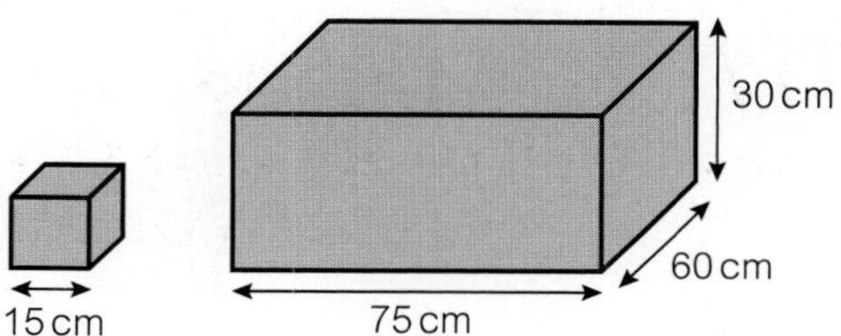

Metric and imperial measures

13 Work out these conversions.

a 5 litres = □ cm^3

b 2.7 litres = □ cm^3

c 3600 cm^3 = □ litres

d 240 cm^3 = □ litres

14 a A butcher receives an order for 10 pounds (lb) of beef mince.
Approximately how many kilograms is this?

b Sean runs 8 miles. How far is this in kilometres?

c Anna orders 900 litres of oil for her central heating oil tank.
How many gallons is this?

d One jelly mould holds 1.5 pints of jelly.
How much jelly is needed for six jelly moulds? Give your answer in litres.

e The central strip of a cricket field between the two wickets has a width of 10 feet.
What is its width in metres?

15 How sure are you of your answers? Were you mostly

☹ Just guessing 😐 Feeling doubtful 🙂 Confident

What next? Use your results to decide whether to strengthen or extend your learning.

Reflect

Challenge

16 Sketch a shape that fits each description. Write the measurements on each shape.

a A triangle with area 32 cm^2

b A parallelogram with area 32 cm^2

c A trapezium with area 32 cm^2.

2 Strengthen

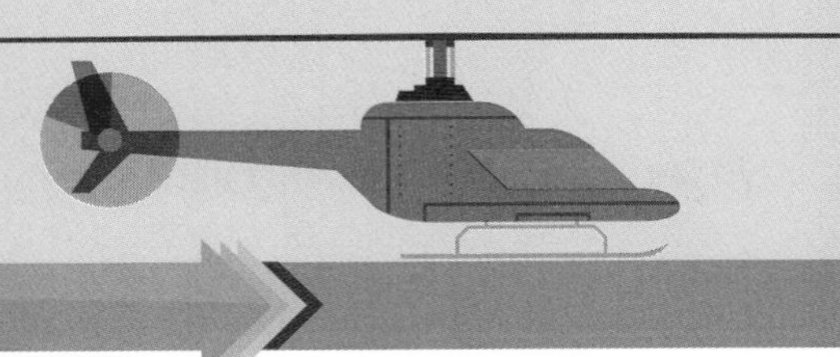

You will:

- Strengthen your understanding with practice.

Areas of shapes

1 For each triangle, write the base length and perpendicular height.

a 6 cm, 10 cm, 8 cm

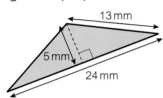

b 13 mm, 5 mm, 24 mm

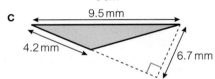

c 9.5 mm, 4.2 mm, 6.7 mm

> **Q1 hint**
> The base length and the perpendicular height must be at right angles (90°) to each other.

2 Use the formula

area of a triangle = $\frac{1}{2}$ × base length × perpendicular height

to work out the area of each triangle in Q1.

> **Q2 hint**
> For part **a**, area = $\frac{1}{2} \times b \times h$
> = $\frac{1}{2} \times 8 \times 6$
> = 4 × 6 = □ cm²

3 Work out the area of this shape.
The working has been started for you.

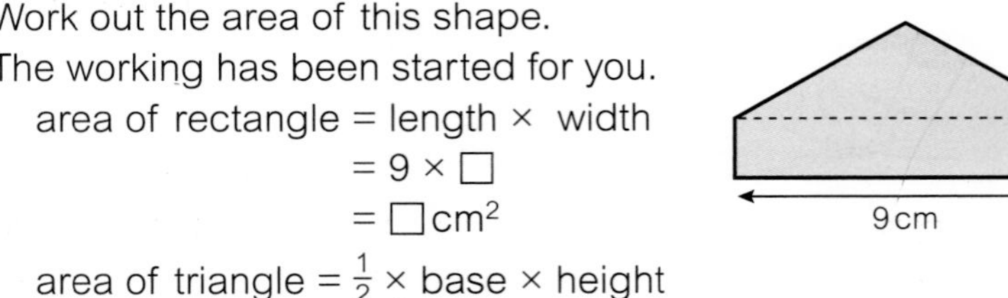

4 cm, 3 cm, 9 cm

area of rectangle = length × width
= 9 × □
= □ cm²

area of triangle = $\frac{1}{2}$ × base × height
= $\frac{1}{2}$ × 9 × □
= □ cm²

total area = area of rectangle + area of triangle
= □ + □
= □ cm²

4 Work out the area of each compound shape.

a

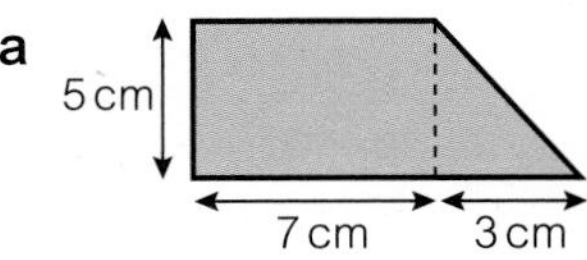

b

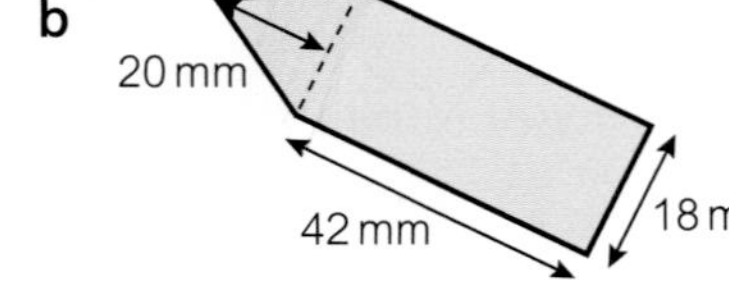

> **Q4a Strategy hint**
> Split the shape into a rectangle and a triangle.

5 Find the area of this parallelogram.
The working has been started for you.

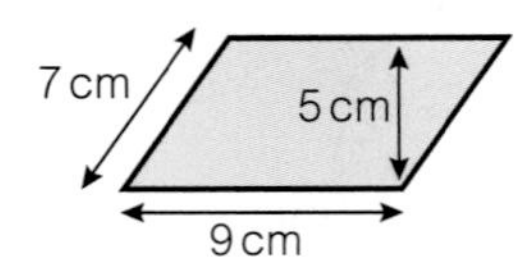

base length = □ cm
perpendicular height = □ cm
area = base × height
= □ × □
= □ cm²

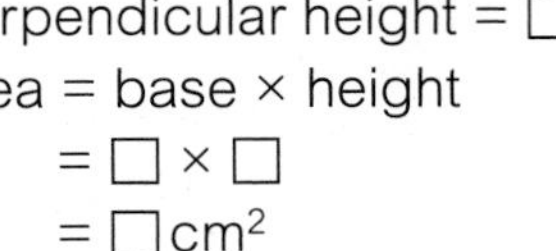

> **Q5 hint**
> How can you tell which is the perpendicular height?

6 Work out the area of each parallelogram.

a

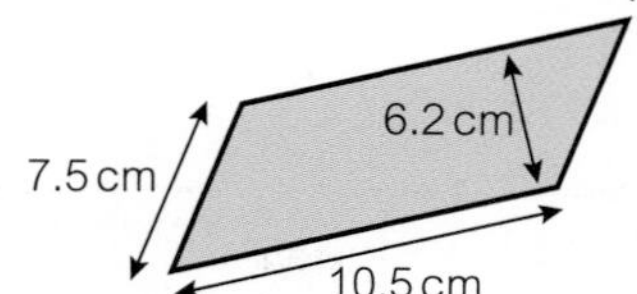

b

12 mm
9 mm
35 mm

7 a Look at these two identical trapezia.

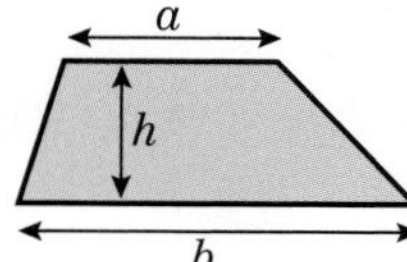

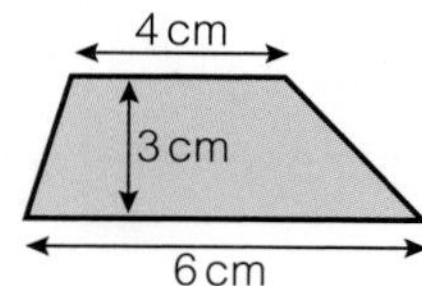

Copy and complete the following.

$a = 4$ cm, $b = \square$ cm, $h = \square$ cm

b Find the area of the trapezium. The working has been started for you.

$$\text{area} = \tfrac{1}{2}(a + b)h$$
$$= \tfrac{1}{2} \times (4 + 6) \times 3$$
$$= \tfrac{1}{2} \times \square \times 3$$
$$= \square \times 3$$
$$= \square\,\text{cm}^2$$

8 Work out the area of each trapezium.

a

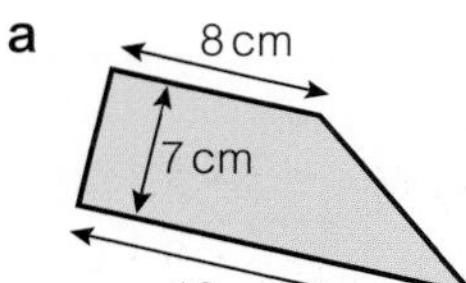

b

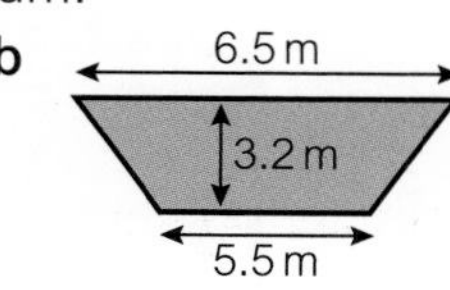

Surface area and volume

1 Which of these nets will fold to make a closed cube?

A

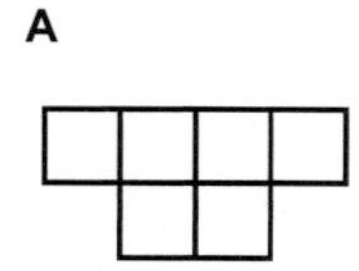

B

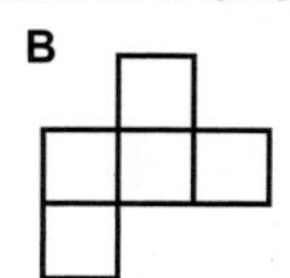

C

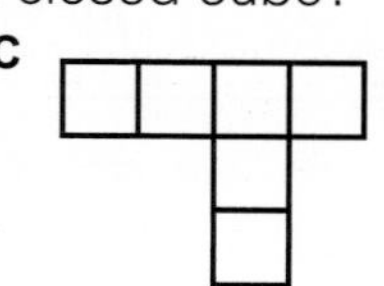

2 The diagram shows a cube of side length 7 cm.
Find the surface area of the cube.

area of one face = 7 × 7 = $\square$ cm^2

surface area of cube = $\square \times \square = \square$ cm^2

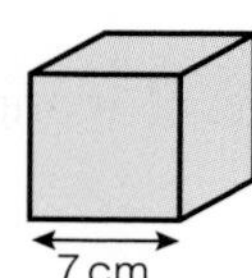

3 Calculate the surface area of a cube with side length 12 mm.

4 Find the surface area of this cuboid.
The working has been started for you.

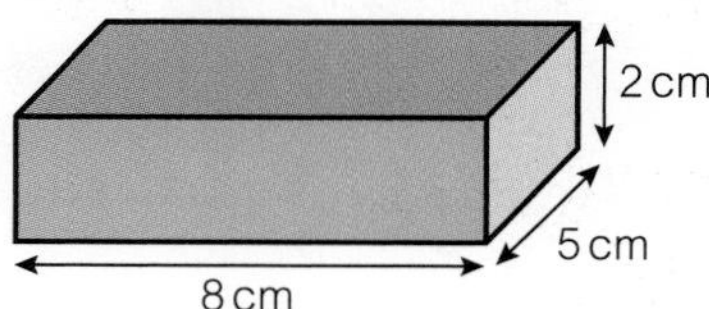

area of front face = 8 × 2 = **16** cm^2

area of right end face = 5 × 2 = **10** cm^2

area of top face = 8 × 5 = $\square$ cm^2

total surface area = **16** + **16** + **10** + **10** + $\square + \square = \square$ cm^2

Q6a hint

Write the base length and perpendicular height. Write the formula for the area. Substitute the numbers into the formula.

Q7 Literacy hint

Trapezia is the plural of trapezium.

Q8 Strategy hint

Write the values of a, b and h. Write the formula. Substitute the numbers into the formula.

Q8b hint

Enter the whole calculation into your calculator, by using the bracket buttons.

Q1 Strategy hint

Draw the shapes and cut them out. Try to fold each one into a cube.

Q2 hint

A cube has six identical faces, so the surface area of a cube = 6 × area of one face.

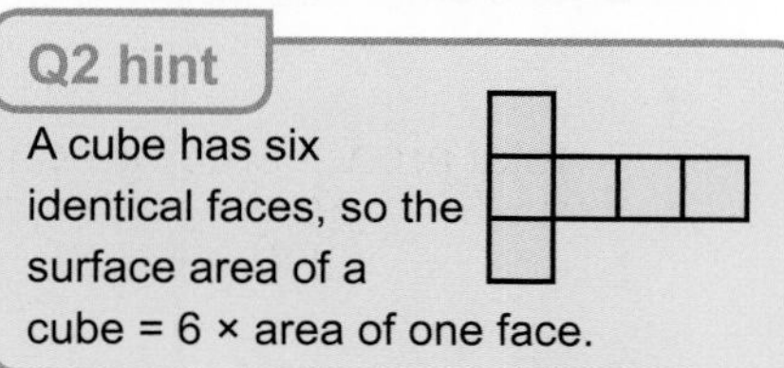

Q3 hint

Find the area of one face first. What units should you use?

Q4 hint

Start by working out the area of the front face, then the end face, then the top face.
Remember that altogether there are three sets of two congruent faces.

5 Work out the surface area of each cuboid.

a

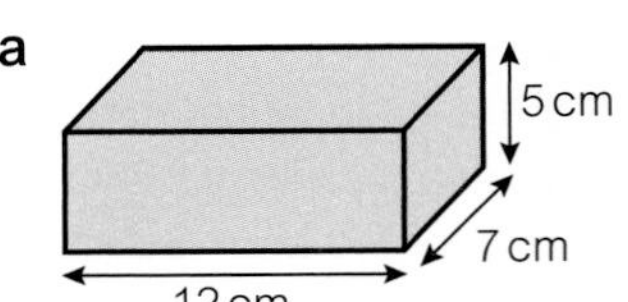

b

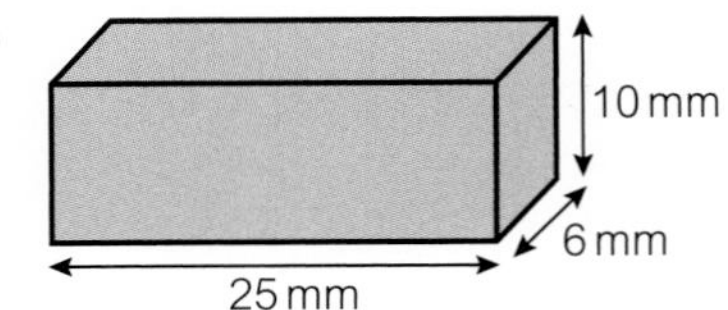

6 Work out the volume of each cuboid in Q5.

7 **Real / Problem-solving** A box holds 12 tins of baked beans as shown.

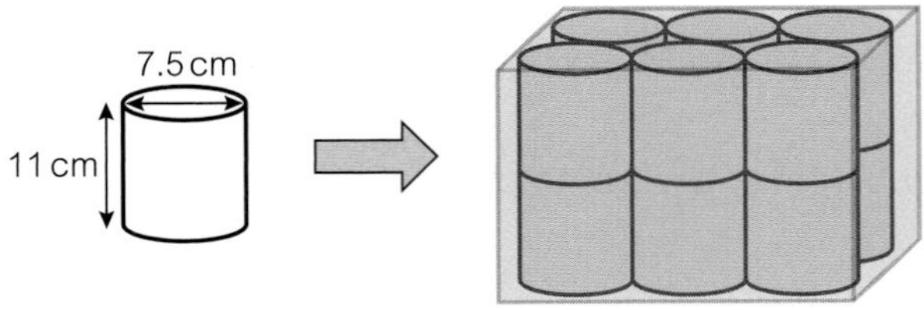

a Work out the surface area of cardboard needed to make the box.

b What is the volume of the box?

Q6 hint

Volume = length × width × height
$= l \times w \times h$
Write down the values of l, w and h. Substitute the numbers into the formula.

Q7 hint

Use the dimensions of the tin to work out the length, width and height of the box, then work out the surface area of the box.

Metric and imperial measures

1 Work out these conversions.

a 3 litres = □ cm^3

b 7 litres = □ cm^3

c 4000 cm^3 = □ litres

d 9000 cm^3 = □ litres

Q1a hint

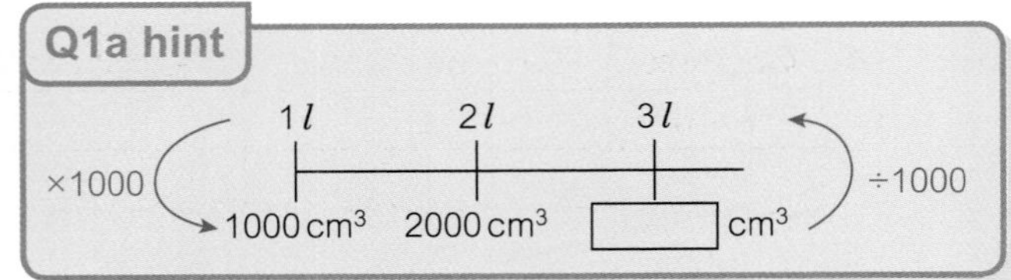

2 Work out these conversions.

a 4.5 litres = □ cm^3

b 8.7 litres = □ cm^3

c 2600 cm^3 = □ litres

d 840 cm^3 = □ litres

Q2a hint

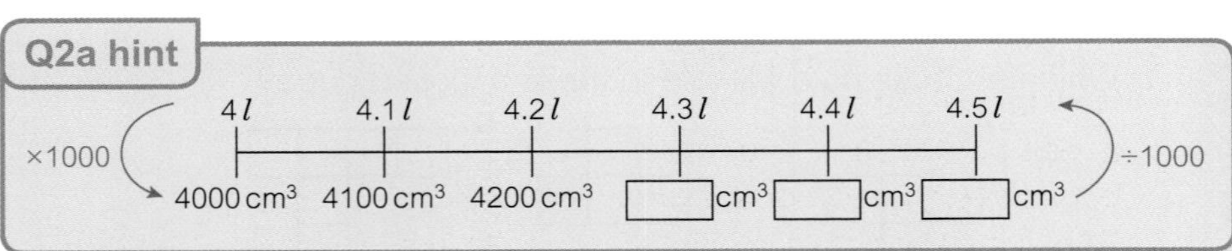

3 Work out these conversions.

a 3 feet ≈ □ cm

b 600 cm ≈ □ feet

c 2.5 feet ≈ □ cm

d 4 litres ≈ □ pints

e 7 pints ≈ □ litres

f 22.5 litres ≈ □ gallons

g 6.2 gallons ≈ □ litres

Q3a hint

÷30 cm 30 60 90 cm ×30
feet 1 2 3 feet

Q3b–g hint

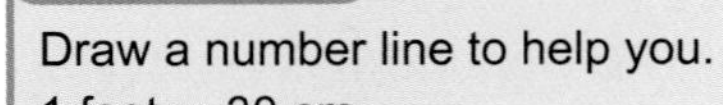

Draw a number line to help you.
1 foot ≈ 30 cm
1 litre ≈ 1.75 pints
1 gallon ≈ 4.5 litres

4 Work out these conversions.

a 7.2 miles ≈ □ km

b 22.4 km ≈ □ miles

c 11 pounds ≈ □ kg

d 7.2 kg ≈ □ lb

Q4 hint

Draw a number line to help you.
1 mile ≈ 1.6 km
1 kg ≈ 2.2 lb

Enrichment

1 **Problem-solving** Work with a partner to answer these questions.

a The diagram shows a white square and 4 yellow triangles on a 3 by 3 square grid.

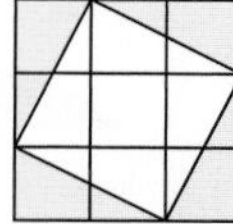

i Work out the area of the square grid.

ii Work out the area of the triangles.

iii Work out the area of the white square by subtracting the area of the triangles from the area of the square grid.

b Repeat part **a** for these diagrams, and for two similar diagrams of your own.

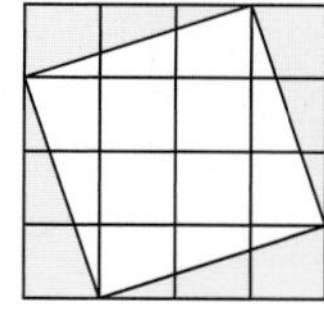

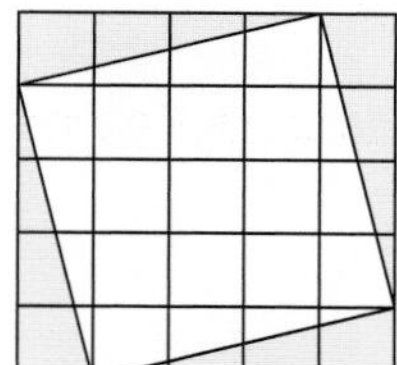

c Copy and complete this table to show all your results.

Grid size	Base of triangle	Height of triangle	Area of white square
3 × 3	2	1	

d What do you notice about the base and height of each triangle and the area of the white square?

2 **Real / Reasoning** An electric car travels 25 metres every second. How far will it travel in

a one minute (give your answer in metres)

b one hour (give your answer in kilometres)?

Ellie knows her electric car can travel 140 km before the battery runs out. She wants to make a journey of 90 miles.

c Will the car battery run out before she gets there? Explain your answer.

3 **Reflect** In this unit you have had to do lots of different things to find the answers to questions.

Write these in order, from the one you found easiest to the one you found hardest:

A Knowing which is the perpendicular height in a shape

B Using a formula to find the area of a shape

C Working out what the net of a 3D solid will look like

D Finding the surface area of a cuboid

E Knowing when to multiply and when to divide when converting measures.

Write a hint, in your own words, for the one you found the hardest.

2 Extend

You will:

- Extend your understanding with problem-solving.

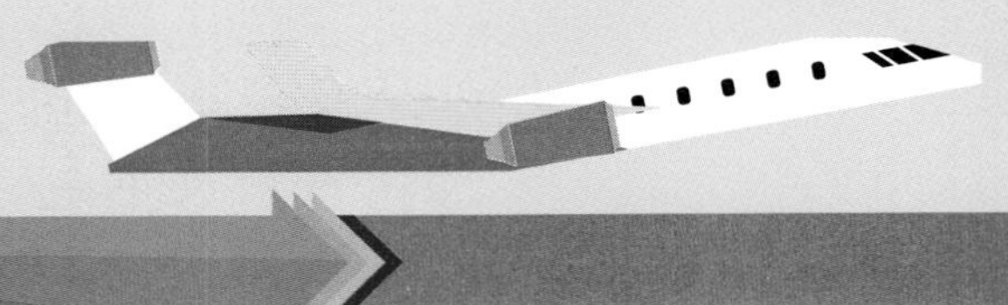

1 A cube has a total surface area of 8.64 cm^2. Work out
 a the area of one face of the cube
 b the side length of the cube.

Q1a hint
A cube has six identical faces.

2 **Problem-solving** The diagram shows two cubes.
The side length of the larger cube is 4 cm.

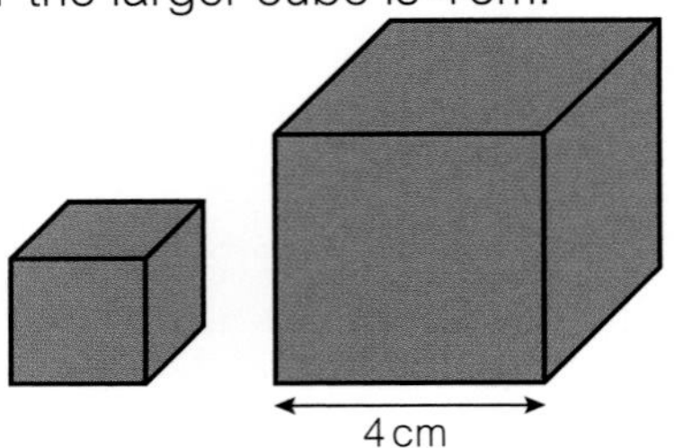

The ratio of their surface areas is 1 : 4.
Work out
 a the surface area of the smaller cube
 b the side length of the smaller cube.

Q2a Strategy hint
Work out the surface area of the larger cube first.

3 **Problem-solving** A red cuboid has length 6 cm, width 3 cm and height 2 cm.
A blue cuboid has length 8 cm and width 2 cm.
The red and blue cuboids have the same surface area.
Work out the height of the blue cuboid.

Q3 Strategy hint
Draw a sketch of each cuboid and label the missing height h. Then work out the surface area of the red cuboid.

4 **Problem-solving** The diagram shows a square company logo.
Work out the area of blue in the logo.

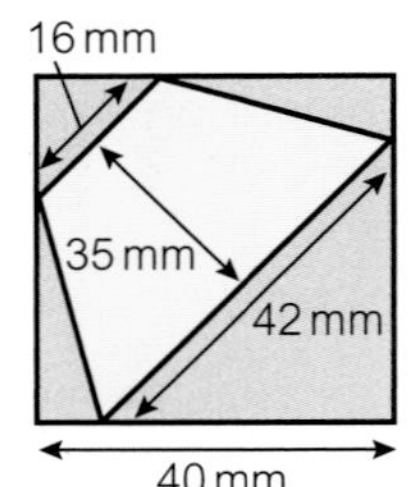

Q4 hint
Work out the area of the square and the area of the trapezium.

5 **Reasoning** The diagram shows a trapezium.
Dave says, 'If I double the height of the trapezium, the area of the trapezium will also double.'
Is he correct? Explain how you worked out your answer.

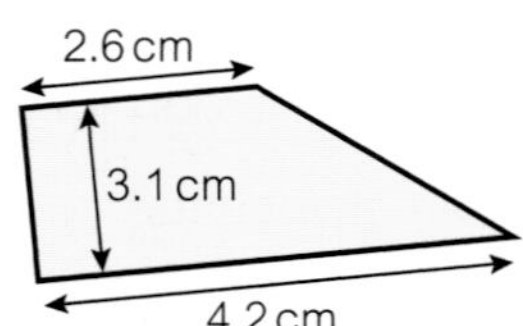

Q6 Literacy hint
A counter example is one example that proves the statement is wrong.

6 **Reasoning** Caroline says, 'If I double the length of one of the parallel sides of a trapezium, but keep the other parallel side and the height the same, the area of the trapezium will also be doubled.'
Show, using a counter example, that she is wrong.

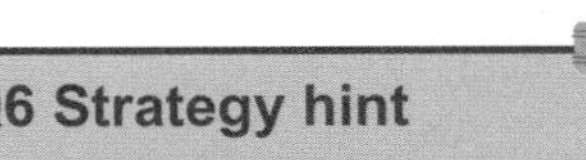

Q6 Strategy hint
Draw your own trapezium to test Caroline's statement.

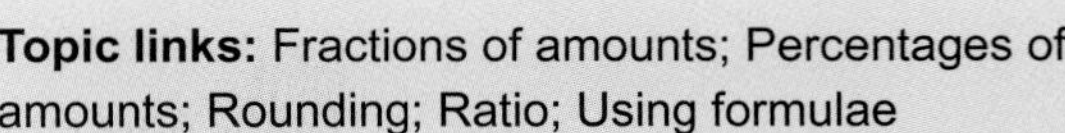

Topic links: Fractions of amounts; Percentages of amounts; Rounding; Ratio; Using formulae

Subject links: Science (Q17)

7 **Problem-solving** This trapezium and this parallelogram have the same area.

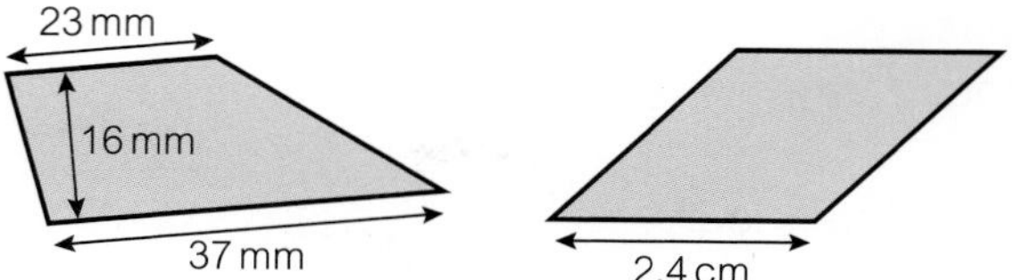

What is the perpendicular height of the parallelogram?

> **Q7 Strategy hint**
> Make sure all measurements are in the same units.

8 **Problem-solving** The diagram shows a foldaway camping bowl. It has four sides in the shape of congruent trapezia. The bottom of the bowl is a square. Work out the total surface area of the bowl.

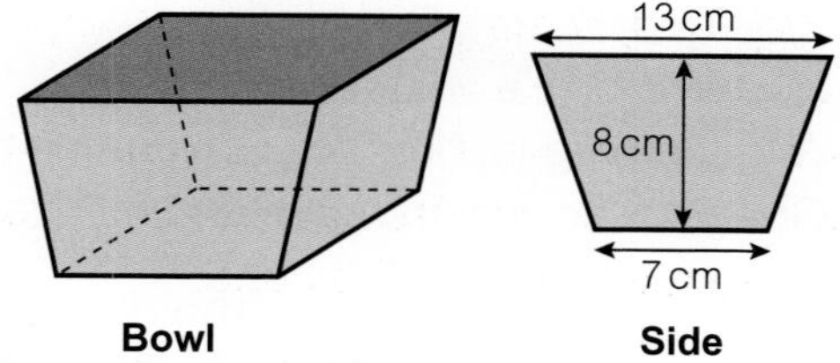

Bowl **Side**

9 **Problem-solving** A water trough is in the shape of a cuboid. It has length 1.5 m, width 0.7 m and height 0.8 m.

a Write the dimensions of the trough in centimetres.

Water is put into the trough. The depth of the water is three quarters of the height of the trough.

b Work out the volume of the water in the trough in cm^3.

c Work out the capacity of the water in the trough in litres.

10 **Problem-solving / Finance** Gareth has an oil tank that is approximately the shape of a cuboid.

It has length 1.8 m, width 80 cm and height 90 cm. It contains oil to a depth of 25 cm.

a Can he fit 1000 litres more into his oil tank? Explain your answer.

Gareth orders oil to fill his tank to 90% full.

b How much oil does he order to the nearest litre?

The price of oil is 69.8p per litre if you order 1000 litres or more, and 70.2p per litre if you order less than 1000 litres.

c How much does he pay for this oil?
Give your answer in pounds to the nearest penny.

> **Q10a Strategy hint**
> Draw a diagram to help you.

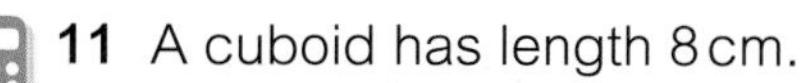

11 A cuboid has length 8 cm.
The width of the cuboid is three quarters of its length. The height of the cuboid is 30% of its length.
Work out the surface area of the cuboid.

12 **Problem-solving** A cuboid has length, width and height in the ratio 4 : 5 : 3. The total of the length, width and height is 96 mm.
Work out the surface area of the cuboid.

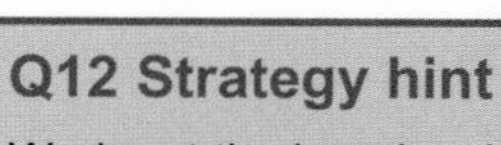

> **Q12 Strategy hint**
> Work out the length, width and height of the cuboid first, by sharing 96 mm in the ratio 4 : 5 : 3.

13 **Problem-solving** This cube and cuboid have the same volume.
Work out the side length of the cube.
Give your answer to the nearest millimetre.

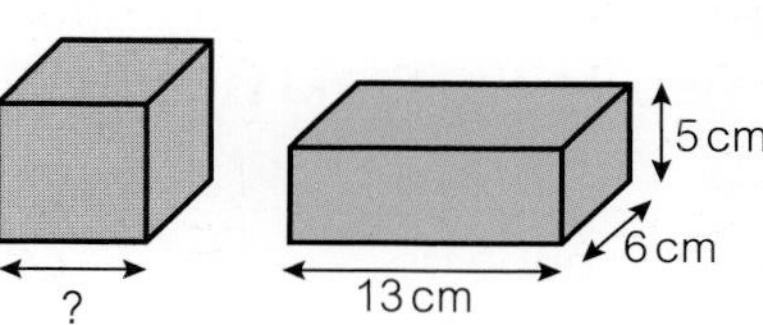

14 **Problem-solving** A gold bar is in the shape of a cuboid with length 150 mm, width 45 mm and height 45 mm.
The bar is melted and made into cubes with side length 12 mm.
How many cubes of gold can be made from the cuboid?

> **Q14 hint**
> The answer must be the largest whole number you can make.

15 One type of helicopter can travel at 140 miles per hour.
It uses an average of 40 gallons of fuel per hour.
A second helicopter can travel at 210 kilometres per hour.
It uses an average of 190 litres of fuel per hour.

a Which helicopter travels the fastest?
b Which helicopter uses the most amount of fuel per hour?

16 **Problem-solving** A tap drips every second into a square sink 40 cm wide and 17 cm deep.
30 drips have a volume of 10 ml.
With the plug in, how long before the sink overflows?
Give your answer in hours and minutes.

Q16 hint
Start by working out the capacity of the sink.
Use 1 cm^3 = 1 ml.

17 **STEM / Problem-solving** The diagram shows the percentage composition of whole milk.

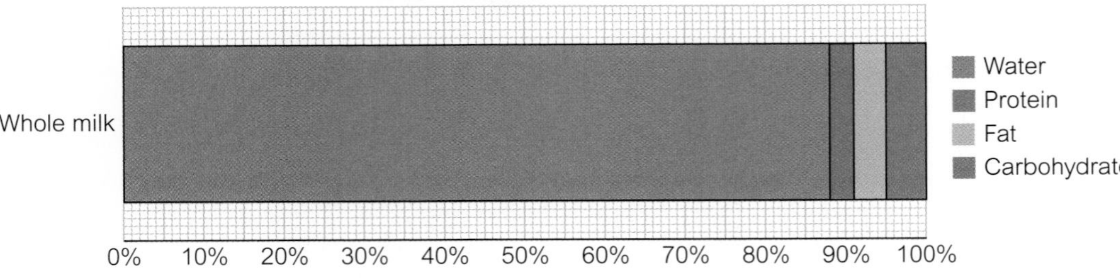

A farm produces 500 gallons of whole milk per day.

a How many litres of fat is contained in 500 gallons of whole milk?

To make skimmed milk, 92.5% of the fat in whole milk is removed.

b How many litres of skimmed milk is made from 500 gallons of whole milk?

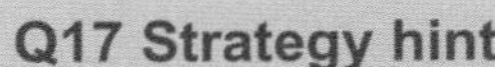

Q17 Strategy hint
Start by changing 500 gallons to litres. Then use the chart to find the percentage of fat in whole milk.

18 The diagram shows a cuboid with volume 31.5 cm^3.
Work out the length of the cuboid.

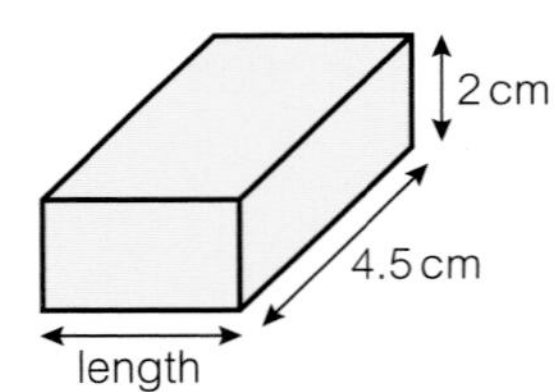

19 Make two accurate copies of this trapezium on squared paper.

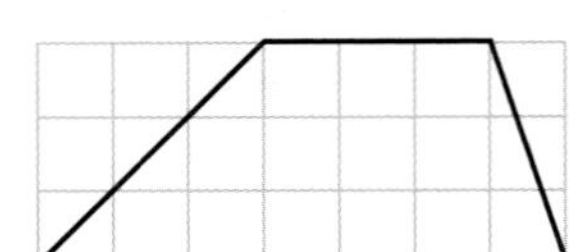

a Cut out both shapes and put them together to make a parallelogram.
b Find the area of the parallelogram.
c Halve it to find the area of the trapezium.
d Write a formula connecting the area (A), the height (h) and the lengths of the parallel sides (a and b) of the trapezium.
e Use your formula to check the area you found in part **c**.

20 A cube has a volume of 64 cm^3.
The cube is cut in half to make two cuboids.
What is the surface area of one of the cuboids?

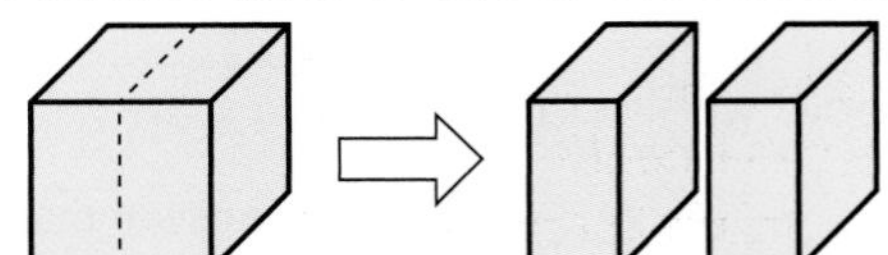

21 The diagram shows a shape made from cuboids.
Find the total surface area of the shape. The working has been started for you.

Base cuboid

area front and back = □ cm²
area right and left ends = □ cm²
area bottom = □ cm²
area top = 9 × □ + 3 × □ = □ cm²

Top cuboid

area front and back = □ cm²
area right and left ends = □ cm²
area top = □ cm²

total surface area = □ cm²

Discussion How else could you work out the total surface area of this shape?

Q21 hint

Why don't you use the whole area of the top face in the base cuboid?

22 Calculate the surface area of each 3D shape.

a

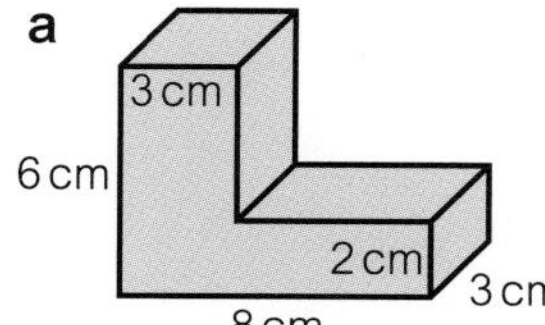

b

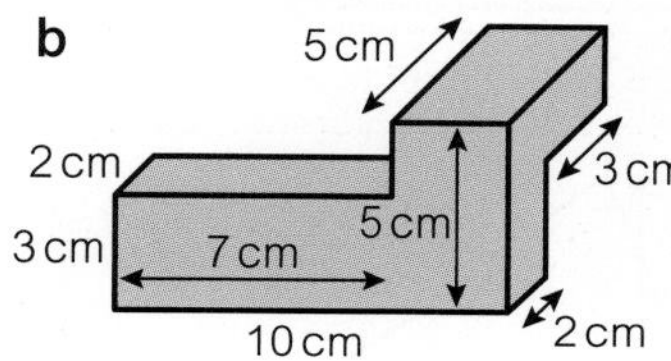

c

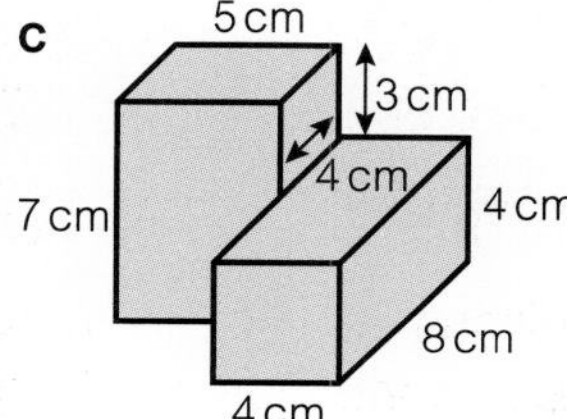

23 **Problem-solving** The blue triangle has an area of 3.6 cm².

The area of the green triangle is 40% of the area of the blue triangle.

Work out the height of the green triangle.

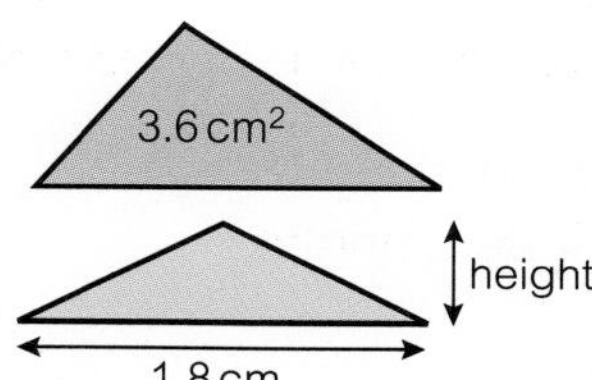

Investigation **Problem-solving / Reasoning / Modelling**

Khalid makes a cake and covers it on all sides in icing.
His friend says 'Wow! There's as much icing as there is cake!'
Khalid's iced cake is a cuboid 18 cm tall, 10 cm wide and 12 cm long.
The icing is 1 cm thick.

1 Copy and complete the working to show that the volume of icing is equal to to volume of the cake.
volume of iced cake = □ cm³
volume of cake = (8 – □) × (10 – □) × (12 – □) = □ cm³
so volume of icing = □ – □ = □ cm³

Part 1 hint

The cake is iced on the top and bottom so you need to subtract 2 × icing thickness from the height of the cake.

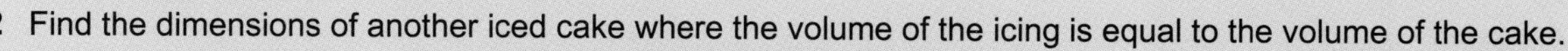

2 Find the dimensions of another iced cake where the volume of the icing is equal to the volume of the cake.

3 What are the dimensions of a cube-shaped cake cake where the volume of icing is equal to the volume of cake?

24 **Reflect** Look back at Q6. It asked you for a 'counter example'.
What did this counter example show about Caroline's statement?
In what sort of situation might you need to prove a statement is untrue?
Could you use a counter example? Explain.

Reflect

2 Unit test

Log how you did on your Student Progression Chart.

1 Work out these conversions.

a 9 litres = □ cm^3

b 0.8 litres = □ cm^3

c 12 000 cm^3 = □ litres

d 950 cm^3 = □ litres

2 The diagram shows a cube of side length 6 cm.
Work out the surface area of the cube.

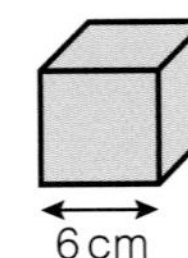

3 Calculate the surface area of this cuboid.

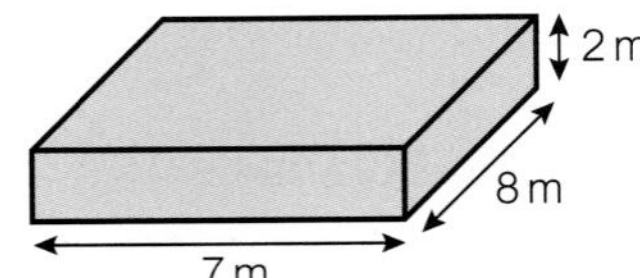

4 Work out the area of this triangle.

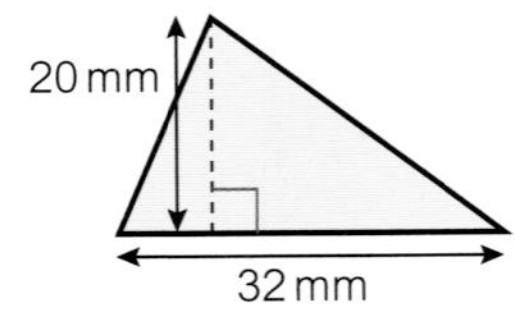

5 These two triangles have the same area.

a Work out the area of the green triangle.

b Work out the height of the blue triangle.

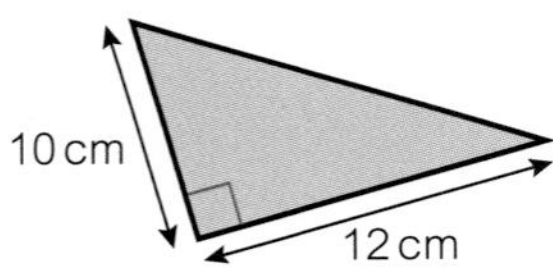

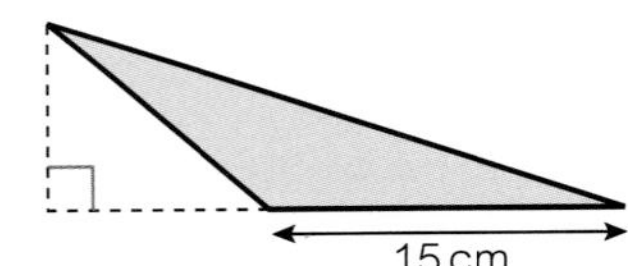

6 Work out the area of this shape.

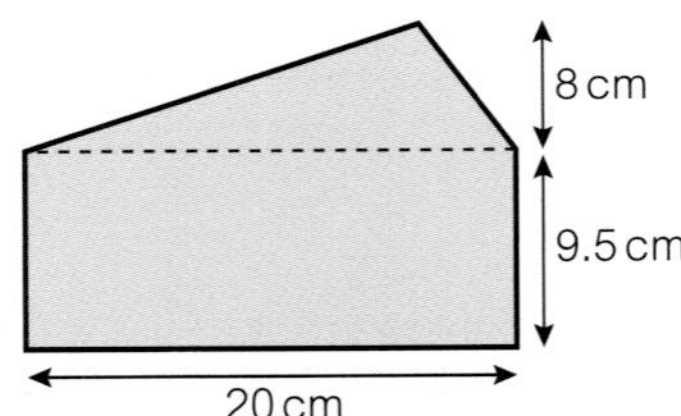

7 Work out these conversions.

a 8.5 cm^2 = □ mm^2

b 60 000 cm^2 = □ m^2

8 Work out the area of each shape.

a A parallelogram

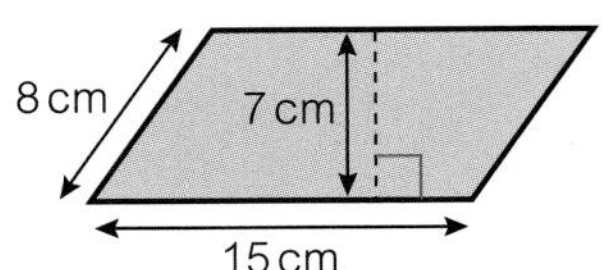

b A trapezium.

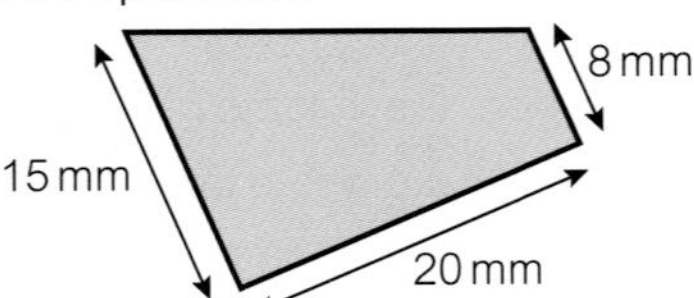

9 The diagram shows the dimensions of an eyeshadow box.
What volume of eyeshadow does it hold? Give your answer in mm^3.

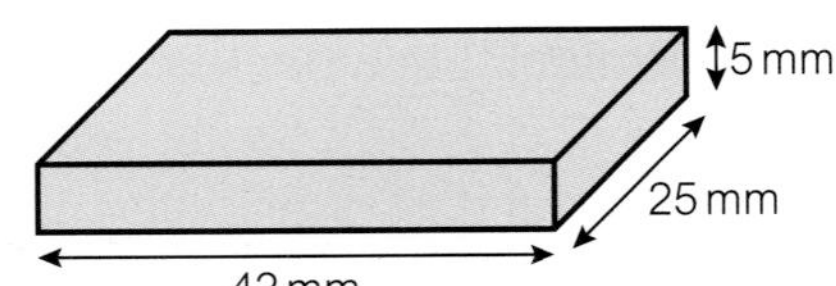

10 Write these conversions.

a 1 foot (ft) ≈ □ cm   b 1 mile ≈ □ km   c 1 kg ≈ □ pounds (lb)

d 1 litre ≈ □ pints   e 1 gallon ≈ □ litres

11 Rob takes part in a 12 mile charity fun run.
How far is the fun run in kilometres?

12 A recipe for Spanish paella uses 4 pints of chicken stock.
How much stock is this in litres?

13 The diagram shows a shape made up of cuboids. Work out

a the volume   b the surface area.

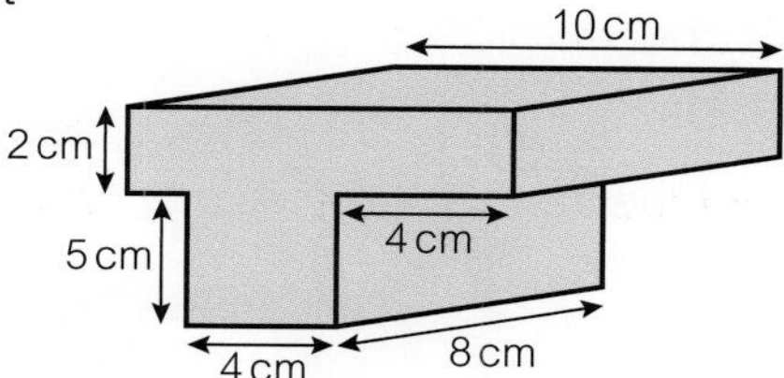

14 Work out the volume of a cube with side length 3.6 cm.

15 An open gift box is a cuboid. It has length 18.5 cm, width 9.4 cm and height 6.2 cm.
Work out the area of cardboard needed to make the open box.

16 A barrel of oil holds approximately 35 gallons.
How much oil is in 50 barrels? Give your answer in litres.

17 The diagram shows a cuboid with volume 5760 mm^3.
Work out the width of the cuboid.

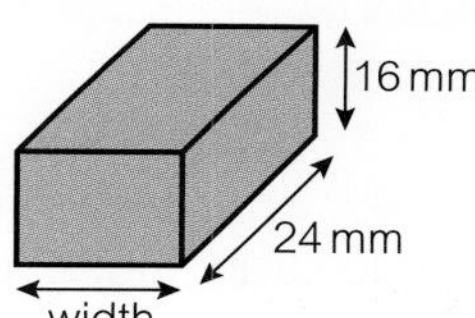

Challenge

18 The box for a wireless router measures 12 cm by 7.5 cm by 8 cm.
Boxes of wireless routers are packed into a larger box for transportation.
The larger box measures 98 cm by 32 cm by 40 cm.

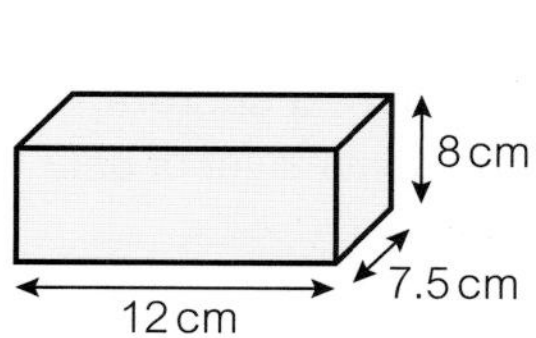

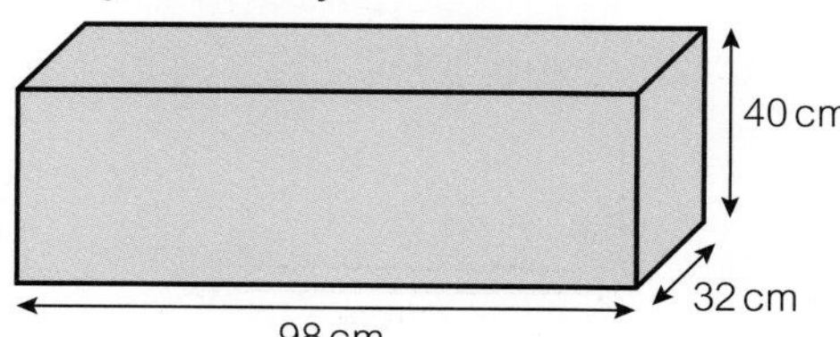

a What is the greatest number of wireless router boxes that will fit into the larger box?

b What volume of empty space will be left in the box?

c Work out the dimensions of a box that will hold 60 wireless router boxes with no wasted space.

19 **Reflect** Write a heading, 'Five important things about area and volume'.
Now look back at the work you have done in this unit, and list the five most important things you have learned.
You might include

- formulae
- conversions
- methods for working things out
- mistakes to avoid (with tips on how to avoid them in future).

Reflect

3 Statistics, graphs and charts

MASTER
Check P68
Strengthen P70
Extend P74
Test P78

3.1 Pie charts

You will learn to:
- Interpret pie charts
- Draw pie charts.

CONFIDENCE

Why learn this?
Workers in the tourist industry use pie charts to show which attractions are most popular.

Fluency
- Work out
  120 + 90 + 50
  360 − 100 − 60 − 40
- How many degrees are there in a full circle?

Explore
How could a car sales company use pie charts to show its sales?

Exercise 3.1

Warm up

1 Use a ruler and protractor to draw these angles.
  a 60° b 110°

2 Work out
  a $\frac{1}{4}$ of 360 b $\frac{1}{6}$ of 360 c 50% of 180 d 30% of 360.

3 The **pie chart** shows the languages Year 8 chose to learn.

Year 8 languages

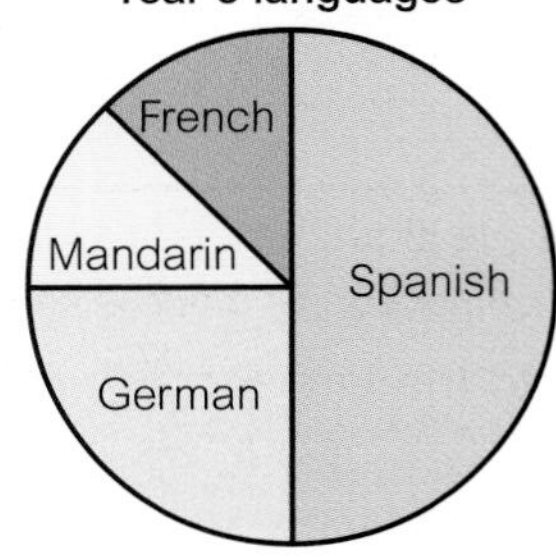

Key point
A **pie chart** is a circle divided into slices called **sectors**. Each sector represents a set of data.

  a Which language was most popular?
  How do you know?
  b What fraction of the students chose
    i Spanish
    ii German
    iii French
    iv Mandarin?
  c There are 280 students in Year 8.
  Work out the number of students who chose each language.

Topic links: Angles, Fractions, Percentages

Subject links: Geography (Q7), Computing (Investigation)

4 Real The pie chart shows the approximate percentages of metals in a 2012 Olympic gold medal.

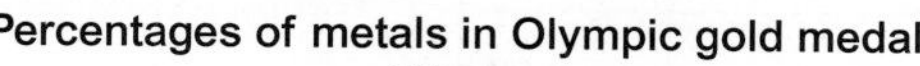

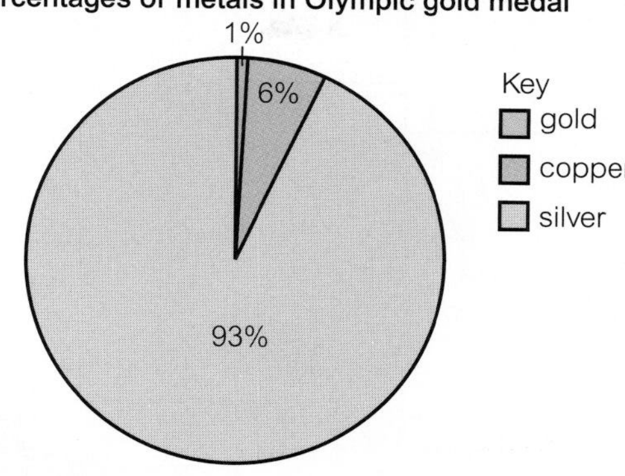

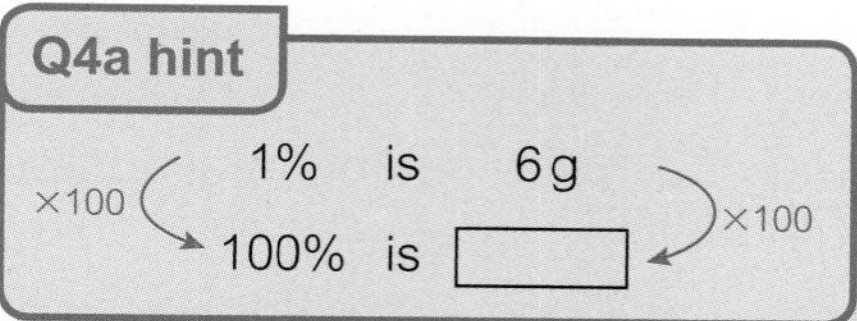

Q4a hint
×100
1% is 6 g
100% is
×100

Each 2012 gold medal contains 6 grams of gold.

a What is the mass of a 2012 gold medal?

b What fraction of the medal is copper?
Give your answer in its simplest form.

c Gold costs approximately £40 per gram.
What is the value of gold in the medal?

Worked example

Draw a pie chart to show this data on students' lunch choices.

Lunch choice	Frequency
sandwiches	35
salad bar	15
hot meal	22

Total number of students = 35 + 15 + 22 = 72 — The total number of students is the total frequency.

÷72: 72 students is 360°
1 student is 360° ÷ 72 = 5° — Work out the angle for one student.

Sandwiches $35 \times 5 = 175°$ — Work out the angle for each lunch choice.

Salad bar $15 \times 5 = 75°$

Hot meal $22 \times 5 = 110°$

Check: 175 + 75 + 110 = 360 — Check that the angles add up to 360°.

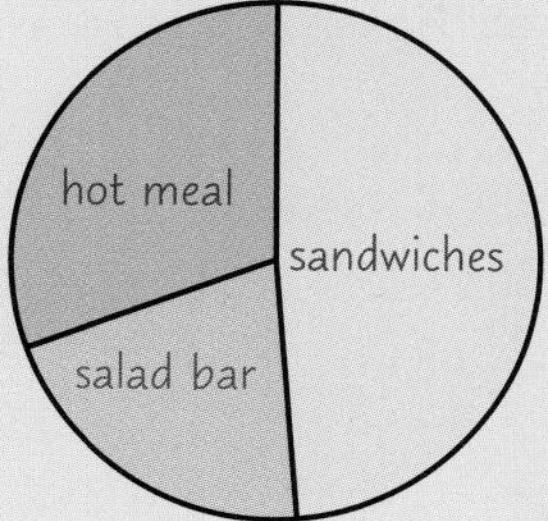

Draw the pie chart.
Label each section or make a key (you do not have to label the angles).
Give your pie chart a title.

Literacy hint

A **radius** is a line from the centre of a circle to the edge.

5 The table shows the percentages of sales in a bakery one month.

Item	Percentage
bread	50%
cakes	20%
pies	20%
pasties	10%

a What angle in a whole circle represents
i 50% **ii** 10% **iii** 20%?

b Draw a pie chart of the data.

Q5b hint

Draw a circle. Draw in a radius. Then use a protractor to draw the angles. Label the sections.

6 The table shows students' sport choices.

Sport	Frequency	Angle
cricket	36	
tennis	24	
rounders	30	
Total		360°

a Work out the total number of students.

b Copy and complete to work out the angle for one student:
☐ students is 360°,
1 student is 360° ÷ ☐ = ☐°

c Work out the angle for each sport. Check that the angles add up to 360°.

d Draw the pie chart. Remember to give it a title and label it (or give it a key).

Q6a hint
The total number of students is the total frequency.

7 **Problem-solving** For her geography project, Lucy asked shoppers in the town centre how far they had travelled to the shops that day.

Distance travelled (d miles)	Frequency
$0 \leqslant d < 3$	6
$3 \leqslant d < 6$	9
$6 \leqslant d < 9$	4
$9 \leqslant d < 12$	5

a Draw a pie chart to show her data.

b Complete these sentences from Lucy's report.

i The modal distance travelled to the shops is _____.

ii More than half the shoppers had travelled less than _____.

iii Just under 25% of shoppers had travelled more than _____.

Discussion Where in the table would you record a distance of exactly 3 miles? … exactly 6 miles?

Q7 hint
$0 \leqslant d < 3$ means a distance between 0 and just under 3 miles.
$3 \leqslant d < 6$ means between 3 and just under 6 miles.

Investigation — **Problem-solving**

1 Use a spreadsheet to draw a pie chart for this data on the first languages spoken by people using the internet.
English 27%, Chinese 24%, Spanish 8%, Japanese 5%, Portuguese 4%, German 3%, Arabic 3%, Russian 3%, Korean 2%, Other 21%

a Input the data.

b Select the cells containing the data.

c Click the **Insert tab** on the top menu and select **Pie**.

d Try 2D and 3D pie charts.

e Give your pie chart a title.

2 Save your pie chart, then move the German, Arabic, Russian and Korean data to the 'Other' section.
Create and save a new pie chart.
Which pie chart is easier to read?
Discussion What do you think is the maximum number of sectors for a pie chart to be able to read it clearly? Why?

3 Create and save a new pie chart showing 'English' and 'Other'.
Discussion Is two sections enough for a pie chart? Explain your answer

Explore

8 **Explore** How could a car sales company use pie charts to show its sales?
What have you learned in this lesson to help you answer this question?
What other information do you need?

Reflect

9 **Reflect** Rosie says that fractions help you to interpret pie charts (as in Q3).
What other areas of mathematics help you to interpret pie charts?
What maths skills do you need to draw pie charts?

3.2 Using tables

You will learn to:

- Calculate the mean from a frequency table
- Design and use two-way tables
- Design and use tables for grouped data.

Why learn this?
Sorting data into tables can help you see patterns.

Fluency
Find the mean, median, mode and range of
0, 4, 7, 4, 3, 4, 2, 1

Explore
How many cheesecakes should a chef make for 100 diners, at lunchtime and at dinnertime?

Exercise 3.2

1 The table shows the numbers of books customers borrowed from a library over one hour last Tuesday.

Number of books	Frequency
1	7
2	10
3	8
4	6
5	1

a How many people borrowed books during that hour?

b How many people borrowed fewer than four books?

c What was the modal number of books borrowed?

d What was the range?

Worked example

Jack asked students in his class how many pets they had.
Here are his results. Work out the mean.

Number of pets	Frequency	Total number of pets
0	7	$0 \times 7 = 0$
1	8	$1 \times 8 = 8$
2	6	$2 \times 6 = 12$
3	3	$3 \times 3 = 9$
4	1	$4 \times 1 = 4$
Total	25	33

Add a column to the table to work out the total numbers of pets.

Work out the total frequency (number of people in the survey) and the total number of pets.

mean = $33 \div 25 = 1.32$

mean = total number of pets ÷ number of people

2 The table shows the numbers of goals scored in netball matches in one season.
Work out the mean.

Goals scored	Frequency
0	3
1	8
2	5
3	3
4	1

3 **Real / STEM** In science, a primary school class grew pea plants and then counted the numbers of peas in a pod.

a What is the modal number of peas in a pod?

b What is the range?

c Work out the mean number of peas in a pod.

Number of peas	Frequency
0	2
1	2
2	9
3	7
4	6
5	11
6	3

4 **Problem-solving** The label on a matchbox says, 'Average contents 32'.
The quality control department counted the contents of some matchboxes one day.
Is the label on the matchbox correct?
Discussion Which average should you use for 'Average contents'? Does it matter?

Number of matches	Frequency
29	5
30	21
31	21
32	22
33	14
34	12
35	2

5 This **two-way table** shows the numbers of tickets sold at a cinema.

	Standard seats	Luxury seats	Total
Adult	39	33	72
Child	15	9	
Total	54		

a Work out the total number of luxury seat tickets sold.

b How many child tickets were sold?

c How many tickets were sold altogether?

d What fraction of the tickets sold were for children?

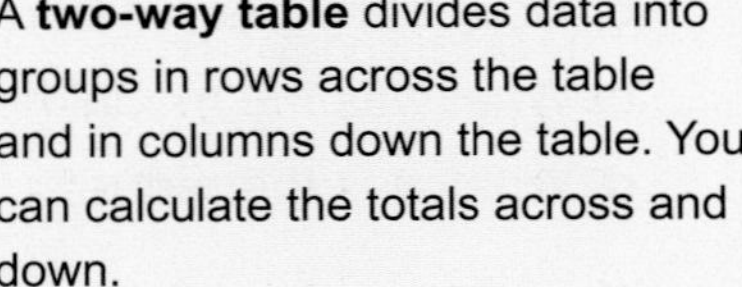

Key point

A **two-way table** divides data into groups in rows across the table and in columns down the table. You can calculate the totals across and down.

Q5a hint

Use the 'Luxury seats' column.

Q5b hint

Use the 'Child' row.

6 The table shows the numbers of members of a salsa dance club.

	Beginners	Intermediate	Advanced	Total
Men	33	36		90
Women			38	110
Total	65			

a Copy and complete the table.

b How many men are in the advanced group?

c How many men are above beginner level?

d Which level has the greatest difference in numbers of men and women?

e What percentage of the total membership is women at advanced level?

Subject links: Science (Q3, Q8)

7 **Reasoning / Finance** Tim records the food sold in his café one weekend.

a Which food is most popular on

i Saturday ii Sunday?

	Saturday	Sunday	Total
Sandwiches	25	21	
Salads	12	9	
Fish and chips	7	6	
Cakes	13	27	
Total			

b Tim makes a profit of

- 35p on each sandwich
- 50p on each salad
- £1.30 on each portion of fish and chips
- 40p on each cake.

Which is his most profitable item over this weekend?

c Tim wants to cut a menu item on Sundays. Which should he cut? Explain why.

Q7c hint

Look at the profit for each item on Sunday.

Discussion How could a spreadsheet help you with Q7?

8 **STEM** In science, tutor group 8B measured the lengths of pea pods they had grown.
Daisy started this table for the results.

Length, l (cm)	Tally	Frequency
$0 \leqslant l < 2$		
$2 \leqslant l < 4$		
$4 \leqslant l < 6$		
$6 \leqslant l < 8$		

a The first class includes all lengths up to, but not including, 2.0 cm.
Which class contains the length 2.0 cm?

b i Copy the table and tally these lengths in cm.
5.7, 2.0, 3.7, 6.1, 5.0, 2.4, 6.8, 4.5, 6.8, 3.7, 4.0, 5.6, 6.3, 4.9, 6.0, 4.1

ii Fill in the frequency column.

c Which is the modal class?

Discussion Can you use the frequency table to work out the exact range of the pod lengths?

9 These are the times taken, in seconds, to stack and unstack a set of 10 plastic cups.
8.2, 10.9, 13.5, 14.6, 12.7, 8.1, 9.5, 11.3, 20.0, 12.7,
9.9, 10.6, 15.4, 18.2, 14.7, 9.5, 10.8, 12.5, 19.4, 16.7

a Record this data in a grouped frequency table with no more than five classes.

b Which is the modal class?

c Estimate the range.

Q9a hint

Make sure your classes are of equal size.

10 **Explore** How many cheesecakes should a chef make for 100 diners, at lunchtime and dinnertime?
Look back at the maths you have learned in this lesson. How can you use it to answer this question?

11 **Reflect** Freddie and Claudia are talking about tables.
Freddie says, 'Tables show information in columns and rows.'
What do you think of Freddie's definition of a table? Is it true for all the tables in this lesson?
Claudia says, 'Tables are everywhere. Click Menu on our TV remote control. It shows you a table.'
Where else do you see tables displaying information in everyday life?

3.3 Stem and leaf diagrams

You will learn to:

- Draw stem and leaf diagrams for data
- Interpret stem and leaf diagrams.

Why learn this?
A stem and leaf diagram gives a quick, detailed overview of a set of data.

Fluency

- Work out the median of 1, 2, 2, 2, 2, 3, 4, 4, 4, 5
- Find the mode and range.

Explore
How rich is the average billionaire?

Exercise 3.3

1 Priya has written 10 data values in order.
1, 1, 2, 3, 5, 7, 8, 8, 8, 9
She says, 'For ten data values in order, the median is the fifth one.'
Is she correct? Explain your answer.

2 These sets of data are written in order.
 i 3, 5, 7, 7, 8, 9, 9, 10, 11
 ii −5, −3, 0, 1, 2, 4, 7, 8, 10, 11, 13, 14, 15, 17, 20, 22, 25, 27
For each set
 a count the number of values, n
 b work out $\frac{n+1}{2}$ to find the middle value(s)
 c write down the median.

Key point
In a set of 9 data values, the median is the $\frac{9+1}{2}$ = 5th one.
In a set of 10 data values, the median is the $\frac{10+1}{2} = \frac{11}{2}$ = 5.5th one.
In a set of n data values, the median is the $\frac{n+1}{2}$th one.

Worked example

Here are the heights of some tomato seedlings (in cm).
2.8, 3.4, 4.5, 4.1, 4.3, 2.7, 1.6, 3.2, 1.9, 2.5
Construct a stem and leaf diagram for this data.

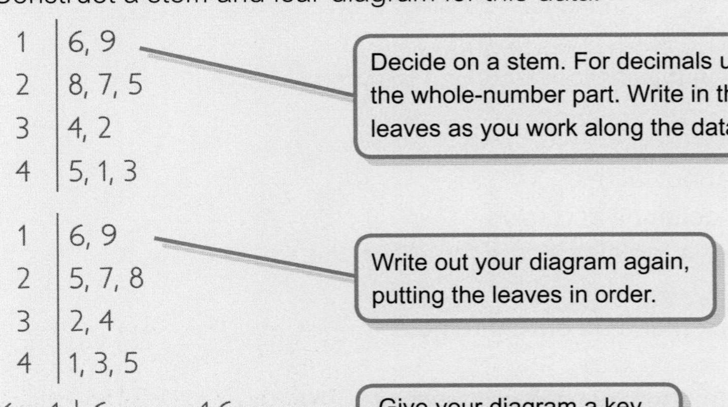

1	6, 9
2	8, 7, 5
3	4, 2
4	5, 1, 3

1	6, 9
2	5, 7, 8
3	2, 4
4	1, 3, 5

Key: 1 | 6 means 1.6 cm

Decide on a stem. For decimals use the whole-number part. Write in the leaves as you work along the data list.
Write out your diagram again, putting the leaves in order.
Give your diagram a key.

Key point
A **stem and leaf diagram** shows numerical data split into a 'stem' and 'leaves'.
The key shows you how to read the values.

Topic links: Percentages, Bar charts

3 The numbers of visitors each day to a stately home were
61, 52, 65, 77, 79, 84, 86, 91, 85, 70, 64,
53, 77, 56, 68, 73, 92, 85, 87, 78, 90

a Construct a **stem and leaf diagram** for this data.

b Problem-solving Use your diagram to answer these questions.

i How many days was the stately home open?

ii On how many days were there more than 70 visitors?

The manager calculates that the house needs at least 65 visitors each day to make a profit.

iii On what percentage of days did it make a profit?

Discussion What assumption did you make to answer part **b i**? Was this assumption reasonable?

Q3a hint

Use the 'tens' digit as the stem. Remember the key.

4 The stem and leaf diagram shows the heights of Year 8 students, measured to the nearest centimetre.

Stem	Leaf
14	6, 9
15	1, 1, 2, 3, 5, 5, 5, 6
16	2, 3, 4, 5, 5, 5, 7, 9, 9
17	0, 2, 4

Key: 14 | 6 means 146 cm

Find

a the mode **b** the range **c** the median.

Discussion Why didn't you need to write the data in order before finding the middle one?

Discussion Which average can you find most easily from a stem and leaf diagram?

Q4c hint

The median is the $\frac{n+1}{2}$th value.

5 Finance / Problem-solving Jay owns a newsagent's. He recorded the amounts his customers spent one morning.

Stem	Leaf
0	65, 87
1	08, 12, 36, 88, 97
2	40, 52, 56, 68, 87, 95
3	05, 15, 20, 35, 38, 40, 46, 62, 77, 99
4	39, 68

Key: 1 | 08 means £1.08

Jay wants to increase the 'average' spend by £1 per customer.
He puts a special offer of 'Chocolate bars, 3 for a £1' by the till.
He recorded the amounts spent the next morning.

Stem	Leaf
0	92
1	12, 18, 36, 52
2	36, 40, 75, 99
3	15, 19, 24, 36, 42, 49, 51, 60, 66, 85, 90
4	04, 39, 78, 82

Key: 1 | 36 means £1.36

Has the special offer increased the average spend by £1?

Q5 Strategy hint

Which average will you choose? Compare for the two diagrams.

6 **Real** At the end of a secretarial course, students were tested on their typing speeds for

- number of words per minute typing their own text (Composition)
- number of words per minute when typing words spoken to them (Transcription).

This back-to-back stem and leaf diagram shows their results.

Transcription		Composition
9, 6, 5	2	1, 3, 4, 5, 7
9, 7, 6, 3	3	0, 2, 2, 3, 3, 4, 4, 5, 7, 8, 8, 9
8, 8, 7, 7, 7, 6, 5, 5, 4, 3, 0	4	1, 6, 7
4, (2)	(5)	

Key: 1 | 2 | or | 2 | 1 means 21 words per minute

Q6 hint

The circled value is 52.

a The course leader says, 'Most of the transcription scores are between 40 and 49.'
Write a sentence like this for the composition scores.

b Work out the median and range for

i composition

ii transcription.

c Write two sentences comparing the median and the range for composition and transcription.

Q6c hint

You could begin with, 'The median score for transcription is □'.

Investigation — Problem-solving

1. Put the visitor data from Q3 into a grouped frequency table.
2. Draw a bar chart for the data. Remember to label your axes and give your chart a title.
3. Which of the parts in Q3 can you answer from your bar chart?
   If there are any you cannot answer, explain why not.
4. Can you work out a median from a bar chart?
5. **a** Which is better, a stem and leaf diagram or a bar chart? Write your reasons in a table.

Stem and leaf is better for	Bar chart is better for
	Colourful diagrams

   b Is there anything they are equally good for?

Part 1 hint

Use classes 50–59, 60–69 etc.

7 **Explore** How rich is the average billionaire?
Is it easier to explore this question now you have completed the lesson?
What further information do you need to be able to answer this? Who is 'the average billionaire'?

8 **Reflect** Hannah, Sam and Tilly discuss how they use worked examples.
Sam says, 'I read the question, then the answer, then all the note boxes telling me what to do.'
Hannah says, 'I only read the note boxes and bits of the answer when I get stuck.'
Tilly says, 'I read the question, then the first part of the answer and its notes. Then I read the next bit of the answer and its notes, and so on.'
Describe how you read the worked example for this lesson.
Try reading it again in different ways (like Sam, Hannah and Tilly).
Which way do you think is best? Why?

3.4 Comparing data

You will learn to:

- Compare two sets of data using statistics or the shape of the graph
- Construct line graphs
- Choose the most appropriate average to use.

Why learn this?
Companies compare their performance with other companies to see if they are doing better than the competition.

Fluency

- What does it tell you when one set of data has a larger range than the other?
- What percentage of the data is less than the median?

Explore
Why does the UK government use the median salary to describe average income, instead of the mean?

Exercise 3.4

1 Here are the quarterly profit figures for two small businesses.

	1st quarter	2nd quarter	3rd quarter	4th quarter
Business A	£5324	£9637	£14 658	£5017
Business B	£8471	£9365	£8852	£10 345

a For each business, work out

i the mean quarterly profit **ii** the range.

b Write two sentences comparing the profits of the two businesses.

c **Problem-solving** One of the businesses makes ice cream. Which one do you think it is?

Q1 Literacy hint
The quarterly profits are the profits for a quarter of the year (3 months). 1st quarter is January–March, and so on.

Q1b hint
Write one sentence comparing the means and one comparing the ranges.

2 **Real / Reasoning** The graphs show the scores of the winning and losing teams each week in the TV quiz University Challenge.

a One line shows the winning team's scores. Which one?

b In which week(s) was the difference between the winning and losing scores

i the greatest

ii the smallest?

c Min says, 'The winning teams' scores are all higher than the losing teams' scores.' Is she correct? Explain your answer.

Discussion Did you need to read exact values from the graph to answer these questions?

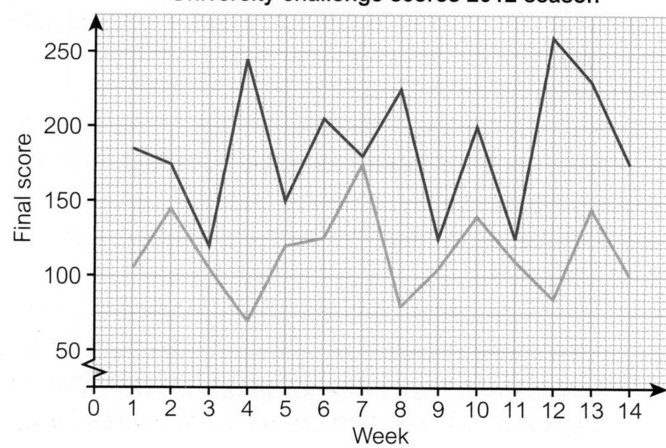

Warm up

3 The manager of a shoe shop keeps a spreadsheet record of all the women's shoes sold over a month.

	A	B	C	D	E	F	G	H	I	J	K	L
1	**Smarter shoes - March sales, women's shoes**											
2	Size	3 1/2	4	4 1/2	5	5 1/2	6	6 1/2	7	7 1/2	8	8 1/2
3	Pairs sold	0	12	9	11	21	24	38	22	12	5	0
4												

a Which shoe size was the mode?

b What was the median shoe size?

The spreadsheet calculates that 6.1 is the mean shoe size sold.

The manager uses the averages to help her decide which size shoes to order.

c Which size should she order most of? Which average should she use?

Discussion How useful is the mean shoe size? How could she use the range to help her decide what sizes to order?

4 The table shows two boys' results in an Under-15 Long Jump competition.

	1st jump	2nd jump	3rd jump	4th jump
Alex	5.27 m	5.19 m	2.78 m	5.40 m
Dan	5.01 m	5.12 m	5.15 m	5.08 m

a From the results in the table, which boy do you think can jump the longest distance?

b Calculate the mean distance for each boy.

c Work out the median distance for each boy.

d Which average, mean or median, best represents each boy's performance?

e **Reasoning** Which value affected Alex's mean distance? Why didn't it affect the median?

Q4e Literacy hint

A data value that doesn't fit the pattern of the other values is called an outlier.

5 **Real** The table gives the mean monthly temperatures (°C) in Moscow and Barbados over one year.

	Jan	Feb	Mar	Apr	May	Jun	Jul	Aug	Sept	Oct	Nov	Dec
Barbados	25	25.3	25	26.3	27	27	26.7	27	27	26.7	26.3	25
Moscow	−8	−7	−2	5	12	15	17	15	10	3	−2	−6

a Draw a line graph to show both sets of temperatures.
Start your axes like this.

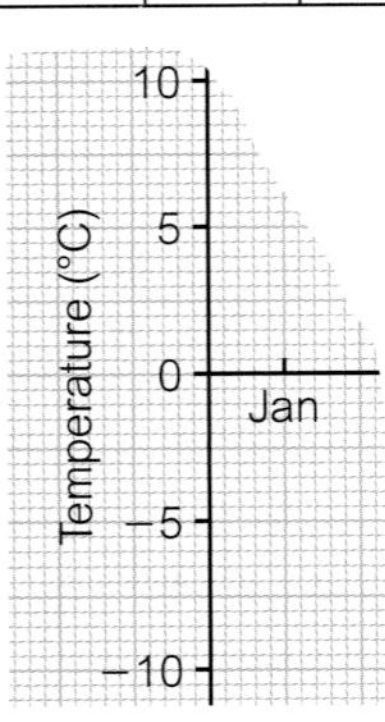

b Write two sentences about your graph, comparing the temperatures in Barbados and Moscow.
You could use some of these words: warmer, colder, maximum, minimum, range, extreme, temperate.

Subject links: Geography (Q5)

6 The pie charts show the ages of patients at two different dental surgeries.

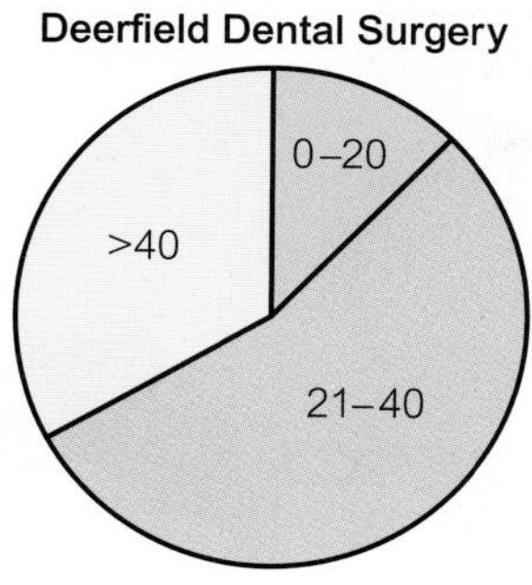

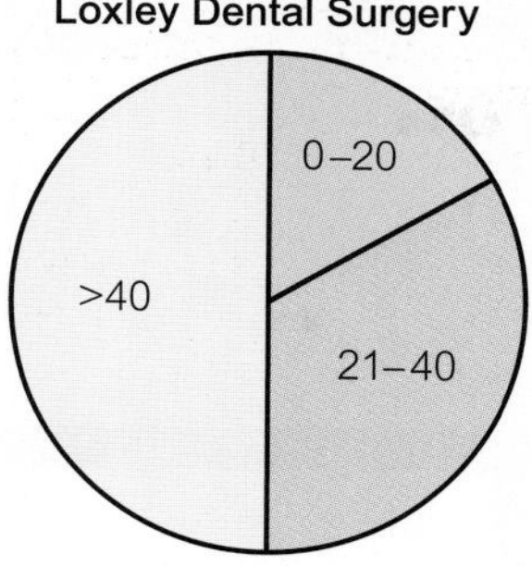

a Which surgery has

i the greatest proportion of patients over 40

ii the lowest proportion of patients under 20?

Loxley Dental Surgery has 1500 patients. Deerfield Dental Surgery has 2400 patients.

b Which surgery has

i the greatest number of patients over 40

ii the lowest number of patients under 20?

Discussion What do you need to know to compare the numbers of patients in each pie chart section?

7 **Finance** Here are the annual salaries of eight people working in a small company.

£27 000, £15 500, £23 750, £16 000, £18 950, £31 000, £18 200, £75 000

a Which salary do you think is the managing director's?

b Work out

i the mean salary

ii the median salary.

c How many people in the company earn less than the mean?

d How many people earn less than the median?

e Which best represents the average salary for this company – the median or the mean?

f Which average would best suit the needs of

i the managing director, who wants to attract more staff to the company

ii the staff, who want a pay rise?

8 **Explore** Why does the UK government use the median salary to describe average income, instead of the mean?

What have you learned in this lesson to help you answer this question?

What other information do you need?

9 **Reflect** In this lesson, there were three discussion questions.

Look at each one again. Did the discussion help you with your mathematics learning? Explain your answer.

Explore

Reflect

CONFIDENCE

3.5 Scatter graphs

You will learn to:

- Draw a scatter graph
- Draw a line of best fit on a scatter graph
- Describe types of correlation.

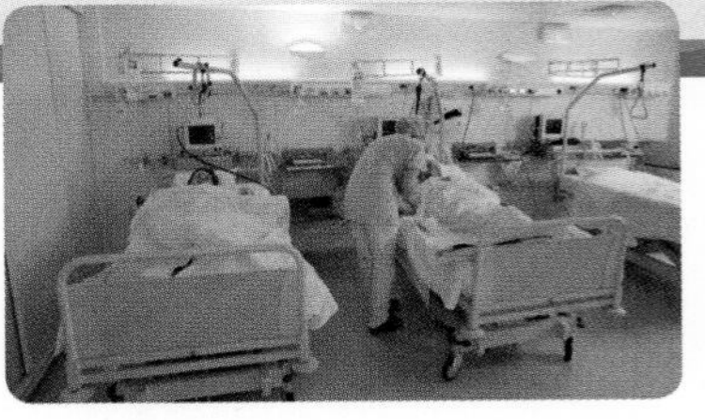

Why learn this?
A scatter graph can be used to monitor patients and decide who should have surgery first.

Fluency
What are the coordinates of the points A, B, C and D?

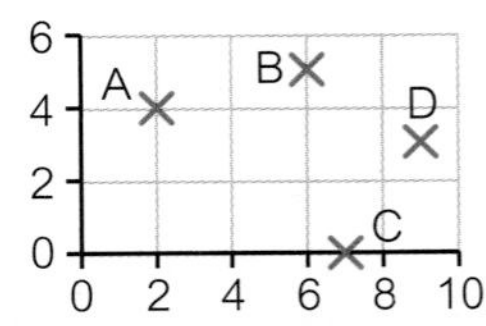

Explore
Is there a link between access to electricity and life expectancy?

Exercise 3.5

Warm up

1 Plot these points on a coordinate grid.
A (20, 9) B (10, 12) C (14, 20) D (28, 0) E (16, 22)

Q1 hint
Look at the values you need to plot. Make sure these values will fit on your axes.
Plot the points with crosses.

Key point
A **scatter graph** plots two sets of data on the same graph to see if there is a relationship or **correlation** between them. This might be a **negative correlation**, a **positive correlation** or there might be **no correlation**.

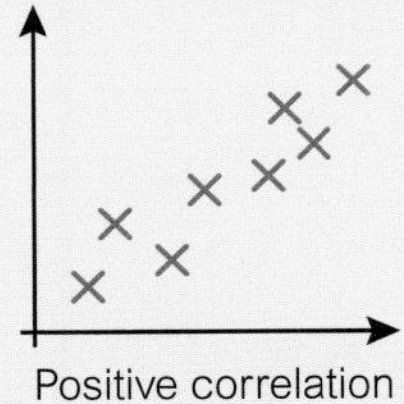

Positive correlation

Negative correlation

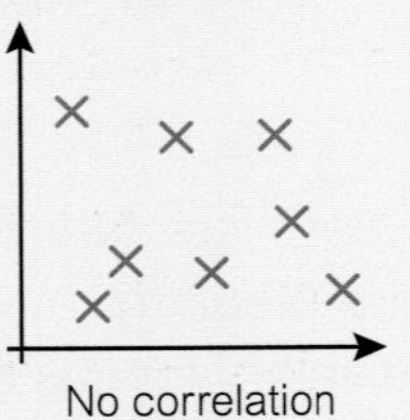

No correlation

2 Each month, Hugo recorded the number of umbrellas he sold and the number of days it rained.
He plotted this scatter graph of his data for six months.

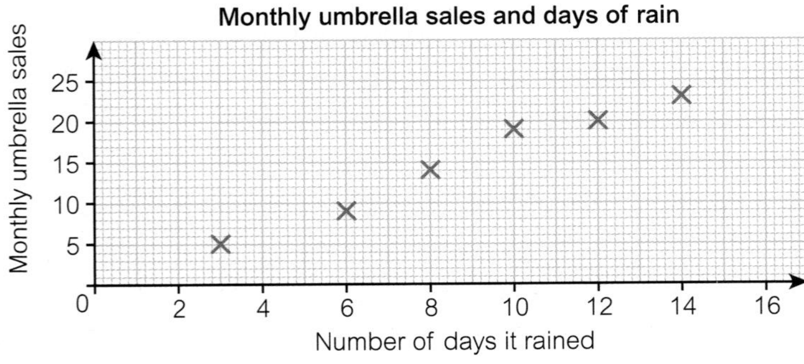

a When it rained for eight days in a month, how many umbrellas did he sell?

b How many days did it rain in the month when he sold 19 umbrellas?

c Which word fits in both the gaps in this sentence?
'The _______ days it rained, the ______ umbrellas he sold.'

Discussion What other word would fit in both gaps in the sentence?
Do you think the relationship between number of days it rained and umbrella sales is likely?

Topic links: Scales, Coordinates

Subject links: Science (Q4), Geography (Q5)

3 Real Describe the correlation shown in each graph.

a

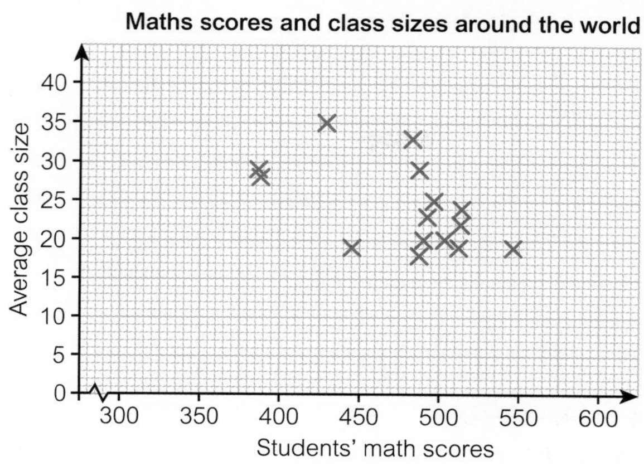

b

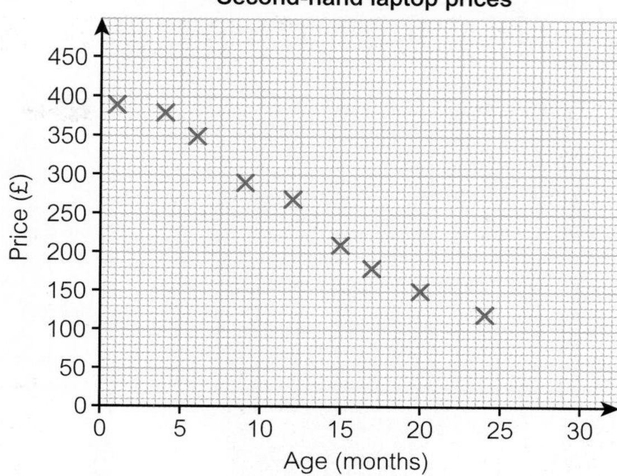

Copy and complete these sentences.

c '______ and ______ do not appear to be related.' **d** 'As laptops get older, their ________ __________.'

4 STEM / Real A healthcare trust wanted to reduce the number of patients who developed an infection in hospital. They put alcohol handrub at the entrances to the wards to encourage people to clean their hands regularly. They produced this scatter graph.

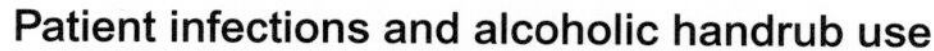

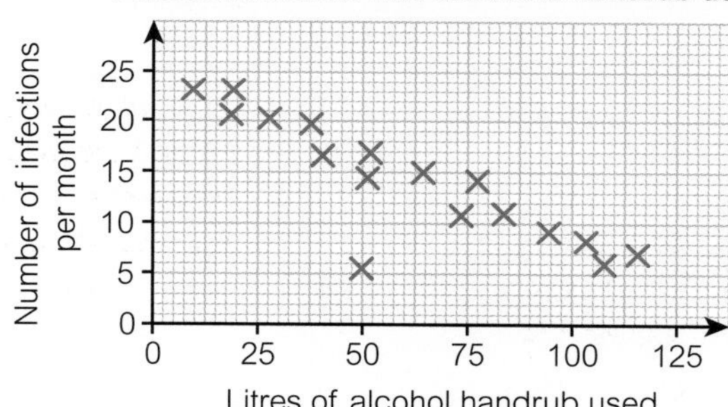

a What type of correlation does this scatter graph show?

b One of the alcohol handrub values was not copied correctly. Which one do you think this was? Explain why.

c Problem-solving Does the data suggest that increasing the amount of alcohol handrub used will reduce the number of infections? Explain your answer.

Discussion What should you do if one piece of data does not seem to fit?

5 Real The table shows data from 15 countries on mothers' employment and child poverty.

Percentage of mothers employed	63	71	77	46	85	50	44	51	57	22	61	67	65	36	56
Percentage of children living in poverty	15	14	4	9	8	17	25	12	20	28	10	21	8	11	25

Source: Child poverty, http://www.oecd.org/els/family/, Copyright OECD

a Plot a scatter graph to show this data with 'Percentage of mothers employed' on the horizontal axis and 'Percentage of children living in poverty' on the vertical axis.

b What type of correlation does your scatter graph show?

c Write a sentence to explain what the graph shows about the relationship between the proportion of mothers who work and child poverty.

You could start with, 'As the proportion of mothers who work increases…'

Q5a hint

You could enter the data into a spreadsheet as a vertical table, select it, then insert a scatter graph.

6 **Problem-solving** Three students drew lines of best fit on their graphs. Whose line best represents the relationship between the age and price of second-hand laptops? Explain why.

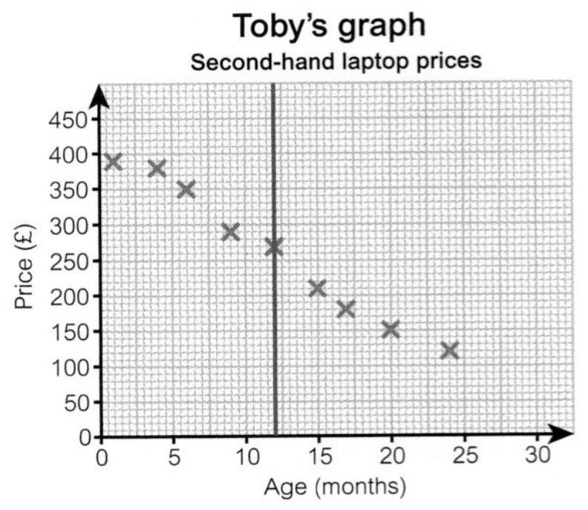

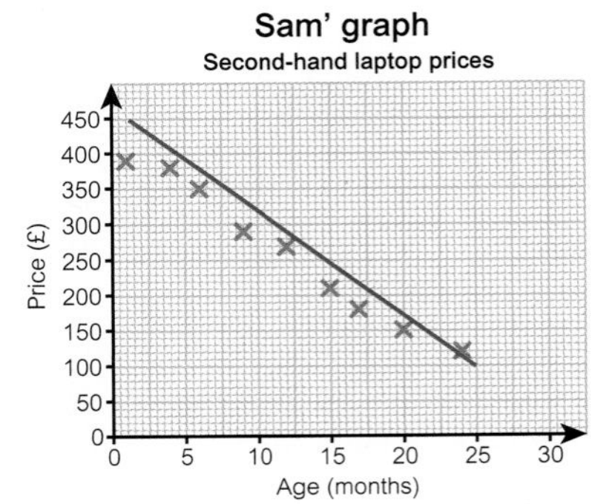

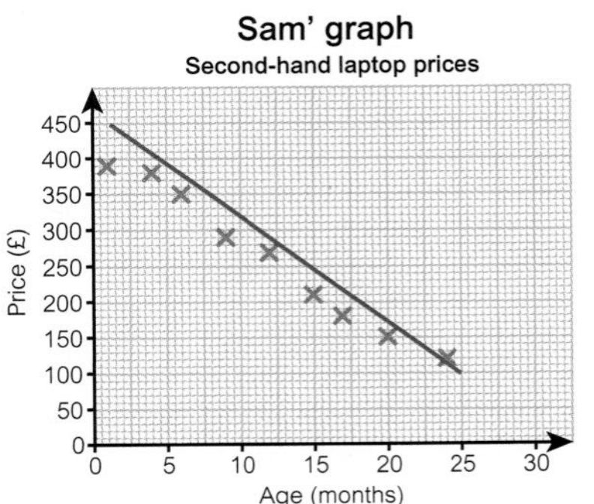

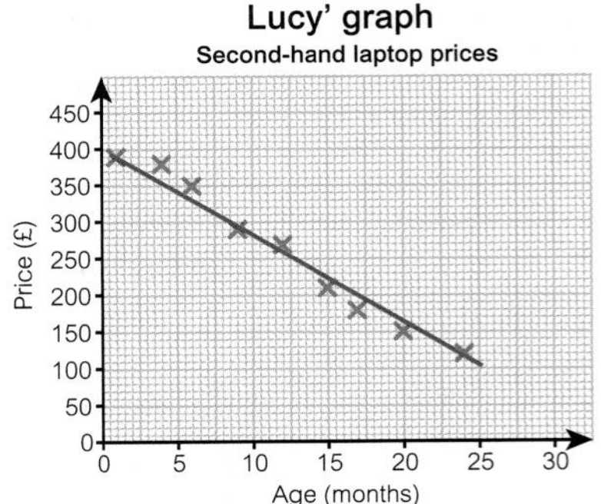

Key point

A **line of best fit** shows up the relationship between two sets of data. There should be the same number of crosses on each side of the line. There may or may not also be crosses on the line.

Discussion Does a line of best fit go through (0, 0) sometimes, always or never?

7 Draw a line of best fit on the graph you drew in Q5.

Q7 hint

Whose line best follows the 'shape' of the data? Check the number of crosses on each side.

Investigation **Problem-solving**

Is there any correlation between any of these data sets taken from a group of children?
You could use a spreadsheet to draw scatter graphs.

Age (years)	6	7	8	9	10	11	12	13	14	15
Height (cm)	115	122	130	132	138	142	147	156	165	170
Number of siblings	3	2	5	1	4	2	1	0	3	1
Number of letters in name	5	5	9	3	7	4	3	3	6	3

Where there is a correlation, do you think there is a real-life relationship between the two sets of data?

Explore

8 **Explore** Is there a link between access to electricity and life expectancy?
Is it easier to explore this question now you have completed the lesson?
What further information do you need to be able to answer this?

Reflect

9 **Reflect** Think about the different ways to display data.
- Which is the easiest to read and understand? Why?
- Which is the hardest to read and understand? Why?
- Which is the easiest to draw? Why?
- Which is the hardest to draw? Why?

Q9 hint

Think back to Year 7 too.

3.6 FINANCE: Misleading graphs

You will learn to:
- Interpret graphs and charts
- Explain why a graph or chart could be misleading.

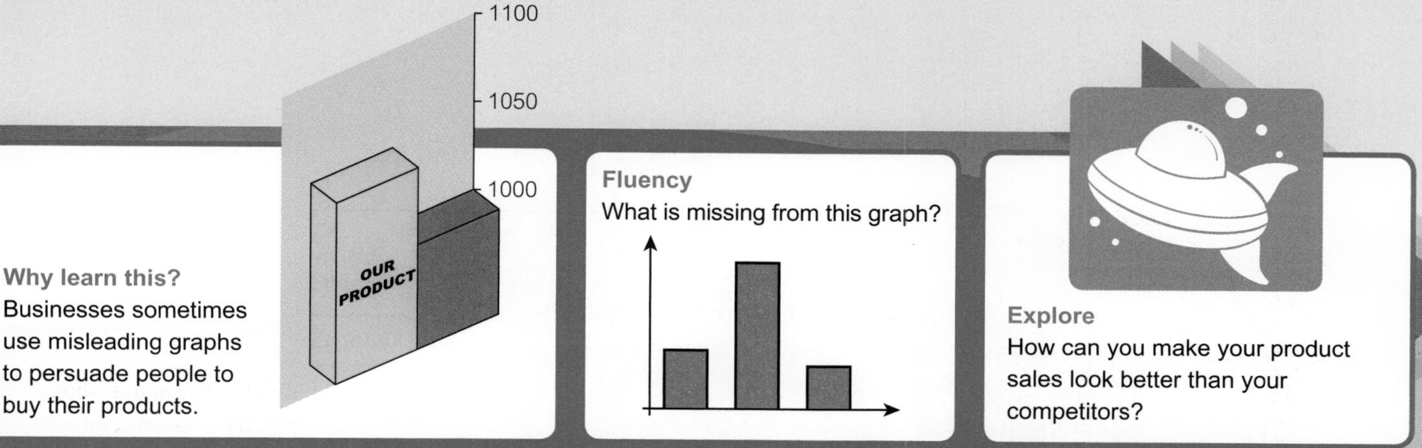

Why learn this?
Businesses sometimes use misleading graphs to persuade people to buy their products.

Fluency
What is missing from this graph?

Explore
How can you make your product sales look better than your competitors?

Exercise 3.6: Financial graphs

Key point
Before you read values from a graph or chart
- read the title
- read the axis labels
- read the scales.

You cannot draw accurate conclusions from an inaccurate graph.

1 Naomi asked some Year 8 students their favourite type of film. She made this pictogram to show the results.

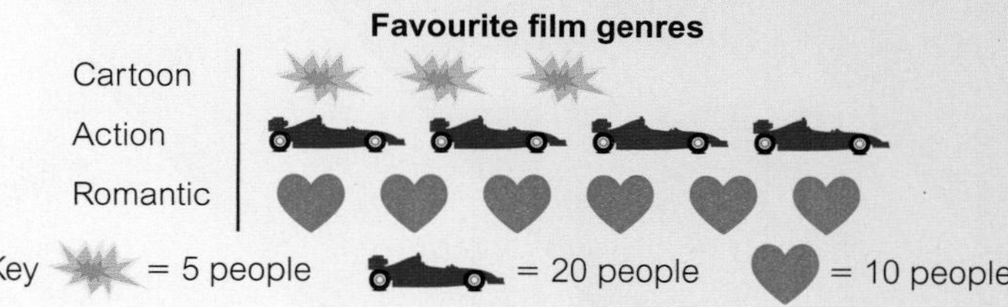

a Naomi says, 'The pictogram shows that Romantic films are the most popular.' Is she correct? Explain.

b What is misleading about the symbols Naomi has used?

c Redraw the pictogram using only one type of symbol to represent the same quantity in each row.

Key point
Changing the scale can make a graph look very different.

2 **Finance / Real** The table and the graph show the average price of a 1 kg loaf of white bread from 1914 to 2004.

1914	1947	1958	1970	1978	1990	2000	2004
1p	2p	4p	8p	32p	64p	70p	90p

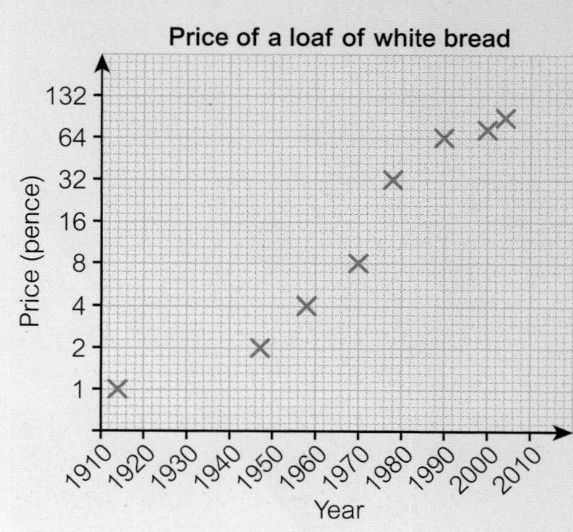

a What is unusual about the vertical scale on the graph?

b What do you think the graph would look like with a vertical scale, 0, 10, 20, 30, 40, ….?
Draw the graph to check your prediction.

c Which graph shows the real increase in price from 1914 to 2004 most clearly?

Discussion How does using a scale with unequal steps affect the graph?

Warm up

3 **Finance** Here are two graphs showing the same sales figures for Hilary's hat shop.

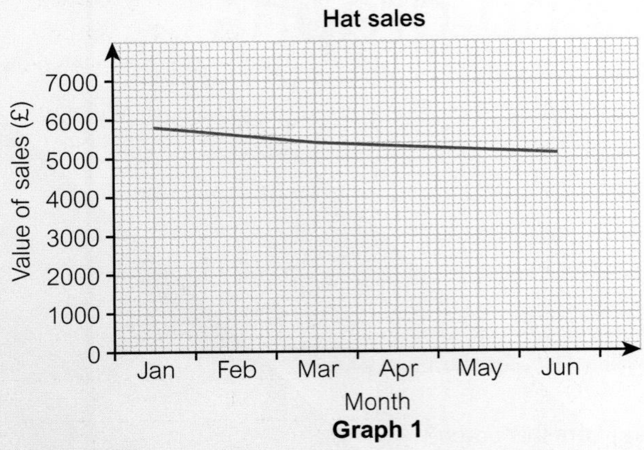

Graph 1

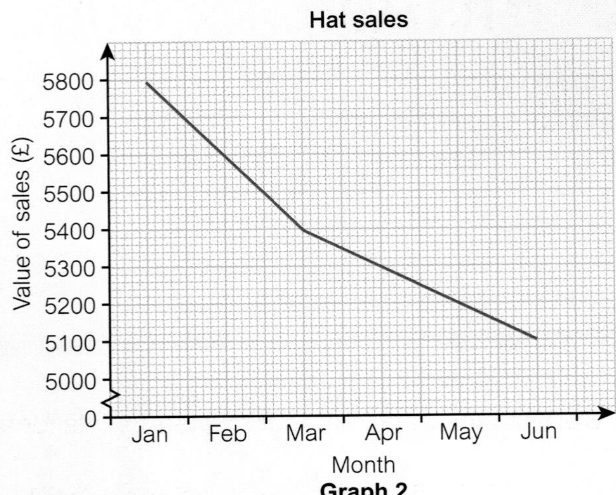

Graph 2

a Hilary says, 'Sales are very slightly down.' Which graph is she using?

b Her bank manager says, 'There has been a massive decrease in sales.' Which graph is he using?

c What is the actual fall in sales?

d Work out the actual fall as a percentage of the January sales figure.

Discussion Do the figures show a massive fall in sales?

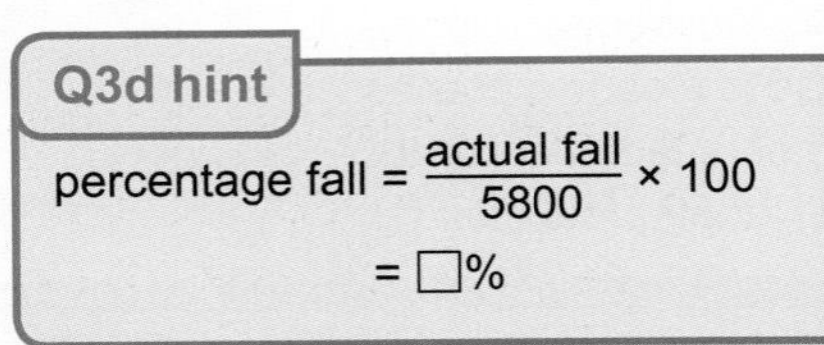
Q3d hint

$$\text{percentage fall} = \frac{\text{actual fall}}{5800} \times 100$$

$= \square\%$

4 **Real / STEM** These two graphs show the increase in mobile tablet use in the UK between 2011 and 2013.

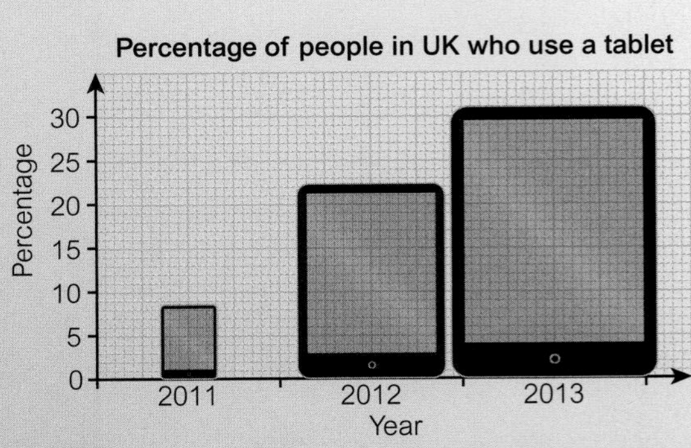

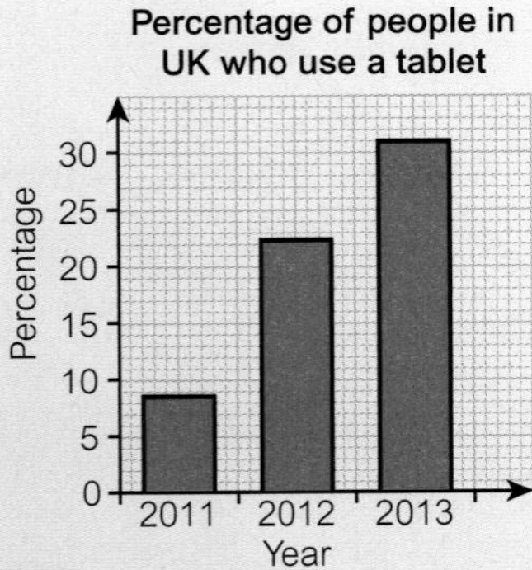

a Which graph shows the increase in the percentage of people using tablets most clearly?

b Which graph appears to show the biggest increase in tablet use?

Discussion How does the graph make the increase look bigger?

5 There are at least three reasons why this pie chart is misleading. Write all the reasons you can find.

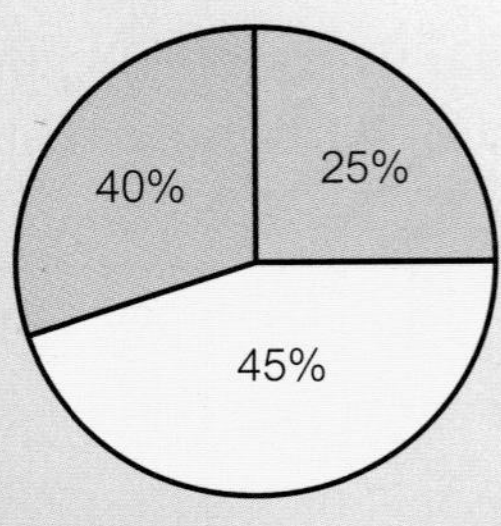

6 **Explore** How can you make your product sales look better than your competitors'?
What have you learned in this lesson to help you answer this question?
What other information do you need?

7 **Reflect** List five ways that graphs can mislead you.
You could begin with, 'It is misleading when different symbols are used on the same ____________.'

Explore

Reflect

3 Check up

Log how you did on your Student Progression Chart.

Averages and range

1 The frequency table shows the numbers of merit points Hetty won each week, in two terms.

a Find the mode.

b Work out the range.

c Work out the mean number of merit points for a week.

Number of merit points in a week	Frequency
0	5
1	7
2	9
3	6
4	3

2 Ali worked out these statistics for his merit points.
mean 1.95, range 7

a Write sentences to compare Ali's mean and range with Hetty's in Q1.

b The team with most merit points wins a prize. Who would you rather have on your team, Ali or Hetty? Explain why.

Tables

3 This table shows ages and genders of members of a tennis club.

	Under 18	18–40	Over 40	Total
Male	10		55	95
Female		38		
Total	40			200

a How many members are males over 40?

b How many members are females under 18?

c Copy and complete the table.

d How many members are over 40?

e What percentage of members are under 18?

4 The table shows the masses, in grams, of some newly-hatched chicks.

Mass, m (g)	Frequency
$0 \leqslant m < 30$	8
$30 \leqslant m < 40$	13
$40 \leqslant m < 50$	14
$50 \leqslant m < 60$	6

a How many chicks were weighed in total?

b Which is the modal class?

c Estimate the range.

d These three masses were missed out of the table.
36 g, 42 g, 40 g
When they are put in the table, will the modal class change? Explain your answer.

Charts and graphs

Car colours in a car park

other

blue

red

silver

black

5 This pie chart shows the colours of cars in a car park one morning.

  a Which colour is the mode?

  b Kai says, 'There are more silver cars than all the others put together.' Is he correct? Explain.

  c There were 18 black cars in the car park. How many cars were there altogether?

6 Draw a pie chart to show Hetty's merit points in Q1.

7 This stem and leaf diagram shows students' marks in a maths test.

  a What is the lowest mark?

  b Work out the range.

  c What is the modal mark?

  d Find the median mark.

  e Students who scored less than 35 had to re-sit the test. How many students had to do this?

Stem	Leaf
2	6, 7, 9
3	0, 5, 7, 8, 8, 9
4	1, 3, 6, 6, 9
5	2, 4, 6, 8, 9, 9, 9
6	0, 2, 4, 8, 8
7	1, 5, 8, 8

Key: 3 | 2 means 32 marks

8 Ms Barber plotted her students' maths test scores against the number of homeworks they completed in this scatter graph.

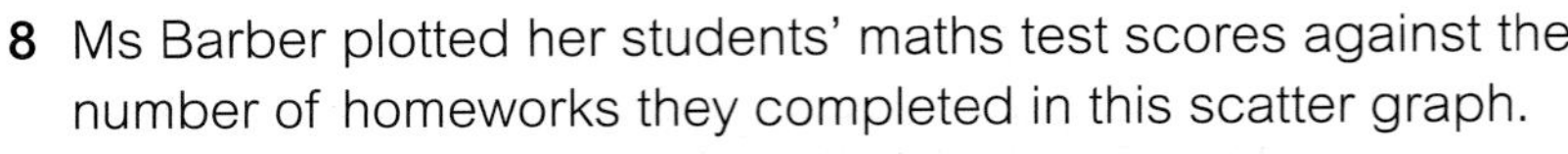

Maths test scores and number of homeworks

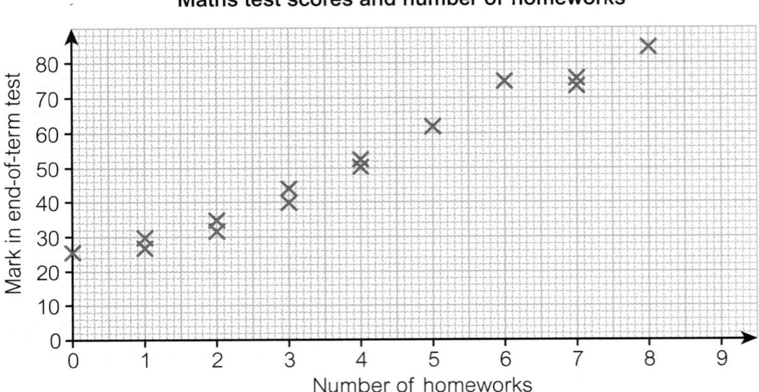

  a What type of correlation does this scatter graph show?

  b What word is missing from this sentence about the graph?

  'Students who complete more homeworks get __________ marks.'

Reflect

9 How sure are you of your answers? Were you mostly

Just guessing Feeling doubtful Confident

What next? Use your results to decide whether to strengthen or extend your learning.

Challenge

10 a Design a two-way table to record any information you choose.

  b In pencil, write numbers in all the cells so that the totals all add up correctly.

  c Rub out some of your numbers so that you can still work out the missing values from the ones that are left.

  d What is the smallest number of values you can keep so that someone else could work out the rest?

  e Give your table to a partner to see if they can fill in the gaps.

Q10a hint

You could design one with 3 groups along the top and 2 down the side like the one in Q3, or you could design your own.

Q10d hint

Try rubbing out another value. Can you still work out the missing ones?

3 Strengthen

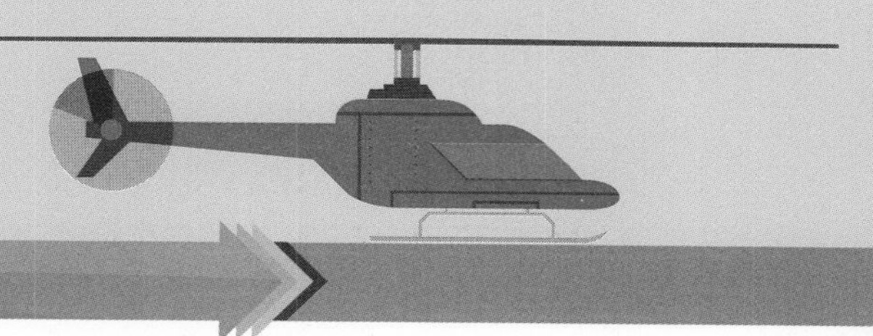

You will:
- Strengthen your understanding with practice.

Averages and range

1 Real Ten families live down a street. Here are the numbers of children in those families.

1, 3, 5, 2, 3, 2, 0, 2, 2, 3

a Find the mode.

b Work out the range.

c Check that the total number of children is 23.

d Work out the mean number of children per family.

Q1d hint

Finding the mean is like sharing out the children equally between the families.

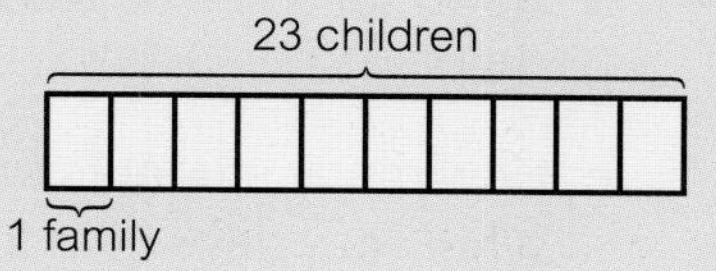

2 Real The frequency table shows the numbers of children in families in another street.

Number of children	Frequency
0	3
1	6
2	10
3	4
4	1

a How many families have no children?

b How many families have more than two children?

c How many families are there altogether?

d Find the mode.

e Work out the range of the number of children.

f Copy and complete this table.

Number of children	Frequency	Total number of children
0	3	0 × 3 = 0 children
1	6	
2	10	2 × 10 = 20 children
3	4	
4	1	
	Total number of families ☐	Total number of children ☐

g Work out the mean number of children for each family.

Q2b hint

Add the number with three children and the number with four children.

Q2d hint

The mode is the most common number of children. What is the highest frequency? What number of children has this frequency?

Q2f hint

Ten families have two children each. This makes 20 children in those families.

3 Here are two people's marks in three rounds of a quiz.

Flo: 7, 7, 6 Jim: 10, 0, 4

a Who scored highest in two of the three rounds?

b Whose results are the most consistent?

c Work out the range for Flo and for Jim.

d Write down the missing word from this sentence.

'The ________ the range, the more consistent the results.'

e Who would you like on your team – Flo or Jim? Explain why.

Q3b Literacy hint

Consistent means more or less the same every time.

Q3d hint

Choose from 'smaller' and 'larger'.

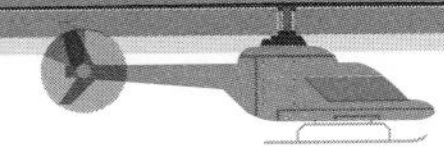

4 Real / Problem-solving Here are Pat's and Sam's marks in their maths homeworks this term.

Pat: 8, 2, 9, 6, 10, 1, 3, 10 Sam: 7, 8, 7, 7, 6, 7, 8, 8

a Work out
   i the median mark and range for Pat
   ii the median mark and range for Sam.
b Write a sentence to compare the medians.
c Write a sentence to compare the ranges.
d Reasoning Who would be the better person to help you with your maths homework? Explain your answer.

Q4c hint
Who had the smaller range and the more consistent marks?

Tables

1 Copy this table of instruments played by Year 8s and 9s.

	Flute	Violin	Trumpet	Total
Year 8	13	10	6	ii
Year 9	12	i	iv	iii
Total		18	v	53

a How many Year 8 students play the flute?
b How many Year 9 students play the flute?
c How many students in total play the flute? Write your answer in the correct space in the table.
d Find the number 6 in this table.
   Copy and complete: '6 students in Year ____ play the ____.'
e Find the number 18 in the table. What does this number tell you?
f Work out the rest of the values in the table, in the order i, ii, iii, iv, v, and write them in.
g How many Year 9s play the trumpet?
h How many Year 8 and 9s play the flute, violin or trumpet?

Q1e hint
You could begin: '18 students …'

2 This two-way table shows information about the animals treated in a vet's surgery.

	Male	Female	Total
Rabbit	4		10
Cat		8	
Dog	6		13
Total	15		

a Copy the table and fill in the missing values.
b How many cats were treated?
c What is the total number of animals treated?
d What fraction of the total number of animals treated were cats?
e What fraction of the animals treated were male dogs?
f Reasoning Jack says, 'The same number of cats and dogs were treated.' Is he correct? Explain your answer.

Q2a hint
Look for a row or column with only one value missing.

Q2d hint
$$\frac{\text{number of cats treated}}{\text{total number of animals treated}}$$

Q3 Literacy hint
9″ means 9 inches.

3 Problem-solving A pizza takeaway asked its customers, 'Which is your favourite pizza?'
These are the possible options.
9″ margherita 12″ pepperoni 9″ four cheese
12″ four cheese 12″ margherita 9″ pepperoni
Design a table the takeaway could use to tick people's choices.

Q3 hint
What are the different sizes? What are the different flavours? Remember to put in an end column and a bottom row for the totals.

4 Which of these distances, d (km), are in the set $5 \leqslant d < 10$?
6 km, 3.5 km, 4 km, 6.5 km, 10 km, 9 km, 5 km, 10.5 km

5 Here are the masses of turkeys on sale in a butcher's shop.
10.5 kg, 15.2 kg, 16.0 kg, 14.7 kg, 11.0 kg,
10.9 kg, 14.0 kg, 13.2 kg, 15.9 kg, 17.5 kg

a What does $10 \leqslant m < 12$ kg mean?

b Copy the table.
Tally the masses into it.
Complete the frequency column.

c Which is the modal class?

Mass, m (kg)	Tally	Frequency
$10 \leqslant m < 12$		
$12 \leqslant m < 14$		
$14 \leqslant m < 16$		
$16 \leqslant m < 18$		

Q4 hint

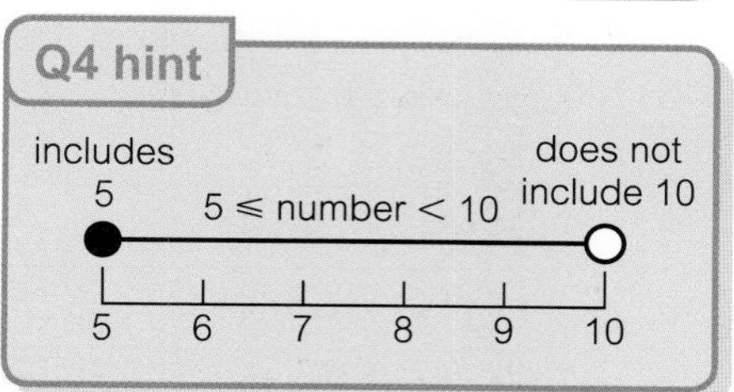

Q5c hint

Write the class like this:
□ kg $\leqslant m <$ □ kg.

Charts and graphs

1 This pie chart shows the meals people ate in a restaurant.
What fraction of the people ate

a chicken b fish c lamb

d vegetarian e chicken or fish?

Vegetarian
Lamb
Chicken
Fish

Q1a hint

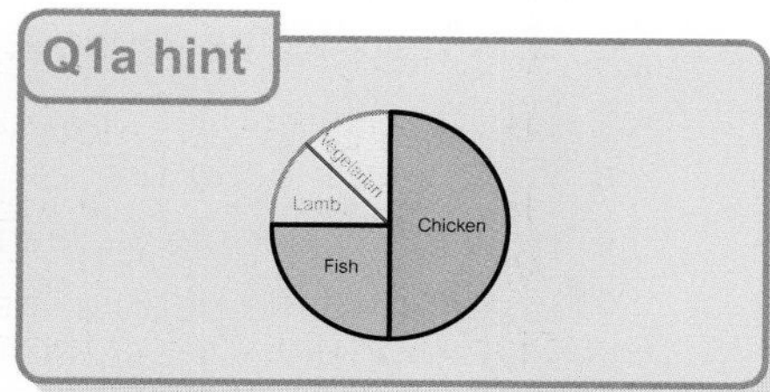

2 The table shows the numbers of different types of fish in a lake.

Type of fish	Frequency
carp	20
rudd	10
tench	40
bream	10

a How many fish are there in the lake in total?

b What fraction of the fish in the lake are carp?

c What fraction of the fish are

i rudd ii tench iii bream?

d Use the fractions you found in parts **b** and **c** to help you draw a pie chart.

Q2b hint

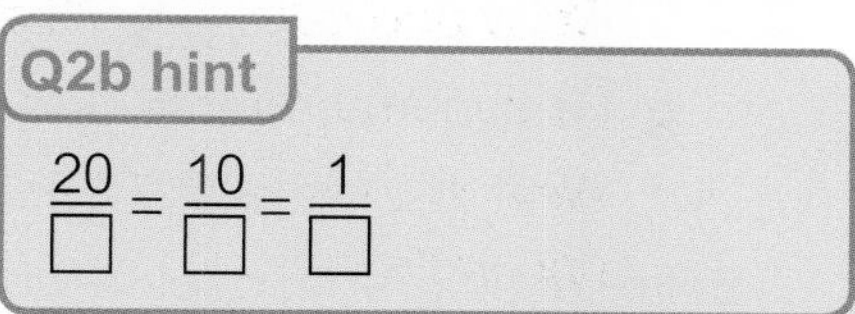

$\frac{20}{\square} = \frac{10}{\square} = \frac{1}{\square}$

Q2d hint

You could start with a circle like this.

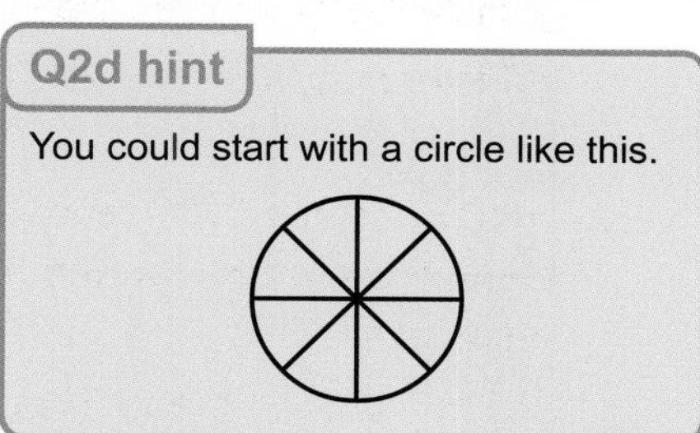

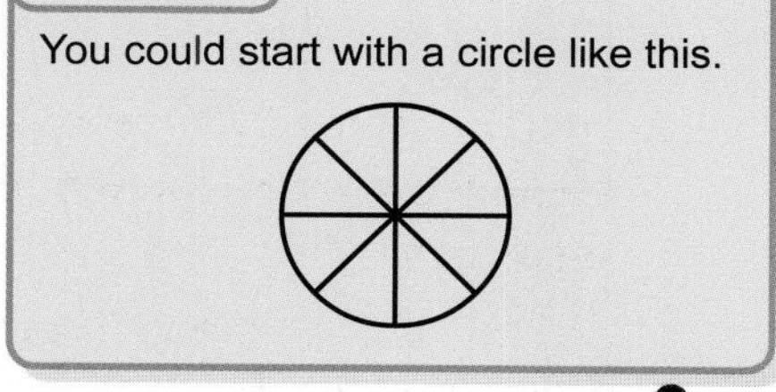

3 A travel company asked 180 people where they went for their holiday.
The table shows their answers.

Holiday	Frequency
UK	100
Spain	45
India	20
USA	15
Total	180

a When you divide a circle into equal sectors to show 180 people, how many degrees represent one person?

b Copy and complete this, to work out the angle for 100 people:

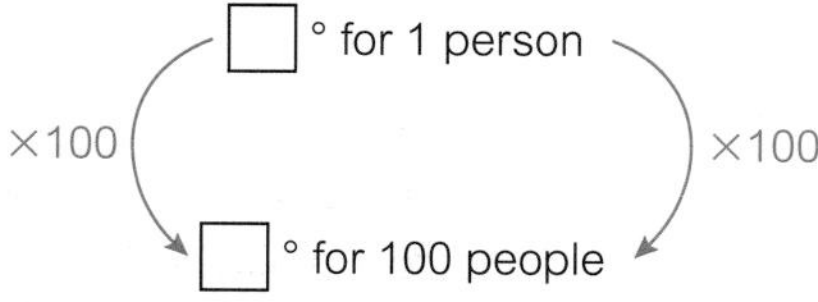

c Work out the angles for 45, 30 and 15 people.

d Draw a pie chart to show the holiday data.

Q3a Literacy hint

A sector is like a slice of the pie.

Q3a hint

There are 360° at the centre of a circle. 360° ÷ □ = □

Q3d hint

Draw a circle. Draw a vertical line from the centre to the top edge. Draw the first angle. Move your protractor round to the edge of your first sector. Draw the next angle.

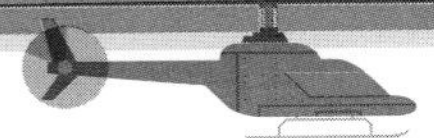

4 **a** Copy the table. Fill in the missing values.

	Number on middle counter	(number of counters + 1) ÷ 2
① ② ③ ④ ⑤	3	(5 + 1) ÷ 2 = 6 ÷ 2 = 3
① ② ③ ④ ⑤ ⑥ ⑦		
① ② ③ ④ ⑤ ⑥ ⑦ ⑧ ⑨ ⑩ ⑪		

b Show how to work out the number on the middle counter in a set of 25 counters, numbered 1 to 25.

5 The stem and leaf diagram shows the ages of people using a swimming pool one day.

2	2, 7, 9
3	3, 4, 5, 7
4	0, 5, 6, 7, 8
5	1, 1, 1, 4, 6, 7
6	0, 3, 5, 5, 7,
7	1, 3

Key: 3 | 8 means 38

a What does 4 | 0 mean?
b How many people in their 40s were in the pool?
c How old was the youngest person in the pool?
d What was the mode?
e How many people were in the swimming pool?
f Imagine all the people lined up in age order, holding numbers 1, 2, 3, 4, 5, …
What number would the 'middle' person be holding?
g Use your answer to part **f** to help you find the median age from the stem and leaf diagram.

Q5b hint
How many values are in the 4 | … row?

Q5d hint
The mode is one of the ages.

Q5f hint
The 1st person is 22, the 2nd person is 27 and so on.

6 For each graph, decide whether it shows positive correlation, negative correlation or no correlation.

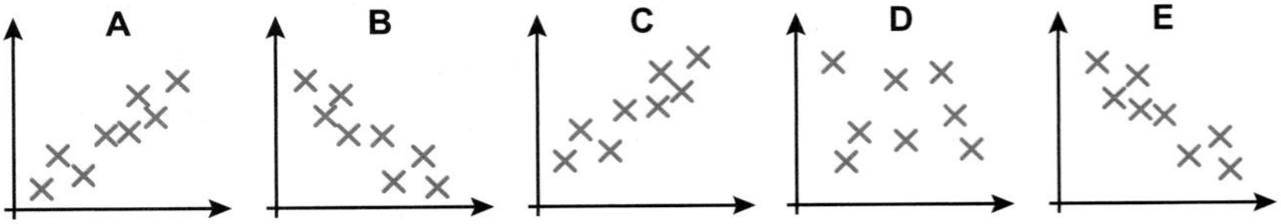

Q6 hint
Positive correlation – looking from (0, 0), the points go 'uphill': the values are increasing.
Negative correlation – looking from (0, 0), the points go 'downhill': the values are decreasing.
No correlation – the points are not close to a straight line, uphill or downhill.

Enrichment

1 Real Here are the 2005 to 2013 World Record times, in seconds, to solve a 3 × 3 × 3 Rubik's cube.
9.55, 10.36, 5.55, 11.75, 9.77, 6.18, 8.72, 11.13, 7.08,
6.77, 6.24, 9.18, 6.65, 10.48, 9.86, 7.03, 5.66

Source: http://www.recordholders.org/en/list/rubik.html

a Problem-solving Which time is the 2013 World Record?
b Tally the times into a grouped frequency table. Use the classes $5 \leqslant t < 7$, $7 \leqslant t < 9$, $9 \leqslant t < 11$ and so on.
c Draw a bar chart for the times.
d How many of the World Record times are less than 9 seconds?

Q1a hint
To be a World Record, the time has to be faster than any previous time.

Q1c hint
Time is a continuous measurement, so there should be no gaps between the bars in your chart.

Reflect

2 **Reflect** For these Strengthen lessons, copy and complete these sentences.
I found questions ______ easiest. They were on _________ (List the topics.)
I found questions ________ most difficult. I still need help with ________ (List the topics.)

3 Extend

You will:

- Extend your understanding with problem-solving.

1 **Problem-solving** Sushma is doing a survey to find out what people enjoy at the theatre.
Here is part of her questionnaire.

How old are you?
under 16 ☐ 16–25 ☐ 26–45 ☐ over 45 ☐
Which of these have you seen at a theatre in the past year? Tick all that apply.
Stand up comedy ☐ Musical ☐ Drama ☐ Other ☐

When she has collected in her questionnaires, Sushma wants to put all the results into a table.

a Design a table she could use to show all this information.

b Which averages can she find from her table?

2 **Real** The pie chart shows the government's recommendations for healthy eating.
An active teenager needs about 2400 calories per day.
How many of these calories should be from

a non-dairy protein

b fruit and vegetables?

An active man needs 3000 calories per day.
How many of these calories should be from

c milk and dairy foods

d starchy foods?

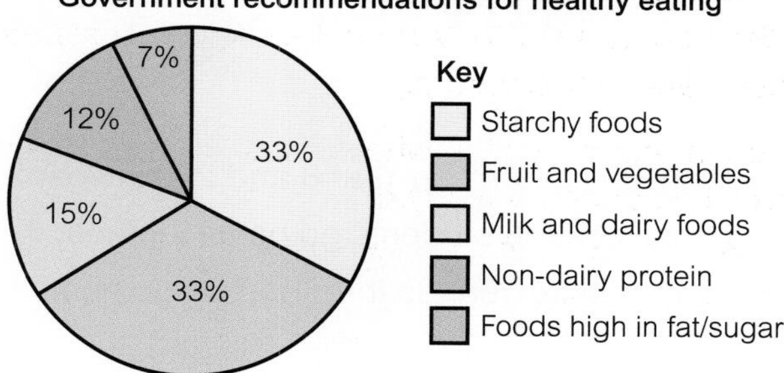

Key point

The **assumed mean** is a sensible estimate for the mean.

Worked example

Work out the mean of 102, 105, 95, 100, 92 using an **assumed mean**.

102 105 95 100 92
differences from 100 +2 +5 −5 0 −8 = −6
−6 ÷ 5 = −1.2
100 + −1.2 = 98.8

The values are all close to 100, so assume the mean is 100. Work out the differences from 100.

Add up the 5 differences and divide by 5 to find the mean difference.

Add the mean difference to the assumed mean.

3 **Real** To set his pedometer, Jay needs to work out his stride length.
He walks eight steps across sand, and then measures each one.
Here are his results.
96 cm, 100 cm, 108 cm, 97 cm, 101 cm, 98 cm, 103 cm, 105 cm
Use an **assumed mean** to calculate his mean stride length.

Q3 hint

Use the method in the worked example.

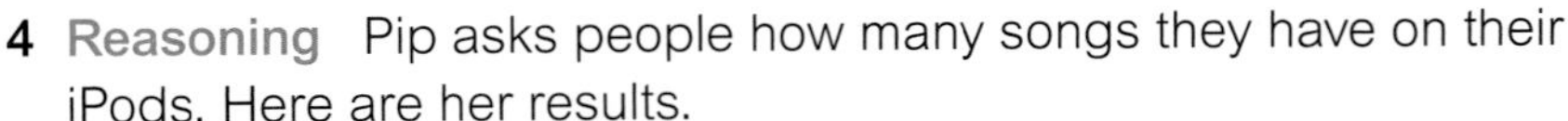

4 **Reasoning** Pip asks people how many songs they have on their iPods. Here are her results.

503, 495, 502, 501, 500, 490, 496, 504,
495, 492, 504, 502, 497, 496, 501, 502

a What value could you use for an assumed mean?

b Use this value to calculate the mean.

c Find the mode.

d Does the mean or the mode better represent the data? Explain your answer.

> **Q4d hint**
> Is the mode roughly in the middle of the data values?

5 **Problem-solving** The pie charts show Year 8 and Year 9 students' lunch choices.

Year 8 lunch choices

go home
hot lunch
sandwiches

Year 9 lunch choices

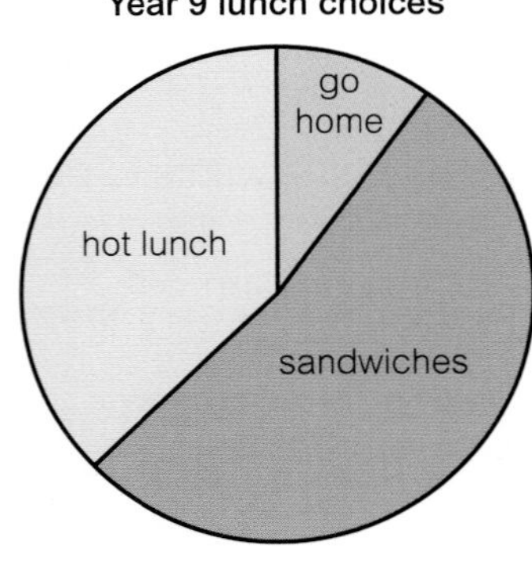

There are 180 students in Year 8 and 220 in Year 9.

a How many Year 8 students go home for lunch?

b Zoe says, 'More Year 9s than Year 8s go home for lunch.'
Is she correct?
Show your working.

> **Q5 Strategy hint**
> Measure the angles of the sectors for 'go home'.
> Work out how many students they represent.

6 **Real** The table shows the mean monthly rainfall, in mm, in Mumbai and London.

Month	Jan	Feb	Mar	Apr	May	Jun	Jul	Aug	Sep	Oct	Nov	Dec
Mumbai	0.6	1.5	0.1	0.6	13.2	574.1	868.3	553.0	306.4	62.9	14.9	5.6
London	82.9	60.3	64.0	58.7	58.4	61.8	62.6	69.4	69.7	91.7	88.2	87.2

a Draw two line graphs for this data, on the same axes.
Put the months on the horizontal axis.
The vertical axis for rainfall will have to go from 0 to 870 mm.

b For how many months of the year is London wetter than Mumbai?

c What happens to the rainfall in Mumbai in the monsoon season (June to September)?

d Compare the rainfall in the two cities using the mean monthly rainfall and the range for each.

> **Q6a hint**
> You could use a spreadsheet.

> **Q6d hint**
> Write a sentence comparing the means and a sentence comparing the ranges.

7 **Real / Reasoning** The pie charts show visitor numbers for different British tourist attractions in 1981 and 1999.

a Write three sentences comparing the percentages of visitors at the different attractions in 1981 and 1999.

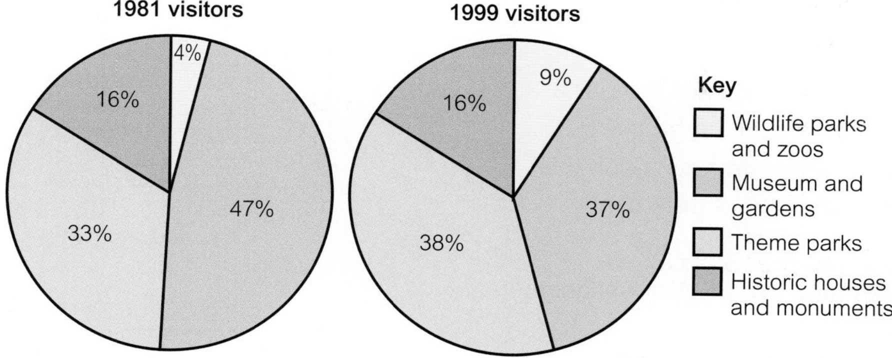

b A newspaper article commenting on these pie charts in 1999 said, 'More people visited museums and gardens in 1981 than in 1999.' Explain why this statement could be incorrect.

Q7a hint
You might like to use some of these words: increase, decrease, stayed the same.

Q7b hint
What do you need to know to work out how many people visited museums and gardens each year?

8 **Real** Here are the fastest eight women's and men's times for the 5000 m in the London 2012 Olympics.

Women 15:04.25, 15:04.73, 15:05.15, 15:05:79, 15:10.66, 15:11.59, 15:12.72, 15:17.88

Men 13:41.66, 13.41.98, 13.42.36, 13:42.99, 13.43.83. 13.45.04, 13.45.30, 13:45.37

a What was the fastest women's time, in minutes and seconds?

b Compare the men's and women's times, using the means and the ranges.

Q8a hint
16:05.36 means 16 minutes, 5.36 seconds.

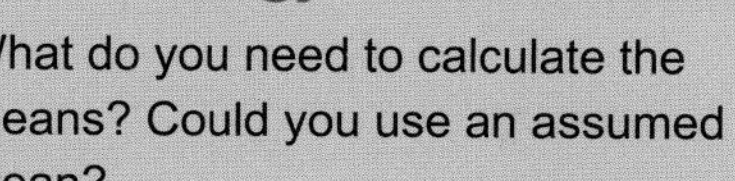

Q8b Strategy hint
What do you need to calculate the means? Could you use an assumed mean?
Round your means to the nearest tenth of a second.

9 Here are the numbers of pages in the books entered for a literature prize.

125, 200, 316, 412, 517, 627, 196, 256, 358, 420, 464, 562, 446, 376, 137, 294, 327, 488, 534, 496, 382, 584, 367, 578

a Draw a stem and leaf diagram for the data.

Use the key '1 | 25 means 125 pages'.

b How many books were entered for the prize?

c What percentage of the books had over 500 pages?

d Draw a grouped frequency table for this data. Use the classes $100 \leqslant p < 200$, $200 \leqslant p < 300$ etc.

e Use the stem and leaf diagram and your frequency table to find

i the median number of pages

ii the mean number of pages

iii the range

iv the modal class(es).

10 STEM / Modelling To test how a copper tank would expand in high temperatures in a power station, a copper bar 10 m long was heated. Its length was recorded at different temperatures. The results were plotted on this scatter graph.

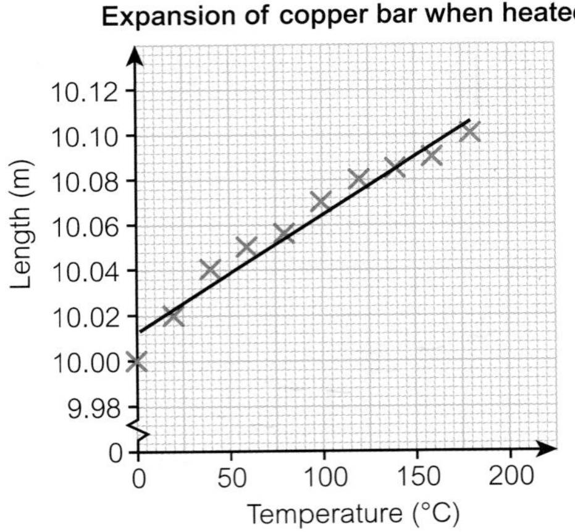

a Describe the correlation shown by the graph.

b What happens to the length of the copper bar as the temperature increases?

c Use the line of best fit to predict the length of the bar at

i 20 °C **ii** 110 °C.

d Using your answers from part **c**, estimate how much the bar would increase in length when heated from room temperature (20 °C) to 110 °C.

11 Modelling Some Year 9 students took two English assessments – writing and comprehension.

Here are their results.

Student	A	B	C	D	E	F	G	H	I	J	K	L	M
Writing	64	59	78	82	42	76	43	absent	15	38	45	68	72
Comprehension	60	absent	72	88	36	80	49	85	27	37	51	65	76

a Draw a scatter graph for this data. Put writing marks on the horizontal axis and comprehension marks on the vertical axis.
Ignore the data for students B and H.

b Draw a line of best fit on your graph.

c Describe the relationship between the marks for writing and marks for comprehension.

d Use your line of best fit to predict the

i comprehension marks for student B **ii** writing marks for student H.

Investigation

Problem-solving

1 From this bar chart, which age group appears to have the most accidents?
Here is the original car accident data.

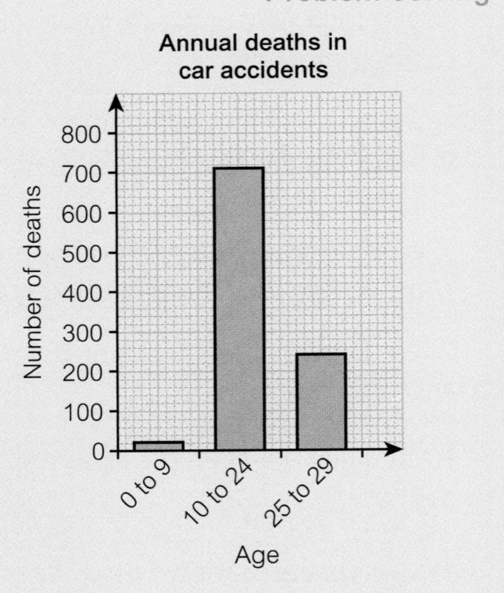

Age, a (years)	Frequency
$0 \leqslant a < 5$	21
$5 \leqslant a < 10$	23
$10 \leqslant a < 15$	48
$15 \leqslant a < 20$	327
$20 \leqslant a < 25$	332
$25 \leqslant a < 30$	241

Source: RAC Foundation 'Mortality statistics and road traffic accidents in the UK'

2 **a** Draw a bar chart to show this data.
Use a horizontal axis like this.

0, 0 5 10 15 20 25 30, Age

b From your bar chart, which age group appears to have the most accidents?

c Why is the first bar chart misleading?

3 Design a poster showing people how to spot misleading graphs.

Reflect

12 **Reflect** Q6 uses data that climate scientists might use. It also uses these maths topics: line graphs, mean and range.
List all the other maths topics you have used in these Extend lessons.
How might climate scientists use these maths topics too?

3 Unit test

Log how you did on your Student Progression Chart.

1 The pie chart shows the different birds seen in a garden one day.
In total 72 birds were seen.
How many of them were
- a starlings
- b sparrows
- c goldfinches?

Birds in a garden

2 A survey about shopping habits asked people how many items they had bought online that week.
Here are the results.

Items bought online	Frequency
0	5
1	8
2	12
3	10
4	8
5	2

- a Work out the range
- b What is the mode?
- c Work out the mean. Give your answer to one decimal place.

3 The table shows the amounts two families spent on their weekly food shop over one year.

	Mean	Median	Range
Smith family	£85	£82.50	£38
Jones family	£75	£81	£24

- a Write two sentences comparing the amounts the two families spent on food.
- b Explain why there is unlikely to be a modal value for a family's weekly food shop.

4 Draw a pie chart to show the online shopping data in Q2.

5 Here are the prices of some mobile phones in one shop.
£129.99, £118.95, £95.99, £92.50, £329.99
- a Work out the mean, median and mode. Give your answers to the nearest penny.
- b Which average best represents the prices of phones in the shop?

6 A chicken farmer recorded the mass of eggs laid one morning.
58.5 g, 61.3 g, 55.2 g, 58.6 g, 49.1 g, 45.2 g, 64.7 g, 61.2 g, 55.0 g, 59.5 g
Copy and complete the grouped frequency table for the data.

Mass, m (g)	Tally	Frequency
$45 \leqslant m < 50$		

7 Learner drivers take a hazard perception test as part of their driving theory exam.
The stem and leaf diagram shows some learner drivers' reaction times in the test.

Stem	Leaf
10	5, 7
11	0, 4, 9
12	6, 6, 8, 9
13	2, 5, 5, 6, 8
14	1, 3, 3

Key: 10 | 7 means 10.7 seconds

a What is the range?

b What is the median?

8 The scatter graph shows prices and ages of second-hand cars.

a What type of correlation does it show?

b What happens to the price of a car as it gets older?

c Explain how you could use this graph to predict the price of a 7-year-old car.

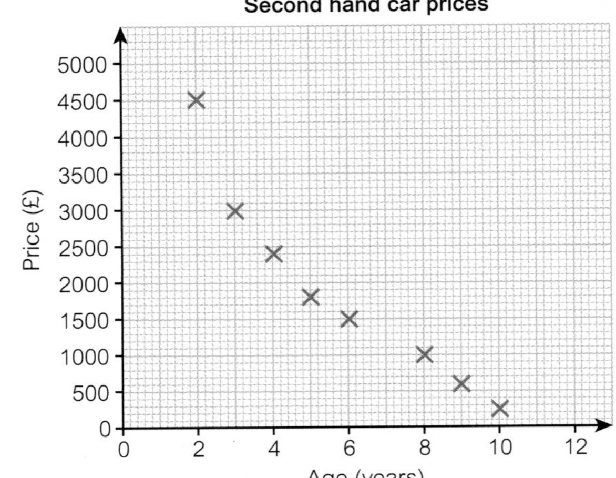

Challenge

9 **Real / Modelling**

75% of 5–18 year olds get pocket money	Average pocket money is £5.75 per week.	Approximately 10 million children aged 5–18 in the UK

Source: http://www.aviva.com/

Use these facts to estimate the total pocket money UK parents pay per week.

10 Write down five numbers with

a a median less than the mean

b a median greater than the mean

c a mode less than the mean.

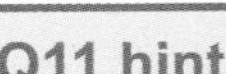

Q10 Strategy hint
Try different values.

Reflect

11 **Reflect** Think back to when you have struggled to answer a question in a maths test.

a Write two words that describe how you felt.

b Write two things you could do when you're finding it hard to answer a question in a maths test.

c Imagine you have another maths test and you do the two things you wrote in your answer to part **b**.
How do you think you might feel then?

Q11 hint
Look back at questions in this test, or previous tests as a reminder.

4 Expressions and equations

MASTER

Check P95 | Strengthen P97 | Extend P101 | Test P105

4.1 Algebraic powers

You will learn to:
- Understand and simplify algebraic powers
- Substitute values into formulae involving powers.

CONFIDENCE

Why learn this?
Einstein's famous formula $E = mc^2$ pops up everywhere, from T-shirts to album covers.

Fluency
- What is the square of 5? … the cube of 4?
- What does $4c$ mean?
- Simplify $w + w$, $3w + p - 2w$

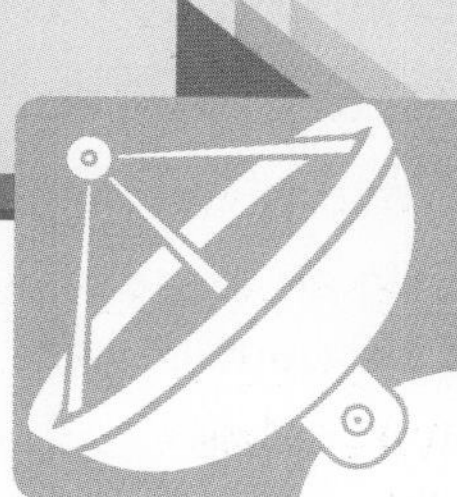

Explore
How much energy does a moving car have?

Exercise 4.1

Warm up

1 Write these **products** using **index notation**.
  a $2 \times 2 \times 2 \times 2 \times 2$
  b $2 \times 2 \times 2 \times 10 \times 10$
  c $3 \times 3 \times 3 \times 10$
  d $5 \times 5 \times 10 \times 10 \times 10$

> **Key point**
> **Index notation** means to write a product using **powers**. For example, $3 \times 3 \times 2$ is written $3^2 \times 2$.

2 Simplify these expressions.
  a $5p - p$
  b $3 \times 2v$
  c $5x - 2x + 3y$
  d $2u + 3 + 3u$
  e $10t + 4s + 5 - 6t$
  f $s \times t \times 2$
  g $4p \times 3q$
  h $2b \times 3c \times 4d$

3 Write each product as a **power**.
  a $d \times d$
  b $m \times m \times m$
  c $c \times c \times c \times c$
  d $t \times t \times t \times t \times t \times t$

4 Write each power as a product.
  a n^3
  b x^2
  c w^5
  d u^{10}
  e 10^4
  f 2^6

5 Simplify these. Write each answer using powers.
  a $3 \times f \times f$
  b $e \times e \times 7 \times e$
  c $3n \times 2n \times 5n \times n$
  d $c \times c \times c \times d \times d$
  e $m \times n \times n$
  f $r \times s \times r \times s \times r$
  g $3m \times 2n \times 4n \times m$
  h $2e \times 3f \times 4g \times e \times e \times g$

> **Key point**
> In algebra we write numbers first and then letters.
> $3m \times n \times 2n = 3 \times m \times n \times 2 \times n$
> $= 3 \times 2 \times m \times n \times n$
> $= 6 \times m \times n \times n$
> $= 6mn^2$

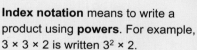

6 a Copy and complete this table.

n	1	3	4		9			
$2n$							24	60
n^2				49		121		

b Is there a difference between $2n$ and n^2? Explain your answer.

c Are there any values for which $2n$ and n^2 are the same?

Discussion Is there a difference between $3n$ and n^3?

7 Problem-solving / Real A square solar panel has a side of length s metres. Write your answers to these questions using powers.

Q7a Strategy hint
Sketch the panel.

a Write an expression for the area of the solar panel.

b Write an expression for the total area of a row of
- **i** 10 panels
- **ii** n panels
- **iii** $2n$ panels.

Q7b Strategy hint
Try using a number instead of s to help you see what you need to do.

c What is the total area of an array of
- **i** 5 rows of 10 panels
- **ii** 10 rows of n panels?

d i For a small solar panel, $s = 60$ cm. Use your expression from part **b i** to work out the area of a row of 10 panels.

ii For a large solar panel, $s = 90$ cm. Use your expression from part **c i** to work out the area of 5 rows of 10 panels.

8 a Write an expression for the volume of each cuboid.

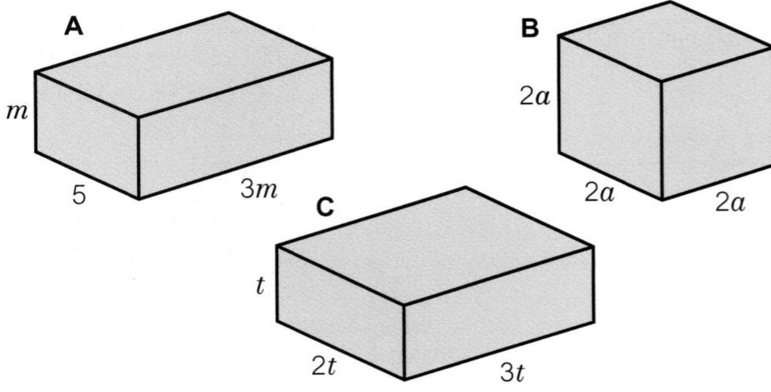

b Work out the volume of cuboid C when $t = 4$ cm.

Q8b hint
Substitute the value of t into your expression.

9 Real / Modelling The population P of a country in four years' time will be approximately $P = Cr^4$ where C is the current population and r is the growth multiplier. Estimate the population in four years' time of

a Liberia, where $C = 4\,100\,000$ and $r = 1.05$

b the Cook Islands, where $C = 20\,000$ and $r = 0.98$.

Discussion Is the formula $P = Cr^{20}$ a good model for predicting the population in 20 years' time?

Q9 Literacy hint
The growth multiplier is worked out by looking at how a country's population has changed over time.

Topic links: Area, Volume

Subject links: Geography (Q9), Science (Q13)

10 Simplify these.

a $a^2 + a^2 + a^2$

b $m^3 + m^3 + m^3 + m^3 + m^3$

c $a^2 + a^2 + b^2 + b^2 + b^2$

d $e^2 + e^2 + e^4$

e $y^5 + y^5 + y^3 + y^3$

f $5a^3 - 2a^3$

g $2p + 3p^2 + 5p^2 + 7p$

h $3h^2 + 4b^3 + 2b^3 + 5h^2$

Q10a hint
How many lots of a^2 are there?

Q10d hint
e^2 and e^4 are *not* like terms.

Investigation

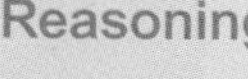

Reasoning

To work out $a^2 \times a^3$ write a^2 and a^3 as products: $a \times a \times a \times a \times a$.

1 Use the same method to write each product as a single power.

$a^2 \times a^4$

$a^3 \times a$

$a^5 \times a^2$.

Find and explain the rule for multiplying powers of the same letter.

2 Use $b^2 \times b^5 = b^7$ and $x^3 \times x^2 = x^5$ to work out these divisions.

$b^7 \div b^5 =$

$b^7 \div b^2 =$

$x^5 \div x^2 =$

$x^5 \div x^3 =$

Find and explain the rule for dividing powers of the same letter.

Discussion What is $x^3 \div x$? What is the power of the second x?

11 Simplify these.

a $p^2 \times p^5$

b $k^3 \times k^2$

c $a^5 \times a$

d $3 \times m^2 \times m^3$

e $4c^3 \times c$

f $5e^3 \times 2e^2$

g $6s^2 \times 3s$

h $5g \times 2g$

Q11d hint
Simplify the powers first: $m^2 \times m^3$

Q11f hint
Rearrange the product:
$5 \times e^3 \times 2 \times e^2 = 5 \times 2 \times e^3 \times e^2$

12 Simplify these.

a $e^7 \div e^2$ b $a^8 \div a^3$ c $3d^6 \div d^3$

d $8m^3 \div m^2$ e $4t^8 \div t^5$ f $6r^2 \div r^2$

Discussion In the expression $4n^2$, do you square the 4 as well?

Q12b hint
Simplify the powers first: $d^6 \div d^3$

13 **Explore** How much energy does a moving car have?
Is it easier to explore this question now you have completed the lesson?
What further information do you need to be able to answer this?

14 **Reflect** Kevin asks, 'Are the results of $x^2 \times x^2$ and $x^2 + x^2$ the same or different?'
Answer Kevin's question, then explain your answer.

Q14 hint
Substitute $x = 3$ into each expression. Do you get the same or different results? Why?

4.2 Expressions and brackets

You will learn to:
- Expand brackets
- Make and simplify algebraic expressions.

CONFIDENCE

Why learn this?
Physicists calculate quantities using formulae involving brackets.

Fluency
- Work out $4 - 10$, $-4 \times (-2)$, $3 \times (-5)$, $-(-6)$, $2 \times 5 - 3 \times 3$
- Simplify $2 \times 3a$, $c \times 5$, $-4 \times 2f$, $d \times d$, $5p \times p$, $3m \times 2n$

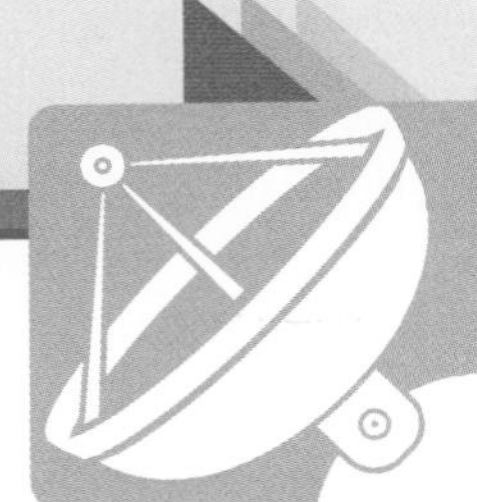

Explore
How can you estimate the total weight of a delivery of boxed eggs?

Exercise 4.2

Warm up

1 Write an algebraic expression for each of these.
 a the sum of a and 2
 b 6 more than s
 c double m
 d 4 less than e.

2 Simplify these.
 a $4a + 3a + 6b - 2b$
 b $2p + 5 - 2 + 5p$
 c $2m - 5m$
 d $3d - 4 - 7d + 6$

Q2c hint
$2 - 5 = -3$

3 Expand and simplify these.
 a $2(m - 7)$
 b $3(5s + 2)$
 c $4(h + 3) + 2(h - 3)$
 d $2(e - 3) + 5(2e + 1)$

4 Copy and complete these.
 a $m \div 5 = \frac{\square}{\square}$
 b $\frac{8}{d} = \square \div \square$
 c $2e \div 3 = \frac{\square}{\square}$
 d $\frac{u - 3}{3} = \square \div \square$

Key point

Division can be written as a fraction.
For example, $a \div 3$ can be written $\frac{a}{3}$.

Worked example

A cup contains b grams of sugar. A teaspoon holds 5 g of sugar.
Write an expression for the number of

a teaspoons of sugar in a cup of sugar

$b \div 5 = \frac{b}{5}$

b teaspoons of sugar in 3 cups of sugar

1 cup $= \frac{b}{5}$, so 3 cups $= 3 \times \frac{b}{5} = \frac{3b}{5}$

c cups in a 2 kg bag of sugar.

2 kg = 2000 g, $2000 \div b = \frac{2000}{b}$

Topic links: Measures

5 A tin weighs t grams and contains f grams of tomatoes.

a Write an expression for the total weight of one tin of tomatoes.

b Write an expression with brackets for the total weight of n tins.

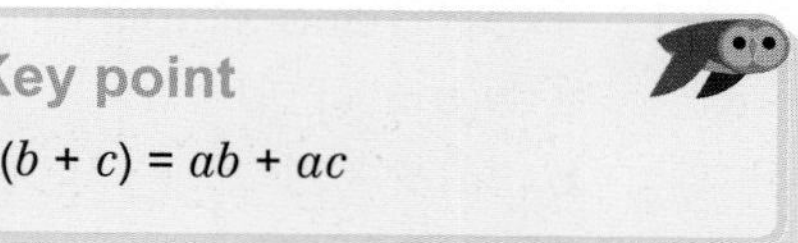

6 a The usual shop price of a T-shirt is £m.
In a sale, the shop reduced the price by £3.
Write an expression for the new price.

b The shop sold 8 T-shirts.
Write an expression for the total amount of money they received.

Discussion How can you turn your expression into a formula?

7 **Real** The diagram shows two kinds of antenna made from metal tubing.
Lengths are in metres.
Write a simplified formula for the total length T of tubing in

a a type A antenna

b a type B antenna

c two type A antennas

d three type B antennas

e two type A and three type B antennas.

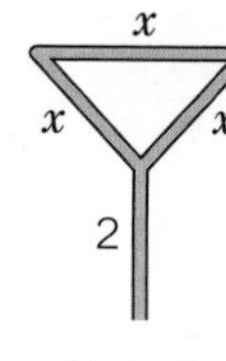

Type A

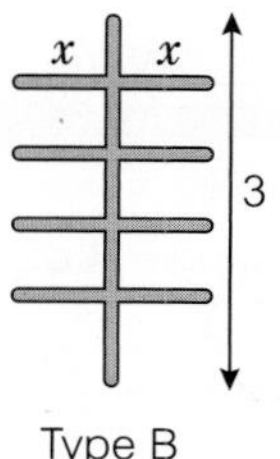

Type B

8 **Problem-solving**

a A bottle holds x millilitres of anaesthetic. A syringe holds 100 ml.
Write an expression for

i the number of syringes that can be filled from a bottle

ii the number of syringes that can be filled from 3 bottles.

b There is d ml of anaesthetic in a drop.
Write an expression for the number of drops in a 600 ml bottle.

Q5a Strategy hint

Try using a number instead of x to help you see what you need to do.

9 Expand and simplify these.

a $-3(2c - 5)$ b $-2(4t + 3)$ c $-5(2 - s)$

d $-10(-1 - x)$ e $-(y + 2)$ f $-(3m - 5)$

Discussion If you multiply a bracket by a negative number, what happens to the signs of the terms inside the bracket?

Q9a hint

Work out $-3 \times 2c + -3 \times -5$

10 Expand and simplify these.

a $10 - 2(c + 3)$ b $8 - 2(b + 2)$

c $12 - 3(n - 1)$ d $8f - 3(f - 2)$

e $9u + 10 - 2(u + 4)$ f $3p - 4 - 2(p - 5)$

g $6(b + 3) - 2(b + 2)$ h $6(i - 4) - 3(i - 3)$

Q10a hint

Work out $-2(c + 3)$ first, then add 10.

11 **Problem-solving** A glass has a capacity of v millilitres. It is filled with 50 ml of cordial and topped up with water. Jo opens some cordial and a full 2 litre bottle of water and serves 8 glasses of drink.

a Write an expression for the amount of water in one glass.

b Write an expression with brackets for the water left in the bottle.

c Expand and simplify your expression in part **b**.

d Calculate the volume of water left when v = 250 ml.

Q11 hint

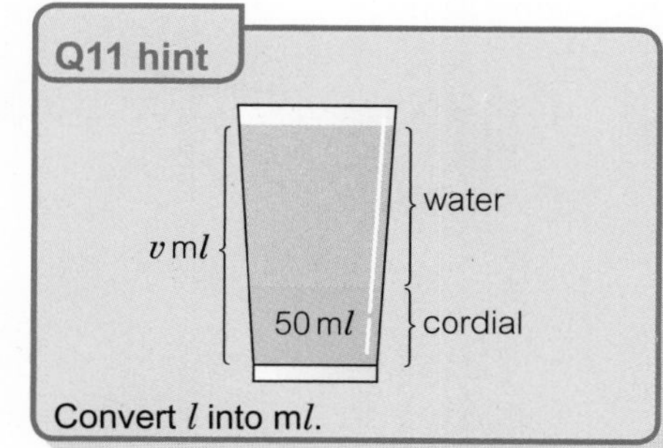

Convert l into ml.

12 Expand and simplify these.

a $p(p + 4)$

b $3d(d - 2)$

c $4a(2a + 3)$

d $-2g(3 - 5g)$

e $m(3m - 4) + 5m$

f $8d^2 + 3d(d - 4)$

g $2s(s + 4) + 3(2s - 2)$

Investigation — Problem-solving / Reasoning

Start with two sticks 100 cm long. Cut x cm from each stick.

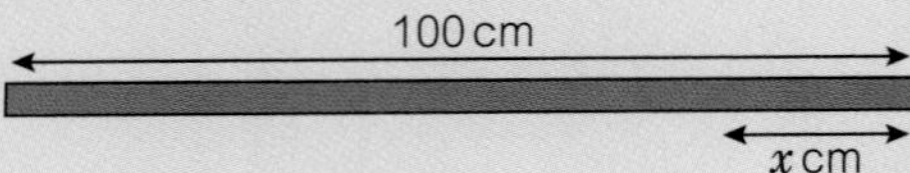

1 Arrange the four pieces into a rectangle like this:

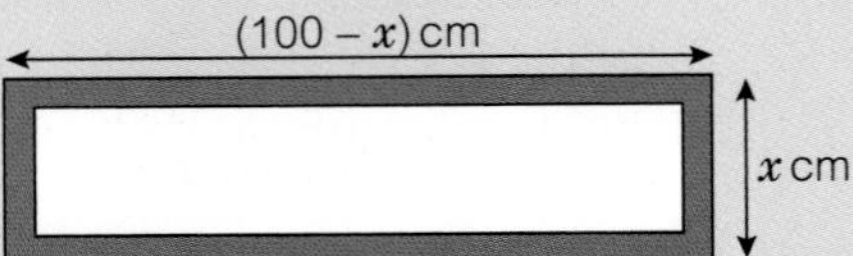

Write a simplified expression for its perimeter and for its area.

2 Now start with four sticks 100 cm long. Cut x cm from each stick and arrange the pieces into a rectangle. You don't have to use all of the pieces.

a How many different rectangles can you make?

b How many different expressions for the area and perimeter are there?

c Work out the perimeter and area of each rectangle when x = 20 cm.

3 Explore the perimeter and area of other shapes that can be made using the same pieces.

Explore

13 **Explore** How can you estimate the total weight of a delivery of boxed eggs?
Is it easier to explore this question now you have completed the lesson?
What further information do you need to be able to answer this?

Reflect

14 **Reflect** Write a definition, in your own words, for

- expand
- simplify.

Compare your definitions with those written by others in your class.
Can you improve your definitions?

Q14 hint

Look back at questions where you were asked to expand and simplify. What did you do?

4.3 Factorising expressions

You will learn to:
- Factorise expressions.

CONFIDENCE

Why learn this?
The HM Revenue & Customs website uses complex calculations involving brackets to work out how much tax a person owes.

Fluency
- What are the factors of 6   15   24?
- Expand $5(a + 1)$, $2(m - 3)$, $3(2x + 1)$, $c(c + 3)$

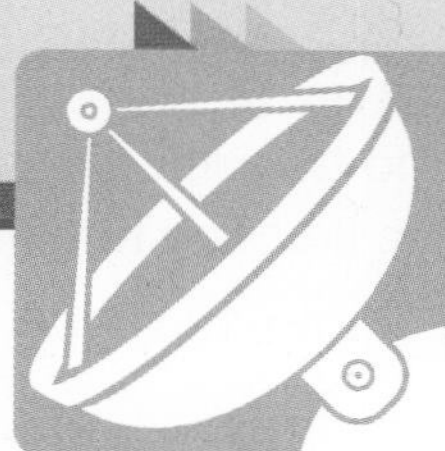

Explore
How much will each member of a four-person band receive for selling their latest album online to 1000 of their fans?

Exercise 4.3

Warm up

1 Copy and complete these.

a $6a = \square \times 2a$ b $12p = \square \times 3p$ c $18u = 6 \times \square u$
d $100i = 4 \times \square i$ e $-8m = \square \times 4m$ f $-14w = 7 \times \square w$

2 What is the highest common factor (HCF) of each pair of numbers?

a 6 and 3 b 8 and 12 c 30 and 20 d 12 and 18

Worked example

Find the common factor of the terms 6 and $3a$.

$6 = \mathbf{3} \times 2$, so **3** and 2 are factors of 6.
$3a = \mathbf{3} \times a$, so **3** and a are factors of $3a$.
The common factor is **3**.

Key point
Expanding removes brackets from an expression.
Factorising inserts brackets into an expression

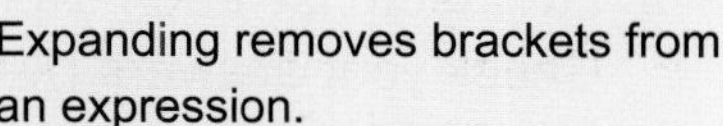

To factorise $5a + 10$, write the common factor of its terms, 5, outside the brackets. This is called 'taking out the common factor'.

3 Find the common factor of each pair of terms.

a 6 and $8m$ b $5a$ and 10 c $7y$ and 7
d $6m$ and $9n$ e $10d$ and $4e$ f pq and pr

4 Copy and complete these **factorisations**. Check your answers.

a $12 + 15m = 3(\square + 5m)$
b $8 + 10c = 2(\square + 5c)$
c $14 - 21a = 7(\square - \square a)$
d $6 + 9w = \square(2 + 3w)$
e $20h - 10 = 10(\square h - \square)$
f $12n + 6 = 6(\square + \square)$
g $5a - 10 = \square(\square - \square)$
h $14u + 7v = \square(\square + \square)$

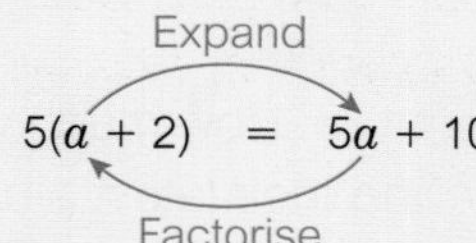

Q4 Strategy hint
Check your factorisation by expanding the brackets.

5 Factorise each expression. Check your answers.

a $15 + 10h$ b $3i + 6$ c $4c - 10$ d $6m - 8$
e $7d + 7$ f $2m - 2$ g $3s - 9t$ h $5 + 5k$

Q5e hint
$7d + 7 = \square(\square + 1)$

6 **Real / Reasoning** Last year, Gareth paid £e each month for electricity. This year his monthly payment went down. His total bill for the first 5 months is given by the expression £$5e - 35$. Factorise $5e - 35$.
Discussion What does the expression in the brackets represent?

7 Find the HCF of each pair of terms.
The first one has been done for you.

a 6 and $12a$ The common factors of 6 and $12a$ are 3 and 6. The HCF is 6.

b 10 and $20b$ c $8a$ and 12 d $9p$ and 18
e $4a$ and $12b$ f $16i$ and $24j$ g $15h$ and 30

8 Factorise each expression completely. Check your answers.

a $12 + 16h$ b $30m - 15$ c $6s + 18$
d $20m - 100$ e $27p + 36$ f $8c + 12d$
g $15k - 45t$ h $24r + 36s$ i $40n - 120p$

Discussion Is $2(2x + 4)$ factorised completely? How can you tell?

Key point
To factorise an expression completely, write the HCF of its terms outside the bracket.

Investigation **Reasoning**

1 Start with the number n. Multiply it by 4 and add 12. Write down an expression for this new number and fully factorise it.
2 Divide your factorised expression by 4.
3 Ask a classmate to think of a number, multiply it by 4, add 12, divide the result by 4 and then tell you the answer. How does your expression in part **2** show how to quickly find the number your classmate first thought of?
4 a Starting with n, make your own set of instructions that result in a factorised expression.
b Write down the instructions for a classmate to follow. Write down the secret solution.
Check that your trick works before trying it out on a classmate.

9 Fully factorise each expression.
Check your answers by expanding the brackets.

a $2p + p^2$ b $g^2 - g$ c $h + h^2$
d $m - 3m^2$ e $4d + 6d^2$ f $12v^2 - 9v$

Q9b hint
$\square(g - \square)$

Q9e hint
Find the HCF of the numbers and letters.

Explore

10 **Explore** How much will each member of a four-person band receive for selling their latest album online to 1000 of their fans?
Is it easier to explore this question now you have completed the lesson?
What further information do you need to be able to answer this?

Reflect

11 **Reflect** At the end of lesson 1.5, you defined 'factor'. (If you didn't do it, or if you cannot find it, then write a definition of 'factor' now.)
Use your definition of factor to help you write a definition, in your own words, of 'highest common factor (HCF)'.
Use your definition of HCF to help you write a definition, in your own words, of 'factorising'. Be as accurate as possible.
How did your factor and HCF definitions help you to define factorising?

4.4 One-step equations

You will learn to:
- Find the inverse of a simple function
- Solve simple equations using function machines
- Solve real-life problems using equations.

Why learn this?
Engineers need to solve equations to analyse electronic circuits.

Fluency
Complete these number facts:
- 3 + 2 = 5, so 5 − 3 = □ and 5 − 2 = □
- 6 × 3 = 18, so 18 ÷ 3 = □ and 18 ÷ 6 = □
- 8 ÷ 2 = 4, so 8 = 4 × □

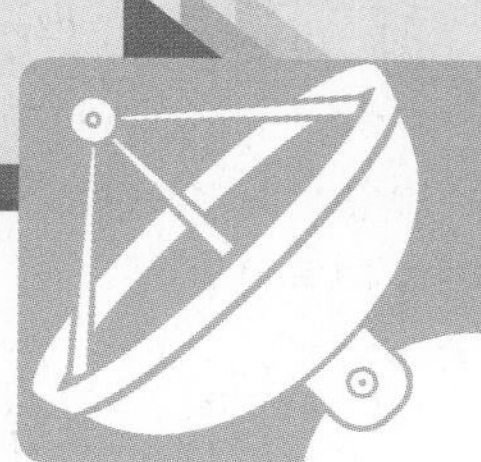

Explore
How fast will you need to cycle to travel around a square block in 5 minutes?

Exercise 4.4

1 Copy and complete these function machines.

a
input 7 → ? → 5 output
input 8 → ? → 6
input 9 → ? →

b
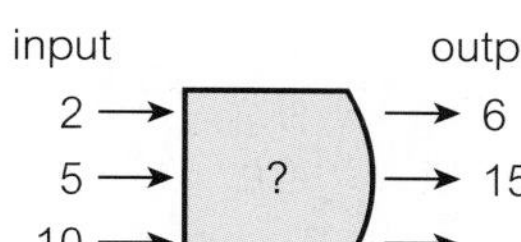

c
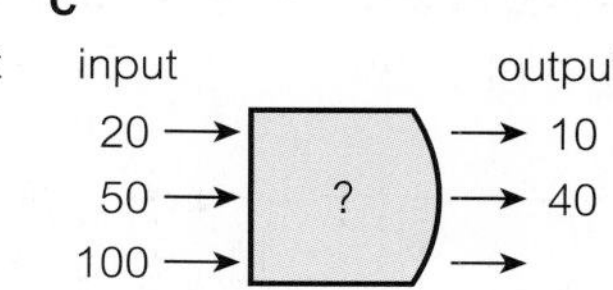

2 Write the correct operation for these statements.

a 97 − 48 = 49
- **i** 49 □ 48 = 97
- **ii** 97 □ 49 = 48

b 29 + 63 = 92
- **i** 92 □ 63 = 29
- **ii** 92 □ 29 = 63

c 4 × 17 = 68
- **i** 68 □ 17 = 4
- **ii** 68 □ 4 = 17

d 128 ÷ 16 = 8
- **i** 16 □ 8 = 128
- **ii** 128 □ 8 = 16

3 Write down the inverse for each **function** machine.

a
4 → ×2 → 8
4 ← □ ← 8

b
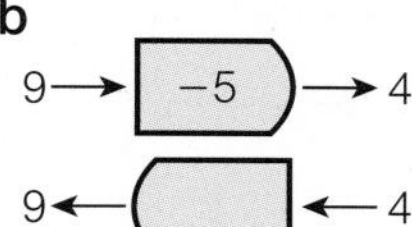

c
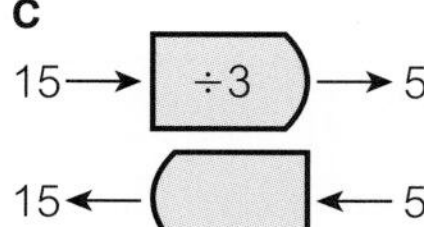

d
8 → +3 → 11
8 ← □ ← 11

Key point

A **function** is a rule that changes one number into another.
The function +3 adds 3 to a number.

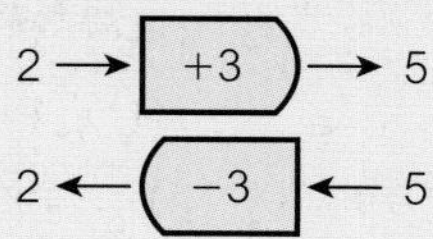

The **inverse function** is −3 because it reverses the effect of the function +3.

4 Use the **inverse function** to find each missing input.

a
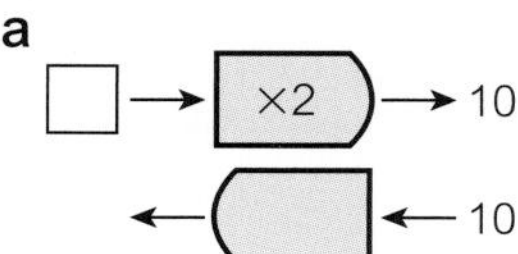

b
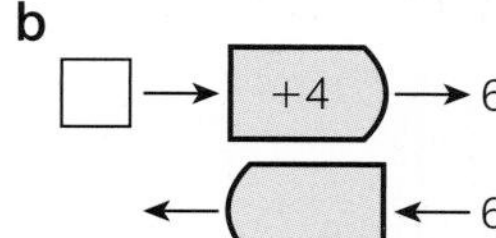

c
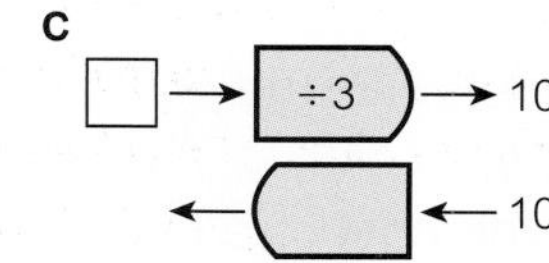

Worked example

Solve the equation $x + 3 = 7$. Check your solution.

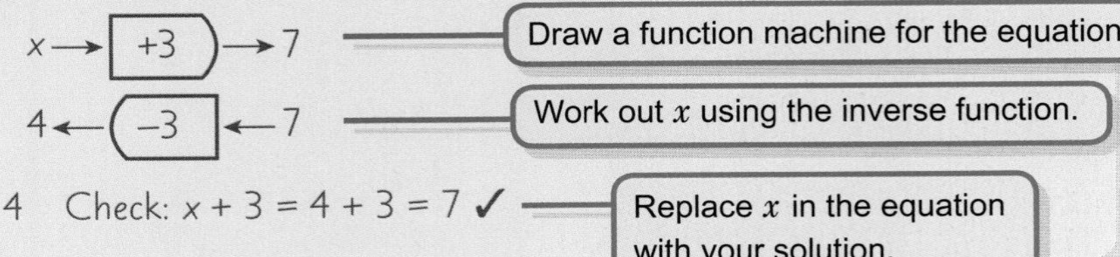

$x = 4$ Check: $x + 3 = 4 + 3 = 7$ ✓ — Replace x in the equation with your solution.

Key point

An **equation** contains an unknown number (a letter) and an '=' sign. To **solve** an equation means to work out the value of the unknown number.

5 **Solve** these **equations**. Check your **solutions**.

a $x + 6 = 11$ b $b - 3 = 6$ c $\frac{u}{2} = 7$

d $\frac{m}{4} = 3$ e $5g = 20$ f $0.5a = 3$

Discussion What is the difference between an equation and a formula?

Q5c hint

$u \rightarrow \boxed{\div 2} \rightarrow 7$

6 a $m + 2 = h$ Find m when $h = 6$.

b $p = \frac{v}{6}$ Find v when $p = 2$.

c $H = j - 4$ Find j when $H = 7$.

d $V = IR$ Find R when $I = 2$ and $V = 12$.

e $S = \frac{d}{t}$ Find d when $S = 22$ and $t = 10$.

7 Solve these equations using function machines.

a $-3 = a - 7$ b $5d = 0$ c $7e = -14$

d $-2n = 10$ e $-4r = -24$ f $2h = -3$

Q7a hint

Turn the equation around to make $a - 7 = -3$

Q7d hint

n is being multiplied by the negative number −2.

Worked example

Bianca cuts 10 cm off a belt of length d cm.

a Write an expression for the new length of the belt.

$d - 10$

b The new length of the belt is 75 cm.
Write an equation involving d.

$d - 10 = 75$

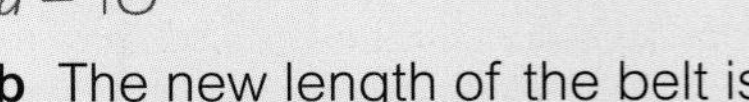

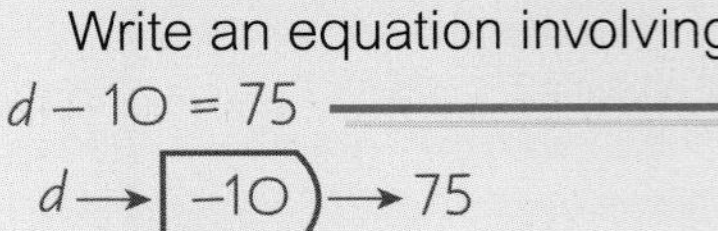

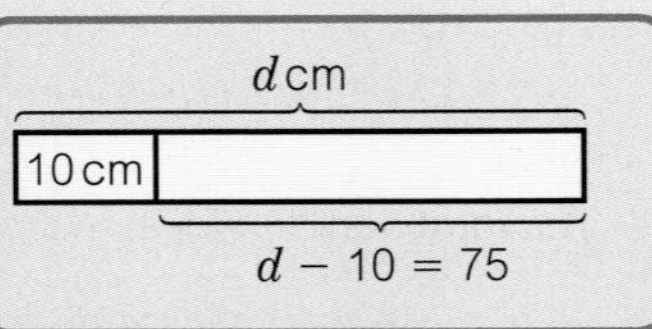

c Solve your equation to find the original length of the belt.

$d = 85$ Check: $85 - 10 = 75$ ✓

The original length of the belt was 85 cm.

8 Jafar adds 12 more characters to a tweet of t characters.

a Write an expression for the new length of the tweet.

b The new length of the tweet is 122 characters.
Write an equation involving t.

c Solve your equation to find the original length of the tweet.

9 **Real** A pair of hiking socks costs £h. The cost of 3 pairs is £12.

a Write an equation involving h.

b Solve your equation to find the cost of a pair of hiking socks.

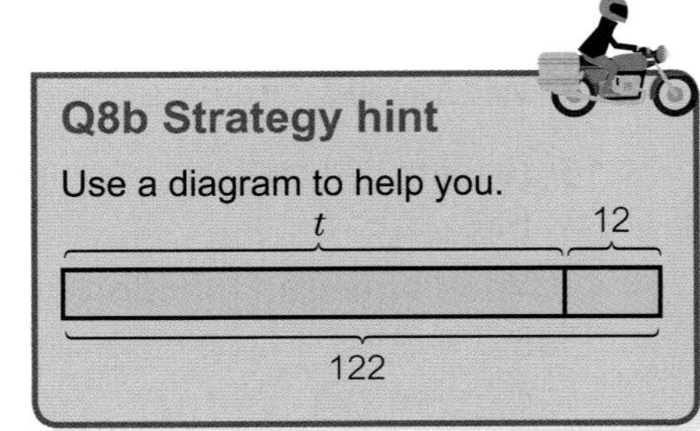

Topic links: Measures, Area, Perimeter, Angles

10 A carton of juice contains j ml. It is shared equally between 8 people. Each person receives 150 ml.

a Write an equation involving j.

b Solve your equation to find the total volume of juice.

11 Sharon sold 12 CDs from her collection of m CDs. She now has 35 CDs.

a Write an equation involving m.

b Solve your equation to find the size of her original collection.

12 Simplify the left-hand side of each equation. Then solve the equation.

a $2d + 3d = 20$ **b** $2 \times 5a = 60$

c $2c + 2c + 4c = 16$ **d** $6g - 2g = 12 + 6$

Q12a hint

Combine the like terms $2d$ and $3d$ first.

13 **Problem-solving** You are given some information about each diagram.

a

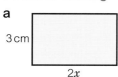

Area = 24 cm²

b

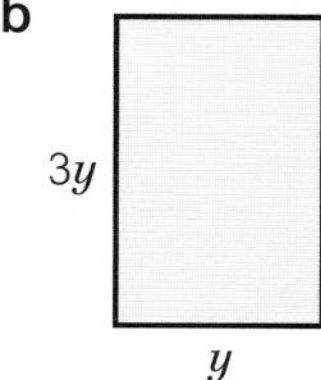

Perimeter = 40 cm

c

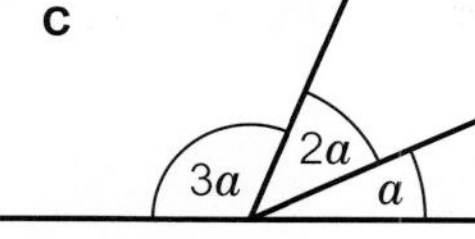

For each diagram, write an equation and solve it to find the unknown quantity.

Investigation **Reasoning / Problem-solving**

All of these regular polygons have perimeter 360 cm.

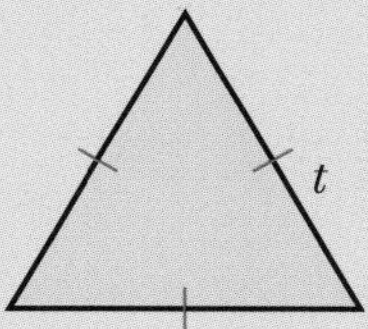

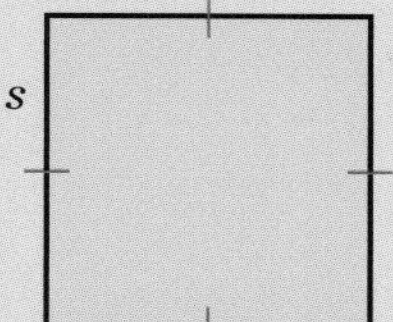

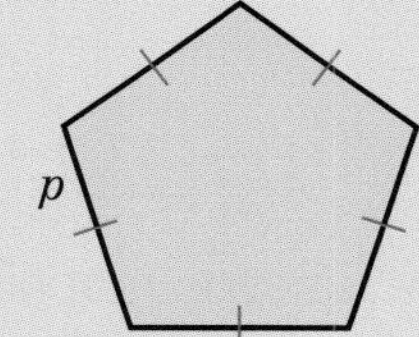

1. Write and solve an equation for each shape, to find the side length of the triangle, square and pentagon. Use the same method to find the side length of a regular hexagon, octagon and decagon with perimeter 360 cm.
2. Two congruent regular hexagons are joined along a side to make a shape with perimeter 120 cm. Solve an equation to find the length of one side.
3. Three congruent regular hexagons are joined at one of their vertices (corners) to make a shape with perimeter 240 cm. Solve an equation to find the length of one side.
4. Join together other regular polygons with the same length sides. Work out the length of a side when the perimeter of your shape is 360 cm.

14 **Explore** How fast will you need to cycle to travel around a square block in 5 minutes?
Is it easier to explore this question now you have completed the lesson?
What further information do you need to be able to answer this?

15 **Reflect** Write the steps you take to solve equations like the ones in this lesson.
You could begin, 'Step 1: Simplify the left-hand side, if needed.'
Beside each step, show whether you found that step OK (☺) or difficult (☹).
Ask a friend or your teacher to help you with any difficult steps.

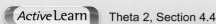

Explore

Reflect

4.5 Two-step equations

You will learn to:

- Solve two-step equations using function machines
- Solve real-life problems using equations.

Why learn this?
You can work out the cost of a unit of electricity from a bill if you know the standing charge.

Fluency

- Work out $2 \times 4 + 1$, $6 \times 3 - 5$, $-2 \times 4 + 3$
- Simplify $2d + 1 + 3d + 5$
- Expand and simplify $2(v + 2)$

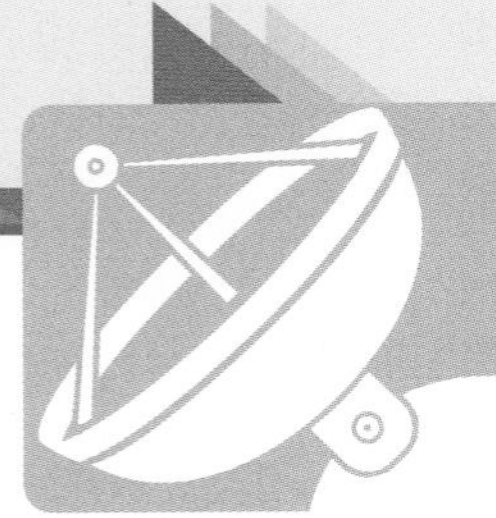

Explore
What is the largest square-shaped field that can be enclosed using a roll of barbed wire?

CONFIDENCE

Warm up

Exercise 4.5

1 Work out the outputs of the function machines.

a
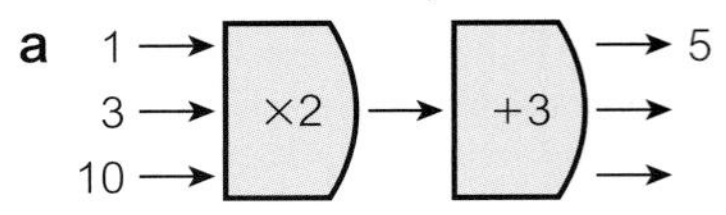

b
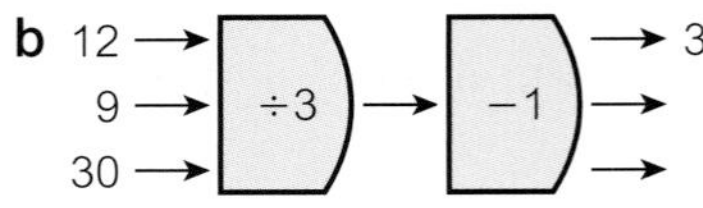

c
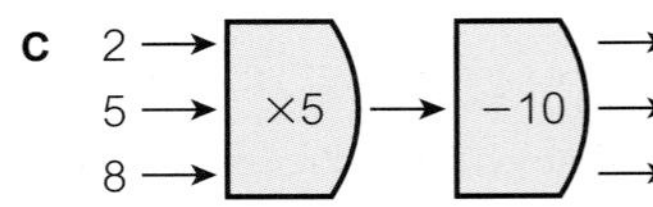

2 Work out the value of x.

a x → [÷2] → 13 **b** x → [+1] → 5 **c** x → [−5] → 23

Q2 hint
Work from right to left.

3 Copy and complete the inverse function machines.

a 3 → [×2] → [+5] → 11
3 ← [ ] ← [ ] ← 11

b 8 → [÷4] → [−1] → 1
8 ← [ ] ← [ ] ← 1

c 5 → [×10] → [+5] → 55
5 ← [ ] ← [ ] ← 55

Worked example

Solve the equation $2a + 1 = 9$ using a function machine.
Check your solution.

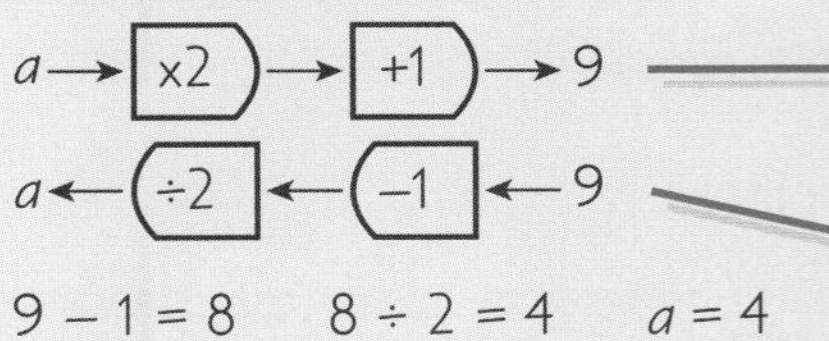

Using priority of operations, a is multiplied by 2 first, then 1 is added.

Reverse the function machine to find the input a.

$9 - 1 = 8$ $8 \div 2 = 4$ $a = 4$

Check by substituting $a = 4$ back into $2a + 1$.
Check: $2a + 1 = 2 \times 4 + 1 = 8 + 1 = 9$ ✓

4 Solve each equation using a function machine. Check your solutions.

a $3x + 4 = 25$ **b** $4b - 10 = 30$ **c** $5n + 2 = 37$
d $10 = 2d - 4$ **e** $2w + 10 = 2$ **f** $-2u + 8 = 20$
g $4 + 3k = 28$ **h** $10h - 7 = 11$ **i** $14 = 3m - 1$

Q4d hint
Rewrite the equation with '= 10' on the right-hand side.

Q4f hint
u is multiplied by −2.

Topic links: Straight-line graphs, Area, Perimeter; Algebra (graphs, Q5)

5 Here is a table of values for the graph of $y = 2x + 3$.

a Write an equation involving n.

b Solve your equation to find n.

x	1	3	n
y	5	9	15

6 **Problem-solving** Firework rockets cost £f each and Catherine wheels cost £2 each.

a Write an expression for the total cost of 7 rockets and a Catherine wheel.

b The cost of 7 rockets and a Catherine wheel is £30 altogether. Use your answer to part **a** to write an equation.

c Solve your equation to find the cost of a rocket.

7 **Problem-solving** Andrew makes a treehouse using 12 planks of length c metres and an extra 2 metres. He used 38 m of wood altogether.

a Write an equation involving c.

b Solve your equation to find the length of a plank.

8 Simplify the left-hand side of each equation. Then solve the equation. Check your solutions.

a $3d + 2d + 8 = 23$
b $4p + 1 + 2p + 3 = 28$
c $5a - 2 + 3a + 4 = 18$
d $10b - 3b + 6 - 12 = 22$
e $2(m + 3) = 8$
f $5(2s - 1) = 25$
g $2(3w + 2) = 16$
h $4(5h - 3) = 48$
i $2(1 + 3t) = 32$
j $3(n + 3) - 2 = 16$
k $4(g - 2) + 3g = 34$
l $5(3u + 5) - 7u = 65$

Q8a hint
Combine the like terms first.

Discussion In parts **e–i**, do you need to expand the brackets? Could you solve these another way?

9 **Problem-solving** The diagram shows two lawns A and B. Lengths are in metres.

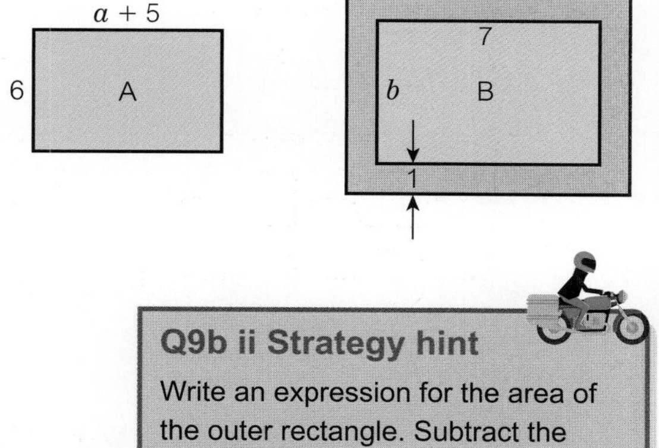

a The area of lawn A is 48 m^2.

i Write an expression for the area in terms of a and using brackets.

ii Write an equation and solve it to find a.

iii Write down the length of lawn A.

b Lawn B is surrounded by a path of width 1 m.

i Write an expression for the area of the lawn.

ii Write an expression for the area of the path.

iii The area of the path is 26 m^2. Write an equation and solve it to find b.

Q9b ii Strategy hint
Write an expression for the area of the outer rectangle. Subtract the area of the lawn.

10 **Explore** What is the largest square-shaped field that can be enclosed using a roll of barbed wire?
Is it easier to explore this question now you have completed the lesson?
What further information do you need to be able to answer this?

11 **Reflect** Look back at the steps you wrote for solving equations at the end of lesson 4.4.
In this lesson you have solved more complex equations.
Choose an equation from this lesson.
Do the steps for solving equations that you wrote at the end of lesson 4.4 work for this equation too? If not, rewrite your steps.
Check that they work for another equation from this lesson.

Explore

Reflect

4.6 The balancing method

You will learn to:
- Solve equations using the balancing method.

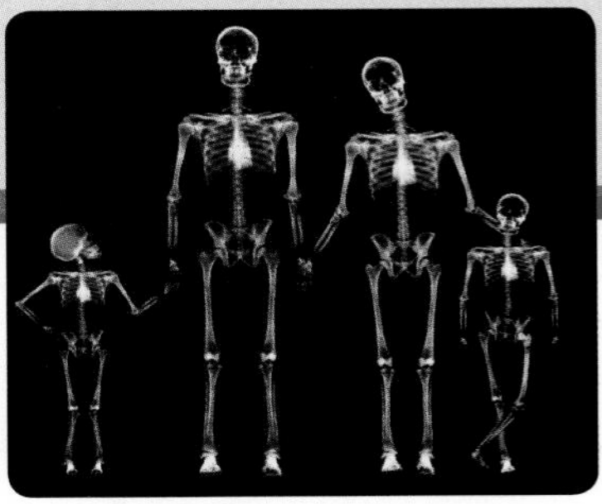

Why learn this?
You can use a formula to estimate the height of a person from the length of the femur leg bone.

Fluency
- Simplify $4p - p$, $5m + 7 - 3m$
- What is the inverse of -3, $\times 4$, $\div 7$, $+2$?

Explore
What is the pre-sale price of an item if the sale price means you can now buy 5 for the price of 4?

Exercise 4.6

1 Simplify these.
   a $5c + 10 + 3c - 7$ b $5(z + 3)$ c $7k - 3(k + 4)$
   d $4(t - 6) + 2(t + 12)$ e $3(5r + 2) - 2(2r + 1)$ f $18p - (15p - 14)$

Worked example

Solve the equation $x + 3 = 8$.

$x + 3 = 8$ — Visualise the equation as balanced scales.

$x + 3 - 3 = 8 - 3$ — The inverse of + 3 is − 3. Do this to both sides.

$x = 8 - 3$
$x = 5$ — Simplify both sides to find x.
Check: $x + 3 = 5 + 3 = 8$ ✓

Key point
In an equation, the expressions on both sides of the equals sign have the same value. You can visualise them on balanced scales.

$x + 3 = 5$

The scales stay balanced if you do the same operation to both sides. You can use this **balancing method** to solve equations.

2 Use the **balancing method** to solve each equation. Check your answers.
   a $m + 8 = 10$ b $d - 7 = 6$ c $3a = 21$
   d $5k = 20$ e $-4g = 12$ f $\frac{n}{4} = 6$
   g $\frac{t}{10} = 3$ h $18 = 6d$ i $\frac{p}{-2} = 4$

   Discussion How could you use this method to solve a two-step equation like $3y + 5 = 17$?

3 The formula $C = 20n$ gives the total cost C of n pencils, in pence. Solve an equation to find the number of pencils bought for £1.80.

Topic links: Straight-line graphs, Area, Perimeter

4 Solve each equation using the balancing method.

a $2m + 5 = 11$ b $4t - 3 = 21$ c $3k + 10 = 70$

d $50 = 5h + 15$ e $46 = 10 + 4w$ f $17 = 5 + 3p$

Q4a hint

Subtract 5 from both sides.
Then divide both sides by 2.

5 Reasoning The length y metres of a train is given by $y = 6x + 8$, where x is the number of carriages.

a A train has a length of 50 m.

i Write down an equation involving x.

ii Solve the equation to find the number of carriages.

b $y = 6x + 8$ has been plotted on the graph.

i Find the point on the red line where $y = 50$.
Read off the number of carriages.
Is this the same as your solution in part **a**?

ii Solve an equation to find the number of carriages in a train of length 20 m. Check your answer on the graph.

c Use the graph to find the length of a train with no carriages.
What part of the train might this be?
Which part of the equation represents this information?

d What does $6x$ in the equation represent?

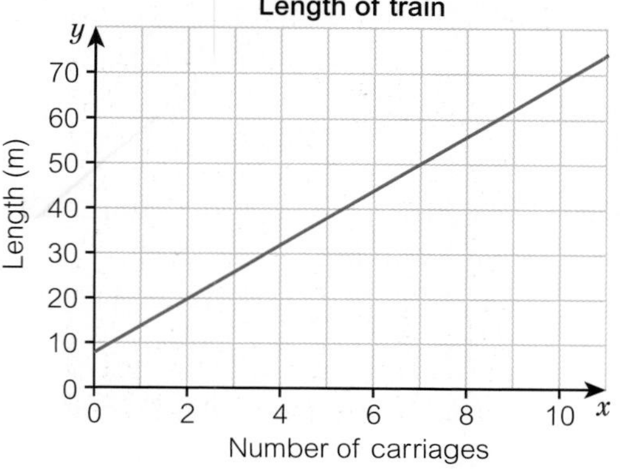

Key point 

When there is an unknown on both sides, use the balancing method to get unknowns on one side only.

6 Solve these equations. Check your answers.

a $6x = 3x + 6$ b $7u = 2u + 20$

c $6m + 4 = 5m + 12$ d $5c + 14 = 8c - 1$

e $4(d + 1) = d + 10$ f $3(2n + 3) = 2n + 21$

g $10s - 2 = 4(s + 7)$ h $2(3v + 1) = 5(v + 2)$

Q6 hint

Expand any brackets first. Then subtract the smaller unknown from both sides.

Investigation **Reasoning / Problem-solving**

This square has the same perimeter as the rectangle.

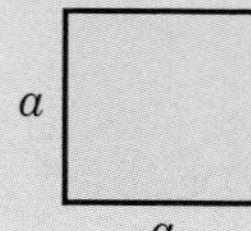

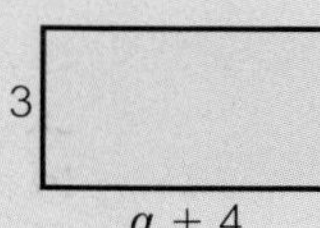

1 Write down an equation using a.

2 a Solve the equation.

b Work out the lengths of the sides of the rectangle.

3 Replace 3 and 4 with two other whole numbers. Repeat parts **1** and **2**.
What do you notice about the value of a?

7 Explore What is the pre-sale price of an item if the sale price means you can now buy 5 for the price of 4?
Is it easier to explore this question now you have completed the lesson?
What further information do you need to answer this?

8 Reflect Do the steps for solving equations that you wrote at the end of lesson 4.5 work for equations with an unknown (a letter) on both sides of the '=' sign? If not, rewrite them.
Check that your steps work for solving equations from lessons 4.4, 4.5 and 4.6.

Q8 hint

You may have to write some extra steps.

4 Check up

Log how you did on your Student Progression Chart.

Powers, expressions and formulae

1 a Write $m \times m \times m \times m$ as a power.
b Write b^6 as a product.
c Write each product using index notation.
i $a \times a \times a \times c \times c$ ii $2n \times 3n \times 4n$

2 The formula for the total surface area A of a cube of side d is $A = 6d^2$. Calculate the surface area when $d = 7.5$ cm.

3 Simplify these expressions.
a $w^2 \times w^3$ b $y \times y^2$ c $4 \times g^3 \times 3 \times g^3$
d $c^6 \div c^2$ e $v^3 \div v$ f $5 \times e^4 \div e^3$

4 Simplify these expressions.
a $s^2 + s^2 + s^2 + s^2$ b $2a^2 + 5b^2 - 2b^2 + a^2$ c $4p^3 + 3p + 2p^3$

5 a Write a simplified formula for the area A cm² of this rectangle.

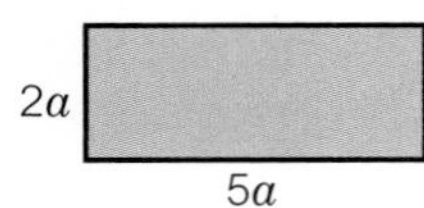

b Use your formula to find A when $a = 4$ cm.

6 a Write an expression for the volume of each cuboid.

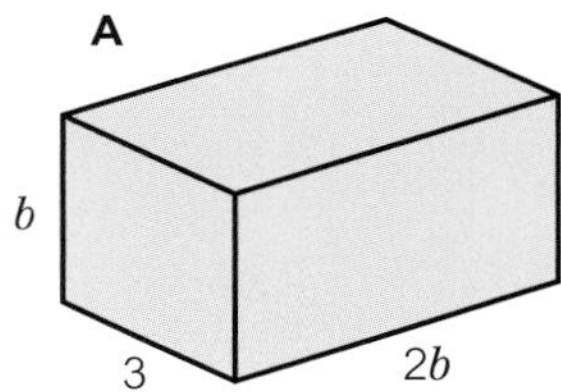

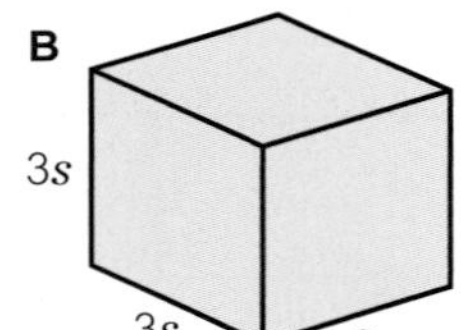

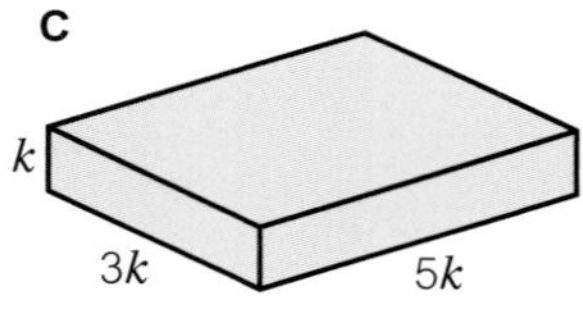

b Work out the volume of cuboid C when $k = 3$ cm.

7 An ice cube tray is filled with w ml of water. It makes 15 ice cubes.
a Write a formula for the volume V ml of water in an ice cube.
b Use your formula to find V when $w = 450$ ml.
c Write a formula for the total volume V of n ice cubes.

8 A £120 bill for a meal is divided equally between n people. Write an expression for the amount each person pays.

Brackets

9 Expand these expressions and simplify where possible.
a $m(2 + n)$ b $2b(b - 3)$ c $-4(2t + 5)$
d $5u - 2(u - 3)$ e $4(r - 1) - 2(r + 2)$ f $c(4c + 3) - c$

10 a Write the highest common factor of $8n$ and $12m$.
b Factorise $8n + 12m$ completely.

11 Factorise these expressions.

a $8s - 8$ b $12 + 4m$ c $3h + 9$

d $100 - 50t$ e $54p + 18r$ f $30j - 42q$

g $k - k^2$ h $16v^2 - 4v$ i $15a^2 + 25a$

Equations

12 Solve these equations.

a $h - 7 = 12$ b $\frac{w}{2} = 10$ c $-4m = 24$

d $3a + 2 = 20$ e $2(d + 5) = 12$ f $3r - 2 = r + 8$

g $5(c - 2) = 2(c + 1)$ h $3(x + 2) = 4x - 1$ i $2(5 - n) = 10n + 4$

13 The formula $v = at$ gives the speed v metres per second (m/s) of a sports car after t seconds. Use the formula to find t when $a = 11$ and $v = 110$ m/s.

14 Solve each equation by working out the unknown length.

a $5(x + 3) = 20$ b $9(x + 2) = 63$ c $6(x + 2) + 4 = 28$

x
3
5
total area = 20

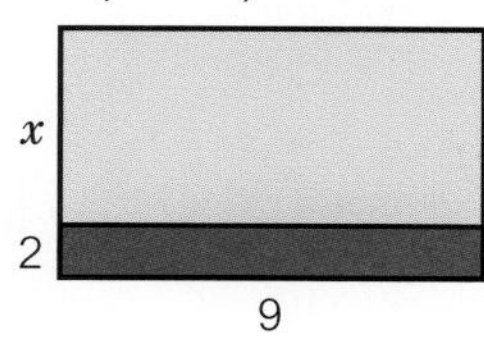

total area = 63

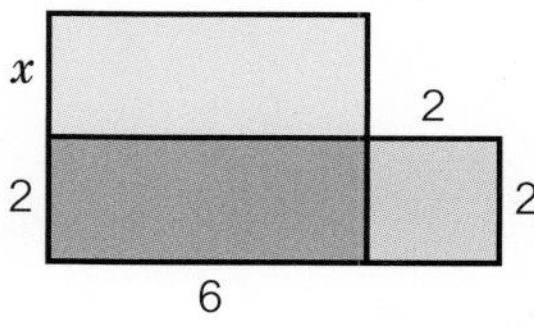

15 A bolt has a mass of 20 g and a nut has a mass of n g.

a Write an expression with brackets for the total mass of 5 nuts and 5 bolts.

b The total mass of 5 nuts and 5 bolts is 125 g.
Solve an equation to find the mass of a nut.

16 How sure are you of your answers? Were you mostly

☹ **Just guessing** 😐 **Feeling doubtful** ☺ **Confident**

What next? Use your results to decide whether to strengthen or extend your learning.

Reflect

Challenge

17 A rectangular paving slab has a width of 1 metre and a length of x metres.

a Write an expression for the perimeter of a slab.

b A straight path of width 1 m is made by joining four slabs.
Write an expression for the perimeter of the path.

c A 1 m wide path made of six slabs encloses a rectangular growing area. Write an expression for

i the outer perimeter of the path

ii the inner perimeter of the path

iii the total perimeter of the path.

d Repeat part **c** for a path made using eight slabs.

e Write a formula for the total perimeter of a 1 m wide path made of an even number of slabs.

f A rectangular growing area has a perimeter of 8 m and is enclosed by a 1 m wide path of eight slabs.
Solve an equation to find the length of a slab.

Q17c hint

Here is one of two possible arrangements.

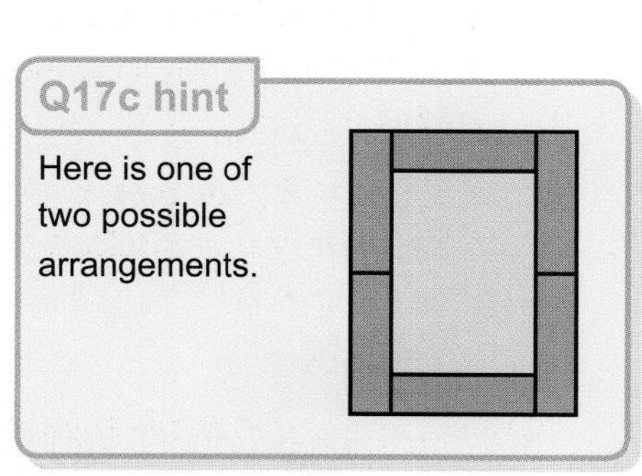

4 Strengthen

You will:

- Strengthen your understanding with practice.

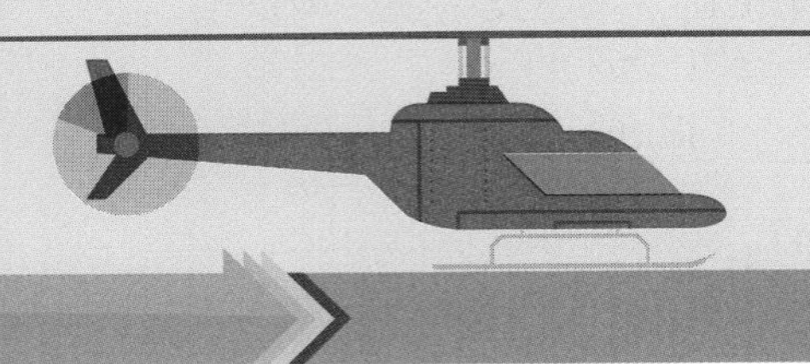

Powers, expressions and formulae

1 Simplify these.

a $c + c + c + c$

b $c \times c \times c \times c$

c $h + h + h$

d $h \times h \times h$

e $m \times m \times m \times m \times m$

f $m + m + m + m + m$

2 Simplify each expression by adding like terms only.

a $c^2 + c^2 + c^2$

b $m^3 + m^3$

c $2n^2 + 3n^2$

d $3a^2 + 2a^2 + 4b^2$

e $2u^3 + 5w^3 + 2w^3$

f $4n^5 - 2n^5 + 3d^2 - 2d^2$

g $a^2 + a^2 + 4a$

h $5g^2 - 2g^2 + 2g^3$

3 Write each power as a product.

a $u^5 = \square \times \square \times \square \times \square \times \square$

b a^2

c d^3

4 Write each product using powers.

a $4 \times t \times t$

b $5 \times a \times a \times a$

c $g \times g \times g \times g \times g \times 2$

d $3 \times e \times 2 \times e$

e $5 \times m \times 2 \times m \times m$

f $2n \times 4n$

g $3d \times 2d \times 2d$

h $-3t \times 5t$

5 Write each product using powers.

a $e \times e \times e \times d \times d$

b $s \times s \times t \times t \times t$

c $e \times f \times e$

d $p \times p \times q \times p \times p$

Q1a hint

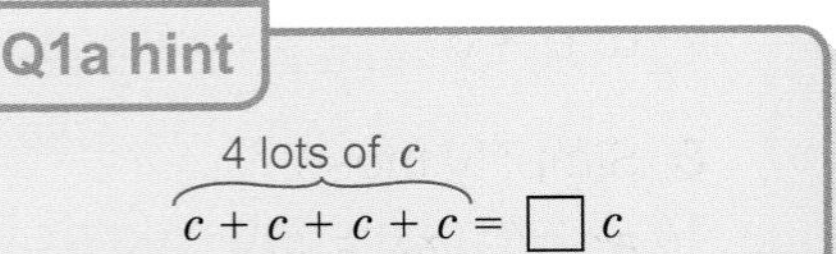

Q1b hint

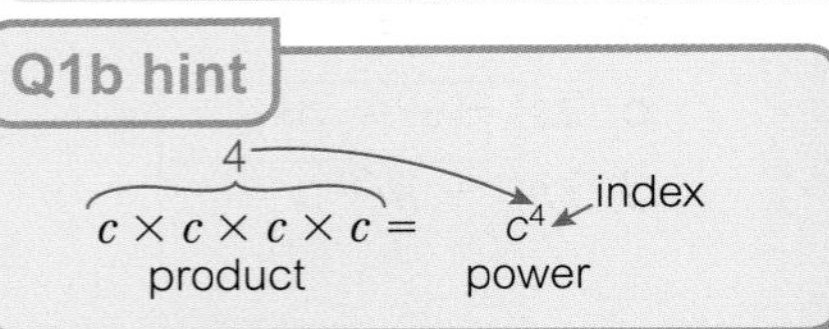

Q2a hint

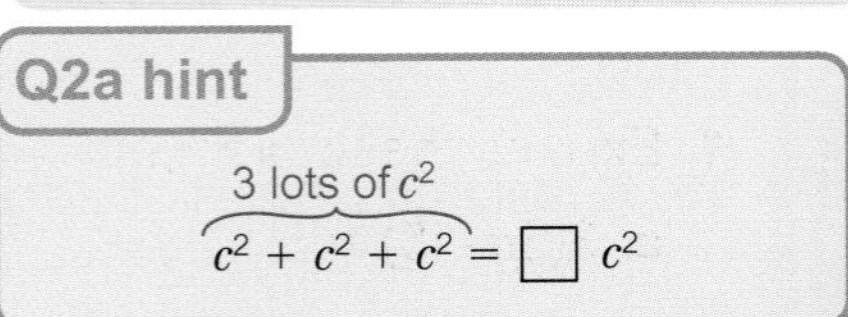

Q2d hint

like terms

$3a^2 + 2a^2 + 4b^2 = \square\, a^2 + 4b^2$

Q2g hint

a^2 means $a \times a$, so a^2 and a are *not* like terms.

Q4a hint

Work out $t \times t$ first. Write the number, then $t^\square$.
Don't write × in the answer.

Q4h hint

Multiply the numbers −3 × 5.

Q5a hint

$e^\square \times d^\square = e^\square d^\square$

Topic links: Straight-line graphs

6 Simplify these.

a $4d^3 \times d^5$ b $p^2 \times 3p$ c $-5n \times 2n^3$ d $-2g^2 \times -3n^2$

Q6a hint

$d^3 \times d^5 = d^{\square}$

7 Copy and complete these.

a i $m^2 = \square \times \square$

ii $m^3 = \square \times \square \times \square$

iii $m^2 \times m^3 = m^{\square + \square} = m^{\square}$

b i $b^3 = \square \times \square \times \square$

ii $b^4 = \square \times \square \times \square \times \square$

iii $b^3 \times b^4 = b^{\square + \square} = b^{\square}$

Simplify these.

c $a \times a^3$ d $c^2 \times c^2 \times c^2$

8 Simplify these.

a $m^7 \div m^4 = m^{\square - \square} = m^{\square}$

b $h^6 \div h^2 = h^{\square}$

c $3s^5 \div s^3 = 3s^{\square}$

d $7m^5 \div m^2$

Q8b hint

What do you multiply h^2 by to get h^6?

Brackets

1 Expand these brackets. The first one has been done for you.

a $3(3g - 5) = 3 \times 3g + 3 \times -5 = 9g - 15$

b $-3(4d + 2)$

c $-2(n + 3)$

d $-4(3c - 2)$

e $-5(2p - 3q)$

Q1 hint

Multiply the term outside the brackets by both terms inside the brackets.
Use the rule: multiplying same signs gives +, different signs gives −.

Q1b hint

Work out $-3 \times 4d$ and -3×2.
Add the results together.

2 Simplify these expressions.

a $5(a + 1) + 3(a + 2)$

b $3(2m + 3) + 4(2m - 3)$

c $5(c + 2) - 3(c + 2)$

d $4(n - 2) - 2(n + 1)$

e $6t - 2(t + 3)$

f $8m - 3(m - 2)$

Q2a hint

Expand each set of brackets.

$\underbrace{5(a + 1)}_{5a + 5} + \underbrace{3(a + 2)}_{3a + 6}$

Q2c hint

$5(c + 2) - \underbrace{3(c + 2)}_{-3 \times \square + -3 \times \square}$

3 Expand these brackets.

a $a(b + 2) = a \times \square + a \times \square =$

b $u(v + 4)$

c $m(n + 3p) = m \times \square + m \times \square =$

d $g(5h + d)$

e $2e(3f - g) = 2e \times \square + 2e \times \square =$

f $4t(2u - 3w)$

Q3e hint

Remember to include the sign for g.

4 Expand and simplify if possible. Each answer will include a power.

a $a(a + 5)$

b $3p(p - 4)$

c $2d(3d + 1) + 7d$

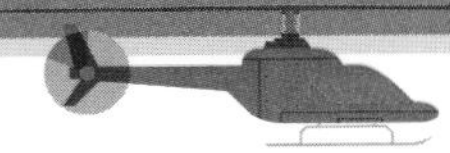

5 Factorise these expressions completely.
Check your answers by expanding the brackets.

a $8a - 12b$
b $5m + 10$
c $7p - 7q$
d $3w - 12t$
e $10p + 4k$
f $12r + 16s$
g $10t - 20u$
h $24a + 36b$

Q5a hint
Take out the highest common factor (HCF).
$8a - 12b$
$= \square \times 2a - \square \times 3b$
$= \square \times (2a - 3b)$

Q5f hint
Make sure you take out the *highest* common factor of 12 and 16.

6 Factorise these expressions completely.
Check your answers by expanding the brackets.

a $6m^2 + 15m = 3m(\square + \square)$
b $4a^2 - 6a$
c $7u^2 + 14u$
d $16d^2 - 24d$

Q6a hint
The HCF of 6 and 15 is 3.
The HCF of m^2 and m is m.
So $3m$ is the HCF of $6m^2$ and $15m$.
$3m \times \square = 6m^2$
$3m \times \square + 15m$

Equations

1 Solve these equations using function machines. Check your solutions.

a $x + 2 = 7$

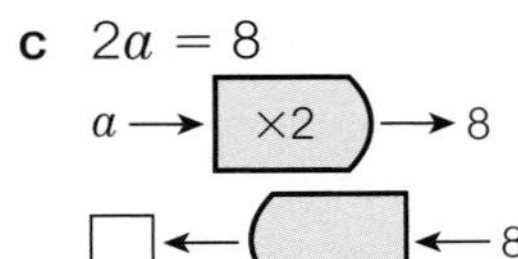

b $x - 5 = 3$
$x \rightarrow [-5] \rightarrow 3$
$\square \leftarrow [\ \ ] \leftarrow 3$

c $2a = 8$
$a \rightarrow [\times 2] \rightarrow 8$
$\square \leftarrow [\ \ ] \leftarrow 8$

d $a \div 3 = 5$
$a \rightarrow [\div 3] \rightarrow 5$
$\square \leftarrow [\ \ ] \leftarrow 5$

Q1a hint
The inverse of + 2 is $\square$ 2

2 Solve these equations using the balancing method. Check your solutions.

a $x + 4 = 12$
b $x - 2 = 7$
c $a + 10 = 15$
d $c - 1 = 5$
e $4p = 12$
f $5t = 30$
g $m \div 2 = 7$
h $\frac{e}{4} = 3$

Q2a hint
You can use a function machine to help you find the inverse function.

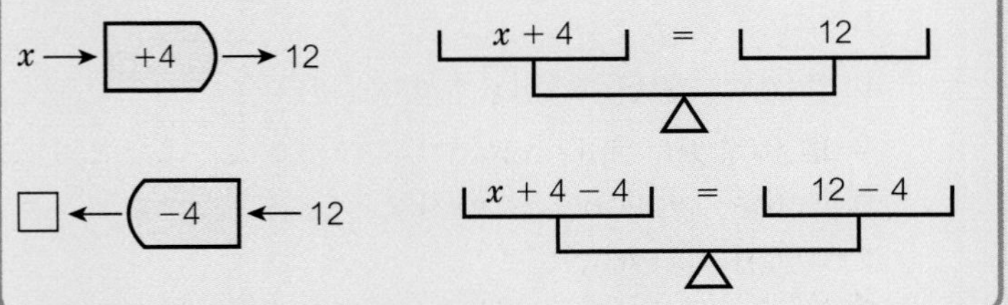

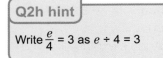

Q2h hint
Write $\frac{e}{4} = 3$ as $e \div 4 = 3$

3 Solve these equations.
  a $2x + 5 = 13$
  b $3y - 2 = 10$
  c $4a + 10 = 30$
  d $2c - 1 = 5$
  e $2(t + 1) = 8$
  f $3(2d - 1) = 15$

Q3a hint

You can use a function machine to help you find the first inverse function and the second inverse function.

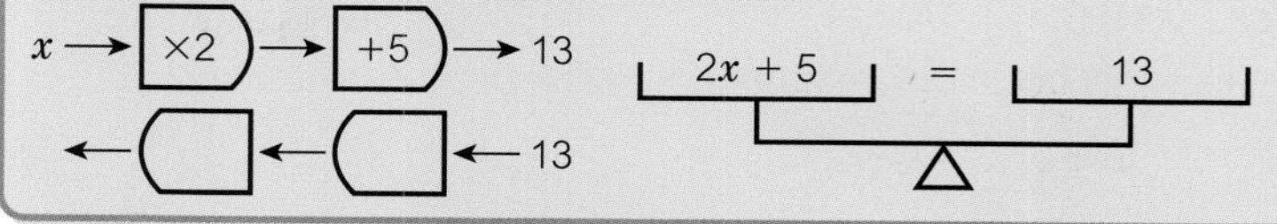

4 Solve these equations.
  a $5s = 2s + 12$
  b $10r = 9r + 3$
  c $7p - 2 = 4p + 4$
  d $8f + 2 = 3f + 12$

Q3e hint

Expand the brackets first.

5 Solve these equations. Expand the brackets first.
  a $6g = 2(g + 4)$
  b $5v = 3(v + 2)$
  c $6(n - 1) = 5n + 4$
  d $2(5h + 1) = 6h + 2$

Q4a Strategy hint

Use the balancing method when the unknown is on both sides of the equation.

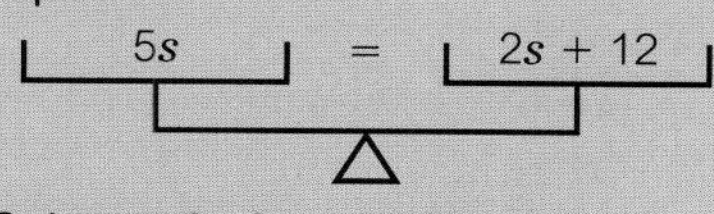

Subtract $2s$ from both sides.

Q4c hint

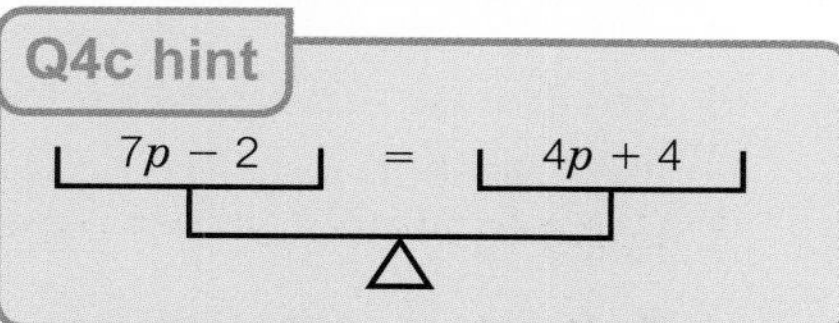

Enrichment

1 **Problem-solving** Esther and Vic live on the same floor in a block of flats.
  a Esther takes 10 seconds to go up a floor using the stairs.
  Write an expression for the time she takes to walk up n floors.
  b Vic uses the lift, which takes 5 seconds to go up a floor.
  He has to wait 30 seconds for the lift to arrive.
  Write an expression for the time he takes to go up n floors.
  c Esther and Vic arrive at their floor at the same time.
    i Write an equation to show this.
    ii Solve the equation to find the floor they live on.

Q1c i hint

Make your answers to parts **a** and **b** equal.

2 **Problem-solving / Reasoning** A truck travels y miles on x gallons of petrol. The formula $y = 20x$ can be used to calculate y.
  a How far can the truck travel on 4 gallons of petrol?
  b The truck travels 60 miles.
  Solve an equation to find how much petrol it used.
  c The graph of $y = 20x$ is shown.
    i Write the coordinates of the points A, B and C.
    ii Which point shows the answer to part **a**?
    iii Which point shows the solution to part **b**? Explain why.

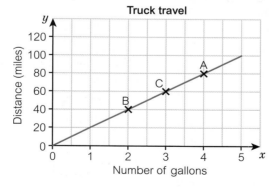

Truck travel

y: Distance (miles) 0, 20, 40, 60, 80, 100, 120
x: Number of gallons 0, 1, 2, 3, 4, 5
A, B, C

  d What does the number 20 mean in the equation $y = 20x$?

Q2b hint

Replace y in the formula by 60 and solve the equation.

3 **Reflect** Anna says, 'Algebra is just like arithmetic really, but when you don't know a number, you use a letter.'
Is Anna's explanation a good one? Explain your answer.

Reflect

4 Extend

You will:

- Extend your understanding with problem-solving.

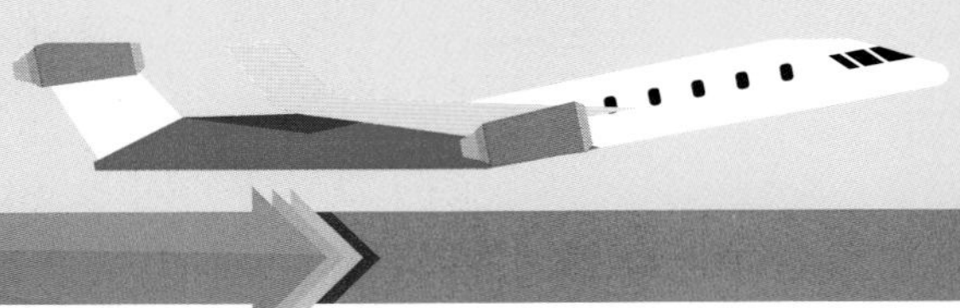

1 **Problem-solving** A roll of wallpaper covers an area of 50 m² and has a width of 2 m. Work out the length of the wallpaper.

2 The area of each shape is given. Solve an equation to find the unknown length of each shape.

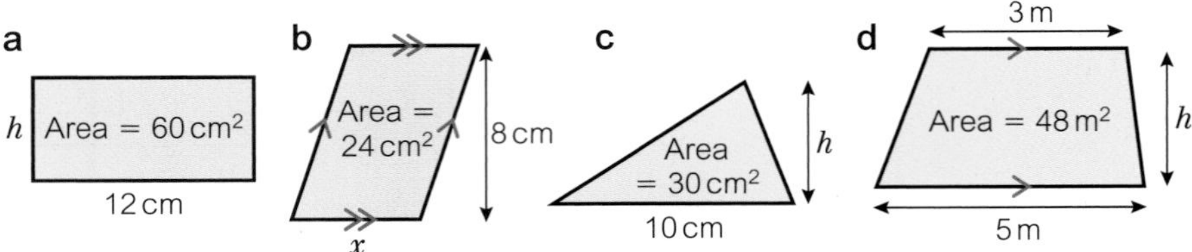

3 **Reasoning** The cost £y for repairing a washing machine is given by the equation $y = 20x + 30$, where x is the number of hours the repair takes.

a A repair costs £110.

i Write an equation involving x.

ii Solve the equation to find the number of hours the repair takes.

b $y = 20x + 30$ has been plotted on the graph.

i Explain why point A gives the solution to the equation in part **a**.

ii Point B gives the solution to the equation $20x + 30 = \square$. Complete the equation.

c Solve an equation to find how long a repair costing £115 takes. Check your answer on the graph.

Discussion Which method gives the more accurate answer?

d What does the number 30 mean in the equation $y = 20x + 30$?

e What does the number 20 mean in the equation $y = 20x + 30$?

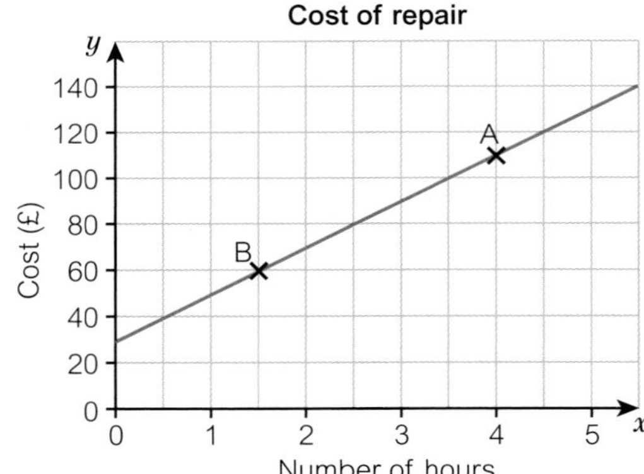

4 **Finance / Reasoning / Modelling** The formula $C = 10n + 5$ can be used to find the cost, in £, of ordering n umbrellas online, including postage and packing.

a i Explain what the number 10 means in the formula.

ii Explain what the number 5 means in the formula.

b Gavin ordered some umbrellas for £35.

i Write an equation involving n.

ii Solve the equation to find how many umbrellas Gavin ordered.

Topic links: Area, Straight-line graphs, Volume, Capacity, Mean

Subject links: Science (Q14, Q15)

c **i** Copy and complete the table of values for $C = 10n + 5$.

n	0	2	4	6	8
C					

ii Plot a graph using the data.

d **i** Mark the point on your graph where $C = 35$.

ii How does this point show the answer to part **b ii**?

e Use your graph to solve the equation $75 = 10n + 5$.
Check your answer by solving the equation.

Discussion Is the formula $C = 10n + 5$ a good model for the cost of ordering any number of umbrellas?

Q4c hint

Put n on the horizontal axis and C on the vertical axis.

5 **Problem-solving** The diagram shows a partly covered swimming pool.
The dimensions are in metres.

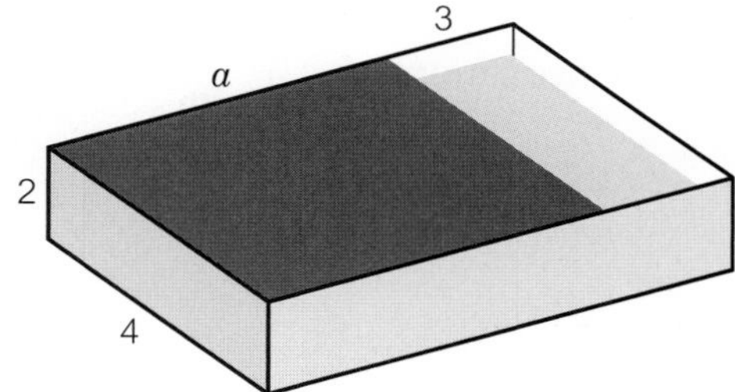

a Write an expression for the volume of water the pool holds, using brackets.

b The pool holds $180\,m^3$. Solve an equation to find the value of a.

6 **Problem-solving** A rectangle has a length of $4a + 2$ and a width of 3.

a Write an expression for the area of the rectangle.

b Work out the length of a rectangle with the same area but a width of 2.

Q6b hint

Factorise the expression in part **a**.

7 **Reasoning** The diagram shows two cubes A and B.

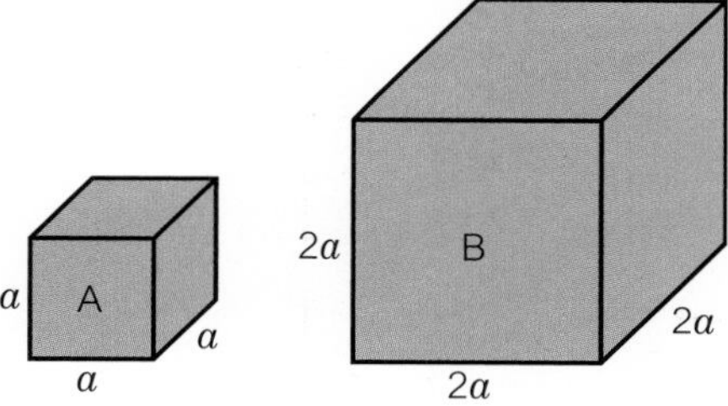

a Write a simplified expression for

i the volume of cube A

ii the volume of cube B.

b Copy and complete this statement:
Volume of cube B = $2^{\square}$ × volume of cube A.

c Cube C has a side of length $3a$.

i Write a simplified expression for the volume of cube C.

ii Write a statement comparing the volume of cube C to the volume of cube A.

iii Calculate the volume of cube C when $a = 4.5\,cm$.

d Cube D has a side of length na, where n is a positive integer.

i Write a simplified expression for the volume of cube D.

ii Write a statement comparing the volume of cube D to the volume of cube A.

iii Calculate the volume of cube D when $a = 25\,cm$ and $n = 7$.

8 Problem-solving Three buckets A, B and C have capacities of d, $d + 2$ and $2d + 1$ litres. The total capacity of buckets A and C is equal to the total capacity of two buckets B.

a Write an equation involving d.

b Solve your equation to find d.

c Find the capacity of each bucket.

9 Solve these equations. Check your solutions.

a $\frac{m}{4} + 3 = 8$ b $\frac{t}{5} + 1 = 3$ c $\frac{u}{10} - 5 = 20$ d $15 + \frac{x}{4} = 17$

Q9a hint

Start by subtracting 3 from both sides.

10 Solve these equations. Check your solutions.

a $\frac{2n}{5} = 8$ b $\frac{5x}{4} = 10$ c $\frac{4u}{3} = 12$ d $\frac{3n}{100} = 30$

Q10a hint

Write $\frac{2n}{5}$ as $2n \div 5$, then multiply both sides by 5.

11 Finance The simple interest £I earned in a year on an investment of £A at a rate of r% interest is given by the formula $I = \frac{rA}{100}$.

a Fauzia invested £250 and earned £20 interest. Substitute these amounts into the formula.

b Work out the rate of interest.

c Jack earned £8.50 in a year with a 2% interest rate. What was his investment?

12 STEM The pressure P, volume V and temperature T of a gas are related by the formula $\frac{PV}{T} = 6$.

Use the formula to find the value of V when $P = 3$ and $T = 40$.

13 STEM An elastic string has natural length l metres.
When the string is stretched by x metres, the tension T newtons is given by the formula $T = \frac{60x}{l}$.

Use the formula to work out x when $T = 24$ newtons and $l = 15$ m.

14 Simplify these.

a $-10t \times 3t^3$ b $-2a \times -3a^2$ c $m^2 \times m^3 \div m^4$

d $c^5 \times c \div c^2$ e $u^4 \div u^2 \times u^3$ f $\frac{p^6}{p^2}$

g $r^4 \times \frac{r^5}{r^3}$ h $\frac{s^4}{s} \times s^3$ i $4w^3 \times 2w^2 \div w$

j $d^6 \div -d^3 \times d^7$ k $2b^4 \times 3b \times b^3 \times 4b^2$ l $4x^4 \times -5x^2 \times -3x$

15 Expand these.

a $(5m)^3$ b $(10a)^2$ c $(2c)^4$ d $(3pq)^2$

Q15a hint

Work out $5m \times 5m \times 5m$.

16 Expand and simplify these.

a $a(a^2 + 2a - 3)$ b $4b(b^2 + 5b + 2)$

c $2c(3c^2 + 2c - 5)$ d $4p(3p^2 - 2) + p^2 + 5p$

e $5m(2m^2 + 3m) + 4m(5m + 1)$ f $3(2s + t) + 5(s + 4t)$

g $4(2m + 3n) + 3(m - 2n)$ h $6d(d - e) - 3d(2d - 3e)$

Q16d hint

Expand the brackets and then collect like terms.

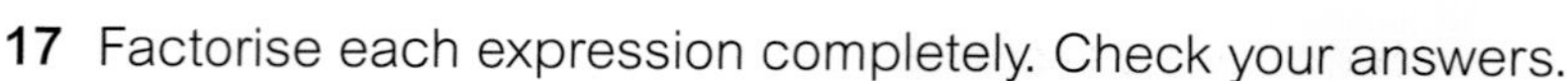

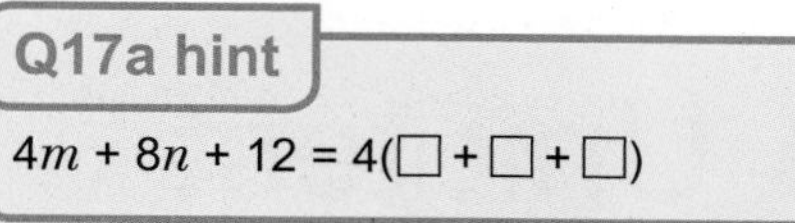

17 Factorise each expression completely. Check your answers.

a $4m + 8n + 12$ b $15a - 10b + 20c$
c $12p + 24q - 30$ d $-14k - 7j - 28f$
e $mn + ma + ms$ f $8ab - 10ac + 10ae$
g $6d^2 - 9d - 12$ h $a^3 + a^2 + a$

Q17a hint
$4m + 8n + 12 = 4(\square + \square + \square)$

18 A bag of paint balls was divided equally between four players. After Karen had used three paint balls, she had two left. Solve an equation to find the number of paint balls in the bag.

Q18 Strategy hint
Let n be the number of paint balls in the bag.

Worked example

Solve the equation $\frac{2a+1}{3} = 5$.

$(2a + 1) \div 3 = 5$ — $\frac{2a+1}{3}$ can be written $\frac{(2a+1)}{3}$ or $(2a + 1) \div 3$.

$(2a + 1) \div 3 \times 3 = 5 \times 3$ — $\times\ 3$ is the inverse of $\div\ 3$.

$2a + 1 = 15$

$2a + 1 - 1 = 15 - 1$

$2a = 14$

$2 \times a \div 2 = 14 \div 2$

$a = 7$

19 Solve these equations. Check your solutions.

a $\frac{h+2}{5} = 3$ b $\frac{m-5}{4} = 2$
c $\frac{2b+5}{3} = 7$ d $\frac{3k-4}{2} = 4$

20 Problem-solving

a Write an expression for the mean of the two numbers $3x$ and 11.
b The mean of the two numbers is 16. Solve an equation to find x.

21 Solve these equations.

Q21c hint
Add $5m$ to both sides.

a $2e + 5 = 5e - 7$ b $3(b - 2) = 4(b - 3)$
c $12 - 5m = m$ d $28 - 4m = 3m$
e $2p = 12 - 2p$ f $15 - 3n = 7 - n$
g $7 - 2s = 10 - 5s$ h $2(3 - a) = a$
i $\frac{3d+11}{4} = d + 2$ j $7 - z = \frac{8z-1}{3}$

22 The perimeter of rectangle A is 5 more than the area of rectangle B. Solve an equation to find the value of a.

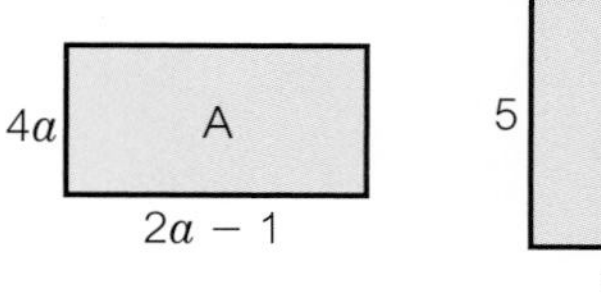

23 Reflect Which do you find easier, working with expressions or equations? Explain why.

Reflect

4 Unit test

Log how you did on your Student Progression Chart.

1 Solve these equations.

a $t + 3 = 11$ b $\frac{y}{3} = 7$ c $-5a = 20$

2 The distance d m a cyclist has travelled after t seconds at a speed of s m/s is given by the formula $d = st$.
Find the value of t when $s = 4$ m/s and $d = 60$ m.

3 On a car journey, four people shared the cost £P of the petrol.
Write an expression for the amount each person paid.

4 Solve the equation $2d - 3 = 17$.

5 The price of a sweat band in SportsPlus is £t.
The price of the same sweat band in Jenco's is £1 more.

a Write an expression for the total cost of four sweat bands from SportsPlus.

b Write an expression with brackets for the total cost of three sweat bands from Jenco's.

c Three sweat bands from Jenco's cost the same as four from SportsPlus.
Solve an equation to find the price of a sweat band in SportsPlus.

6 Solve these equations.

a $3(m - 2) = 9$ b $4r + 5 = 2r + 11$ c $2(b + 5) = 3b + 8$

7 Solve the equation $5(c - 2) = 2(c + 1)$.

8 Expand these expressions. Simplify where possible.

a $c(2b + 5)$ b $3u(u + 1)$ c $-2(t - 3)$

d $5(m + 2) - 3(m - 2)$ e $u(3u - 2) + 6u$ f $2(3a + b) - 2(a - b)$

9 Simplify these expressions.

a $w^3 + w^3$ b $2h^2 + 3h^2 + 4h$ c $4a^2 + 5ab - a^2 - 3ab$

10 Expand $a(a^2 + a + 4)$.

11 A company logo is made using three squares of side a cm.

a Write an expression for

i the area of one square

ii the total area of the logo.

b Use your answer to part **a** to find the total area of the logo when $a = 4$ cm.

c Write a formula for the total area A of a new logo made using

i 4 squares ii 5 squares iii n squares.

12 a Write $c \times c \times c \times c \times c$ as a power.

b Write m^4 as a product.

c Write each product using index notation.

i $p \times p \times t \times t \times t$ ii $5a \times 2a \times a$

13 Simplify these expressions.

a $d^3 \times d^2$ b $c^6 \div c$ c $s^3 \times \frac{s^4}{s^2}$ d $(3c)^2$

14 **a** **i** Write the highest common factor of $8a$ and 16.
ii Factorise completely $8a + 16$.
b Factorise completely
i $12s + 8t$ **ii** $4w^2 - 6w$ **iii** $6pe + 12pc - 9pt$

15 Solve these equations.
a $\frac{x-2}{3} = 4$ **b** $\frac{g}{3} + 2 = 7$ **c** $\frac{2b}{5} = 6$ **d** $\frac{3h}{-2} = 9$

16 Solve these equations.
a $\frac{4p+2}{5} = 10$ **b** $\frac{-2+3s}{5} = 5$ **c** $\frac{10-6x}{4} = 1$ **d** $\frac{9+t}{2} = 2t$

17 **STEM** The strength H of a magnetic field is given by the formula $H = \frac{nI}{L}$.
Use the formula to find I when $H = 1000$, $n = 100$ and $L = 0.2$.

18 36 sparklers are divided equally between n people.
a Write an expression for the number of sparklers each person receives.
b Each person receives two sparklers.
Write an equation and solve it to find the number of people.

19 **Problem-solving** Two bottles of juice are mixed with 600 ml of fizzy water.
The mixture fills 10 glasses.
a Write an expression for the volume a glass contains.
b Each glass contains 300 ml.
Solve an equation to find the volume of juice a bottle contains.

Challenge

20 Find numbers to complete the power pyramids.
a For pyramid A, multiplying two adjacent powers on the same row gives the power above.
b For pyramid B, dividing two adjacent powers on the same row gives the power below.
c Use both rules to complete pyramid C.
d Replace a^{13} in pyramid C with a higher power of your own and try again.

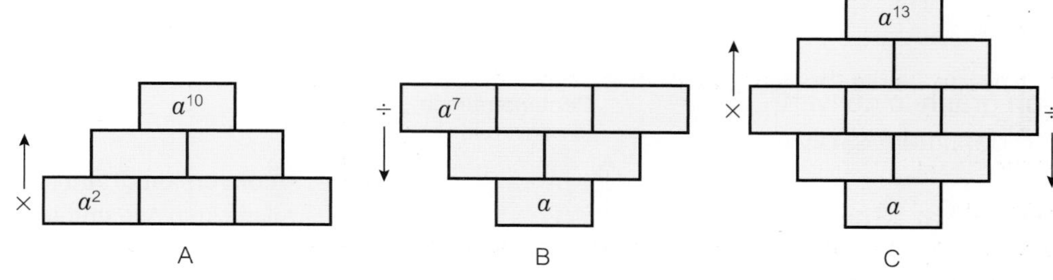

21 **Reflect** This may be the first time you have done any algebra since Year 7.
Choose A, B or C to complete each statement.

In this unit, I did ..	**A** well	**B** OK	**C** not very well.
I think algebra is ...	**A** easy	**B** OK	**C** difficult.
When I think about doing algebra, I feel ...	**A** confident	**B** OK	**C** unsure.

If you answered mostly As and Bs, are you surprised that you feel OK about algebra? Why?
If you answered mostly Cs, look back at the questions in the lessons that you found most tricky. Ask a friend or your teacher to explain them to you. Then complete the statements above again.

Reflect

5 Real-life graphs

MASTER | Check P122 | Strengthen P124 | Extend P129 | Test P133

5.1 Conversion graphs

You will learn to:

- Draw, use and interpret conversion graphs.

CONFIDENCE

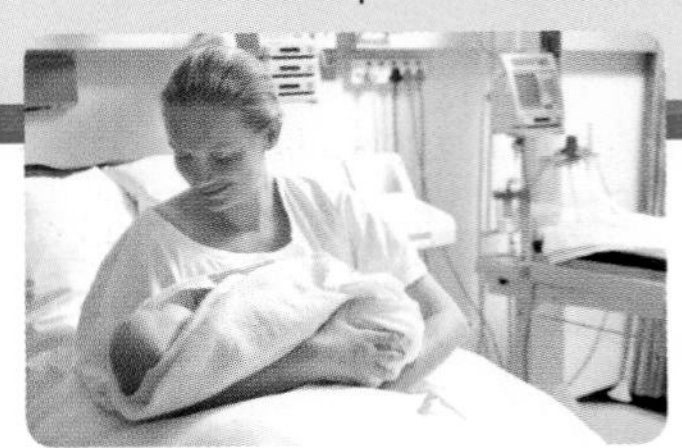

Why learn this?
Some health professionals use conversion graphs to convert a newborn baby's weight from kilograms to pounds and ounces.

Fluency
Work out the missing numbers.

- 5 miles ≈ 8 km, so 15 miles ≈ □ km
- £10 ≈ €12, so £40 ≈ € □
- 4 pints ≈ 2 litres, so 20 pints ≈ □ litres

Explore
Is it cheaper to buy an iPad® in the UK or France?

Exercise 5.1

Warm up

1 Copy and complete.

a 1 cm = □ mm　**b** 1 kg = □ g　**c** 1 m = □ cm
d 1 l = □ ml　**e** 1 km = □ m

2 Work out the value of one small square in each of these scales.

a
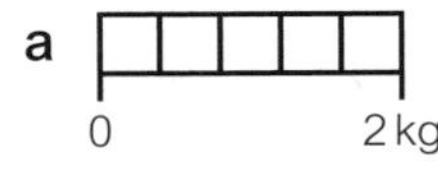

b

c
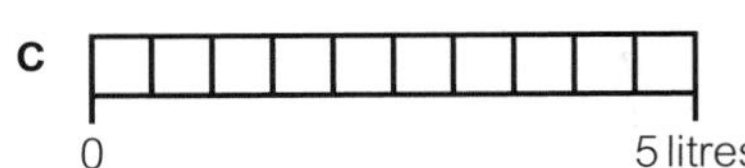

d

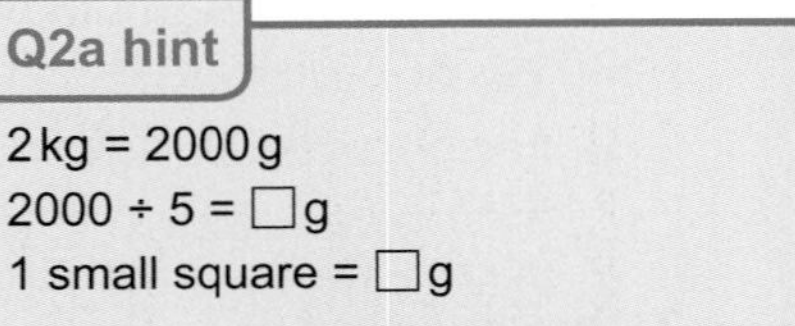

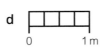

Q2a hint
2 kg = 2000 g
2000 ÷ 5 = □ g
1 small square = □ g

3 Here is a **conversion graph** to convert between inches and centimetres, giving approximate values.
The green arrows show that 20 cm is approximately the same as 8 inches.
Use the graph to convert

a 10 cm to inches
b 35 cm to inches
c 6 inches to centimetres
d 11 inches to centimetres

Discussion How can you use this graph to convert 70 cm into inches?

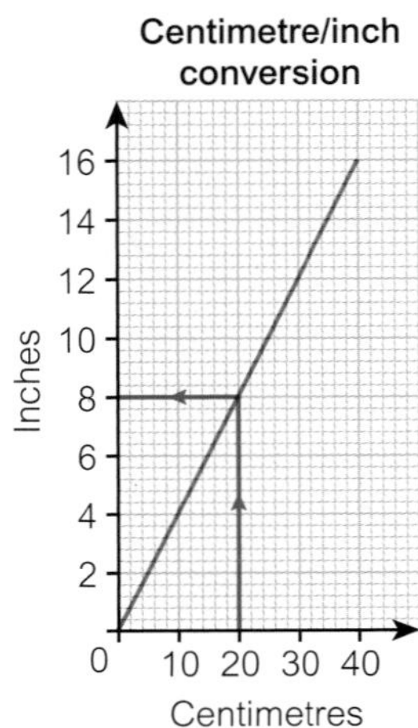

Key point
A **conversion graph** converts values from one **unit** to another.

Topic links: Coordinates, Imperial and metric measures

Subject links: Science (Q5)

4 The graph shows the currency conversion between British pounds (£) and US dollars ($).

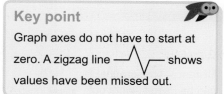

a Use the graph to convert

i £5 to dollars ii $4 to pounds iii $12 to pounds.

b Use your answers to part **a** to convert

i $40 to pounds ii £15 to dollars.

Discussion Why do currency conversion graphs always go through (0, 0)?

Dollar/pound currency conversion

Pounds (£)

Dollars ($)

5 **STEM** The table shows three temperatures in degrees Celsius (°C) and degrees Fahrenheit (°F).

°C	70	80	90
°F	158	176	194

a Copy these axes onto graph paper.

b Plot the points from the table on the grid and join them with a straight line.

c Nitrogen chloride has a boiling point of 160°F. What is its boiling point in °C?

d Nitric acid has a boiling point of 83°C. What is its boiling point in °F?

e Which has the higher boiling point, nitrogen chloride or nitric acid?

Discussion Is a temperature of double 70°C the same as double 158°F?

Key point

Graph axes do not have to start at zero. A zigzag line shows values have been missed out.

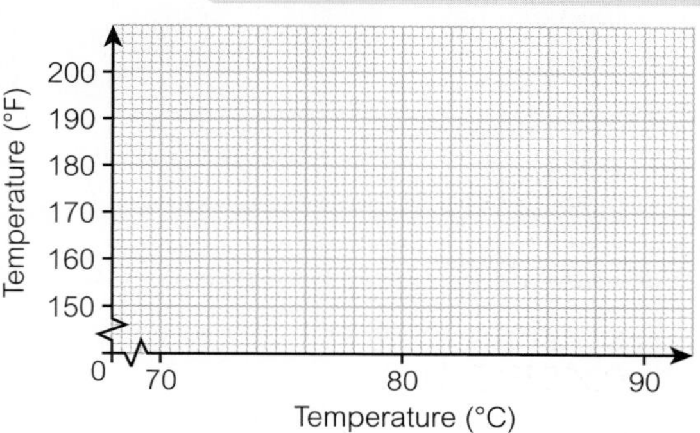

Investigation

The graphs show the currency conversion between British pounds (£) and New Zealand dollars (NZD), and New Zealand dollars (NZD) and Danish krone (DKK).

1 Use the graphs to work out the value of

a £5 in DKK

b 72 DKK in £.

2 Draw a conversion graph between British pounds (£) and Danish krone (DKK).

3 Check your graph is correct by converting values in £ to DKK using your graph, and also these two graphs.

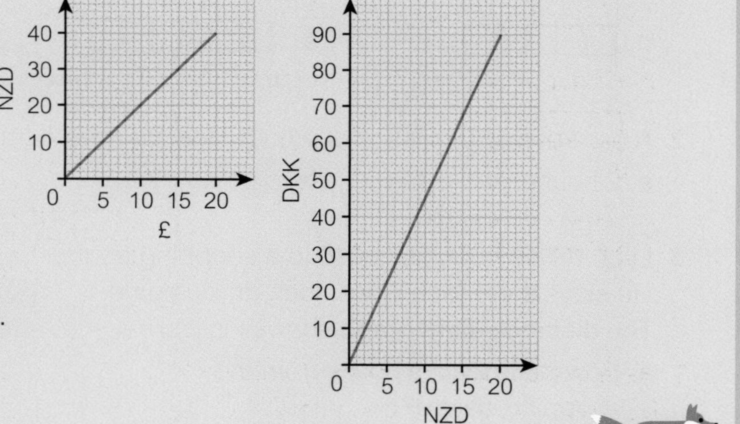

6 **Explore** Is it cheaper to buy an iPad® in the UK or France?
Is it easier to explore this question now you have completed the lesson?
What further information do you need to be able to answer this?

7 **Reflect** After this lesson, Caroline says, 'In Q4a i, I almost read 5 on the euros axis, instead of on the pounds axis.'
She wrote down:

Conversion graphs: be careful to read the correct axis.

Look back at the questions you answered in this lesson.
Write your own 'be careful to' list for conversion graphs.

Explore

Reflect

5.2 Distance–time graphs

You will learn to:
- Interpret a distance–time graph
- Draw a simple distance–time graph
- Draw and use graphs to solve distance–time problems.

CONFIDENCE

Why learn this?
Distance–time graphs can be used to work out journey times and help plan deliveries.

Fluency
A car travels 30 miles in 1 hour. How far does it travel in
- $\frac{1}{2}$ an hour
- 20 minutes?

Explore
What story does this distance–time graph tell you?

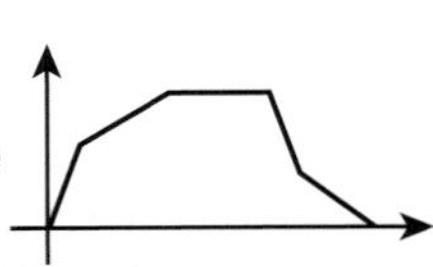

Exercise 5.2

Warm up

1 Work out the value in minutes of one small square in each of these scales.

a 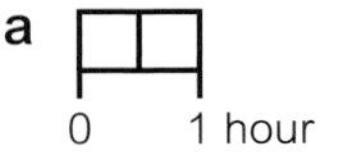

b 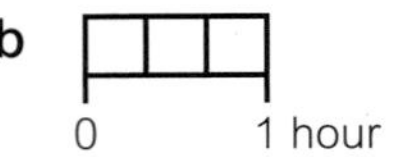

c 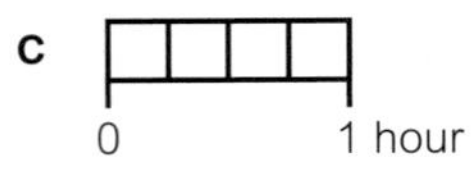

d 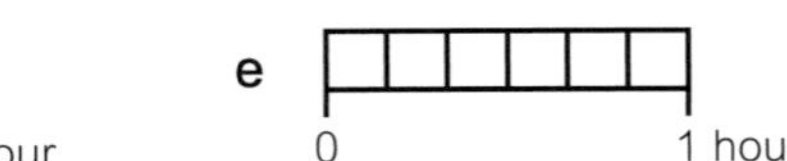

e 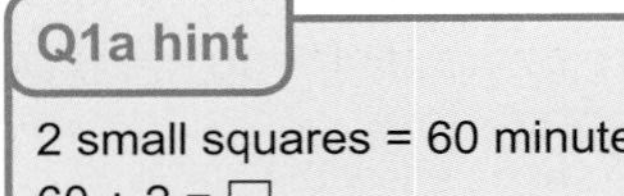

Q1a hint
2 small squares = 60 minutes
60 ÷ 2 = □
1 small square = □ minutes

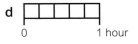

2 A car travels 50 miles in one hour. How far does it travel in

a 2 hours b $\frac{1}{2}$ an hour?

Key point
A **distance–time graph** represents a journey. The vertical axis represents the **distance** from the starting point. The horizontal axis represents the **time** taken.

3 Liam drives from his house to a shopping centre. He stays there for a while, then drives home. The **distance–time graph** shows his journey.

a How far is Liam's house from the shopping centre?

b What time does Liam arrive at the shopping centre?

c How long does he take to drive to the centre?

d How long does he stay at the shopping centre?

e How long does he take to drive home?

f **Reasoning** When was he driving fastest? How can you tell this from the graph?

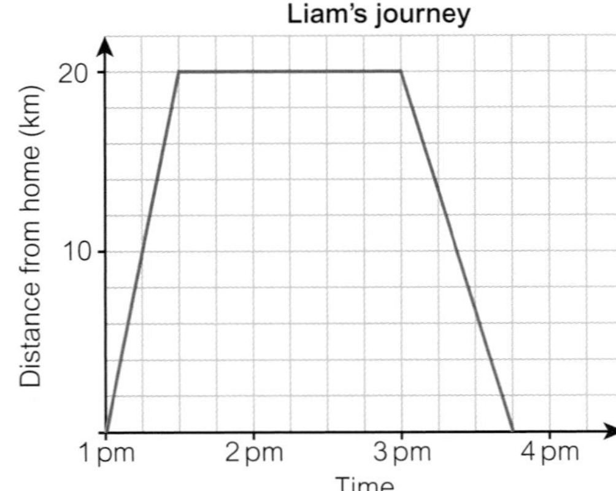

Q3b hint
Four small squares represent 1 hour.

Topic links: Time

4 Peter walks to the post office. He stops to chat to a friend on the way home.
The graph shows his journey.

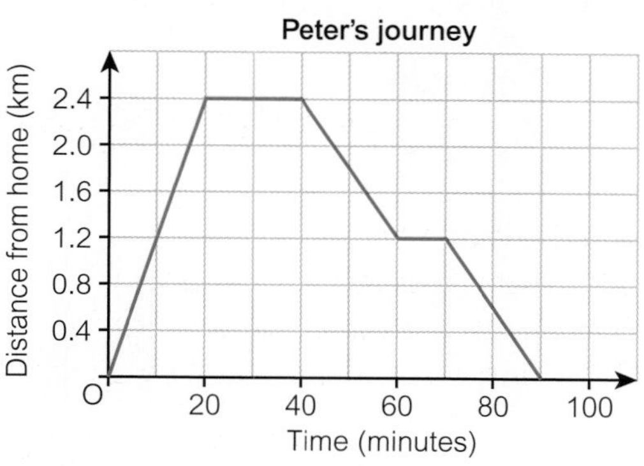

a How far away is the post office from Peter's house?
b How long does Peter spend at the post office?
c How long does Peter spend chatting to his friend?
d How long does it take for Peter to get from his house to the post office?
e How long does it take for Peter to get from the post office back to his house?
f When is Peter walking fastest?

Discussion What happened to Peter's distance from home between 60 and 70 minutes?

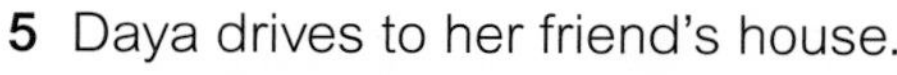

5 Daya drives to her friend's house.
She drive 125 km in 2.5 hours. Then she stops for a half-hour break. She then drives 75 km in 1 hour and arrives at her friend's house.
a On graph paper draw a horizontal axis from 0 to 4 hours and a vertical axis from 0 to 200 km. Draw a distance–time graph to show Daya's journey.
b During which part of her journey was she travelling fastest?

Key point

On a distance–time graph the **gradient** (steepness) of the line represents the **speed** of the journey.

6 Geoff leaves home at 8 am and jogs 5 km to work. It takes him $\frac{3}{4}$ of an hour. He leaves work at 4 pm and jogs 2 km further away from home to see his friend. This takes him 15 minutes. He spends $\frac{1}{4}$ of an hour with his friend, then jogs directly home. He arrives there at 6 pm.
a Draw a distance–time graph to show Geoff's journey.
b During which part of his journey is Geoff jogging the quickest?

7 One evening Clare walks to the cinema.
The graph shows her journey.

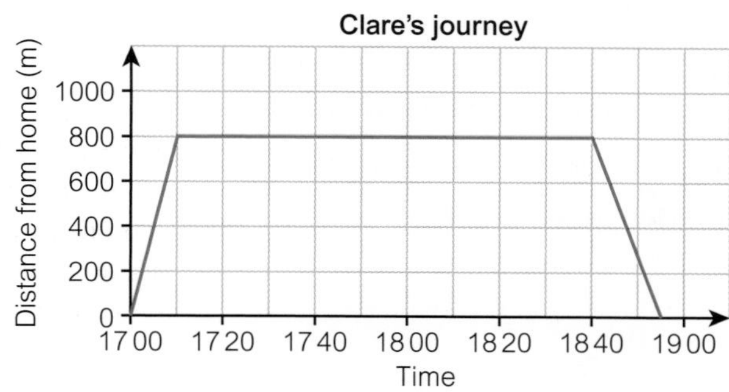

a How far is the cinema from Clare's home?
b How far does Clare walk in total?

Q7b hint

She walks to the cinema and back again.

8 The graph shows two bus journeys. One bus leaves Bath at 11 am and travels to Newport. The other bus leaves Newport at 11 am and travels to Bath.
a Which line shows the Bath to Newport bus?
b What time does each bus arrive?
c Which is the quicker bus journey?

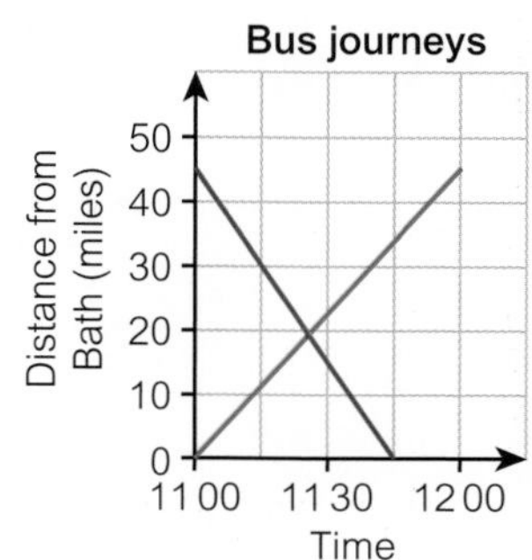

Q8b hint

The vertical axis shows the distance from Bath.

9 Katy and Aaron take part in a sponsored cycle ride. The graph shows their journeys.

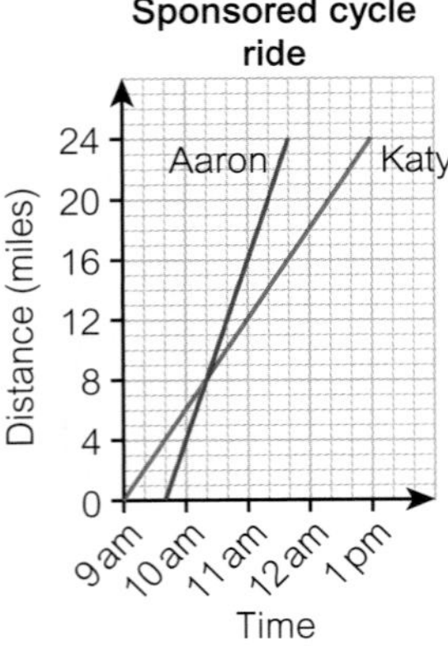

a How far is the cycle ride?

b How long does it take Katy to complete the cycle ride?

c At what time does Aaron set off?

d How long does it take Aaron to complete the cycle ride?

e At what time does Aaron overtake Katy?

Q9c hint

Three small squares represent 1 hour.

Q9e hint

At what time do the two lines cross?

Investigation **Reasoning**

In rally racing, drivers race between two set places.

Design a route for a rally race. You could include some curves and some straight sections, and use different road surfaces. Drivers will slow down for curves and speed up for straight sections, and they will drive faster on tarmac than on gravel. Sketch a distance–time graph for your race.

10 **Explore** What story does this distance–time graph tell you?

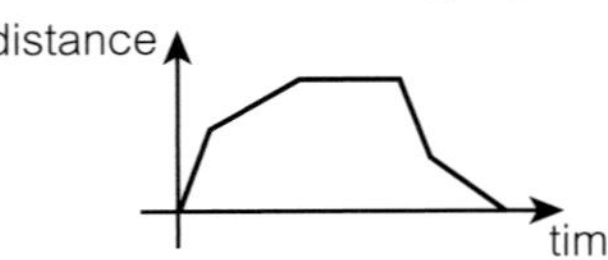

Look back at the maths you have learned in this lesson. How can you use it to answer this question?

11 **Reflect** You have seen lines like this on distance–time graphs:

Describe, in your own words, what each type of line tells you.

What if lines A and B were steeper? What would each of them tell you then?

What if lines A and B were less steep? What would each of them tell you then?

Would there ever be a line like line D on a distance-time graph?

Explain your answer.

D

Explore

Reflect

5.3 Line graphs

You will learn to:

- Draw and interpret line graphs.

Why learn this?
You can look at the graphs of rainfall and temperature for a holiday destination to help you decide the best time to go.

Fluency
Work out the missing numbers in these sequences.

- 4, 8, □, 16
- £500, £750, □, £1250

Explore
How do scientists use a climate graph to help recognise climate change?

Exercise 5.3

Warm up

1 The graph shows an approximate conversion of inches to millimetres.
Copy this table. Use the graph to complete it.

Inches	1	5	3.2		
Millimetres				50	120

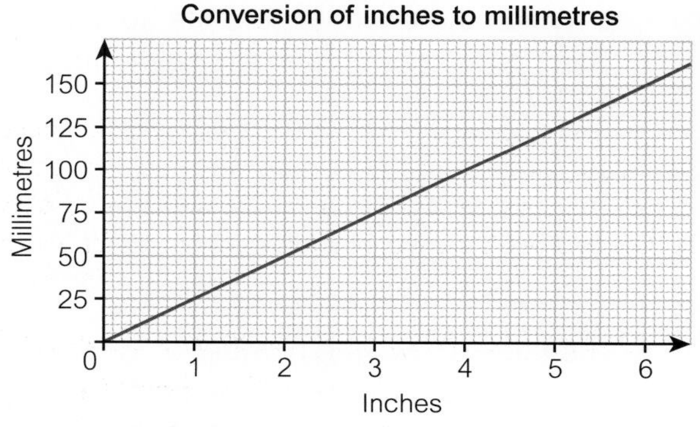

2 **Reasoning** The table shows how much Becky earned every two years from 2004 to 2012.

Year	2004	2006	2008	2010	2012
Amount earned (£)	8600	9000	9200	10 800	10 000

a Copy these axes onto graph paper.

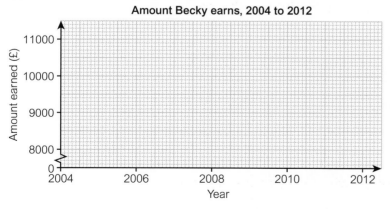

Amount Becky earns, 2004 to 2012

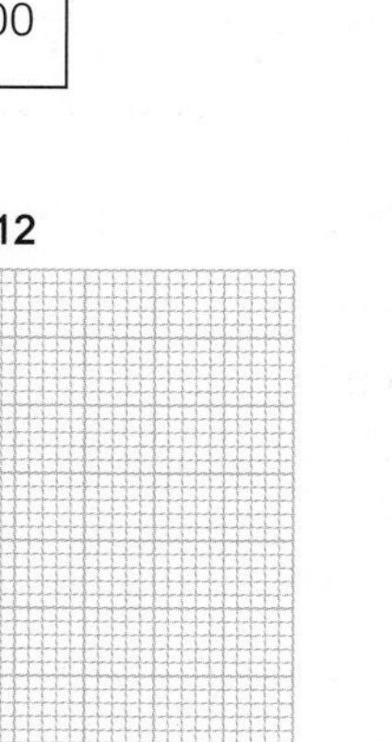

b Plot the points from the table on the graph. Join them with straight lines to draw a **line graph** for this data.

c Estimate the amount Becky earns in 2011.
Explain why this is only an estimate.

Discussion Could you use the graph to predict what Becky will earn in the future?

Discussion Why is there a break in one axis but not the other?

Key point
Line graphs can be used to see how quantities change over time.

3 **Finance** The graph shows the average price of silver, in US dollars ($) per ounce, from 2000 to 2012.

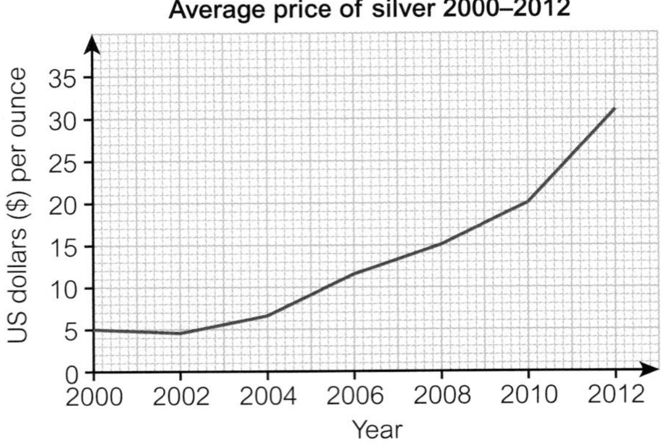

a What was the average price of silver in 2010?

b Work out the increase in price between

  i 2008 and 2010   ii 2004 and 2006.

c Between which years was the biggest increase? How can you tell this from the graph?

d Estimate the price of silver in 2005.

e Describe the change in the price of silver from 2000 to 2012. Include information such as when the price increased and decreased, between which years the increase was smallest and largest, etc.

4 **Real / Reasoning** Gary is planning an outdoor activity holiday in the Lake District. The table shows the average temperature each month in the Lake District.

Month	Jan	Feb	Mar	Apr	May	Jun	Jul	Aug	Sep	Oct	Nov	Dec
Temperature (°C)	4.4	4.4	6.1	8.1	11.0	13.6	15.6	15.1	12.9	10.0	6.8	4.5

a Draw a line graph of this data. Label the axes and give the graph a title.

b Which three months are the hottest?

This graph shows the average monthly rainfall in the Lake District.

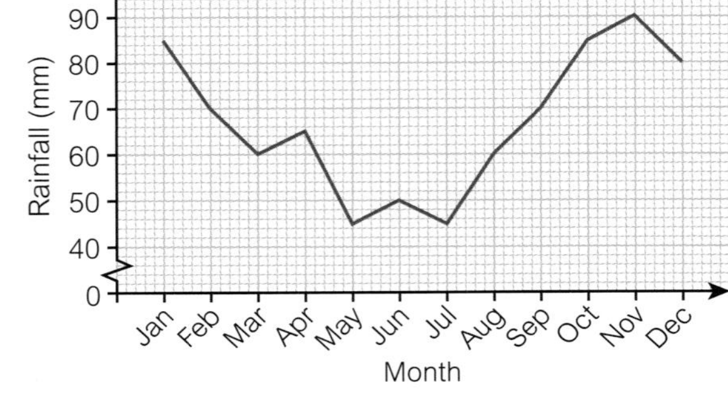

c Which three months are the driest?

d Use both graphs to decide when you think Gary should take his outdoor activity holiday in the Lake District. Explain your answer.

5 The table shows the number of visitors to a theme park from May to October. All the numbers are given to the nearest thousand.

Month	May	Jun	Jul	Aug	Sep	Oct
Number of visitors (thousands)	12	15	22	28	14	11

a Copy these axes onto graph paper.

Number of visitors (thousands)
0
10
15
20
25
30
May
Jun
Jul
Aug
Sep
Oct
Month

b Plot the points from the table on the graph. Join them with straight lines.

c The difference between the visitor numbers in September and October was 3000.

  i Between which two months was the greatest difference in visitor numbers?

  ii Work out this difference.

Explore

6 **Explore** How do scientists use a climate graph to help recognise climate change?
Is it easier to explore this question now you have completed the lesson? What further information do you need to be able to answer this?

Reflect

7 **Reflect** In this lesson, Q2 asked you to discuss. Think about the discussions you had. Did they help you? Describe how.
Think back to other mathematics lessons. When else has discussion been useful to you? Describe how.

5.4 Complex line graphs

You will learn to:

- Interpret information from a complex real-life graph, read values and discuss trends.

Why learn this?
A company that makes swimsuits can use previous years' sales and weather graphs to predict how many swimsuits they need to make next year.

Fluency
What number is halfway between these pairs of numbers?

- 20 and 25
- 2000 and 4000
- 1996 and 2000

Explore
What trends could a business look for in graphs?

Exercise 5.4

1 The graphs show students' average scores in tests over one year in different subjects.

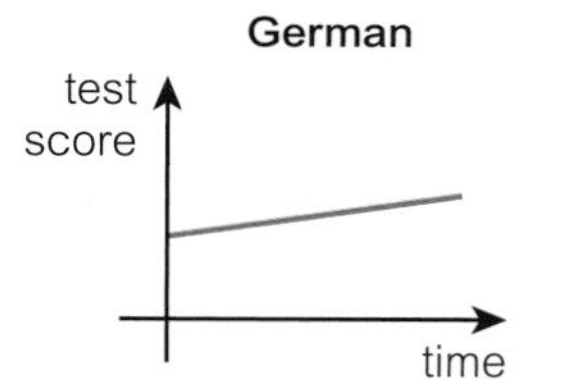

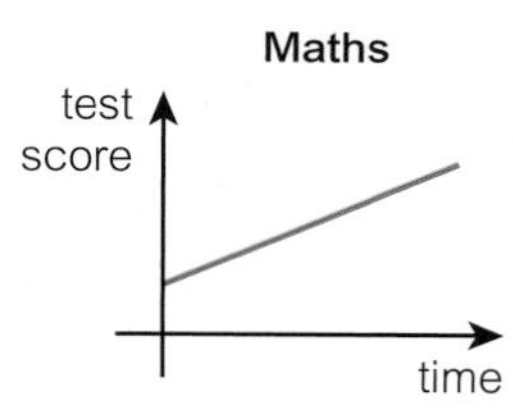

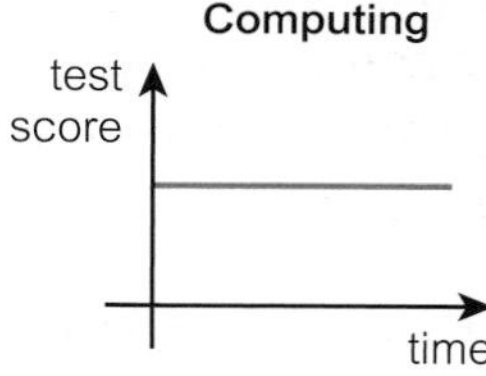

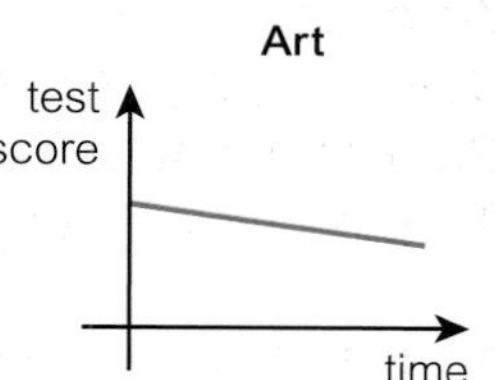

In which subject are scores

a falling **b** increasing the fastest **c** staying the same?

2 Ali decides to have a bath. The line graph shows the level of water in the bath over time.
Match each point on the graph, labelled 1 to 9, with the description cards, A to I.

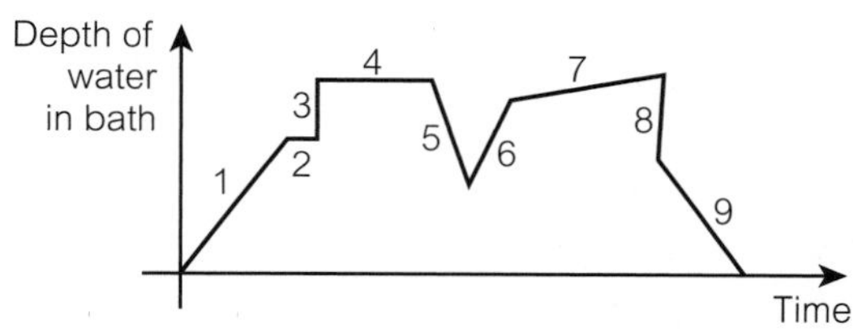

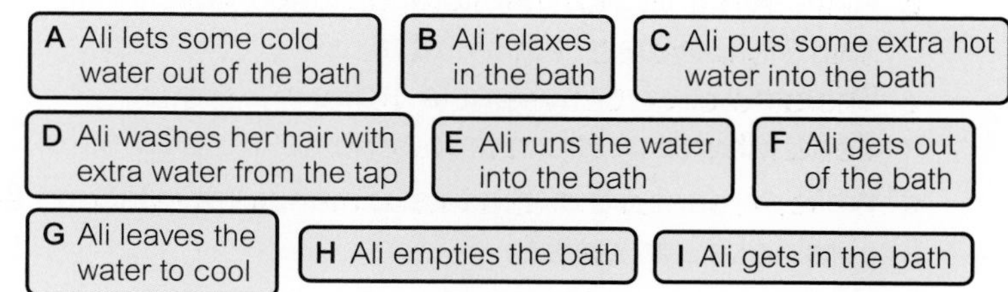

A Ali lets some cold water out of the bath
B Ali relaxes in the bath
C Ali puts some extra hot water into the bath
D Ali washes her hair with extra water from the tap
E Ali runs the water into the bath
F Ali gets out of the bath
G Ali leaves the water to cool
H Ali empties the bath
I Ali gets in the bath

3 A company sells music singles.
The graph shows the sales of CD singles and digital singles over time.

a When did the company sell the most CD singles?
b When did the company sell the most digital singles?
c When did digital singles first sell more than CD singles?
d How do you think the graphs for CD singles and digital singles might continue?

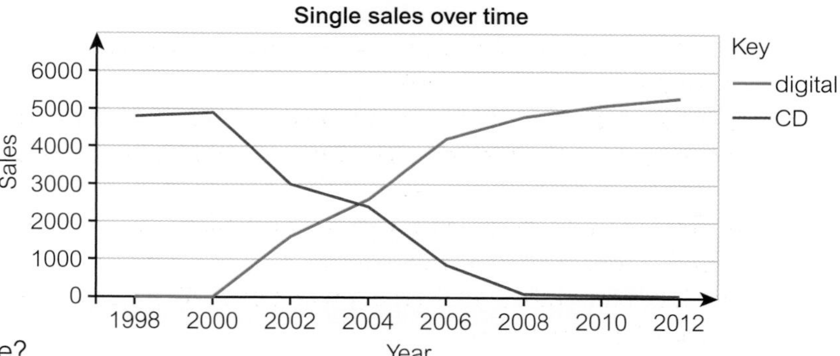

4 **Real / Reasoning** The graph shows the number of visitors to three UK attractions between 2008 and 2012.

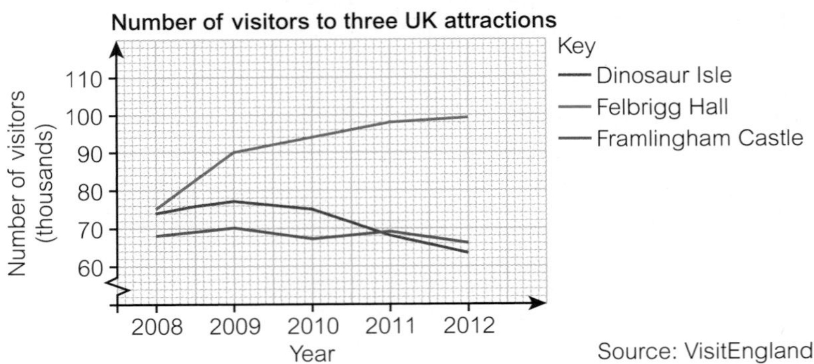

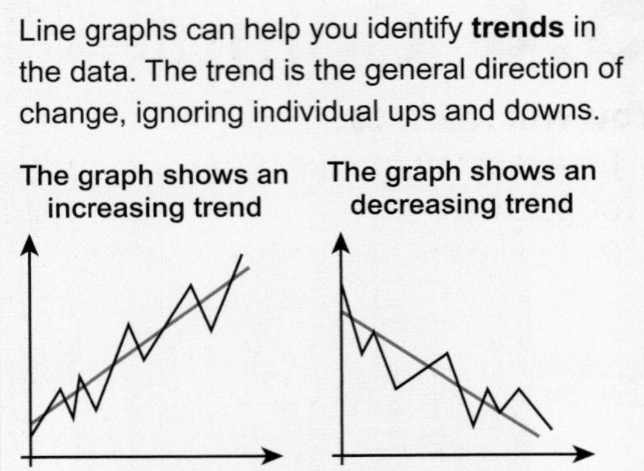

a How many visitors visited each attraction in 2008?

b Describe the trend in visitor numbers to Felbrigg Hall. Use the words increasing or decreasing.

c Describe the trend in visitor numbers to Dinosaur Isle.

d Is it possible to describe a trend in visitor numbers to Framlingham Castle?

e Use the graph to predict the number of visitors to each attraction in 2013. Explain how you made your predictions.

Key point
Line graphs can help you identify **trends** in the data. The trend is the general direction of change, ignoring individual ups and downs.
The graph shows an increasing trend
The graph shows an decreasing trend

Discussion How accurate are your predictions for Q4 part **e**?

5 **Real / Problem-solving / Reasoning** The graph shows the total distance travelled using different types of transport in the UK. Information was taken every 10 years from 1970 to 2010.

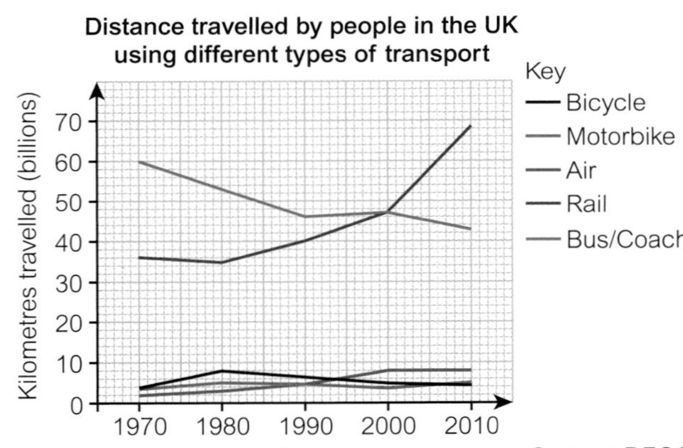

a Describe the trends in the distance travelled by each type of transport.

b In 1970, what distance was travelled by

i bicycle ii bus/coach?

The 'Cars, vans and taxis' category is missing from the graph. In 1970, 297 billion kilometres were travelled by cars, vans and taxis.

c What percentage of the total distance travelled in 1970 was by cars, vans and taxis? Give your answer correct to 1 decimal place.

In 2010, 656 billion kilometres were travelled by cars, vans and taxis.

d What percentage of the total distance travelled in 2010 was by cars, vans and taxis? Give your answer correct to 1 decimal place.

e Describe how the use of cars, vans and taxis has changed between 1970 and 2010.

Q5c Strategy hint
Use the graph to work out the distance travelled by each type of transport first, then find the total.

6 **Explore** What trends could a business look for in graphs?
Is it easier to explore this question now you have completed the lesson?
What further information do you need to be able to answer this?

7 **Reflect** This lesson asked you to interpret information from some complex real-life graphs.
Which questions were easiest for you to answer? What made them easier?
Which questions were hardest for you to answer? What made them harder?

Explore

Reflect

5.5 STEM: Graphs of functions

You will learn to:

- Discuss and interpret line graphs and graphs of functions from a range of sources
- Plot the graphs of a function derived from a real-life problem.

Why learn this?
Scientists draw graphs to show the results of experiments. Graphs can show trends and meanings that may not be clear from just looking at data.

Fluency
Use the formula $y = 4x$ to work out the values of y when

- $x = 5$
- $x = 9$
- $x = 15$

Explore
How long does a snap-and-shake light stick last?

Exercise 5.5 Graphs in science

1 A cat is tracked to show its movements during 24 hours.
  a What time did the cat leave in the morning?
  b Write a short description of the cat's movements during the day.

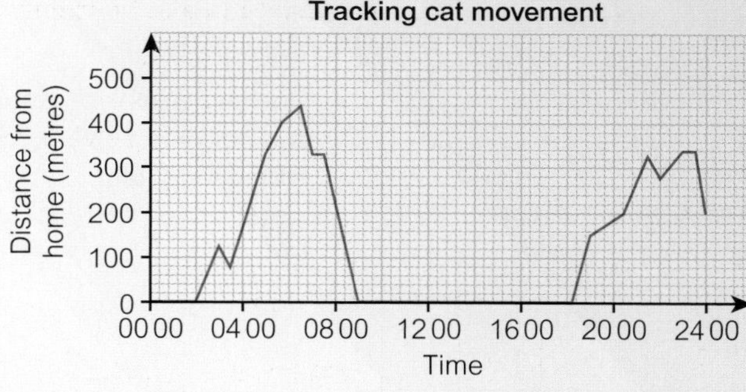

Key point
You can **interpret** graphs from real-life situations by reading values and suggesting what they mean.

Q2 Literacy hint
A 'newton' is a unit of force.

2 **STEM / Reasoning / Problem-solving** In an experiment, a 25 cm length of fishing line was tested to see when it would break. The graph shows the tension in the line as the line was stretched.
  a How much tension was needed to stretch the line by 1 cm?
  b By how many centimetres was the fishing line stretched when the tension was 20 newtons?
  c How far had the fishing line been stretched when it broke? Explain how you can tell from the graph when this happened.
  On the fishing line packaging, it says that the line is expected to break when it is stretched with a weight of 11 lb.
  d Use this formula to work out the tension in a line stretched with a weight of 11 lb.
    tension (newtons) = 10 × mass in kilograms
  e Did the line break before or after the breaking strain stated on the packaging? Explain your answer.

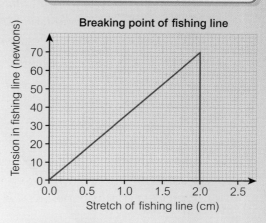

Breaking point of fishing line

Tension in fishing line (newtons): 0, 10, 20, 30, 40, 50, 60, 70
Stretch of fishing line (cm): 0.0, 0.5, 1.0, 1.5, 2.0, 2.5

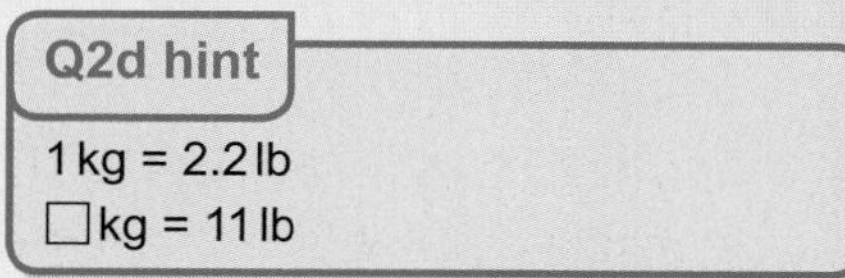

Q2d hint
1 kg = 2.2 lb
□ kg = 11 lb

Warm up

3 **STEM / Reasoning** The graph shows the growth rate of yeast at different temperatures.

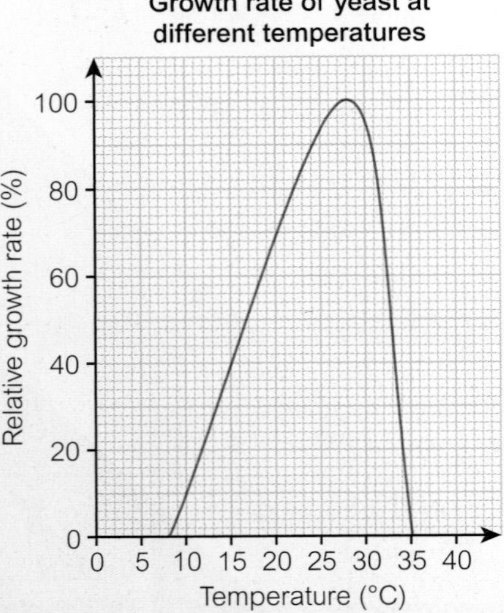

a At what temperature does yeast start growing?

b At what temperatures does yeast reach 40% of its maximum growth rate?

c Describe what happens to the growth of the yeast at

i 28°C **ii** 35°C

Discussion Is the amount of yeast increasing or decreasing when the graph shows a decrease in the percentage growth rate?

4 **STEM / Modelling / Problem-solving** When an ice cube is left at room temperature for 15 minutes, the formula to work out the approximate amount of ice that melts is

melt water (ml) = 0.0002 × surface area of cube (mm^2)

The table shows the side lengths of five different size ice cubes.

Ice cube	Side length (mm)	Surface area (mm^2)	Melt water (ml)
1	10	$6 \times 10^2 = \square$	$0.0002 \times \square = \square$
2	15		
3	20		
4	25		
5	30		

a Copy and complete the table.

b On graph paper, draw a horizontal axis from 0 to 5500 and a vertical axis from 0 to 1.1. Label the horizontal axis 'Surface area (mm^2)' and the horizontal axis 'Volume of melt water (ml)'. Give your graph a title.
Plot the points from part **a** on the graph.

c Use your graph to work out

i the amount of melt water from a cube of side length 18 mm.

ii the side length of a cube that produced 0.87 ml of melt water. Give your answer correct to the nearest millimetre.

Key point

Drawing graphs of real-life situations can help you solve problems and understand data.

Q4a hint

surface area of cube = 6 × area of one face

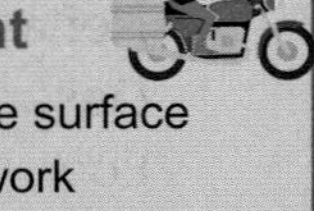

Q4c ii Strategy hint

Use the graph to find the surface area of the cube, then work backwards to find the side length of the cube.

Topic links: Using formulae, Surface area

Subject links: Science (Q2–Q5)

STEM

5 STEM / Modelling To activate a chemical light stick, you bend the tube and shake it. At 15 °C the light stick gives off 2 lumens of light. For each 10 °C increase in temperature the number of lumens doubles.

a Copy and complete this table showing the temperature and the number of lumens.

Temperature (°C)	15	25	35	45
Number of lumens	2	4		

b Draw a graph to show the number of lumens at different temperatures. Plot 'Temperature (°C)' on the horizontal axis and 'Number of lumens' on the vertical axis.

c Use your graph to estimate

i the number of lumens a light stick will give off at 30 °C

ii the temperature at which the light stick will give off 10 lumens.

Q5 Literacy hint
A lumen is a measure of the brightness of a light. The greater the number of lumens, the brighter the light.

Q5b hint
Plot the points from your table, then join them with a smooth curve.

Q5b Strategy hint
It is easier to draw a curve with your hand 'inside' it and moving outwards. Turn your paper round so you can draw the curve comfortably.

6 STEM / Reasoning Scientists added sulphuric acid to a metal and measured the volume of gas released over time. Then they repeated this at different temperatures. The graph shows their results.

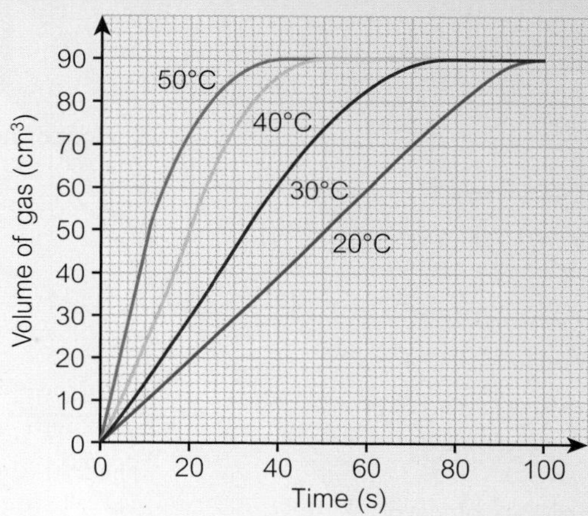

a What volume of gas did all the reactions release?

b At 20 °C, what volume of gas was released up to 60 seconds?

c How long did it take to release this volume of gas at
i 30 °C **ii** 40 °C **iii** 50 °C?

d How does increasing the temperature affect the speed of the reaction?

Q6a hint
Use the correct units for volumes of gas.

Q6c hint
Read values from the graphs as accurately as possible.

7 Explore How long does a snap-and-shake light stick last?
Is it easier to explore this question now you have completed the lesson?
What further information do you need to be able to answer this?

8 Reflect In this lesson you looked at lots of science graphs.
Describe two graphs you have drawn or used in science lessons.
Look back at what you have learned in this unit so far.
Which of these skills have you already used in science?

Explore

Reflect

5.6 More real-life graphs

You will learn to:

- Discuss and interpret linear and non-linear graphs from a range of sources
- Solve real-life problems by drawing graphs.

CONFIDENCE

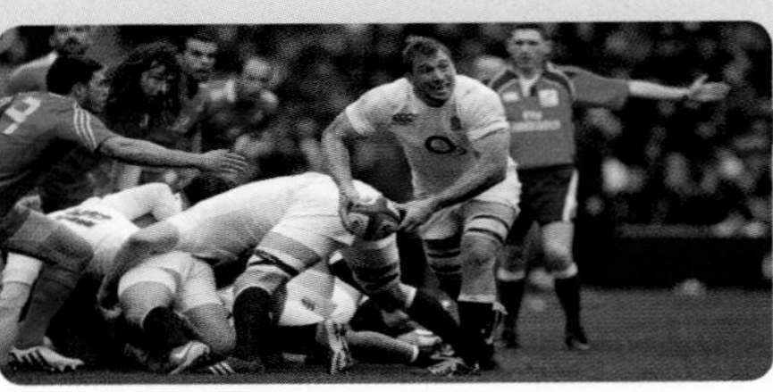

Why learn this?
Professional rugby players use graphs showing data from GPS trackers to display their movement around the pitch during a match.

Fluency
In which of these two distance–time graphs was the person travelling faster?

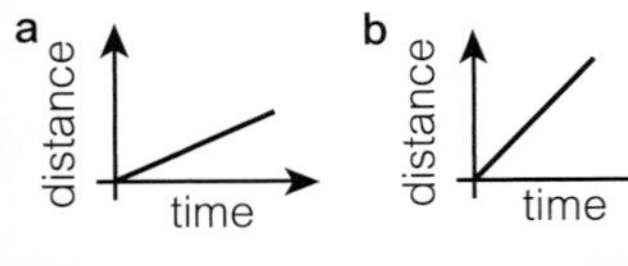

Explore
What would an altitude graph look like for a skier?

Exercise 5.6

Warm up

1 The graph shows the cost of printing hoodies.
The printing company charge a one-off set-up cost, and then a price per printed hoodie.

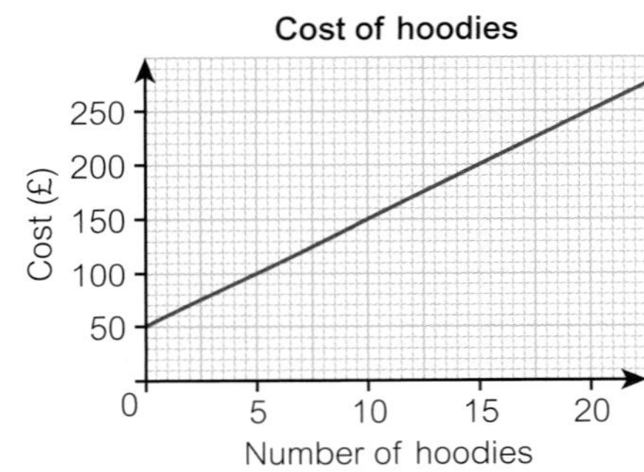

a How many hoodies can you get for
 i £110
 ii £175?

b A judo club orders 17 hoodies. How much should they sell them to their members for, to cover the cost of printing?

2 **Real / Problem-solving / Reasoning** Dave is self-employed.
He does gardening and house maintenance.
The graph shows his charges for jobs.

Key point
A **linear graph** is a graph that is made up of a straight line.

a How much does Dave charge for
 i 3 hours of gardening ii $4\frac{1}{2}$ hours of house maintenance?

b What do the values at 0 hours on the graph represent?

c How much does Dave charge per hour for gardening?

d How much does Dave charge per hour for house maintenance?

e Dave visits Mr Smith and does $7\frac{1}{4}$ hours of gardening. How much does he charge him?

f Dave visits Mrs Anderson and does $3\frac{1}{2}$ hours of house maintenance and 3 hours of gardening. How much do you think he should charge her?
Explain your answer.

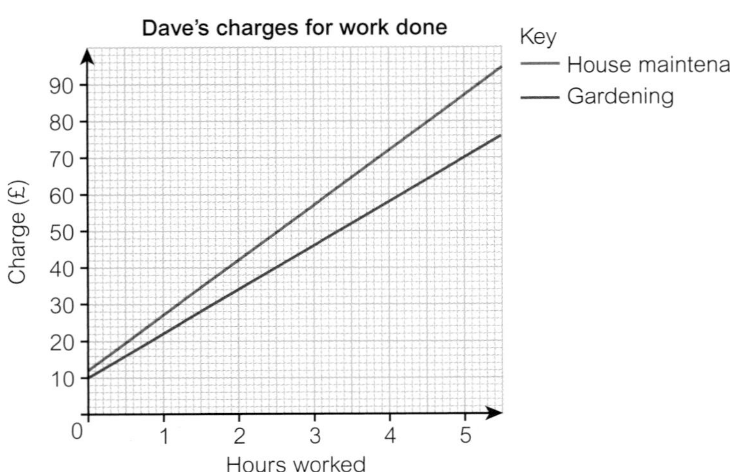

Topic links: Time

3 **Real** The graph shows the amount a plumber charges his customers.

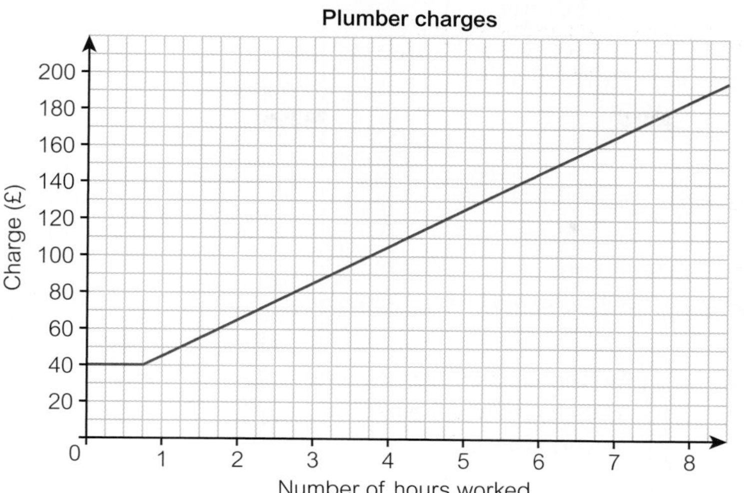

a How much does the plumber charge for

i 1 hour's work

ii $6\frac{3}{4}$ hours' work?

b The plumber charges a call-out fee.

i How much is the call-out fee?

ii How many minutes of work are included in the call-out fee?

iii How much does the plumber charge per hour after the initial call-out fee?

> **Key point**
>
> A **non-linear graph** is not a straight line.

4 The graph shows how the depth of water in this container changes over time, when water is poured in at a steady rate.

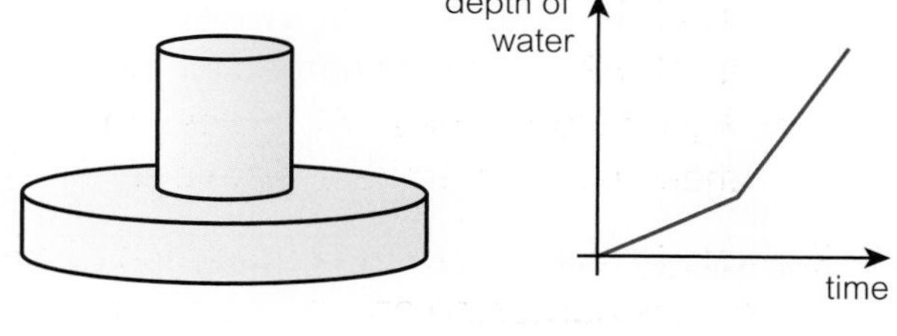

a Which bit of the container fills fastest, the wide part or the narrow part?

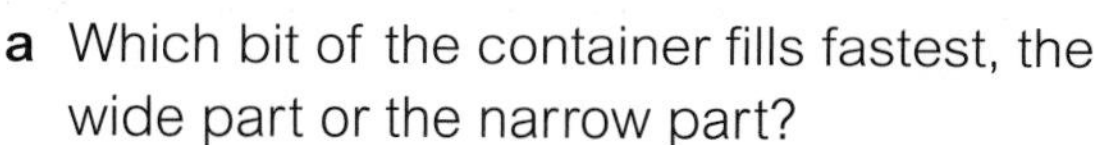

b How can you tell when it is filling fastest from the graph?

c Match each of the graphs to the correct container.

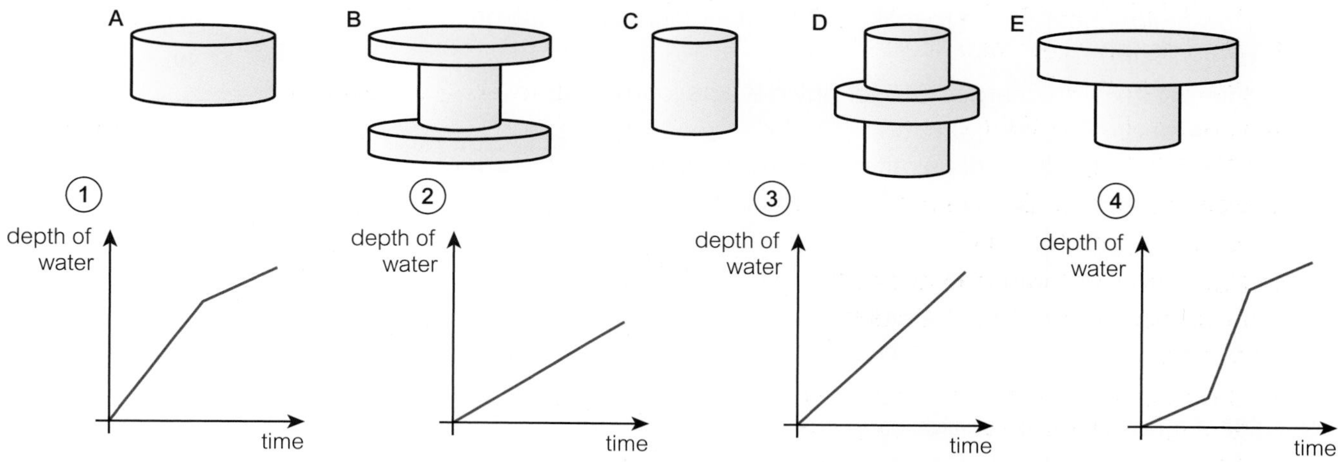

d Which container has not been matched to a graph? Sketch a depth–time graph for this container.

5 **Reasoning** A fielder throws a cricket ball to a wicket keeper. The graph shows the height above the ground of the cricket ball.

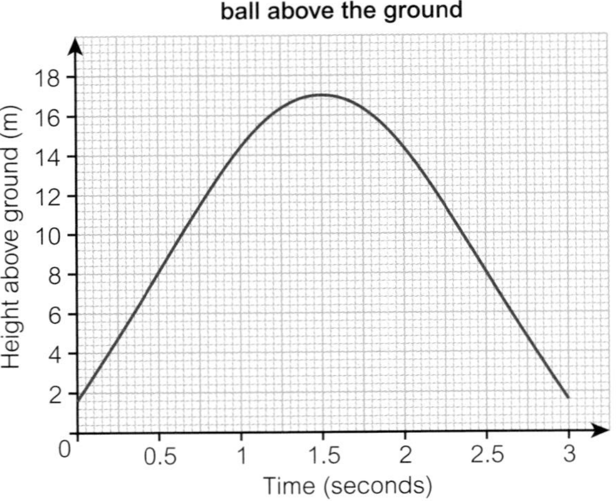

- **a** How high is the ball above the ground after
  - **i** 1 second
  - **ii** 2.3 seconds?
- **b** What was the highest point above the ground that the ball reached?
- **c** Explain why the ball does not go below 1.6 m.
- **d** After how many seconds is the ball 12 m above the ground?
  Explain why there are two answers to this question.

6 **Reasoning** A shop owner buys 250 pens. He sells 40 on Monday, 30 on Tuesday, 35 on Wednesday, 45 on Thursday, 25 on Friday, and 40 on Saturday.

- **a** Draw a line graph of the number of pens in stock during the week.
- **b** The shop is closed on Sunday. The shop owner buys 100 more pens. How many pens are now in stock?
- **c** Has the shop owner bought enough pens?
  Explain your answer.

Q6a hint

Put 'Days of the week' on the horizontal axis and 'Number of pens in stock' on the vertical axis.

7 **Real / Finance / Problem-solving** A taxi firm charges according to the number of minutes a journey takes.
The table shows their charges for their three different tariffs.

Tariff 1	Daytime (6 am–8 pm)	£2.40 plus 85p per minute
Tariff 2	Evening (8 pm–10 pm)	£2.40 plus £1 per minute
Tariff 3	Night-time (10 pm–6 am)	£2.40 plus £1.15 per minute

- **a** Draw a line graph showing the cost of taxi journeys up to 20 minutes long. Use a different line for each tariff.
- **b** What is the cost of a 5-minute journey at 2.30 pm?
- **c** How much cheaper is it to make a 12-minute journey at 9.45 pm than at 10.15 pm?

A different taxi firm charges £15 for any daytime journey up to 20 minutes long.

- **d** Use your graph to work out after how many minutes it is cheaper to use the second taxi firm than the first taxi firm.

Q7a hint

Use the table to work out the cost of a 20-minute journey on each tariff. The line for each tariff will start at (0 minutes, £2.40).

Explore

8 **Explore** What would an altitude graph look like for a skier?
Is it easier to explore this question now you have completed the lesson?
What further information do you need to be able to answer this?

Reflect

9 **Reflect** Look back at the graphs in this lesson.
The graph for Q2 is a straight line. The graph for Q5 is a curve.
Write, in your own words, why you think some real-life graphs are straight lines and some real-life graphs are curves.

5 Check up

Log how you did on your Student Progression Chart.

Line graphs

1 The graph shows the number of UK airline passengers, in millions, every 2 years between 2001 and 2011.

a How many airline passengers were there in

i 2003 ii 2011?

b In which years were there 124 million passengers?

c Estimate the number of airline passengers in 2010.

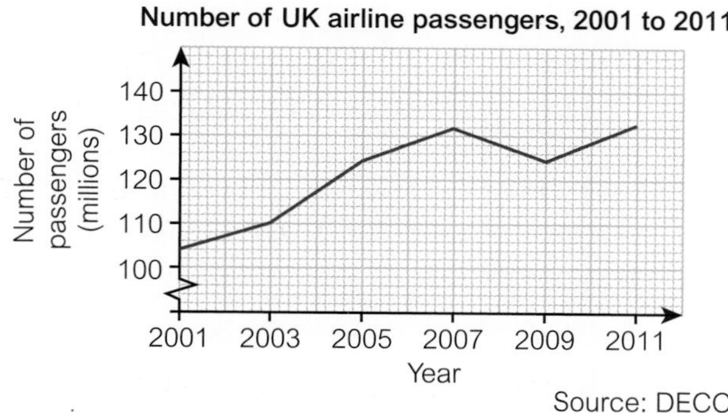

2 The graph shows the percentage of seats occupied on UK airline flights between 2003 and 2011.

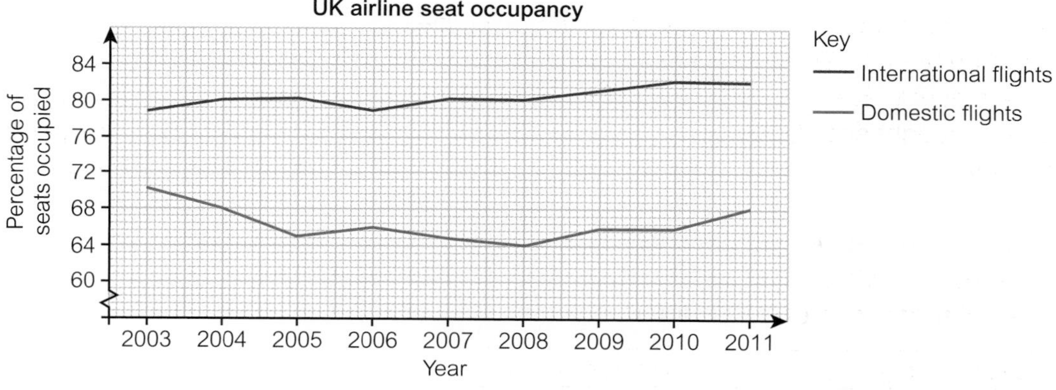

a Amanda says, 'In 2003, 69% of domestic flight seats were occupied.' Is she correct? Explain your answer.

b Which year had the smallest percentage of domestic flight seats occupied?

c Which year had the smallest difference in the percentage of domestic flight and international flight seats occupied?

d Describe the trend in the percentage of international flight seats occupied.

Conversion and distance–time graphs

3 On one day the conversion rate from GB pounds to Thai baht was £1 = 50 baht.

a Copy and complete this table of values.

£	0	5	10
Baht	0		

b On graph paper draw a horizontal axis from £0 to £10 and a vertical axis from 0 baht to 500 baht.
Plot the points from the table and join them with a straight line.

c Use your conversion graph to complete these conversions.

i £3.50 = □ baht ii 460 baht = £□

4 Gemma visits her sister. She stops to fill up her car with petrol on the way.
The graph shows her journey.

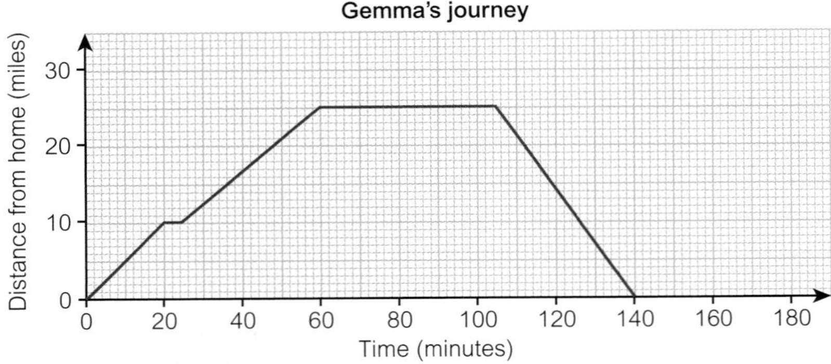

a How far away from Gemma does her sister live?

b How long does Gemma spend at the petrol station?

c How long does Gemma spend at her sister's house?

d How long does it take Gemma to get home from her sister's house?

e On which part of the journey is Gemma driving fastest?

Real-life graphs and graphs of functions

5 A vet charges a £40 call-out fee plus £20 per quarter hour.

a Copy and complete this table showing the total cost for different call-out times.

Length of call out (hours)	0	$\frac{1}{2}$	1	2	3
Total cost (£)	40				

b Draw a graph to show the total cost of a call out for up to 3 hours.
Plot 'Length of call out (hours)' on the horizontal axis and 'Total cost (£)' on the vertical axis.

c Use your graph to work out the total cost of a call out that lasts $2\frac{3}{4}$ hours.

6 The graph shows the average length of baby boys from 0 to 24 months.

a What is the average length of a baby boy aged 3 months?

b At what age does an average baby boy reach 76 cm?

c Daniel is 15 months and has a length of 78 cm. Is he longer or shorter than average?

d During which 6-month period does a baby boy grow fastest: 0–6, 6–12, 12–18 or 18–24 months?
Explain how you can tell this from the graph.

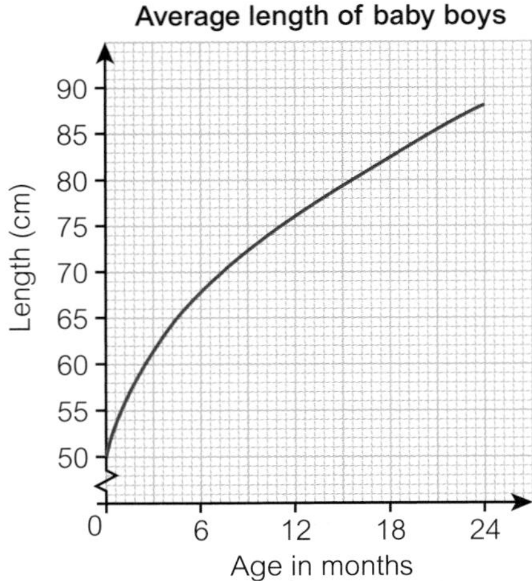

Reflect

7 How sure are you of your answers? Were you mostly
Just guessing Feeling doubtful Confident
What next? Use your results to decide whether to strengthen or extend your learning.

Challenge

8 Sketch a distance–time graph from the time you left home this morning to arriving at your first lesson. Plot 'Time' on the horizontal axis and 'Distance travelled (km)' on the vertical axis.

5 Strengthen

You will:

- Strengthen your understanding with practice.

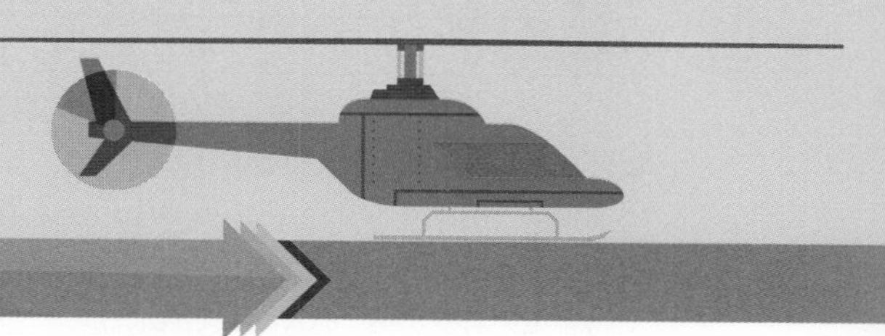

Line graphs

1 Real The line graph shows the total number of game consoles owned by households in a UK town.

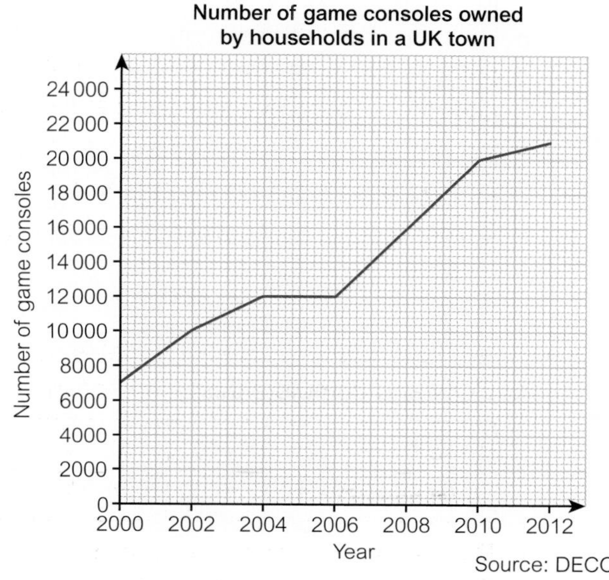

a Look at the scale on each axis. Copy and complete these statements.

  i Five small squares on the horizontal axis represent ☐ year.

  ii One small square on the vertical axis represents ☐ game consoles.

b How many game consoles were owned by households in the town in

  i 2002 **ii** 2012?

c In which year were 18 000 game consoles owned by households in the town?

d During which years did the number of game consoles owned by households in the town stay the same? How is this shown on the graph?

2 Real The line graph shows the average number of kilometres travelled by car per person in the UK.

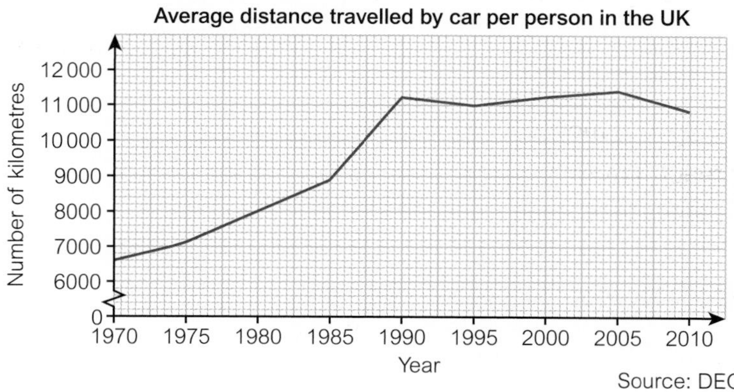

a Look at the scale on each axis.

  i How many squares on the horizontal axis represent one year?

  ii What does '8000' mean, on the vertical axis?

  iii What does one small square on the vertical axis represent?

b What was the average distance travelled by car per person in

  i 1980 **ii** 1990?

c In which year was the average distance travelled by car per person 7100 km?

d Which year had the highest average distance travelled by car per person?

Q2a ii hint

Read the label for the vertical axis.

Q2d hint

In which year did the graph reach its highest point?

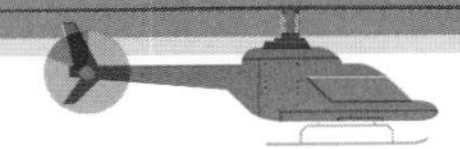

3 **Real** The table shows the number of laptops owned by households in the UK.

Year	2000	2002	2004	2006	2008	2010	2012
Laptops (millions)	2	2	3	5	9	17	27

Source: DECC

a Draw a line graph of this data.
Plot 'Year' on the horizontal axis from 2000 to 2012.
Plot 'Number of laptops (millions)' on the vertical axis from 0 to 30.
Write the title on your graph.

b Describe the trend in the number of laptops owned by households in the UK.

c Use your graph to estimate the number of laptops owned by households in the UK in

i 2007   ii 2011.

Q3a hint

On the horizontal axis use a scale of 10 small squares = 2 years.
On the vertical axis use a scale of 5 small squares = 5 million.

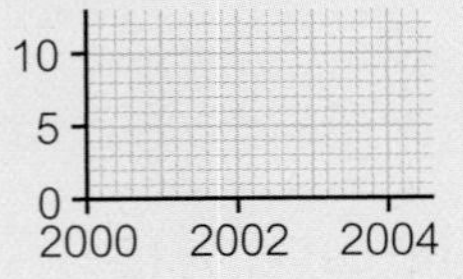

Q3b hint

Are the numbers of laptops increasing or decreasing?

4 **Real** The graph shows the average maximum daytime and minimum night-time temperatures in Keswick, Cumbria.

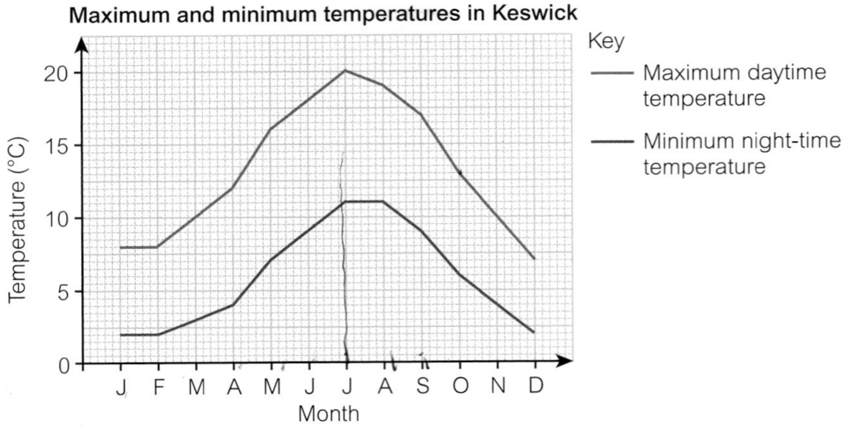

a What does S stand for on the horizontal axis?

b Which month had the highest maximum temperature?

c Which months had the lowest minimum temperature?

d In October, what was the average

i maximum temperature   ii minimum temperature?

e In which month was the smallest difference between the maximum and minimum temperatures?

Q4 Strategy hint

Before you answer questions about a graph

- read the title
- read the axes labels
- read the key
- look at the axes scales.

Q4b hint

In which month did the red line reach its highest point?

Q4e hint

In which month is the gap between the red line and the blue line smallest?

Conversion and distance–time graphs

1 **Real** The conversion graph shows the approximate conversion of feet to metres.

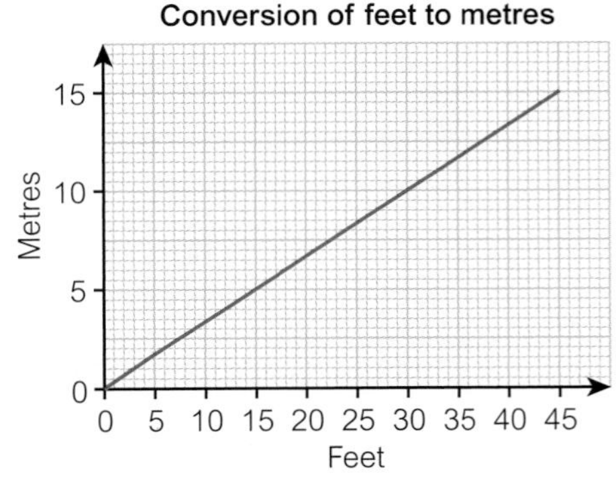

Q1 Literacy hint

The plural of foot is feet.

a Look at the scale on each axis.

i How many feet does one small square represent?

ii How many metres does one small square represent?

b Copy and complete these conversions. The symbol '≈' means 'is approximately equal to'.

i 3 feet ≈ ☐ metre

ii 25 feet ≈ ☐ metres

iii 12 metres ≈ ☐ feet

iv 4.5 metres ≈ ☐ feet

c Use the graph to convert 75 feet into metres.

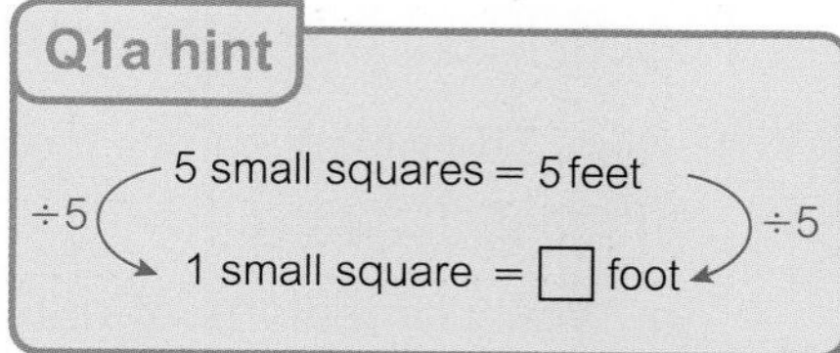

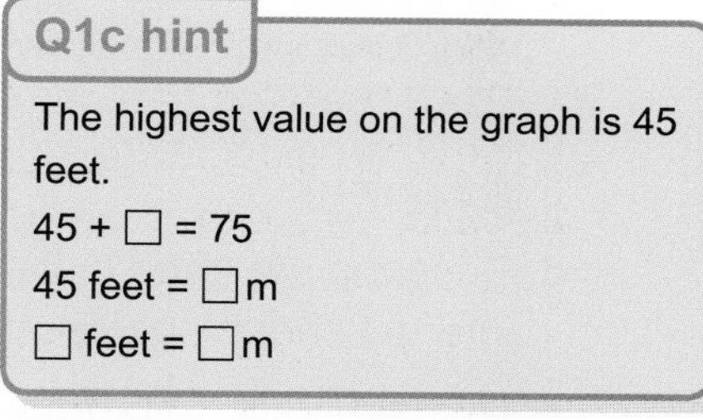

Q1c hint
The highest value on the graph is 45 feet.
45 + ☐ = 75
45 feet = ☐m
☐ feet = ☐m

2 Real On one day the conversion rate from GB pounds to South African rand was £1 = 15 rand.

a Copy and complete this table of values.

£	0	5	10
Rand	0		

b On graph paper draw a horizontal axis from £0 to £10 and a vertical axis from 0 rand to 150 rand. Plot the points from the table on the graph and join them with a straight line.

c Use your conversion graph to complete these conversions.

i £3 = ☐ rand **ii** 120 rand = £ ☐

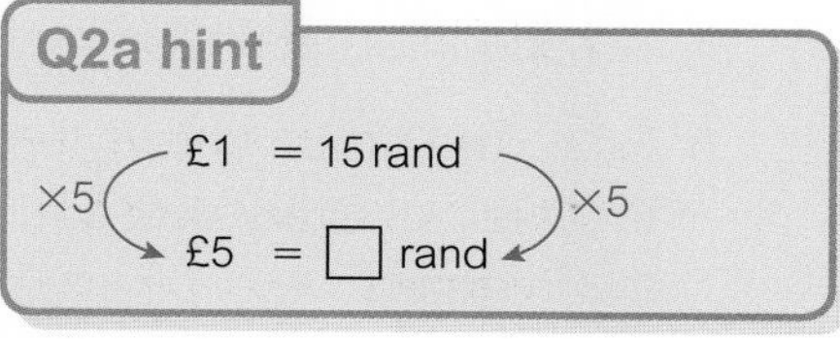

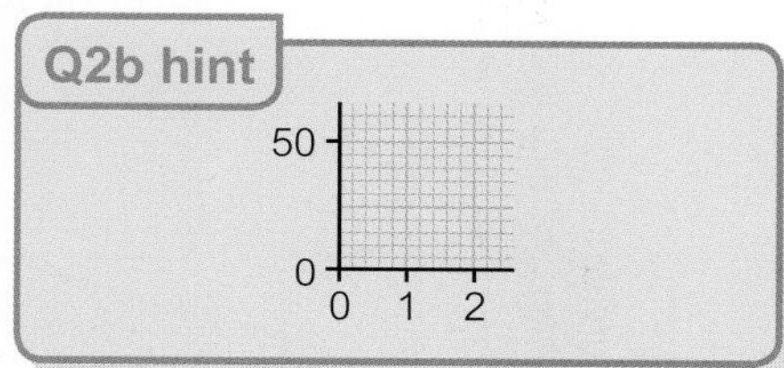

3 Peter goes to the shop by car. The graph shows his journey.

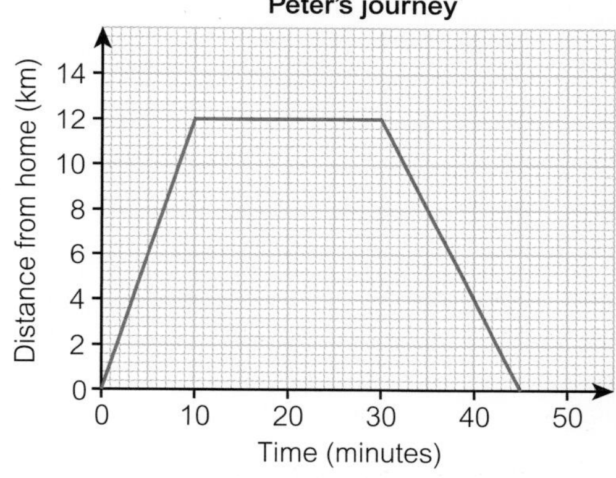

a How can you tell from the graph when Peter is at the shop?

b How long does it take Peter to get to the shop?

c How long does Peter spend at the shop?

d How long does it take Peter to get home from the shop?

e Which part of the journey was quickest?

f Peter leaves home at 10 am. What time does he get home?

Q3a hint
When he is inside the shop, his distance from home stays the same.

Q3c hint
Time spent at the shop is the difference between the arrival time and leaving time.

Q3e hint
How long did he take to drive to the shop? And home from the shop?

4 This is a description of Helena's journey on Monday.
She sets off from home at 0800. She walks 3 miles to the swimming pool and arrives at 0845. She stays at the swimming pool for 1 hour. She leaves the swimming pool and walks a further 1 mile in 15 minutes to arrive at work. She stays at work until she leaves at 1330. She then walks another 5 miles to her mum's house. She arrives at 1500.

a What is the total number of miles that Helena walked?

b Draw a distance–time graph to show Helena's journey. Use squared paper. On the horizontal 'Time (hours)' axis, use a scale of 4 squares = 1 hour. On the vertical 'Distance (miles)' axis, use a scale of 2 squares = 1 mile. Give your graph a title.

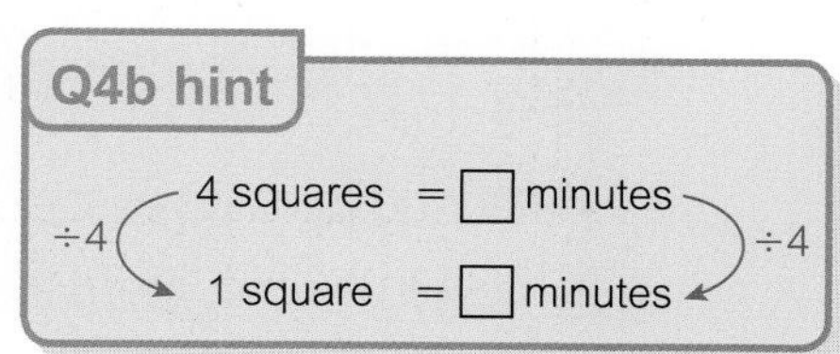

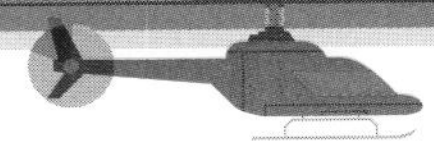

Real-life graphs and graphs of functions

1 **Real** The graph shows the percentage of adults in the UK who use internet shopping.

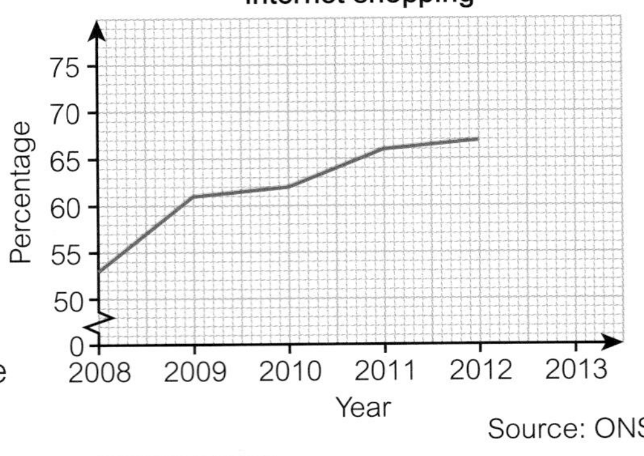

a What percentage of adults used internet shopping in 2009?

b By what percentage did the number of adults using internet shopping increase between 2010 and 2011?

c Between which two years was the biggest increase in internet shopping?

d Describe the trend in the percentage of adults in the UK who use internet shopping. Use the words 'increasing' or 'decreasing'.

e Use the graph to predict the percentage of adults in the UK who used internet shopping in 2013.

Q1b hint

increase = 2011 percentage − 2010 percentage

2 **Real** The graph shows the percentage of adults in the UK who use the internet every day, and the percentage of adults who never use the internet.

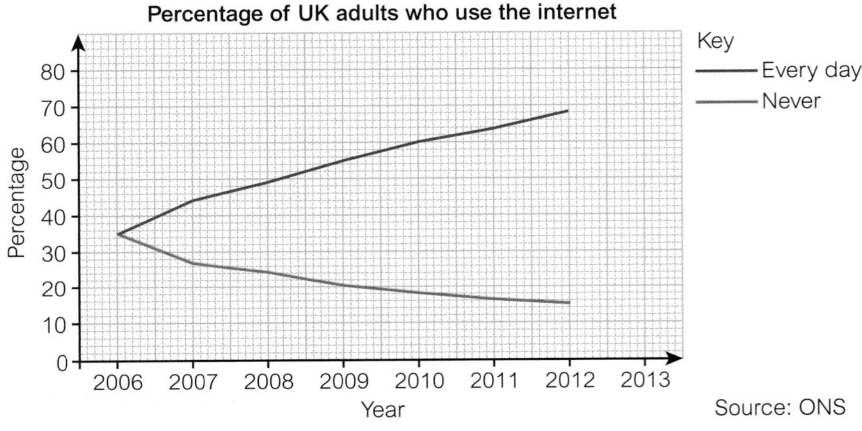

a What percentage of adults used the internet every day in

i 2006

ii 2012?

b Eloise says, 'The percentage of adults who use the internet every day has almost doubled from 2006 to 2012.' Is she correct? Explain your answer.

c Craig says, 'The percentage of adults who never use the internet has more than halved from 2006 to 2012.' Is he correct? Explain your answer.

d Describe the trend in the percentage of adults in the UK who

i use the internet every day

ii never use the internet.

e Use the graph to predict the percentage of adults in the UK in 2013 that

i use the internet every day

ii never use the internet.

Q2a hint

Use the key to choose the correct graph line.

Q2c hint

Read from the graph the percentages of adults who never used the internet in 2006 and 2012.

3 A beach shop hires out kayaks. They charge £6 per half hour.

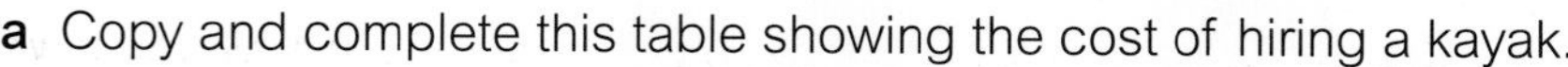

a Copy and complete this table showing the cost of hiring a kayak.

Rental time (hours)	0	$\frac{1}{2}$	1	4
Cost (£)	0			

b Draw a graph to show the cost of renting a kayak for up to 4 hours. Plot 'Rental time (hours)' on the horizontal axis, from 0 to 4 hours. Plot 'Cost (£)' on the vertical axis, from 0 to £50. Add a title.

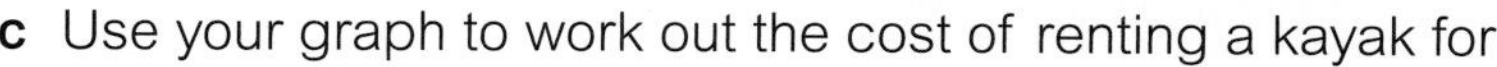

c Use your graph to work out the cost of renting a kayak for

i 3 hours

ii $1\frac{1}{2}$ hours.

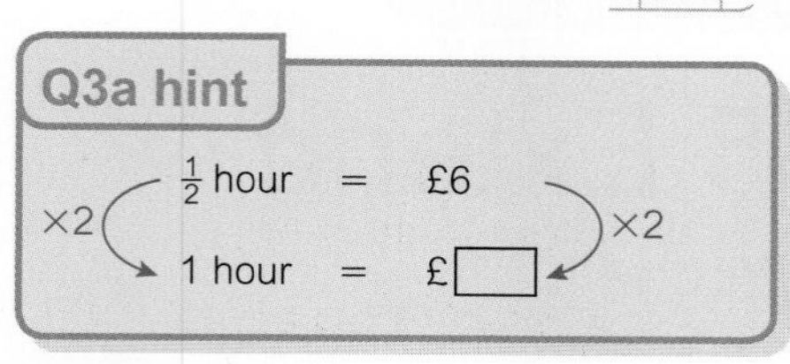

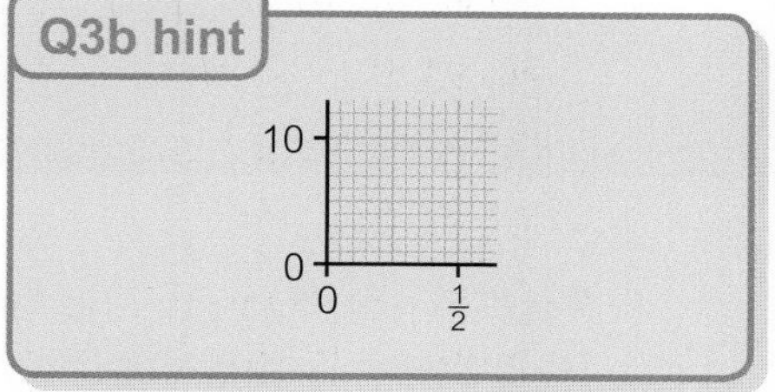

Enrichment

1 **Finance** The graphs show the conversion of ounces to grams and the cost of gold on a particular day.

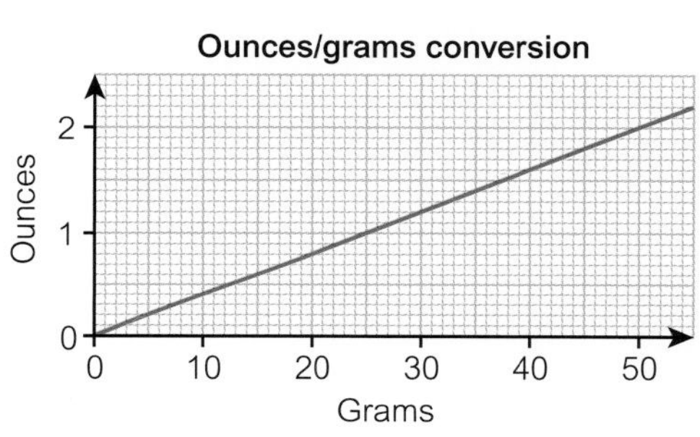

a How much does 1.2 ounces of gold cost?

b A piece of gold costs £1050. What does it weigh in ounces?

2 The graph shows the number of T-shirts sold by a shop during the first 6 months of the year.
Write 'True' or 'False' for each statement. Use readings from the graph to explain.

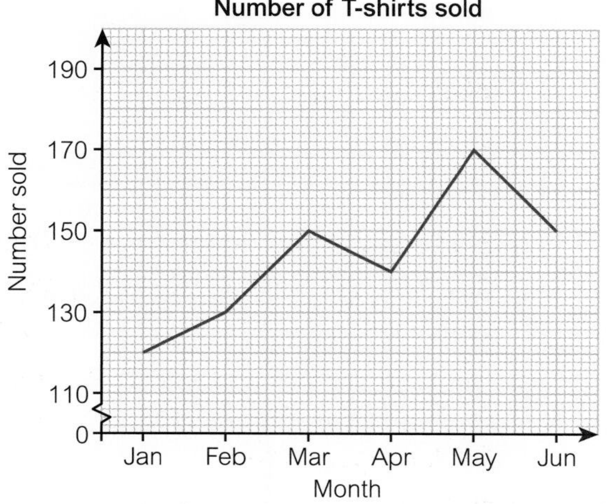

a The number of T-shirts sold in February was double the number sold in January.

b The highest number of T-shirts sold was in May.

c The greatest increase in sales was between February and March.

d The greatest decrease in sales was between May and June.

e The mean number of T-shirts sold per month is 150.

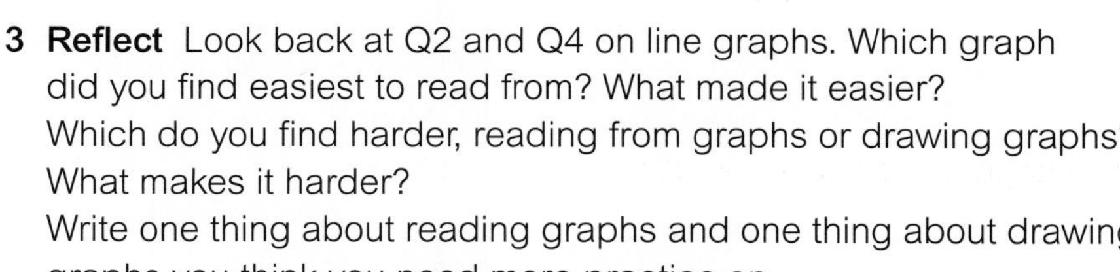

3 **Reflect** Look back at Q2 and Q4 on line graphs. Which graph did you find easiest to read from? What made it easier?
Which do you find harder, reading from graphs or drawing graphs? What makes it harder?
Write one thing about reading graphs and one thing about drawing graphs you think you need more practice on.

Reflect

5 Extend

You will:

- Extend your understanding with problem-solving.

1 Real In hospital, patients are asked to describe their pain on a scale of 0 to 10. Their answers are recorded, and staff can then decide what pain relief is needed. This is the pain scale used.

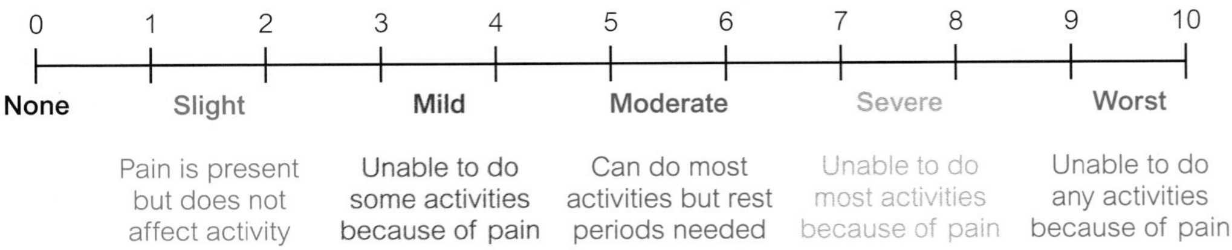

This graph shows the pain levels of a patient over the first 10 days after an operation.

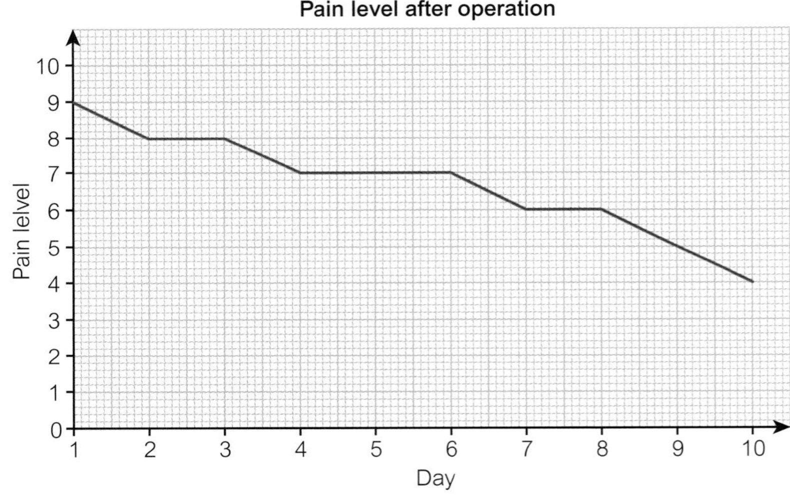

a Describe fully the pain levels of this patient over the first 10 days after the operation.

b Is it possible to predict the pain levels of this patient for days 11 and 12? Explain your answer.

Q1a hint

Include words and numbers from the pain scale above.

2 **a** Use the fact that 1 gallon ≈ 4.5 litres to draw a conversion graph for gallons to litres. Make sure your graph goes up to 5 gallons.

b Use your graph to complete these conversions

i 3.5 gallons ≈ □ litres

ii 0.2 gallons ≈ □ litres

iii 1 litre ≈ □ gallons

iv 12.5 litres ≈ □ gallons

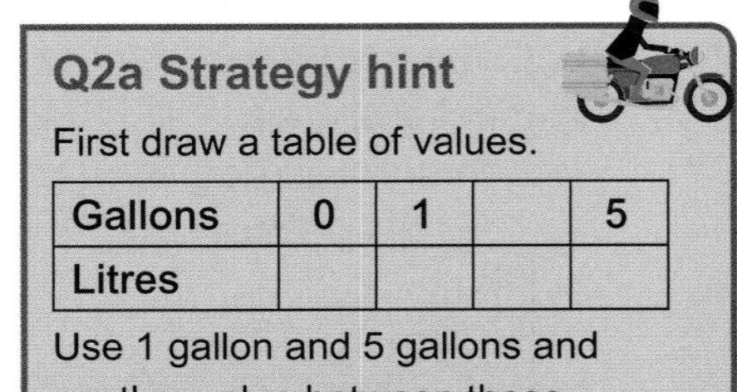

Q2a Strategy hint

First draw a table of values.

Gallons	0	1		5
Litres				

Use 1 gallon and 5 gallons and another value between those.

Topic links: Percentages, Sequences, Using formulae, Time

Subject links: Science (Q6), PE (Q3, Q4)

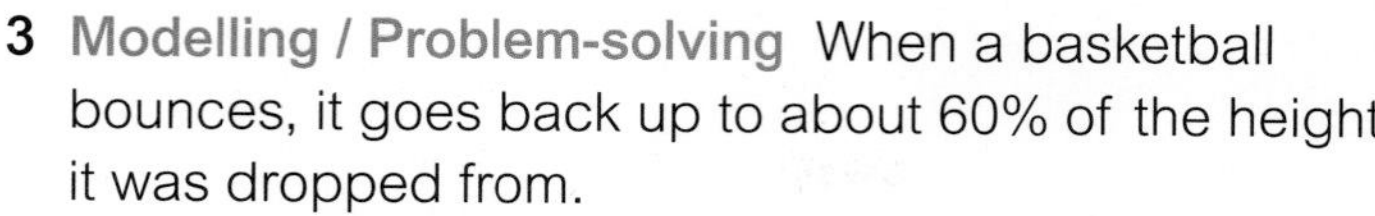

3 **Modelling / Problem-solving** When a basketball bounces, it goes back up to about 60% of the height it was dropped from.

A basketball is dropped from a height of 2 m.

a Copy and complete this table showing the height of a basketball after four bounces.
Round each answer to the nearest centimetre.

Dropped from	2 m
1st bounce	$0.6 \times 2 = 1.2$ m
2nd bounce	$0.6 \times 1.2 = 0.72$ m
3rd bounce	
4th bounce	

A power-ball is dropped from a height of 10 m.
The graph shows the height of the ball after two bounces.

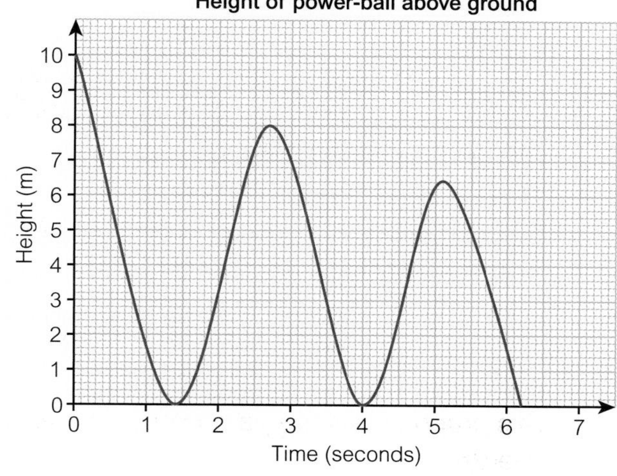

b Copy and complete this table showing the height of a power-ball after four bounces.

Use the graph to complete the table for 0, 1 and 2 bounces. Then use these heights to work out the percentage that the power-ball bounces back each time.

Number of bounces	0	1	2	3	4
Height (m)					

4 Said and Chan take part in a triathlon competition.
They have to swim, then cycle, then run.
The graph shows their results.

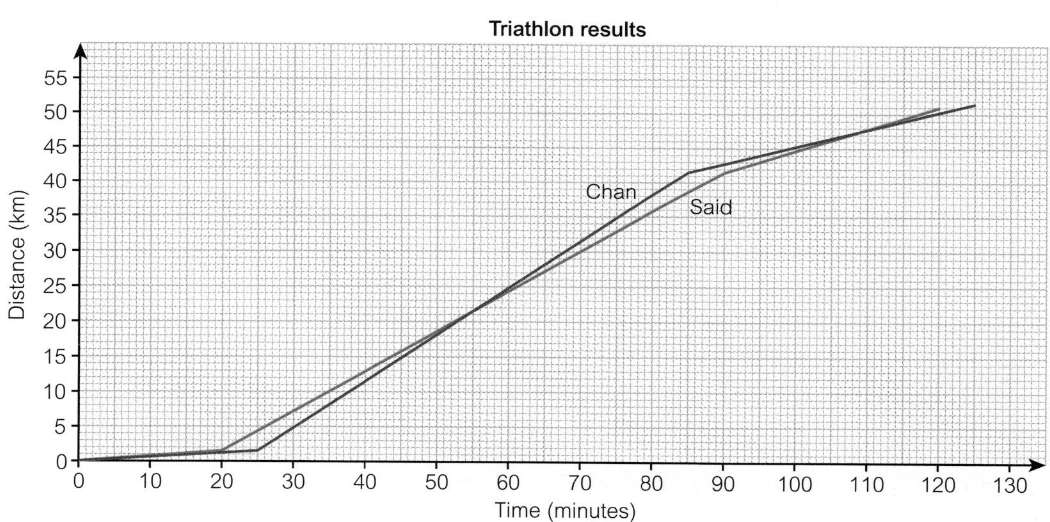

a **i** Who is in the lead after the swim?

ii Who is in the lead after the cycle?

iii Who wins the triathlon?

b Copy the table. Fill in the distances for swim, cycle and run.

c Fill in the times for Said and Chan.

	Distance (km)	Said's time (minutes)	Chan's time (minutes)
Swim			
Cycle			
Run			
Total			

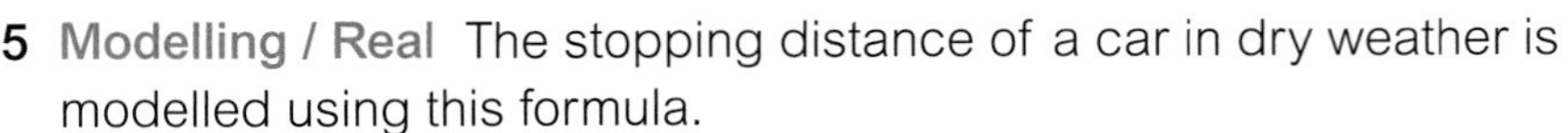

5 **Modelling / Real** The stopping distance of a car in dry weather is modelled using this formula.

$d = \frac{x^2}{20} + x$, where d is the stopping distance in feet, and x the speed of the car in miles per hour (mph).

a Copy and complete this table showing the stopping distances at different speeds.

Speed of car, x (miles per hour)	0	10	20	30	40	50	60	70
Stopping distance, d (feet)	0	15						

b Draw a graph to show the data in the table. Plot 'Speed of car (mph)' on the horizontal axis, and 'Stopping distance (ft)' on the vertical axis. Plot your points and join them with a smooth curve.

c Use your graph to estimate the stopping distance of a car travelling at 55 mph.

d A car needs to stop before it hits a wall 20 feet away. What is the fastest speed it can be travelling at to stop in time?

e What is the difference in the stopping distance of a car travelling at 20 mph and 30 mph?

f **Reasoning** Do you think this mathematical model will work in all weather conditions? Explain your answer.

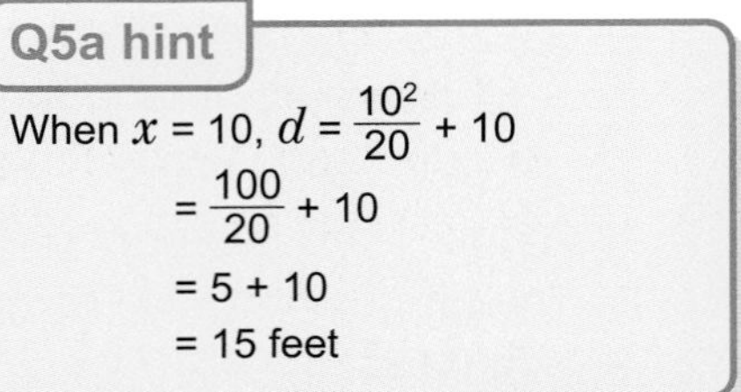

Q5a hint

When $x = 10$, $d = \frac{10^2}{20} + 10$

$= \frac{100}{20} + 10$

$= 5 + 10$

$= 15$ feet

Key point

Some graphs are more accurate and realistic when the points are joined with a smooth curve rather than straight lines.

6 **STEM** A car was tested to see how long it took to accelerate to a speed of 50 metres per second (m/s). It was also tested to see how long it took to stop when the brakes were applied. The graph shows the results of the test.

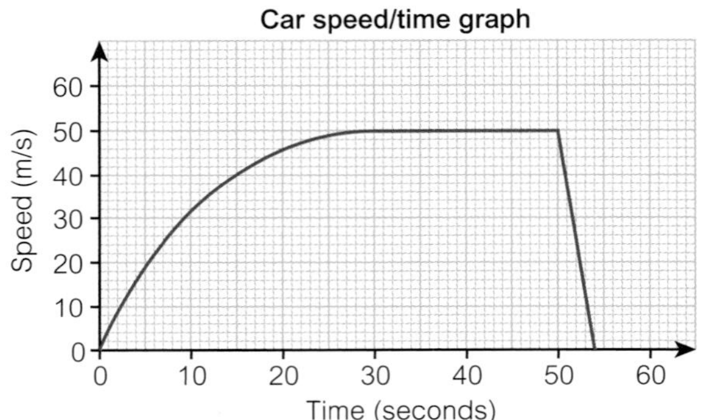

a How many seconds did it take the car to reach a speed of 50 m/s?

b What was the approximate speed of the car at 10 seconds?

c For how many seconds did the car travel at 50 m/s?

d How many seconds did the whole test take?

e How many seconds did it take for the car to stop once the brakes were applied?

7 **Reasoning** A BASE jumper jumped off a building 300 m high. He fell for a certain distance, and then opened his parachute before coming to land. The graph shows his height above ground during the first 13 seconds of his jump.

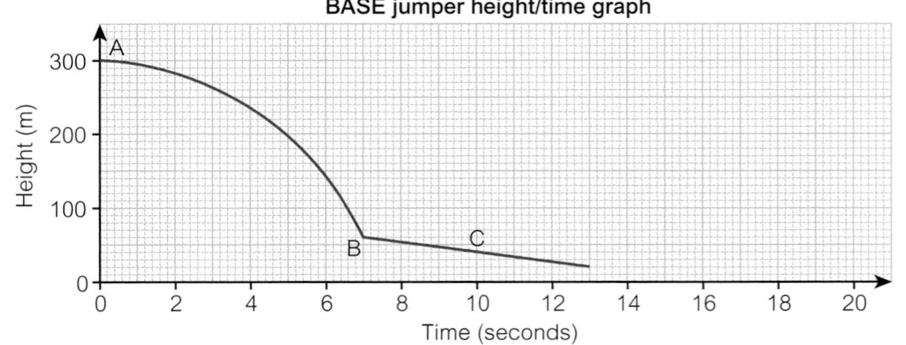

a Match points A, B and C to these statements.
  i Descending with parachute open
  ii Jumping off building 300 m high
  iii Opening parachute.

b At what height did the BASE jumper open his parachute? Explain how you can tell this from the graph.

c How many seconds does it take the BASE jumper to descend 20 m once he has opened his parachute? Explain your answer.

d How many seconds after he jumped do you think he will land? Explain your answer.

8 Hannah goes on holiday by car.
The distance–time graph shows the five sections of her journey.

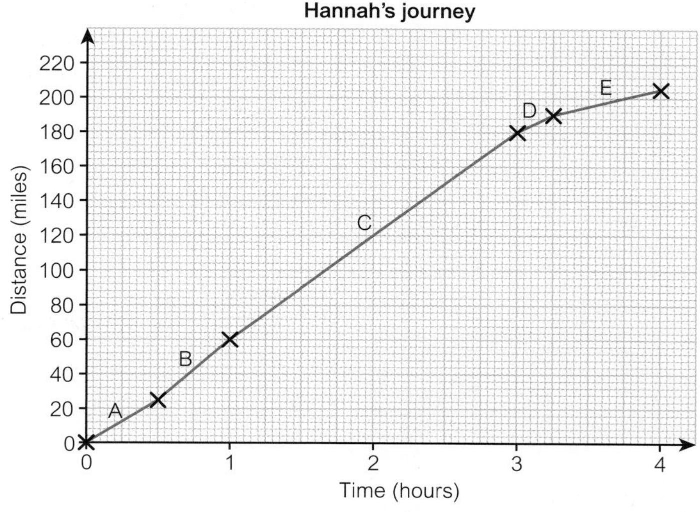

Copy and complete this table.

Section	Distance (miles)	Time taken	Speed (miles per hour)
A	25 − 0 = 25	30 minutes	50
B	60 − 25 = 35		
C			
D			
E	205 −		

Q8 hint

In section A of her journey she travels 25 miles in 30 minutes.
If she carried on at this speed she would travel 50 miles in 1 hour.
So her speed for this section of the journey is 50 miles per hour.

9 **Reasoning** Vase A and vase B hold the same amount of water.
They are both filled with water at the same steady rate.
The graph shows the depth of water in each vase over time.

Vase A

Vase B

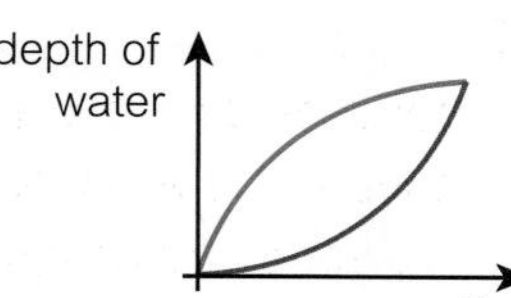

a In which vase will the water level rise faster at first?

b Which line graph is for vase A and which is for vase B? Explain your answers.

10 **Reflect** Look again at Q1. Why might doctors want to graph a patient's pain?
Look again at Q4. Why might athletes want to graph their performance?
Look again at Q6. Why might automotive engineers want to graph a car's time to reach 50 m/s and time to stop?

Reflect

5 Unit test

Log how you did on your Student Progression Chart.

1 The graph shows the number of CD players owned by households in the UK, every 2 years from 2000 to 2012.

a How many CD players were owned by households in the UK in

i 2002

ii 2008?

b In which year did CD player ownership peak?

c Estimate the number of CD players owned by households in the UK in 2011.

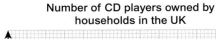

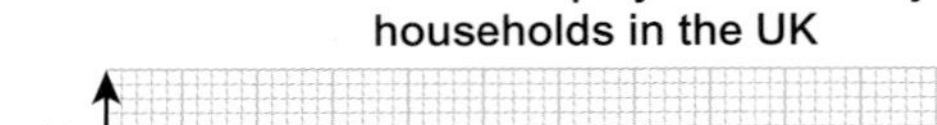

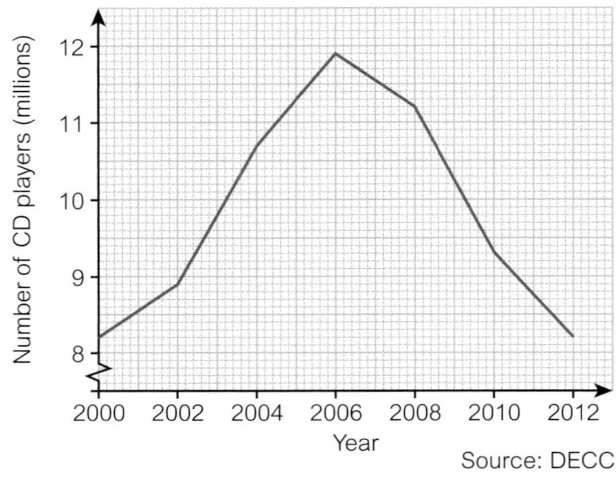

2 The table shows the average temperature inside a centrally heated home, every 10 years from 1970 to 2010.

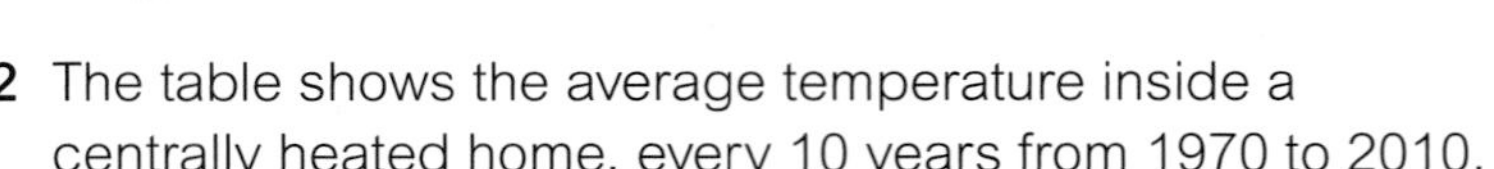

Year	1970	1980	1990	2000	2010
Inside temperature (°C)	13.7	14.4	16.7	18.0	16.9

Source: DECC

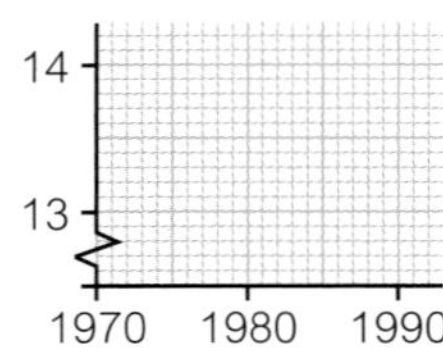

a Draw and complete the line graph of this data.

b Describe the trend in the average temperature inside a centrally heated home.

3 One teaspoon has a capacity of 5 ml.

a Copy and complete this table.

Teaspoons	0	1	2	5
ml	0			

b Copy these axes onto graph paper.

c Plot the points from the table on the graph and join them with a straight line.

d Use your conversion graph to complete these conversions.

i 3.5 teaspoons = ☐ ml

ii 21 ml = ☐ teaspoons

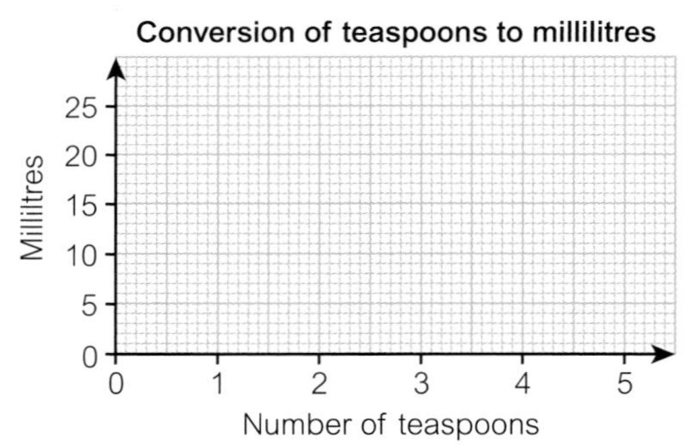

4 On Saturday, Raj walks from home to visit a friend. Later in the day he walks from his friend's house to collect his bike from the repair shop. He then cycles directly home.

The graph shows Raj's journey.

a At what time does Raj arrive at his friend's house?

b How long does he stay at his friend's house?

c How far does he walk from his friend's house to the repair shop?

d On which part of the journey is Raj travelling fastest?

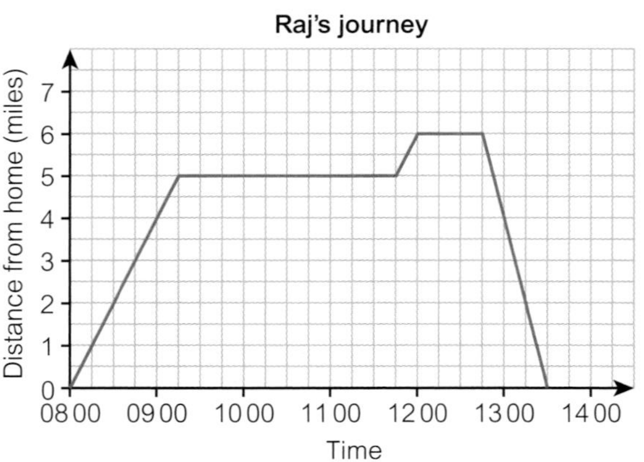

5 The graph shows the average mass of a kitten up to 15 weeks old.

a What is the average mass of a kitten aged 7 weeks?

b At what age does an average kitten reach a mass of 1 kg?

c Sham has a kitten that is 9 weeks old. It has a mass of 750 g.
Is its mass more or less than average?

d During which 5-week period does a kitten's mass increase fastest?
Explain how you can tell this from the graph.

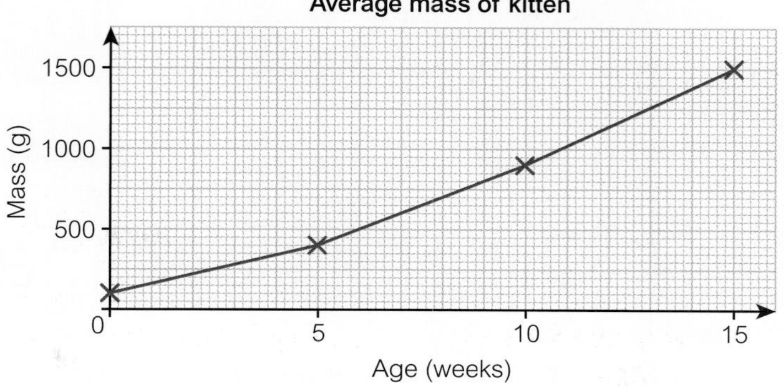

6 The graph shows the percentage change in the population of swallows and starlings in the UK from 1994.

a Describe the trend in the swallow population in the UK.

b What was the percentage increase in the swallow population in 2004?

c What do you predict the percentage change will be in the swallow population by 2014?

d Describe the trend in the starling population in the UK.

e What was the percentage decrease in the starling population in 2012?

f What do you predict the percentage change will be in the starling population by 2014?

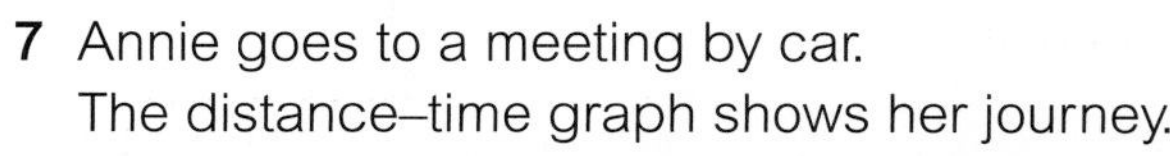

7 Annie goes to a meeting by car.
The distance–time graph shows her journey.

a How long did Annie's meeting last?

b Which was the fastest part of Annie's journey?

c What was Annie's speed

i from the office to the meeting

ii from the meeting back to the office?

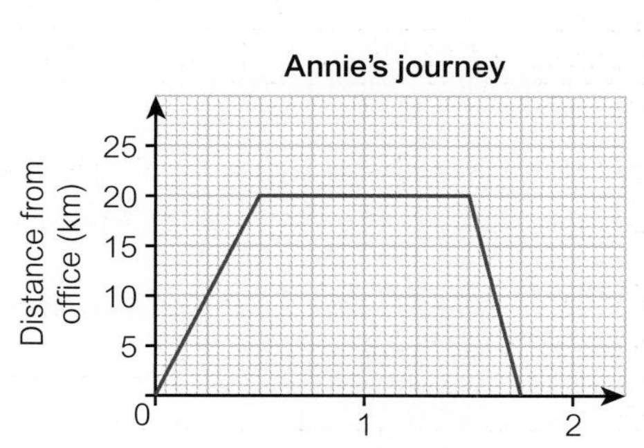

Challenge

8 The graph shows the height above the ground of a rollercoaster over time. Write a description of the ride for a marketing brochure.

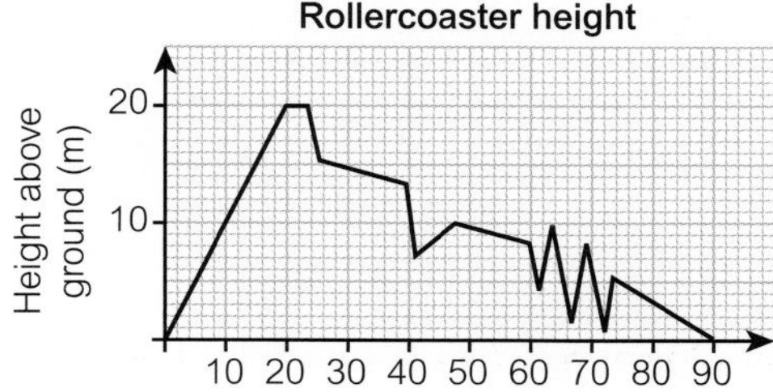

Q8 hint

You can include in your description the different sections of the ride, e.g. fastest section, highest section, scariest section, steepest section …

9 **Reflect** Look carefully at the numbers and words used in this unit test. Now copy and complete this spider diagram to show all the different areas of mathematics that you had to use in each question. Write a sentence about how much mathematics you know and can do.

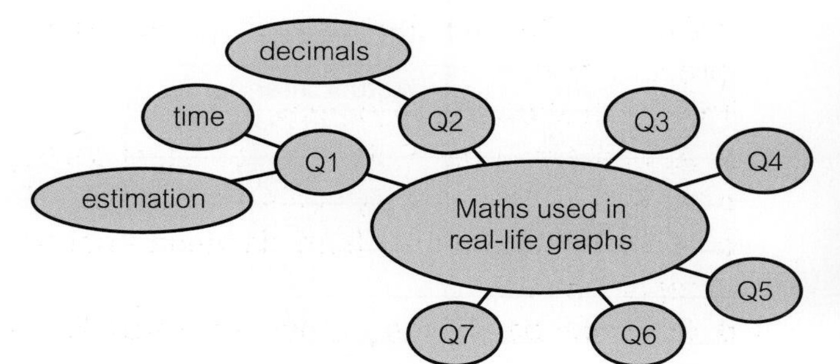

Reflect

6 Decimals and ratio

MASTER | Check P149 | Strengthen P151 | Extend P155 | Test P159

6.1 Ordering decimals and rounding

You will learn to:

- Round numbers to an appropriate degree of accuracy
- Order positive and negative numbers, including decimals.

CONFIDENCE

Why learn this?
We don't often use precise values in our day-to-day conversations.

Fluency
7.4, 7.7, 7.1, 7.6, 7.8

- Which of these decimals are closer to 7 and which are closer to 8?
- How do you decide whether to round up or down?
- Which symbol, < or >, should go between the numbers 7.4 and 7.7?

Explore
How many votes were cast in the X Factor final?

Exercise 6.1

Warm up

1 Round each number to the nearest 100.

a 245 **b** 878 **c** 495
d 523 **e** 1449 **f** 67

2 Write each number in words.

a 4013 **b** 23 527 **c** 146 005 **d** 1 529 400

3 Rearrange these numbers in *ascending* order.
27, 14, 103, −11, 83, 10.1, −10.1, 38.9

Q3 Literacy hint
Ascending order means in order of size with the lowest number first.

4 Round each number to the nearest 1000.

a 2455 **b** 5199 **c** 12 875
d 45 812 **e** 546 848 **f** 623 399

5 Round each number to the nearest 10 000.

a 84 562 **b** 47 487 **c** 9458
d 48 099 **e** 754 397 **f** 873 822

Key point
To round to the nearest 10 000, look at the digit in the thousands column.

6 **Real** This table shows the total attendance at five Premier League football teams' grounds in the 2007/08 season.
Round each value to the nearest 100 000.

Team	Actual attendance
Arsenal	1 141 335
Aston Villa	760 560
Chelsea	786 549
Everton	702 142
Liverpool	827 111

Key point
To round to the nearest 100 000, look at the digit in the ten thousands column.

Topic links: Metric measures

Subject links: Geography (Q11, Q14)

7 Round each number to two decimal places.

a 2.536 b 7.489 c 5.083

d 6.199 e 45.157 f 23.007

Key point

To round a decimal to two decimal places (2 d.p.), look at the digit in the third decimal place.

8 Write each set of decimal numbers in *ascending* order.

a 1.093, 0.08666, 1.232, 0.20071, 0.1258

b 4.227, 4.051, 4.234, 4.735, 3.292

c 0.7113, 0.0732, 7.001, 0.7499, 7.0932

Key point

When ordering decimals, look at the place value of each digit.

$0.3 = \frac{3}{10}$, $0.03 = \frac{3}{100}$

So 0.3 is larger than 0.03.

9 Rearrange these numbers in *descending* order.

24.457, 25.645, 22.961, 24.833, 25.622

10 Rearrange each set of numbers in *ascending* order.

a −8.12, −0.89, −5.76, −3.11, −1.88

b −0.125, −0.845, −0.149, −0.135, −0.0122

c −0.033, −0.0309, −0.0342, −0.0325, 0.0324

Q8 Literacy hint

Ascending order means getting bigger. **Descending order** means getting smaller.

Worked example

Write 1 662 682 as a decimal number of millions to one **decimal place**.

1 662 682 = 1.662682 million — Write as a decimal number of millions.

1.7 million — Round to 1 decimal place (1 d.p.)

Key point

To save writing all the zeros, you can write

1 000 000 as 1 million

2 500 000 as 2.5 million.

11 **Real** The table shows the populations of 10 capital cities in Europe. Write each population as a decimal number of millions to one decimal place.

City	Actual population
Moscow	11 541 000
London	8 174 100
Berlin	3 520 000
Madrid	3 233 527
Rome	2 792 508
Paris	2 268 265
Budapest	1 728 718
Vienna	1 552 789
Prague	1 227 332
Dublin	1 045 769

12 Round each number to three decimal places.

a 4.5391 b 29.7965 c 69.0852

d 85.8008 e 72.7576 f 3.2567

Key point

To round a decimal to three decimal places, look at the digit in the fourth decimal place.

13 **Reasoning / Real** In a restaurant the tips are divided equally between the workers.

Work out how much each worker receives each day.

Day	Mon	Tue	Wed	Thu	Fri	Sat	Sun
Total tips (£)	55	68	71	86.50	94	124.50	100
Number of workers	6	7	6	8	7	12	9

Discussion Did you round up or down? Explain.

14 **Real** The graph shows the population of the UK between 2004 and 2012.

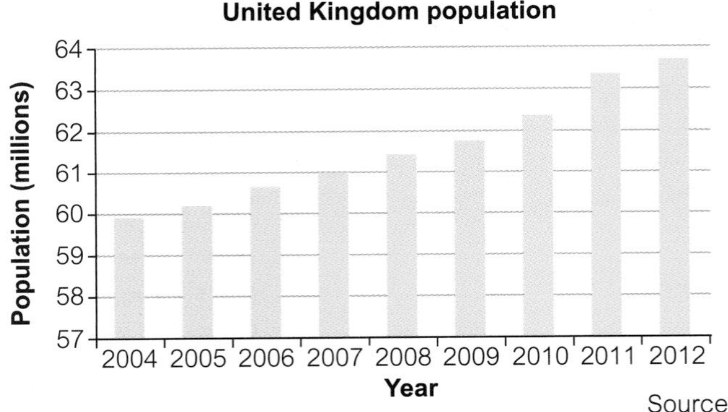

a Describe what happened to the UK population between 2004 and 2012.
b What was the population in 2005 to the nearest million?
c In which years was the population 61 million to the nearest million?

15 Copy and complete these. Put the correct sign, < or >, between each pair of numbers.

a 1.064 □ 1.022 b 6.242 □ 6.224
c 7.737 □ 7.739 d 0.06852 □ 0.06812

16 Rearrange these numbers in *descending* order.
−0.029, −0.0205, −0.092, −0.0925, −0.052,
−0.0209, −0.0592, −0.095, −0.0529

17 Work out the length of one side of a square with perimeter

a 10 cm b 24.3 cm
c 13.65 cm d 1.526 km

Round all your answers to an appropriate degree of accuracy.

Key point
For most calculations, an appropriate degree of accuracy is a value you can measure accurately.

18 Copy and complete these. Put the correct sign, < or >, between each pair of numbers.

a −2.078 □ −2.087 b −8.27 □ −8.72
c −6.26 □ −6.25 d −0.0532 □ −0.0530

Investigation Real / Finance

Petrol and diesel are sold by the litre. The price is often given to one decimal place.
For example, you might see petrol at 132.9p per litre.
Actual prices need to be rounded when the customer has finished pumping fuel.

1 Choose some volumes of petrol in whole numbers of litres.
Will the price need to be rounded up or down?
2 Why do you think petrol stations give the price as a decimal number of pennies?

Part 1 hint
Try 2 litres, 5 litres, 10 litres.

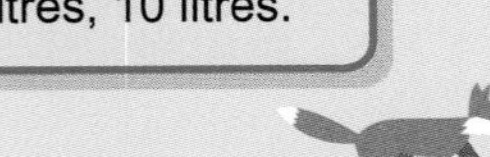

19 **Explore** How many votes were cast in the X Factor final?
Is it easier to explore this question now you have completed the lesson?
What further information do you need to be able to answer this?

20 **Reflect** In this lesson you have been doing lots of work with decimals.
Imagine someone had never seen a decimal point before.
How would you define it?
How would you describe what it does?
Write a description in your own words.
Compare your description with others in your class.

6.2 Place-value calculations

You will learn to:
- Multiply larger numbers
- Multiply decimals with up to two decimal places
- Multiply any number by 0.1 and 0.01

Why learn this?
Metric measurements use decimals. You need to calculate with decimals to find lengths and areas.

Fluency
- What does the '1' represent in 0.1 and 0.01?
- How do you write 0.3 and 0.07 as fractions?

Explore
Does multiplying one number by another always make it bigger?

Exercise 6.2

Warm up

1 Work out
  a 45 × 7
  b 53 × 28
  c 32 × 17
  d 267 × 15

2 Work out
  a 63 × 10
  b 182 × 100
  c 430 ÷ 10
  d 4300 ÷ 100

3 Estimate these by rounding one or both numbers.
  a 50 × 0.8
  b 5.3 × 7
  c 19.9 × 0.5
  d 134 × 11

4 Copy and complete.

```
   137
 × 245
 _____
        ← 137 × 5
        ← 137 × 40
 _____  ← 137 × 200
 _____  ← Add these together
```

Worked example

Work out 2.6 × 3.2

Estimate: 3 × 3 = 9

```
     2 6
 ×   3 2
 _______
     5 2
 + 7 8 0
 _______
   8 3 2
```

Use a standard method to work out 26 × 32

2.6 × 3.2 = 8.32

Use your estimated answer to see where to put the decimal point.

5 Work out

a 3.7×2.2 b 2.5×4.2 c 7.22×3.1

d 3.46×8.9 e 8.94×0.32 f 4.04×8.2

Discussion For each part, count the number of digits after the decimal point in both numbers in the question.
Do the same for the answer. What do you notice?

Q5 hint
Estimate first.

6 **Real** A car can travel 13.8 kilometres on 1 litre of petrol.
How far can it travel on 8.8 litres of petrol?

7 Follow these steps to work out 3.26×5.12

a Estimate the answer.

b Work out 326×512

c Decide where to position the decimal point.

8 Use the multiplication facts given to work out the answers.

a $12 \times 17 = 204$. Work out 1.2×1.7

b $36 \times 14 = 504$. Work out 3.6×0.14

c $108 \times 4 = 432$. Work out 10.8×0.04

d $36 \times 72 = 2592$. Work out 0.36×7.2

Q8a hint
The answer will have the digits 204.
Where do you put the decimal point?

9 Work out

a 36×0.1 b $36 \div 10$ c 45×0.1

d $45 \div 10$ e 107×0.1 f $107 \div 10$

Discussion What do you notice?

10 Work out

a 8.6×0.1 b 11.6×0.1 c 0.53×0.1

11 a Copy and complete.

$29 \times 1 = \square$

$29 \times 0.1 = \square$

$29 \times 0.01 = \square$

b **Reasoning** What division calculation is equivalent to '× 0.01'?

12 Work out

a 3621×0.01 b 4568×0.01 c 88.6×0.01

d 11.6×0.01 e 534×0.01 f 683×0.01

13 **Problem-solving** A factory makes 3.5 silk flowers every second.

a Each flower uses 60.3 cm of silk.
How many metres of silk are used in one minute?

b Each flower has a 0.325 m wire stem.
A hotel orders 275 silk flowers.
What length of wire is needed?

Topic links: Multiplying and dividing by 10 and 100, Metric measures, Area

14 Work out the area of each shape.

a

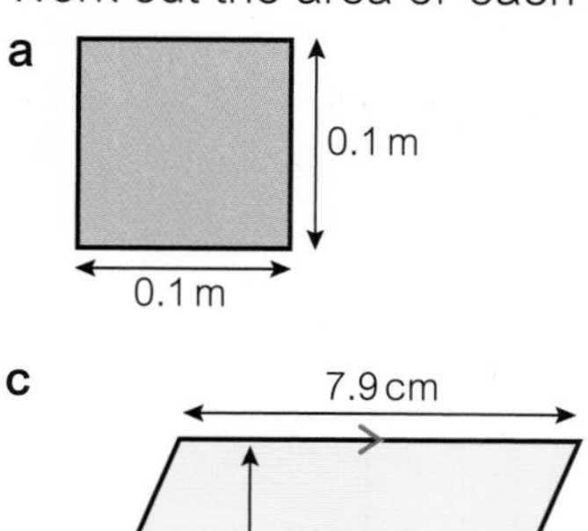

b

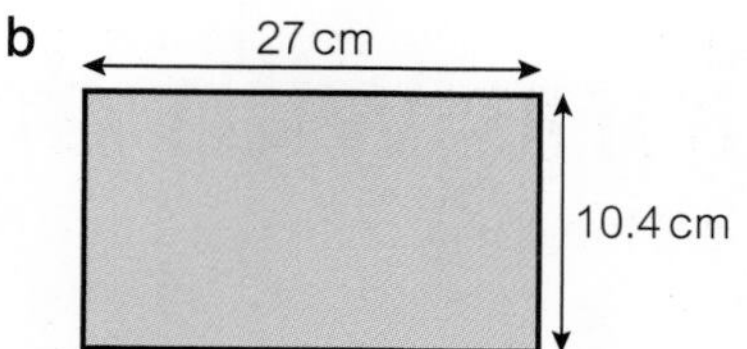

c

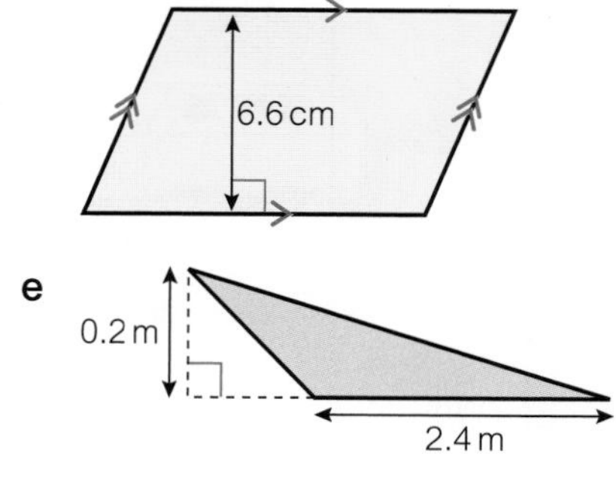

d

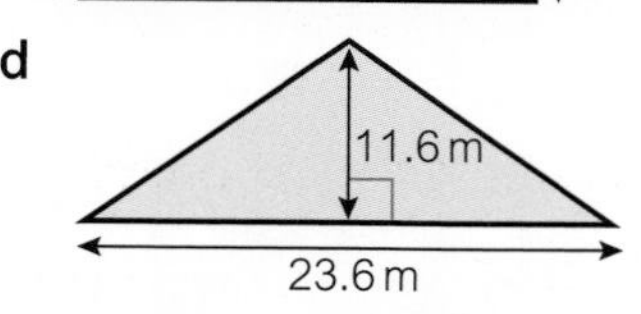

e

0.2 m

2.4 m

f

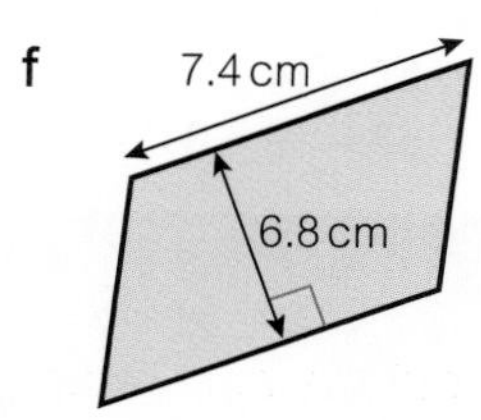

15 **Real / Problem-solving** Anita is planning to paint the walls of her living room.

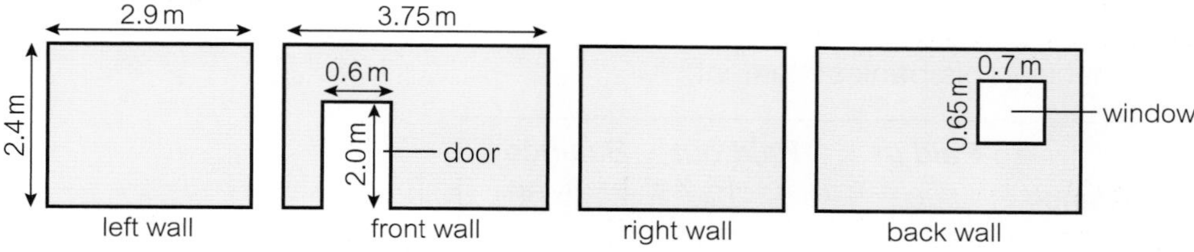

Anita needs 0.1 litres of paint to paint each 1 m^2.
How much paint will she need to paint all the walls?

16 **Explore** Does multiplying one number by another always make it bigger?
Choose some sensible numbers to help you explore this situation.
Then use what you have learned in this lesson to help you answer the question.

17 **Reflect** Look back at Q5. At the end of this question you discussed a mathematical 'rule'.
The rule tells you where to put the decimal point in the answer when multiplying decimals.
Write the 'rule' in your own words.
Why do you think the rule was at the end of the question and not at the beginning?
What would you do to multiply two decimals, if you couldn't remember the rule?

6.3 Calculations with decimals

You will learn to:
- Add and subtract decimals of any size
- Multiply and divide by decimals
- Divide by 0.1 and 0.01

CONFIDENCE

Why learn this?
We need to calculate using decimals when dealing with money and measurements.

Fluency
Work out
- 57 – 14 – 23
- 63 – 12 – 31

Explore
Why does a sharp axe cut better than a blunt one? Think about the area of the cutting surface.

Exercise 6.3

Warm up

1 **Finance** Billy has been checking his bank statement.

Date		*Paid in*	*Paid out*	*Balance*
16/09/2013	*Start balance*			£125.68
	Water bill		£23.75	
	Electricity		£17.29	
	Lotto	£10.00		
	Mobile		£15.99	
	Wages	£256.75		
17/09/2013	*End balance*			

What is the balance of Billy's account after his wages are paid in?

Q1 Literacy hint
Your **bank balance** is the amount of money in your account.

2 Work out
a 4.83 × 2.7 **b** 2.45 × 3.32

3 Use a written method to calculate
a $3\overline{)294}$ **b** $23\overline{)943}$

4 Work out
a 36 ÷ 12 and 3.6 ÷ 1.2 **b** 72 ÷ 8 and 7.2 ÷ 0.8
c 484 ÷ 4 and 4.84 ÷ 0.04 **d** 625 ÷ 25 and 6.25 ÷ 0.25

Discussion What do you notice? How does this help you work out 8.1 ÷ 0.9 and 0.64 ÷ 0.08 without a calculator?

5 Work out
a 6.3 ÷ 0.7 **b** 4.8 ÷ 0.6 **c** 12.1 ÷ 1.1
d 0.28 ÷ 0.07 **e** 0.9 ÷ 0.03 **f** 14.4 ÷ 0.12

Topic links: Written multiplication and division, Metric measures,

Subject links: Science (Q7, Q9)

Worked example

Work out 67.8 ÷ 1.2

×10 (1.2)67.8 → 12)678) ×10

1.2 has one decimal place, so multiply both numbers by 10.

$$12\overline{)6\,7^7 8.^6 0} = 56.5$$

Work out the division.

Check: 12 × 56.5 ≈ 10 × 60 = 600

Key point

To divide by a decimal, multiply both numbers by a power of 10 (10, 100, …) until you have a whole number to divide by.
Then work out the division.

6 Work these out using a written method.
Give your answers to one decimal place where appropriate.

a 18.9 ÷ 0.09 **b** 39 ÷ 0.75 **c** 131.72 ÷ 0.37
d 348 ÷ 5.8 **e** 43.32 ÷ 0.3 **f** 82.3 ÷ 6.25
g 367 ÷ 2.4 **h** 0.556 ÷ 3.6 **i** 72.5 ÷ 0.7

Discussion 'Dividing a number by a number less than 1 gives you an answer larger than the first number.' Is this statement true?

Q6f hint

You will need to work out the second decimal place and then round, rather than just stopping at the first decimal place.

7 **STEM** A scientist has 27.9 g of substance X.
He needs to divide it into samples for testing.
Each testing dish holds 2.4 g.
How many testing dishes does the scientist need?

8 Work out

a 3241 + 306.192 + 2.308 **b** 806.5 – 21.33 – 95
c 3150.14 – 88.6 + 27.2031 **d** 3096 + 108.7 + 0.204 – 3.14

Q8a hint

Keep the decimal points in line.

```
  3241
   306.192
+    2.308
__________

__________
```

9 **STEM / Problem-solving** Suzie is testing a beaker of water.
She removes these samples for analysis.

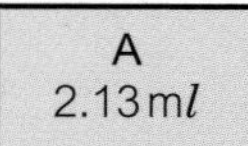

A	B	C	D
2.13 ml	0.005 ml	3.075 ml	0.321 ml

a There is 32.4 ml in the beaker after samples A and B are removed. How much water was originally in the beaker?

b How much water is left in the beaker after all samples are removed?

10 **Real / Problem-solving** A skateboard factory makes boards from sheets of plywood. The factory checks the area of plywood wasted each week. One week the total waste was 28.75 m^2 over the five days the factory was open.

Day	Waste
Monday	4.35 m^2
Wednesday	5.4 m^2
Thursday	6.14 m^2

a How much plywood was wasted on Tuesday and Friday?

On Friday 2.4 m^2 more plywood was wasted than on Tuesday.

b How much was wasted on Tuesday?

11 Work out

a 2.724×3.25 b 4.59×2.764
c 8.91×5.126 d 7.261×9.28
e 6.903×0.425 f 23.241×7.26

Q11a hint

Set out in columns, e.g.

```
  2724
×  325
------

------
```

12 a Work out the volume of this cuboid.

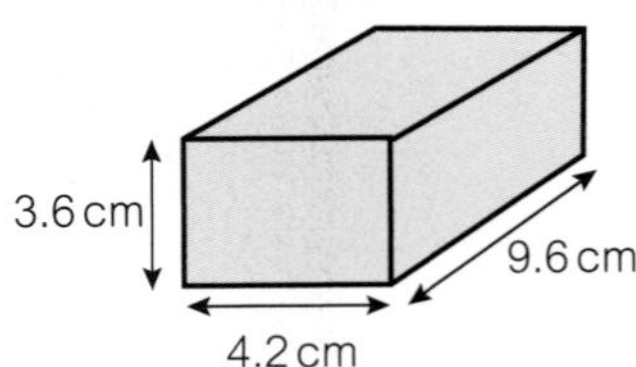

b Another cuboid has a volume of $35.52\,m^3$.
Its length is 4 m and its width is 2.4 m.
What is its height?

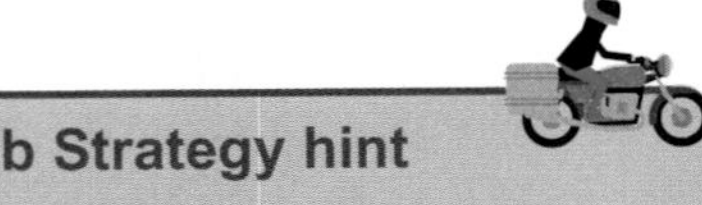

Q12b Strategy hint

Make a sketch.

13 Work out

a $15 \div 0.1$ b $2.6 \div 0.1$ c $85.3 \div 0.01$
d $572 \div 0.01$ e $7.6 \div 0.01$ f $0.3 \div 0.1$

Investigation — Reasoning

1 Choose a number.
Carry out these operations on your number.
×100 ×10 ×0.1 ×0.01 ÷100 ÷10 ÷0.1 ÷0.01

2 Repeat part **1** with another number.

3 Are any of these operations equivalent?
Use your answers to parts **1** and **2** to complete these rules.
×100 is equivalent to □
□ is equivalent to ÷0.1
□ is equivalent to ÷10
×0.01 is equivalent to □

4 What do you think the rules are for
a ×0.001 b ÷0.001?
Test your rules.

14 **Explore** Why does a sharp axe cut better than a blunt one?
Look back at the maths you have learned in this lesson.
How can you use it to answer this question?

15 **Reflect**

a What happens when you divide a positive number by a number between 0 and 1?

b What happens when you multiply a positive number by a number between 0 and 1?

c Write your own 'What happens when …?' question and answer it.

Q15 hint

a Look back at some of the calculations you did in Q5.

b Look back at some of the calculations you did in lesson 6.2.

6.4 Ratio and proportion with decimals

You will learn to:
- Use ratios involving decimals
- Solve proportion problems.

Why learn this?
Increasing or decreasing quantities in proportion does not always give us whole numbers.

Fluency
3 : 5 6 : 9 5 : 16 14 : 21
12 : 19 30 : 45 4 : 9
Which of these ratios are equivalent to 2 : 3?

Explore
Why do some old TV programmes have space at the sides of the screen?

Exercise 6.4

Warm up

1 Write each ratio in its simplest form.
  a 8 : 4 **b** 12 : 3 **c** 15 : 25
  d 4 : 18 **e** 7 : 49 **f** 40 : 60

2 **a** Share £20 in the ratio 2 : 3.
  b Share £36 in the ratio 4 : 5.
  c A piece of rope 24 m long is cut in the ratio 5 : 3.
  How long is each piece of rope?

Worked example

Share £114 between Alice, Bert and Chen in the ratio 5 : 2 : 1.

5 + 2 + 1 = 8 parts — First find out how many parts there are in total.
£114 ÷ 8 = £14.25 per part — Find out how much one part is worth.
Alice: 5 × £14.25 = £71.25 — Multiply the amount that one part is worth by each value in the ratio.
Bert: 2 × £14.25 = £28.50
Chen: 1 × £14.25 = £14.25
Check: £71.25 + £28.50 + £14.25 = £114

3 Share each quantity in the ratio given.
  a £108 in the ratio 2 : 3 : 4 **b** £486 in the ratio 1 : 3 : 5
  c £510 in the ratio 1 : 2 : 3 **d** £242 in the ratio 1 : 2 : 3 : 5
  e 429 m in the ratio 2 : 3 : 6 **f** 468 kg in the ratio 3 : 6 : 7
  g 591 km in the ratio 1 : 2 : 4 : 5 **h** £1032 in the ratio 3 : 5 : 9

Discussion How should you round when working with ratios in money? What about kg? Why?

4 Simplify each ratio into a whole number ratio in its simplest form.
  a 40 : 28.5 **b** 70 : 51.2 **c** 25.5 : 17 **d** 28.6 : 5.15

Q4a hint
Simplify using powers of 10.
28.5 has one decimal place, so multiply both sides of the ratio by 10, then simplify.

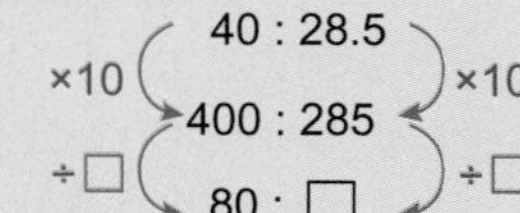

Topic links: Multiplying and dividing by 10 and 100, Metric measures, Imperial measures

5 **Real / Problem-solving** 2p coins used to be made from a mix of copper, tin and zinc in the ratio 95 : 3.5 : 1.5.

a A 2p coin had a mass of 7 g. What were the masses of copper, tin and zinc in the coin?

b Sally had £1 in 2p pieces. What was the total mass of the coins?

6 **Real** Turquoise paint is made by mixing blue, green and yellow in the ratio 2.5 : 1.4 : 0.1.

Copy and complete the table to show how much of each colour is needed to make the quantities shown.

Size	Blue	Green	Yellow
1 litre			
1.5 litres			
2.5 litres			

Q6 hint

Simplify the ratio into whole numbers. Then share the amount of paint in the new ratio.

7 **Real / Reasoning** A photo-printing service offers the following picture sizes:

6 × 4 inches, 7 × 5 inches, 8 × 6 inches, 10 × 8 inches, 12 × 8 inches.

A digital camera takes photographs in the ratio 3 : 2.

Which sizes of photo can be printed from this camera?

8 **STEM** The aspect ratio describes the ratio 'width : height' of an image.

Most modern televisions have an aspect ratio of 16 : 9.

How high would screens be with these widths?

a 32 cm **b** 30.5 cm **c** 41.7 cm **d** 44.3 cm

How wide would screens be with these heights?

e 27 cm **f** 17.5 cm **g** 26.4 cm **h** 35.2 cm

Q8 hint

A screen 16 cm wide would be 9 cm tall.

9 **Reasoning** The triathlon is a race where competitors swim, cycle and run. Four recognised lengths of race are shown in the table below.

Race	Swim	Cycle	Run
Sprint	0.75 km	20 km	5 km
Olympic	1.5 km	40 km	10 km
Half Ironman	1.9 km	90 km	21.1 km
Ironman	3.8 km	180.2 km	42.2 km

a What proportion of the Sprint triathlon is running?

b Cycling is Tom's strongest sport. Which race or races would give him the best chance of winning?

Q9a hint

First find the total distance of the race. Then write the proportion for 'run' as a fraction, and simplify.

Explore

10 **Explore** Why do some old TV programmes have space at the sides of the screen?

What have you learned in this lesson to help you answer this question? What other information do you need?

Reflect

11 **Reflect**

a Look back at Q5a. Write all the steps you took to work out the answer.

b Look back at Q9. Write the steps you took to work out the answer.

c Lou says, 'Question 5 was about ratio. A ratio compares one part to another part. Question 9 was about proportion. A proportion compares one part to the whole thing.'

Is Lou correct?

Q11c hint

Use your steps for Q5a and Q9 to help you.

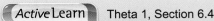

6.5 STEM: Using ratios

You will learn to:
- Solve engineering problems using ratio and proportion
- Use unit ratios.

Why learn this?
Most machines have gears, and gears depend on ratios.

Fluency
Simplify each ratio.
4 : 7 4 : 8 6 : 16
5 : 20 3 : 5 24 : 28
Can all the ratios be simplified?

Explore
How do mountain bikes get up steep hills?

Exercise 6.5: Engineering ratios

1 Divide each quantity in the ratio given.
   a 567 kg in the ratio 5 : 1
   b 486 metres in the ratio 3 : 2
   c £7816 in the ratio 2 : 3 : 5

2 Simplify each ratio into a whole number ratio in its simplest form.
   a 5.2 : 4.5 **b** 8.2 : 6.3
   c 8.5 : 2.25 **d** 2.56 : 1.37

3 Wood's metal is an alloy made from bismuth, lead, tin and cadmium.
Mixing these amounts will make 1 kg of Wood's metal.

bismuth	500 g
lead	250 g
tin	125 g
cadmium	125 g

How much of each metal is needed to make 2.5 kg?

Worked example

A new TV has aspect ratio of 16 : 9. Express this as a **unit ratio**.
Give your answer to two decimal places.

÷9 (16 : 9 → 1.78 : 1) ÷9 — Divide both sides of the ratio by the smallest number, 9

Key point
You can compare ratios by writing them as **unit ratios**. In a unit ratio, one of the two numbers is 1.

4 Write each ratio as a **unit ratio**.
Give each answer to a maximum of two decimal places.
   a 9 : 5 **b** 11 : 4 **c** 17 : 33 **d** 11 : 23

5 **Real** Over the years, images have been shown in many different rectangular shapes, usually expressed as aspect ratios, width : height.

a Convert each aspect ratio to a unit ratio.

i 5 : 3 (European widescreen)
ii 3 : 2 (35 mm film)
iii 8 : 5 (computer screen)
iv 4 : 3 (cathode ray tube TV)
v 37 : 20 (US widescreen)
vi 12 : 5 (cinema widescreen)

b Which of these ratios shows the widest picture?

6 **Real / STEM** Engine performance can be compared by looking at the ratio of power to weight. A high power-to-weight ratio means a car will accelerate (or perform) well.
Find the ratio of power to weight for each of these cars as a unit ratio.

Q6 hint
Use a calculator to work out $\frac{\text{power}}{\text{weight}}$ and round to a whole number.

Car	Power (kW)	Weight (tonne)	Power : weight (unit ratio)
Chevrolet Corvette	476	1.51	315 : 1
Caparo T1	429	0.47	
Caterham Superlight R500	196	0.51	
Ariel Atom 500	373	0.55	
Ferrari F12	544	1.63	
Porsche GT2RS	456	1.37	

Discussion Which car has the best performance?

7 **Real / STEM** Most modern bikes have a variety of gears, with a number of different-sized cogs.
A road-racing bike has a front cog at the pedals with 53 teeth and a choice of 5 cogs at the rear.

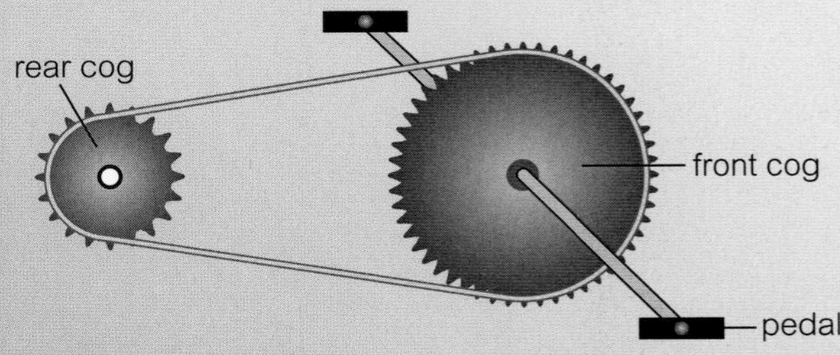

One turn of the pedals turns the front cog once.

Key point

26 teeth

52 teeth

In engineering, gears are used to change speeds. These two cogs are connected by a chain and have equal sized teeth. Each turn of the large cog makes the small cog turn twice, because 1 × 52 = 2 × 26.

Copy and complete the table to work out the number of turns the rear wheel will make when the pedals are turned once for different gears.

Front cog teeth	53	53	53	53	53
Gear	1	2	3	4	5
Rear cog teeth	32	25	19	14	11
Ratio of front teeth to rear teeth	53 : 32				
Unit ratio	1.66 : 1				
Number of rear wheel turns per turn of the pedals	1.66				

8 **Real / STEM** Some cyclists prefer fixed wheel bikes, with no gears. Typically a front cog has 50 teeth and a rear cog has 20 teeth.

a What is the ratio of front cog teeth to rear cog teeth?

b How many times does the rear wheel turn for every turn of the pedals?

A typical road bike travels 195.3 cm for every rotation of the rear wheel.

c How many times must a cyclist turn the pedals to travel 1 km?

9 **Real / STEM** Although not as visible, cars use gears in the same way as bikes. Different gear ratios (number of turns in the engine : number of turns in the wheels) make the wheels travel different distances for each revolution in the engine.
In a typical car each revolution of the wheels is about 2 m.

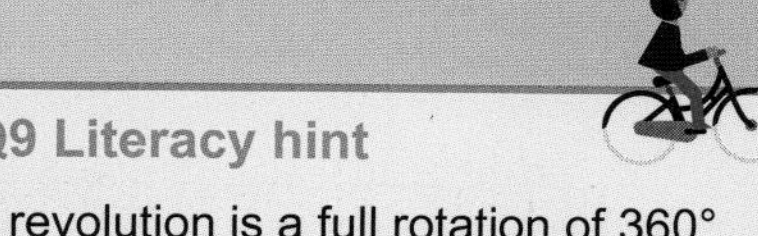

Q9 Literacy hint
A revolution is a full rotation of 360°.

Gear	Turns in the engine : turns in the wheels
1st	2.97 : 1
2nd	2.07 : 1
3rd	1.43 : 1
4th	1 : 1
5th	0.84 : 1
6th	0.56 : 1

a Explain why 6th gear is the fastest gear.

b How many revolutions of the engine does it take to travel 1 km in 6th gear?

10 **Real / Problem-solving** Clocks and watches with hands also have gears.
What is the gear ratio of the minute hand to the second hand?

11 **Explore** How do mountain bikes get up steep hills?
Is it easier to explore this question now you have completed the lesson?
What further information do you need to be able to answer this?

12 **Reflect** In this lesson you answered lots of real problem-solving questions. This is different from some other lessons in this unit where you worked out lots of calculations (as in lesson 6.2).
Which type of lesson do you like best? Explain.

6 Check up

Log how you did on your Student Progression Chart.

Ordering and rounding

1 Copy and complete these. Put the correct sign, < or >, between each pair of numbers.

a 7.152 □ 7.251 b 4.0531 □ 4.0501 c 0.6091 □ 0.6901

2 Write each number as a decimal number of millions to 1 decimal place.

a 7 500 000 b 4 250 000 c 85 650 000

3 Rearrange these decimal numbers in *ascending* order.

5.9281 5.90113 5.0982 5.9408

4 Rearrange these temperatures in *descending* order.

−30.5 °C −31.03 °C −31.3 °C −30.01 °C

5 Round each number to three decimal places.

a 7.1335 b 108.44958

Place-value calculations

6 81 × 56 = 4536

Use this multiplication fact to work out these.

a 8.1 × 56 b 0.81 × 560 c 56 × 8100

7 Work out

a 708 × 0.1 b 41 × 0.01 c 6.11 × 0.01

8 Jane says that she can use an equivalent calculation to find the answer to 4.03 ÷ 0.1

What calculation could she do?

9 Work out

a 734 ÷ 0.1 b 174 ÷ 0.01 c 253 ÷ 0.01

10 To paint an area of 1 m^2, you need 0.1 litres of emulsion paint.

What is the maximum area that you can paint with 1 litre of paint?

Decimal calculations

11 Ollie bought these items.

Milk £1.48

Bacon £2.75

Bread 89p

Juice £1.68

Low fat spread £1.49

What is the total cost?

12 Serpil has £456.56 in her bank account.
She pays her water bill of £21.69 and her phone bill of £15.99.
A shop refunds her £42.25.
How much is in her bank account now?

13 Work out

a 506.23 − 71.6 + 28.603 **b** 4999 + 235.6 + 0.037 − 34.89

14 Work out

a 6.8 × 4.3 **b** 1.25 × 8.6 **c** 3.46 × 2.18

15 Work out

a 64 ÷ 0.8 **b** 38 ÷ 2.5 **c** 185 ÷ 1.25

Ratio and proportion with decimals

16 Write each ratio in its simplest form.

a 10 : 2.5 **b** 4.8 : 3

17 Share each quantity in the ratio given.

a 6.5 kg in the ratio 2 : 3

b 451 litres in the ratio 2 : 4 : 5

c £1000 in the ratio 1 : 3 : 5

18 A small pot of custard has 3.3 g of protein, 18 g of carbohydrate and 7.1 g of fat.

a What proportion of the custard is fat?

b A large pot weighs 3.5 times as much.
How many grams of protein does the large pot contain?

19 Write each ratio as a unit ratio.

a 7 : 5 **b** 5 : 18

20 **How sure are you of your answers? Were you mostly**
Just guessing **Feeling doubtful** **Confident**
What next? Use your results to decide whether to strengthen or extend your learning.

Reflect

Challenge

21 A string factory makes 1563.25 m of string each day.
One ball of string uses 6.5 m.

a How many balls of string does the factory make in one day?

b How many balls of string does the factory make in a week (Monday to Friday)?

22 Work out 1 ÷ 0.7
Write your answer to six decimal places.
Repeat for 2 ÷ 0.7, 3 ÷ 0.7, 4 ÷ 0.7, and so on.
What do you notice?
What happens if you work out 1 ÷ 1.4, 2 ÷ 1.4, and so on?

6 Strengthen

You will:
- Strengthen your understanding with practice.

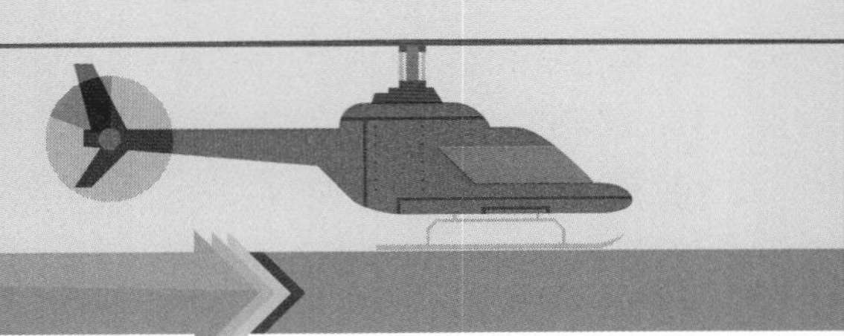

Ordering and rounding

1 Round each number to the nearest 1000.
a 14 526 **b** 47 851 **c** 39 205 **d** 83 764

2 The number of cars entering the London Congestion Zone is recorded each day during the week.

Day	Mon	Tue	Wed	Thu	Fri	Sat	Sun
Number of cars	174 567	158 211	162 421	143 896	136 491	168 504	123 855

Round each number to the nearest 10 000.

3 Round each number to one decimal place.
a 3.67 **b** 14.56 **c** 2.06 **d** 3.65

4 Round each number to two decimal places.
a 5.128 **b** 4.865 **c** 12.476 **d** 26.048

5 Real In a time trial in a velodrome (cycling track), riders complete 1 km on their own as fast as they can. Here are the times (in seconds) for seven riders.
A 54.194, B 53.696, C 55.103, D 53.656, E 54.725, F 59.308, G 50.514
Who came first, second and third in this race?

6 Write each number as millions.
Parts **a** and **d** have been done for you.
a 2 000 000 = 2 million **b** 8 000 000 = □ million
c 12 000 000 = □ million **d** 8 600 000 = 8.6 million
e 7 400 000 = □ million **f** 15 700 000 = □ million

7 Real These are Sunday night TV viewing figures.

Programme	Viewers
Downton Abbey	9 623 145
By Any Means	3 450 238
Countryfile	6 285 016
The Crane Gang	926 818
X Factor	9 528 586

Round each number to a decimal number of millions to one decimal place.

Q1a Strategy hint
Draw a number line to help.
14 000 14 500 15 000

Q2 Strategy hint
Draw a number line to help.
170 000 175 000 180 000

Q3a Strategy hint
You can use number lines for decimals too. 3.6 3.65 3.7

Q4a Strategy hint
Use a number line.
5.120 5.125 5.130

Q5 Strategy hint
List the times in a column with the decimal points lined up.
Look at the whole number parts first, then the tenths, …

Q7 hint
9 623 145 = 9.623 145 million
= 9.□ million (1 d.p.)

Topic links: Area, Volume, Measures

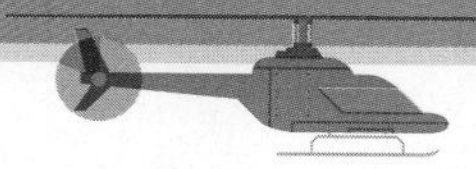

8 Rearrange these numbers in *ascending* order (smallest first).
7.29, 7.88, 7.605, 7.325, 7.52, 7.22, 7.292, 7.50, 7.4, 7.61
7.22, 7.29, ... 7.88

9 Rearrange these numbers in *descending* order (largest first).
−7.13, −6.68, −4.80, −1.48, −7.3, −0.98, −1.62, −5.05, −4.2, −2.18

10 A satellite tracking device measures distances on Earth in kilometres to four decimal places.

Distance A	18.8177 km
Distance B	17.2264 km
Distance C	15.8191 km
Distance D	15.0941 km
Distance E	12.6015 km

Round each distance to three decimal places.

11 Copy and complete these. Put the correct sign, < or >, between each pair of decimal numbers.

a 6.6 □ 6.13 **b** 4.4 □ 4.51 **c** 6.5 □ 6.405
d 5.1 □ 5.368 **e** 5.21 □ 5.201 **f** 15.45 □ 15.445

12 The diagram shows a rectangular flower bed.

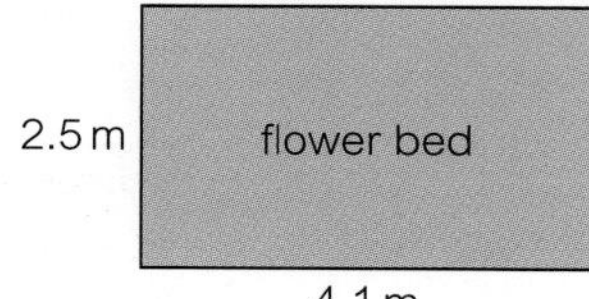

a Which is the best estimate to use for the calculation 2.5 × 4.1?

3 × 4.1 2.5 × 4 3 × 4

b Work out 25 × 41

c Use your answers to parts **a** and **b** to work out 2.5 × 4.1 to give you the area of the flower bed.

13 Petrol costs £1.37 per litre.
How much does 24.5 litres of petrol cost?

Q8 hint
Use a number line to help.
7.00 7.50 8.00

Q10 hint
Look at the 4th decimal place to decide whether to round up or down.

Q11 hint
Decide which number is greater.
Put the wider end of the symbol next to the greater number.

Q11a Strategy hint
Look at the whole numbers first, then the tenths, then the hundredths, …

Q12a Strategy hint
What is easy to multiply but close to the original numbers?

Q13 hint
1 Estimate.
2 Work out 137 × 245.
3 Put in the decimal point.
4 Round answers in pounds to two decimal places.

Place-value calculations

1 Here is a spider diagram for 27 showing the links between multiplying and dividing by powers of 10.
Draw a spider diagram like this for 157.

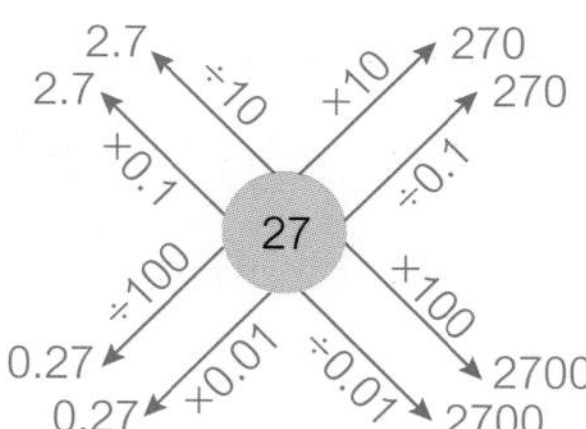

2 Draw a similar spider diagram for each of these numbers.
a 57 **b** 101 **c** 45.2 **d** 2.8

3 Multiply each number by 0.1
a 9.06 **b** 4.73 **c** 6.43

4 Multiply each number by 0.01
a 3.42 **b** 1.14 **c** 7.36
d 6.214 **e** 57.972 **f** 61.03

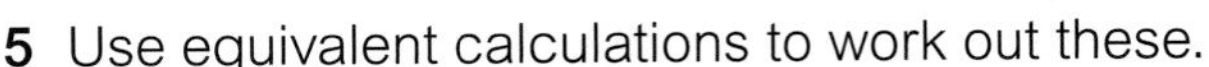

5 Use equivalent calculations to work out these.
- a 5.28×0.1
- b $9.75 \div 100$
- c $7.51 \div 0.1$
- d $0.98 \div 0.01$
- e 0.43×0.01

Q5 Strategy hint
Look at the spider diagram on page 152.
'×10' is equivalent to '÷0.1'
'×0.1' is equivalent to '÷10'

6 $3.2 \times 4.6 = 14.72$

Use this multiplication fact to work out these.
- a 32×4.6
- b 32×46
- c 0.32×4.6
- d 0.32×0.46

Q6a hint
×10 ($3.2 \times 4.6 = 14.72$ → $32 \times 4.6 = \square$) ×10

7 $0.25 \times 58 = 14.5$

Use this multiplication fact to work out these.
- a 2.5×5.8
- b 25×58

Decimal calculations

1 Work out these additions. Use a written method.
- a $7.58 + 8.2$
- b $9.75 + 12.4$
- c $1.245 + 2.03$
- d $5.102 + 789.2$

2 Work out these subtractions. Use a written method.
- a $21.5 - 9.87$
- b $28.4 - 0.015$
- c $1235.4 - 1.245$
- d $5.1548 - 0.0145$

3 Work out these divisions. Use a written method.
Give your answers to one decimal place where appropriate.
- a $24.32 \div 3.2$
- b $1221.42 \div 4.2$
- c $64\,953 \div 1.4$
- d $81.45 \div 6.5$

Q1a hint
Always line up the decimal points when adding in columns.

```
   7 . 5 8
 + 8 . 2
 ---------
     .
 ---------
```

Q2a hint
Always line up the decimal points when subtracting in columns.

```
  ¹2¹⁰1 .¹⁴5¹0
 −    9 . 8 7
 -------------
    1 1 . 6 3
 -------------
```

Q3a hint
It is easier to divide by a whole number.

×10 ($24.32 \div 3.2$ → $243.2 \div 32$) ×10

Ratio and proportion with decimals

1 A piece of rope is 8.5 m long. Josie cuts it in the ratio 3 : 2.
How long will each piece be?

2 A piece of wood is 12.6 m long. Alex cuts it in the ratio 4 : 3 : 1.
How long will each piece be?

3 Tips at a hotel are shared between the receptionists, porters and cleaners in the ratio 2 : 4 : 5.
The total tips for two days were

Saturday	£90.75
Sunday	£278.96

How much did each group receive on each day?

Q1 hint
There are five parts.
8.5 ÷ 5 gives the length of one part.

8.5 m
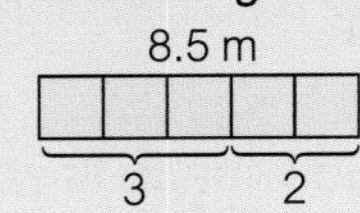
3 2

Q2 hint
12.6 m
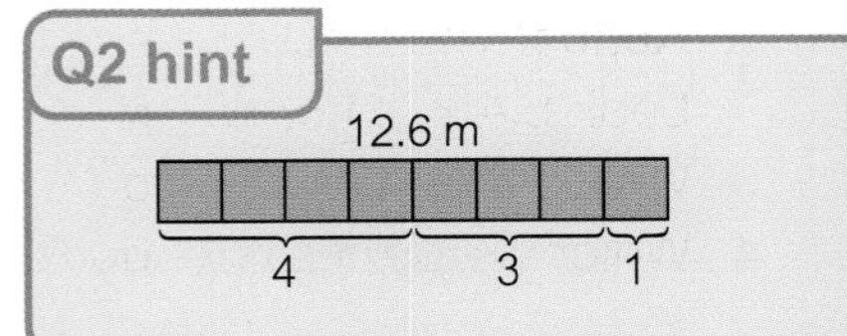
4 3 1

4 Simplify each ratio.
- a 6.5 : 3
- b 8.5 : 3
- c 4.8 : 2
- d 5.4 : 6.6

5 A recipe serves 12 people.
How much of each ingredient would you need to serve 15 people?

Ingredient	12 people	15 people
flour	250 g	
eggs	4	
sugar	200 g	
butter	175 g	
milk	150 ml	

6 Modern digital cameras take pictures in a rectangular shape.
The ratio of width to height is 3 : 2.
Copy and complete the table to show the missing dimensions.
Give your answers to one decimal place.

Width of image	Height of image
6 cm	
	10 cm
	15 cm
	24 cm
18.5 cm	
16.4 cm	
	35.6 cm

Q4 Strategy hint

Choose a number to multiply by that will give a whole number.

×2 6.5 : 3 ×2
13 : 6

Q5 Strategy hint

Work out the amounts for one person first.

Q6 hint

W : H
3 : 2
×? 6 : □

W : H
3 : 2
□ : 10 ×?

Enrichment

1 **Reasoning** All three pictures have their sides in the same ratio.

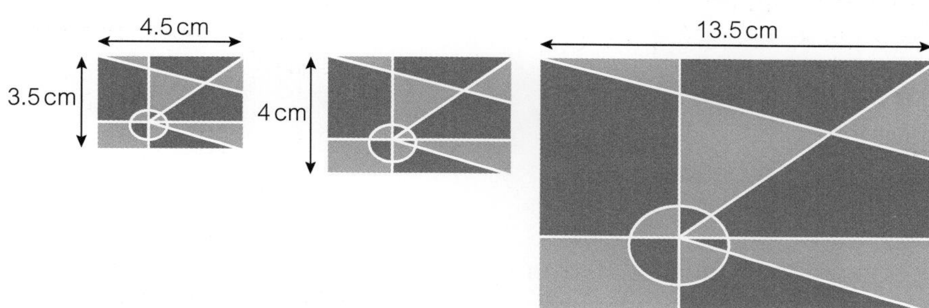

- a Work out the missing lengths.
- b Work out the area of each picture.
- c How many times bigger is the area of the largest picture than the area of the smallest one?

2 **Reflect** The hints in these Strengthen lessons used lots of diagrams.
Look back at the diagrams in the hints.
Which diagrams did you find most useful? Why?
Which diagrams did you find least useful? Why?

Reflect

6 Extend

You will:

- Extend your understanding with problem-solving.

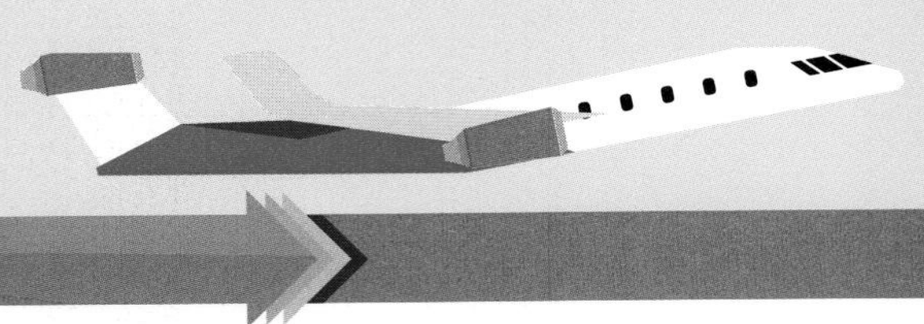

1 **Real** The tables show the heights of the world's highest mountains (in feet). Round each height to the nearest thousand feet.

Mountain	Height (feet)
Everest	29 021
K2	28 244
Kangchenjunga	28 162
Lhotse	27 932
Makalu	27 758

Mountain	Height (feet)
Cho Oyu	26 899
Dhaulagiri	26 788
Manaslu	26 775
Nanga Parbat	26 650
Annapurna	26 538

Discussion How useful is this rounded data?

2 **Problem-solving** Donna, Shakira and Myles are going out for a meal. They decide to put their money together. Donna has £13.50, Shakira has £18.20 and Myles has £22.75.
The prices of their food are given in the table below.

Item	Donna	Shakira	Myles
drink	£1.95	£1.95	£1.95
starter	£2.95	£2.95	£2.50
main	£6.95	£7.75	£7.95
dessert	£3.50	£3.50	£3.50

a How much is the total bill?
b Could Donna afford to pay for all her own food if they hadn't pooled their money?
c They leave a tip of 10% of the bill. How much is this?
d How much money do they have left?
e They share the remaining money equally between them. How much do they get each?

3 **Real** The tables show the drainage areas (in km^2) of 10 river basins.

River basin	Drainage area (km^2)
Nile	3 254 555
Amazon	6 144 727
Yangtse	1 722 155
Mississippi	3 202 230
Yenisei	2 554 482

River basin	Drainage area (km^2)
Yellow River	945 000
Ob	2 970 000
Parana	2 582 672
Congo	3 730 000
Amur	1 929 981

Write each area in millions to one decimal place. The first one has been done for you.

Nile: 3.3 million km^2

Discussion Do you think some of these are rounded values? Explain.

Topic links: Percentages, Measures, Bar charts, Volume

Subject links: Geography (Q1, Q3), Science (Q6)

4 The tables show the amounts of money spent by a local council.

Item	Amount
road maintenance	£14 454 001
salaries	£11 771 908
community services	£7 912 748
building works	£7 003 404

Item	Amount
media services	£6 746 849
waste recycling	£4 444 025
health services	£4 251 390
housing	£3 334 303

a Rewrite each amount in millions to one decimal place.

b Draw a bar chart to show this data.

5 **Modelling / Problem-solving** A football pitch can be any length between 90 m and 120 m, and any width between 45 m and 90 m to the nearest metre. What is the minimum area of a football pitch?

Q5 hint

90 m to the nearest metre could be as short as 89.5 m

6 **Reasoning** The nearest planet to Earth is Venus.
Both planets orbit the Sun.
The orbit of Earth varies between 147 million km and 152 million km away from the Sun.
The orbit of Venus varies between 107 million km and 109 million km away from the Sun.
These measurements are given to the nearest million km.

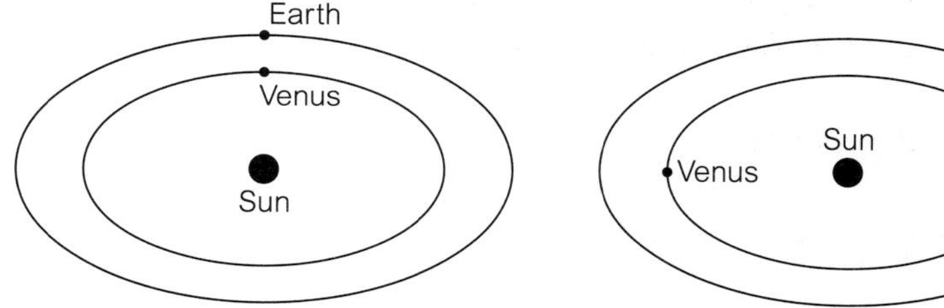

Assume that both planets lie in the same plane and orbit the Sun at different speeds.

a What is the closest possible distance between them?

b What is the furthest possible distance between them?

7 **Real / Finance** Bank statements show overdrawn balances as negative numbers.
These students are all overdrawn. Two bank balances are missing.

Student	Bank balance (£)
Lily	−65.94
Mia	
Freya	−72.31
Maya	−12.62
Arjan	−12.84

Student	Bank balance (£)
Josh	−47.15
Luke	−17.03
Ali	−22.67
Junior	−5.82
Lincoln	

a Mia owes the most. Write a possible balance for Mia's account.

b Lincoln owes the least. Write a possible balance for Lincoln's account.

8 Liquid medicines can be measured in centilitres or millilitres.

a Change these doses from ml to cl.

i 25 ml **ii** 50 ml **iii** 60 ml **iv** 125 ml

b A bottle contains 1 litre of medicine.
How many of each dose from part **a** could you get from the bottle?

Q8 hint

10 ml = 1 cl
1 litre = 1000 ml

9 **STEM** Prescription medicine doses are measured in grams and milligrams.
A high dose tablet of ibuprofen has 600 mg of active ingredient.
a How much is this in grams?
A tablet with 600 mg of active ingredient weighs 2.4 g in total.
b How much of the tablet is *not* active ingredient?

Q9 hint

1000 mg = 1 g

10 **Real** Nurses frequently carry out calculations using ratios to convert between units.
A doctor prescribes 200 mg of ibuprofen.
The medicine is in a container that has 500 mg of ibuprofen dissolved in 40 ml of water.
How much of the liquid should the nurse give to the patient so they take the correct dose of ibuprofen?

11 **Reasoning** Work out
a 105 ÷ 5
b 105 × 0.2
c 425 ÷ 5
d 425 × 0.2
e Copy and complete.
÷10 is equivalent to ×0.1
÷5 is equivalent to □
÷0.2 is equivalent to □
÷2 is equivalent to □
÷4 is equivalent to □

Q11e hint

Use your answers from parts **a** to **d** to help you.

12 **Real** 5 g of grass seed covers a 10 m by 10 m square.
a How many m^2 will 5 g cover?
b How many grams do you need to cover a football pitch that is 110 m × 60 m?

13 **Problem-solving** Ramiz is thinking of assembling a bike from spare parts bought from an online retailer.
The prices of the main items are given in these tables.

Part	Price
frame	£495.00
wheels (each)	£112.49
gears	£37.99
brakes (each)	£53.75
saddle	£20.99

Part	Price
seat pillar	£47.36
handlebars	£39.96
tyres (each)	£43.75
chain	£11.89
inner tubes (each)	£4.49

a How much would making such a bike cost?
Postage and packing adds 10% to the price.
b How much will it cost to have all the components delivered?
A similar new bike in a bike shop costs £1150.
c Which would be cheaper, and by how much?

14 A cereal box is 19.6 cm wide, 7.2 cm deep and 27.5 cm high.
a What is the volume of the cereal box?
b All three dimensions are halved. What is the ratio of the volume of the small box to the volume of the original one?

15 8 km is approximately 5 miles.
a How many miles is each km?
b How many km is each mile?

16 **Finance**

a On a particular day £200 is worth €229.

  i How much is £1 worth in euros?

  ii How much is €1 worth in pounds?

b On another day £50 is worth $79.

  i How much is £1 worth in dollars?

  ii How much is $1 worth in pounds?

17 Use suitable equivalent calculations to work out these.

a 3.5×62	**b** 1.6×125	**c** 2.25×848
d 1.5×4682	**e** 1.8×4235	**f** 6.25×488

Q17a hint

3.5 is equivalent to $\frac{7}{2}$

Multiplying by 3.5 is the same as multiplying by 7 and dividing by 2.

18 Use a calculator to work out

a $4.2^2 \times (3.6 + 1\frac{1}{2})$ **b** $\frac{9}{4} \times 3.5 + 8.4^2$

c $6^3 + 4.2^2 + 1.1^2 + \frac{4}{5}$ **d** $(2.6 + 3.2)^2 \times (\frac{3}{4} + 1.12)^2$

19 **Finance** Banks use interest rates as a way to charge people for borrowing money.

The charge you pay is a percentage of the amount you borrow.

For example, Clare borrows £10 000 at an interest rate of 5% per year.

At the end of the year she is charged £10 000 × $\frac{5}{100}$ =

£10 000 × 0.05 = £500 interest.

Ajmal has borrowed £200 000 from the bank to buy a house, at an interest rate of 3.2% per year.

a How much interest will he pay if he borrows the money for a year?

b He pays the bank £850 per month. How much does he owe the bank at the end of the first year?

20 Copy and complete these. Put the correct sign, < or >, between each pair of numbers.

a −30.58 □ −33.9	**b** −23.69 □ −18.93
c −85.93 □ −66.47	**d** −13.87 □ −82.57
e −66.43 □ −25.07	**f** −40.02 □ −25.83
g −39.93 □ −39.929	**h** −4.59 □ 4.61

Investigation **Modelling**

Estimate the volume and the surface area of a typical adult.

Use a cuboid as a model.

You may wish to use measuring equipment to help you.

Use a sensible degree of accuracy for all your measurements and calculations.

21 **Reflect** What kind of jobs might need the maths skills you have used in these Extend lessons?

Look back at the questions to help you. For example, Q19 asked you to work out interest on a loan. Someone working as a financial advisor needs these skills.

6 Unit test

Log how you did on your Student Progression Chart.

1 Round each amount to two decimal places.

a £66.255 **b** £134.0875 **c** £236.625

2 This table shows the distance between London and four other large cities.
Round each distance to the nearest 1000 km.

From	To	Distance
London	Auckland	18 327 km
London	Tokyo	9582 km
London	Buenos Aires	11 102 km
London	Los Angeles	8778 km

3 Round each number to three decimal places.

a 4.7913 **b** 37.0004 **c** 21.4897

4 Work out

a 26.1 + 9.65 **b** 10 − 1.72 **c** 9.4 + 6.57 − 11.46

5 Work out

a 345 × 0.62 **b** 3.5 × 0.15 **c** 0.05 × 0.64

6 Long rolls of cloth need to be cut in the ratio 5 : 1 : 2.
How long is the longest piece of cloth from a roll 48 m long?

7 Rearrange these numbers in *ascending* order.
45.39, 45.18, 45.275, 45.33, 66.5, 66.39

8 Work out

a 36 ÷ 0.1 **b** 419 ÷ 0.01 **c** 4.8 ÷ 0.6

d 48 ÷ 0.08 **e** 8.4 ÷ 0.2 **f** 0.63 ÷ 0.3

9 Rearrange these numbers in *ascending* order.
−9.31, −9.78, −9.57, −9.3, −9.53, −9.511, −9.9

10 Simplify each ratio.

a 12 : 16.8

b 1.5 : 7.5

11 Sophie mixes acid and water in the ratio 2 : 5.2
She makes 288 m*l* of the mixture.
How much acid and how much water did she mix?

12 Ben makes orange paint by mixing red, yellow and white paint in the ratio 20 : 16 : 1.5.
How much of each colour does he need to make 1.5 litres of orange paint?

13 471 × 34 = 16014

Use this multiplication fact to work out

a 4.71 × 0.34

b 0.471 × 34

c 47.1 × 0.034

d 0.471 × 0.34

14 50 inches is about the same distance as 127 cm.
What is the ratio of inches to cm?
Give your answer as a unit ratio.

15 Work out

a 54.18 × 6.7

b 78.03 ÷ 1.7

16 Copy and complete these. Put the correct sign, < or >, between each pair of numbers.

a 40.43 □ 58.57

b 68.6 □ 66.79

c 87.62 □ 87.43

d −7.62 □ −7.7

e −6.145 □ −6.154

f −9.803 □ −9.088

17 John's savings account pays 2.5% interest per year.
John has £500 in savings.
How much interest will he have earned after 1 year?

Challenge

18

0.12	0.86	1.188	12.5
5.04	27.5	9	0.7
11.3	6.3	0.1	33
51.3	2.97	10.7	10.8

Each of the numbers in the blue rectangle can be made by adding, subtracting, multiplying or dividing some or all of these decimal numbers.

0.3	0.4	1.4	9.9	3.6	6.2	5.7

a You can use each number a maximum of once in each calculation.
Make as many of the numbers from the blue rectangle as you can.
Keep a note of the calculations you do to avoid duplication.

b Following the same rules:
What is the highest number you can make?
What is the lowest number you can make?
What is the number closest to zero you can make?

19 **Reflect** Look back at the questions in this unit test.
Which took the shortest time to answer? Why?
Which took the longest time to answer? Why?
Which took the most thought to answer? Why?

Reflect

7 Lines and angles

MASTER | Check P175 | Strengthen P177 | Extend P181 | Test P185

7.1 Quadrilaterals

You will learn to:
- Classify quadrilaterals by their geometric properties
- Solve geometric problems using side and angle properties of special quadrilaterals.

CONFIDENCE

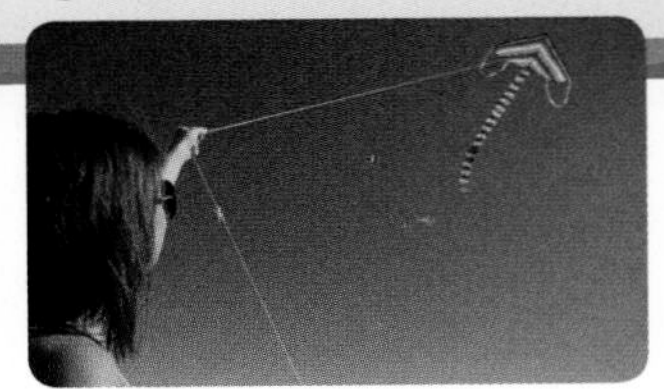

Why learn this?
Kite designers change the angles in the designs of their kites to make faster, better models.

Fluency
- What do the angles in a quadrilateral add up to?
- Subtract each of these from 180: 30 70 55
- Subtract each of these from 360: 170 210 65

Explore
How is a square drawn on a sphere different from one drawn on paper?

Exercise 7.1

Warm up

1 Copy and complete this table showing the number of lines of symmetry and order of rotational symmetry of these quadrilaterals.

Quadrilateral	Square	Rectangle	Parallelogram	Rhombus	Kite	Trapezium	Isosceles trapezium
Number of lines of symmetry							
Order of rotational symmetry							

Key point

The properties of a shape are facts about its sides, angles, diagonals and symmetry.
Here are some of the properties of the special quadrilaterals that you should know.

Square	• all sides are equal in length • opposite sides are parallel • all angles are 90° • diagonals bisect each other at 90°	Rectangle	• opposite sides are equal in length • opposite sides are parallel • all angles are 90° • diagonals bisect each other
Rhombus	• all sides are equal in length • opposite sides are parallel • opposite angles are equal • diagonals bisect each other at 90°	Parallelogram	• opposite sides are equal in length • opposite sides are parallel • opposite angles are equal • diagonals bisect each other
Kite 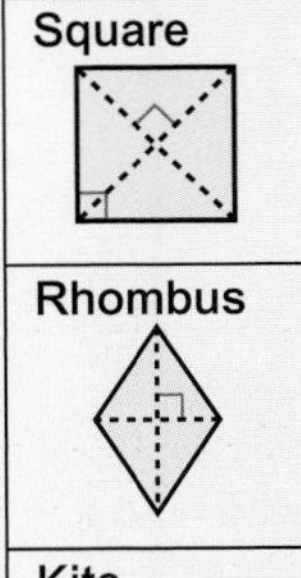	• 2 pairs of sides are equal in length • no parallel sides • 1 pair of equal angles • diagonals bisect each other at 90°	Trapezium 	• 1 pair of parallel sides
		Isosceles trapezium  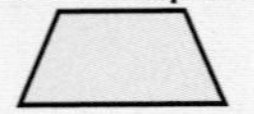	• 2 sides are equal in length • 1 pair of parallel sides • 2 pairs of equal angles

Topic links: Coordinates

Subject links: Design and technology (Q5, Q6)

2 Name each quadrilateral being described.

a My opposite sides are parallel and equal in length. None of my angles are 90°.

b I have one pair of parallel sides, and two sides the same length.

c I have one pair of equal angles, and no parallel sides.

d All my angles are 90°. My **diagonals bisect** each other, but not at 90°.

Q2 Literacy hint

A **diagonal** is a line that joins two opposite vertices of a shape. When diagonals **bisect** each other, they cut each other in half.

Discussion Is this shape a trapezium?

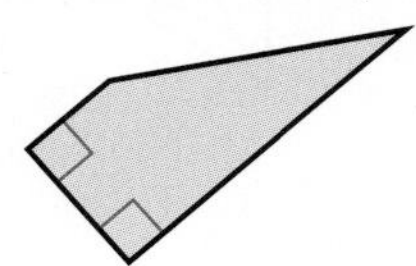

3 **Problem-solving** Draw a coordinate grid on squared paper with both axes going from 0 to 10. Plot these points.

A (1, 1), B (3, 1), C (10, 1), D (4, 4), E (6, 4),
F (1, 7), G (3, 7), H (5, 7), I (9, 7), J (6, 10)

Which four points can you join to make each of these quadrilaterals?

a rectangle

b trapezium

c parallelogram

d square

e kite

Worked example

In this parallelogram, one of the angles is 55°.
Work out the sizes of the other angles.

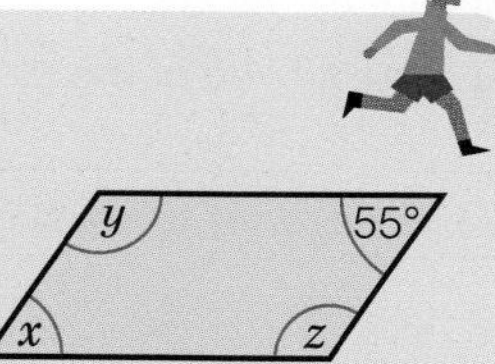

$x = 55°$ (opposite angles of a parallelogram are equal)

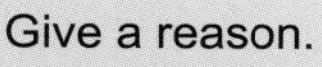

$360 - 55 - 55 = 250°$ (angles in a quadrilateral sum to 360°)

$250 \div 2 = 125°$ (opposite angles of a parallelogram are equal)

$y = 125°$ and $z = 125°$

4 One of the diagonals has been drawn in this rectangle.

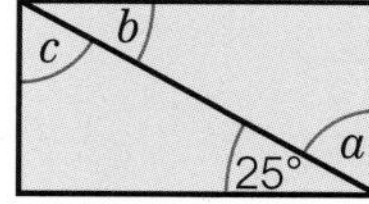

Work out the sizes of angles a, b and c. Give a reason for each answer.

5 Lowri uses this rhombus and parallelogram in her patchwork quilt design.

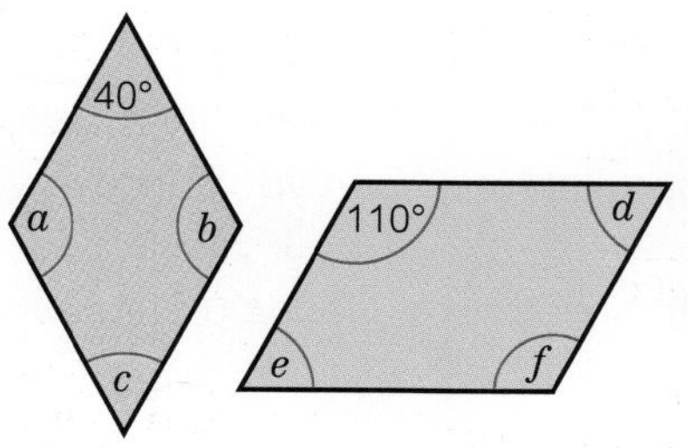

a Work out the sizes of the angles marked with letters. Give a reason for each answer.

b Draw a sketch to show how these shapes will tessellate.

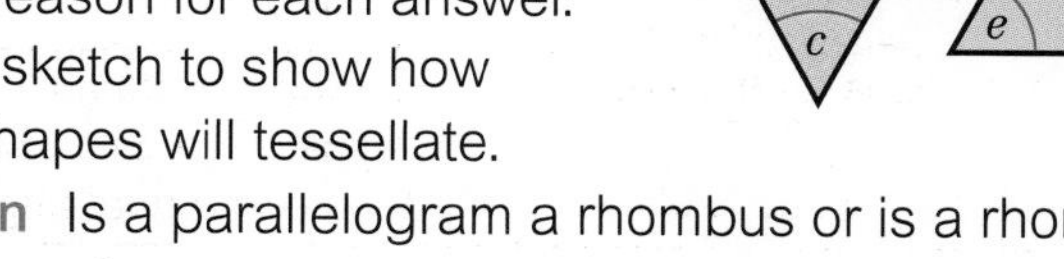

Q5 hint

Shapes tessellate if they make a repeating pattern with no gaps.

Discussion Is a parallelogram a rhombus or is a rhombus a parallelogram?

6 **Real** Anil designs a kite on his computer.
The diagram shows some of the angles.
Work out the sizes of angles a, b and c.
Give a reason for each answer.

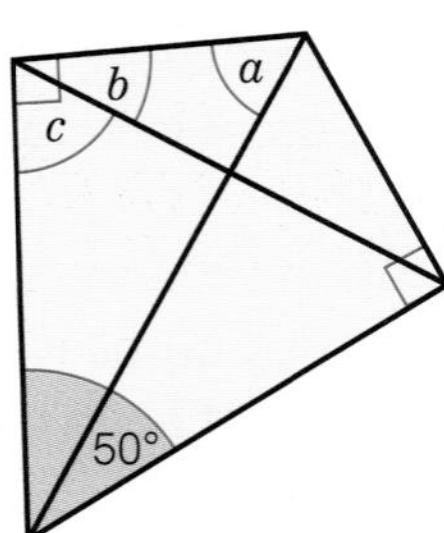

Investigation **Problem-solving**

The diagram shows the pieces of a Tangram puzzle.

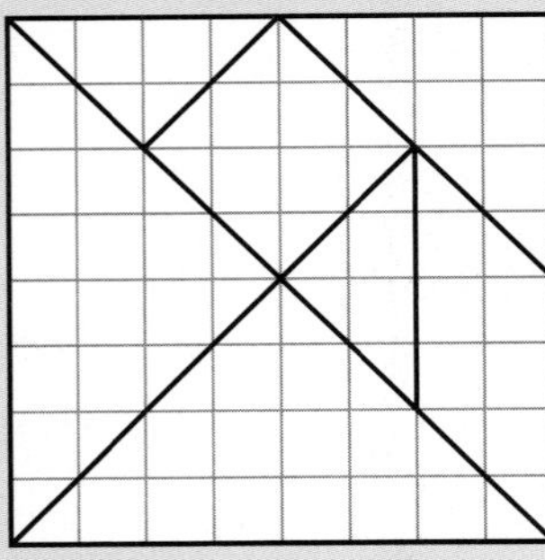

Copy the diagram on squared paper.
Cut out all the pieces.

1 Work out two different ways that you can use two of the pieces to make a trapezium.

2 Work out two different ways that you can use two of the pieces to make a parallelogram.

3 Work out how you can use all of the pieces to make each of these shapes.
   a rectangle
   b parallelogram
   c trapezium
   d triangle
   e hexagon

Explore

7 **Explore** How is a square drawn on a sphere different from one drawn on paper?
Is it easier to explore this question now you have completed the lesson?
What further information do you need to be able to answer this?

Reflect

8 **Reflect** Frankie says that to identify a shape, he begins by asking himself these questions.
- Are its sides straight?
- Are any sides equal in length?
- Are the equal sides next to each other, or opposite?

Write down all the questions you ask yourself to identify a shape.
Test your questions on some quadrilaterals. Can you improve your questions?
Compare your questions with other people's. Can you improve your questions?

7.2 Alternate angles and proof

You will learn to:
- Identify alternate angles on a diagram
- Understand a proof that the sum of the angles of a triangle is 180° and of a quadrilateral is 360°.

Why learn this?
Snooker players use angle properties to help plan their next shot.

Fluency
Which numbers are missing from these statements?
- The sum of the angles on a straight line is □°.
- The sum of the angles in a triangle is □°.

Explore
What is a mathematical proof?

Exercise 7.2

1 Work out the size of each angle marked with a letter.

a 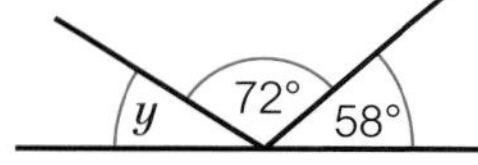

b 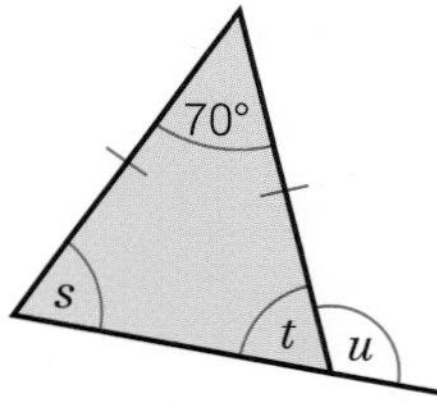

c 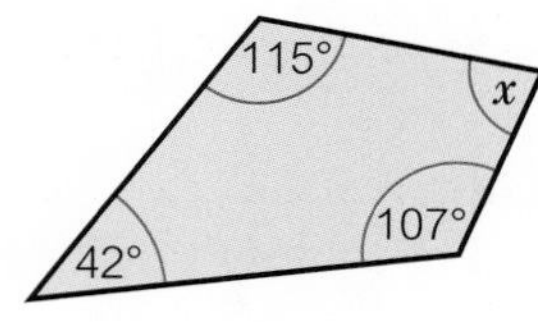

2 Work out the size of angle x in each case.

a 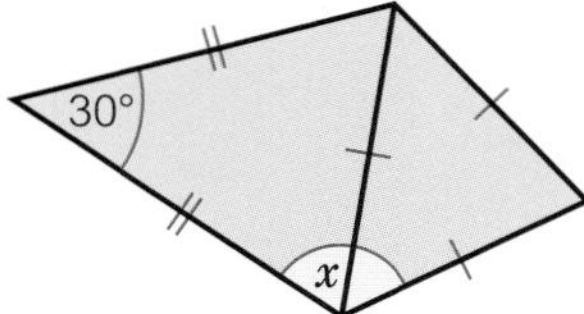

b 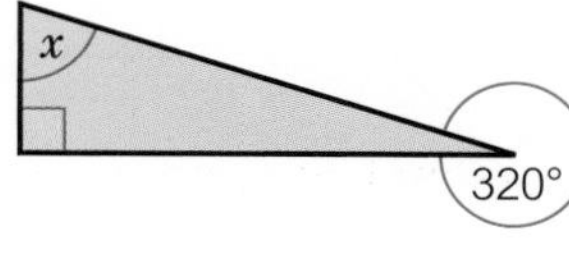

c 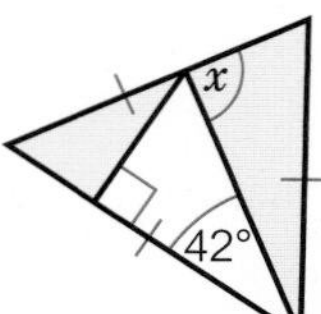

3 The diagram shows a line crossing two parallel lines and angles labelled a, b, c and d.

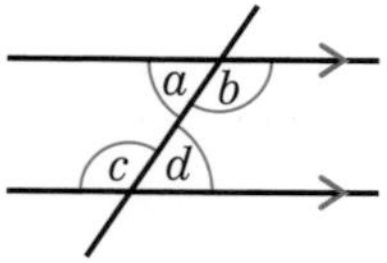

a and d are **alternate angles**.
a and d are the same size.

b and c are alternate angles.
b and c are the same size.

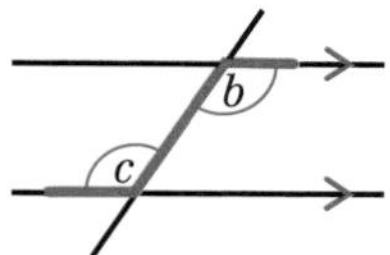

Now look at this diagram.
Write down two pairs of alternate angles.

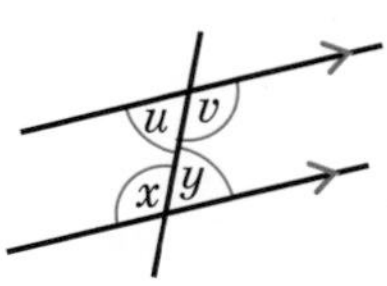

Key point
We show parallel lines using arrows.

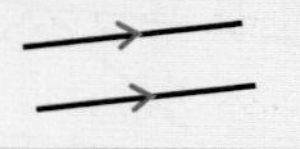

Key point
When a line crosses two parallel lines it creates a 'Z' shape.
Inside the Z shape are **alternate angles**. Alternate angles are equal.

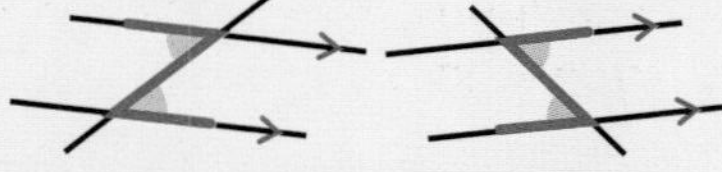

Alternate angles are on different (alternate) sides of the diagonal line.

4 The diagram shows two lines crossing parallel lines. Copy and complete these statements.

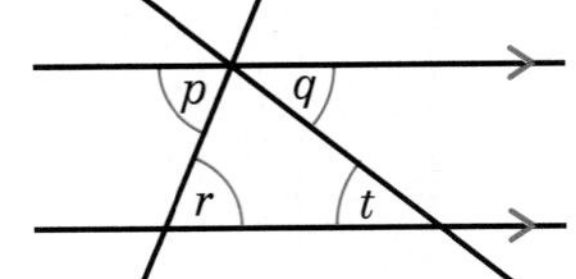

a Angle r and angle □ are alternate angles.

b Angle t and angle □ are alternate angles.

c Angle □ is the same size as angle q.

d Angle □ is the same size as angle p.

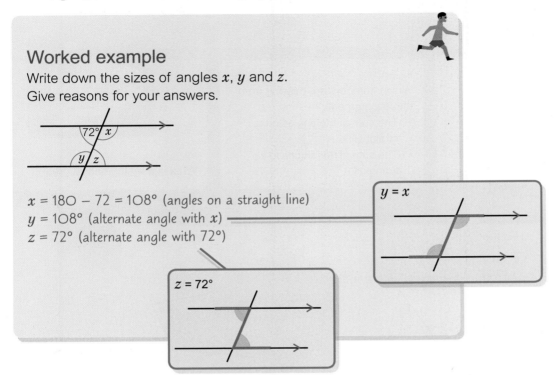

Worked example

Write down the sizes of angles x, y and z.
Give reasons for your answers.

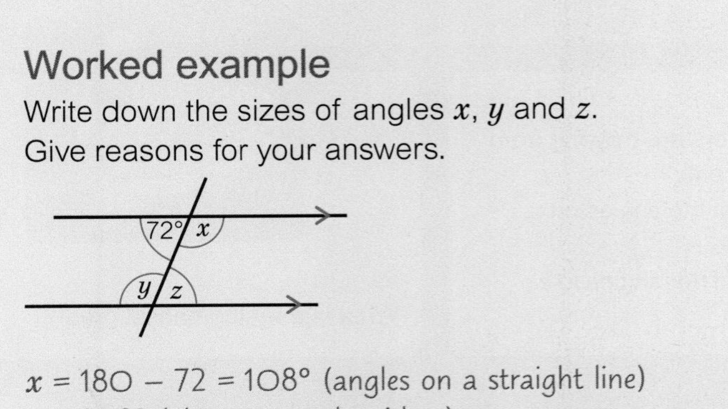

$x = 180 - 72 = 108°$ (angles on a straight line)
$y = 108°$ (alternate angle with x)
$z = 72°$ (alternate angle with 72°)

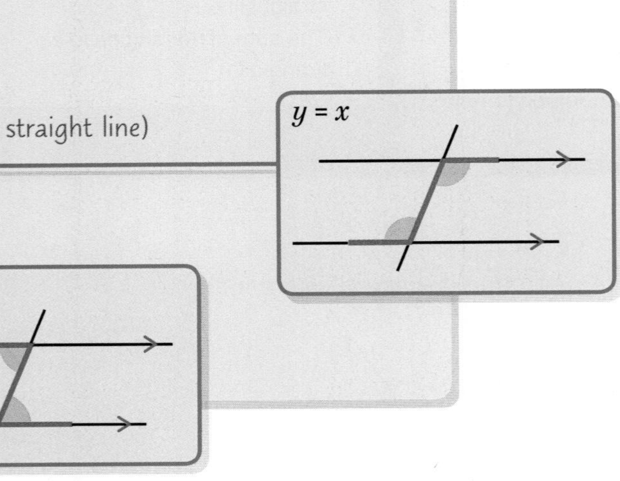

5 Write down the sizes of the angles marked with letters. Give a reason for each answer.

a

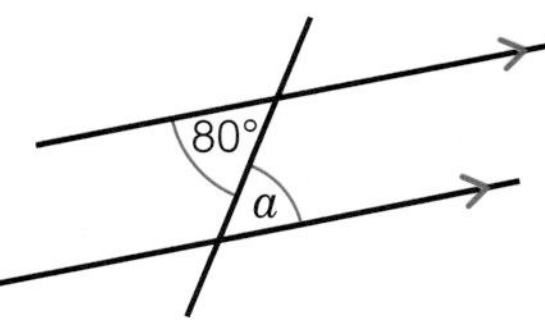

b

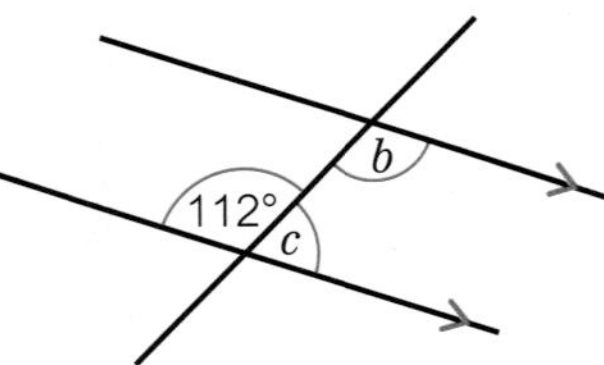

c

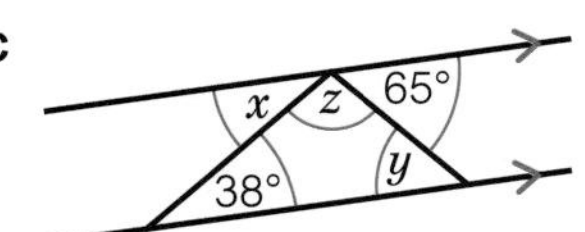

d

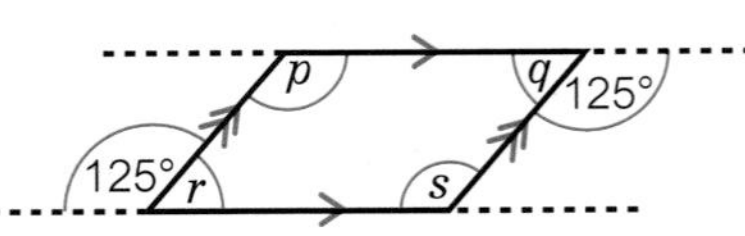

Discussion What angle facts about parallelograms have you shown in part **d**?

6 **Problem-solving** In this diagram, angles a and b are in the ratio 5 : 7.

Work out the size of angle c. Give a reason for your answer.

Topic links: Ratio, Writing formulae

7 **Reasoning** Sketch a copy of this diagram.

Copy and complete these sentences that **prove** that the angles in a triangle add up to 180°.

a Angle x is equal to angle □ as they are alternate angles.

b Angle y is equal to angle □ as they are __________ angles.

c $x + b + y = \square°$ because they lie on a __________ line.

d Since $x = a$ and $y = \square$

$x + b + y = \square + b + \square$

so $a + b + c = \square°$.

e This proves that the angles in a triangle sum to □°.

Key point

It is not enough to show that a theory works for a few values. You need to **prove** it works for all values. A **proof** uses logical reasoning to show a theory is true.

8 **Reasoning** Sketch a copy of this diagram.
The quadrilateral has been split into two triangles.
Copy and complete this **proof** to show that the angles in a quadrilateral add up to 360°.

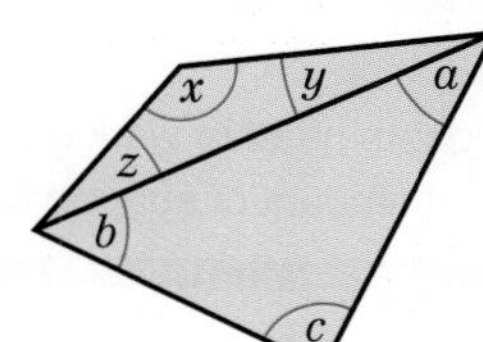

$x + y + z = \square°$ because the sum of the angles in a triangle is □°.

$a + b + c = \square°$ because the sum of the angles in a triangle is □°.

$x + y + z + a + b + c = \square°$

This proves that the angles in a quadrilateral sum to □°.

Investigation

Reasoning

1 For each diagram, answer these questions.

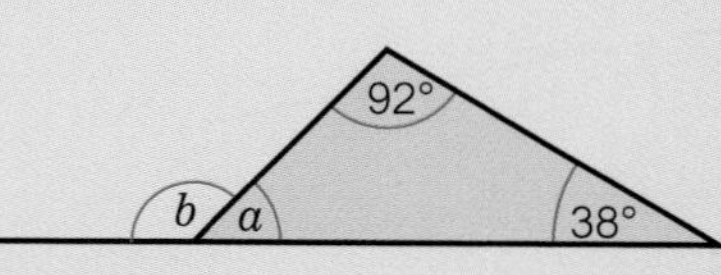

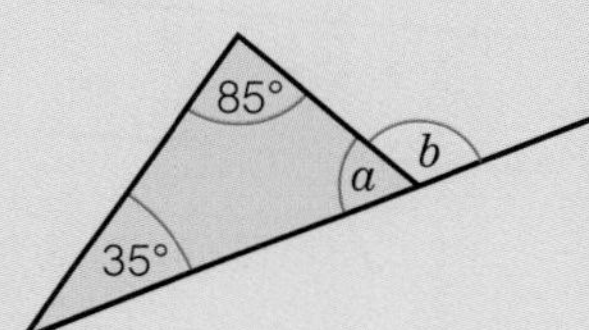

a Work out the sum of the two given angles in the triangle.

b Work out the size of angle a.

c Work out the size of angle b.

2 What do you notice about your answers to parts **1a** and **1c**?

3 Will this be true for every triangle? Explain why.

4 Draw two triangles of your own to test your answer.
Choose your own values for angles c and d, then work out a and b.

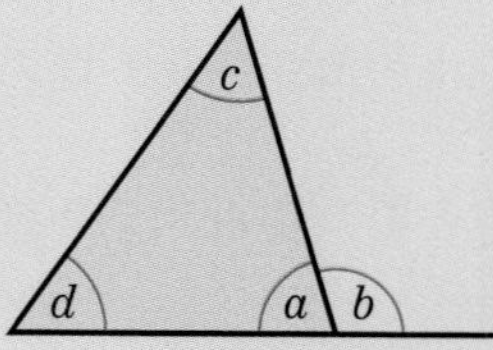

5 Copy and complete the formula: $b = \square + \square$.

9 **Explore** What is a mathematical proof?
Is it easier to explore this question now you have completed the lesson?
What further information do you need to be able to answer this?

10 **Reflect** Marco says, 'A mathematical proof is an argument that convinces people something is true.'
Read each line of the proofs you worked on in Q7 and Q8.
How does the way they are written help to convince people?

Q10 hint

What type of language are the proofs using? How are they set out? Why is algebra used?

Explore

Reflect

7.3 Geometrical problems

You will learn to:
- Solve geometrical problems using side and angle properties of triangles and quadrilaterals
- Identify corresponding angles
- Solve simple problems using properties of angles in parallel and intersecting lines.

CONFIDENCE

Why learn this?
Bridge designers need to work out angles to provide the maximum amount of support for a bridge.

Fluency
Identify the pairs of alternate and vertically opposite angles in these parallel lines.

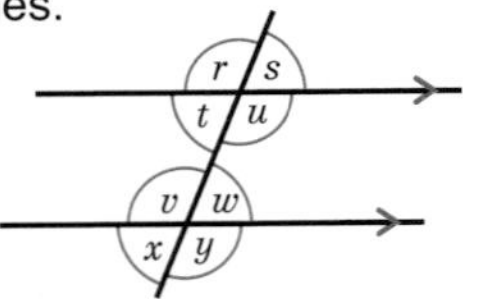

Explore
Why are triangles used in construction?

Exercise 7.3

Warm up

1 Work out the sizes of the angles marked with letters.

a
25°
y
x
z

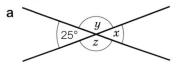

b

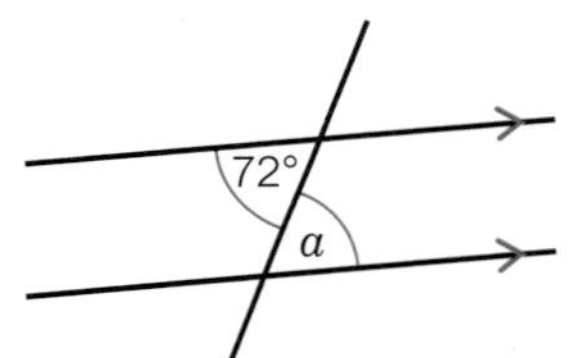

c

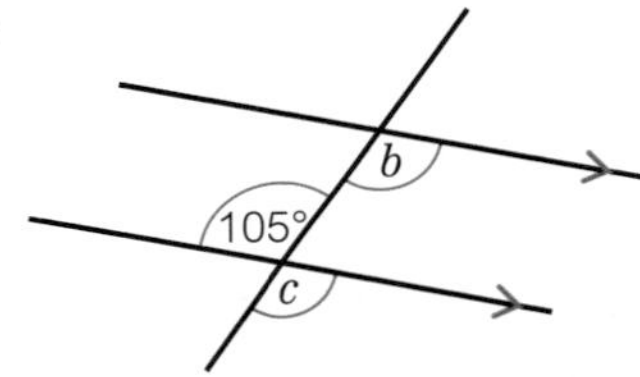

2 Name each quadrilateral being described.

a My opposite sides are parallel and my opposite angles are equal. My diagonals bisect each other at 90°.

b I have one pair of parallel sides. All my sides are different lengths.

c All my angles are 90°. My diagonals bisect each other at 90°.

d I have two pairs of equal sides, but they are not parallel.

3 Work out the sizes of the angles marked with letters.

a

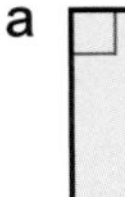

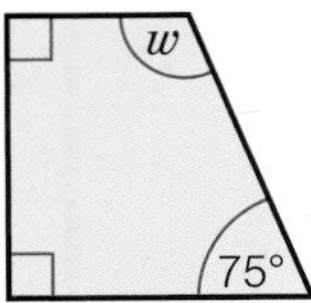

b

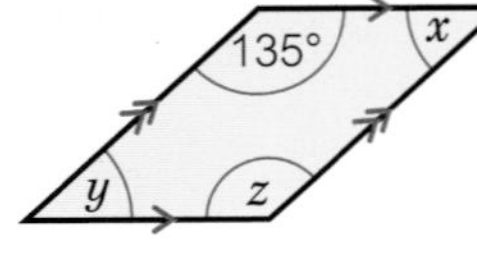

c

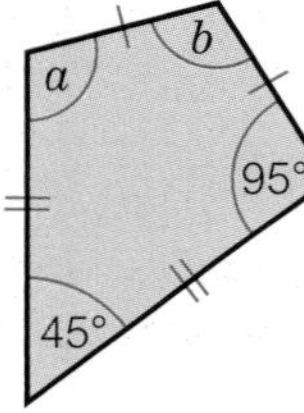

d

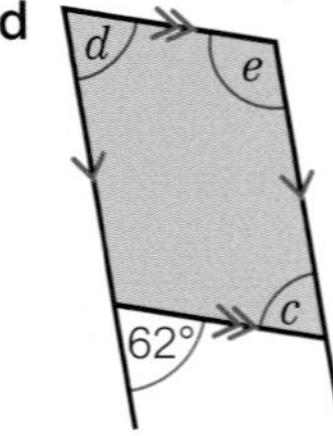

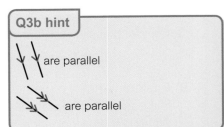

Q3b hint

are parallel

are parallel

Topic links: Ratio, Symmetry

4 **Real** The diagram shows the road markings on a 'no parking' zone. Work out the sizes of angles x and y.

Q4 hint

Use angles on a straight line to work out x, then properties of a parallelogram to work out y.

5 The diagram shows part of the design of a safety gate. The wooden bars form isosceles triangles and rhombuses. Work out the sizes of angles a, b, c and d.

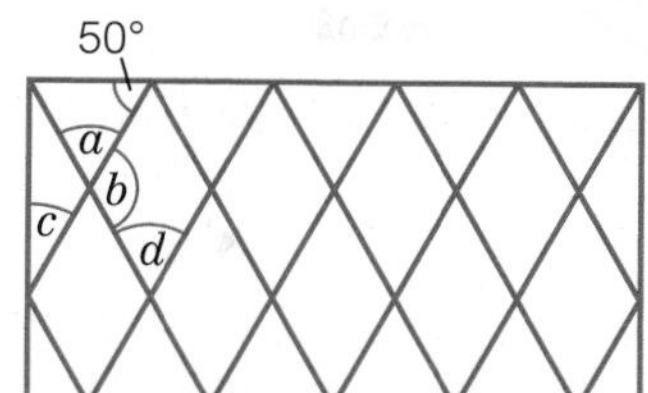

6 **a** Quadrilateral ABCD is called an arrowhead. Copy and complete these statements

- **i** AD is equal in length to ☐.
- **ii** AB is equal in length to ☐.
- **iii** ∠BAD = ∠☐
- **iv** ABCD has ☐ line(s) of symmetry and rotational symmetry of order ☐.

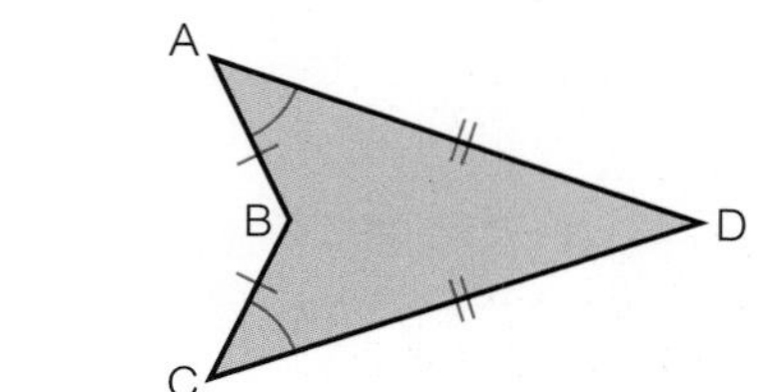

b In this arrowhead ∠KJM = 40° and ∠JKM = 35°. Calculate the size of these angles.

- **i** ∠KLM
- **ii** ∠KML
- **iii** ∠JML

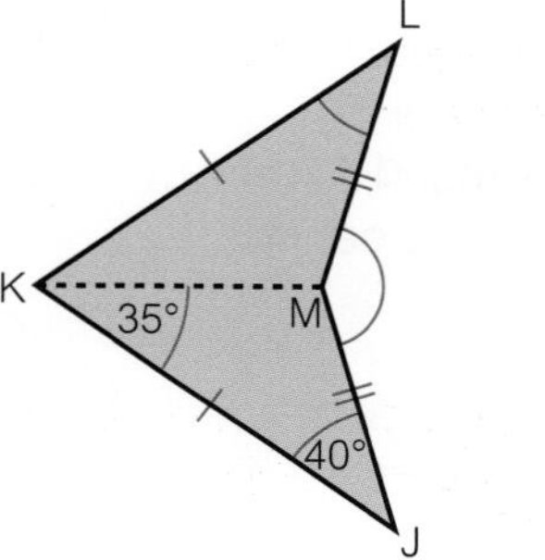

7 **Problem-solving** The diagram shows a chevron road sign. A chevron is made from two congruent parallelograms.

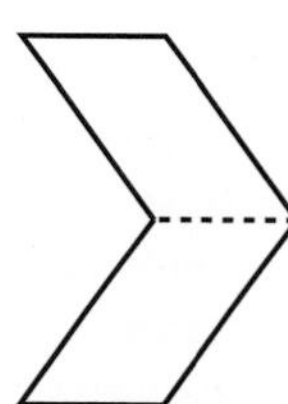

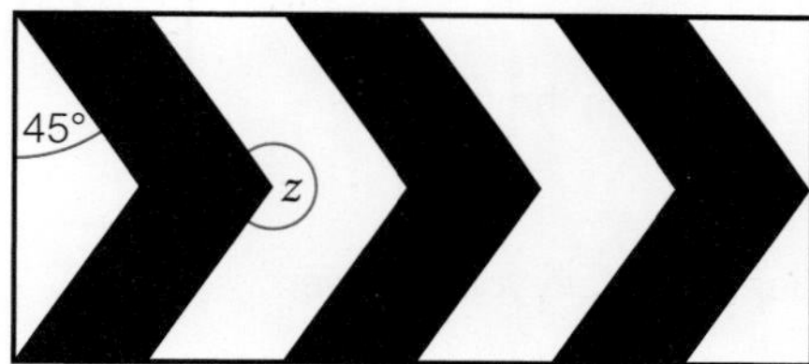

Work out the size of angle z.

Worked example

Write down the sizes of angles x, y and z. Give reasons for your answers.

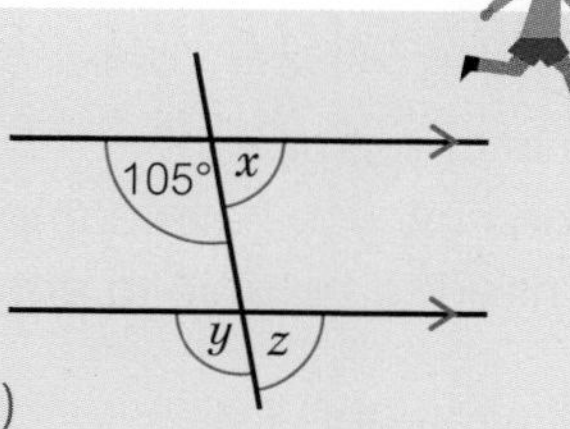

$x = 180 - 105 = 75°$ (angles on a straight line)
$y = 105°$ (corresponding angle with 105°)
$z = 75°$ (corresponding angle with x)

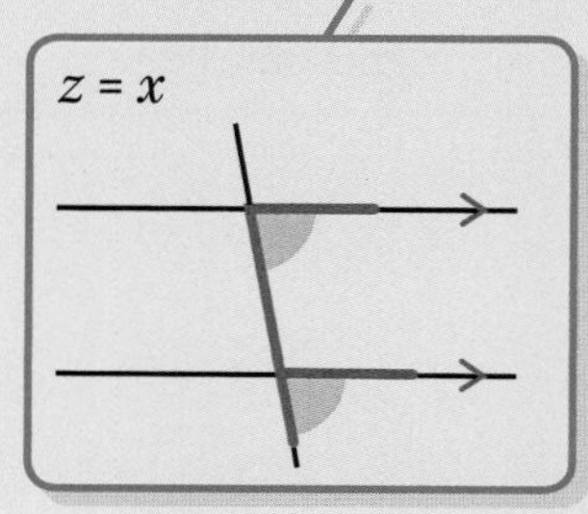

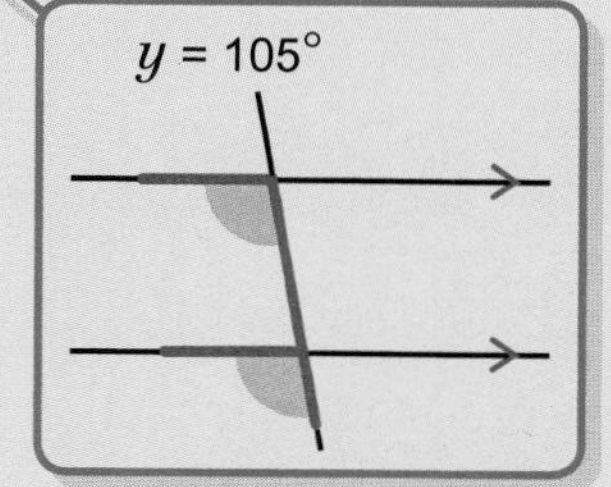

Key point

When a line crosses two parallel lines it creates an 'F' shape. There are **corresponding angles** on an F shape. Corresponding angles are equal. Corresponding angles are on the same (corresponding) side of the diagonal line.

8 Write down the sizes of the angles marked with letters. Give a reason for each answer.

a

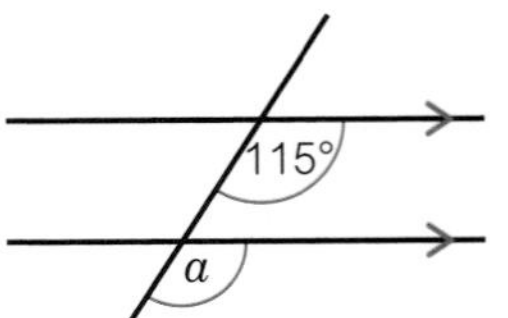

b

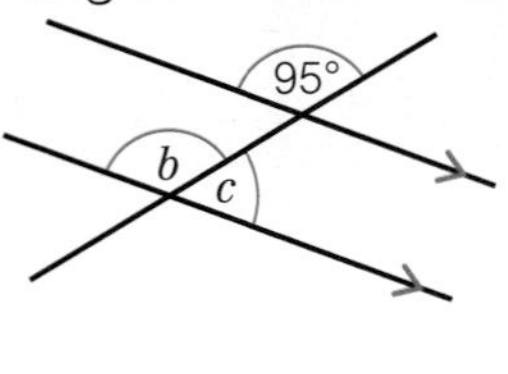

c

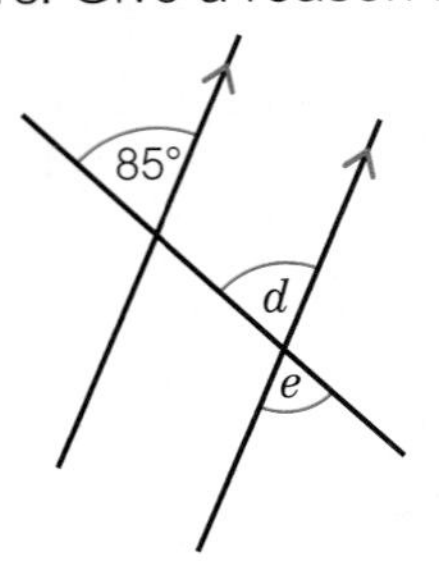

d

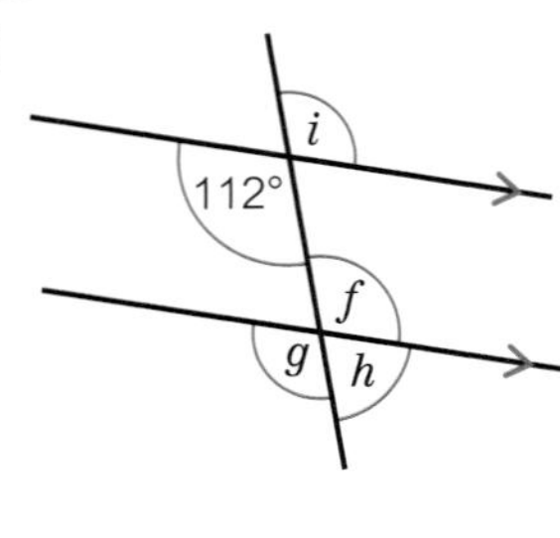

Discussion The capital letter F has corresponding angles.
What other capital letters have corresponding angles?

9 Write down the sizes of the angles marked with letters. Give a reason for each answer.

a

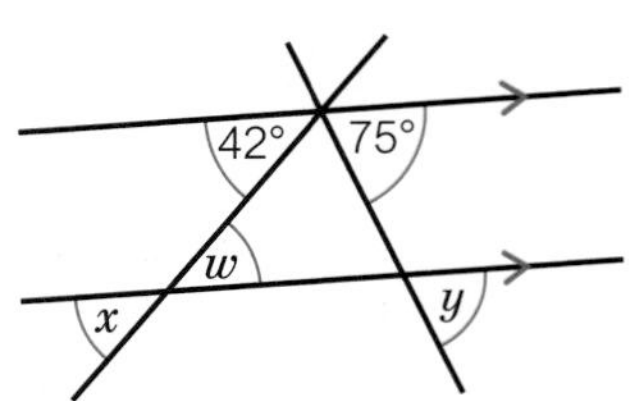

b

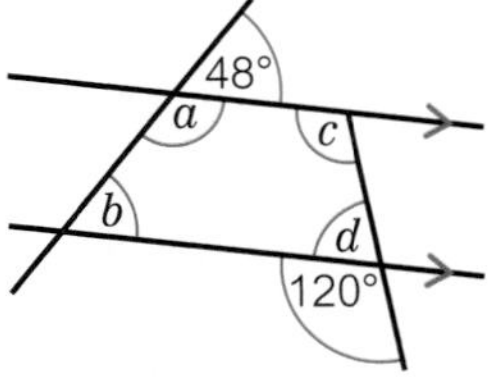

c

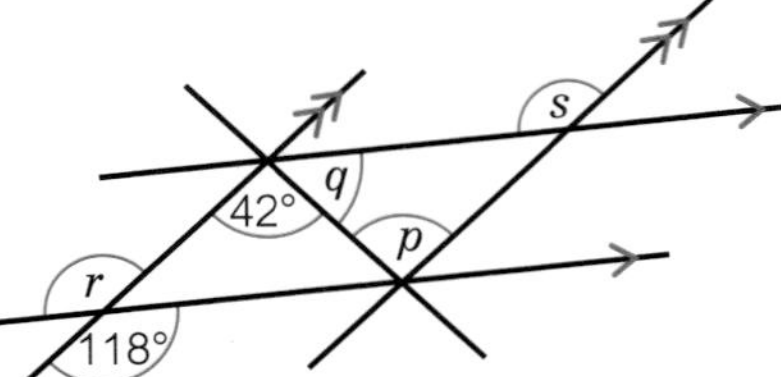

10 **Reasoning** Look at this diagram. Explain why WX and YZ cannot be parallel lines.

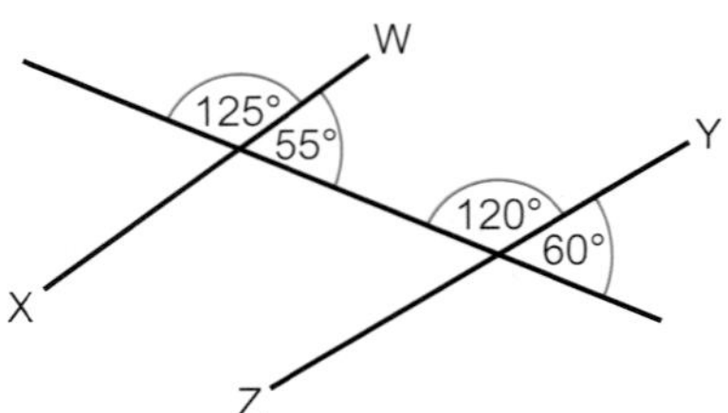

Q10 Strategy hint
Are there any corresponding angles?

Investigation — Reasoning

This diagram shows an isosceles triangle drawn inside a square.
The base of the triangle is the base of the square.
The top of the triangle divides the top of the square in the ratio 1 : 1, i.e. it is the midpoint.

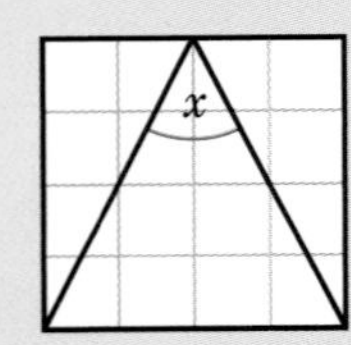

1. Make a copy of the diagram on squared paper.
2. With a protractor, measure the size of angle x.
3. Will angle x always be the same, whatever the size of the square? Explain your answer.
4. Draw different squares to test your answer to part 3.
5. Investigate further to see whether angle x is always the same for different size squares when the top of the triangle divides the top of the square in different ratios, e.g. 1 : 2, 1 : 3 or 1 : 4.

Explore

11 **Explore** Why are triangles used in construction?
Is it easier to explore this question now you have completed the lesson?
What further information do you need to be able to answer this?

Reflect

12 **Reflect** After the lesson Otmane wrote this list.

To solve shape and angle problems, look out for
- right angles (marked with a small square)
- parallel lines (marked with arrows)
- alternate angles (alternate sides of any line that crosses parallel lines)

Look back at the questions you answered in this lesson.
Write your own 'Look out for' list.

Q12 hint

You could begin your list with the same points as Otmane.

7.4 Exterior and interior angles

You will learn to:
- Calculate the sum of the interior and exterior angles of a polygon
- Calculate the interior and exterior angles of a polygon.

Why learn this?
People who design footballs need to work out the angles in the pieces to make sure they fit together correctly.

Fluency
- What is 180 multiplied by each of these numbers?
  2 3 4 5 6
- What is special about a regular polygon?

Explore
What different shapes can you use to tile walls?

Exercise 7.4

1 Work out the sizes of the angles marked with letters.

a

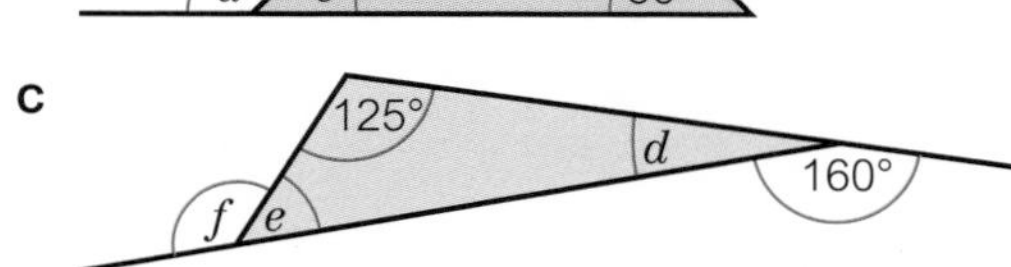

b

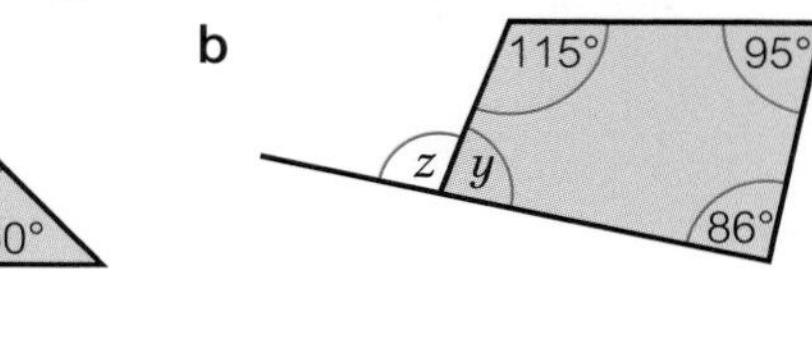

c

Warm up

Investigation — Reasoning

You can work out the sum of the interior angles in a polygon by dividing the polygon into triangles.
A diagonal divides a quadrilateral into two triangles.
The sum of the interior angles in a quadrilateral = 2 × 180° = 360°.

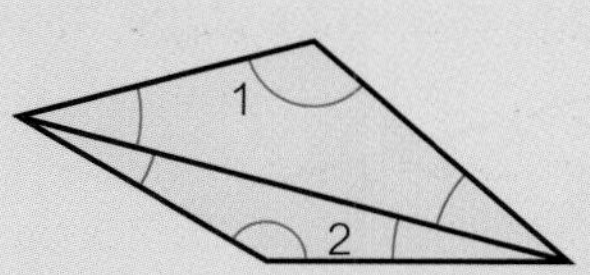

1 Draw a pentagon and divide it into triangles using diagonals.
The diagonals must all start from the same vertex (corner) of the pentagon.

2 Copy and complete:
A pentagon divides into ☐ triangles.
The sum of the interior angles in a pentagon = ☐ × 180° = ☐°.

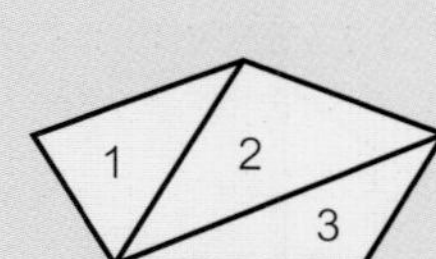

3 Use the same method to work out the sum of the interior angles in a hexagon.

4 Copy and complete this table.

Shape	triangle	quadrilateral	pentagon	hexagon
Number of sides	3	4	5	6
Number of triangles	1	2	3	☐
Sum of interior angles	180°	360°	☐°	☐°

5 Describe in words how to work out the number of triangles from the number of sides.

6 Describe in words how to work out the sum of the interior angles from the number of sides.

7 Write a formula to work out the sum of the interior angles, S, for a polygon with n sides.

8 Use your formula to work out the sum of the interior angles of a 20-sided polygon.

2 For each **irregular polygon**, work out

i the sum of the interior angles

ii the size of the angle marked with a letter.

a

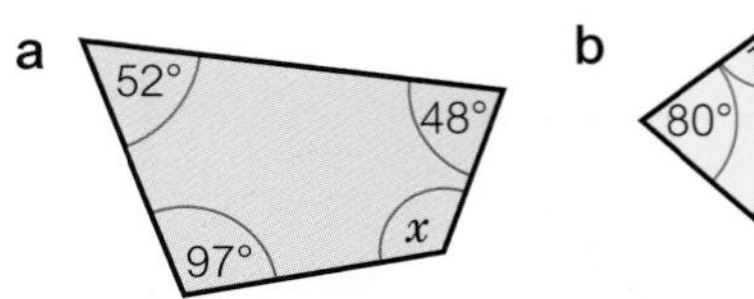

b

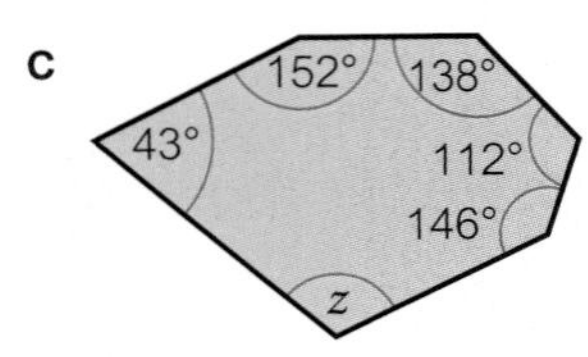

c 152°, 138°, 43°, 112°, 146°, z

Discussion Is the sum of the interior angles of a regular pentagon the same as for an irregular pentagon?

Key point

In an **irregular polygon** sides are not equal lengths and angles are not equal.

Q2b hint

The shape has 5 sides so it is a pentagon.

3 Reasoning **a** For each polygon, work out the size of each exterior angle, and then the sum of the exterior angles.

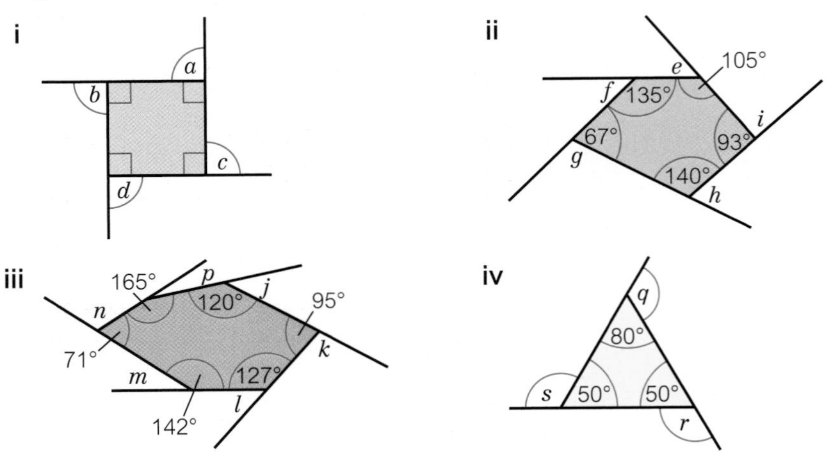

b What do you notice about the sum of the exterior angles for each shape?

c Copy and complete:

The sum of the exterior angles of a polygon is ☐°.

Discussion Is the sum of the exterior angles of a regular polygon the same as for an irregular polygon?

4 Reasoning **a** Work out the missing exterior angles for each of these polygons.

i

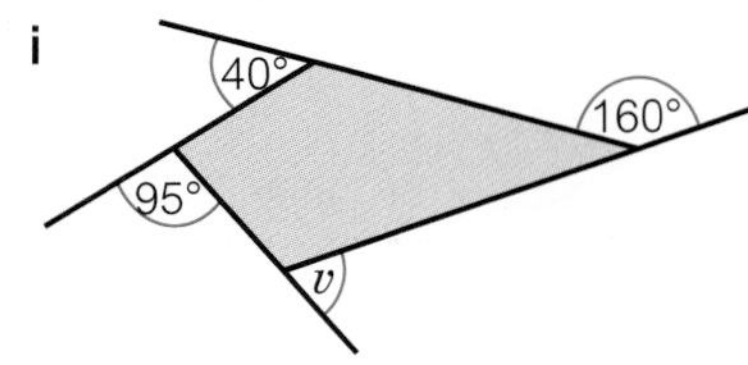

ii

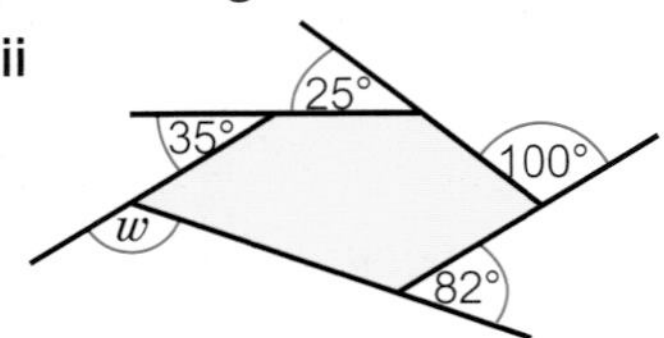

iii

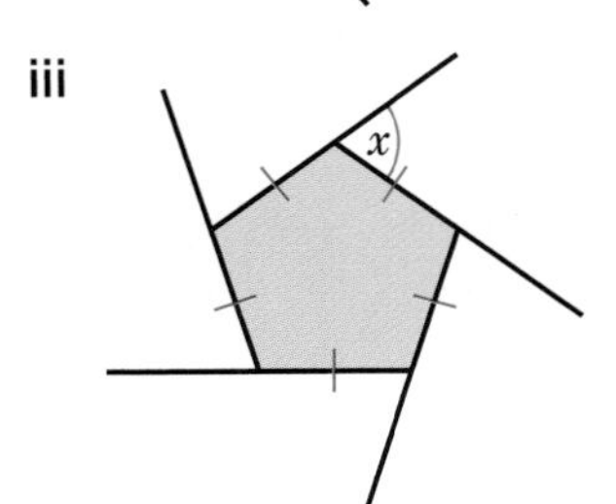

iv

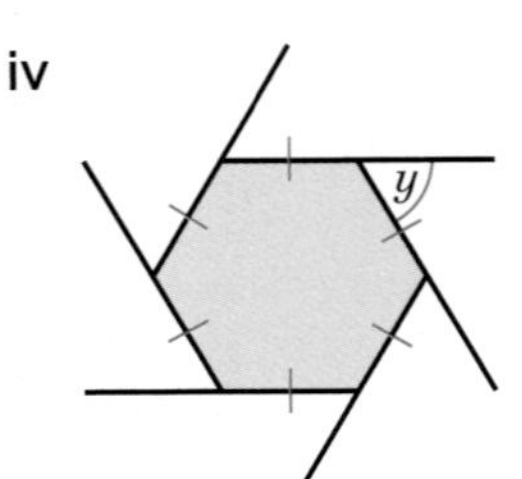

Q4a iii hint

In a regular polygon, all the interior angles are the same size.
What does this tell you about the exterior angles?

b Use your answer to part **a** to describe in words how to work out the exterior angle of a regular polygon. Remember that the exterior angles are all the same size. Also, there are the same number of exterior angles as there are sides.

c Write a formula to work out the exterior angle of a regular polygon with n sides.

d Write a formula to work out the interior angle of a regular polygon when you know the exterior angle.

Topic links: Writing and using formulae

Subject links: Computing (Q7)

Worked example

Work out the sizes of the exterior and interior angles of a regular nonagon.

Exterior angle $= \frac{360°}{9} = 40°$ — Sum of exterior angles = 360°
There are 5 equal angles.

Interior angle $= 180° - 40° = 140°$

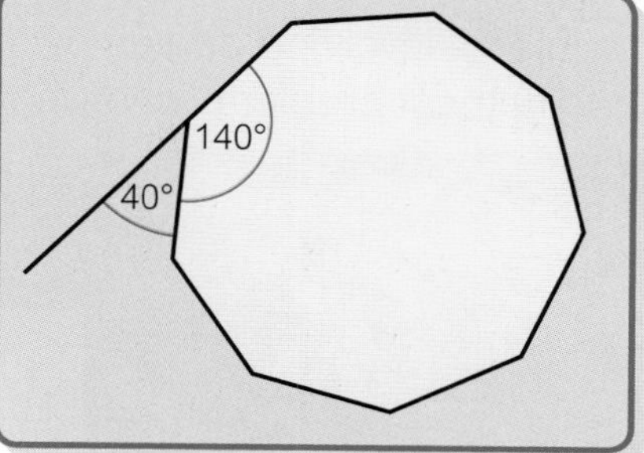

5 For each regular polygon, work out

i the exterior angle **ii** the interior angle.

a equilateral triangle

b decagon (10-sided polygon)

c regular 16-sided polygon

Q5 Strategy hint
Sketch the shape and an exterior angle.

6 A children's roundabout is in the shape of an octagon.
Work out the sizes of angles a, b and c.

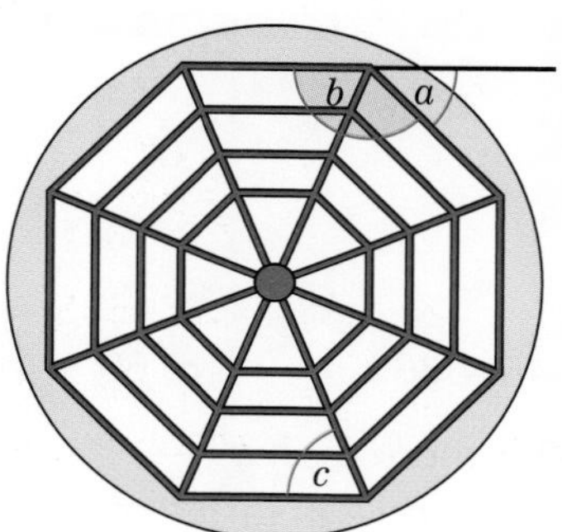

Q6 hint
Angle c is half the size of angle b.

7 **Real / STEM** A computer programmer writes a program to create a 12-sided regular polygon. Each side of the polygon is 50 mm.
After each length of 50 mm the programmer gives the angle through which the pointer must turn anticlockwise to start the next side.
The diagram shows the first three sides.

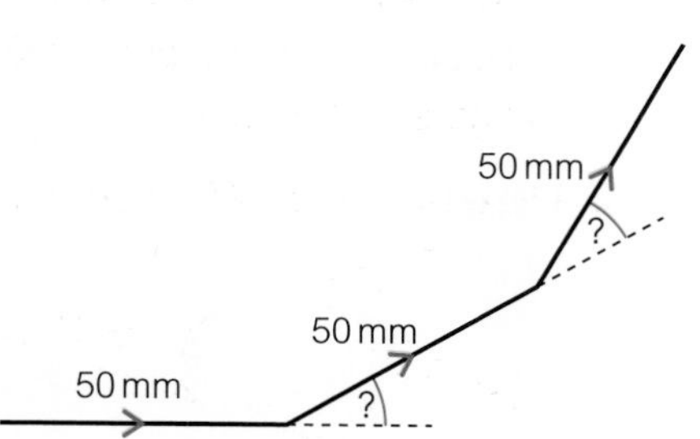

a What is the angle that the pointer needs to turn through?

b What angle would the pointer need to turn through to create a regular nonagon (9 sides)?

8 **Problem-solving / Reasoning** A regular polygon has an exterior angle of 24°. How many sides does the polygon have?
Explain how you worked out your answer.

Q8 Strategy hint
360° ÷ □ = 24°

9 **Explore** What different shapes can you use to tile walls?
Is it easier to explore this question now you have completed the lesson?
What further information do you need to be able to answer this?

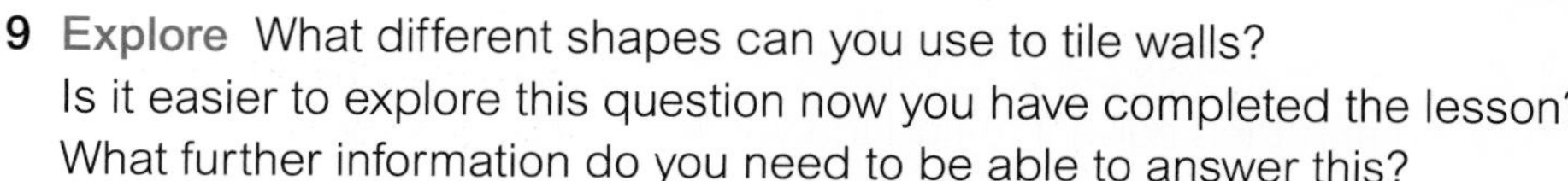

10 **Reflect** Write down the steps for finding the sum of the interior angles of any polygon. You might begin with, 'Step 1: count the number of sides'. Do your steps work to find the interior angles of one of the regular polygons in Q5?
If not, rewrite your steps for any regular polygon.
Now write down the steps to find the exterior angle of any regular polygon.

Q10 hint
Use your answers to Q5 to help you.

Explore

Reflect

7.5 Solving geometric problems

You will learn to:
- Solve problems involving angles by setting up equations
- Solve geometrical problems showing reasoning.

CONFIDENCE

Why learn this?
Engineers use the properties of shapes to help them solve problems, for example the result of different forces acting on an object.

Fluency

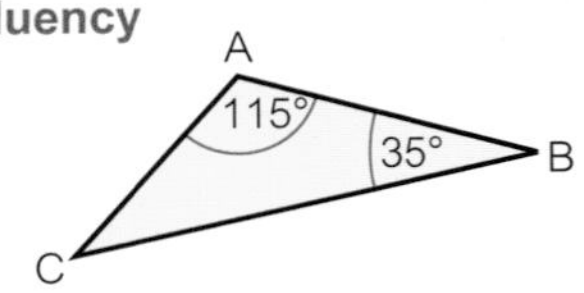

What is
- ∠CAB
- ∠ABC
- ∠ACB

Explore
Four squares will fit around a point. How many other different types of quadrilaterals will fit around a point?

Exercise 7.5

Warm up

1 Solve these equations.
a $5x + 30 = 180$ **b** $8x - 40 = 360$ **c** $60 + 4x = 90$

2 An angle is y. Another angle is 30° more than y.
a Write an expression for the larger angle in terms of y.
b Write an expression for the total of the two angles. Simplify your expression.

Worked example

Work out the value of x in this diagram.

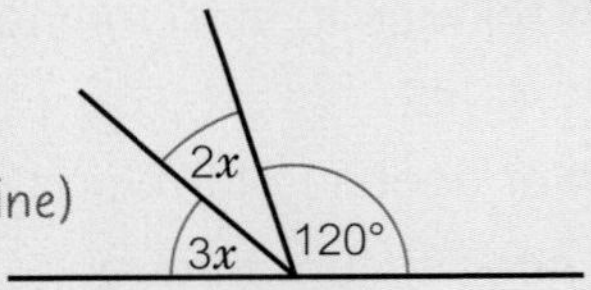

$3x + 2x + 120 = 180°$ (angles on a straight line)
$5x + 120 = 180$
$5x = 180 - 120$
$5x = 60$
$x = \frac{60}{5} = 12°$

Give a reason.

Simplify by collecting like terms.

Check: $3x = 3 \times 12 = 36°$, $2x = 2 \times 12 = 24°$, $36 + 24 + 120 = 180°$ ✓

Key point
You can solve a problem by setting up an equation and solving it. The phrase 'in terms of' tells you which letter to use.

3 For each diagram, write an equation and then solve it to find the value of x. Check that your answers are correct.

a

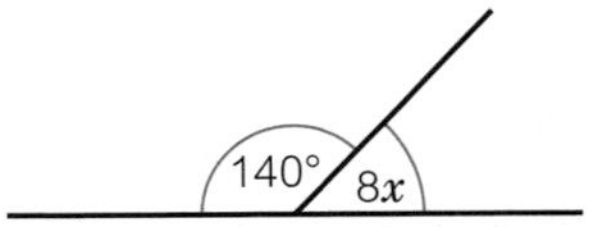

b

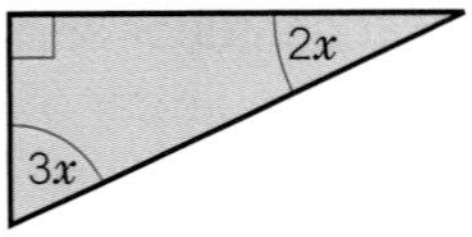

c

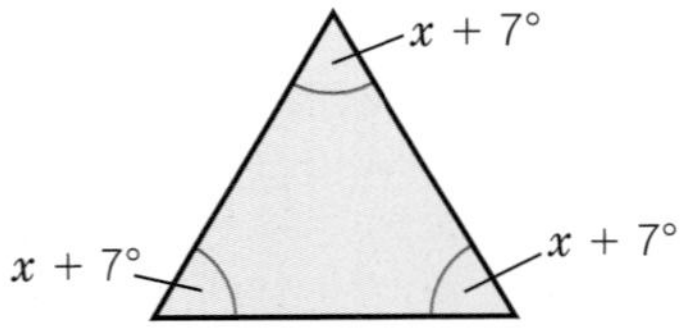

Discussion Is there more than one equation that you can write for part **c**?

Topic links: Solving equations, Ratio

4 The diagram shows a quadrilateral.
   a Write an equation in terms of x for the sum of the angles.
   b Solve your equation to find the value of x.
   c Write down the sizes of the four angles in the quadrilateral.

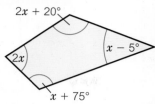

> **Q4 hint**
> Simplify your equation by collecting like terms.

5 **Problem-solving** In triangle ABC, ∠ABC is twice the size of ∠BAC and ∠BCA is three times the size of ∠BAC.
Work out the sizes of the three angles in the triangle.

> **Q5 Strategy hint**
> Sketch a diagram of triangle ABC. Label ∠BAC as x then write an expression for each of the other angles in terms of x. Write an equation and then solve it.

6 **Problem-solving** In the isosceles trapezium ABCD, ∠DAB is three times the size of ∠ADC.
Work out the sizes of the angles in the trapezium.

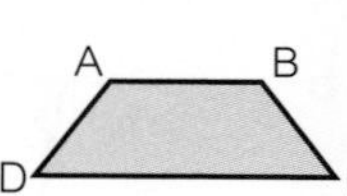

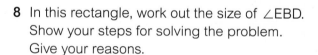

> **Q6 Strategy hint**
> Let ∠ADC = x.

7 The diagram shows a kite.
Copy and complete the steps in the working and reasoning, to find the size of angle y.

∠ADC = ☐ (symmetry of kite)

112 + ☐ + ☐ + ∠BAD = 360°
(angles in a quadrilateral)

∠BAD = ☐

∠ABX = ∠ADX = y (ABD is isosceles triangle)

$y + y +$ ☐ = 180° (angles in a triangle)

$y =$ ☐

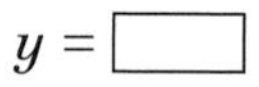

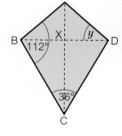

8 In this rectangle, work out the size of ∠EBD.
Show your steps for solving the problem.
Give your reasons.

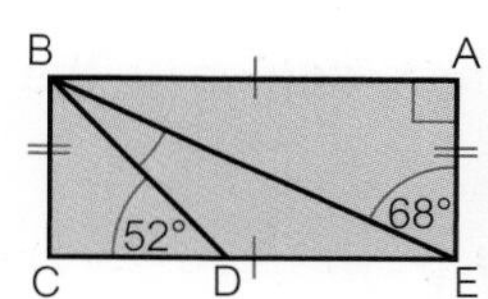

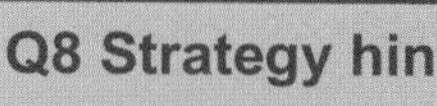

> **Q8 Strategy hint**
> Sketch the diagram. Label the angles as you work them out.

9 Work out the sizes of angles a, b, c and d.
Give your reasons.

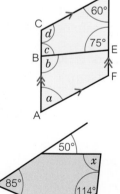

10 **Problem-solving** The diagram shows an irregular pentagon.
Angles x and y are in the ratio 3 : 2.
Work out the sizes of angles x and y.
Explain your reasoning.

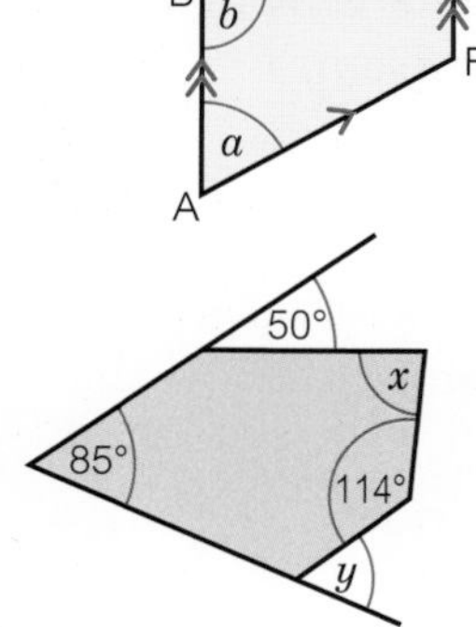

> **Q10 Strategy hint**
> Work out the sum of the interior angles of a pentagon first.

11 **Explore** Four squares will fit around a point.
How many other different types of quadrilaterals will fit around a point?
Is it easier to explore this question now you have completed the lesson?
What further information do you need to be able to answer this?

12 **Reflect** Q5 had a hint to sketch a diagram.
Did you sketch the diagram? Did it help you? Explain.
Did the diagrams in the other questions help?

Explore

Reflect

7 Check up

Log how you did on your Student Progression Chart.

Solving geometrical problems

1 Work out the sizes of the angles marked with letters, stating any angle facts that you use.

a

b

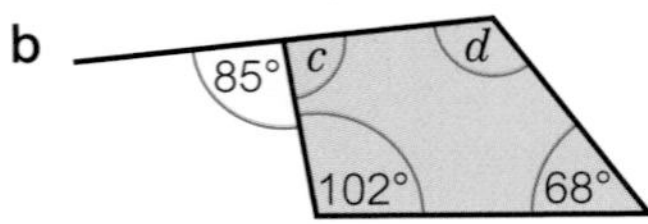

c

d

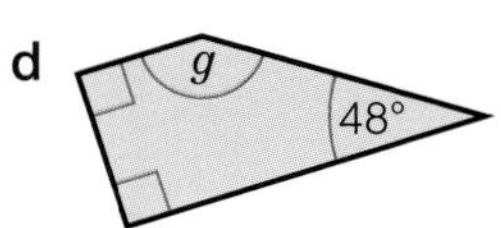

e

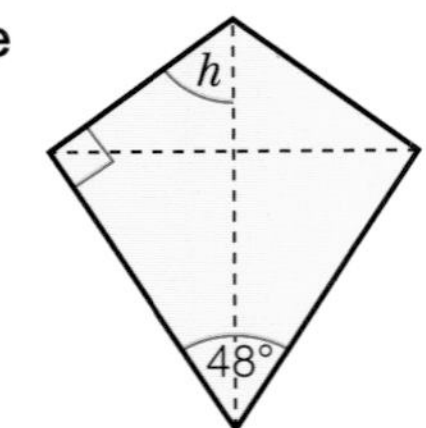

2 The diagram shows a straight line.

a Write an equation in terms of x.

b Solve your equation to find the value of x.

c Write down the sizes of the three angles on the straight line.

3 The diagram shows a triangle.

a Write an equation in terms of x.

b Solve your equation to find the value of x.

c Write down the sizes of the three angles in the triangle in order of size, starting with the smallest.

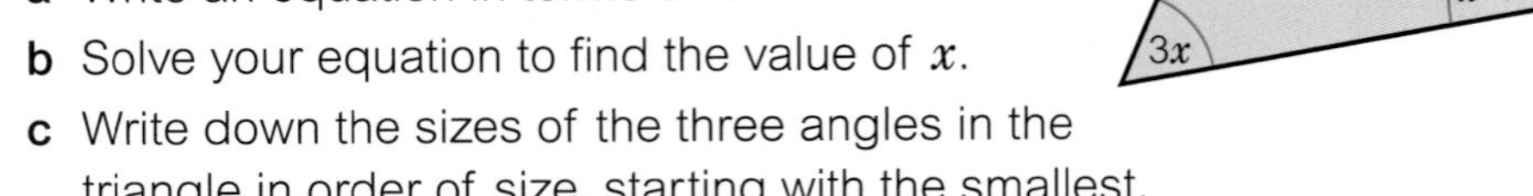

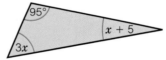

4 In this rectangle, calculate the size of ∠BCE.
Show your steps for solving the problem.
Give your reasons.

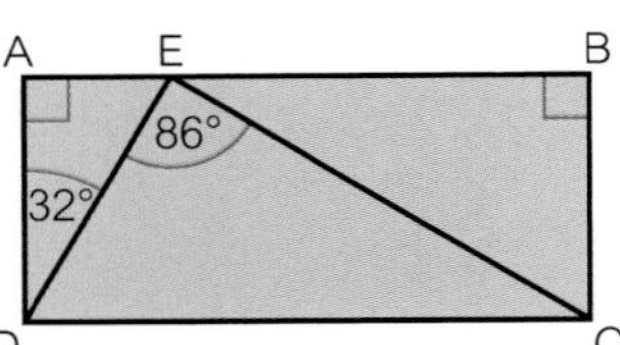

5 The diagram shows a trapezium and an isosceles triangle.
Work out the sizes of angles a, b and c.
Give your reasons.

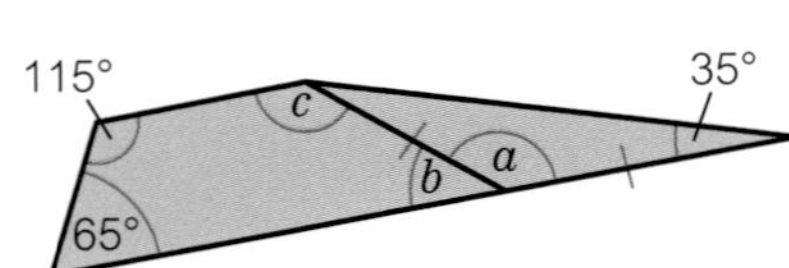

Parallel lines

6 Work out the size of angle x in each diagram. Give your reasons.

a

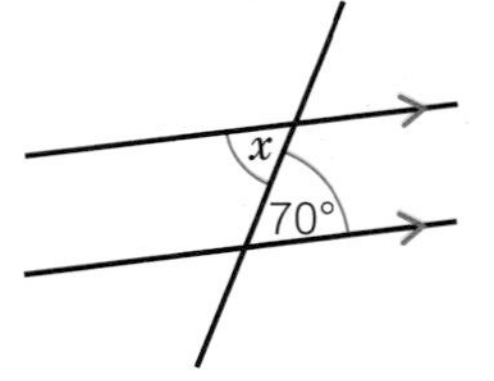

b

c

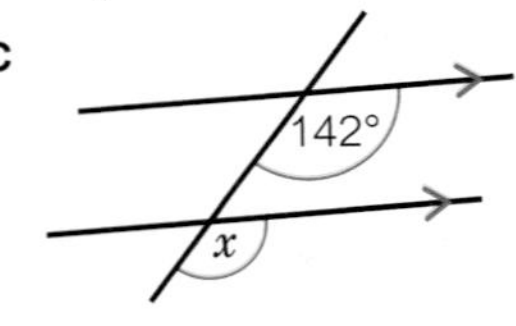

d

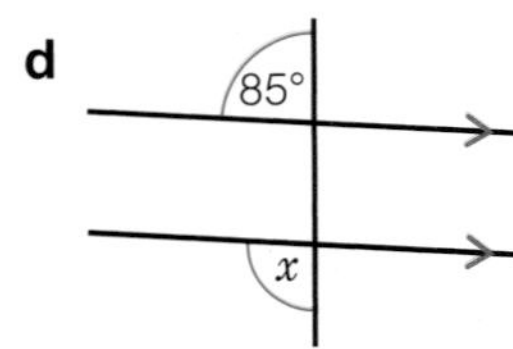

7 Work out the sizes of the angles marked with letters in these diagrams.
Give your reasons.

a

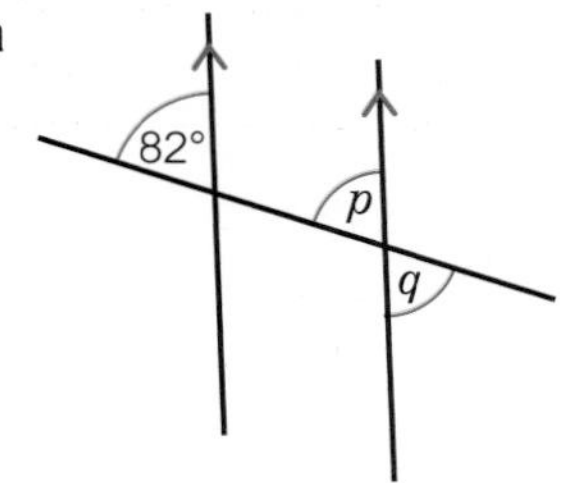

b

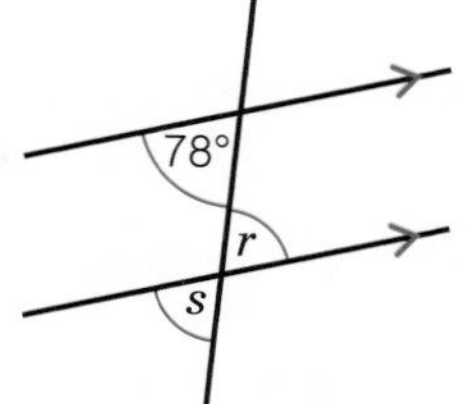

c

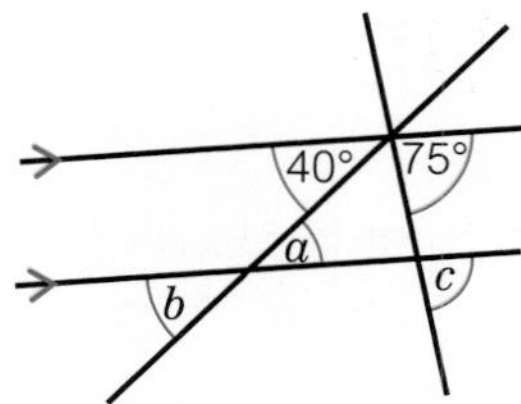

d

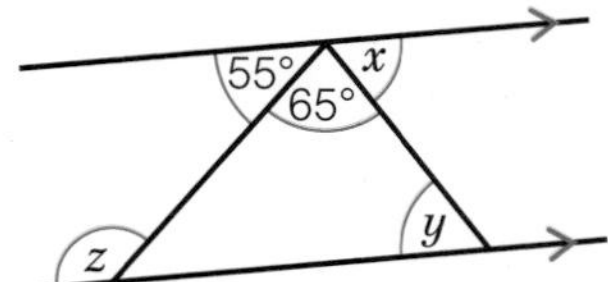

e

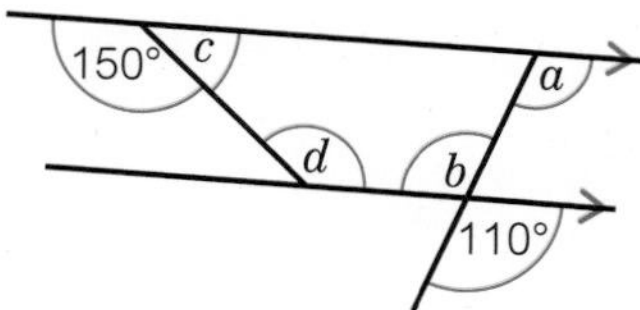

Interior and exterior angles

8 Work out the sum of the interior angles of a pentagon.
You can use this diagram to help.

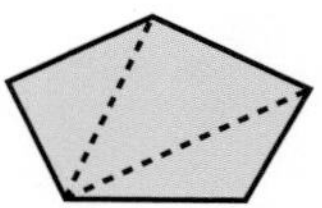

9 The diagram shows an irregular hexagon.

a What is the sum of the interior angles of a hexagon?

b Work out the size of angle z.

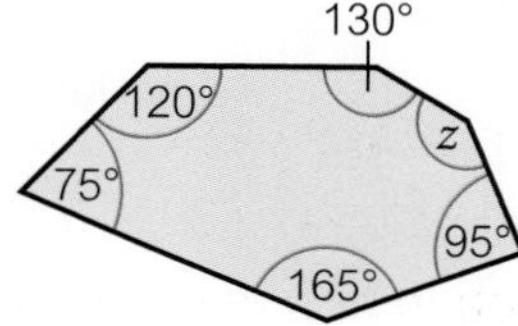

10 The diagram shows a regular hexagon.
Work out the sizes of angles x and y.

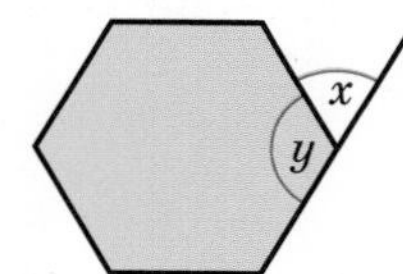

11 How sure are you of your answers? Were you mostly

☹ Just guessing 😐 Feeling doubtful ☺ Confident

What next? Use your results to decide whether to strengthen or extend your learning.

Reflect

Challenge

12 Here are some angle cards.

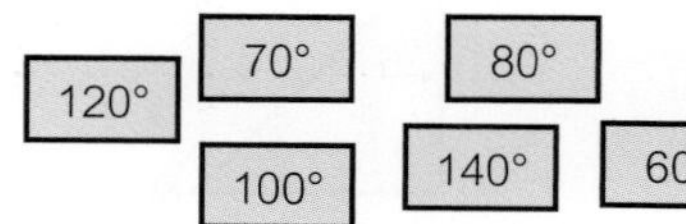

a Make three copies of this diagram.

b Use the angles on the cards to complete the diagram in three different ways. You can use the same card more than once on each diagram.

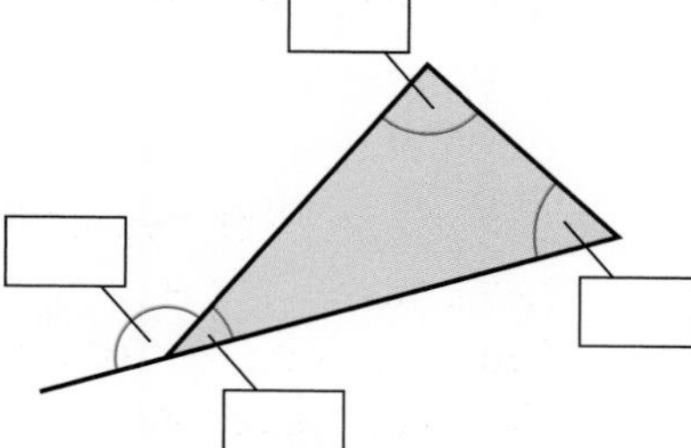

13 The diagram shows two sets of parallel lines.
Write down

a two pairs of alternate angles

b two pairs of corresponding angles

c two pairs of angles that sum to 180°

d two sets of three angles that sum to 180°

e two sets of four angles that sum to 360°

f two sets of six angles that sum to 360°.

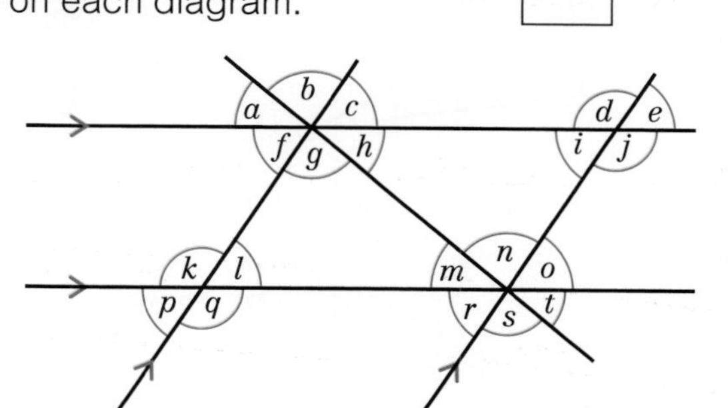

7 Strengthen

You will:

- Strengthen your understanding with practice.

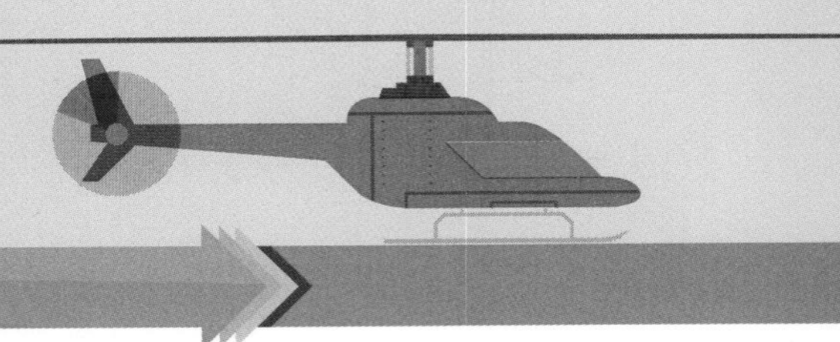

Solving geometrical problems

1 a Copy and complete this statement.

The sum of the angles in any quadrilateral is $\square$°.

b Work out the sizes of the angles marked with letters in these quadrilaterals.

i trapezium

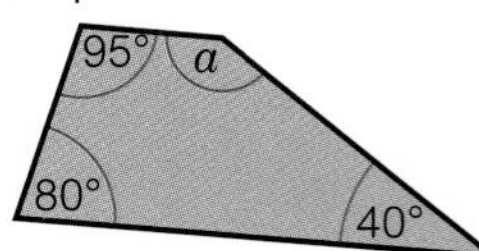

ii parallelogram

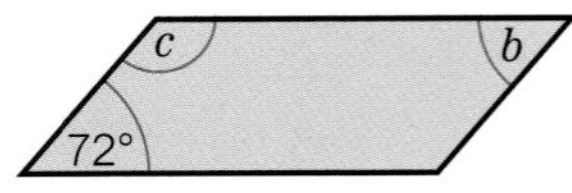

iii rhombus

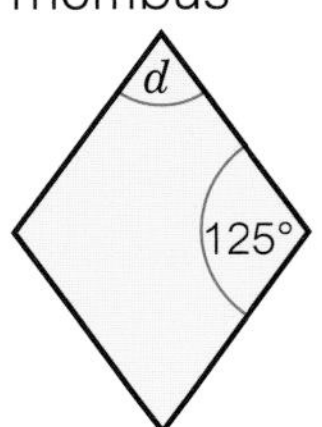

iv kite

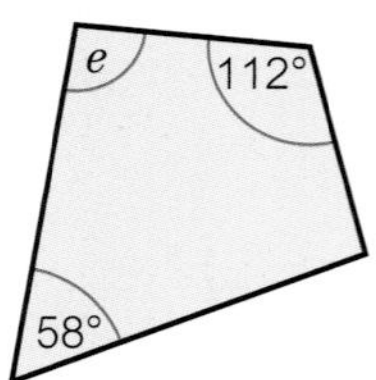

Q1b Strategy hint

1 Look for symmetry.
2 Look for equal angles.

2 The diagram shows triangle ABC.
Work out the size of angle q.

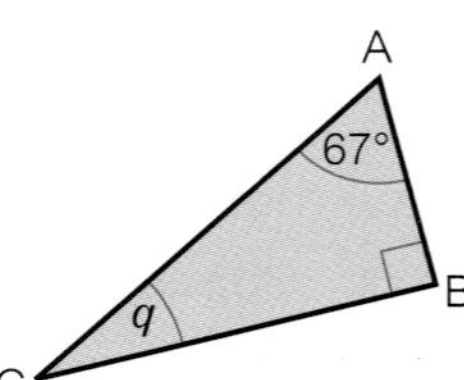

Q2 Strategy hint

Copy the diagram. Work out any angles that you can and then mark them on your diagram.

3 The diagram shows triangle LMN.

a Which two sides are equal?
b What does this tell you about the angles?
c What type of triangle is LMN?
d Work out the size of angle p.

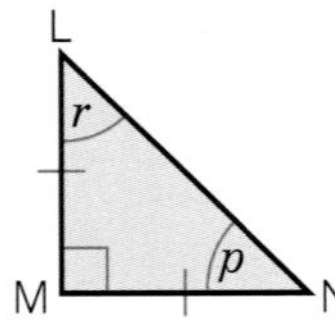
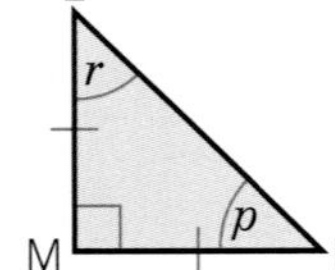

Q3d hint

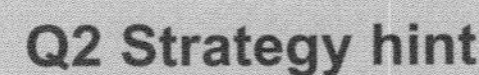

180 – $\square$ = $\square$
$\square$ ÷ 2 = $\square$°

4 Work out the size of angle z in each diagram.

a

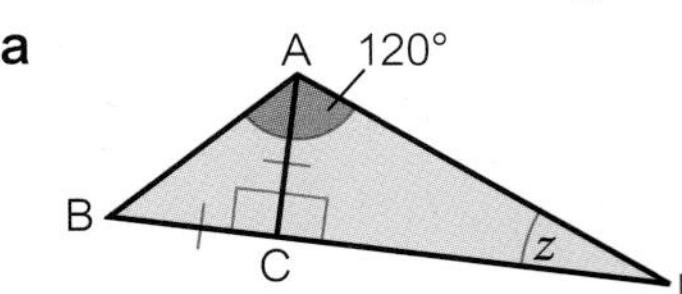

b

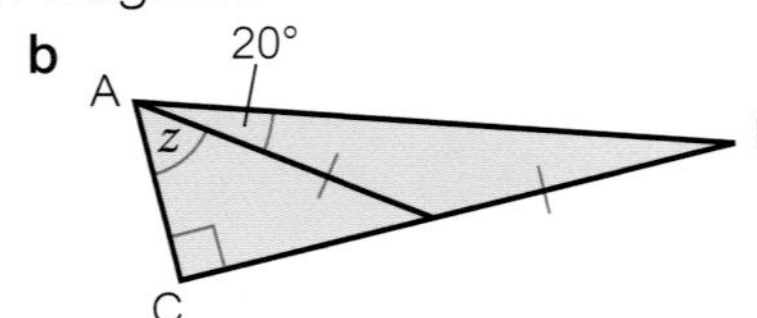

Q4b Strategy hint

Look at the angles you know. How can you use them to work out the other angles?

Q5a hint

Work out angle a first.

5 Work out the sizes of the angles marked with letters, stating any angle facts that you use.

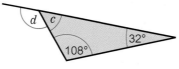

a

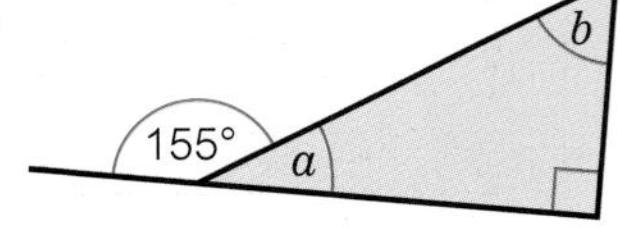

b

d c 108° 32°

c

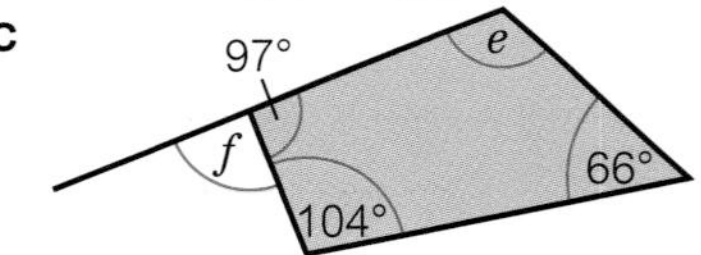

6 Work out the value of x in each of these diagrams.

a

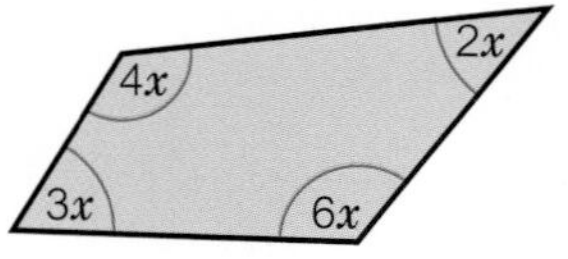

b

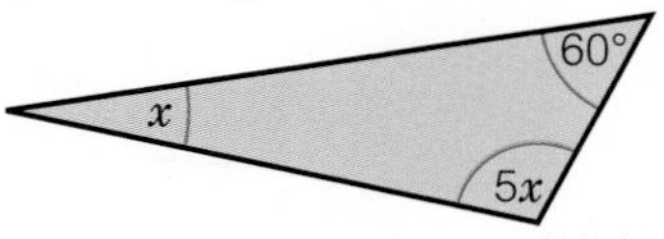

Q6b hint

$x + 5x + 60 = \square$

7 The diagram shows some angles on a straight line.

a Write an equation in terms of x.

b Simplify your equation by collecting like terms.

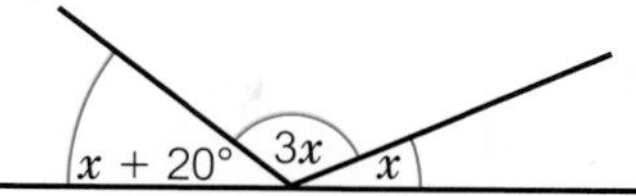

c Solve your equation to find the value of x.

d Write down the sizes of the three angles on the straight line in order of size. Start with the smallest.

Q7a hint

$x + 20 + \square + \square = \square$

8 The diagram shows a quadrilateral.

a Write an equation in terms of x.

b Simplify your equation by collecting like terms.

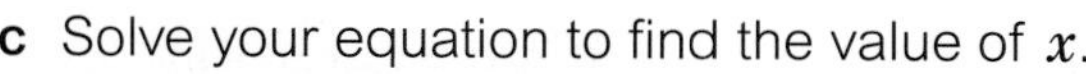

c Solve your equation to find the value of x.

d Write down the sizes of the four angles in the quadrilateral.

Q8a hint

$2x + x - 10 + \square + \square + \square = 360$

9 The diagram shows a parallelogram and an isosceles triangle.

a What is the size of angle a?

b Work out the size of angle b.

c What is the size of angle c?

d Work out the size of angle d.

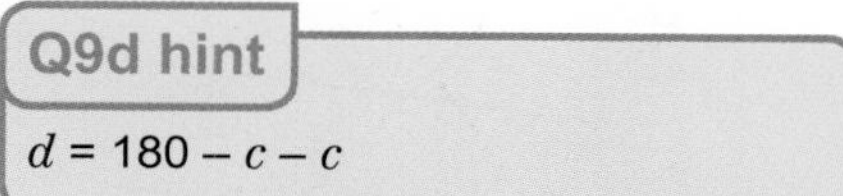

Q9d hint

$d = 180 - c - c$

10 The diagram shows a right-angled triangle and a rhombus.

a Work out the size of angle x.

b Work out the size of angle y.

c Work out the size of angle z.

11 In this rectangle, work out the size of angle CED. Show your steps for solving this problem and explain your reasoning.

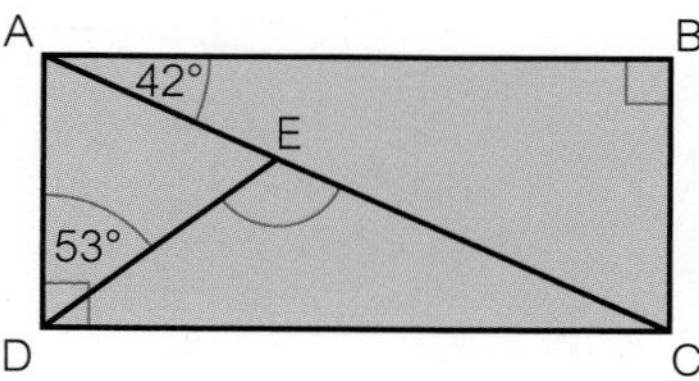

Q11 Strategy hint

Copy the diagram. Work out any angles you can and mark them on the diagram.

Parallel lines

1 The diagram shows a set of parallel lines.

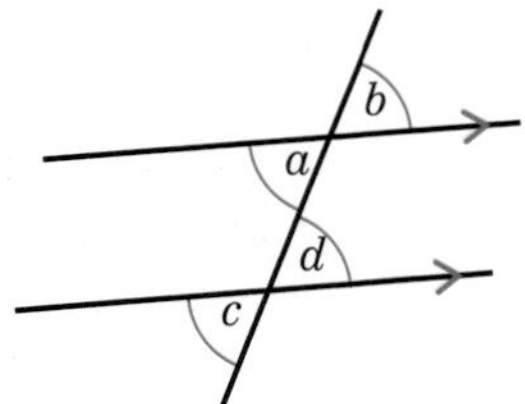

Copy and complete these statements using words from the box.

a a and b are ______________ angles.

b a and d are ______________ angles.

c a and c are ______________ angles.

d b and d are ______________ angles.

e c and d are ______________ angles.

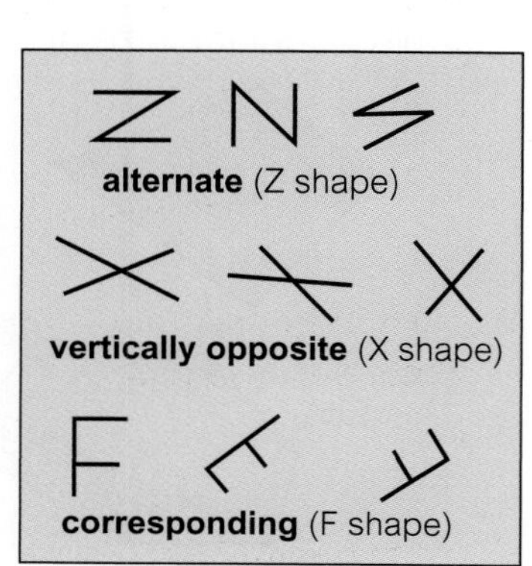

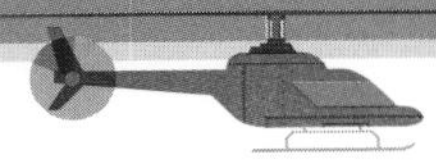

2 Write down the size of angle x in each of these diagrams.
Give a reason for each answer.

a

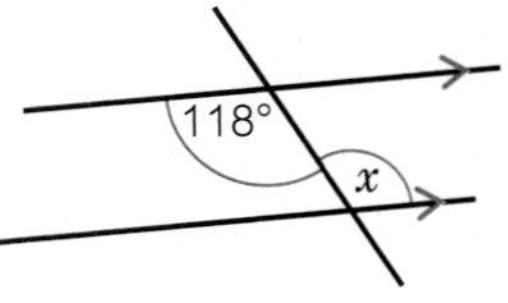

b

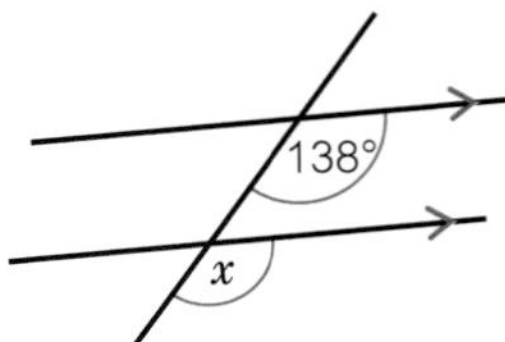

c

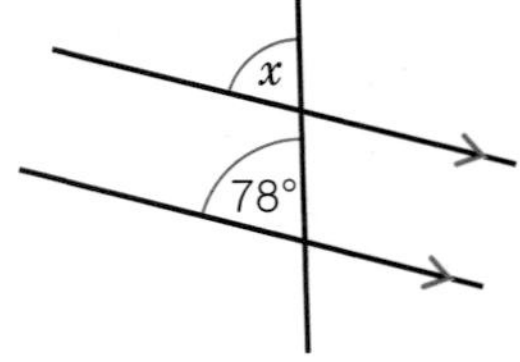

d

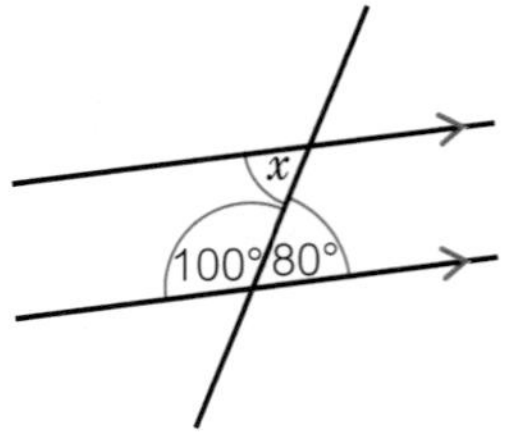

3 Write down the sizes of angles c and d in each of these diagrams.
Give a reason for each answer.

a

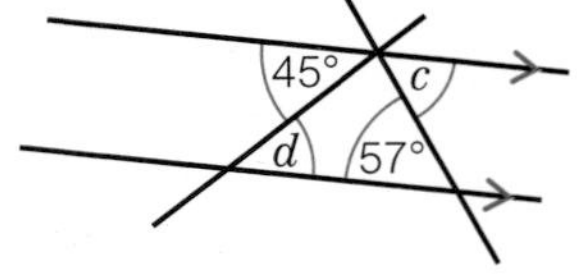

b

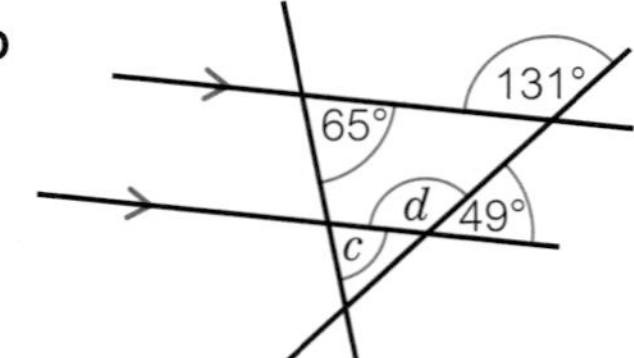

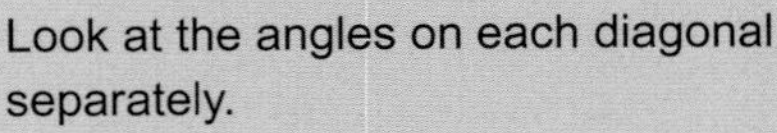

Q3a Strategy hint

Look at the angles on each diagonal separately.

c

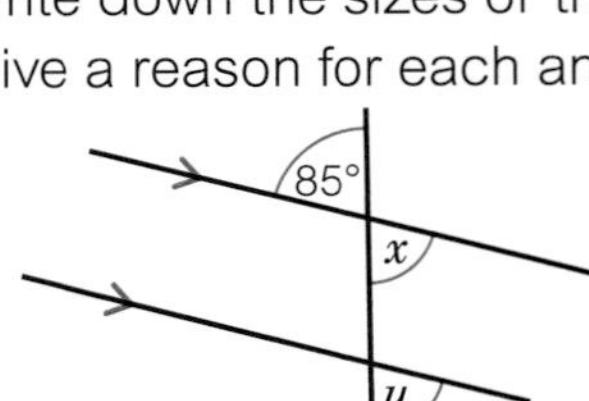

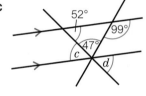

4 Write down the sizes of the angles marked with letters in each of these diagrams.
Give a reason for each answer.

a

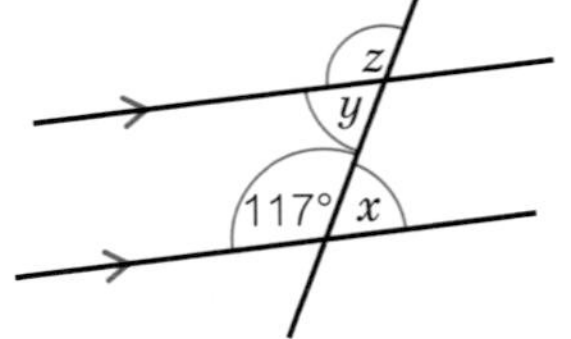

b

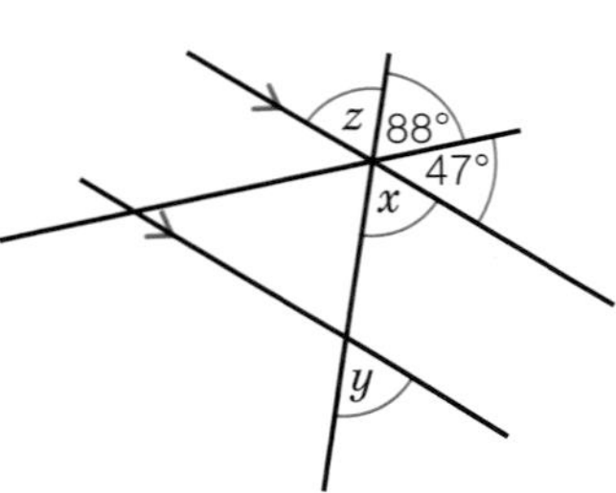

c

z 88° 47° x y

Interior and exterior angles

1 **i** Sketch each shape.
ii Divide each shape into triangles using diagonals from the same vertex.
iii Work out what the angles in each shape add up to.
iv Work out the size of angle x.

a

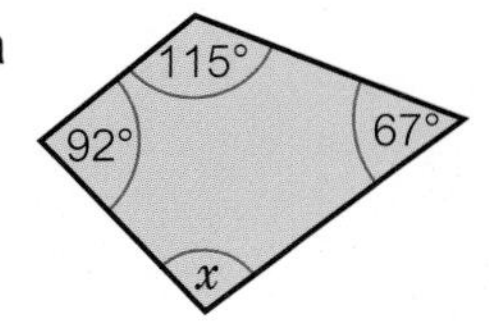

b

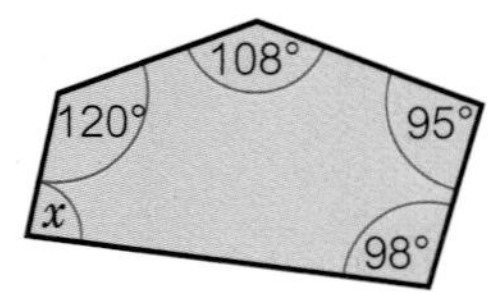

c

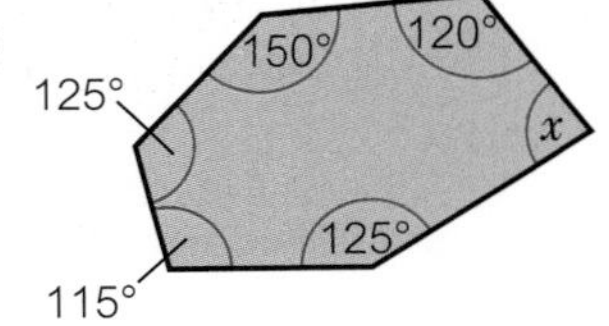

Q1a hint

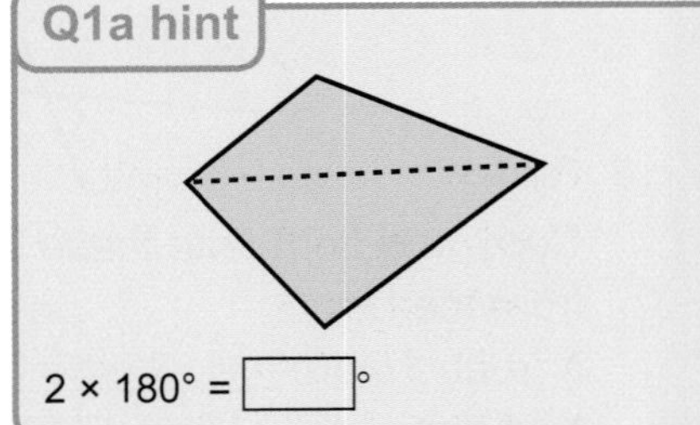

2 × 180° = ☐°

2 The diagram shows an irregular hexagon. Work out the size of angle x.

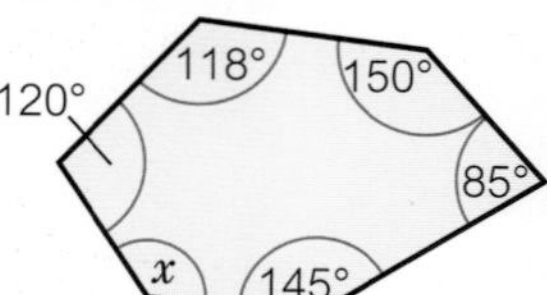

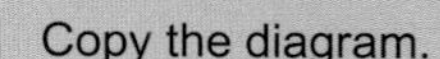

Q2 Strategy hint

1. Copy the diagram.
2. Divide the shape into triangles.
3. Work out what the angles add up to.
4. Find the missing angle.

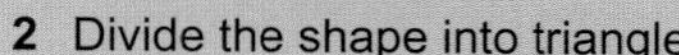

3 The diagram shows a regular pentagon.

a What do you know about the angles in a regular polygon?

b Work out the size of the exterior angle x.

c Work out the size of the interior angle y.

Q3b hint

Use the formula:
exterior angle of regular polygon $= \dfrac{360°}{\text{number of sides}}$

Q3c hint

The exterior angle and the interior angle lie on a straight line.

4 The diagram shows a regular hexagon. Work out the sizes of angles a and b.

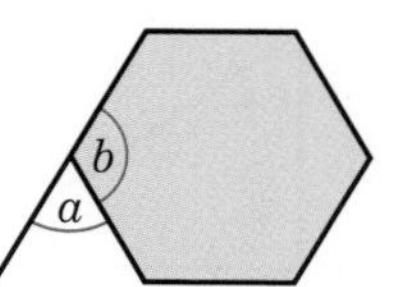

Q4 hint

a is the exterior angle and b is the interior angle.

Enrichment

1 Decide whether each of these statements is *always true*, *sometimes true* or *never true*.

If the statement is *always true* or *sometimes true*, draw a diagram to show it.

If the statement is *never true*, explain why.

For example: 'A trapezium has two right-angles'.
Sometimes true

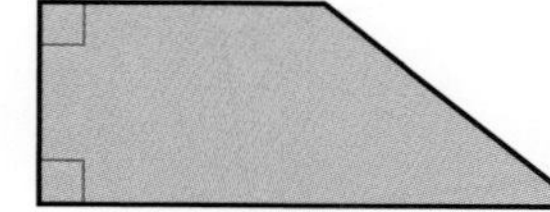

a All the angles in a triangle are less than 90°.

b Two angles in a triangle are each more than 90°.

c All the angles in a quadrilateral are less than 90°.

2 **a** The diagram shows an equilateral triangle inside a square.
Show that $x = 30°$.

b The diagram shows a square inside a regular pentagon.
Work out the size of angle y.

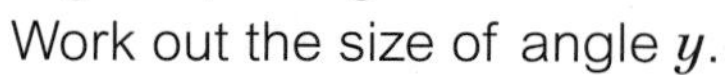

c The diagram shows a regular pentagon inside a regular hexagon.
Work out the size of angle z.

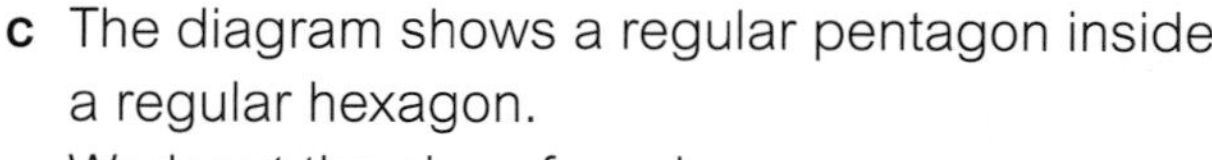

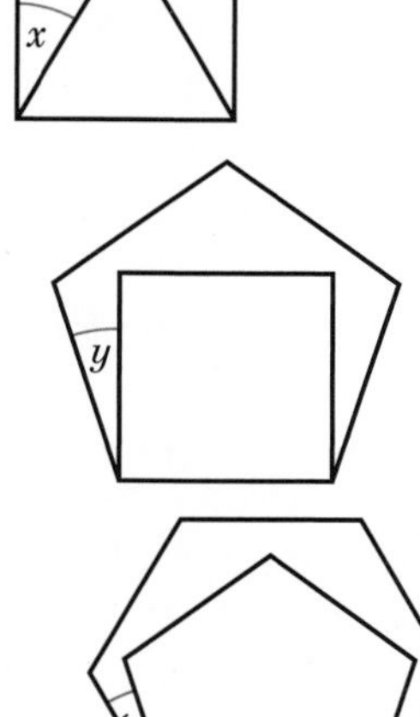

3 **Reflect** These Strengthen lessons cover these topics:

- solving geometrical problems
- parallel lines
- interior and exterior angles.

Which topic did you find easiest? Write one thing about this topic you fully understand and you are sure about.
Which topic did you find hardest? Write one thing about this topic you still do not understand or you are not sure about.

Q3 hint

Show what you have written to a friend or your teacher. Ask them to explain to you the thing you did not understand.

Reflect

7 Extend

You will:

- Extend your understanding with problem-solving.

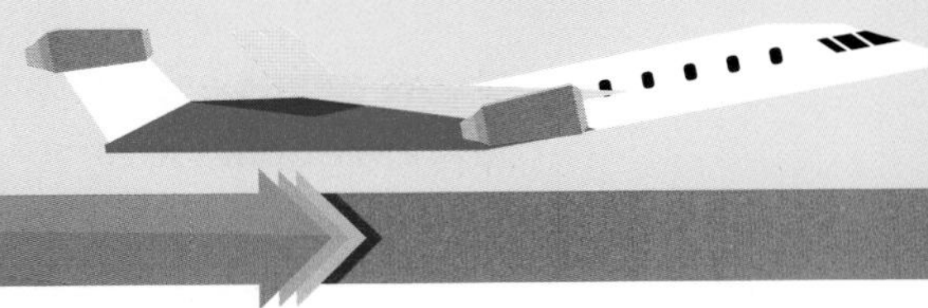

1 The diagram shows triangle ABC.

a Work out the value of x.

b Show how to check your value of x is correct.

c Work out the size of angle y.

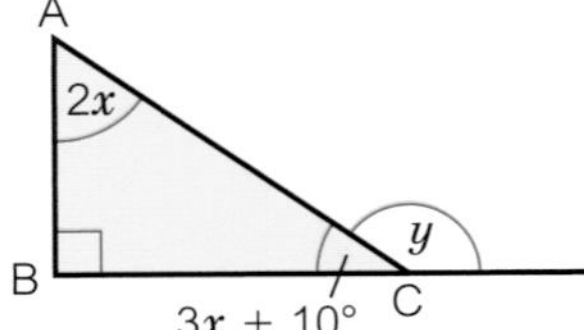

> **Q1b hint**
> Work out the size of ∠BAC and ∠ACB.

2 Problem-solving The diagram shows quadrilateral ABCD.
Work out the size of ∠CDE.

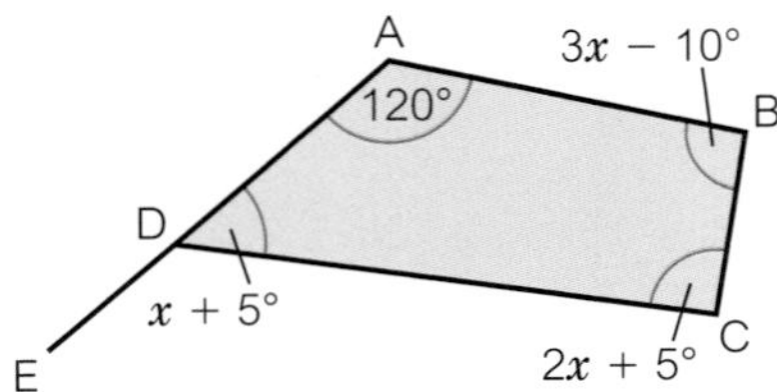

> **Q2 Strategy hint**
> Write an equation in terms of x.
> Solve your equation to find the value of x.

3 Problem-solving In triangle ABC, ∠ABC is 20° more than ∠BAC and ∠BCA is 50° less than ∠BAC.
Work out the size of the smallest angle in the triangle.

> **Q3 Strategy hint**
> Sketch a diagram of triangle ABC. Label ∠BAC as x then write an expression for each of the other angles in terms of x.

4 Real / Problem-solving Irena makes jewellery.
The diagram shows the design of a gold pendant.
It has four gold arms inside a gold oval.
The angles between the arms inside the pendant double each time.
Work out the sizes of the angles between the four arms.

5 STEM The diagram shows a ramp in a multi-storey car park.
For this sort of ramp, angle k must be less than 9.5°.
An engineer measures the angle at the top of the ramp.
It is 189°.

a Work out the size of angle k.

b Is angle k less than 9.5°?

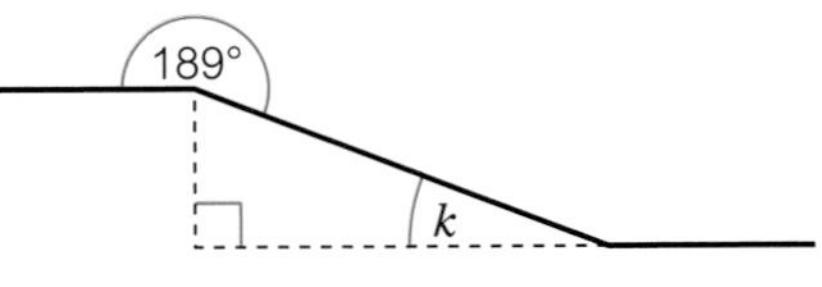

6 Problem-solving The diagram shows a star made from four kites.
Work out the size of angle z.

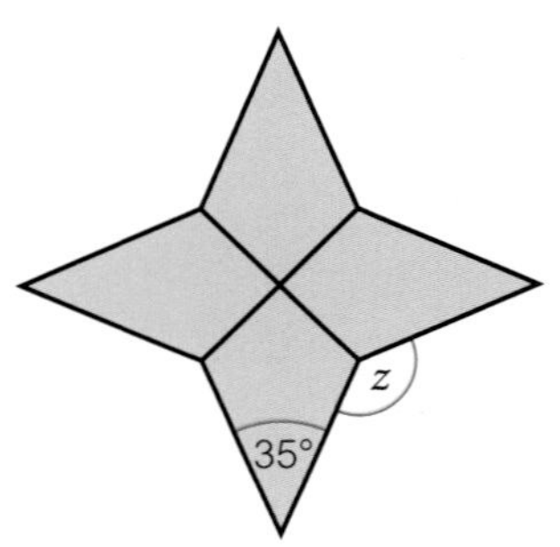

> **Q6 Strategy hint**
>
> 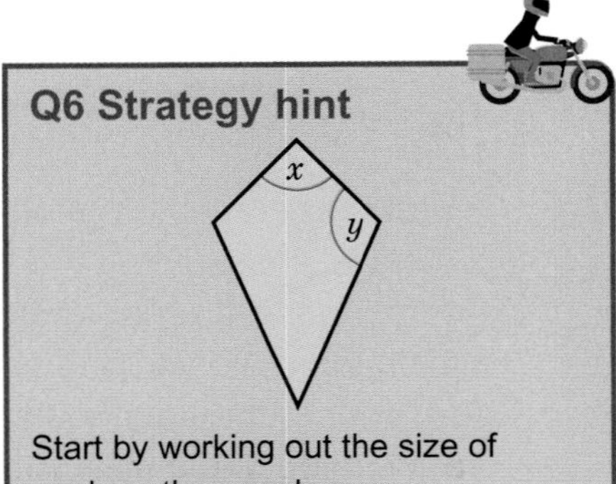
>
>
> Start by working out the size of angle x, then angle y.

Topic links: Solving equations, Ratio, Sequences, Coordinates, Fractions, Using formulae

7 **Real / Problem-solving** Marcin makes metal wall art by overlapping shapes around a point. He starts with one rhombus, then overlaps the next one by dividing the angle at the base in the ratio 2 : 1.

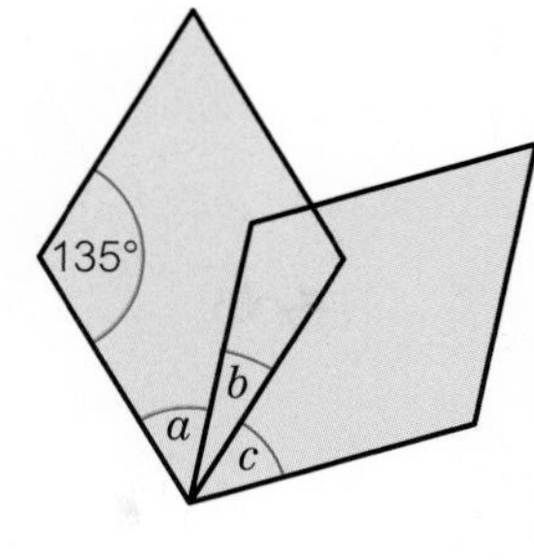

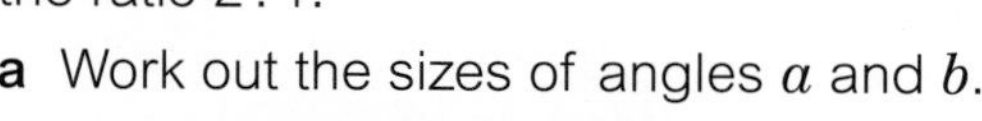

a Work out the sizes of angles a and b.

b Show that angle c is 30°.

Q7b hint

c = small angle in rhombus – angle b

Marcin continues the pattern, overlapping each rhombus by the same amount each time.

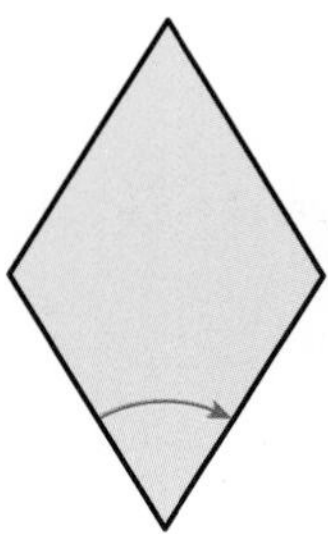 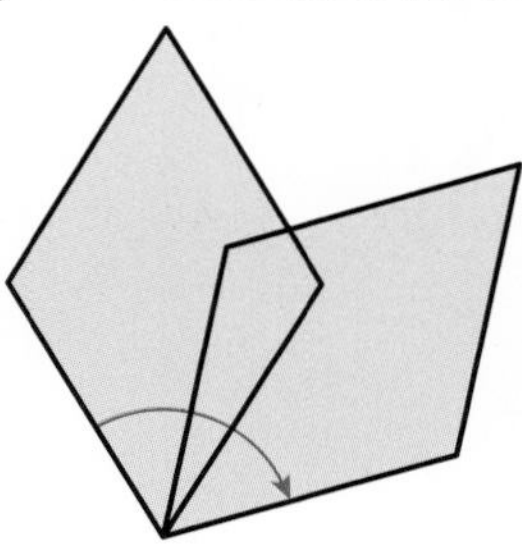 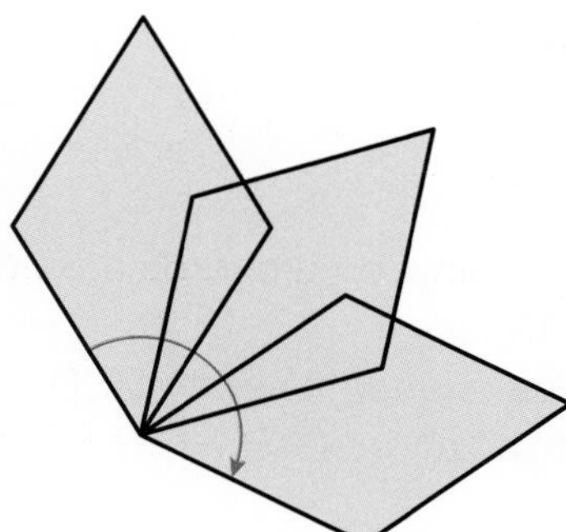

The table shows the total angle used around the centre point each time an extra rhombus is added.

Number of rhombuses	1	2	3	4	5
Total angle	45°	75°			

c Copy and complete the table.

d What is the term-to-term rule for the 'Total angle' sequence of numbers?

e The pattern is complete when the final rhombus overlaps behind the first rhombus.
How many rhombuses will Marcin need to complete the pattern?

8 **a** What is the sum of the angles in a pentagon?
Explain how you worked out your answer.

The diagram shows a pentagon.

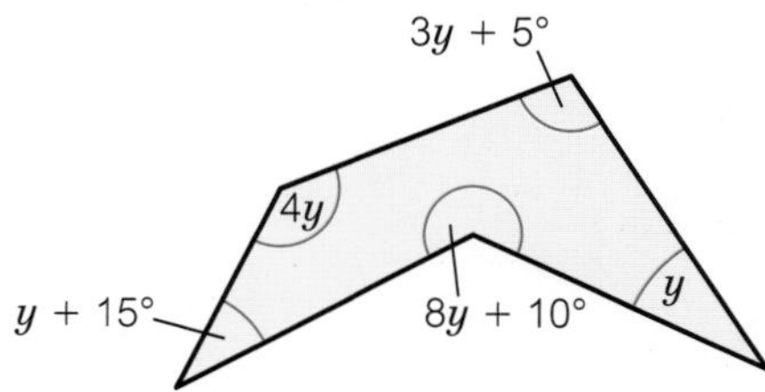

b Work out the value of y.

c Work out the sizes of all the angles in the pentagon.

d Show how to check that your answers to part **c** are correct.

Q8d hint

The sum of the angles in part **c** should equal your answer to part **a**.

9 The diagram shows two regular octagons.

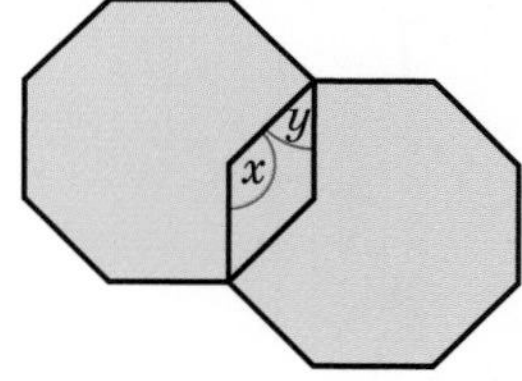

a Work out the size of angle x.

b Work out the size of angle y.

10 **Problem-solving** The diagram shows a regular hexagon overlapping with a regular pentagon.
Work out the size of angle y.

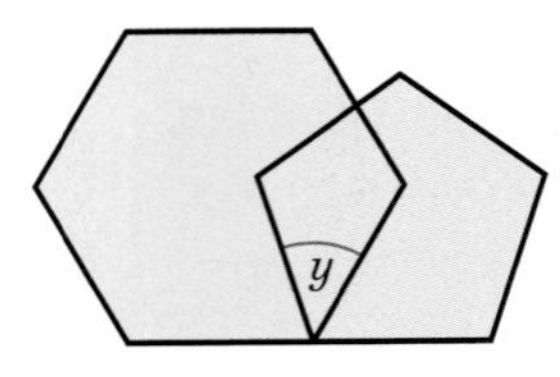

Q10 Strategy hint

Make a copy of the diagram. Start by working out the exterior angles of the polygons and write them on your diagram.

11 **Problem-solving** The diagram shows six congruent trapezia that fit exactly around a point.
Work out the size of angle a. Explain your reasoning.

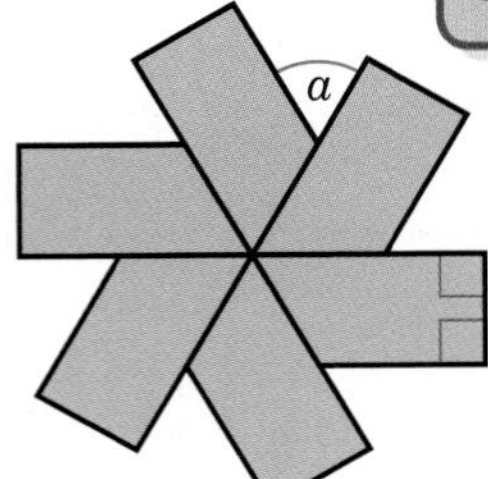

12 **Problem-solving** **a** Plot these points on a coordinate grid:
A(1, 2), B(1, 4), C(3, 6) and D(3, 0).

b Join the points in order to make quadrilateral ABCD.

c Write down the sizes of ∠ADC and ∠DAB.

13 The diagram shows two lines intersecting a pair of parallel lines. Work out the sizes of angles a to g. Give reasons for each.

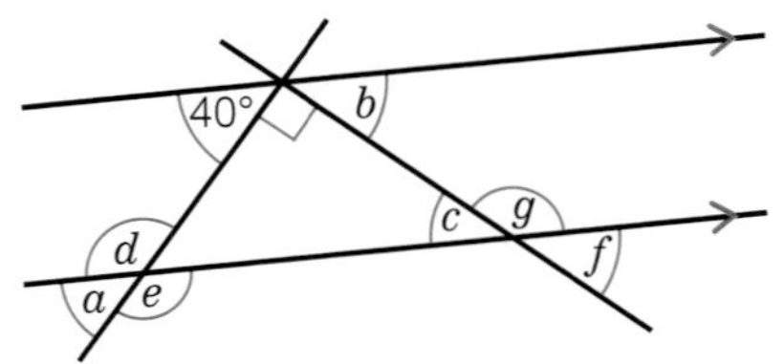

14 Work out the value of x in each diagram.

a

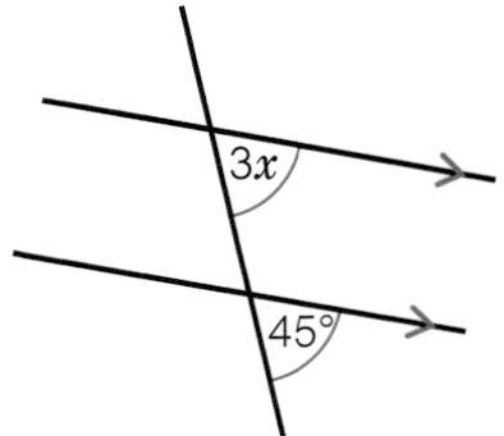

b

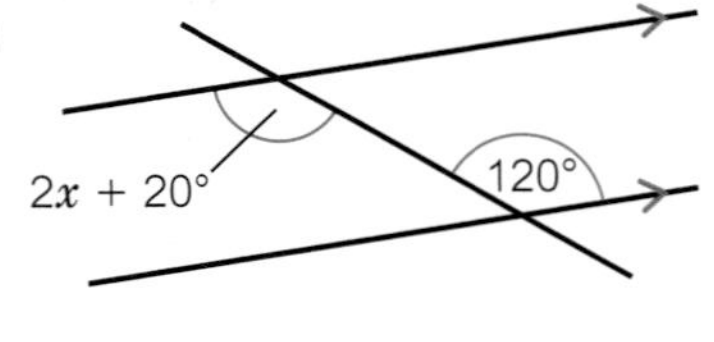

c

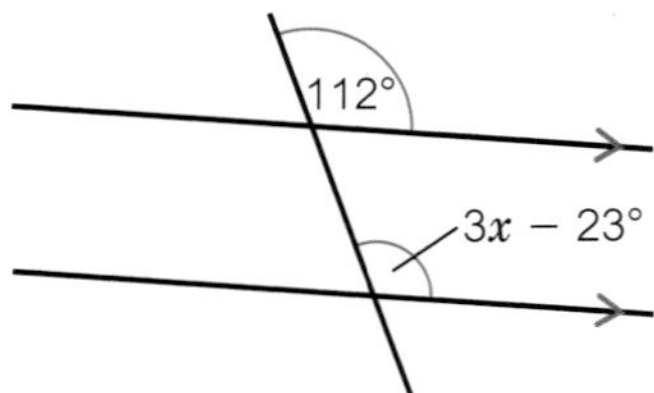

Q14 hint

For each part, write an equation and then solve it.

15 **Problem-solving** In the diagram, $\angle BAC = \frac{1}{4}\angle BAD$.
Work out the size of ∠ACD.
Explain your reasoning.

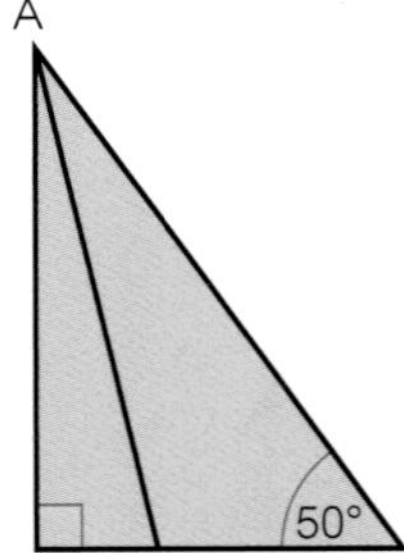

16 **Problem-solving** The diagram shows four congruent kites that fit exactly around a point.
Angle x is double the size of angle y.
Work out the sizes of angles x and y.
Explain your reasoning.

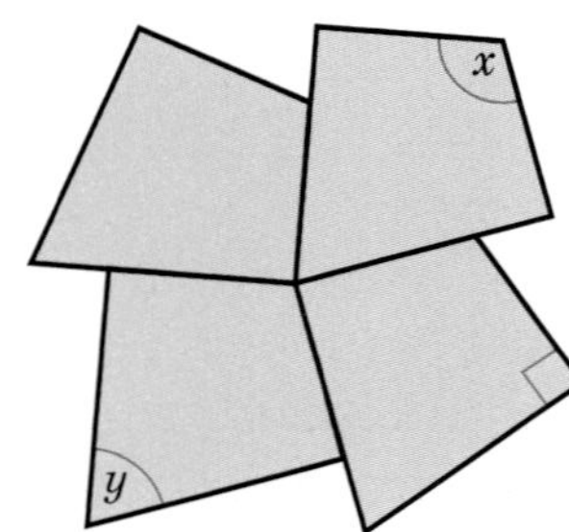

17 STEM / Reasoning The diagram shows a three-stage ramp into a car park.
Recommendations for a three-stage ramp are:

- stages 1 and 3 have an angle of less than 3.6° with the horizontal
- stage 2 has an angle of less than 7.1° with the horizontal.

An engineer measures the angles shown on the diagram.
Does this ramp meet the recommendations? Explain your answer.

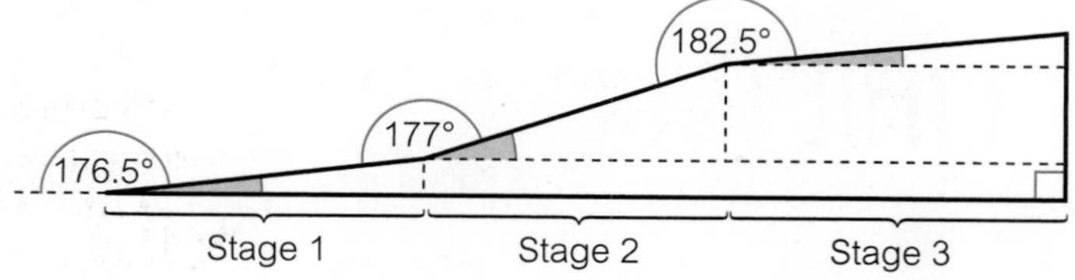

Q17 Strategy hint
Start with stage 1 and work through one stage at a time. Find the angle of each stage with the horizontal (shown in blue) and decide if the ramp meets the recommendations.

18 Problem-solving

a A regular polygon has an exterior angle of 18°.
  i How many sides does the polygon have?
  ii Work out the size of each interior angle.

b A regular polygon has an interior angle of 168°.
  How many sides does the polygon have?

19 Reasoning Callie says it is not possible to draw a polygon that has interior angles that sum to 1500°.
Is she correct. Explain your reasoning.

Investigation — Problem-solving

1 Work out the sizes of the angles marked with letters.

a

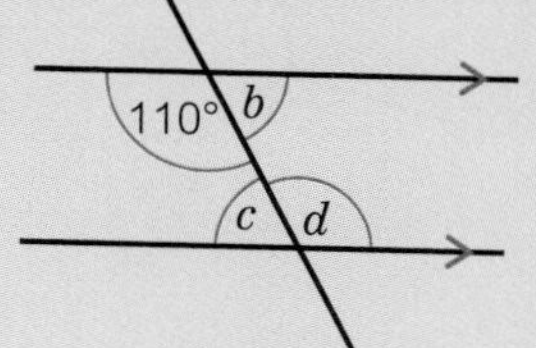

b

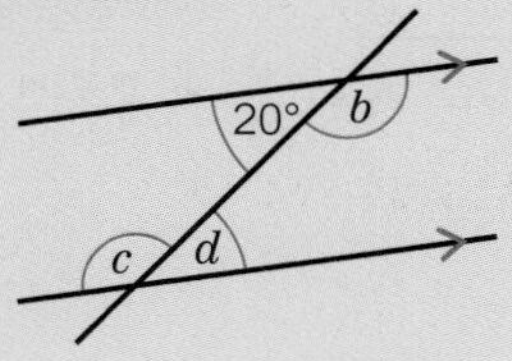

2 a Using your answers to part 1, what can you say about the angles in this diagram?
b Copy and complete: $a + c = \square°$ and $b + d = \square°$.

3 What can you say about the sum of the angles marked x and y in this trapezium?

4 Will the same be true for any quadrilateral that has parallel sides? Explain your answer.

5 Check your answer by drawing diagrams.

20 Reflect Look back at the questions you answered in these Extend lessons.
Find a question that you could not answer straightaway, or that you really had to think about.
While you worked on this question:

- What were you thinking about?
- How did you feel?
- Did you keep trying until you had an answer? Did you give up before reaching an answer, and move on to the next question?
- Did you think you would get the answer correct or incorrect?

Write down any strategies you could use to help you stay calm when answering tricky maths questions. Compare your strategies with other people's.correct

Reflect

7 Unit test

Log how you did on your Student Progression Chart.

1 Work out the size of angle y in each diagram.

a
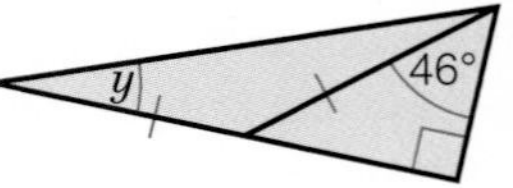

b
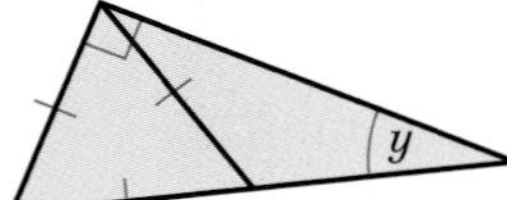

2 Work out the sizes of the angles marked with letters. State any angle facts that you use.

a
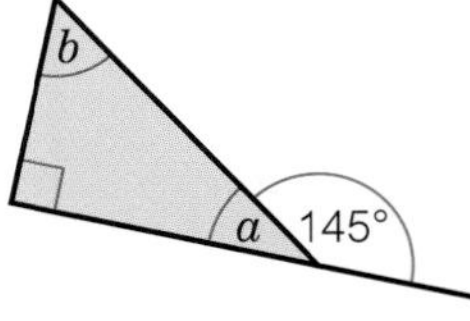

b
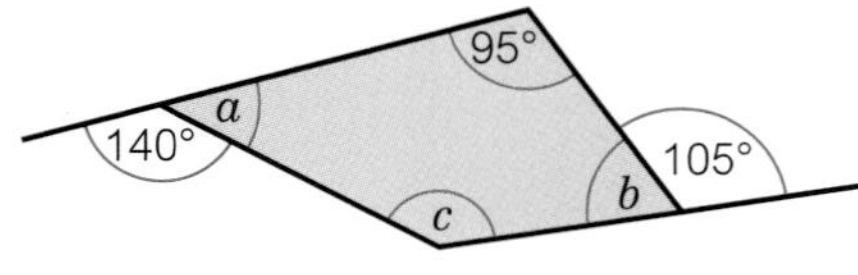

3 Work out the sizes of the angles marked with letters. State any angle facts that you use.

a
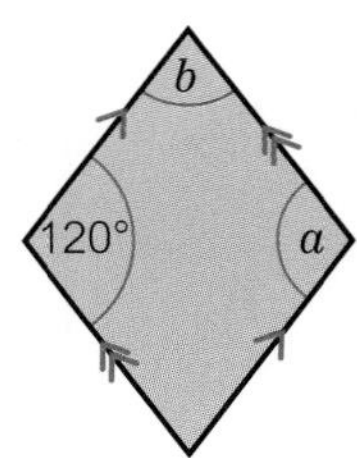

b
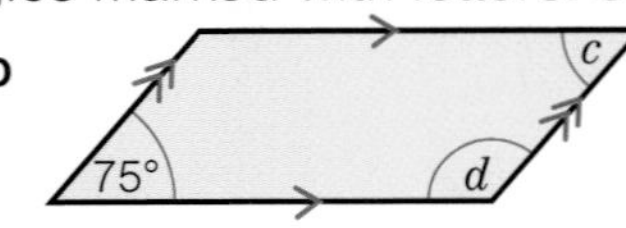

c
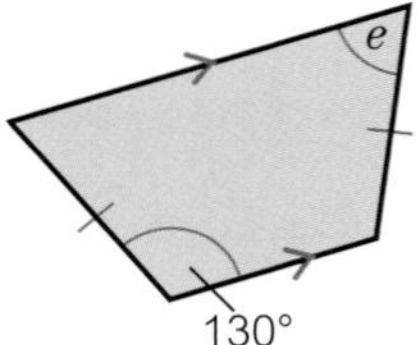

4 The diagram shows some angles on a straight line.
Work out the value of x.

5 The diagram shows a quadrilateral.
  a Work out the value of x.
  b Write down the sizes of the four angles in the quadrilateral.

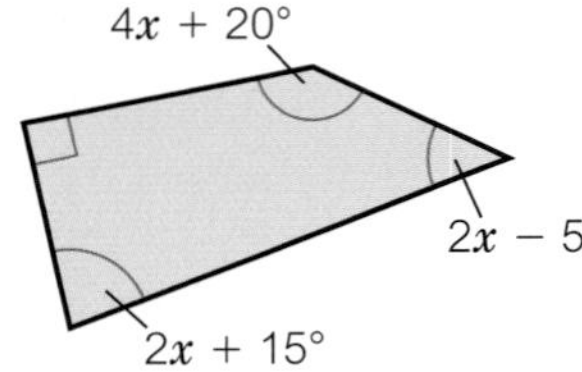

6 The diagram shows a kite and a right-angled triangle.
Work out the size of angle w.

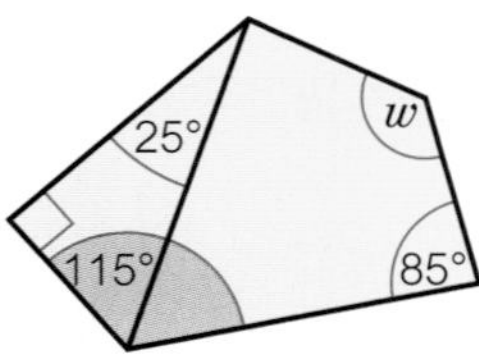

7 a Copy and complete these statements.
  i The angles in a triangle add up to □°.
  ii The angles in a quadrilateral add up to □°.
  iii The angles in a pentagon add up to □°.
  iv The angles in a hexagon add up to □°.
  b The diagram shows an irregular hexagon. Work out the size of angle m.

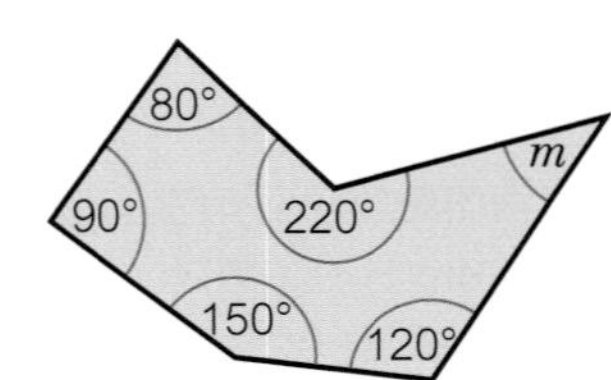

8 Work out the sizes of the angles marked with letters.
Give a reason for each answer.

a

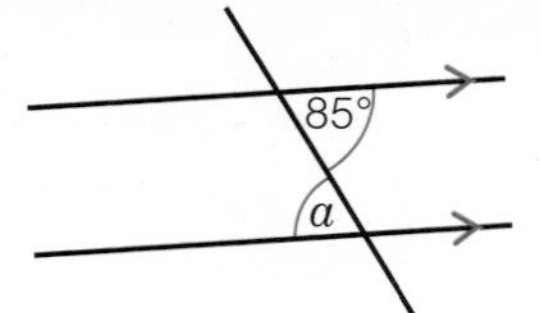

b

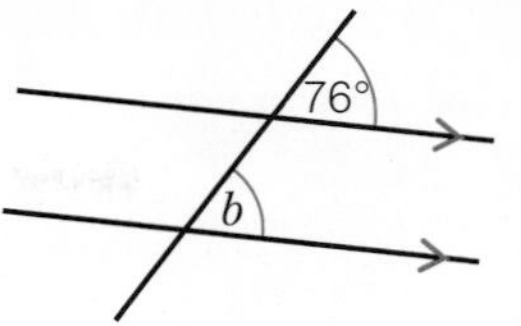

c

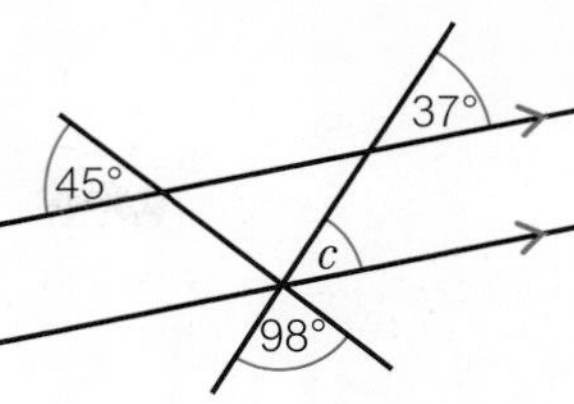

9 The diagram shows a trapezium, ABCD.

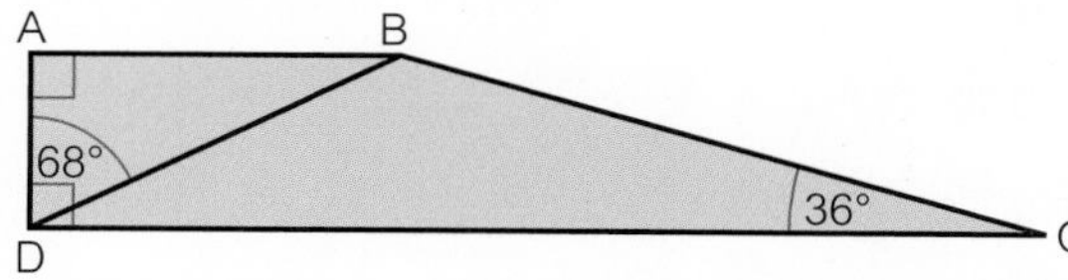

Work out the size of ∠DBC. Show your steps for solving this problem and explain your reasoning.

10 The diagram shows a regular octagon.
Work out the sizes of angles x and y.

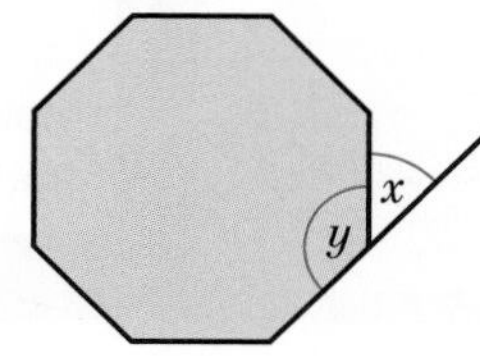

11 **a** The exterior angle of a regular polygon is 36°.

i How many sides does the polygon have?

ii Work out the size of each interior angle.

b The interior angle of a regular polygon is 165°.
How many sides does this polygon have?

Challenge

12 A tessellation is a pattern of repeated shapes with no gaps in between.
These diagrams show some different tessellations.

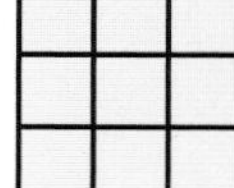

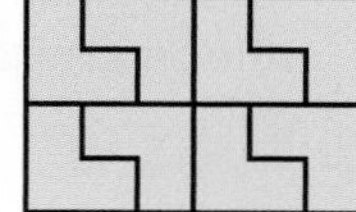

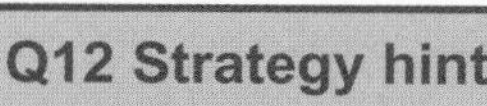

Q12 Strategy hint
Draw a diagram to help you explain each answer.

a Do all quadrilaterals tessellate?

b Do all triangles tessellate?

c Which regular polygons will tessellate?

d Some regular polygons will not tessellate.
Do they tessellate with other shapes?

13 **Reflect** Which of these statements best describes your work on lines and angles in this unit?

- I did the best I could.
- I could have tried harder.

Why did you choose that statement?
Was it true for every lesson?
Write down one thing you will do to make sure you do the best you can in the next unit.

8 Calculating with fractions

8.1 Adding and subtracting fractions

You will learn to:
- Add and subtract fractions with any size denominator.

CONFIDENCE

Why learn this?
Statisticians subtract fractions to work out the probability of something not happening.

Fluency
Work out
- $\frac{1}{5}+\frac{3}{5}$
- $\frac{5}{8}-\frac{1}{8}$
- $\frac{10}{17}+\frac{1}{17}$
- $\frac{4}{7}-\frac{3}{7}$
- $1-\frac{1}{3}$

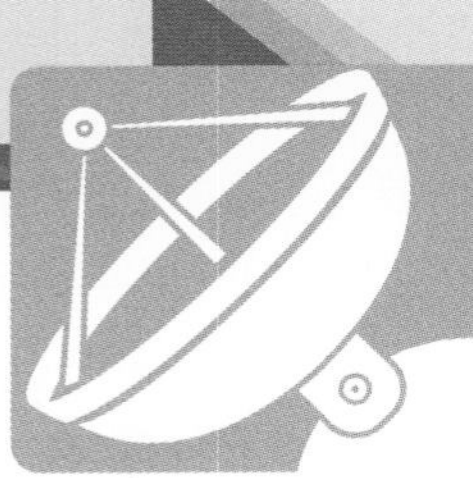

Explore
How did the Ancient Egyptians write fractions over 4000 years ago?

Exercise 8.1

Warm up

1 Write these improper fractions as mixed numbers.

a $\frac{7}{2}$ **b** $\frac{16}{3}$ **c** $\frac{100}{25}$ **d** $\frac{26}{9}$ **e** $\frac{15}{4}$

2 Copy and complete these equivalent fractions.

a $\frac{1}{8}=\frac{\square}{16}$ **b** $\frac{2}{5}=\frac{\square}{10}$ **c** $\frac{5}{6}=\frac{\square}{24}$ **d** $\frac{2}{9}=\frac{\square}{27}$

3 Work out the lowest common multiple (LCM) of

a 6 and 5 **b** 2 and 3 **c** 10 and 8

Key point
To add or subtract fractions write them as equivalent fractions with the same denominator. Use the LCM as the denominator.

Worked example
Work out $\frac{3}{10}+\frac{1}{5}$

$$\frac{3}{10}+\frac{1}{5}=\frac{3}{10}+\frac{2}{10}$$

The LCM of 5 and 10 is 10.

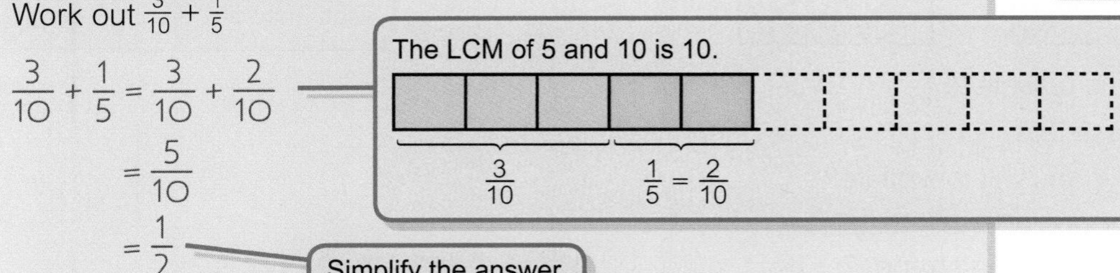

$$=\frac{5}{10}$$

$$=\frac{1}{2}$$

Simplify the answer.

4 Work out

a $\frac{1}{2}+\frac{1}{4}$ **b** $\frac{1}{2}+\frac{1}{4}+\frac{1}{4}$ **c** $\frac{1}{3}+\frac{1}{3}+\frac{1}{3}$

Q4a hint

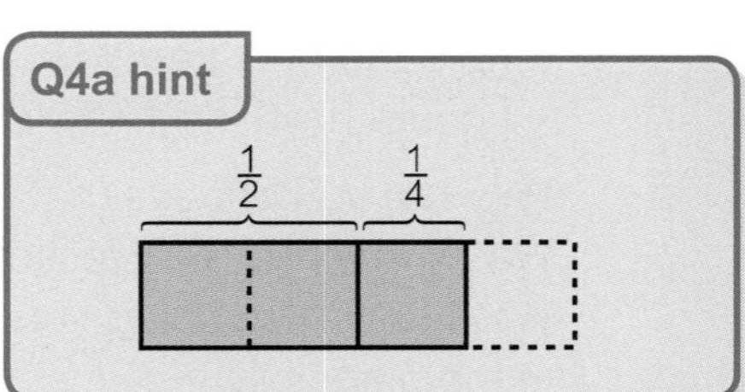

5 Work out

a $\frac{5}{12}+\frac{2}{6}=\frac{5}{12}+\frac{\square}{12}$ **b** $\frac{2}{3}+\frac{1}{12}$ **c** $\frac{1}{3}-\frac{1}{6}$

d $\frac{4}{5}-\frac{3}{10}$ **e** $\frac{1}{6}+\frac{1}{18}$ **f** $\frac{5}{9}-\frac{1}{3}$

Topic links: LCM

6 **Reasoning** Kieran says, '$\frac{2}{3} + \frac{2}{5} = \frac{4}{8}$'

a Use these bars to explain what mistake he has made.

b Work out $\frac{2}{3} + \frac{2}{5}$ by writing both fractions with denominator 15.

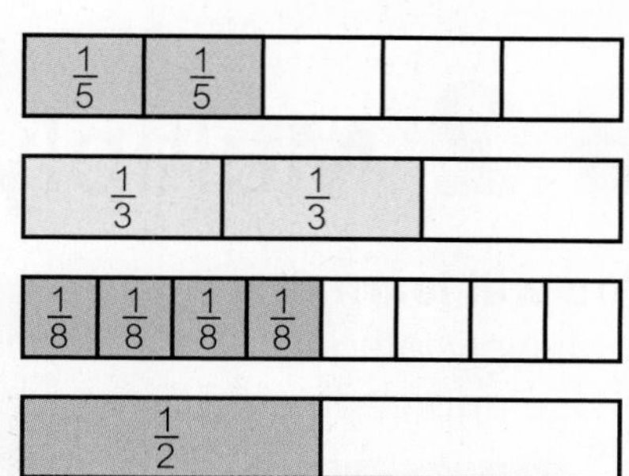

7 Work out

a $\frac{1}{2} + \frac{1}{3} = \frac{\square}{6} + \frac{\square}{6}$
$= \frac{\square}{6}$

b $\frac{2}{3} + \frac{1}{5}$ c $\frac{1}{2} + \frac{1}{7}$ d $\frac{3}{4} - \frac{1}{6}$ e $\frac{13}{20} + \frac{1}{5}$

Q6b hint
Use 15 because it is the LCM of 3 and 5.

8 $\frac{3}{4} - \frac{2}{7} = \frac{13}{28}$ $\frac{3}{4} + \frac{2}{7} = 1\frac{1}{28}$

Use these facts to work out

a $\frac{13}{28} + \frac{2}{7}$ b $1\frac{1}{28} - \frac{3}{4}$ c $\frac{13}{28} - \frac{3}{4}$ d $\frac{13}{28} - \left(\frac{3}{4} - \frac{2}{7}\right)$

9 Use your calculator to work these out.
Write your answers as mixed numbers.

a $\frac{1}{2} + \frac{3}{5} + \frac{1}{4}$ b $\frac{2}{5} - \frac{3}{5} - \frac{9}{10}$ c $\frac{13}{8} + \frac{21}{3}$ d $\frac{11}{2} + \frac{21}{6} - \frac{3}{5}$

Discussion What are the different ways that your calculator can display numbers?

Q9 hint
Use the fraction button on your calculator to enter a fraction.

10 Janinda adds two mixed numbers with different denominators to get $4\frac{1}{3}$.
What two numbers might she have added?

Q10 Strategy hint
Start with a mixed number with some thirds.

11 **Real** Answer these question in fractions of an hour.

a On Monday, Katherine spends $\frac{3}{4}$ of an hour on maths homework and $\frac{1}{2}$ an hour on French homework.
How long does she spend doing homework on Monday?

b On Wednesday, she spends $\frac{2}{3}$ of an hour on art homework and 15 minutes on creative writing.
How long does she spend doing homework on Wednesday?

c This is all of her homework.
How long has she spent in total doing homework this week?

Investigation **Problem-solving / Reasoning**

1 Start at 0. Add $\frac{1}{2}$, then $\frac{1}{4}$, then $\frac{1}{8}$, then $\frac{1}{16}$.

2 Keep going, following the pattern.
Do you ever reach 1?

12 **Explore** How did the Ancient Egyptians write fractions over 4000 years ago?
Is it easier to explore this question now you have completed the lesson?
What further information do you need to be able to answer this?

13 **Reflect** Look back at Q5. What steps did you take to work out these calculations?
You might begin with, 'Step 1: I looked at the denominators and noticed ...'
Do your steps work for Q7? What about Q8?
If not, rewrite your steps so that they work for all the questions in this lesson.

Explore

Reflect

8.2 Multiplying fractions

You will learn to:
- Multiply integers and fractions by a fraction
- Use appropriate methods for multiplying fractions.

CONFIDENCE

Why learn this?
Royalty fees for song-writers are split into twelfths. The publisher multiplies by twelfths to work out the fee for each person or rights holder.

Fluency
Work out
- 15 × 3
- 4 × 6
- 13 × 3
- $\frac{1}{2}$ of 50 ml
- $\frac{1}{3}$ of 12 oz

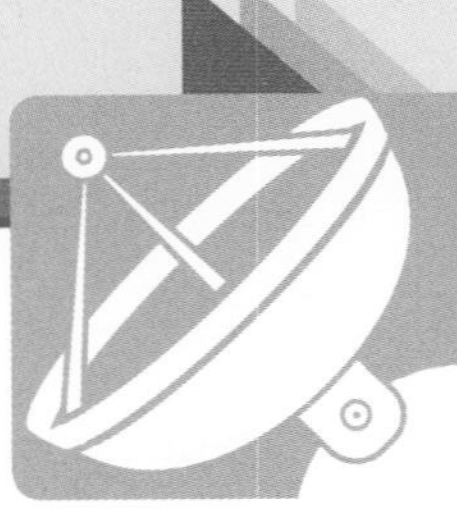

Explore
How many times can you halve a cake before nothing is left?

Exercise 8.2

Warm up

1 Work out

a $\frac{3}{4}$ of 100 kg **b** $\frac{2}{5}$ of 50 cm **c** $\frac{7}{10}$ of 30 ml

2 Simplify these fractions.

a $\frac{4}{12}$ **b** $\frac{15}{25}$ **c** $\frac{8}{36}$
d $\frac{13}{10}$ **e** $\frac{25}{2}$ **f** $6\frac{3}{9}$

3 Work out

a $\frac{4}{5}$ of 30 **b** $\frac{2}{3}$ of 90 **c** $\frac{2}{7}$ of 42 **d** $\frac{3}{10}$ of 10
e $10 \times \frac{2}{5}$ **f** $45 \times \frac{1}{9}$ **g** $16 \times \frac{7}{8}$ **h** $22 \times \frac{4}{11}$

Discussion How are you using multiplying and dividing in these calculations? Does it make a difference if you use the operations the other way around?

Key point
In maths, $\frac{3}{4}$ of 100 is the same as $\frac{3}{4} \times 100$.

Q3e hint
$10 \times \frac{2}{5}$ is the same as $\frac{2}{5} \times 10$.

4 Work out the areas of these shapes. Simplify your answers.

a

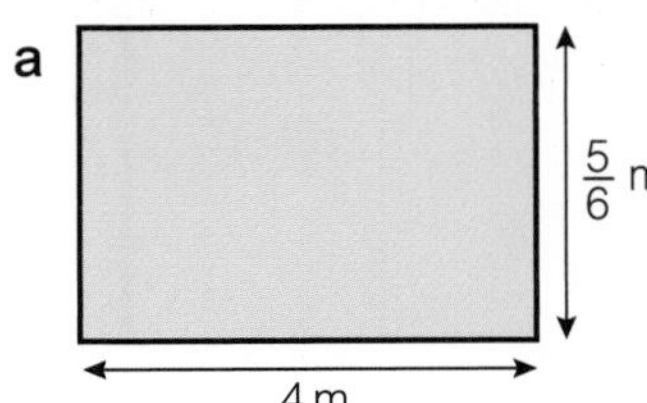

b

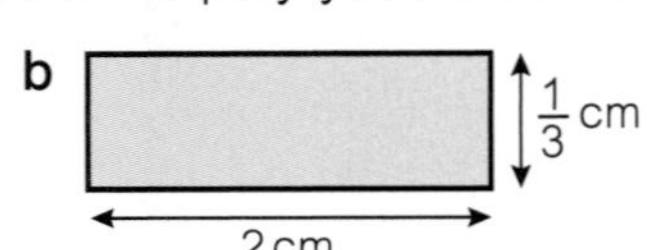

c

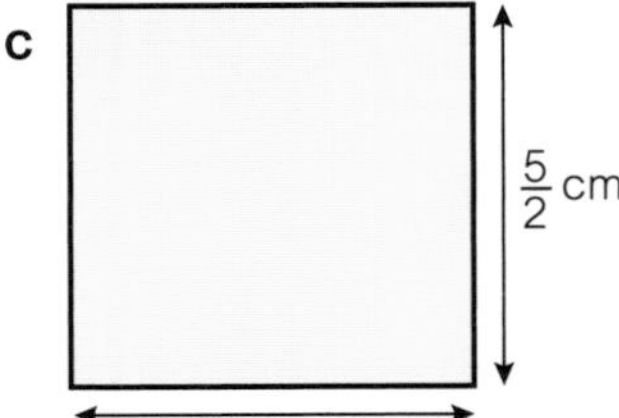

d

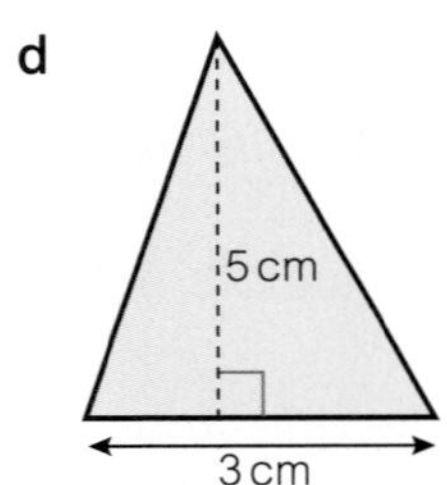

Topic links: Area, Perimeter, Probability, Equivalent fractions and decimals

5 Problem-solving / Reasoning Josh and Bhavika spin this spinner 50 times.

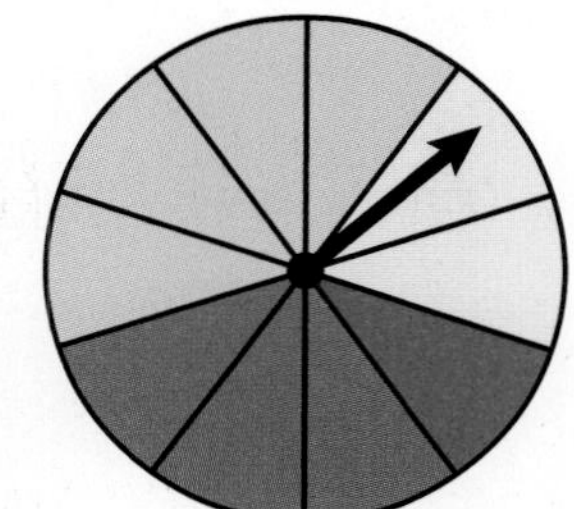

a They want to know how many times to expect the spinner to land on red. Josh says, 'The probability is 0.1, so I'm going to multiply 50 by 0.1.' Bhavika says, 'The probability is $\frac{1}{10}$, so I'm going to multiply 50 by $\frac{1}{10}$.' Will they both get the same answer? Explain.

b How many times should they expect the spinner to land on yellow?

c Bhavika expects the spinner to land on a particular colour 15 times. Which colour?

Worked example

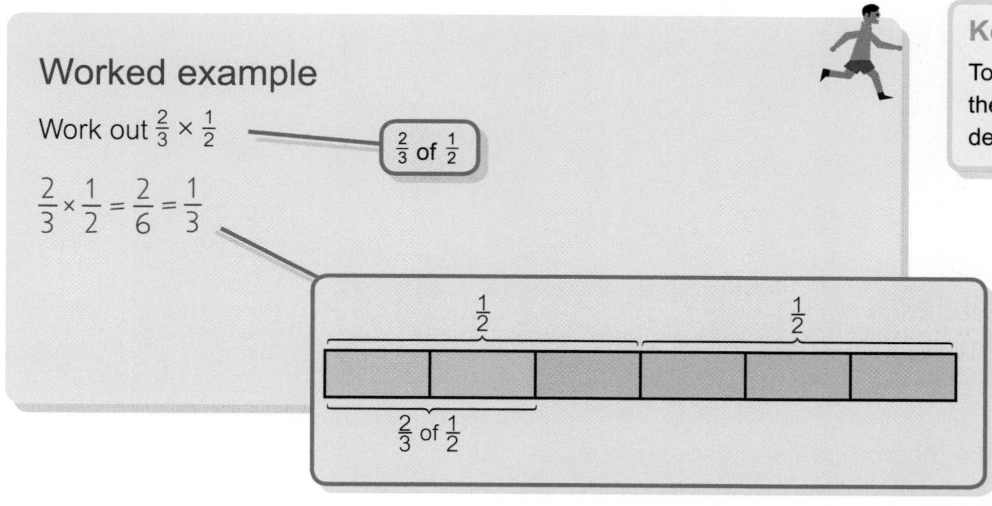

Work out $\frac{2}{3} \times \frac{1}{2}$

$\frac{2}{3}$ of $\frac{1}{2}$

$$\frac{2}{3} \times \frac{1}{2} = \frac{2}{6} = \frac{1}{3}$$

Key point

To multiply two fractions, multiply their numerators and multiply their denominators.

6 Work out these multiplications. Use the fraction wall to check your answers.

1
$\frac{1}{3}$ | $\frac{1}{3}$ | $\frac{1}{3}$
$\frac{1}{6}$ | $\frac{1}{6}$ | $\frac{1}{6}$ | $\frac{1}{6}$ | $\frac{1}{6}$ | $\frac{1}{6}$
$\frac{1}{2}$ | $\frac{1}{2}$
$\frac{1}{12}$ | $\frac{1}{12}$ | $\frac{1}{12}$ | $\frac{1}{12}$ | $\frac{1}{12}$ | $\frac{1}{12}$ | $\frac{1}{12}$ | $\frac{1}{12}$ | $\frac{1}{12}$ | $\frac{1}{12}$ | $\frac{1}{12}$ | $\frac{1}{12}$
$\frac{1}{4}$ | $\frac{1}{4}$ | $\frac{1}{4}$ | $\frac{1}{4}$
$\frac{1}{8}$ | $\frac{1}{8}$ | $\frac{1}{8}$ | $\frac{1}{8}$ | $\frac{1}{8}$ | $\frac{1}{8}$ | $\frac{1}{8}$ | $\frac{1}{8}$

a $\frac{1}{2} \times \frac{1}{2}$ **b** $\frac{1}{3} \times \frac{1}{2}$ **c** $\frac{1}{4} \times \frac{1}{3}$

d $\frac{3}{4} \times \frac{1}{2}$ **e** $-\frac{2}{3} \times \frac{1}{4}$ **f** $-\frac{5}{6} \times \frac{1}{2}$

Q6e hint

Use the rule for multiplying negtive numbers.

7 Work out the areas and perimeters of these squares.

a

b

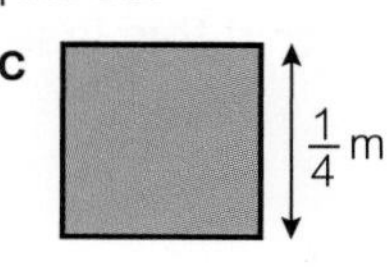

c $\frac{1}{4}$m

8 In 2012, $\frac{1}{20}$ of a council's members were from minority ethnic groups.
Of these, $\frac{1}{3}$ were women.
What proportion of the council were minority ethnic women?

Investigation

Problem-solving

Chris works out $\frac{9}{28} \times \frac{7}{12}$ like this.

$$\frac{9}{28} \times \frac{7}{12} = \frac{9 \times 7}{28 \times 12}$$
$$= \frac{63}{336}$$

Kamran works it out like this.

$$\frac{9}{28} \times \frac{7}{12} = \frac{9 \times 7}{28 \times 12}$$
$$= \frac{{}^{3}\cancel{9} \times \cancel{7}^{1}}{{}_{4}\cancel{12} \times \cancel{28}_{4}}$$
$$= \frac{3}{4} \times \frac{1}{4}$$
$$= \frac{3}{16}$$

1 Did they both get the same answer?

2 Whose method do you prefer? Why?

3 Use your preferred method to work out $\frac{8}{49} \times \frac{7}{24}$.

9 Work these out, using the method from the investigation.

a $\frac{5}{6} \times \frac{9}{10}$
b $\frac{5}{12} \times \frac{6}{15}$
c $\frac{7}{8} \times \frac{4}{7}$
d $\frac{20}{21} \times \frac{3}{10}$
e $\frac{5}{14} \times \frac{6}{15}$
f $\frac{17}{33} \times \frac{11}{34}$

Key point

When you multiply fractions you can rearrange them so they cancel.

Q9a hint

$$\frac{2 \times 9}{3 \times 10} = \frac{2 \times 9}{10 \times 3}$$

10 **Real / Finance** A company pays a fee of £3000 to use a song in an advertisement. There are three people in the band: the writer gets $\frac{4}{12}$ of the fee, the singer gets $\frac{1}{12}$ and the guitarist gets $\frac{1}{12}$.

a What fraction of the fee does the whole band get?

b How much money does each member of the band receive?

11 Work out

a $\frac{2}{3} \times \frac{7}{8}$
b $-\frac{3}{7} \times \frac{7}{12}$
c $\frac{4}{9} \times \frac{2}{9}$
d $-\frac{5}{6} \times \frac{2}{9}$
e $\frac{9}{11} \times \frac{2}{3} \times \frac{11}{20}$
f $\frac{9}{14} \times \frac{3}{18} \times \frac{7}{8}$

Explore

12 **Explore** How many times can you halve a cake before nothing is left? Look back at the maths you have learned in this lesson. How can you use it to answer this question?

Reflect

13 **Reflect** Look back at Q6.
How did you learn how to multiply fractions?
What is good about learning a new mathematics skill this way?
Explain your answer.
Is anything not so good?
What other ways do you like to learn new mathematics skills?

Q13 hint

Did you read the worked example?
Did your teacher explain it to you?

8.3 Fractions, decimals and reciprocals

You will learn to:

- Convert fractions to decimals
- Write one amount as a fraction of another
- Find the reciprocal of a number.

Why learn this?
Opticians add reciprocal fractions to find out what type of lens you need in your glasses.

Fluency
Match each fraction to its decimal equivalent.
$\frac{1}{10}$ $\frac{2}{5}$ $\frac{1}{4}$ $\frac{1}{2}$ $\frac{1}{5}$
0.5 0.4 0.2 0.1 0.25

Explore
How are fractions used in music?

Exercise 8.3

Warm up

1 How many minutes in
a $\frac{1}{4}$ of an hour   b $\frac{1}{5}$ of an hour   c $\frac{1}{3}$ of an hour?

2 Work out
a $\frac{1}{4} \times \frac{1}{6}$ b $\frac{2}{5} \times \frac{3}{7}$ c $\frac{1}{8} \times \frac{2}{3}$ d $\frac{1}{12} \times \frac{6}{7}$

3 Round these decimals to one decimal place.
a 4.27   b 1.09   c 5.32   d 0.85

Worked example

Write 10.25 hours in hours and minutes.

$10.25 = 10\frac{1}{4}$ — Write the decimal as a fraction or mixed number.

10 hours 15 minutes — $\frac{1}{4}$ of an hour = 15 minutes.

4 Convert these to hours and minutes.
a 1.2 hours   b 4.5 hours   c 9.1 hours   d 8.6 hours

Q4a hint
What is $\frac{1}{10}$ of 60 minutes?

5 **Real** Jonty calculates that his flight leaves in 5.5 hours.
a Write 5.5 hours in hours and minutes.
b Jonty has to be at the airport $\frac{3}{4}$ of an hour before his flight leaves. How long is it until he has to be at the airport?

6 Write each saving as a fraction of the original selling price.
Give each answer in its simplest form.
a *save* **25p** *originally* **£3.50**
b *save* **80p** *originally* **£4**
c *save* **45p** *originally* **£2.40**

Q6 hint
Write both amounts in pence.

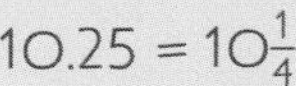

7 **Finance** Marc sells cakes for £1 each at a charity bake sale.
He works out that each cake costs 20p to make.

a What fraction of £1 is the cost per cake?

b What fraction is profit?

8 Use written division to write these fractions as decimals.

a $\frac{2}{5}$ **b** $\frac{3}{10}$ **c** $\frac{3}{8}$ **d** $\frac{7}{5}$ **e** $\frac{9}{4}$

Key point

The line in a fraction means 'divide by'.
To write $\frac{3}{4}$ as a decimal, work out $3 \div 4$.

$$4\overline{)3.{}^{3}0{}^{2}0}\quad = 0.75$$

Investigation **Problem-solving**

1 Jocelyn works out some divisions on her calculator and gets these answers.

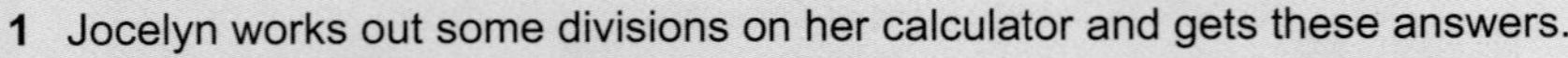

0.333333333 0.8333333333 2.166666667
0.666666667 0.1428571429 1.666666667

a Why does a 7 appear at the end of three of the decimals?

b Match each decimal to one of these fractions. $\frac{1}{7}$ $\frac{1}{3}$ $\frac{5}{3}$ $\frac{2}{3}$ $\frac{5}{6}$ $\frac{13}{6}$

2 Use your calculator to find the fraction equivalent of these recurring decimals.
0.090 909 09… 0.272 727 27… 0.181 818 18…

3 What happens if you press the S⟺D button on your calculator?

9 Write the recurring decimals in the investigation using dot notation.

Key point

A **recurring decimal** contains a digit, or sequence of digits, which repeats itself forever. A dot over the digit shows that it recurs.
$0.\dot{3} = 0.333333\ldots$

10 Work out

a $\frac{4}{5} \times \frac{5}{4}$ **b** $\frac{2}{3} \times \frac{3}{2}$ **c** $\frac{1}{3} \times 3$

Discussion What do you notice about all your answers to Q10 and the fractions in the question?

11 Write your own calculation with two fractions.

$\frac{\square}{\square} \times \frac{\square}{\square} = 1$

Key point

You can write integers (whole numbers) as fractions with a denominator of 1.
Dividing by 1 doesn't change the number.

12 Write down the **reciprocal** of these numbers.

a $\frac{2}{7}$ **b** 5 **c** $\frac{1}{10}$ **d** 8

Key point

The **reciprocal** of a fraction is the 'upside down' fraction.
A number multiplied by its reciprocal is always 1.

13 **Real / STEM** The focal length (f) of the lens in your eye changes depending on the distance of the object you are looking at.
Ruby looks at a book 100 millimetres away.
Use this calculation to work out the focal length of her eye.

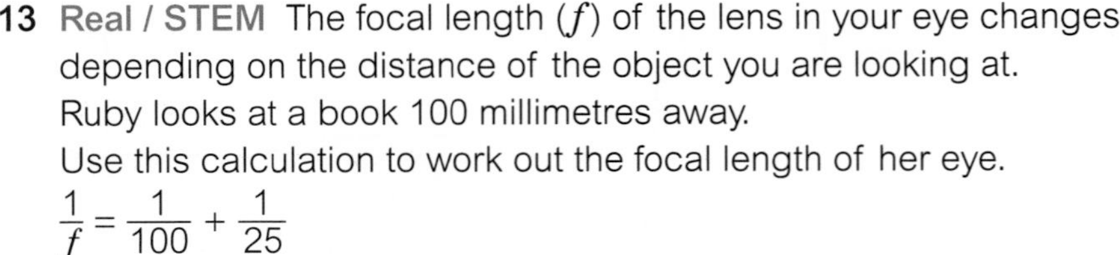

$$\frac{1}{f} = \frac{1}{100} + \frac{1}{25}$$

14 **Explore** How are fractions used in music?
What have you learned in this lesson to help you answer this question?
What other information do you need?

15 **Reflect** Write two new things you have learned in this lesson.
Write down the questions that used these new things.
When you answered these questions, did you make any mistakes?
If so, check that you understand where you went wrong.

Explore

Reflect

Subject links: Science (Q13), Music (Q14)

8.4 Dividing fractions

You will learn to:
- Divide integers and fractions by a fraction
- Use strategies for dividing fractions.

Why learn this?
Lengths and areas in real life are not usually whole numbers, so you need to be able to calculate with fractions and decimals too.

Fluency
How many
- 2s are there in 10
- 5s are there in 10
- 1s are there in 3
- 4s are there in 16?

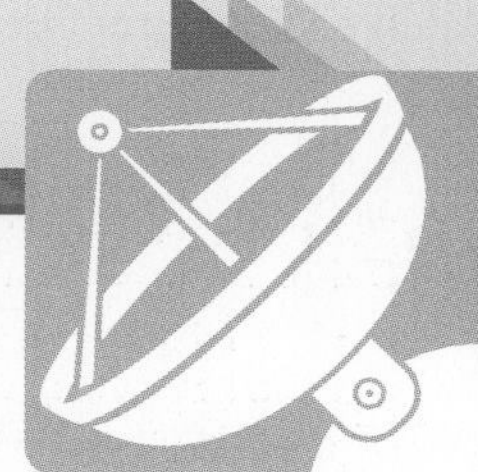

Explore
Why is dividing fractions important when people use imperial measures?

Exercise 8.4

Warm up

1 Find the common factors of each pair of numbers.
- **a** 12 and 9
- **b** 16 and 10
- **c** 27 and 18

2 Work out
- **a** $\frac{1}{4} \times 2$
- **b** $\frac{1}{3} \times \frac{1}{2}$
- **c** $\frac{3}{5} \times \frac{2}{7}$
- **d** $\frac{2}{3} \times \frac{3}{4}$
- **e** $\frac{5}{9} \times \frac{3}{10}$
- **f** $\frac{1}{2} \times -4$
- **g** $-\frac{1}{3} \times -\frac{2}{5}$
- **h** $-\frac{4}{5} \times -\frac{1}{6}$

3 Write a calculation to match each question.
The first one has been done for you.
- **a** How many fifths are there in 1?

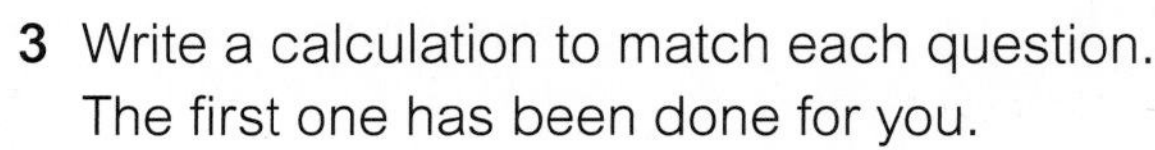
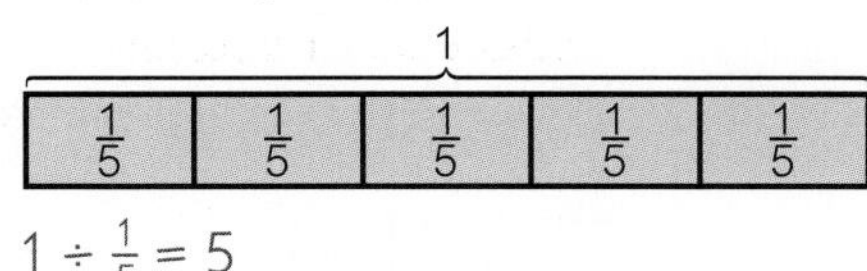

$1 \div \frac{1}{5} = 5$

- **b** How many quarters are there in 1?
- **c** How many thirds are there in 1?
- **d** How many halves are there in 3?
- **e** How many quarters are there in 2?

Key point
A fraction is a type of division. It divides a shape into equal parts.

Q3b hint

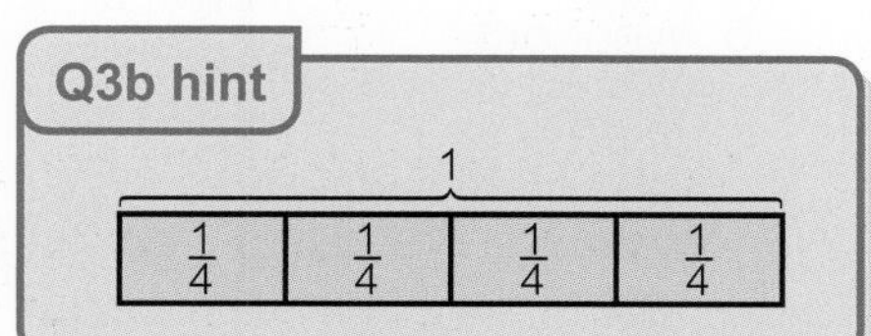

4 Write down the reciprocal of
- **a** $\frac{2}{3}$
- **b** 6
- **c** $\frac{1}{9}$
- **d** $\frac{1}{4}$

Investigation — **Problem-solving**

1 Complete these number patterns.

$2 \div \frac{1}{4} = \square = 2 \times \square$

$3 \div \frac{1}{10} = \square = 3 \times \square$

2 Look at your answers to part **1**. Explain how you use the reciprocal of a fraction to divide.

3 Match each diagram to a calculation and work out the answer.

A $\frac{3}{5} \div \frac{3}{10}$

B $\frac{2}{3} \div \frac{1}{3}$

C $\frac{3}{4} \div \frac{1}{8}$

D $\frac{1}{2} \div \frac{1}{6}$

i
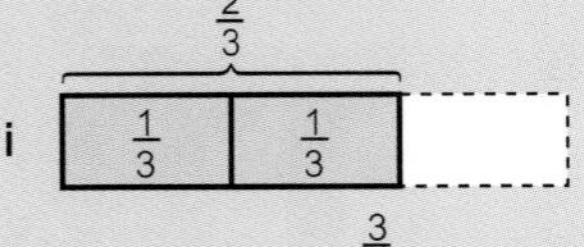

ii
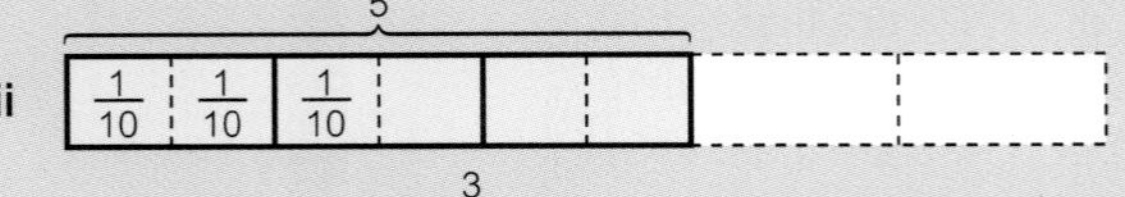

iii $\frac{3}{4}$: $\frac{1}{8}$ $\frac{1}{8}$ $\frac{1}{8}$ $\frac{1}{8}$ $\frac{1}{8}$ $\frac{1}{8}$

iv $\frac{1}{2}$: $\frac{1}{6}$ $\frac{1}{6}$ $\frac{1}{6}$

4 Work out the calculations in part **3** using your rule from part **2**. Does it work?

5 Use your rule to work out

a $\frac{1}{2} \div \frac{1}{3}$

b $\frac{2}{5} \div \frac{1}{4}$

c $\frac{1}{10} \div \frac{3}{4}$

Worked example

Work out $4 \div \frac{2}{9}$

$$4 \div \frac{2}{9} = \frac{4}{1} \times \frac{9}{2}$$

Change to multiplication by the reciprocal.

$$= \frac{{}^{2}\cancel{4} \times 9}{{}_{1}\cancel{2} \times 1}$$

$$= 2 \times 9$$

$$= 18$$

Key point

Dividing by a fraction is the same as multiplying by its reciprocal.

5 Work out

a $12 \div \frac{2}{3}$ **b** $3 \div \frac{3}{7}$ **c** $50 \div \frac{2}{9}$ **d** $18 \div \frac{3}{10}$

e $-20 \div \frac{2}{5}$ **f** $24 \div -\frac{8}{15}$ **g** $-16 \div \frac{4}{9}$ **h** $40 \div -\frac{4}{5}$

Q5 hint

Use the rules for dividing negative numbers.

6 How many $\frac{3}{4}$ pint mugs can you fill from a 6 pint kettle?

7 **Reasoning** Rachelle says, 'Dividing always makes things smaller.' Give a counter example to show why Rachelle is wrong.

Q7 Literacy hint

A counter example is one that shows a statement to be false.

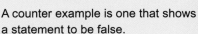

8 Work out

a $\frac{1}{5} \div \frac{1}{3}$ **b** $\frac{2}{9} \div \frac{1}{4}$ **c** $\frac{3}{10} \div \frac{1}{2}$ **d** $\frac{1}{4} \div -\frac{8}{5}$

9 Work out

a $\frac{4}{9} \div \frac{2}{3}$ **b** $\frac{2}{5} \div \frac{8}{15}$ **c** $\frac{9}{20} \div \frac{21}{40}$ **d** $-\frac{7}{12} \div \frac{21}{32}$

10 **Real** Gas bills are sent every quarter year.
How many gas bills will you get in 20 months?

11 **Real** A sewing pattern uses $\frac{5}{8}$ of a yard of fabric for a pair of shorts.
How many pairs could you make from 4 yards?

12 A cake recipe uses $\frac{5}{7}$ of a pound of flour.
How many cakes could you make from 6 pounds of flour?

13 **Problem-solving** Continue these patterns.

a	**b**
$\frac{1}{2} \times 8 = 4$	$\frac{1}{2} \div 8 = \frac{1}{16}$
$\frac{1}{2} \times 4 =$	$\frac{1}{2} \div 4 =$
$\frac{1}{2} \times 2 =$	$\frac{1}{2} \div 2 =$
$\frac{1}{2} \times 1 =$	$\frac{1}{2} \div 1 =$
$\frac{1}{2} \times \frac{1}{2} =$	$\frac{1}{2} \div \frac{1}{2} =$
$\frac{1}{2} \times \frac{1}{4} =$	$\frac{1}{2} \div \frac{1}{4} =$
$\frac{1}{2} \times \frac{1}{8} =$	$\frac{1}{2} \div \frac{1}{8} =$

c Describe and explain the different sequences and patterns you can see.

14 Use your calculator to work out these divisions.

a $\frac{1}{2} \div \frac{6}{5}$

b $\frac{8}{3} \div \frac{2}{3}$

c $\frac{10}{11} \div \frac{5}{2}$

d $\frac{6}{7} \div \frac{1}{2}$

e $\frac{2}{3} \div \frac{8}{3}$

Discussion How can you tell by comparing the two fractions whether the answer is going to be bigger or smaller than the first fraction?

Explore

15 **Explore** Why is dividing fractions important when people use imperial measures?
What have you learned in this lesson to help you answer this question? What other information do you need?

Reflect

16 **Reflect** Part 3 of the investigation used bar models to show dividing by fractions.
Did the bar models help you to understand? Explain your answer.

8.5 Calculating with mixed numbers

You will learn to:

- Use the four operations with mixed numbers.

Why learn this?
Measurements in real life are more likely to be a mixed number than a whole number.

Fluency
Write these improper fractions as mixed numbers.

- $\frac{15}{2}$
- $\frac{10}{7}$
- $\frac{15}{9}$

Explore
Why did people use mixed numbers more in the 1950s?

Exercise 8.5

1 Work out

a $\frac{1}{2} + \frac{2}{3}$ **b** $\frac{3}{4} + \frac{1}{8}$ **c** $\frac{2}{5} - \frac{1}{4}$

d $\frac{3}{10} \times \frac{1}{3}$ **e** $\frac{1}{2} \div \frac{3}{4}$ **f** $\frac{8}{9} \div \frac{1}{3}$

2 a Work out the missing value.

b Work out the perimeter.

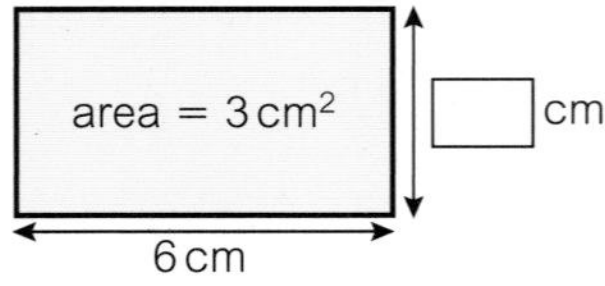

3 Work out these calculations of mixed numbers.
Write the answers in their simplest form.
The first one has been started for you.

a $3\frac{1}{4} + 2\frac{1}{2} = 5 + \frac{1}{4} + \frac{2}{4} =$ **b** $1\frac{1}{2} + 5\frac{1}{3}$ **c** $5\frac{3}{10} + 2\frac{1}{5}$

d $3\frac{2}{3} + 4\frac{4}{5}$ **e** $5\frac{3}{8} + 2\frac{7}{9}$ **f** $2\frac{3}{4} - 1\frac{1}{2}$ **g** $10\frac{1}{8} - 4\frac{1}{10}$

Q3 hint
Add the whole numbers first, then add the fraction parts by writing them with a common denominator.

4 Real / Problem-solving Paul is travelling from Turkey to Iran.

a He spends $2\frac{1}{2}$ hours on the bus. He then travels for $3\frac{3}{4}$ hours by train.
How long does he spend travelling?

b Paul sets off at 1445. The time in Iran is $1\frac{1}{2}$ hours ahead of Turkey.
What time does he arrive at his destination in Iran?

Worked example

Write $5\frac{2}{3}$ as an improper fraction.

$5\frac{2}{3} = \frac{15}{3} + \frac{2}{3}$

$= \frac{17}{3}$

Write the whole number as a fraction with the same denominator as the fraction part.

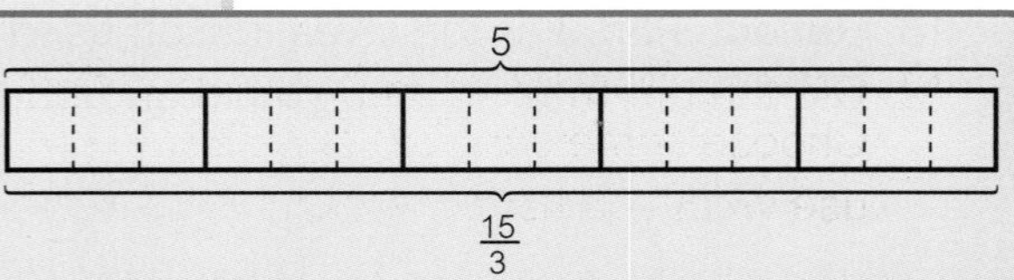

5 Write these mixed numbers as improper fractions.

a $5\frac{1}{2}$ **b** $2\frac{3}{8}$ **c** $9\frac{1}{6}$ **d** $10\frac{3}{4}$

Topic links: Area, Measures

Worked example

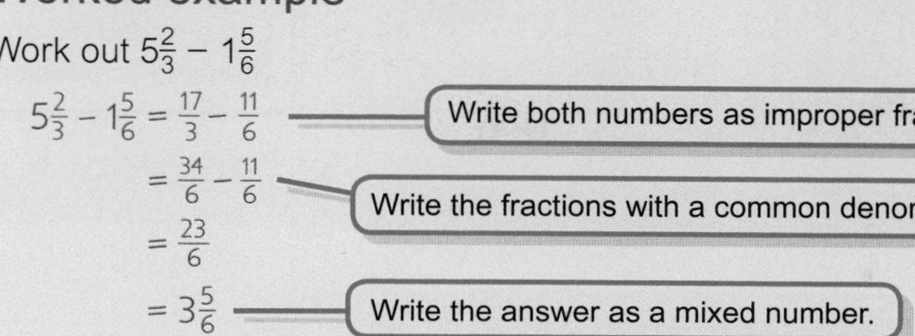

Work out $5\frac{2}{3} - 1\frac{5}{6}$

$5\frac{2}{3} - 1\frac{5}{6} = \frac{17}{3} - \frac{11}{6}$ — Write both numbers as improper fractions.

$= \frac{34}{6} - \frac{11}{6}$ — Write the fractions with a common denominator.

$= \frac{23}{6}$

$= 3\frac{5}{6}$ — Write the answer as a mixed number.

Key point

It is usually easier to write mixed numbers as improper fractions before doing the calculation.

6 Work out these subtractions.

a $3\frac{2}{3} - 2\frac{3}{4}$ **b** $2\frac{2}{5} - 2\frac{3}{10}$ **c** $8\frac{1}{2} - 4\frac{3}{5}$ **d** $2\frac{5}{6} - 5\frac{1}{3}$

e $4\frac{3}{4} - \frac{11}{16}$ **f** $4\frac{3}{7} - 3\frac{1}{3}$ **g** $1\frac{1}{3} - 4\frac{3}{4}$ **h** $3\frac{2}{3} - 5\frac{8}{9}$

7 Sanjay has completed $15\frac{2}{3}$ miles of a $24\frac{5}{7}$ mile race.
How far does he have left to run?

8 Work out

a $2\frac{1}{2} \times 3$ kg **b** $4\frac{1}{10} \times 6$ m **c** $1\frac{3}{5} \times 10$

d $2\frac{1}{2} \times 2\frac{1}{2}$ **e** $3\frac{3}{4} \times 1\frac{1}{3}$ **f** $5\frac{2}{3} \times 2\frac{1}{10}$

Q8a hint

Write mixed numbers as improper fractions before multiplying.

9 **Problem-solving** Mumtaz can swim $1\frac{1}{5}$ times faster than Ethan.
Ethan can swim one length in 30 seconds.
How long will it take Mumtaz to swim one length?

10 Work out the area of this trapezium.

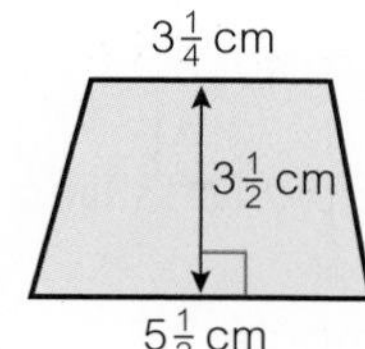

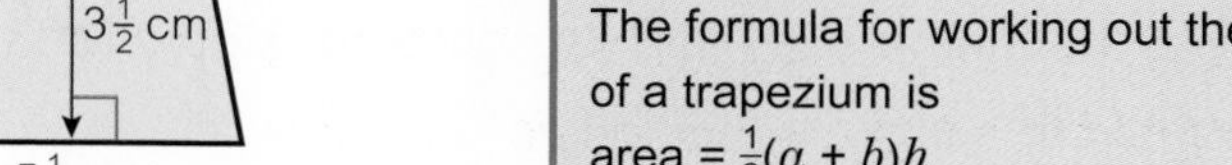

Q10 hint

The formula for working out the area of a trapezium is
area = $\frac{1}{2}(a + b)h$

11 Work out

a $6\frac{1}{4} \div 2$ **b** $9\frac{2}{5} \div 3$ **c** $10\frac{2}{3} \div \frac{1}{2}$

d $2\frac{3}{4} \div \frac{2}{5}$ **e** $15\frac{5}{8} \div \frac{3}{5}$ **f** $4\frac{4}{5} \div \frac{5}{6}$

12 A relay race is $1\frac{1}{4}$ miles. There are three relay runners on the team.
Each person runs the same distance.
How far does each person run?

13 A pancake recipe uses $1\frac{3}{4}$ pints of milk to make 20 pancakes.
How much is needed to make 10 pancakes?

14 Find the lengths of these rectangles.

a area = $6\frac{1}{3}$ m^2, $\frac{3}{4}$ m

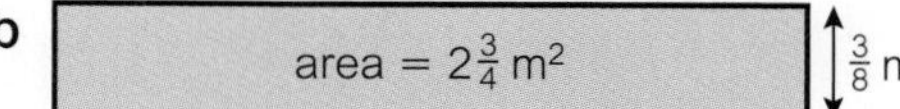

b area = $2\frac{3}{4}$ m^2, $\frac{3}{8}$ m

15 **Explore** Why did people use mixed numbers more in the 1950s?
Choose some sensible numbers to help you explore this situation. Then use what you have learned in this lesson to help you answer the question.

16 **Reflect** What is the same when you calculate with fractions and with mixed numbers? What is different?

Explore

Reflect

8 Check up

Log how you did on your Student Progression Chart.

Adding and subtracting fractions

1 Work these out. Simplify your answers where needed.

a $\frac{1}{5} + \frac{3}{5}$ **b** $\frac{7}{10} - \frac{5}{10}$

c $\frac{5}{12} + \frac{11}{12}$ **d** $\frac{3}{4} - \frac{1}{4}$

e $\frac{47}{21} - \frac{5}{21}$ **f** $\frac{2}{11} - \frac{7}{11}$

g $\frac{3}{25} + \frac{1}{50}$ **h** $\frac{3}{4} + \frac{1}{2}$

2 Theo says, '$\frac{1}{3} + \frac{1}{3} = \frac{2}{6}$'

Simplify $\frac{2}{6}$ and use your answer to explain why Theo has made a mistake.

3 Work out

a $\frac{2}{5} + \frac{1}{3}$ **b** $\frac{5}{21} + \frac{1}{2}$

c $\frac{5}{6} - \frac{1}{3}$ **d** $\frac{4}{5} - \frac{3}{10}$

e $\frac{7}{10} - \frac{2}{3}$ **f** $\frac{1}{2} - \frac{3}{4}$

g $\frac{3}{25} - \frac{1}{3}$

4 $\frac{4}{9}$ of the memory on Harry's computer stores MP3 files.
Video files take up another $\frac{1}{7}$.
How much memory is left on Harry's computer?

Multiplying and dividing fractions

5 Work out

a $\frac{1}{4} \times 20$ **b** $\frac{2}{3} \times -5$ **c** $30 \times \frac{7}{10}$

6 Work out

a $4 \div \frac{1}{3}$ **b** $10 \div \frac{2}{5}$ **c** $7 \div \frac{5}{6}$

7 Work out

a $\frac{1}{2} \times \frac{1}{4}$ **b** $\frac{2}{3} \times \frac{3}{4}$ **c** $\frac{2}{9} \times \frac{2}{5}$ **d** $\frac{6}{11} \times \frac{1}{3}$

8 Write down the reciprocal of these numbers.

a 3 **b** $\frac{1}{5}$ **c** $\frac{2}{7}$

9 Work out these. Give your answers as mixed numbers where needed.

a $\frac{1}{4} \div 6$ **b** $\frac{4}{9} \div 3$

c $\frac{2}{3} \div \frac{1}{15}$ **d** $\frac{5}{13} \div \frac{4}{25}$

e $\frac{1}{25} \div \frac{2}{25}$ **f** $\frac{16}{21} \div \frac{8}{3}$

10 A rectangle is $\frac{4}{5}$m long and $\frac{3}{10}$m wide.

a Calculate the perimeter of the rectangle.

b Calculate the area of the rectangle.

Calculating with mixed numbers and decimals

11 Use a written method to convert these fractions to decimals.

a $\frac{11}{4}$ b $\frac{9}{5}$ c $\frac{5}{8}$

12 Match each fraction to its equivalent decimal.

0.7	0.8	$0.\dot{6}$	$0.\dot{3}$	0.75
$\frac{1}{3}$	$\frac{7}{10}$	$\frac{4}{5}$	$\frac{3}{4}$	$\frac{2}{3}$

13 Write $3\frac{2}{5}$ as an improper fraction.

14 Work out

a $1\frac{3}{5} + 2\frac{1}{10}$ b $5\frac{5}{6} + 2\frac{3}{4}$

c $2\frac{3}{5} - 3$ d $3\frac{4}{5} - 2\frac{2}{3}$

15 Sally says that 4.4 hours is 4 hours 40 minutes. Why is she incorrect?

16 Work out

a $\frac{2}{3} \times 2\frac{1}{2}$ b $-\frac{5}{6} \times 1\frac{1}{3}$

c $\frac{1}{6} \div \frac{1}{2}$ d $2\frac{5}{8} \div \frac{7}{8}$

e $5\frac{1}{2} \div \frac{1}{3}$ f $-2\frac{1}{3} \div 1\frac{2}{3}$

17 How sure are you of your answers? Were you mostly

Just guessing **Feeling doubtful** **Confident**

What next? Use your results to decide whether to strengthen or extend your learning.

Reflect

Challenge

18 Susannah multiplies an integer by a fraction and gets the answer 10.
What two numbers could she have multiplied?

19 Sort these calculations into the two groups.

$4\frac{2}{3} \times 1\frac{1}{5}$	$15\frac{1}{8} - 5\frac{1}{4}$	$1\frac{1}{2} \times 8$	$6\frac{2}{5} + 20\frac{1}{2}$	$1\frac{3}{7} \times 1\frac{1}{7}$	$18\frac{3}{10} - 1\frac{4}{5}$

- Group 1: Write as improper fractions first
- Group 2: Calculate the whole number parts first

8 Strengthen

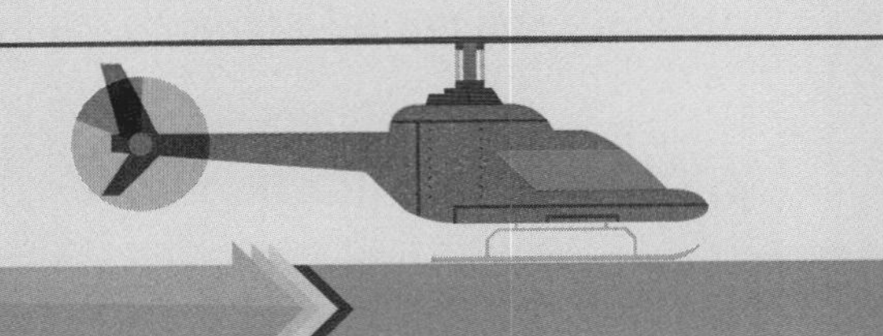

You will:
- Strengthen your understanding with practice.

Adding and subtracting fractions

1 Match each calculation to a diagram and work out the answer.

a $\frac{2}{3}+\frac{1}{3}$ A $\left[\frac{1}{2}\,\middle|\,\frac{1}{2}\right]$

b $\frac{1}{3}+\frac{1}{3}$ B $\left[\frac{1}{2}\,\middle|\,\frac{1}{4}\right]$

c $\frac{1}{2}+\frac{1}{2}$ C $\left[\frac{1}{3}\,\middle|\,\frac{1}{3}\right]$

d $\frac{1}{3}+\frac{1}{6}$ D $\left[\frac{2}{3}\,\middle|\,\frac{1}{3}\right]$

e $\frac{1}{2}+\frac{1}{4}$ E $\left[\frac{1}{3}\,\middle|\,\frac{1}{6}\right]$

2 Use the diagrams and your answers from Q1 to work out

a $1-\frac{1}{2}$ **b** $\frac{2}{4}-\frac{1}{4}$ **c** $1-\frac{2}{3}$

3 **Real** The probability of rolling a 4 on a dice is $\frac{1}{6}$.
What is the probability of not rolling a 4?

4 Add together these fractions by writing them with the same denominator.

a $\frac{1}{3}+\frac{2}{9}$ **b** $\frac{3}{5}+\frac{1}{10}$ **c** $\frac{1}{8}+\frac{3}{4}$ **d** $\frac{2}{15}+\frac{2}{3}+\frac{1}{5}$

5 Work out these fraction subtractions by writing them with the same denominator.

a $\frac{3}{4}-\frac{3}{8}$ **b** $\frac{2}{5}-\frac{3}{10}$ **c** $\frac{5}{6}-\frac{1}{3}$ **d** $\frac{7}{9}-\frac{2}{3}$

6 Copy and complete. The first two have been started for you.

a The lowest common multiple of 2 and 7 is 14.

$\frac{3}{7}+\frac{1}{2}=\frac{6}{14}+\frac{\square}{14}=\frac{\square}{14}$

b The lowest common multiple of 3 and 4 is 12.

$\frac{1}{3}+\frac{1}{4}=\frac{\square}{12}+\frac{\square}{12}=\frac{\square}{12}$

c The lowest common multiple of 10 and 3 is $\square$.

$\frac{3}{10}+\frac{2}{3}=$

7 Work out

a $\frac{5}{8}+\frac{1}{6}$ **b** $\frac{2}{5}-\frac{1}{12}$ **c** $\frac{6}{11}-\frac{2}{3}$

Q4a hint

$\frac{1}{3}=\frac{3}{9}$

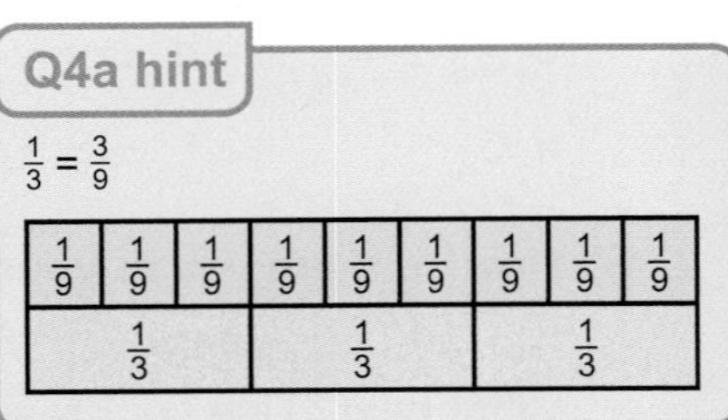

Q5a hint

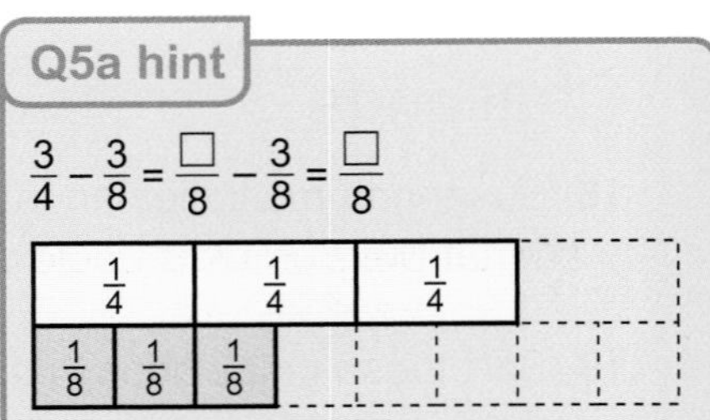

$\frac{3}{4}-\frac{3}{8}=\frac{\square}{8}-\frac{3}{8}=\frac{\square}{8}$

Q7a hint

Use the LCM of the denominators.

Topic links: Probability

8 Marie says, '$\frac{1}{10} + \frac{1}{20} = \frac{2}{30} = \frac{1}{15}$.'

a Explain what mistake she has made.

b What is the correct answer to $\frac{1}{10} + \frac{1}{20}$?

Q8a hint

When you add or subtract fractions the denominators must be the same.

9 Isabelle, Sofia and Tristan enter a competition. If they win, they agree to split the prize like this.

Isabelle: $\frac{1}{3}$ Sofia: $\frac{1}{5}$ Tristan: $\frac{1}{12}$

They give the remainder to charity.

a What fraction would Isabelle and Sofia have between them?

b What fraction of the prize would they give to charity?

c How much more would Isabelle get than Tristan?

Multiplying and dividing fractions

1 Work out

a $5 \times \frac{1}{3} = 5$ lots of $\frac{1}{3} = \frac{1}{3} + \frac{1}{3} + \frac{1}{3} + \frac{1}{3} + \frac{1}{3} = \frac{\square}{3} = \square\frac{\square}{3}$

b $2 \times \frac{1}{7} = \frac{1}{7} + \frac{1}{7} = \frac{\square}{\square}$

c $\frac{3}{5} \times 4 = 4 \times \frac{3}{5} = \frac{3}{5} + \frac{3}{5} + \frac{3}{5} + \frac{3}{5} = \frac{\square}{5} = \square\frac{\square}{5}$

d $\frac{6}{11} \times 3$ e $5 \times \frac{2}{7}$ f $\frac{1}{4}$ of 18 g $\frac{9}{10}$ of 40

2 Work out these multiplications. Simplify the fractions first.

a $\frac{5}{6} \times \frac{3}{5} = \frac{5 \times \square}{6 \times \square} = \frac{\square \times 5}{6 \times \square} = \frac{\square}{6} \times \frac{5}{\square}$

b $\frac{12}{33} \times \frac{11}{4}$ c $\frac{8}{15} \times \frac{5}{24}$ d $\frac{14}{25} \times \frac{10}{7}$ e $\frac{20}{63} \times \frac{9}{10}$

3 a Work out these divisions.

$24 \div 12 =$ $24 \div \frac{1}{2} =$

$24 \div 8 =$ $24 \div \frac{1}{3} =$

$24 \div 2 =$ $24 \div \frac{1}{4} =$

$24 \div 1 =$

b Complete this sentence: 'When the numbers you divide by get smaller, the answer gets ________.'

4 Write down the reciprocals of these numbers.

a $\frac{2}{7}$ b $\frac{3}{4}$ c 5 d 12

e $\frac{1}{3}$ f $\frac{1}{2}$ g $\frac{1}{8}$ h 6

Q4c hint

The reciprocal of a whole number, is $\frac{1}{\text{number}}$.

5 Work out.

a $\frac{3}{5} \div \frac{2}{7} = \frac{3}{5} \times \frac{\square}{2} = \frac{\square}{10}$ b $\frac{8}{9} \div \frac{1}{5} = \frac{8}{9} \times \frac{\square}{1} = \frac{\square}{\square}$

c $\frac{1}{10} \div \frac{2}{3}$ d $\frac{3}{7} \div \frac{1}{6}$ e $\frac{10}{51} \div \frac{2}{5}$

Q5 Strategy hint

Multiply the first number by the reciprocal of the second.

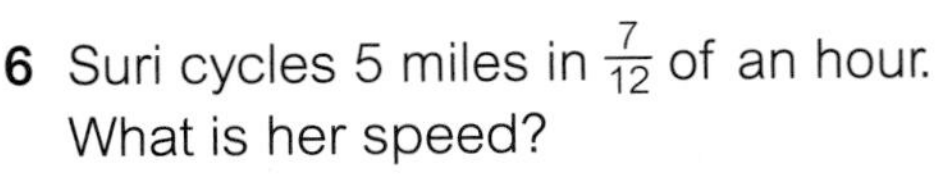

6 Suri cycles 5 miles in $\frac{7}{12}$ of an hour.
What is her speed?

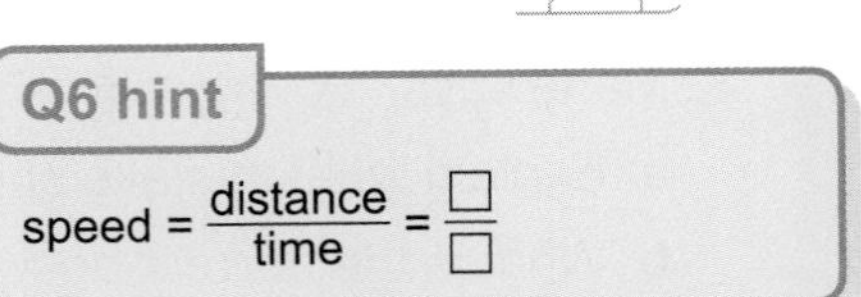

Q6 hint

speed = $\frac{\text{distance}}{\text{time}} = \frac{\square}{\square}$

Calculating with mixed numbers and decimals

1 Match these equivalent fractions and decimals.

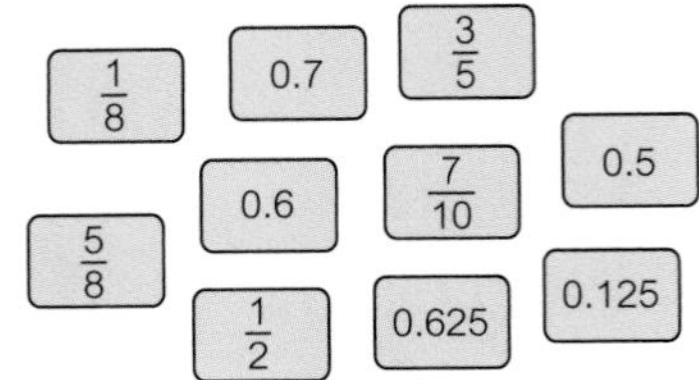

Q1 Strategy hint

$\frac{5}{8} = 5 \div 8 =$

$8\overline{)\square.\square\square\square}$ = $\square.\square\square\square$

The number you divide by goes outside the 'bus stop'.

2 Write the first 5 decimal places of

a $0.\dot{3}$ **b** $0.1\dot{6}$ **c** $0.8\dot{3}$

Q2 hint

The dot shows the digit repeats forever.

3 Convert each fraction to a decimal.
Write recurring decimals using dot notation.

a $\frac{1}{9}$ **b** $\frac{4}{9}$ **c** $\frac{11}{9}$ **d** $\frac{5}{3}$

4 Write these mixed numbers as improper fractions.

a $2\frac{3}{4}$ **b** $3\frac{1}{2}$ **c** $2\frac{5}{6}$

d $5\frac{3}{8}$ **e** $1\frac{1}{10}$ **f** $12\frac{3}{10}$

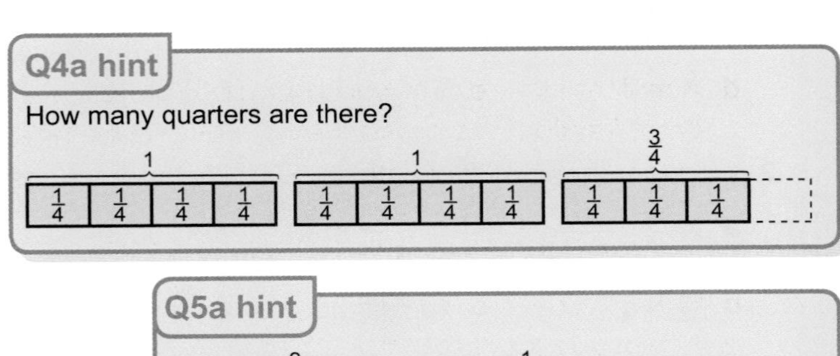

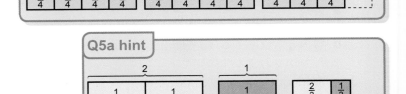

5 Work out these mixed number calculations.

a $2\frac{2}{3} + 1\frac{1}{3}$ **b** $1\frac{2}{5} + 3\frac{1}{5}$

c $5\frac{1}{6} + 2\frac{5}{6}$

Q5a hint

2 — 1 | 1; 1 — 1; $\frac{2}{3}$ | $\frac{1}{3}$

6 Work out

a $1\frac{1}{3} + 2\frac{3}{4}$ **b** $4\frac{3}{10} + 2\frac{1}{5}$

c $3\frac{9}{10} + \frac{1}{7}$ **d** $10\frac{2}{5} + 3\frac{5}{6}$

e $7\frac{1}{8} + 4\frac{15}{16}$

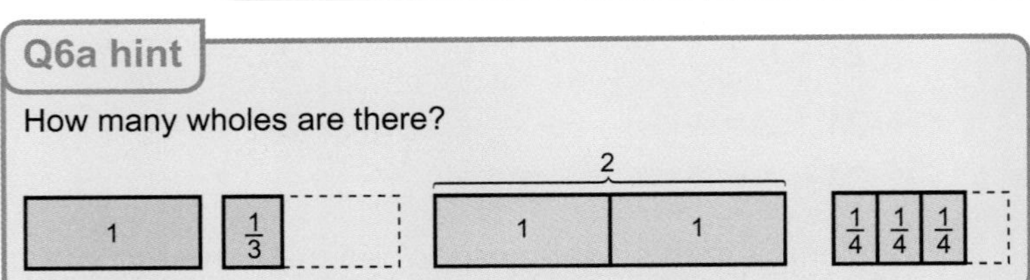

7 Work out these subtractions. Give your answers as mixed numbers.

a $5 - 3\frac{1}{2} = \frac{10}{2} - \frac{\square}{2}$

b $4\frac{2}{3} - 1\frac{1}{3}$ **c** $10\frac{3}{4} - 2\frac{1}{4}$ **d** $5\frac{4}{5} - 2\frac{1}{10}$

e $1\frac{1}{2} - \frac{3}{4}$ **f** $2\frac{3}{7} - 1\frac{7}{10}$

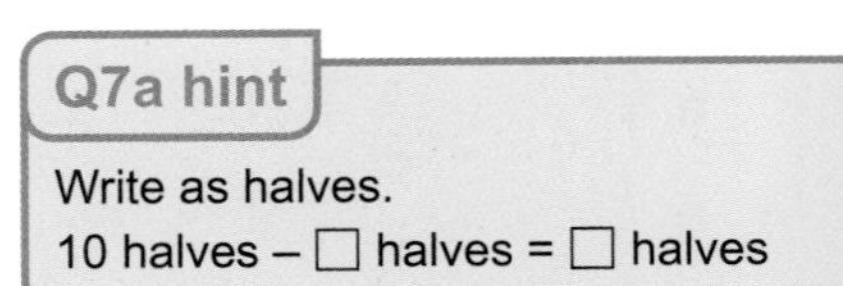

8 Will divides his evening up like this.

Dinner: $\frac{3}{4}$ hour Exercise: 1 hour Homework: 1 hour 30 minutes

a How many hours and minutes has Will scheduled?

b He has 5 hours in total before bed. How much time does he have left?

9 Work out these multiplications. The first one has been started for you.

a $\frac{4}{5} \times 2\frac{1}{3} = \frac{4}{5} \times \frac{\square}{3} = \frac{4 \times \square}{5 \times 3} =$

b $\frac{7}{10} \times 1\frac{2}{3}$ c $\frac{1}{15} \times 2\frac{1}{2}$ d $3\frac{8}{9} \times \frac{1}{6}$ e $1\frac{2}{11} \times 6\frac{1}{3}$

Q9 hint

Write mixed numbers as improper fractions. Give your answers as mixed numbers.

10 Work out these divisions. The first one has been started for you.

a $5\frac{1}{2} \div \frac{1}{2} = \frac{\square}{2} \times \frac{2}{1} = \frac{2 \times \square}{2 \times 1} =$

b $3\frac{2}{11} \div \frac{4}{5}$ c $4\frac{1}{9} \div \frac{2}{3}$ d $12\frac{1}{2} \div \frac{1}{4}$ e $10\frac{1}{3} \div 2\frac{3}{4}$

Enrichment

1 **Finance** Jatin pays $\frac{1}{5}$ of his salary as tax.
He uses $\frac{1}{10}$ of his salary to pay back his student loan.
He pays $\frac{1}{4}$ of his salary into a pension scheme.
What fraction of his salary does he take home?

2 **Real / Problem-solving** Scientists recommend that babies sleep for $\frac{5}{8}$ of the day.

a How many hours should babies sleep for?

b Adults should sleep for 8 hours a day.
What fraction of the day is this?

c A mother sleeps only when her baby does.
What fraction of the day is she awake while her baby sleeps?

3 **Finance / Real** The US stock market used to trade in fractions. Prices were given as eighths of a dollar, instead of in cents.

a How many cents is $\frac{1}{8}$ of a dollar?

b How many cents is $\frac{3}{8}$ of a dollar?

c Shares for one company cost $3\frac{5}{8}$ of a dollar per share.
How many shares could you get for $1125?

d Cleo's shares increased their value by $\frac{1}{2}$. They originally cost her $2\frac{1}{8}$ of a dollar. How much are they now?

Discussion Why do you think the US stock market changed to using decimals?

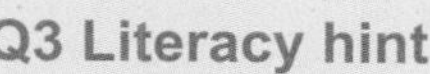

Q3 Literacy hint

There are 100 cents in a dollar.

4 **Reflect** List these tasks (A–F) in order from easiest to hardest.

A Adding and subtracting fractions
B Multiplying fractions
C Dividing fractions
D Adding and subtracting mixed numbers
E Multiplying mixed numbers
F Dividing mixed numbers

Look at the first task in your list (the easiest).
What made it easiest?
Look at the two tasks at the bottom of your list (the hardest).
What made them hardest?
Write hints to help you with the two tasks you found hardest.

Q4 hint

List the letters of the tasks in order. You don't need to write out the descriptions.

8 Extend

You will:

- Extend your understanding with problem-solving.

1 Work out

a $\frac{1}{8} \times \frac{2}{3}$

b $\frac{15}{43} + \frac{1}{10}$

c $\frac{3}{5} \times \frac{20}{81}$

d $\frac{19}{20} - \frac{4}{5}$

2 **Real** The musicians in a band share $\frac{1}{3}$ of a royalty fee for their song. There are six musicians. What fraction of the fee does each musician get?

3 **Finance** This pie chart shows the proportion of workers earning different wages at a company.

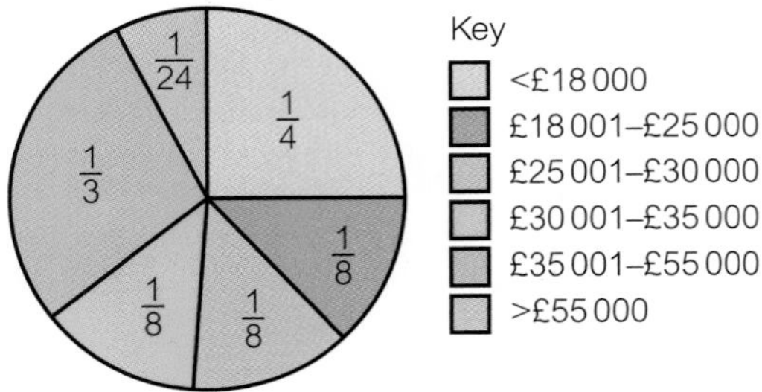

a What fraction of workers earn £25 000 or less?

b What fraction of workers earn more than £30 000?

c What is the modal wage group?

d Write down one problem with the way the information is grouped.

4 **Reasoning** Petra has 10 cakes at her party. She wants to give all 75 guests an equal piece.

a Explain why she won't have enough if she cuts the cakes into sevenths.

b How many pieces should she cut the cakes into?

c How many pieces will she have left over?

5 Work out

a $\left(\frac{1}{2}\right)^2$

b $\left(\frac{1}{4}\right)^2$

c $\left(\frac{2}{3}\right)^2$

d $\sqrt{\frac{16}{25}}$

e $\sqrt{\frac{1}{64}}$

f $\sqrt{\frac{9}{16}}$

6 Use your calculator to work out

a $2\frac{3}{8} + 1\frac{1}{3}$

b $2\frac{3}{4} \times 3\frac{1}{8}$

c $1\frac{1}{3} \div -3\frac{1}{2}$

d $\left(2\frac{1}{4} + 9\frac{1}{5}\right) - \left(\frac{3}{5}\right)^2$

e $\left(5\frac{1}{2} \times 2\right) + \left(1\frac{3}{4} - 1\frac{3}{8}\right)$

f $\left(\frac{9}{10} \div 1\frac{2}{3}\right) \times \left(2\frac{1}{2} + 9\frac{1}{3}\right)$

Topic links: Pie charts, Averages, Area and volume

7 a Complete this magic square so that each row, column and diagonal sums to the same number.

$1\frac{1}{3}$		
	$1\frac{2}{3}$	
$2\frac{2}{3}$		2

b Make your own magic square using fractions.

8 Simplify these fractional ratios.

a $3\frac{1}{2} : \frac{1}{4}$ b $2\frac{1}{5} : \frac{3}{10}$ c $1\frac{3}{4} : 2\frac{1}{6}$

Q8a hint

Multiply both numbers to make them into integers.

9 **Reasoning** The owner of a café calculates that $\frac{2}{3}$ of her customers order cake.
Half the people who order cake have cheesecake.
How many pieces of cheesecake should she have for 60 customers?

10 **STEM / Real** Meteorologists use these ratings to describe the level of cloud cover.

1 Clear: $0–\frac{1}{10}$ cloud cover
2 Scattered: $\frac{1}{10} - \frac{5}{10}$ cloud cover
3 Broken: $\frac{5}{10} - \frac{9}{10}$ cloud cover
4 Overcast: fully covered

A forecast for five days was

Monday: $\frac{1}{4}$ covered
Tuesday: $\frac{3}{5}$ covered
Wednesday: $\frac{3}{4}$ covered
Thursday: $\frac{1}{3}$ covered
Friday: clear sky

a What was the mean amount of cloud cover for the five days?
b Work out the mean of the cloud cover ratings (the numbers 1–4) for the five days.

11 Write down the reciprocals of these numbers.

a $\frac{5}{9}$ b $\frac{3}{2}$ c $4\frac{1}{2}$
d $2\frac{3}{5}$ e $-\frac{3}{2}$ f $-\frac{1}{10}$

12 a What is the product of a number and its reciprocal?
b Does 0 have a reciprocal? Explain.

Q12a hint

'Finding the product' means multiplying.

13 Work out

a $\left(\frac{1}{4}\right)^3$ b $\left(\frac{2}{3}\right)^3$ c $\sqrt[3]{\frac{1}{27}}$ d $\sqrt[3]{\frac{8}{125}}$

14 Work out the missing values.

a
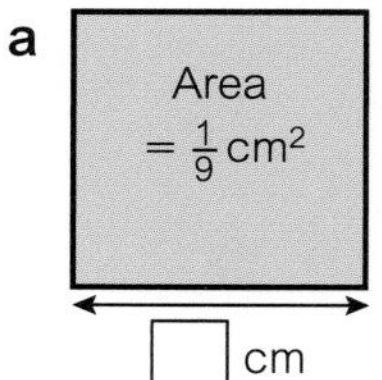

b
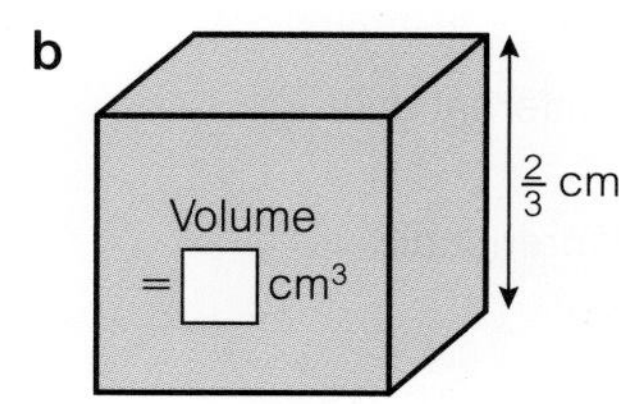

c
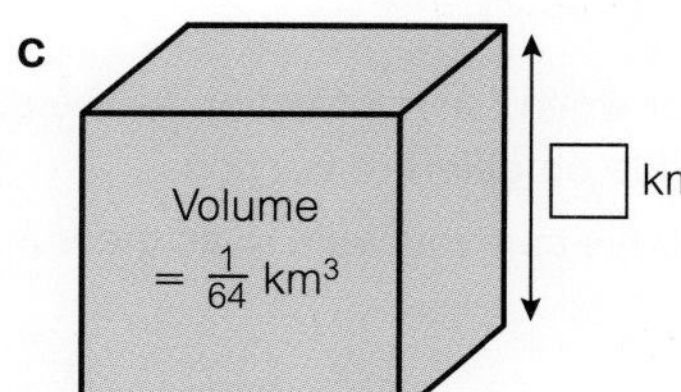

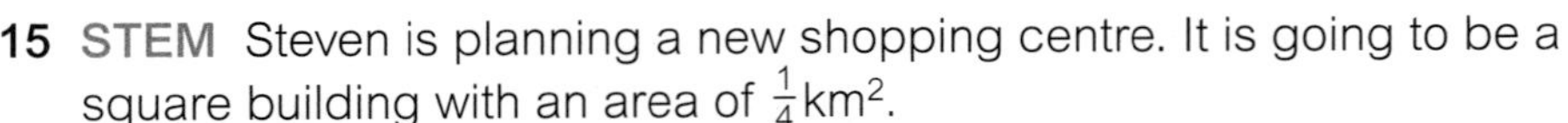

15 STEM Steven is planning a new shopping centre. It is going to be a square building with an area of $\frac{1}{4}$km^2.

a Work out the length of one side of the building.

b What is the length of a path running around the perimeter of the building?

c Steven decides to have cube-shaped seats in the shopping centre. The seats will be $\frac{1}{2}$m high.
Work out the volume of one seat.

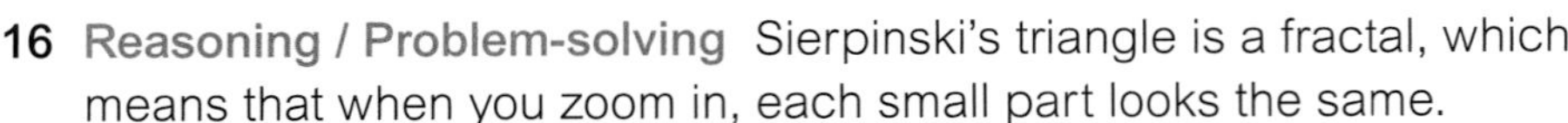

16 Reasoning / Problem-solving Sierpinski's triangle is a fractal, which means that when you zoom in, each small part looks the same.

a This is the first step for making Sierpinski's triangle.

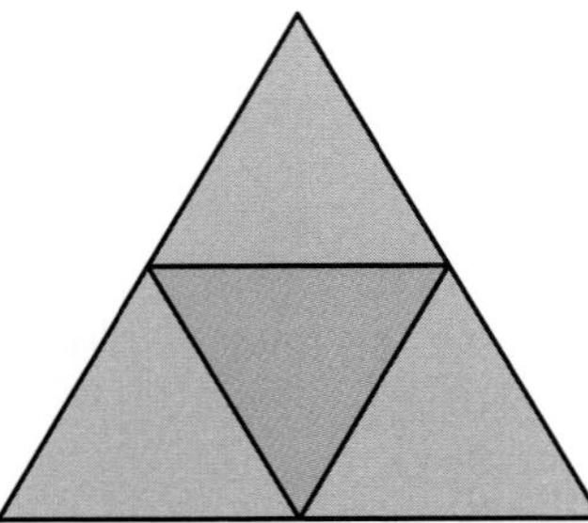

What fraction of this triangle is shaded red?

b This is the second step in Sierpinski's triangle.

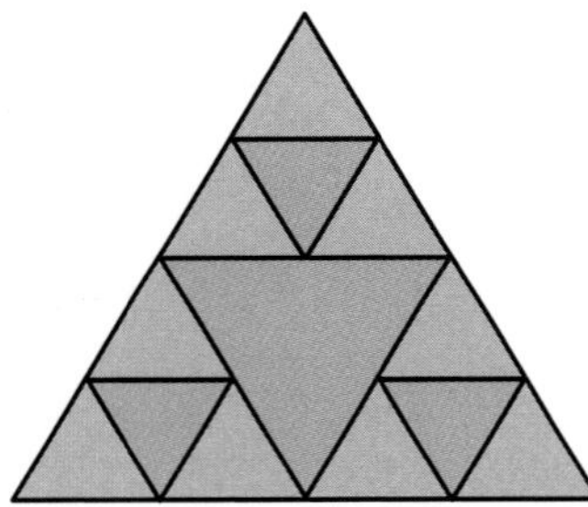

Add the fraction taken up by the big triangle to the fraction taken up by the three smaller triangles to work out the total fraction that is red.

c Draw the third step in Sierpinski's triangle.
Write down the three fractions you need to add together to work out the total fraction that is red.

d Describe the sequence made by the numerators and the sequence made by the denominators.
Discussion Do you think the whole triangle will ever be red?

Q15b hint

Imagine splitting the big red triangle into four smaller triangles. How many smaller triangles are there altogether?

Investigation **Problem-solving**

$\frac{1}{2} = \frac{1}{3} + \frac{1}{6}$

Zoe is trying to find out whether all unit fractions can be written as the sum of two different unit fractions.

She finds that $\frac{1}{9} = \frac{1}{10} + \frac{1}{90}$.

1 Can you find a rule for writing a unit fraction as the sum of two different unit fractions? Test your rule on different fractions.

2 How many different ways can you write $\frac{1}{8}$ as the sum of two different unit fractions?

Key point

A unit fraction is a fraction that has a numerator of 1.

17 **Real** The Ancient Egyptians wrote nearly all of their fractions as unit fractions. They used this eye shape to show '1 over' a number.

a Use this key to translate these fractions.

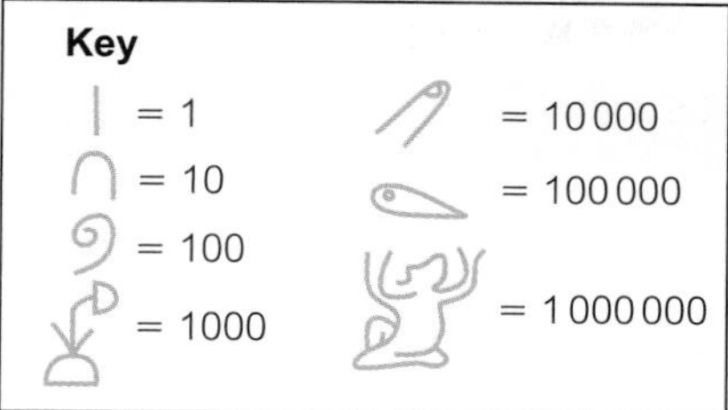

The first one has been done for you.

i $= \frac{1}{10}$ **ii**

iii **iv**

They wrote fractions only as unit fractions (except in special cases).

So, for example, they wrote $\frac{3}{8}$ as because it is $\frac{2}{8} + \frac{1}{8} = \frac{1}{4} + \frac{1}{8}$.

The two fractions were always written separately.

b Use Egyptian fractions to write these.

i $\frac{1}{3}$ **ii** $\frac{1}{8}$

iii $\frac{5}{6}$ **iv** $\frac{3}{4}$

Q17b iii hint

Find different unit fractions that add together to give $\frac{5}{6}$.

18 Johann says, 'If I add 1 to the numerator and denominator of a fraction, the fraction will be bigger than what I started with.'

a Start with $\frac{1}{3}$ and keep adding 1 to the numerator and denominator. What happens? Explain why.
Use a table like this to set out your working.

Fraction	Decimal
$\frac{1}{3}$	0.333...
$\frac{2}{4}$	

Q18a Strategy hint

Converting your fractions to decimals will make it easier to compare them.

b Try starting with $\frac{6}{5}$. What happens? Explain why.

19 **Reflect** The word fraction is used in lots of ways. Here are two examples:

- In everyday English, a fraction means 'a small amount'. When hanging a picture you might 'move it up a fraction' or you might ask someone to 'budge up a fraction' so you can sit beside them.
- In chemistry, the fractionating process separates a mixture into its components.

Write a definition, in your own words, of 'fraction' in mathematics.
What do you think 'fractional ownership' means? When might it be a good idea?

Reflect

8 Unit test

Log how you did on your Student Progression Chart.

1 Work out these multiplications.
a $\frac{1}{5} \times 35$ b $\frac{2}{3} \times -18$
c $45 \times \frac{3}{9}$ d $12 \times \frac{5}{6}$

2 Work out these additions and subtractions.
a $\frac{1}{3} + \frac{1}{6}$ b $\frac{3}{4} + \frac{1}{8}$ c $\frac{3}{4} - \frac{1}{2}$
d $\frac{5}{11} + \frac{5}{10}$ e $\frac{5}{8} - \frac{1}{10}$ f $\frac{3}{11} - \frac{2}{5}$

3 Sarah works for 4 hours a day at a hairdressers.
One day she spent 80 minutes doing admin work.
What fraction of her working day did she spend doing admin work?

4 Alex ran $2\frac{1}{2}$ miles, then swam a further $\frac{3}{4}$ of a mile, then cycled $5\frac{2}{7}$ miles.
How many miles did he travel in total?

5 Write each fraction as a decimal.
a $\frac{3}{4}$ b $\frac{9}{10}$
c $\frac{4}{5}$ d $\frac{5}{8}$

6 Work out
a $3\frac{2}{5} + 4\frac{1}{3}$ b $10\frac{3}{4} + 1\frac{1}{6}$
c $15\frac{5}{6} - 2\frac{1}{3}$ d $3\frac{7}{10} - 6\frac{3}{8}$

7 Work out
a $\frac{3}{4} \times \frac{1}{5}$ b $-\frac{1}{3} \times \frac{5}{6}$
c $\frac{7}{10} \times \frac{2}{3}$ d $-\frac{4}{5} \times -\frac{1}{11}$

8 Work out
a $5 \div \frac{1}{4}$ b $10 \div \frac{2}{3}$
c $8 \div \frac{2}{5}$ d $-5 \div \frac{8}{9}$

9 How many quarters are there in three fifths?
Give your answer as a fraction.

10 Work out
a $3\frac{1}{4} - \frac{1}{2}$ b $2\frac{3}{5} - 1\frac{3}{4}$
c $3\frac{3}{10} - 9\frac{1}{2}$ d $5\frac{2}{3} - 7\frac{6}{7}$

11 Gerry takes $5\frac{1}{2}$ minutes to ice a cake. How long will it take him to ice eight cakes?

12 Work out these multiplications. Give your answers in their simplest form.
a $\frac{5}{12} \times \frac{2}{15}$ b $\frac{3}{10} \times \frac{5}{18}$
c $2\frac{1}{2} \times \frac{4}{25}$ d $3\frac{2}{3} \times \frac{1}{16}$

13 Work out

a $\frac{1}{3} \div \frac{1}{2}$
b $\frac{2}{5} \div \frac{1}{4}$
c $-\frac{3}{4} \div \frac{7}{9}$
d $-\frac{5}{12} \div -\frac{2}{5}$

14 Use these calculations to answer the following additions and subtractions.

$3\frac{2}{5} + 6\frac{3}{4} = 10\frac{3}{20}$ $4\frac{3}{7} - 1\frac{2}{3} = 2\frac{16}{21}$

a $10\frac{3}{20} - 6\frac{3}{4}$
b $2\frac{16}{21} + 1\frac{2}{3}$
c $4\frac{3}{7} - 2\frac{16}{21}$

15 Find the reciprocal of these numbers.

a 5
b 10
c $\frac{1}{2}$
d $\frac{6}{11}$
e $1\frac{1}{2}$
f $3\frac{4}{5}$

16 Work out

a $\frac{3}{8} \div \frac{1}{2}$
b $\frac{2}{5} \div \frac{8}{15}$
c $4\frac{3}{10} \div \frac{18}{21}$
d $2\frac{4}{11} \div \frac{12}{33}$

17 Work out the side length of a square with area

a $\frac{1}{4}\text{cm}^2$
b $\frac{4}{25}\text{cm}^2$

18 Work out the side length of a cube with volume

a $\frac{1}{27}\text{cm}^3$
b $\frac{8}{27}\text{m}^3$

19 Write these fractions as the sum of two different unit fractions.

a $\frac{1}{3}$
b $\frac{1}{5}$

Challenge

20 a Fold a square of paper in half three times.
What fraction have you split it into?

b Find as many different ways as you can of folding the square into eight equal pieces.

c How many sections would the paper be split into if you folded it in half seven times?

Discussion There is a common belief that the maximum number of times you can fold a piece of paper in half is seven.
Do you think it's true?

d Is there a way of folding the paper into 10 equal pieces?

Q20c hint

You could draw a diagram to try different methods instead of folding the paper each time.

21 **Reflect** In this unit, did you work:

- slowly
- at average speed
- quickly?

Did you find the work easy, OK or hard?
How did that affect how fast you worked?
Is it always good to work quickly? Explain your answer.
Is it always bad to work slowly? Explain your answer.

Reflect

9 Straight-line graphs

MASTER | Check P222 | Strengthen P224 | Extend P229 | Test P233

9.1 Direct proportion on graphs

You will learn to:

- Recognise when values are in direct proportion
- Plot graphs and read values to solve problems.

CONFIDENCE

Why learn this?
Climate scientists plot graphs of sea levels against global temperature to find out the relationship.

Fluency
1 gallon ≈ 4.5 litres: fill in the missing capacities.

- 4 gallons ≈ ☐ litres
- ☐ gallons ≈ 45 litres
- 200 gallons ≈ ☐ litres

Explore
Is the price of coffee in direct proportion to the amount you buy?

Exercise 9.1

Warm up

1 **Real** **a** 1 kg of apples costs £2.40. How much do $2\frac{1}{2}$ kg of apples cost?
b 500 ml of juice costs 60p. How much does 1.25 litres cost?
c In 2013 the exchange rate for pounds to Russian roubles was £1 = 48 roubles. How many roubles would you get for £15?

Key point
When two quantities are in **direct proportion**

- plotting them as a graph gives a straight line through the origin
- when one variable is zero, the other variable will also be zero
- when one variable doubles, so does the other.

2 Which of these graphs show one variable in **direct proportion** to another?

A
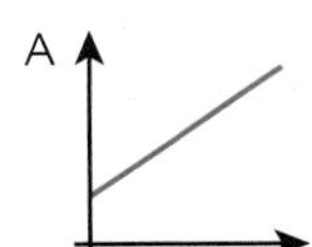
B
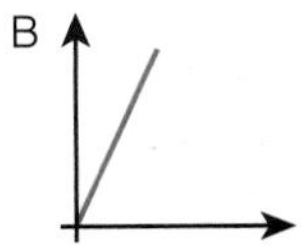
C
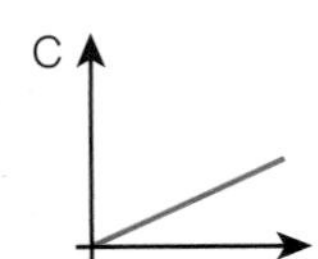
D
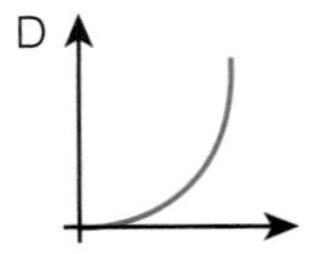
E
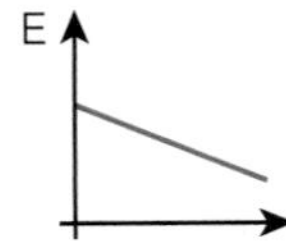

3 **Real / Problem-solving** This line graph shows the price of pick-and-mix sweets by mass.

a How much does 100 g of sweets cost?
b How many grams of sweets would you get for £7.50?
c How much does 350 g of sweets cost?
d How many grams of sweets would you get for £3.60?
e Max is having a party for 30 people. He wants to buy sweets for everyone. He buys 50 g for each person. How much does that cost him?
f How much does the price increase for every extra 100 g of sweets?
g Are the two quantities in direct proportion?

Price of pick-and-mix sweets

Cost (£): 0 1 2 3 4 5 6 7 8 9 10
Mass (g): 0 50 100 150 200 250 300 350 400 450 500 550 600

4 **STEM / Reasoning** A scientist gets these results in an experiment to test the resistance of different lengths of copper wire.

a Are resistance and length in direct proportion for this wire? Explain how you know.

b Use the graph to work out the resistance of these lengths of wire.

i 4 m **ii** 15 m **iii** 30 m

c Use the graph to work out the length of wire with resistance

i 0.01 ohms **ii** 0.25 ohms

Discussion How reliable are your answers to parts **b iii** and **c ii**?

Q4 Strategy hint

The graph doesn't go to 30 m. Use values you know to work out larger values.

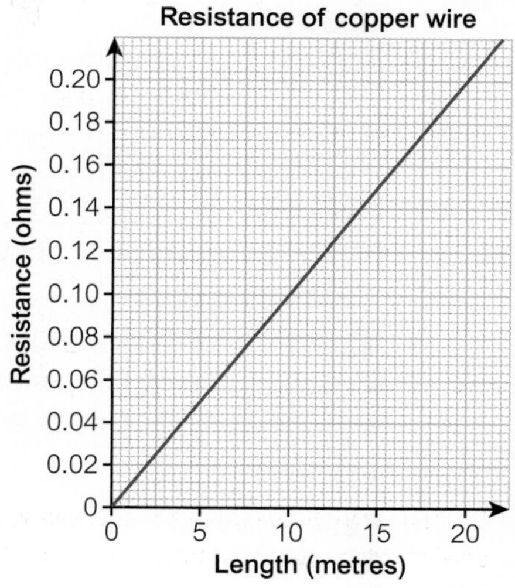

5 **Real / Problem-solving** This graph can be used for converting between a length in metres (m) and a length in feet (ft).

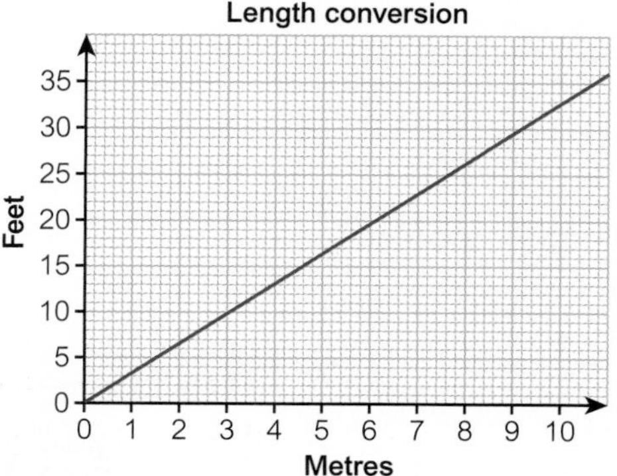

a Convert 6 m to feet.

b Convert 30 feet to metres.

c Which is longer, 4 m or 12.5 feet?

d Stuart is 6 feet tall. Dave is 1.6 m tall. Who is taller?

e Chris needs 75 feet of wallpaper for her room. It is sold in 5 metre rolls. How many will she need to buy to have enough wallpaper?

6 **Real / Reasoning** The table shows some equivalent temperatures in Celsius and Fahrenheit.

Celsius	Fahrenheit
10°	50°
15°	59°
30°	86°

a Plot a line graph for these values.

b Are Celsius and Fahrenheit in direct proportion? Explain how you know.

c What is the freezing point of water in °F?

The Government advises elderly people to keep their living rooms at 21 °C and their bedrooms at 18 °C.

d What are these temperatures in Fahrenheit?

Q6a hint

Plot Celsius on the horizontal axis and Fahrenheit on the vertical axis. Use sensible scales.

Q6c hint

What is the freezing point of water in °C?

7 A car travels at a constant speed of 90 km/h.

a Copy and complete this table for the distance travelled by the car.

Time (hours)	0	1	2
Distance (km)			

b Plot this journey on a distance–time graph.

Another car travels for 1 hour at 100 km/h and then for two hours at 60 km/h.

c Show this journey on your distance–time graph.

d Which graph shows direct proportion?

Discussion When is distance travelled in direct proportion to time taken?

Q7 Literacy hint

'km/h' stands for kilometres per hour or kilometres travelled in every hour.

Q7c Strategy hint

Use different colours when you have two graphs on the same axes.

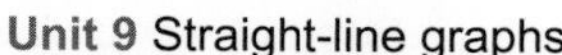

8 **Real / Finance** A perfume costs £75 for 50 ml.
The perfume company is planning to sell this perfume in different sized bottles up to 100 ml.

a Plot a line graph to show the price for up to 100 ml of perfume.

b Are the price and volume in ml in direct proportion?

Discussion Why don't companies usually price their goods like this?

Q8a hint

Use a table like this.

Volume in ml		50	
Price		£75	

Choose a factor and a multiple of 50 for two more volume values. Work out the prices.

9 **Real** Posters are sold online for £7.50 each. The postage charge is £2.50 per order.

a Copy and complete this table for the price of buying different numbers of posters.

Number of posters	1	2	10
Price			

b Plot a line graph to show the price for 1, 2 and 10 posters including postage.

c Use your graph to work out the price of 5 posters.

d Is the price of 10 posters twice the price of 5 posters?

e Is the cost of posters as shown in this graph in direct proportion? Explain.

10 **Real** Which of these are in direct proportion?

A Litres and pints

B Temperature measured hourly over 24 hours

C Pounds (£) and dollars

D The distance travelled on a journey at a constant speed

E The distance travelled on a journey at varying speeds

Q10 Strategy hint

Sketch or visualise a graph.

Explore

11 **Explore** Is the price of coffee in direct proportion to the amount you buy?
Is it easier to explore this question now you have completed the lesson? What further information do you need to be able to answer this?

Reflect

12 **Reflect**

a List all the things you have to do to interpret graphs (as in Q3 to Q5).
You may start your list, 'Read values'.

b List all the things you have to do to draw graphs (as in Q6 to Q9).
You may start your list, 'Draw a table of values'.

c Which are you better at, interpreting or drawing graphs?
Explain why.

Topic links: Ratio, Proportion, Exchange rates, Metric /imperial measures
Subject links: Science (Q4)

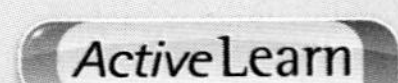 Theta 2, Section 9.1

9.2 Gradients

You will learn to:
- Plot a straight-line graph and work out its gradient.

Why learn this?
When you meet steep hills on the road, you will usually see a road sign showing the gradient.

Fluency
- Complete these coordinate pairs for $y = 4x$.
  (3, □), (□, 24), (10, □), (□, 20), (−2, □), (□, −28)
- Work out these multiplications
  3 × −4, −2 × 5, −7 × 2
  −1 × 4, 3 × −2, −2 × −3

Explore
What does the percentage or ratio shown on a road sign mean?

Exercise 9.2

1 Order these distance–time graphs from the one showing the fastest speed to the one showing the slowest speed.

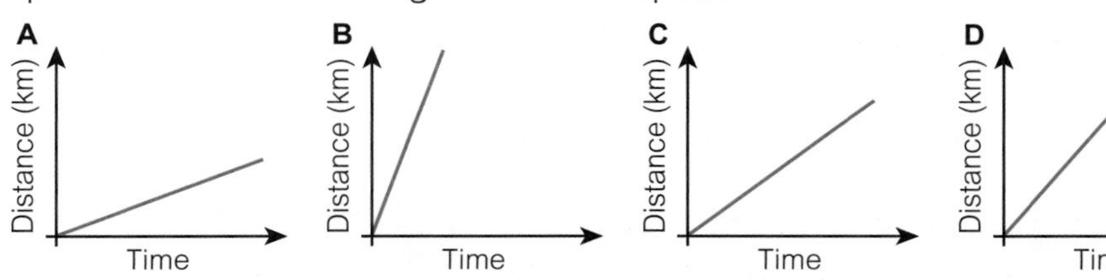

2 **a** Copy and complete this table of values for the equation $y = 2x + 2$.

x	1	2	3	4	5
y	4				

b Complete these coordinate pairs from the table of values.
(1, 4), (2, □), (3, □), (4, □), (5, □)

c **i** Draw a coordinate grid from −3 to 5 on the x-axis and −12 to 12 on the y-axis, and plot the coordinates.

ii Draw a straight line that goes through all the points and extend the line to the edges of the grid.

iii Label the graph with its equation.

d What is the value of y when $x = -3$?

Q2c hint
If your points are not on a straight line, check the table of values.

3 **a** Copy and complete this table of values for the equation $y = 2x - 5$.

x	−2	−1	0	1	2
y	−9				

b Use the same grid as for Q2 to plot the coordinates for $y = 2x - 5$. Join the points in a straight line and label the line.

c What do you notice about the two lines you have drawn?

Warm up

Investigation **Problem-solving**

1 Draw a table of values for $y = 3x$. Plot the graph on a grid with axes from −10 to +10.
2 Plot the graph of $y = 4x$ on the same grid.
3 What do you notice about these two lines? Which one is steeper?
4 What do you think the graph of $y = 2x$ might look like?
Draw a table of values and plot the graph to see if you were correct.
5 On the same grid, plot the graph of $y = -2x$.
6 Compare your graphs of $y = 2x$ and $y = -2x$. What is the same? What is different?

4 a How many squares does line A go up for every one square across?
b How many squares does line A go up for every two squares across?
c How many squares does line A go up for every three squares across?
Discussion What do you notice?
d Is the gradient of line A positive or negative?
e Is the gradient of line B positive or negative?
f How many squares does line B go down for every one square across?
Discussion What is similar about gradients and correlation?

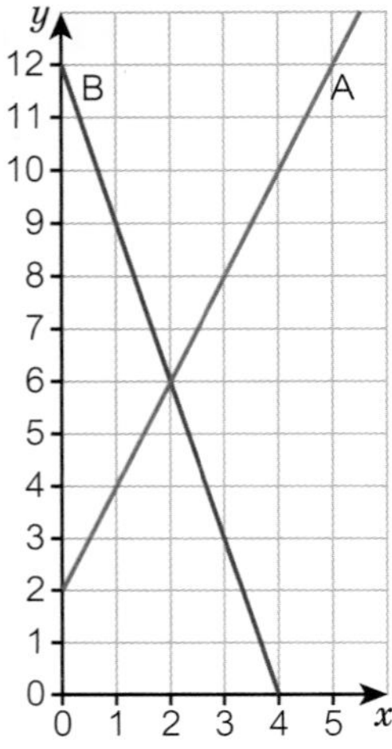

Key point

The steepness of the graph is called the **gradient**.
To find the gradient, work out how many units the graph goes up for every one unit across.

5 Write down the gradients of the lines in Q4.

6 Work out the gradient of each line segment in the diagram.

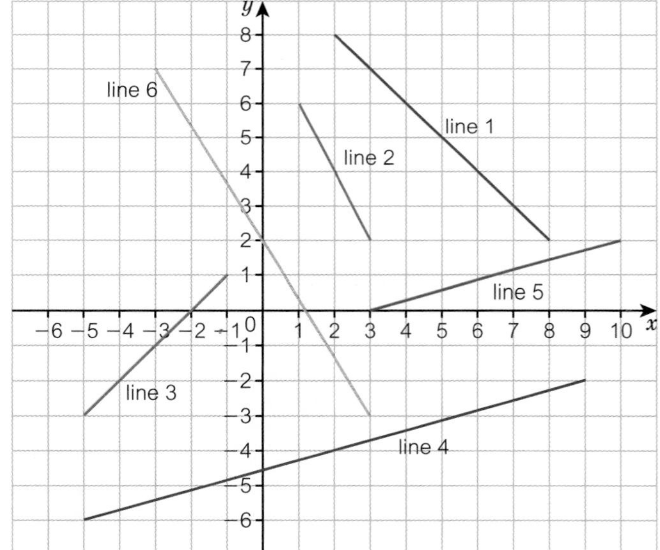

Q6 hint

You will sometimes need to use the whole of the line segment to work out the gradient.
A gradient can be a fraction. Write the fraction in its simplest form.
6 up with 8 across is $\frac{6}{8} = \frac{3}{4}$.
Check whether each gradient is positive or negative.

7 **Reasoning** Find the missing values.
a A gradient of $\frac{1}{2}$ means ☐ up for every 2 across.
b A gradient of $\frac{3}{4}$ means ☐ up for every 4 across.
c A gradient of $\frac{1}{6}$ means ☐ up for every ☐ across.
d A gradient of $-\frac{1}{3}$ means ☐ down for every 3 across.
e A gradient of $-\frac{2}{5}$ means ☐ down for every ☐ across.
f Which of these gradients is for the steepest line? Explain.

Q7 hint

You could sketch these on squared paper.

Topic links: Negative numbers, Simplifying fractions, Ratio, Percentages, Correlation, Substitution

8 Real a Here are some diagrams showing skateboard ramps.
Work out the gradient of each ramp.

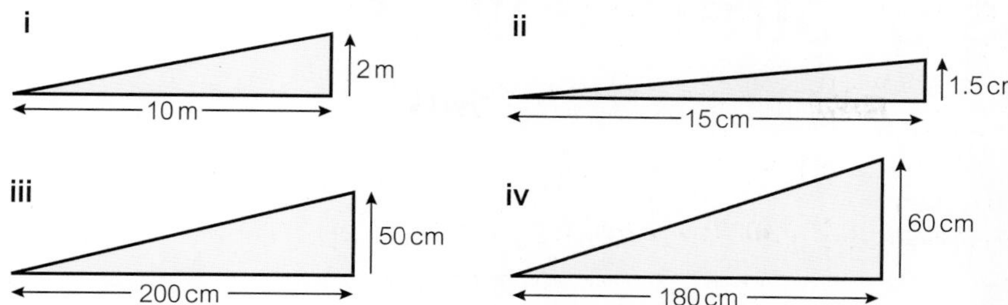

b Write each gradient in part **a** as a percentage.

c Sketch these skateboard gradients on squared paper.

i $\frac{1}{6}$ **ii** $\frac{2}{7}$ **iii** 30% **iv** 12.5%

> **Q8b hint**
> Convert the fraction to a percentage.

> **Q8c iv hint**
> What is 25% as a fraction? Use this to work out 12.5% as a fraction.

9 a Draw a grid from −10 to +10 on both axes. Complete the table of values for each graph. Use the completed tables to plot each graph. Use a different colour for each line.

i $y = x - 1$

x	−2	−1	0	1	2	3
y	−3	−2	−1			

ii $y = 4x + 4$

x	−3	−2	−1	0	1
y			0	4	

iii $y = -2x + 3$

x	−2	−1	0	1	2	3
y	7					

b Work out the gradient of each line.

Discussion What is the connection between the gradient, the sequence of y values and the **coefficient** of x?

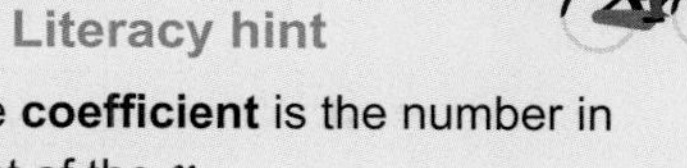

> **Q9 Literacy hint**
> The **coefficient** is the number in front of the x.

10 Explore What does the percentage or ratio shown on a road sign mean?
Look back at the maths you have learned in this lesson.
How can you use it to answer this question?

11 Reflect Some people think of finding the gradient as 'rise over run' or 'upstairs above the corridor'.

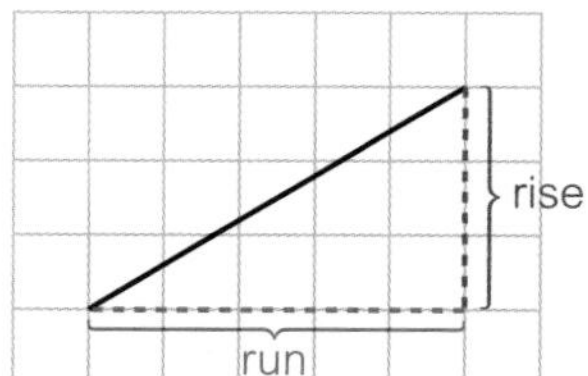

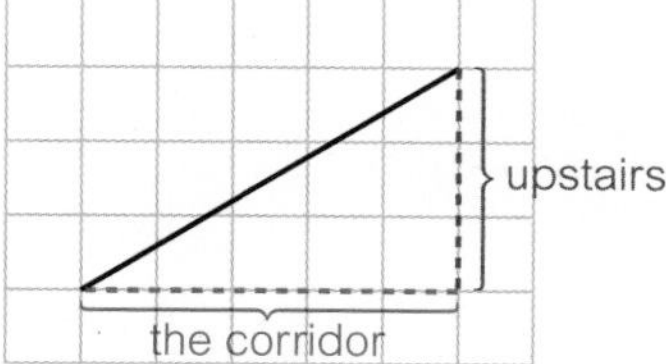

Do you like these ways of remembering how to find the gradient?
Can you think of your own way to remember it?
What else do you use to remember mathematics facts? Compare with your classmates.

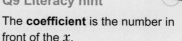

> **Q11 hint**
> Think of rhymes, pictures, …

9.3 Equations of straight lines

You will learn to:
- Plot the graphs of linear functions
- Find midpoints of line segments
- Write the equations of straight-line graphs in the form $y = mx + c$.

CONFIDENCE

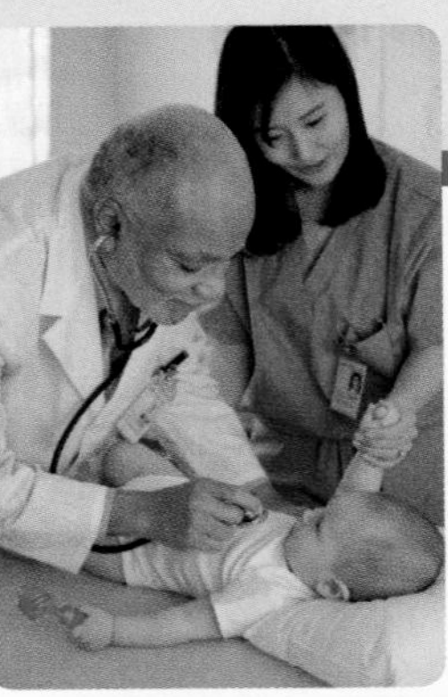

Why learn this?
Doctors use straight-line graphs to estimate body surface area. This helps in working out the correct doses of medicines, especially for small children.

Fluency
Work out
- $\frac{-1 + 1}{2}$
- $\frac{-3 + 5}{2}$

Explore
How do economists use straight-line graphs to work out how much people are spending compared with their income? What can they tell from the graphs?

Exercise 9.3

Warm up

1 Find the midpoint of each line segment.

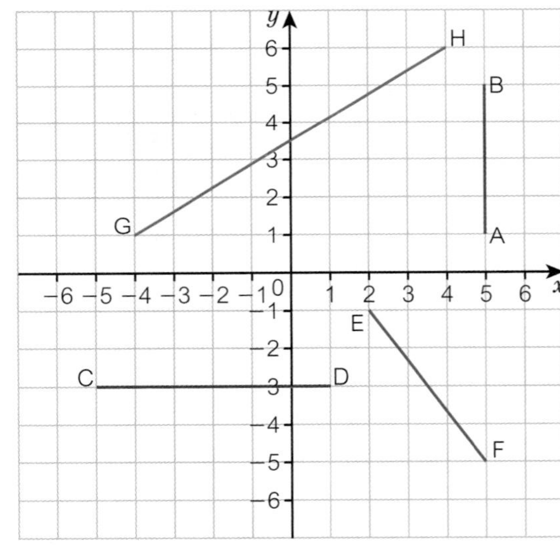

Q1 hint
Write your answers like this.
Line AB has midpoint (___, ___).

2 Which of the lines in Q1 has a positive gradient?
Which has a negative gradient?

3 Work out the midpoint of a line segment AB, where

a A is (0, 2) and B is (4, 10)
b A is (1, 0) and B is (7, −4)
c A is (−3, 8) and B is (2, −4)
d A is (5, −2) and B is (0, −6)

Key point
The midpoint of a line segment is

$\left(\frac{x_1 + x_2}{2}, \frac{y_1 + y_2}{2}\right)$

A (x_1, y_1), B (x_2, y_2)

4 **Reasoning** a Copy and complete this table of values for these equations.

x	−2	−1	0	1	2
$y = 2x$					
$y = 2x + 5$					
$y = 2x - 7$					

b Plot the graphs on the same grid.

c What do you notice about all the lines you have drawn?

d Work out the gradient of each line.

e Copy and complete these sentences.
Lines with the same gradient are ___________.
Parallel lines have the same ______________.

Q4 hint

You could plot these graphs using graph plotting software.

Investigation — Problem-solving / Reasoning

1 Look at the graphs you plotted in Q4. Write the coordinates of the y-**intercept** of each line.

2 Where do you think the graph of $y = 2x + 3$ will be on your grid?

3 Draw a table of values for $y = 2x + 3$. Use this to check your answer to part 2.

4 Draw a table of values for $y = -3x$. Plot the graph.

5 Draw the lines $y = -3x + 1$ and $y = -3x - 2$ on the same grid without working out the table of values.

6 Explain how you know the y-intercept from the equations of lines.

Part 1 hint

The y-**intercept** is where a line crosses the y-axis.

Worked example

Write the equation of

a line A

b line B.

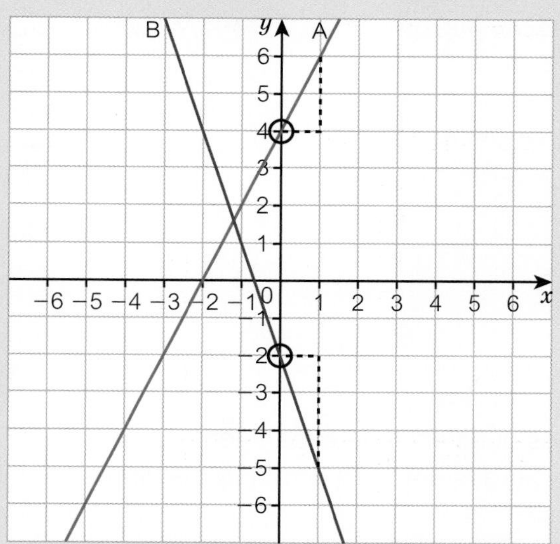

a $y = mx + c$
gradient, $m = 2$
y-intercept is (0, 4), so $c = 4$.
Equation of line A is $y = 2x + 4$.

b $y = mx + c$
gradient, $m = -3$
y-intercept is (0, −2), so $c = -2$.
Equation of line B is $y = -3x - 2$.

5 Reasoning a Work out the gradient and y-intercept for line A.

b Use these to write the equation of line A.

$y = \square x + \square$
↑ gradient ↑ y-intercept

c What are the equations of lines B and C?

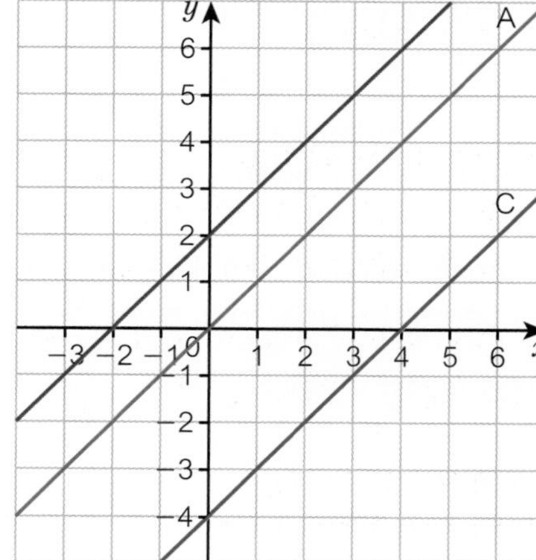

Key point

A **linear equation** generates a straight-line (linear) graph.
The equation for a straight-line graph can be written as
$y = mx + c$
where m is the gradient and c is the y-intercept.

Q5 hint

Use your equation for line A to help you find the equations of lines B and C.

6 Reasoning **a** Match each line to an equation.

$y = x$	$y = 2x + 4$
$y = 3x$	$y = 2x - 1$

b Which lines pass through the **origin**?

c Which line is the steepest?

d Write the equations of the two lines that are parallel.

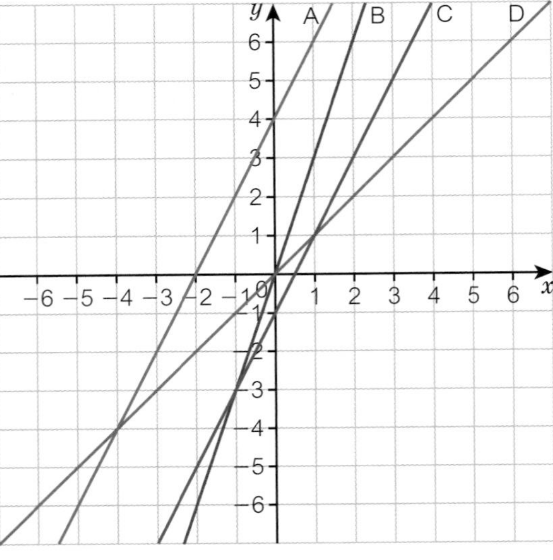

Q6 Literacy hint

The **origin** on a coordinate grid is the point (0, 0).

7 Write the equations of these lines.

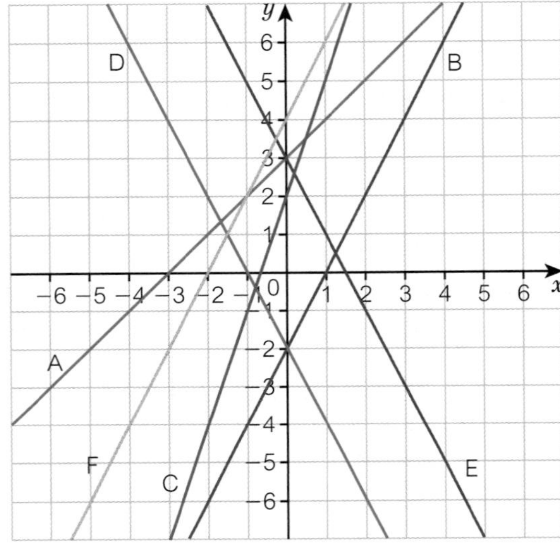

8 STEM Jayne carries out a science experiment.
She puts different voltages across a wire and measures the current.
Here are her results.

Voltage (V)	2	4	6
Current (A)	1	2	3

a Plot the points, with voltage on the horizontal axis and current on the vertical axis. Join the points with a straight line.

b Use your graph to work out the current when the voltage is 5V.

c Write down the equation of the line.

Explore

9 Explore How do economists use straight-line graphs to work out how much people are spending compared with their income?
What can they tell from the graphs?
Is it easier to explore this question now you have completed the lesson?
What further information do you need to be able to answer this?

Reflect

10 Reflect Write down what you think 'linear' means.
$y = mx + c$ is a linear equation.
Write, in your own words, what m and c stand for.
Write hints for how to remember what m and c stand for.

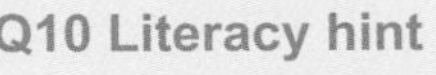

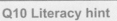

Q10 Literacy hint

Some say that m comes from the French word *monter*, meaning to climb. Others say it comes from the Latin word *modus*, meaning measure.

Topic links: Calculating with negative numbers, Substitution

Subject links: Science (Q11)

Theta 2, Section 9.3

9.4 STEM: Direct proportion problems

You will learn to:
- Identify and describe practical examples of direct proportion
- Solve problems involving direct proportion with or without a graph.

Why learn this?
The stiffness of a bike frame is related to the thickness of the tube walls, amongst other factors.

Fluency
- Use this relationship to convert between kilograms (and grams) and pounds.
  1 kg = 2.2 pounds (lb)
  2 kg = ☐ lb   ☐ kg = 22 lb   ☐ kg = 3.3 lb
- Which bike is heavier: a 9 kg Pennine or an 18 lb 8 oz Brecon?

Explore
Is the strength of a bike frame proportional to its mass?

Warm up

Exercise 9.4 Cycling and bike design

1 **Real** Titanium is a metal used for making bike frames.
One cubic centimetre of titanium has a mass of 4.5 g.
a What is the mass of 200 cm^3 of titanium?
b What volume of titanium was used to make a frame of mass 1.53 kg?

2 **STEM** A designer uses this graph to find the force exerted on a bicycle frame by people of different mass.
a Are force and mass in direct proportion? Explain.
b Find the equation of the graph in the form $y = mx + c$.
c Write a formula linking force (F) and mass (M).
d Use your formula to work out the force exerted by a person with mass
i 30 kg   ii 60 kg   iii 90 kg.

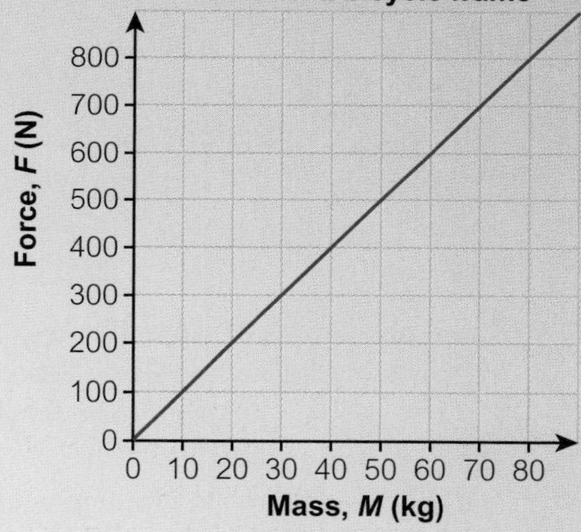

Discussion What do you notice about the forces exerted by 30 kg, 60 kg, 90 kg?

Q2c hint
Replace y with F and x with M.

Worked example

Here are the prices of some bicycle brake parts.

Brake pads	1 pair £1.99	2 pairs £3.75
Brake cable casing	2 metres £4.98	5 metres £12.45

Are the price and quantity in direct proportion for
a brake pads   b brake cable casings?

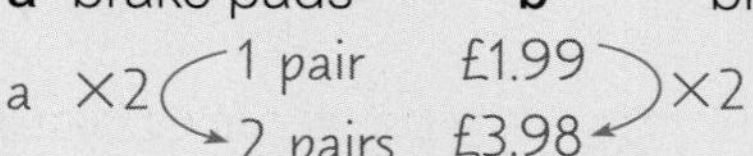

Assume they are in direct proportion. Work out what the other price would be. Do they match?

But two pairs here cost £3.75, so price and quantity are not in direct proportion.

b Price for 1 m is £4.98 ÷ 2 = £2.49. Price for 5 m is 5 times the price for 1 m (£2.49 × 5 = £12.45), so price and quantity are in proportion.

3 **Real** The table shows the temperatures at different heights on Mont Ventoux.

Height above sea level (m)	0	250	500	1000
Temperature drop (°C)	0	1.6	3.2	6.4

a Are height and temperature drop in direct proportion?
b Jay is at 400 m above sea level, and the temperature is 19.3°C. He starts to cycle up the mountain. What is the predicted temperature at the summit (1900 m above sea level)?

4 **Real** Solve these problems. Which of them show direct proportion?
a 1 inch = 2.54 cm. How many centimetres are the same as 24 inches?
b The cost of a hotel phone call is £1 plus 20p a minute. How much will it cost for
i a 5-minute call ii a 10-minute call?
c The cost of 40 litres of petrol is £52.00. How much does 50 litres cost?
d Sarah is paid £54 for 6 hours work. She works for 36 hours. How much does she earn?
e Rich cycled for 2 hours at 25 mph, then for 3.5 hours at 20 mph. How far did he travel?

Q4 hint
If you are not sure, try doubling the values – is the answer also doubled?

5 **Problem-solving / Reasoning** Four cyclists are training for a competition. The distances, in km, travelled by the cyclists each day are
A 2, 7, 12, 17, 22, … B 2, 4, 8, 16, 32, …
C 1, 4, 9, 16, 25, … D 1, 4, 7, 10, 13, …
a Which of these sequences will produce a straight-line graph?
b Are any of these direct proportion relationships? Explain your answer.

Investigation **Problem-solving**

The graph shows the time trial results (to the nearest second) for Bradley Wiggins and Peter Hawkins over a 10-mile course in 2013, plus the results for two amateur cyclists riding the same course.

1 Use values from the graph to work out the average speed of each rider using

$$\text{speed} = \frac{\text{distance}}{\text{time}}$$

2 Now work out the gradient of each line. What do you notice?
3 Which line shows fastest speed? What can you say about its gradient?

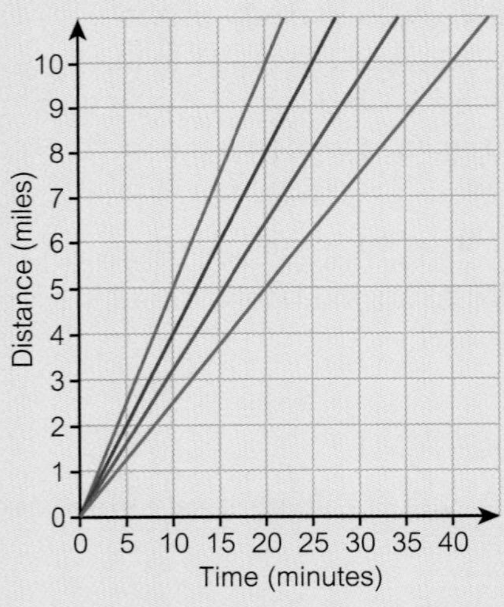

6 **Explore** Is the strength of a bike frame proportional to its mass?
Is it easier to explore this question now you have completed the lesson?
What further information do you need to be able to answer this?

7 **Reflect** Is it easier to solve direct proportion problems with or without a graph? Explain.

Q7 hint
For example, would it be easier or harder to answer Q4 with graphs?

Topic links: Conversion graphs and charts, Sequences, Substitution, Ratio and proportion

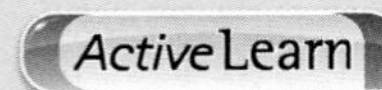

Theta 2, Section 9.4

9 Check up

Log how you did on your Student Progression Chart.

Straight-line graphs

1 a Copy and complete this table of values for the equation $y = 3x + 2$.

x	−2	−1	0	1	2
y					

b Plot the line $y = 3x + 2$ on a coordinate grid like this.

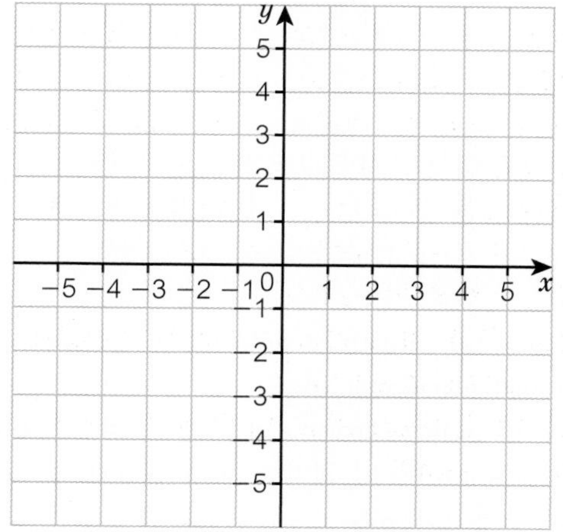

2 a Copy and complete this table of values for the equation $y = x - 3$.

x	−2	−1	0	1	2
y					

b Plot the line $y = x - 3$ on your grid from Q1.

c Which line is steeper, $y = 3x + 2$ or $y = x - 3$?

d Write the coordinates of the y-intercept of the line $y = x - 3$.

3 Work out the gradient of each line.

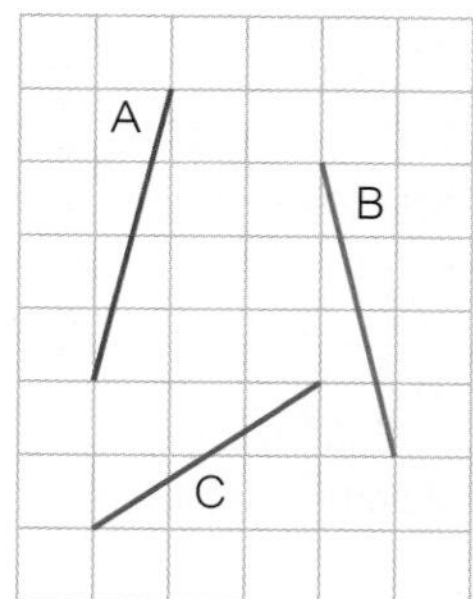

Finding equations of graphs

4 Write the equations of lines A, B and C.

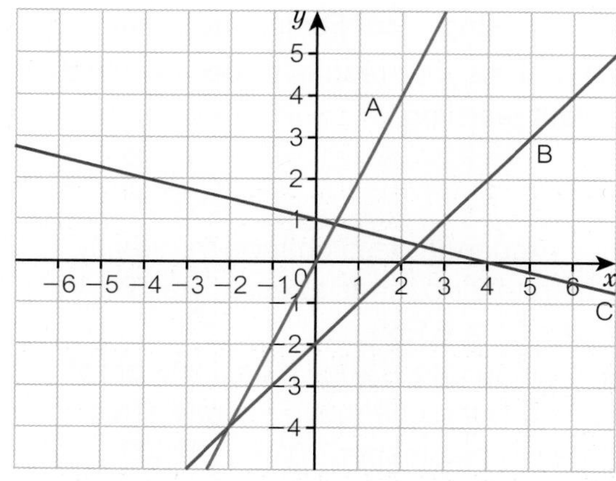

5 Match each line to its equation.

a $y = \frac{1}{2}x$

b $y = \frac{1}{2}x - 5$

c $y = 2x$

d $y = 2x + 5$

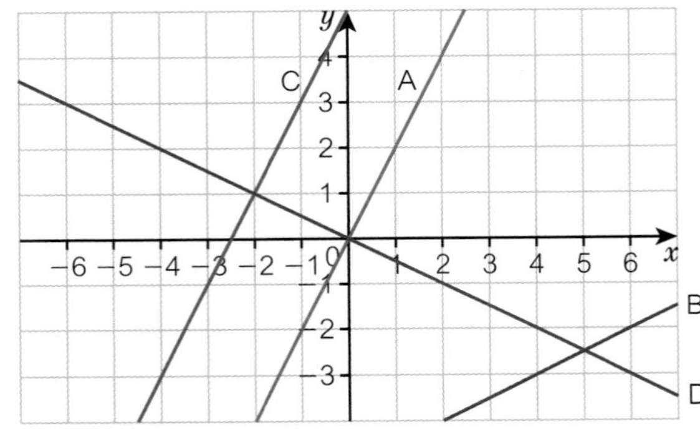

Midpoints

6 Work out the midpoint of the line segment AB where

a A is (3, 6) and B is (7, 2)   b A is (−4, 0) and B is (2, 5)

Direct proportion

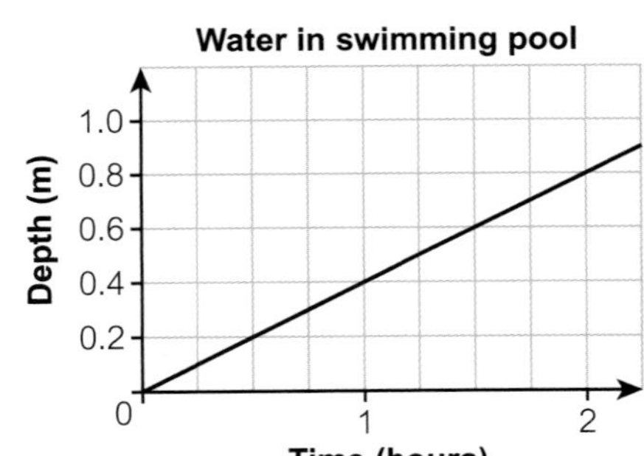

7 The graph shows the depth of water in a swimming pool over time.

a Is the pool filling or emptying?

b Is the depth of water directly proportional to time? Explain.

c How long does it take to fill the pool to a depth of

i 0.5 m   ii 1.6 m?

8 The table shows the prices of different sized packets of rice.

Packet size	Price (p)
250 g	60
500 g	110
1 kg	180

a Draw a graph with size on the horizontal axis and price on the vertical axis.

b Are packet size and price in direct proportion? Explain.

9 In an experiment, different masses are hung on a spring. The amount the spring stretches is measured. Here are the results.

Mass (g)	0	10	15	20
Stretch (cm)	0	4.2	6.3	8.4

Are the mass and stretch in direct proportion? Explain.

Reflect

10 How sure are you of your answers? Were you mostly

Just guessing   Feeling doubtful   Confident?

What next? Use your results to decide whether to strengthen or extend your learning.

Challenge

11 Currency exchange rates change frequently. In 2013 the average exchange rate for pounds to euros was £1 = €1.18, but in the year 2000 it was £1 = €1.65.

If the exchange rate is shown as a line graph with £ on the vertical axis, how does the change in the rate affect the graph?

Which line will be steeper, 2013 or 2000?

9 Strengthen

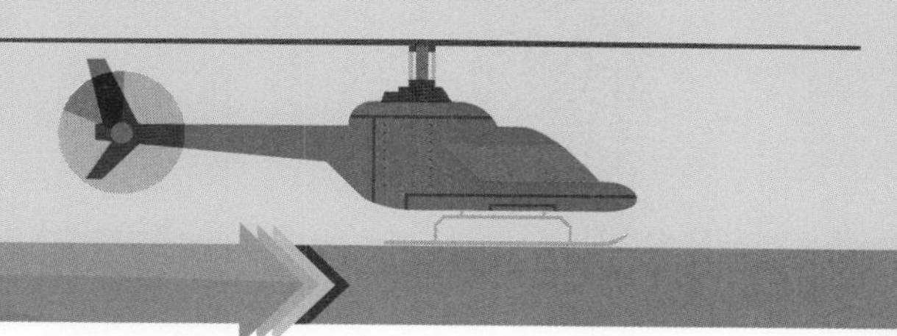

You will:
- Strengthen your understanding with practice.

Straight-line graphs

1 a Which hill is steepest?

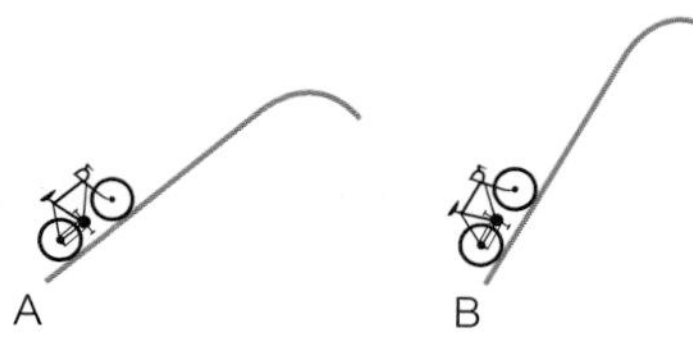

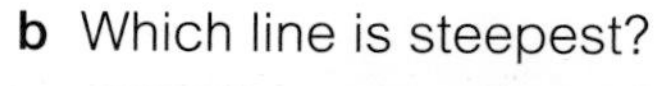

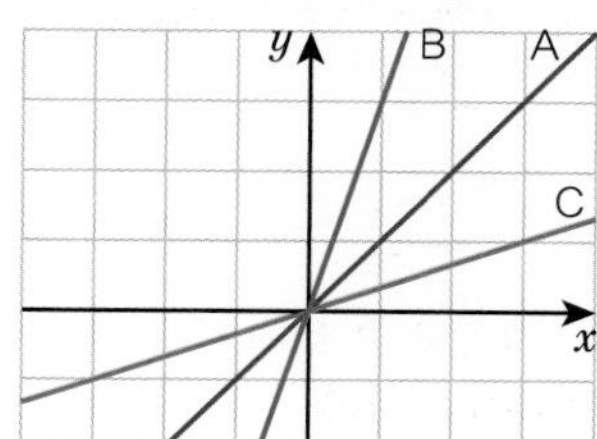

b Which line is steepest?

2 Look at the diagram and then complete these sentences.
The steepness of the graph is called the ____________.
A positive gradient goes ________ from left to right.
A negative gradient goes ________ from left to right.

Q2 hint

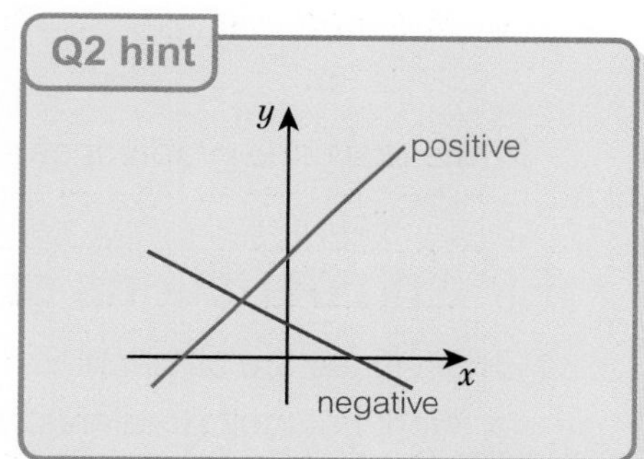

3 a Are the gradients of these lines positive or negative?

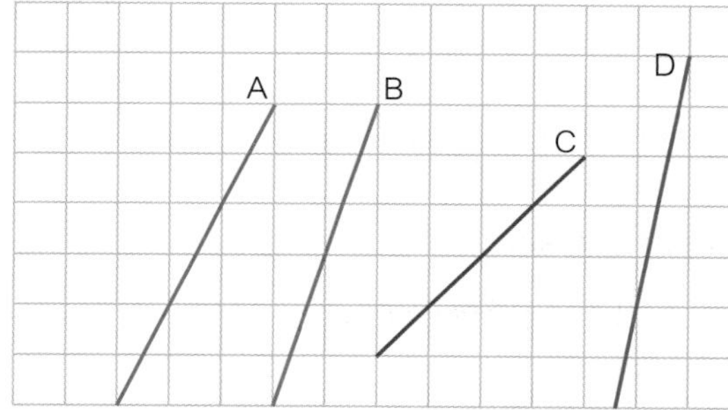
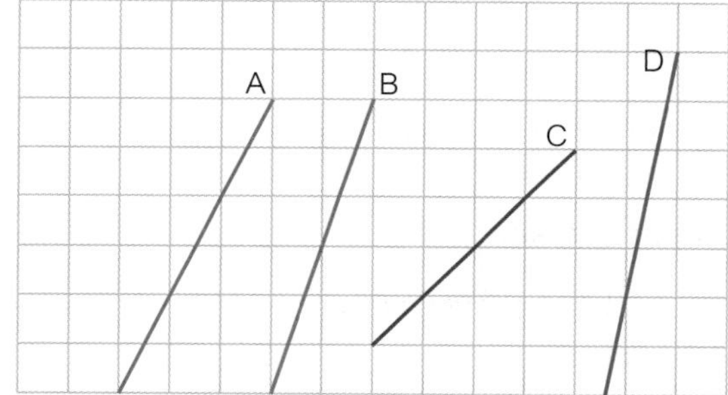

b Choose a point on line A.
Move your finger one square across (to the right).
How many squares does your finger move up to meet line A again?

c Repeat part **b** to work out the gradients of lines B, C and D.

Q3b hint

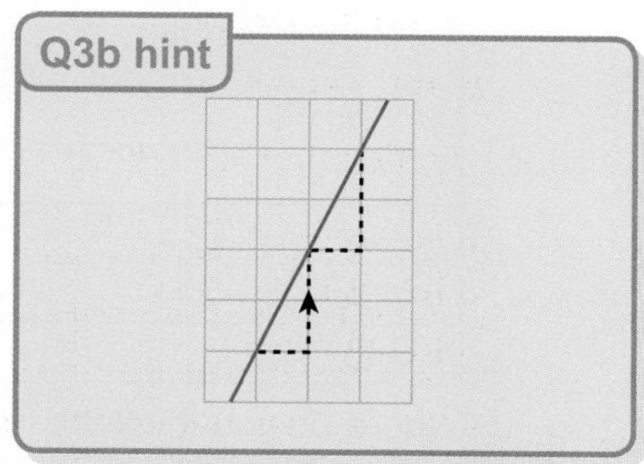

4 a Are the gradients of these lines positive or negative?

b Choose a point on line E.
Move your finger one square across (to the right).
How many squares do you have to move your finger down to meet line E again?

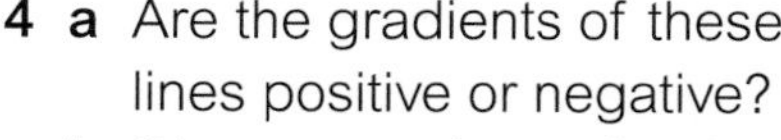

c Repeat part **b** to work out the gradients of lines F and G.

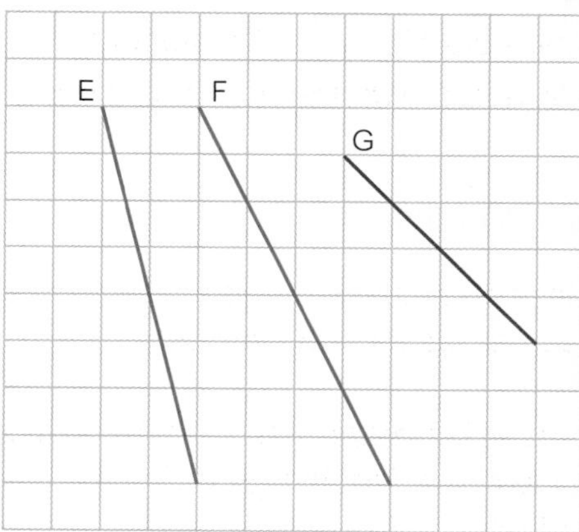

Q4b hint

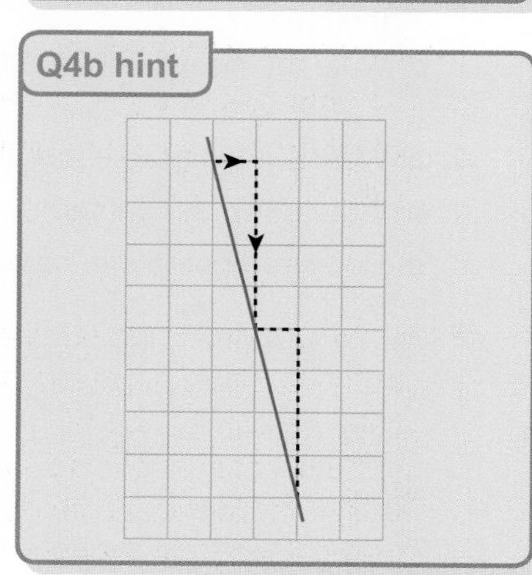

5 Work out the gradients of these graphs by counting the squares up and dividing by the squares across.

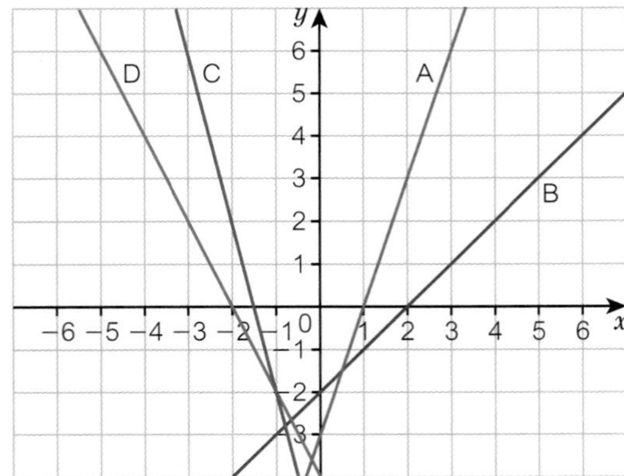

6 What fraction of the side of a square on the grid is each red line?

a 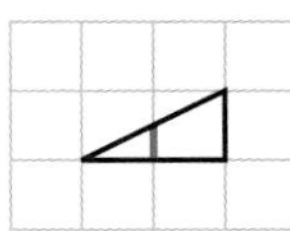 b 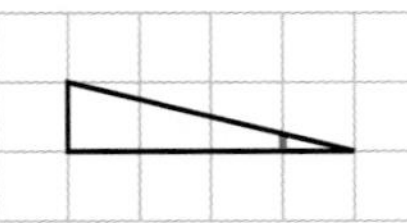 c 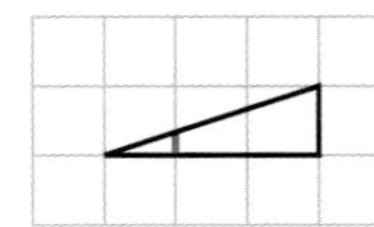

Q6 hint

How many equal steps does it take to go up one whole square?

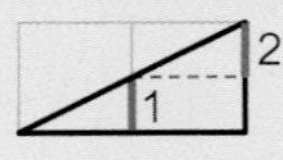

7 These lines have fraction gradients.

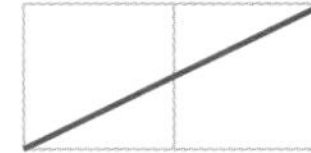   

Write down the gradient of each line.

Finding equations of graphs

1 These lines are all parallel.

a Work out their gradients. What do you notice?

b Copy and complete this table.

Line	y-intercept
$y = 3x + 3$	
$y = 3x + 1$	
$y = 3x$	
$y = 3x - 2$	
$y = 3x - 4$	

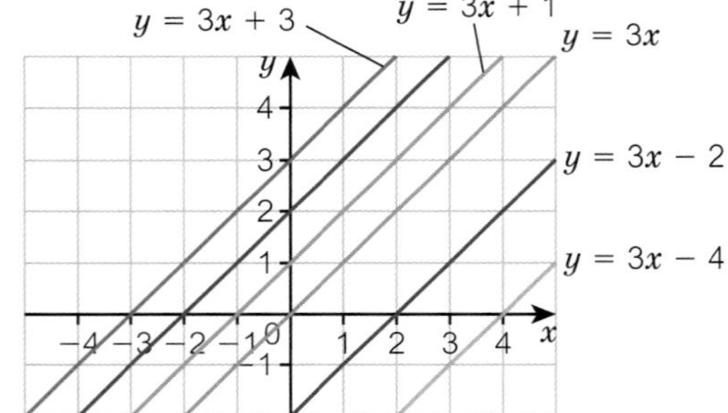

c Where do you think the line $y = 3x + 5$ will cross the y-axis?

d Write the equation of the line that is not labelled.

Q1b hint

The y-intercept is the value where the line crosses the y-axis.

2 a Work out the gradient of this line.

b Write down the y-intercept.

c Copy and complete the equation of the line.

$y = \square x \quad + \quad \square$

gradient $\quad$ y-intercept

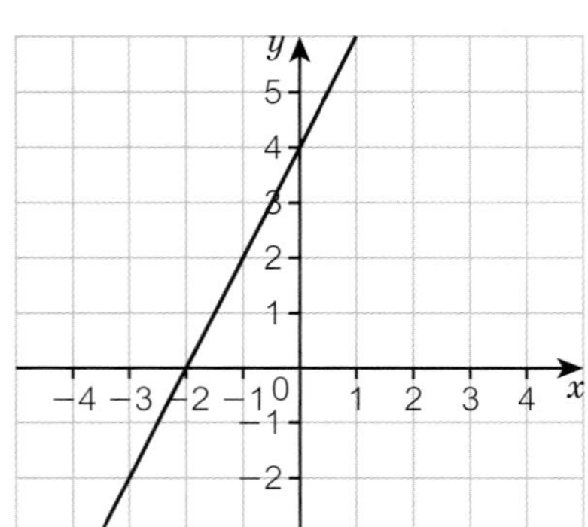

3 Write down the equations of these lines.

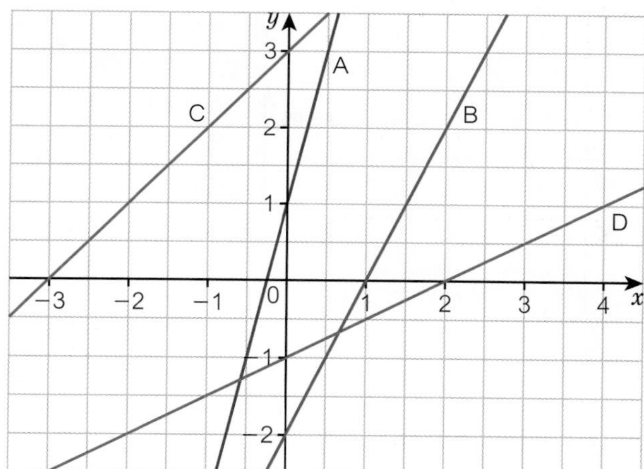

Q3 Strategy hint

Follow the steps in Q2.

Q3 hint

Write '$1x$' as 'x'.

4 Write down the equations of these lines.

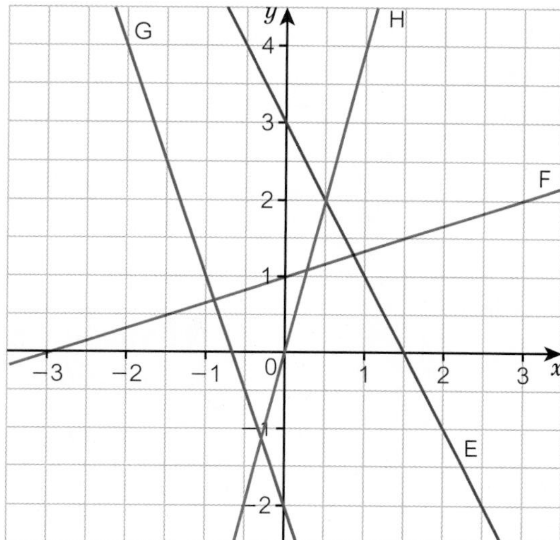

Q4 Strategy hint

First decide if the gradient is positive or negative.

5 Follow these steps to match the graphs to their equations.

$y = -2x + 1$ $\quad$ $y = x + 3$

$y = -\frac{1}{2}x - 2$ $\quad$ $y = 3x + 3$

a Write down the equations that have negative gradients.

b Use the y-intercept to match the two graphs to the equations in part **a**.

c Write down the two equations that have positive gradient.

d Can you use the y-intercept to tell which is which?

e Work out the gradient of one line.

f Match the remaining line and equation.

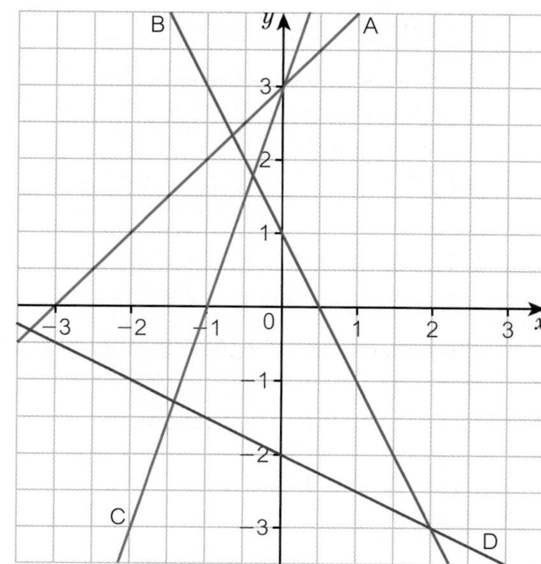

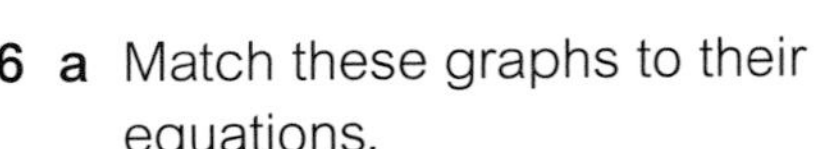

6 a Match these graphs to their equations.

$y = 3x$

$y = -\frac{1}{4}x+2$

$y = -4x + 2$

$y = 3x + 4$

b Which two lines have the same gradient?

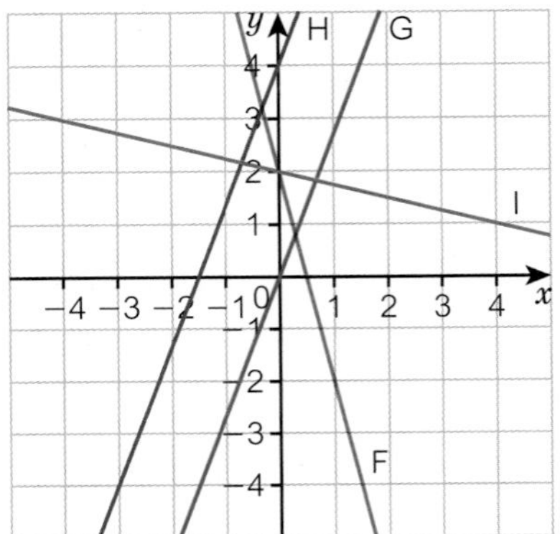

Q6 Strategy hint

Write down the equations that have negative gradient. Look at the y-intercept or find the gradient of one line.

Midpoints

1 a Copy this coordinate grid.

b Draw the line AB with end points A (2,4) and B (6,0) on your grid.

c Label the midpoint of line AB point M.

d Copy and complete the calculation to work out the coordinates of M.

(x, y)
A (2, 4)
B (6, 0)
M (□, □)

$\frac{2+6}{2}$ $\frac{4+0}{2}$

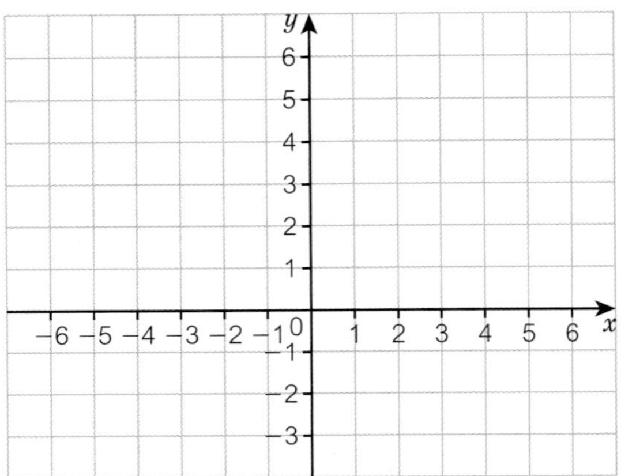

e Check your answer matches the midpoint on the line.

Q2 Strategy hint

Follow the steps in Q1

Q2c hint

Coordinates can include fractions.

2 Work out the midpoints of these lines:

a from E (0, 3) to F (6, 9)

b from G(1, 5) to H (7, 1)

c from I (−1, 4) to J (3, 2)

d from K (7, 4) to L (−3, 0)

e from N (2, 3) to P (3, 9)

f from Q (5, −1) to R (−2, −4)

Direct proportion

1 a Draw a pair of axes like this:

b Draw any straight line through the origin.

c Label your graph 'Direct proportion'.

d Underneath your graph, copy and complete:

When two quantities are in direct proportion their graph is a s_________ l______ through _______.

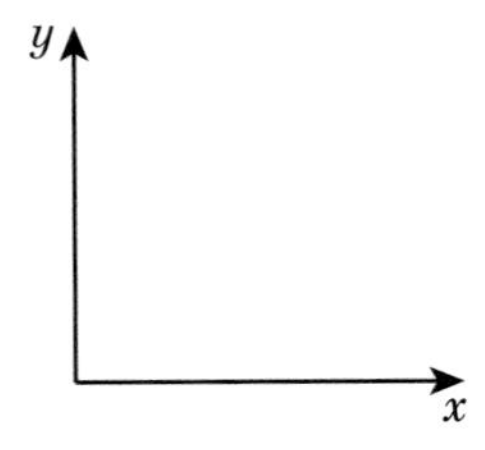

2 **Real** Which of these graphs show direct proportion?

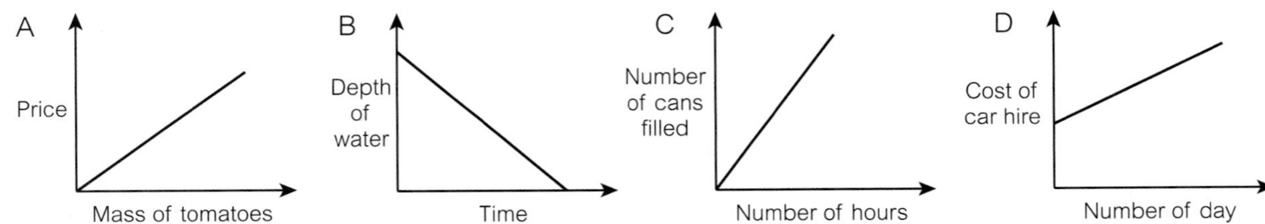

Topic links: Negative numbers, Ratio and proportion, Area and volume

Subject links: Cookery (Enrichment Q2)

3 Real / Problem-solving **a** Copy and complete the conversion table to change gallons to litres.

b Plot a conversion graph to show this information.

c Use the graph to change these between gallons and litres.

i 8 gallons **ii** 18 litres

iii 36 gallons **iv** 76.5 litres

d Are gallons and litres in direct proportion? Explain.

Gallons	Litres
0	0
1	4.5
2	
5	
10	
20	

4 Reasoning Here is a table showing the cost of sending a small parcel by first class post in the UK.

Mass	Cost
up to 1 kg	£5.65
up to 2 kg	£8.90
up to 5 kg	£15.10
up to 10 kg	£21.25

Plot the graph on a coordinate grid. How does the graph show that the mass and the cost are not in direct proportion?

Q4 hint

Plot 'kg' on the x-axis and 'cost in £s' on the y-axis.
Does the line go through (0, 0)?
Is it a straight line or are there different gradients?
Do the other points on the line, in between the plotted points, have any meaning?

5 Are these quantities in direct proportion?

a

Hours worked	Pay
0	£0
1	£16
2	£22
3	£28

b

Texts sent	Cost
0	£0
10	£7
50	£35
100	£70

Q5 Strategy hint

When one value is zero, is the other value zero? When one value is doubled, is the other value doubled?

Enrichment

1 Write a list of 10 items your family pays for each week. You could include groceries, electricity, gas or water, childcare, petrol etc.
Decide for each one if the amount bought is in direct proportion to the price.

2 **a** Plot these points on a coordinate grid and join them to make a triangle.
A (2, 1) B (6, 5) C (−1, 12)
What type of triangle is ABC?

b Extend any lines you need to so that they cross the y-axis.
Write down the equation of the lines AB, BC, CA.

3 Plot points A, B and C from Q2 on a new grid.
Add point D to make a parallelogram, by drawing a line parallel to AB.
Write down the equation of the line CD.

4 **Reflect** Look back at the questions you got wrong in the Check test.
Were they mostly questions about
- equations of lines
- gradients
- direct proportion?

Now look back at the Strengthen questions you answered.
Write down one thing you now understand better.
Is there anything you still need help with?
Ask a friend or your teacher to help you with it.

Reflect

9 Extend

You will:

- Extend your understanding with problem-solving.

1 **Real** An aircraft travels 210 km in half an hour.
How far will it travel in 40 minutes?

2 **Real** It takes $1\frac{1}{4}$ hours to bake 4 potatoes.
How long will it take to bake 6 potatoes?

3 **Real / Problem-solving** It takes 4 men 2 days to build a 10 m section of wall.
How long will it take 2 men to build the next 10 m?

> **Q3 hint**
> Will it take 2 men more or less time than 4 men?

4 **Real** A survival pack contains rations for 6 people for 3 days.
How long will the rations last 9 people?

5 a Write down the gradient of this line.
b Work out the gradient using the formula

$$\text{gradient} = \frac{\text{change in } y}{\text{change in } x}$$

Do you get the same answer?

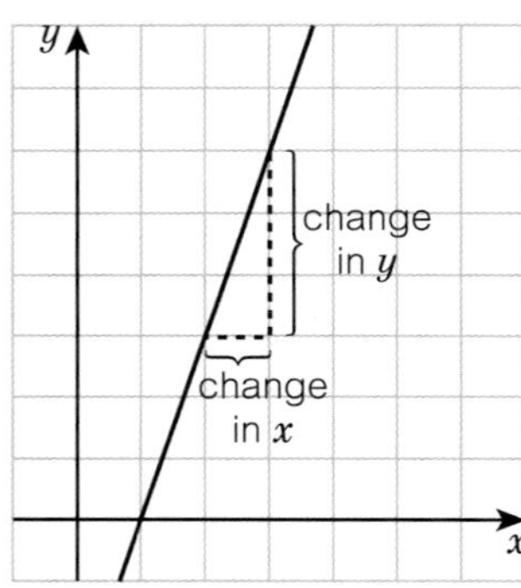

6 Use the formula to work out the gradients of these lines.

$$\text{gradient} = \frac{\text{change in } y}{\text{change in } x}$$

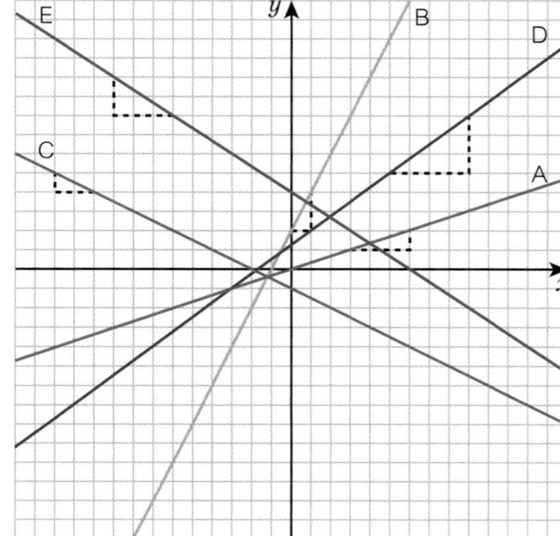

7 This graph converts centimetres to feet.

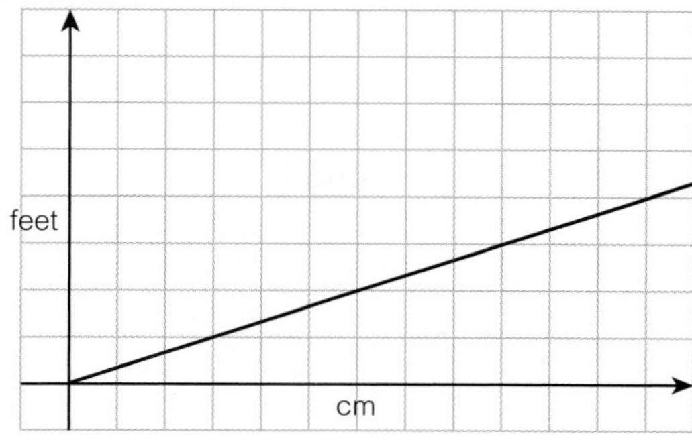

1 foot = 30 cm

a Are cm and feet in direct proportion?

b Work out the gradient of the line.

c Write down the equation of the line.

d 1 foot = 30 cm.
How does the equation show this relationship?

Key point

When the 2 quantities A and B are in direct proportion, A = (a number) × B

Q7c hint

$y = \square x + \square$

8 Write the equations of the graph lines for these equations.

	y	x
a	£1	€1
b	1 kg	2.2 lb
c	1 m	10 cm
d	1 mile	1.6 km

Q8 hint

Look back at Q7.

9 **Real / Finance** Write each statement as an equation showing direct proportion. The first one has been done for you.

a The cost (C) of sending a text message (t) at 7p a text.
$C = 7t$ (Or $C = 0.07t$, if C is in £.)

b The perimeter (P) of a regular hexagon with sides of length k.

c Weekly earnings (E) for 37 hours at y pounds an hour.

d The cost (c) in pounds of x calculators at £5 each.

e The number of miles (m) travelled in 3.5 hours at a speed of y miles per hour.

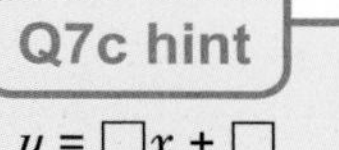

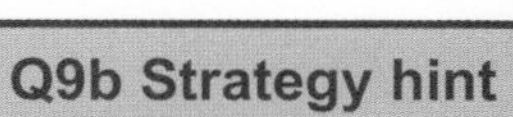

Q9b Strategy hint

Draw a diagram to help you.

10 **Problem-solving / Real / Finance** Describe in a statement what each formula shows. The first one has been done for you.

a $C = 35b$ C is cost in pence, b is number of bananas.
The cost of bananas at 35p per banana.

b $P = 8s$ P is perimeter, s is length of side.

c $W = 9h$ W is wage, h is hours.

d $E = 30w$ E is weekly earnings in pounds, w is hourly rate.

e $d = 60h$ d is distance in miles, h is hours.

11 **Problem-solving** Make up five more formulae that show direct proportion. Swap with a partner to make up a word problem for the formulae.

Q11 hint

$P = 5s$ could be
'What is the total cost in pence of s sweets at 5p each?'
or 'What is the total amount of paint in s 5-litre cans?'
or 'What is the perimeter of a pentagon with sides of length s?'

12 **STEM / Real** There is a link between how soon after a lightning flash you hear the thunder clap and how far away the thunderstorm is. Use the data to plot a graph to show the results. Is the distance of the thunderstorm in direct proportion to the number of seconds it takes to hear it?

Seconds	Miles
3	0.65
5	1.09
8	1.74

Q12 hint

When you have plotted and joined the points, continue the line until it crosses an axis.
Is it a straight line? Does it go through (0, 0)?

13 **STEM** A laboratory measures a pair of variables.

x	3.5	4.5	8
y	21	27	48

a Work out $y \div x$ for each pair.

b Is $y \div x$ the same each time?

c Are y and x in direct proportion?

14 **Problem-solving / Reasoning**

a Match each graph A to D with calculations **i** to **iv**.

i The cost of n phone calls at 40p per minute.

ii The cost of n biscuits at 25p each.

iii The cost of hiring a bike at £5 plus £2 for every hour of hire.

iv Energy cost at £2 standing charge plus 50p per unit.

b Explain how you matched the graphs.

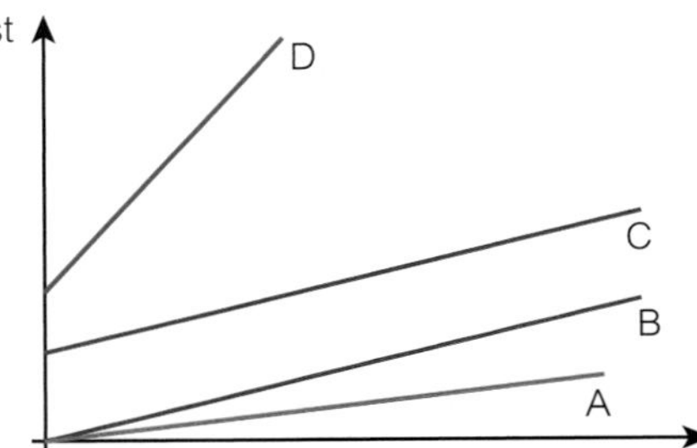

15 Aluminium tubing for bicycle frames is priced per metre.
The price of 1 metre is £x.
Write an expression for the cost of

a 2 metres **b** 5 metres **c** 10 metres.

16 **Real / Problem-solving** Here are the ingredients to make enough dough for 12 slices of pizza.

250 g plain flour
1 teaspoon salt
1 tablespoon caster sugar
10 g dried yeast
2 tablespoons olive oil
180 ml warm water

Ceris wants to make pizza for a sleep-over. She is inviting five friends and wants to provide 5 slices of pizza each, including herself.

a How much flour, dried yeast, oil and water will she need?

b Ceris's granny wants to make enough dough for 36 slices.
She prefers to use imperial measures. 30 g is approximately 1 ounce and 30 ml is approximately 1 fluid ounce.
Work out the amount of each ingredient she will need.

Q16 hint

Teaspoons and tablespoons can be used with both imperial and metric measures, so do not need to be converted.

17 **Problem-solving** **a** It takes Jasmin 30 seconds to fill a 6 litre watering can from her garden tap. The time taken to fill a bucket with water is proportional to the size of the bucket.
How long will it take her to fill a 10 litre watering can?

b In a set of Russian dolls the height is proportional to the width.
The tallest doll is 12 cm tall and 5 cm wide.
The smallest doll is 3 cm tall. How wide is it?

18 **STEM** Here are some results from an experiment.
Which pairs of quantities are in direct proportion?

c	4	6.5	7
d	12	19.5	21

p	2	5	6.5
q	13	25	31

r	2.1	4.5	8.1
s	7.35	15.75	31.59

Q18 hint

Follow the steps in Q13.

19 Which of these pairs of quantities are in direct proportion?

Force, F (newtons)	2	5	8	11
Mass, m (grams)	204	510	816	1122

Area of square	16	25	64	81
Side length	4	5	8	9

Perimeter of square	10	32.8	38.8	44.8
Side length	2.5	8.2	9.7	11.2

Enrichment

20 **a** On a coordinate grid from −10 to +10 on both axes, draw a line in the first quadrant.

b Reflect your line in the y-axis.

c Reflect both lines in the x-axis.

d Do any of the lines have the same gradient?

e Do any of the lines intersect with each other?

f Write the equation of each line.

Q20 hint

The first quadrant is the top right quadrant, and has positive x and y coordinates.

21 **Reflect** Larry enters pairs of coordinates in a spreadsheet like this.

	A	B
1	x	y
2	4	7
3	3	5
4		

In cell B4, he types in the formula **=slope(B2:B3, A2:A3)**
Use what you know about gradients to explain what this spreadsheet formula does.
What answer does Larry get? Test it for yourself in a spreadsheet.

Q21 hint

What does 'slope' mean? What do you think B2:B3 means? What do you think A2:A3 means?

Reflect

9 Unit test

Log how you did on your Student Progression Chart.

1 Five cinema tickets cost £35. How much do 3 tickets cost?

2 Work out the midpoint of the line segment CD where

a C is (5, 2) and D is (11, 8) **b** C is (−2, 1) and D is (0, −4)

3 a Work out the gradient of each line.

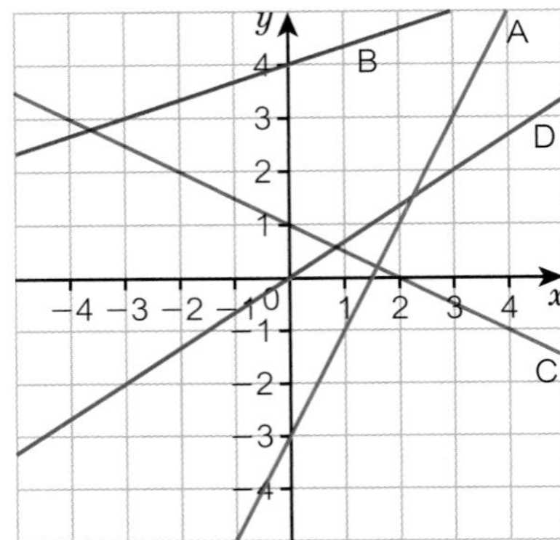

b Work out the equation of each line.

4 The table shows the prices of different masses of building sand.

Mass (tonnes)	1.5	2.1	2.6
Price (£)	45	63	78

a Plot a graph of these values.

b Are the price and mass in direct proportion? Explain.

c What is the price per tonne of sand?

d Write an equation linking price and mass.

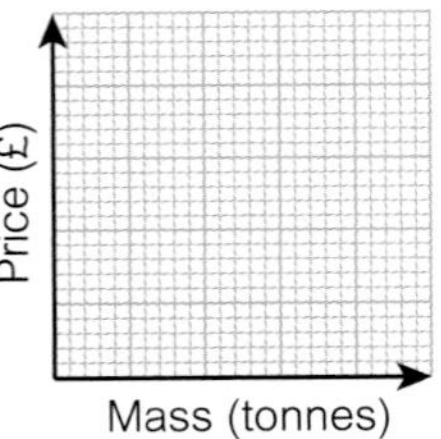

5 It takes 2 women 6 hours to paint a classroom.
How long will it take 3 women to paint a similar classroom?

6 A line EF has midpoint M.
E has coordinates (−1, 3).
M has coordinates ($1\frac{1}{2}$, 7).
Work out the coordinates of F.

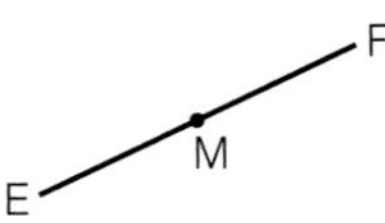

7 Are units of electricity used and cost in direct proportion?
Show your working.

Units used	Cost (£)
50	19.25
100	21.50
200	26.00

8 Match each graph line to its equation.

a $y = 4x + 2$

b $y = \frac{1}{4}x - 2$

c $y = -x + 3$

d $y = -4x + 2$

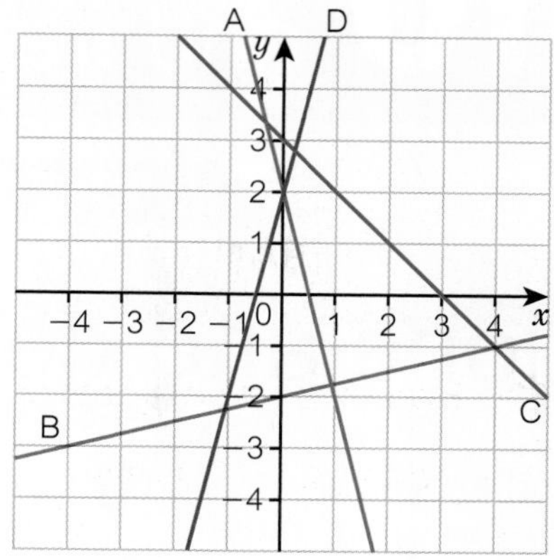

9 For each pair of values of x and y, work out if they are in direct proportion. If they are, write an equation linking x and y.

a

x	4	10	17
y	9.6	23	42.5

b

x	3.1	5.7	11.6
y	11.78	21.66	44.08

Challenge

10 You can convert between grams (g) and ounces (oz) in recipes.
1 oz = 28 g

a Convert 2 oz, 3 oz, 4 oz to grams.
Why isn't 1 oz = 28 g a very practical conversion?
Why do people use 1 oz = 25 g or 1 oz = 30 g instead?

Here are 2 recipes.

Easter biscuits (makes 24)
200 g plain flour
75 g caster sugar
100 g butter
1 egg
50 g currants
25 g candied peel
$\frac{1}{2}$ teaspoon ground cinnamon

Blueberry muffins (makes 12)
9 oz self raising flour
2 oz soft margarine
3 oz caster sugar
6 oz fresh blueberries
grated rind of one lemon
2 eggs
8 fl oz milk

b Convert the Easter biscuit recipe to ounces.

c Convert the muffin recipe to grams. Use 1 fl oz = 30 ml.

d Which ingredients do not need converting?

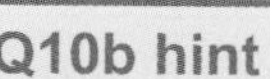

Decide whether to use 1 oz = 25 g or 1 oz = 30 g.

11 Reflect

a How did you find the work in this unit on straight-line graphs?
Easy OK Hard
Explain why.

b Think about your work on fractions in unit 8. Complete the sentence with a word or words from the box.
Questions on straight-line graphs are ____________ questions on fractions.

easier than	as easy as	as hard as	harder than

Explain why.

Reflect

10 Percentages, decimals and fractions

MASTER | Check P247 | Strengthen P249 | Extend P253 | Test P257

10.1 Fractions and decimals

You will learn to:
- Recall equivalent fractions and decimals
- Recognise recurring and terminating decimals
- Order fractions by converting them to decimals or equivalent fractions.

CONFIDENCE

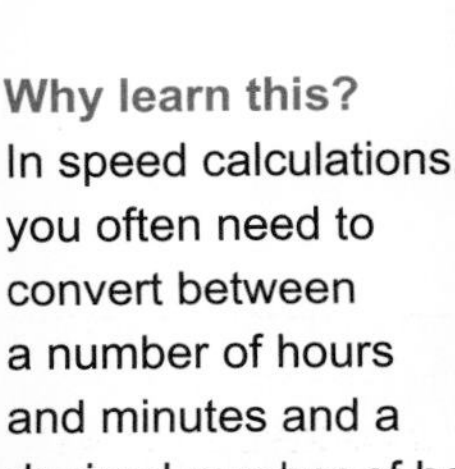

Why learn this?
In speed calculations, you often need to convert between a number of hours and minutes and a decimal number of hours.

Fluency
- Round these numbers to 2 decimal places.
  13.6718
  9.048 812
  0.698
  0.014 887
- What is 1 minute as a fraction of 1 hour?

Explore
How do speed cameras calculate your average speed?

Exercise 10.1

Warm up

1 Work out these divisions. Write your answers as decimals.
- **a** $5\overline{)8}$
- **b** $3\overline{)4}$
- **c** $4\overline{)10}$

2 Copy and complete this table of equivalent fractions and decimals.

Fraction	$\frac{1}{10}$	$\frac{1}{5}$		$\frac{1}{3}$		$\frac{1}{2}$			$\frac{3}{4}$	$\frac{4}{5}$	
Decimal			0.25		0.4		0.6	$0.\dot{6}$			0.9

Q2 hint
Equivalent fractions and decimals have the same value.

3 Which shape has the larger area?

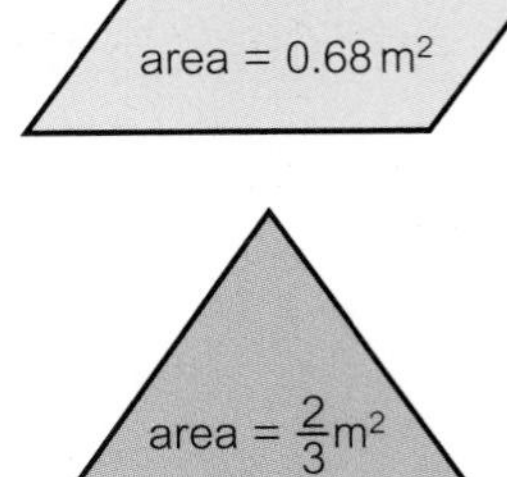

Q3 hint
Convert the fraction into a decimal.

$\frac{1}{3} = 0.333$ (×2) → $\frac{2}{3} = \square$ (×2)

4 Lynn has two dogs, Polly and Deefa.
Polly has a mass of 7.55 kg and Deefa has a mass of $7\frac{3}{5}$ kg.
Which dog is heavier? Explain your answer.

Subject links: Science (Q12, Q17)

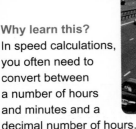

5 Write these **terminating decimals** as fractions in their simplest form.

a 0.49
b 0.78
c 0.362
d 0.256
e 3.24
f 7.125

Key point

A **terminating decimal** ends after a definite number of digits, for example 0.64 and 1.465.

Q5a hint

$0.49 = \frac{49}{\square}$

6 **Reasoning** Shelley converts 0.0675 to a fraction like this.

$$0.0675 = \frac{675}{1000} \overset{\div 25}{=} \frac{27}{40}$$

(÷25 applied to numerator and denominator)

a Explain the mistake that Shelley has made.

b How can you use Shelley's answer to write down the correct conversion?

7 **Reasoning** Jayne spends 1 hour 48 minutes doing her homework one evening.
She says, 'I have spent 1.48 hours doing homework this evening.'
Is she correct? Explain your answer.

Q7 hint

Write 48 minutes as a fraction of an hour, then use division to write it as a decimal.

8 Write these lengths of time as a decimal number of hours.

a 3 hr 30 min
b 1 hr 15 min
c 10 hr 12 min
d 6 hr 45 min

9 Write these **recurring decimals** using dot notation.

a 0.8888…
b 0.363 636…
c 0.422 22…
d 0.305 305 30…
e 0.123 412 341 2…
f 0.633 333…

Key point

In a **recurring decimal**, a dot over the beginning and end of a sequence shows it recurs.
For example,
1.364 364 364 36... is $1.\dot{3}6\dot{4}$.

Investigation

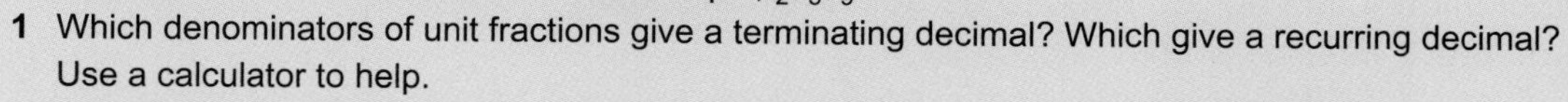

A unit fraction has a numerator of 1, for example, $\frac{1}{2}, \frac{1}{5}, \frac{1}{9}$.

1 Which denominators of unit fractions give a terminating decimal? Which give a recurring decimal? Use a calculator to help.

2 $\frac{1}{5}$ is a terminating decimal. $\frac{2}{5}$ and $\frac{3}{5}$ are multiples of $\frac{1}{5}$. Will all the multiples of $\frac{1}{5}$ also be terminating decimals? Explain your answer.

3 $\frac{1}{3}$ is a recurring decimal. Will all the multiples of $\frac{1}{3}$ also be recurring decimals? Explain your answer.

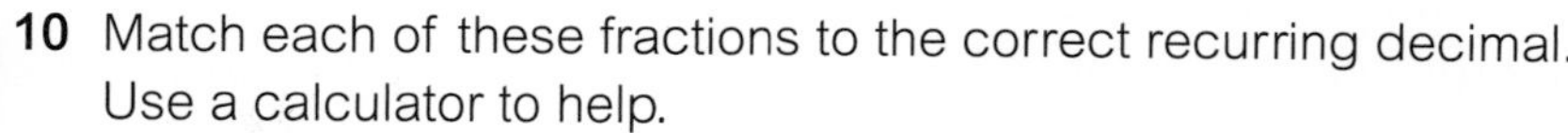

10 Match each of these fractions to the correct recurring decimal.
Use a calculator to help.

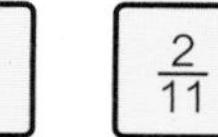

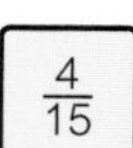

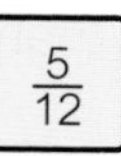

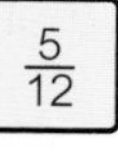

$\frac{5}{9}$ $\frac{2}{11}$ $\frac{4}{15}$ $\frac{5}{12}$

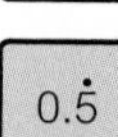

$0.\dot{1}\dot{8}$ $0.41\dot{6}$ $0.2\dot{6}$ $0.\dot{5}$

11 Write these lengths of time as recurring decimals.

a 5 hr 10 min
b 3 hr 20 min
c 7 hr 40 min
d 6 hr 4 min

12 **Problem-solving / STEM** Jarred travels 8 miles in $3\frac{3}{4}$ hours.

a Use the formula speed = $\frac{\text{distance}}{\text{time}}$ to work out his speed in miles per hour. Give your answer to 2 d.p.

b How many minutes will it take Jarred to travel 2 miles?

Q12a hint
Write the time as a decimal.

13 Lilli travels 140 kilometres at 50 kilometres per hour.
Use the formula time = $\frac{\text{distance}}{\text{speed}}$ to work out how long her journey took.
Give your answer in hours and minutes.

14 By converting the fractions to decimals, write these in descending order.

$\frac{1}{2}$ $\frac{3}{5}$ $\frac{5}{8}$ $\frac{1}{3}$ $\frac{5}{12}$

15 Use equivalent fractions to put each set of fractions in order, starting with the smallest.

a $\frac{2}{5}$ $\frac{7}{8}$ $\frac{19}{20}$ $\frac{7}{10}$
b $\frac{11}{14}$ $\frac{3}{4}$ $\frac{1}{2}$ $\frac{3}{7}$
c $\frac{7}{10}$ $\frac{3}{5}$ $\frac{4}{6}$ $\frac{11}{15}$

Q15 hint
Change all the fractions so they have a common denominator, then compare them.

16 Write each of these in descending order

a 0.6 $\frac{19}{30}$ 0.55 $\frac{11}{15}$ 0.7 $\frac{7}{12}$ $\frac{8}{15}$

b $\frac{3}{5}$ 0.9 $\frac{17}{20}$ 0.84 0.625 $\frac{8}{10}$ 0.72

17 Use the decimal equivalent of $\frac{1}{4}$ to work out

a $\frac{1}{8}$ as a decimal
b $\frac{1}{16}$ as a decimal.

Q17a hint
$\frac{1}{8}$ is half of $\frac{1}{4}$

18 Use the decimal equivalent of $\frac{1}{100}$ to work out

a $\frac{1}{200}$ as a decimal
b $\frac{1}{50}$ as a decimal
c $\frac{1}{25}$ as a decimal.

Q18b hint
$\frac{1}{50}$ is double $\frac{1}{100}$.

Explore

19 **Explore** How do speed cameras calculate your average speed?
Is it easier to explore this question now you have completed the lesson?
What further information do you need to be able to answer this?

Reflect

20 **Reflect** This lesson uses a lot of mathematics terminology about decimals and fractions.
For example:

terminating decimals — recurring decimals
unit fractions — equivalent fractions and decimals.

Write a short definition, in your own words, for each term.
Give an example with each definition.
Write any other terminology about decimals and fractions that you know.

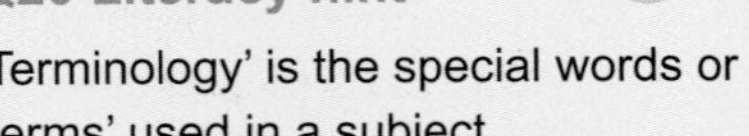

'Terminology' is the special words or 'terms' used in a subject.

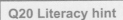

10.2 Equivalent proportions

You will learn to:
- Recall equivalent fractions, decimals and percentages
- Use different methods to find equivalent fractions, decimals and percentages
- Use the equivalence of fractions, decimals and percentages to compare proportions.

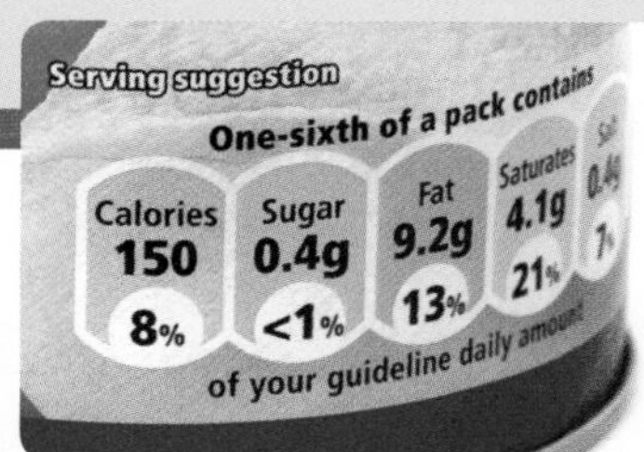

Serving suggestion
One-sixth of a pack contains
Calories 150 8%
Sugar 0.4g <1%
Fat 9.2g 13%
Saturates 4.1g 21%
of your guideline daily amount

Why learn this?
Nutrition information on food labels is often given as proportions in fractions, decimals or percentages.

Fluency
Copy and complete.
- 200 × □ = 1000
- 40 × □ = 1000
- 8 × □ = 1000

Explore
How do businesses use fractions, decimals and percentages to report on efficiency?

Exercise 10.2

1 Write these **proportions** as fractions in their simplest form.

a 15 out of 20 b 9 out of 18 c 40 out of 100
d 16 out of 24 e 10 out of 35 f 20 out of 45

2 Copy and complete this table.

Fraction	$\frac{1}{4}$				$\frac{3}{5}$		
Decimal		0.5		0.2		0.3	
Percentage			75%				100%

3 Copy and complete this table.

Mixed number	$1\frac{1}{2}$				
Decimal		1.7			1.05
Percentage			180%	110%	

Discussion Profits for a business increase by 200%. What does this mean?

Key point
A positive mixed number is greater than 1, so the decimal equivalent is greater than 1 and the percentage equivalent is greater than 100%.
For example, $1\frac{3}{4}$ = 1.75 = 175%.

4 A magazine article states, 'Our number of readers has gone up by 250%.' Write 250% as

a a mixed number b a decimal.

Key point
A **proportion** of a whole can be written as a fraction, decimal or percentage.

5 **Real** In a 25 g portion of cornflakes, 2 g is sugar.

a Write the proportion of sugar in cornflakes as a fraction.

b Write your fraction in part **a** as

i a decimal ii a percentage.

Warm up

6 **Real** Here are the nutrition information panels from two brands of crisps.

Brand A
Per 50 g

Protein	3.0 g
Carbohydrate	26.1 g
Saturated fat	5.2 g
Unsaturated fat	12.3 g
Fibre	3.4 g

Brand B
percentage content

Protein	6.5%
Carbohydrate	53.4%
Saturated fat	13.1%
Unsaturated fat	20.7%
Fibre	6.3%

a Write as a fraction, decimal and percentage the proportion of
i protein **ii** carbohydrate **iii** fibre
in Brand A.

b Which brand has the higher proportion of saturated fat?

c Which brand has the higher proportion of total fat?

7 Write these fractions as decimals and percentages.
The first one has been done for you.

a

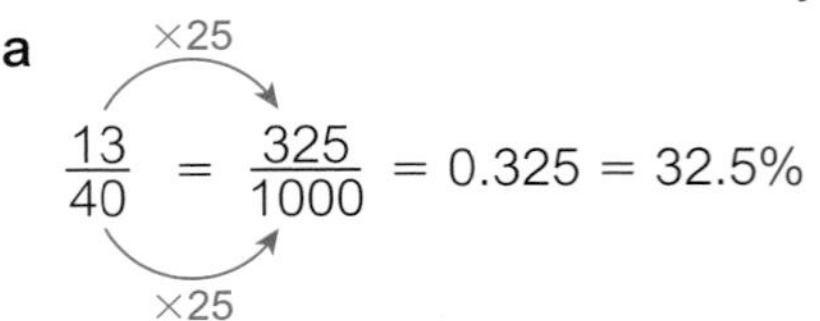

b $\frac{19}{40}$ **c** $\frac{69}{200}$ **d** $\frac{3}{8}$

Key point

Sometimes you might need to use a denominator of 1000 when you convert between fractions, decimals and percentages.

Q7d hint

8 × 125 = 1000

8 Write these percentages as decimals and fractions.
The first one has been done for you.

a

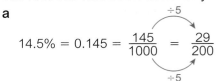

÷5

$14.5\% = 0.145 = \frac{145}{1000} = \frac{29}{200}$

÷5

b 12.5% **c** 42.5% **d** 9.5%

9 **Problem-solving** This yellow rectangle has had a triangle cut out of it.

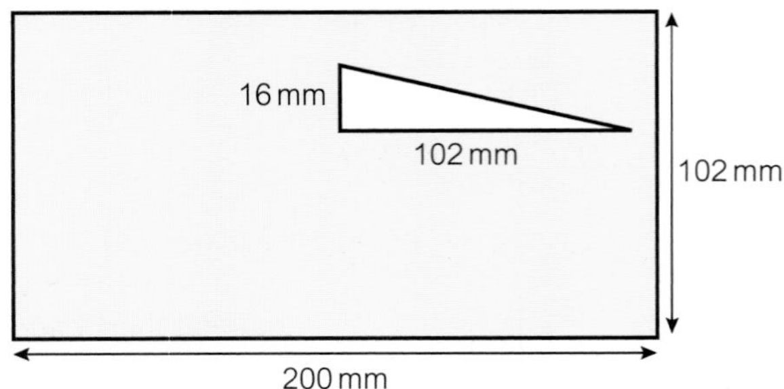

a What fraction of the yellow rectangle is left?

b What percentage of the yellow rectangle is left?

Q9a Strategy hint

Start by working out the area of the rectangle and the area of the triangle.

10 Write these fractions as decimals and percentages.
The first one has been done for you.

a

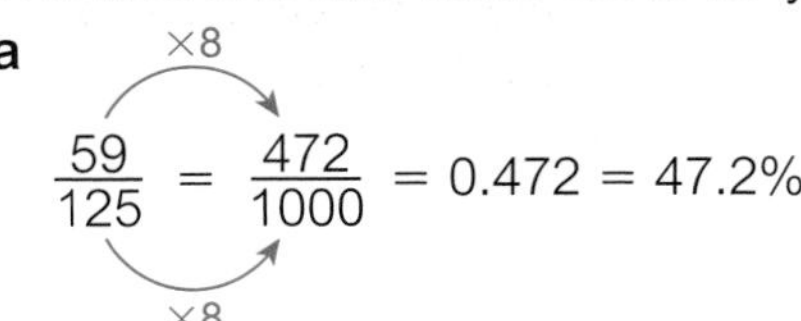

b $\frac{31}{250}$ **c** $\frac{17}{500}$ **d** $\frac{3}{125}$

Topic links: Area, Pictograms

11 Real Geoff, Ishmael and Sumaya run sales teams.
The table shows how many sales pitches each team made, and how many of them they won.
Which sales team won the highest percentage of their pitches?

Team	Pitches	Wins
Geoff	10	7
Ishmael	8	5
Sumaya	12	9

Q11 Literacy hint
A 'sales pitch' is when products are presented to persuade somebody to buy them.

12 Write these percentages as decimals and fractions.
The first one has been done for you.

a

$$34.2\% = 0.342 = \frac{342}{1000} = \frac{171}{500}$$

(÷2 top and bottom)

b 62.4% **c** 2.8% **d** 95.3%

13 Real A business is testing two different methods for delivering goods ordered online to customers.
Method A has 24 dissatisfied customers out of 296.
1% of the Method B customers were dissatisfied.
Which method is better?

14 Problem-solving The pictogram shows the number of ice creams sold over a weekend.

a What fraction of the ice creams sold over the weekend were sold on Sunday?

b What percentage of the ice creams sold over the weekend were sold on Sunday?

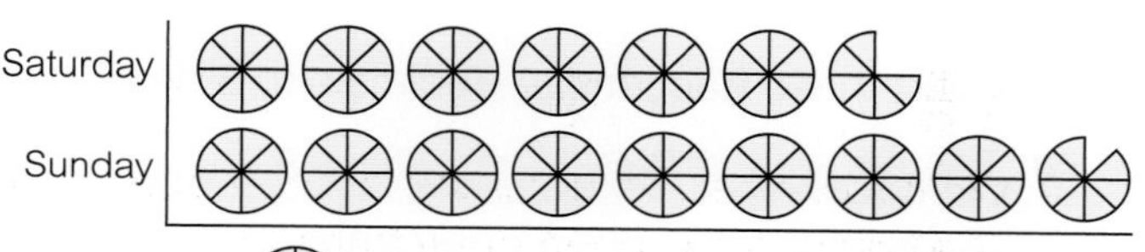

Key: (circle) represents 8 ice creams

Investigation **Problem-solving**

You are given these cards.

Arrange all the cards to make two sets of numbers.
Each set of numbers must have an equivalent fraction, a decimal and a percentage.

15 Explore How do businesses use fractions, decimals and percentages to report on efficiency?
Is it easier to explore this question now you have completed the lesson?
What further information do you need to be able to answer this?

16 Reflect List these tasks (A–E) in order from easiest to hardest.

A Writing a proportion as a fraction (as in Q5 and Q6)
B Writing a fraction as a decimal (as in Q7 and Q10)
C Writing a decimal as a percentage (as in Q7 and Q10)
D Writing a percentage as a decimal (as in Q8 and Q12)
E Writing a decimal as a fraction (as in Q8 and Q12)

Look at the task you placed first (easiest). What made it easiest?
Look at the task you placed last (hardest). What made it hardest?
Write a hint to help you with the task you found hardest.

Q16 hint
Just list the letters of the tasks in order. You don't need to write out the descriptions.

Explore

Reflect

10.3 Writing percentages

You will learn to:
- Express one number as a percentage of another
- Work out a percentage increase or decrease.

CONFIDENCE

Why learn this?
Some businesses give prices without VAT (Value Added Tax). You have to work out for yourself how much VAT you will have to pay.

Fluency
Find 10% and 15% of these amounts.
- £40
- 60 kg
- 120 km

Explore
How much is a car worth when it is 3 years old?

Exercise 10.3

Warm up

1 Convert these fractions to decimals to 3 d.p.
a $\frac{2}{3}$ **b** $\frac{5}{8}$ **c** $\frac{3}{7}$

2 Give these proportions as percentages.
a 15 out of 20 **b** 6 out of 25 **c** 3 out of 5 **d** 3 out of 4

3 Rewrite these statements giving the proportions as percentages.
a 18 out of 60 students use a smartphone.
b 14 out of 50 people are vegetarian.
c 30 out of 80 residents own their home.
d 12 out of 15 items sold cost more than £35.
e 40 out of 300 students drink coffee.

> **Q3 hint**
> Write as a fraction. Change to a decimal, then to a percentage.

4 **Problem-solving** The bar chart shows sales figures for one weekend.

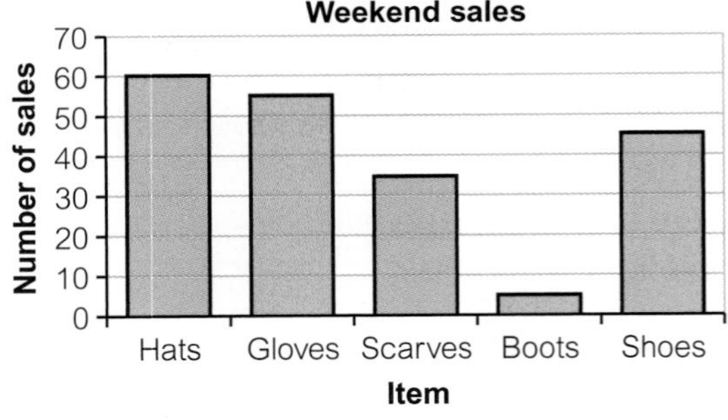

What percentage of the total sales were
a gloves **b** scarves **c** boots and shoes?

> **Q4 Strategy hint**
> Write as a fraction of total sales first.

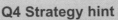

5 A $\frac{1}{2}$ litre bottle of mayonnaise contains 330 ml of fat.
What percentage of the mayonnaise is fat?

> **Q5 hint**
> Make sure the units for both quantities in the fraction are the same.

6 A 1 kg bag of mortar contains 250 g cement, 650 g sand and 100 g lime.
What percentage of the bag is
a cement **b** lime **c** sand and lime?

Topic links: Bar charts

7 Sufjan buys some party lights. They cost £15 plus 20% VAT.
  a Work out 20% of £15.
  b What is the total cost of the party lights?

8 Leela gets a 2% pay rise. Her salary was £25 000.
  What is her new salary?

9 **Finance** Jen buys £400 worth of shares.
  The value of her shares increases by 35%.
  What are her shares worth now?

10 A shirt costs £25. It is reduced in a sale by 10%.
  a Work out 10% of £25. b Work out the sale price of the shirt.

11 **Finance** A company spends £1200 on office furniture and £1800 on computer equipment.
  After 1 year the office furniture decreases in value by 15% and the computer equipment by 33%.
  Work out the value after 1 year of
  a the office furniture b the computer equipment.

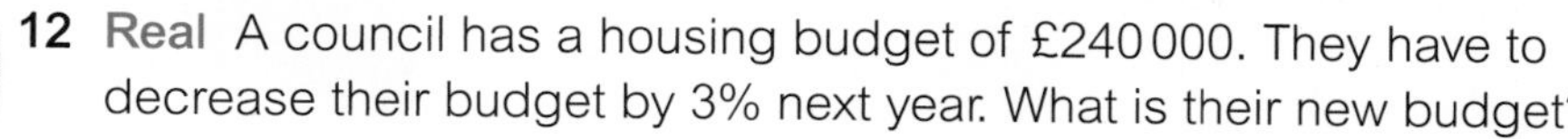

12 **Real** A council has a housing budget of £240 000. They have to decrease their budget by 3% next year. What is their new budget?

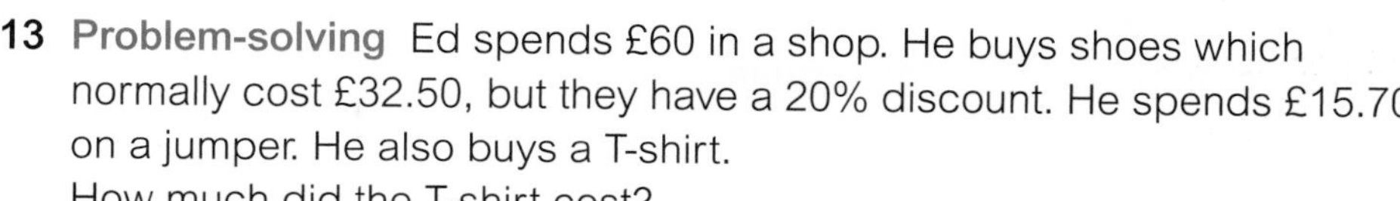

13 **Problem-solving** Ed spends £60 in a shop. He buys shoes which normally cost £32.50, but they have a 20% discount. He spends £15.70 on a jumper. He also buys a T-shirt.
  How much did the T-shirt cost?

Key point

To **increase** an amount by a percentage, you can find the percentage of the amount, then add it to the original amount.

Key point

To **decrease** an amount by a percentage, you can find the percentage of the amount, then subtract it from the original amount.

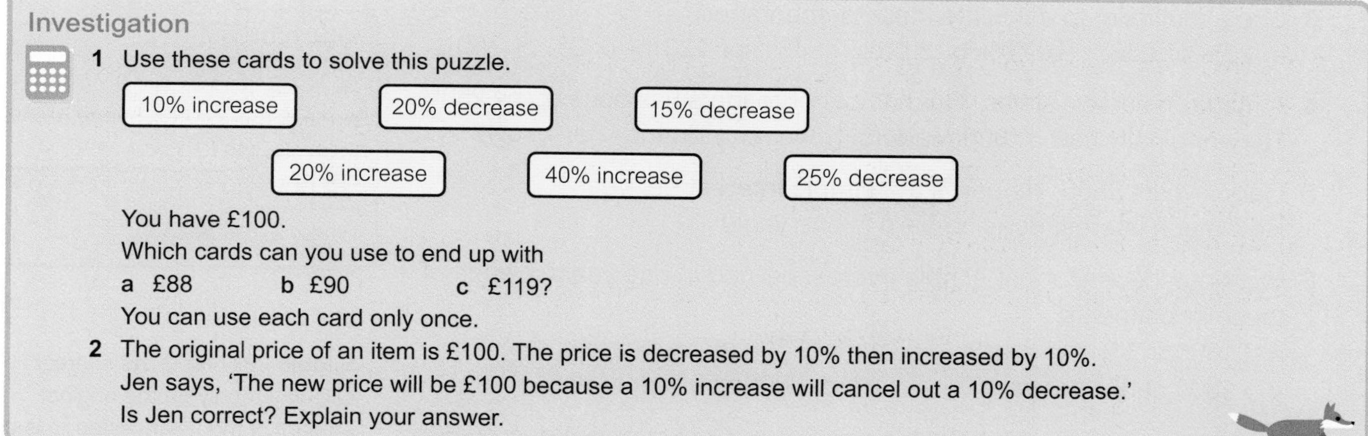

Investigation

1 Use these cards to solve this puzzle.

10% increase	20% decrease	15% decrease
20% increase	40% increase	25% decrease

You have £100.
Which cards can you use to end up with
a £88 b £90 c £119?
You can use each card only once.

2 The original price of an item is £100. The price is decreased by 10% then increased by 10%.
Jen says, 'The new price will be £100 because a 10% increase will cancel out a 10% decrease.'
Is Jen correct? Explain your answer.

14 **Explore** How much is a car worth when it is 3 years old?
  Is it easier to explore this question now you have completed the lesson?
  What further information do you need to be able to answer this?

15 **Reflect**
  Look again at part 1 of the investigation.
  Ellie says, 'I began by working out each card, on its own, for £100.'
  Alec says, 'I worked out the 20% cards first, so I could work with £120 and £80.'
  What did you do first?
  Which is the best first step, Ellie's, Alec's or yours? Why?

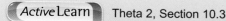

10.4 Percentages of amounts

You will learn to:
- Use a multiplier to calculate percentage increase and decrease
- Use the unitary method to solve percentage problems.

Why learn this?
When you can calculate percentages, you can check your discount is correct.

Fluency
What percentage must be added to each of these to make 100%?
- 90%
- 60%
- 75%
- 45%

Explore
In 2020, how many people in the world will be using the internet?

Exercise 10.4

1 Work out the new amount after a 10% increase.
 a £14 b 240 g c 20p d 110 mm

2 Work out the new amount after a 15% decrease.
 a 50 ml b 44 kg c \$320 d £210

3 Use a multiplier to calculate these percentages.
 a 20% of £56 b 70% of 32 kg c 45% of 120 ml d 8% of 750 g

> **Q3a hint**
> 20% = 0.2, so 20% = 0.2 × £56 = £□

4 A magazine article states, 'Our number of readers has gone up by 250%.' They originally had 30 000 readers. How many do they have now?

5 Gary invests £500. He earns 5% **simple interest** per year.
How much interest does he earn in one year?

> **Q5 hint**
> Work out 5% of £500.

6 Work out the amount of simple interest earned in one year for each of these investments.
 a £1000 at 5% per year b £300 at 2% per year
 c £5000 at 8% per year d £800 at 6% per year

> **Key point**
> **Simple interest** is the interest calculated only on the original amount of money invested. It is the same amount each year.

7 A jacket costs £45. In a sale, the price of the jacket is reduced by 30%.
 a Work out 30% of £45.
 b Work out the sale price of the jacket.
 c Work out 70% of £45.
 d What do you notice about your answers to parts **b** and **c**? Explain.

8 A café increases the cost of drinks by 25%.
It originally charged £1.40 for a glass of fresh juice.
 a Work out 25% of £1.40.
 b Work out the new price of a glass of juice.
 c Work out 125% of £1.40.
 d What do you notice? Explain.

Discussion What multipliers would you use to find a 20% decrease and a 20% increase?

9 Work out these percentage increases and decreases.
Use a multiplier for each one.
a Decrease £150 by 10%.
b Decrease 60 ml by 25%.
c Increase 80 kg by 15%.
d Increase 120 km by 30%.

Q9 hint
a 100% − 10% = □, so multiplier is □.
c 100% + 15% = □, so multiplier is □.

10 **Finance / Problem-solving** Between 2004 and 2013 the price of gold went up by approximately 365%.
In 2004, 1 ounce of gold cost $425. How much did it cost in 2013?

11 **Finance** Karen invests £400 for 3 years at 2.5% simple interest per year.
Work out
a the amount of interest she earns in 1 year
b the amount of interest she earns in 3 years
c the total amount her investment is worth at the end of the 3 years.

Q11 hint
For part **a**, work out 2.5% of £400.
For part **b**, multiply your answer to part **a** by 3.
For part **c**, add your answer to part **b** onto the original £400.

12 **Finance** Mark invests £12 500 for 4 years at 6.75% simple interest.
How much is his investment worth at the end of the 4 years?

Worked example
20% of an amount is £40.
Work out the original amount.

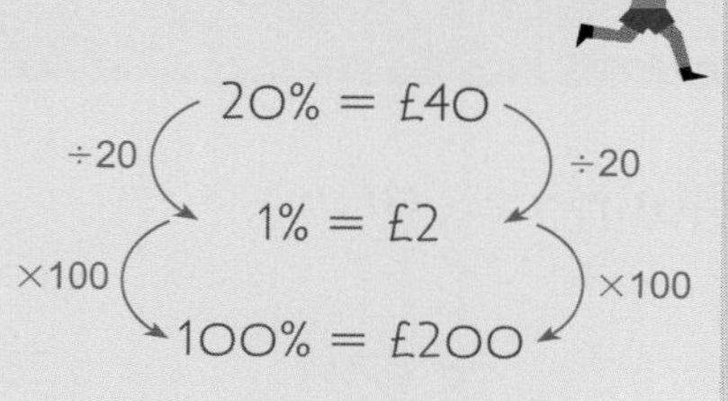

Key point
Sometimes you want to find the original amount after a percentage increase or decrease. You can use the **unitary method**.

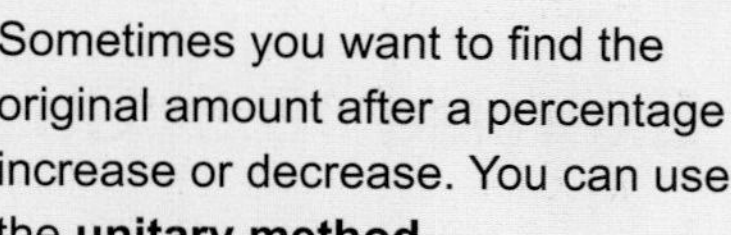

13 Work out the original amount for each of these.
a 30% of an amount is £180.
b 80% of an amount is 320 kg.
c 15% of an amount is 45 litres.
d 120% of an amount is 720 km.
e 165% of an amount is 82.5 cm.

Q13d hint
120% = 720
÷120 ÷120
1% = □

14 The cost of a DVD is reduced by 30%. It now costs £6.30.
How much was it originally?

15 **Real** Sales of fair trade honey products in 2012 were 95% of what they were in 2011. In 2012 sales were £3.6 million.
What were they in 2011?

16 **Explore** In 2020, how many people in the world will be using the internet?
Is it easier to explore this question now you have completed the lesson?
What further information do you need to be able to answer this?

17 **Reflect**
a Write the steps you take to use a multiplier to calculate a percentage.
b Write the steps you take to use a multiplier to calculate
i a percentage increase ii a percentage decrease.
c Can you use your answers to part **b** to write one set of steps that work for percentage increase and percentage decrease?

Q17 hint
Describe what a multiplier is.

Explore

Reflect

10.5 FINANCE: Solving problems

You will learn to:

- Use strategies for calculating fractions and decimals of a given number
- Use mental strategies of conversion and equivalence of fractions, decimals and percentages to solve word problems mentally.

CONFIDENCE

Why learn this?
Being able to calculate mentally means you can quickly calculate costs to ensure you don't get overcharged or short-changed.

Fluency
Write 6 as a percentage of
- 12
- 24
- 30
- 48

Explore
How much money are you likely to make in one year if you invest £1000?

Exercise 10.5: Cost of living

Warm up

1 Write each decimal as a fraction.
a 0.5 b 0.2 c 0.75 d 0.8 e 0.25 f 0.4

2 Write each percentage as a fraction.
a 50% b 30% c 10% d 24% e 45% f 5%

3 Finance Monique and Alicia share a flat together. Monique pays $\frac{3}{5}$ of the bills, Alicia pays $\frac{2}{5}$. Their council tax bill is £120 per month.
a How much does Monique pay?
b How much does Alicia pay?
c Show how to check your answers to parts **a** and **b** are correct.

Key point
You can use different **strategies** to work out fractions and decimals of amounts mentally. You can use **jottings** to help.

Investigation — Problem-solving

1 Here are three ways of working out 20% of £150.
- Find 10% and double it
- 0.2 × £150
- Find $\frac{2}{10}$ of £150

Which two of these are equivalent?
Which is quickest?

2 Work out $\frac{1}{20}$ of 46.

3 Work out $\frac{1}{10}$ of 46 and halve it. What do you notice?

4 Work out $\frac{1}{12}$ of 90.

5 Work out $\frac{1}{3}$ of 90 and find a quarter. What do you notice?

4 Finance / Real Suzie gets paid £30 000 a year. She doesn't pay tax on the first £10 000. Suzie's tax rate is 20%. How much tax does she pay?

5 Finance / Problem-solving An MP3 player was reduced by 40% in January.
Prices were further reduced by $\frac{1}{4}$ of the January price in February.
The original selling price of the MP3 player was £50. What is the sale price in February?

Topic links: Pie charts

6 **Finance / Problem-solving** Leah wants to buy a moped.
She sees this advert.
She decides to pay the deposit and monthly payments.

BRAND NEW MOPED FOR SALE!
Cash Price £1200
OR
Deposit of 25% of cash price plus
10 monthly payments of £102

a How much is the deposit?

b How much does she pay in total?

c How much extra does she pay using this method rather than paying by cash?

d How much extra does she pay as a percentage of the cash price?

Discussion What different mental strategies can you use to find 25% of an amount?

Q6d hint
Write the extra amount as a fraction of the cash price. Simplify the fraction, then change it into a percentage.

7 **Finance / Reasoning** The pie charts show the proportions of the average weekly household expenditure that were spent on different items in 2004 and in 2010.

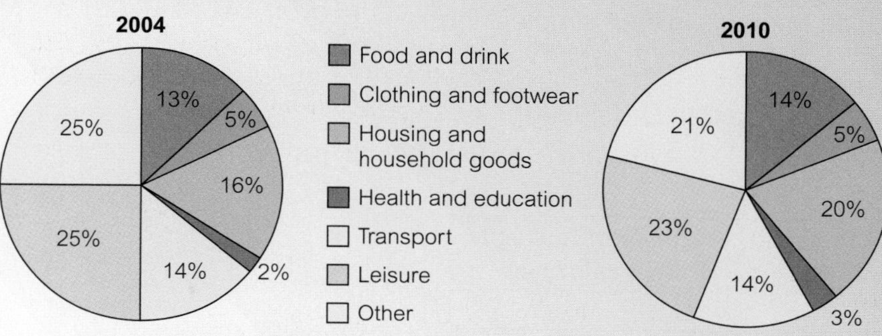

a i Which items had the same proportion of the weekly household expenditure in 2004 and in 2010?

ii Was the same amount of money spent on the items in your answer to part **i** in 2004 and 2010? Explain your answer.

b Which item has had the biggest increase in proportion from 2004 to 2010?

In 2004 the total average weekly household expenditure was £430.

c In 2004, how much was spent each week on Leisure?

In 2010 the total average weekly household expenditure was £480.

d In 2010, how much was spent on Clothing and footwear?

e What is the increase in the actual amount of money spent on Housing and household goods from 2004 to 2010?

f Has the actual amount of money spent on Leisure decreased or increased from 2004 to 2010? Explain your answer.

Q7e hint
Work out the amounts spent in 2004 and in 2010, then find the difference.

8 **Explore** How much money are you likely to make in one year if you invest £1000?
Is it easier to explore this question now you have completed the lesson?
What further information do you need to be able to answer this?

9 **Reflect** In this lesson, the first key point says, 'You can use jottings to help.'
What are 'jottings'?
Look back at your answers to the questions in this lesson.
Did you use jottings? How? Did they help? Explain.

10 Check up

Log how you did on your Student Progression Chart.

Fractions, decimals and percentages

1 Copy and complete this table.

Fraction			$\frac{2}{5}$				$1\frac{3}{4}$	
Decimal	0.1			0.3		1.6		
Percentage		20%			70%			150%

2 Write these terminating decimals as fractions in their simplest form.

a 0.54 **b** 0.665 **c** 2.36

3 The residents of three streets were surveyed to find out if they would like a skate park nearby.
The table shows the results of the survey.

Street	Number of residents surveyed	Number of residents that said 'yes'
Elm Street	25	7
Oak Street	50	13
Ash Street	20	5

a For each street write the proportion of residents who said 'yes' as a

i fraction of those surveyed

ii percentage of those surveyed.

b In which street did the greatest proportion of residents say 'yes'?

4 Write these in descending order.

$\frac{1}{4}$ 0.4 $\frac{3}{8}$ 4% $\frac{1}{3}$ $\frac{7}{20}$ 30% 0.75

5 Copy and complete this table. Write the fractions in their simplest form.

Fraction	Decimal	Percentage
$\frac{9}{40}$		
	0.135	
		15.5%

Percentage problems

6 A $\frac{1}{2}$kg box of cornflakes contains 490 g of corn.
What percentage of the contents of the box is corn?

7 A mirror costs £18 plus 20% VAT.

a Work out 20% of £18.

b What is the total cost of the mirror?

8 A tennis racket costs £30. It is reduced in a sale by 15%.
Work out the sale price of the tennis racket.

9 Work out these percentage increases and decreases.

a Increase £72 by 60%
b Decrease 250 g by 28%
c Decrease 420 ml by 2%
d Increase 45 kg by 11%

10 Mo invests £650 for 4 years at 3% simple interest per year.
Work out

a the amount of interest she earns in 1 year
b the amount of interest she earns in 4 years
c the total amount her investment is worth at the end of the 4 years.

11 Amir wants to buy a 3D TV. He sees this advert.

3D TV for Sale!
Cash Price £800
or
Deposit of 30% of Cash Price
plus 10 monthly payments of £60

He decides to pay the deposit and monthly payments.

a How much is the deposit?
b How much does he pay in total?
c Which method is cheaper and by how much?

12 The cost of a jumper was reduced by 40%.
It now costs £33.
How much was the original price?

13 How sure are you of your answers? Were you mostly
Just guessing   Feeling doubtful   Confident
What next? Use your results to decide whether to strengthen or extend your learning.

Reflect

Challenge

14 a Write one fraction with a denominator of 25, one with a denominator of 50 and one with a denominator of 200.
b Write each of your fractions in part **a** as a decimal and a percentage.
c Write your fractions in part **a** in order of size, starting with the smallest.

15 Fill in some possible percentages and amounts in this spider diagram.

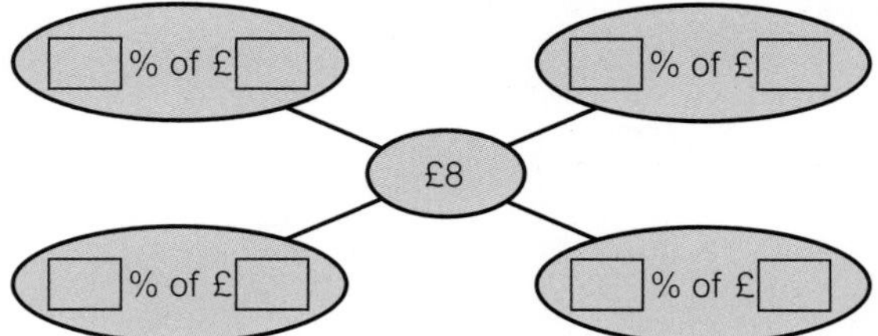

16 Part of the print on this sale sticker has been smudged.

Give three examples of what the original price and percentage off could be.

10 Strengthen

You will:
- Strengthen your understanding with practice.

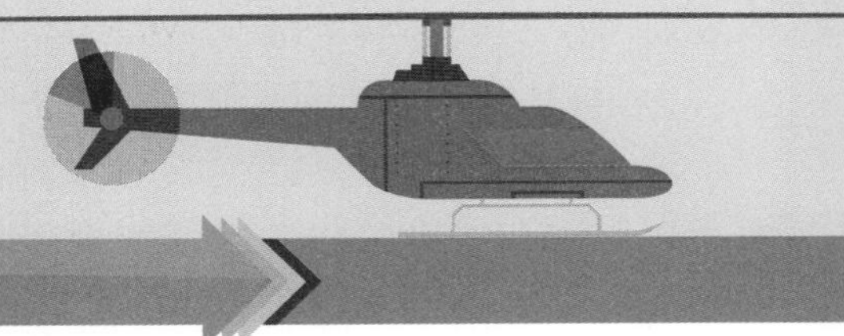

Fractions, decimals and percentages

1 Copy and complete this diagram.

Fraction	0	$\frac{1}{10}$	$\frac{1}{5}$	$\frac{3}{10}$	$\frac{2}{5}$	$\frac{1}{2}$	___	___	___	___	1
Decimal	0	0.1	___	___	___	0.5	___	___	___	___	1
Percentage	0	10%	___	___	___	___	___	___	___	___	100%

Q1 hint
Fill in the decimals and percentages first, then the fractions. Write each fraction in its simplest form.

2 Write these mixed numbers as a decimal and as a percentage.
- **a** $2\frac{4}{5}$
- **b** $1\frac{3}{10}$
- **c** $5\frac{3}{4}$
- **d** $7\frac{1}{5}$

Q2 hint
Use the number lines in Q1.
$2\frac{4}{5} = 2.\square$ and $200\% + \square\% = \square\%$

3 Write an equivalent mixed number and decimal or percentage for each of these.
- **a** 3.7
- **b** 9.5
- **c** 410%
- **d** 940%

Q3a hint
$3.7 = 3 + 0.7 = 3\frac{\square}{\square}$
$3.7 = 300\% + 70\% = \square\%$

4 Write these terminating decimals as fractions or mixed numbers in their simplest form.
- **a** 0.64
- **b** 0.82
- **c** 8.44
- **d** 0.725
- **e** 0.484

Q4a hint

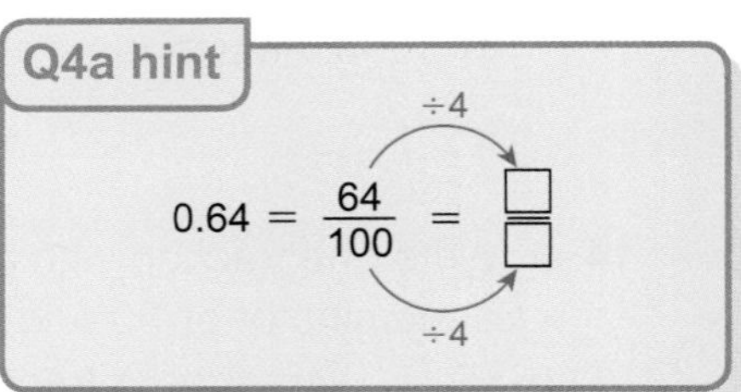

Q4d hint

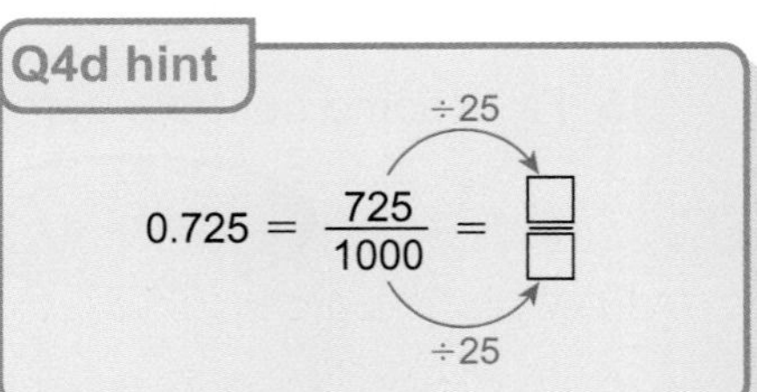

5 Fifteen out of 45 members of a knitting club are children.
- **a** What fraction are children?
- **b** What percentage are adults?

6 The members of three dog training clubs were surveyed to find out if they fed their dog a certain brand of food.
The table shows the results of the survey.

Club	Number of members surveyed	Number of members that said 'yes'
Perfect Pooches	20	16
Cool K9s	10	7
Delightful Dogs	25	21

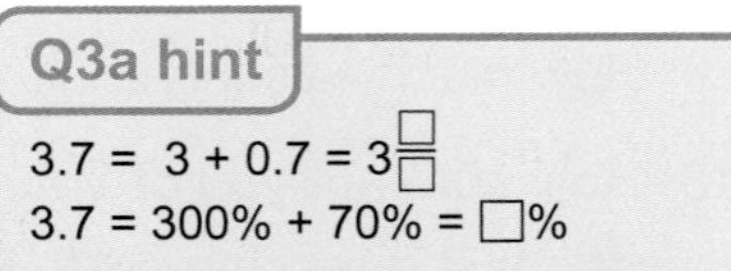

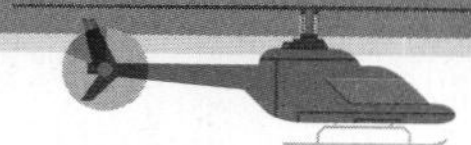

a How many in Cool K9s said 'yes'?
b How many Perfect Pooches members were surveyed?
c For each club write the proportion of members who said 'yes' as a
 i fraction of those surveyed
 ii percentage of those surveyed.
d In which club did the greatest proportion of members say 'yes'?

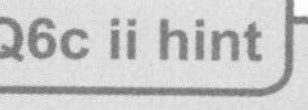

Q6c ii hint

$\frac{\text{number that said yes}}{\text{number surveyed}}$

$= \frac{\square}{\square} \times \square = \square\%$

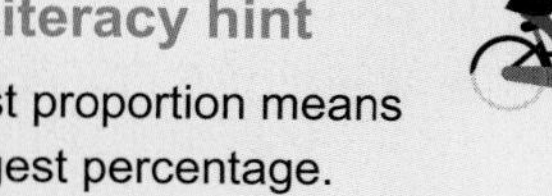

Q6d Literacy hint

Greatest proportion means the biggest percentage.

7 Convert these fractions to decimals using a calculator.
Write each answer correct to 2 decimal places.

a $\frac{3}{7}$
b $\frac{2}{3}$
c $\frac{20}{9}$
d $\frac{35}{11}$

Q7a hint

8 a Write these in descending order.
$\frac{3}{4}$ $\frac{7}{8}$ $\frac{3}{5}$ $\frac{11}{15}$ $\frac{13}{20}$

b Write these in ascending order.
$\frac{2}{15}$ $\frac{1}{3}$ $\frac{3}{8}$ $\frac{7}{10}$ $\frac{15}{22}$

c Write these in ascending order.
$\frac{2}{5}$ 0.25 30% $\frac{3}{8}$ 35%

d Write these in decending order.
$\frac{8}{15}$ 50% 0.55 $\frac{3}{5}$ 47%

Q8 hint

Convert them to decimals first.

9 a Write each of these as an equivalent fraction with a denominator of 1000, as a decimal, and as a percentage.
 i $\frac{37}{200}$
 ii $\frac{430}{500}$
 iii $\frac{11}{40}$
 iv $\frac{23}{40}$

b Write each of these fractions as a percentage.
 i $\frac{87}{200}$
 ii $\frac{325}{500}$

Q9a i hint

1000 ÷ 200 = 5, so 200 × 5 = 1000

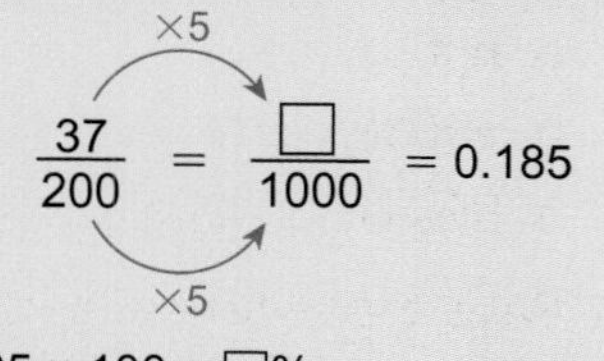

$\frac{37}{200} = \frac{\square}{1000} = 0.185$ (×5)

0.185 × 100 = □%

Q9a iii hint

1000 ÷ 40 = 25, so 40 × 25 = 1000

Q9b hint

Write each as a fraction with denominator 1000, then write as a decimal, then change to a percentage.

10 Write these percentages as

a decimals
 i 54%
 ii 29%
 iii 100%
 iv 44.5%

b fractions
 i 13%
 ii 12%
 iii 95%
 iv 92.5%

c decimals and fractions
 i 16%
 ii 75%
 iii 30%
 iv 72.5%

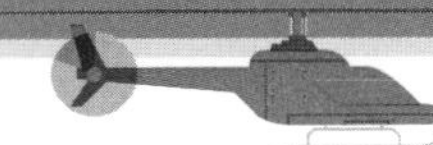

Percentage problems

1 Rewrite these statements giving the numbers as percentages.
   a 12 out of 20 students like PE.
   b 13 out of 25 members of a judo club are girls.
   c 32 out of 50 members of a boxing club are boys.
   d 2 out of 10 students have a cat.
   e 4 out of 5 DVD purchases are made online.

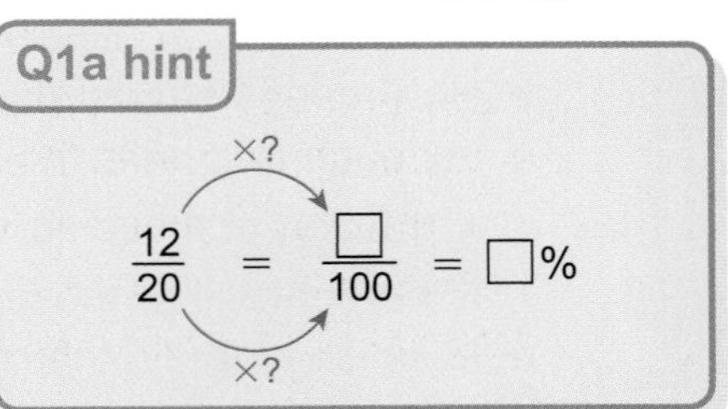

2 For each of these, write the first amount as a percentage of the second amount.
   a 48 cm out of 1 m
   b 15 mm out of 5 cm
   c 300 ml out of 2 litres
   d 750 m out of 3 km
   e 130 g out of 0.5 kg

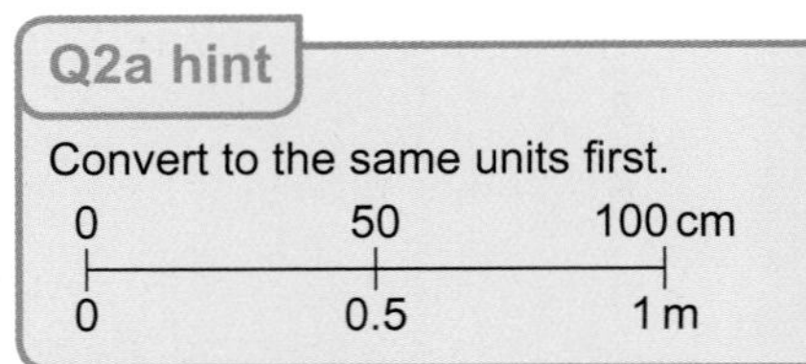

Q2a hint
Convert to the same units first.
0
50
100 cm
0
0.5
1 m

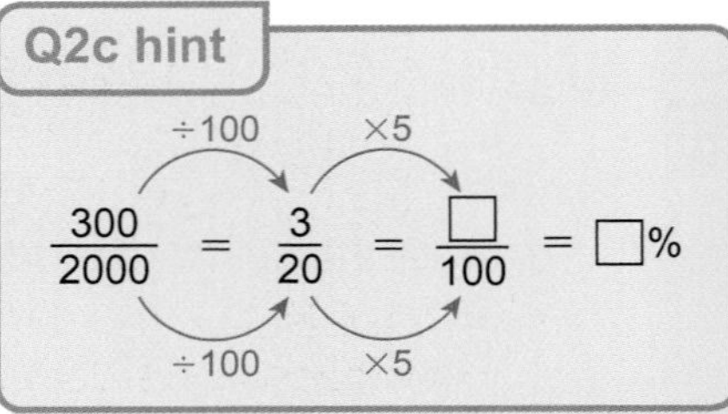

3 Increase these amounts by the given percentage.
   a £46 by 20%
   b £60 by 10%
   c £80 by 15%
   d £56 by 25%

Q3a hint

Work out 10%.
Double it to find 20%.
Add it to £46.

4 Decrease these amounts by the given percentage.
   a £85 by 5%
   b £90 by 10%
   c £20 by 30%
   d £72 by 15%

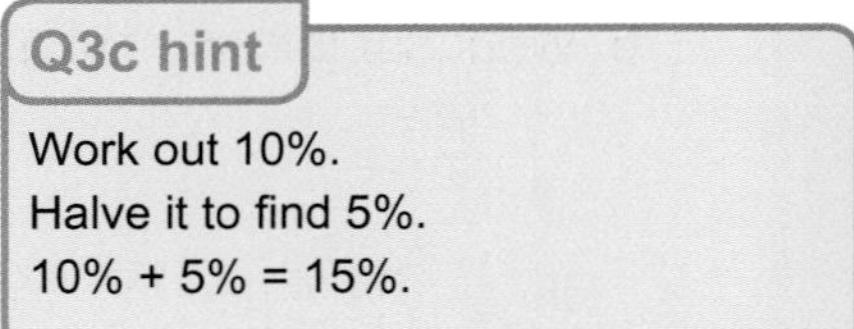

5 Use a multiplier to calculate these percentages.
Show your working.
   a 40% of £150
   b 65% of 550 g
   c 8% of 560 ml
   d 120% of 68 litres

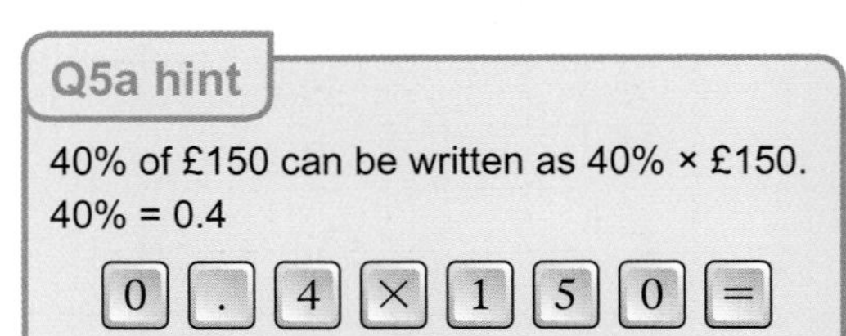

Q5a hint
40% of £150 can be written as 40% × £150.
40% = 0.4
0 . 4 × 1 5 0 =

6 7% means $\frac{7}{100}$. Convert 7% to a decimal like this.

Write each of these percentages as a decimal.
   a 3%
   b 4.5%
   c 6.2%
   d 4.75%

7 **Finance** Sita invests £800 for 3 years at 4% simple interest per year. Copy and complete the workings to find out how much her investment is worth at the end of the 3 years.
interest after 1 year = 4% of £800 = 0.04 × £800 = ☐
interest after 3 years = 3 × ☐ = ☐
total value of investment = £800 + ☐ = ☐

8 **Finance** Work out how much each of these simple interest investments is worth at the end of the number of years given.
a £400 for 4 years at 3.5% per year
b £650 for 5 years at 4.2% per year
c £1200 for 6 years at 5.8% per year

Q8 hint
Use the workings in Q7 to help you.

9 **Finance / Reasoning** Sarah wants to buy a car. She sees this advert.

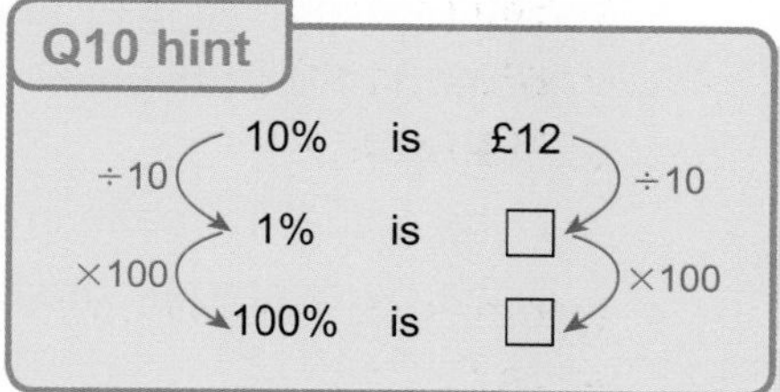

NEW CAR FOR SALE!
CASH PRICE £8000
OR
DEPOSIT OF 40% OF CASH PRICE
PLUS 20 MONTHLY PAYMENTS OF £280

She decides to pay the deposit and monthly payments.
a How much is the deposit?
b Which method of payment is more expensive? By how much?

Q9b hint
Work out the total cost of the deposit and monthly payments. Is this more or less than £8000?

10 10% of an amount is £12.
a Work out 1% of the amount.
b Work out 100% of the amount.

Q10 hint

÷10	10%	is	£12	÷10
	1%	is	☐	
×100	100%	is	☐	×100

11 5% of an amount is 30 g.
a Work out 1% of the amount.
b Work out the original amount.

Q11b hint
The original amount is 100%.

Enrichment

1 **Finance** The value of a house could increase or decrease each year.
a Copy and complete the table to show the value of this house over a five-year period.

Year	Value at start of year	Percentage change	Value at end of year
1st	£120 000	10% increase	£132 000
2nd	£132 000	15% increase	
3rd		20% decrease	
4th		25% increase	
5th		15% decrease	

b What is the difference in the value of the house at the start of the 1st year and the end of the 5th year?

2 **Reflect** Julie says, 'Working with fractions, decimals and percentages is all about multiplying and dividing.'
Look back at the questions you answered in these strengthen lessons.
Write down two questions where you had to multiply to find an answer.
Write down two questions where you had to divide to find an answer.
Write down two questions where you had to multiply *and* divide to find an answer.

Reflect

10 Extend

You will:

- Extend your understanding with problem-solving.

1 Finance / Real Fatima invests £5000 for 5 years.

a Copy and complete the table showing the value of her investment at the end of each year.

Year	Value at start of year	Percentage change	Value at end of year
1st	£5000	20% increase	£6000
2nd	£6000	8% increase	
3rd		12% decrease	
4th		10% increase	
5th		3% decrease	

b Compare the value of her investment at the start of the 1st year and the end of the 5th year.
Work out

i the actual increase in her investment

ii the percentage increase in her investment.

Q1b ii hint

Percentage increase $= \frac{\text{actual increase}}{\text{original amount}} \times 100$

2 Reasoning These offers are given by three supermarkets for the same packet of biscuits.

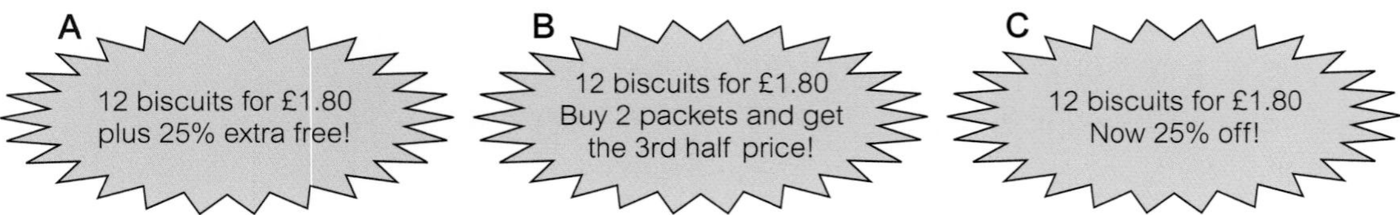

A
12 biscuits for £1.80
plus 25% extra free!
B
12 biscuits for £1.80
Buy 2 packets and get
the 3rd half price!
C
12 biscuits for £1.80
Now 25% off!

Which supermarket gives the best offer?
Explain how you made your decision.

3 STEM Green gold is made from 75% gold, 20% silver and 5% copper. To make a deep green gold, the amount of gold stays the same, the silver is reduced by 25%, the copper is increased by 20% and the rest is cadmium.

Q3 hint

For silver, find 25% of 20%, then take it away from 20%.

a Copy and complete this table showing the percentage content of deep green gold.

	Gold	Silver	Copper	Cadmium
Percentage	75%			

b What fraction of deep green gold is

i gold ii silver iii copper iv cadmium?

Write each fraction in its simplest form.

4 **Problem-solving** The brown cube has a side length of 7 cm.

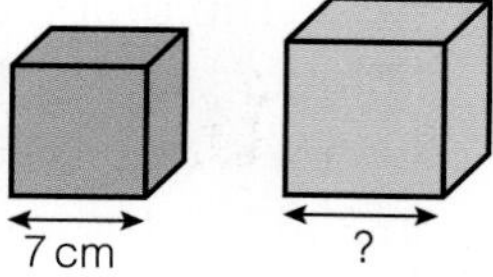

a Work out the surface area of the brown cube.

The surface area of the green open cube is 85% greater than the surface area of the brown cube.

b Work out the side length of the green cube. Give your answer to the nearest millimetre.

5 **Modelling / Reasoning** A factory makes scooters.
It has four production lines, A, B, C and D.
The table shows the numbers of perfect scooters and defective scooters produced on each production line on one day.

Production line	Number of perfect scooters	Number of defective scooters	Fraction of scooters that are defective
A	460	40	
B	543	57	
C	370	30	
D	279	21	

a Copy and complete the table to show the fraction of scooters that are defective on each production line.
Write each fraction in its simplest form.

b Write the fractions from the table in order of size starting with the smallest.

c **i** Which production line is producing the lowest proportion of defective scooters?

ii Do you think this is the best production line? Explain your answer.

d The company model their total production figures on production line A.
Do you think this is a good production line to use?
Explain your answer.

Q5b hint

Write the fractions with a common denominator or convert them to decimals or percentages.

Q5c ii hint

Compare the proportion of defective scooters as well as the number of perfect scooters produced.

6 Write these in ascending order.

1.4% $\frac{4}{5}$ 0.7% 1.1% $\frac{1}{20}$ $\frac{3}{85}$ 4.1% $\frac{1}{68}$

7 **STEM / Modelling** Harry carried out an experiment to measure the increase in the number of bacteria on food.
At 8 °C, he found that the number of bacteria increased by 40% every $\frac{1}{2}$ hour.

a Copy and complete this table to show the number of bacteria on the food between 10 00 and 13 00.
Write each answer to the nearest whole number.

Time	10 00	10 30	11 00	11 30	12 00	12 30	13 00
Number of bacteria	100	140					

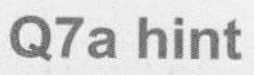

Q7a hint

100 × 1.4 = 140
140 × 1.4 = □

b Draw a graph to show the data in the table.
Plot 'Time' on the x-axis, and 'Number of bacteria' on the y-axis.
Plot your points and join them with a smooth curve.

c Use your graph to

i estimate the number of bacteria on the food at 10 45

ii estimate the time at which the number of bacteria reached 500.

d The food in a fridge should be kept at a temperature of 4 °C.
Do you think you could use the results from this experiment to model the bacteria growth on food in a faulty fridge?

8 **Real** The graph shows the percentage change in visitor numbers to Tintagel Castle.
It shows that in 2009 there were 18% more visitors than in 2008. It shows that in 2010 there were 4% fewer visitors than in 2009.

a In 2011, what was the percentage change in visitor numbers from 2010?

b In 2010 there were approximately 190 000 visitors. Approximately how many visitors were there in 2011? Give your answer to the nearest 1000.

c Approximately how many visitors were there in 2012? Give your answer to the nearest thousand.

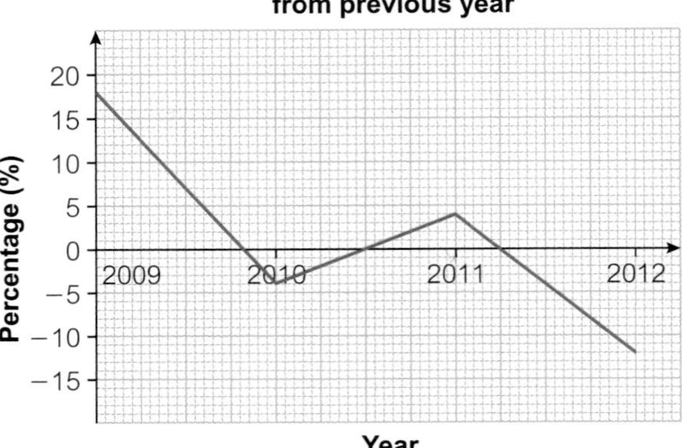

Source: Visit England

9 **Finance** Kim puts £1250 into an investment that pays 4.85% simple interest per year.
She takes the money out after 4 years and 3 months.
What is the value of her investment when she takes her money out?
Give your answer to the nearest penny.

Q9 hint
In the final year she only gets 3 months' worth of the yearly amount.

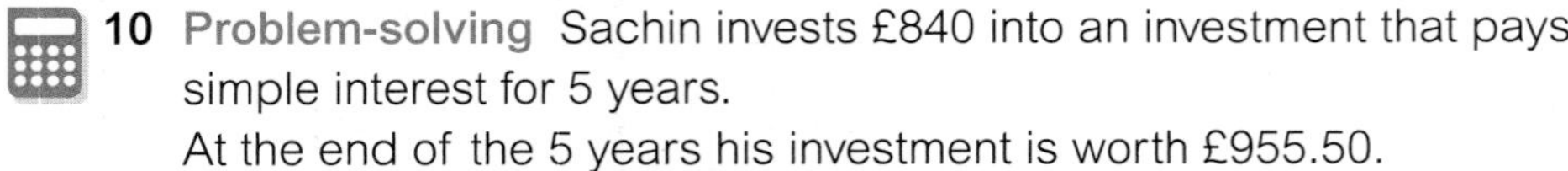

10 **Problem-solving** Sachin invests £840 into an investment that pays simple interest for 5 years.
At the end of the 5 years his investment is worth £955.50.
What is the yearly simple interest percentage?

Q10 Strategy hint
Work backwards through the problem.

11 **Finance / Problem-solving** Moira puts some money into low risk and high risk investments in the ratio 3 : 1.

a What fraction of her money does she put into

i the low risk investments **ii** the high risk investments?

The total amount she invests is £600.

b How much money does she put into

i the low risk investments **ii** the high risk investments?

Moira makes 4% on her low risk investments and 12% on her high risk investments.

c How much money does she make overall?

12 **Problem-solving** The area of the blue triangle is 25% more than the area of the yellow triangle.
Work out a possible base length and height of the blue triangle.

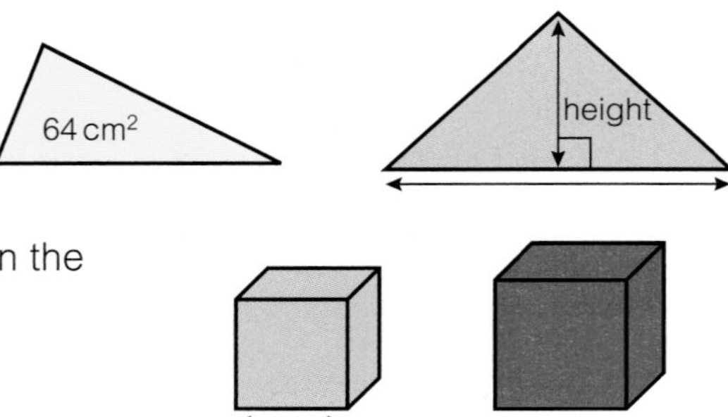

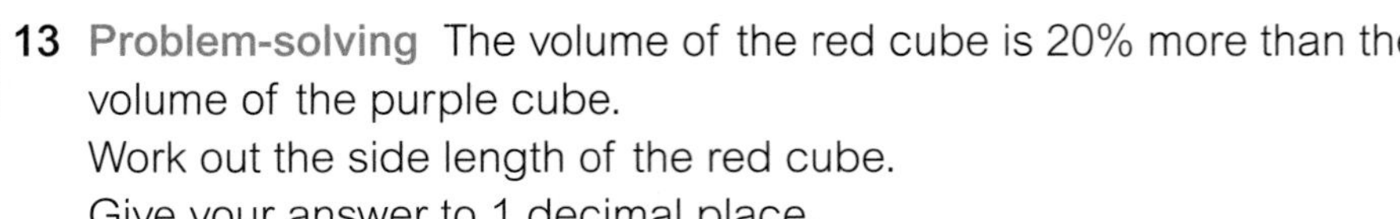

13 **Problem-solving** The volume of the red cube is 20% more than the volume of the purple cube.
Work out the side length of the red cube.
Give your answer to 1 decimal place.

14 Here is a sequence of numbers.
200, 160, 128, 102.4, …
Each term in the sequence is 80% of the previous term.
The term-to-term rule is 'multiply by 0.8'.

a Write down the first four terms in each of these sequences.

i First term is 400, each term in the sequence is 30% of the previous term.

ii First term is 80, each term in the sequence is 120% of the previous term.

Topic links: Bar charts, Real-life graphs, Proportion, Ratio, Surface area, Area, Volume, Sequences

Subject links: Science (Q3, Q7)

Look at this sequence of numbers.
300, 180, 108, 64.8, …

b Copy and complete these statements.

i The term-to-term rule is 'multiply by ☐'.

ii Each term in the sequence is ☐% of the previous term.

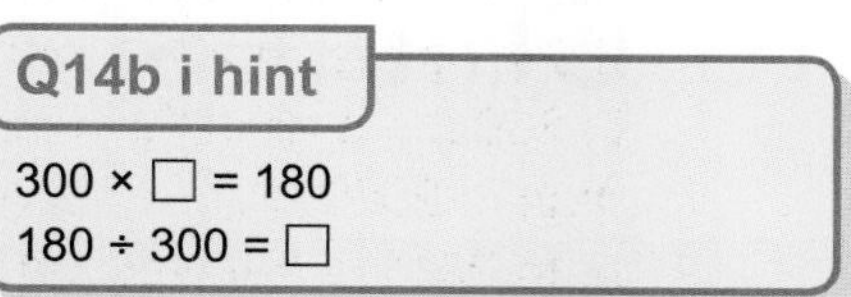

c Work out the term-to-term rule for each of these sequences.

i 60, 30, 15, 7.5, …

ii 800, 560, 392, 274.4, …

iii 20, 32, 51.2, 81.92, …

iv 60, 75, 93.75, …

d **Problem-solving** Work out the missing terms in this sequence.
☐, 550, 605, ☐, 732.05, …

15 The bar chart shows the percentage of the people over the age of 65 in a village who use the internet for shopping.

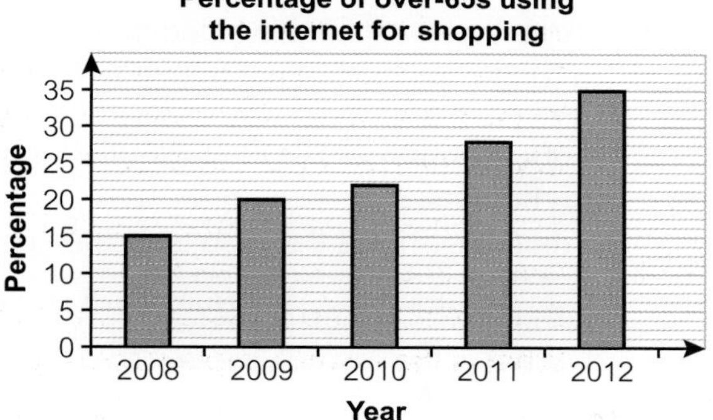

a In 2008 there were 200 people over the age of 65 in the village.
How many used the internet for shopping?

b Between 2008 and 2012 the number of people over the age of 65 increased by 20%.

i How many people over the age of 65 were living in the village in 2012?

ii How many of these used the internet for shopping?

c Use your answers to parts **a** and **b ii** to work out

i the actual increase in the number of over-65s using the internet for shopping between 2008 and 2012

ii the percentage increase in the number of over-65s using the internet for shopping.

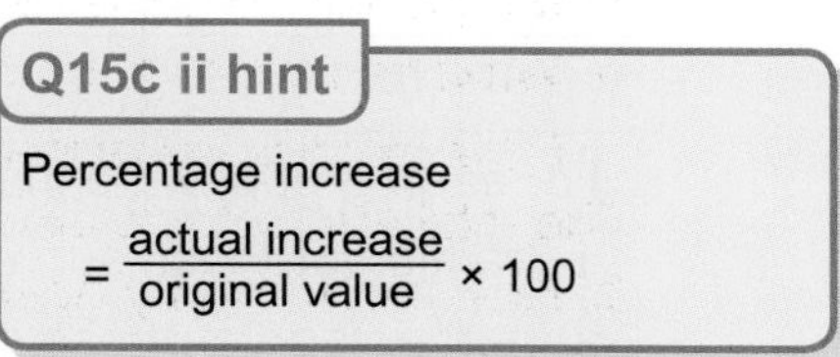

Q15c ii hint
Percentage increase
$= \frac{\text{actual increase}}{\text{original value}} \times 100$

Investigation — Problem-solving

1. Sketch a cuboid 6 cm by 4 cm by 2 cm.
2. Sketch a second cuboid with one side length that is 50% bigger than the first cuboid.
3. Work out the volume of both cuboids.
4. Work out the percentage increase in the volume of the first cuboid. What do you notice?
5. Test that this percentage increase is the same if you make one of the other side lengths of the first cuboid 50% bigger.
6. What happens to the percentage increase in volume if you make two of the side lengths of the first cuboid 50% bigger? What about all three lengths?

16 **Reflect** These extend lessons had questions on percentages used by

- supermarkets for advertising (as in Q2)
- manufacturers for quality control (as in Q5)
- tourism for monitoring visitor numbers (as in Q8).

List how three other types of business might use percentages.

Reflect

10 Unit test

Log how you did on your Student Progression Chart.

1 Write the missing fractions, decimals and percentages in this table.

Fraction		$\frac{9}{10}$				$1\frac{3}{5}$
Decimal	0.75				1.3	
Percentage			25%	275%		

2 Write these terminating decimals as fractions in their simplest form.

a 0.28 **b** 0.255 **c** 4.42

3 Three groups of students were surveyed to find out if they liked a new brand of milkshake.

The table shows the results of the survey.

Group	Number of students surveyed	Number of students who liked the milkshake
A	100	72
B	50	37
C	200	142

a For each group, write the proportion of students who liked the milkshake as a

  i fraction of those surveyed

  ii percentage of those surveyed

b Which group had the greatest proportion of students who liked the milkshake?

c Which group had the greatest proportion of students who didn't like the milkshake?

4 A one litre carton of fruit drink is made from 350 ml of mango juice, 400 ml of orange juice, and some mandarin juice.

What percentage of the fruit drink is

a mango juice **b** orange juice **c** mandarin juice?

5 A kayak costs £320 plus 20% VAT.

a Work out 20% of £320.

b What is the total cost of the kayak?

6 Write these fractions in descending order.

$\frac{9}{11}$ $\frac{4}{5}$ $\frac{7}{8}$ $\frac{3}{4}$ $\frac{13}{16}$

7 Copy and complete this table. Write the fractions in their simplest form.

Fraction	Decimal	Percentage
$\frac{131}{200}$		
	0.525	
		2.5%

8 A CD player costs £60. It is reduced in a sale by 35%.
Work out the sale price of the CD player.

9 Jatin gets a pay rise of 8%. His old salary was £22 000.
What is his new salary?

10 a 10% of an amount is 6.2 kg. Work out the original amount.
b 40% of an amount is 96 m. Work out the original amount.

11 The same computer is on sale in two different shops.

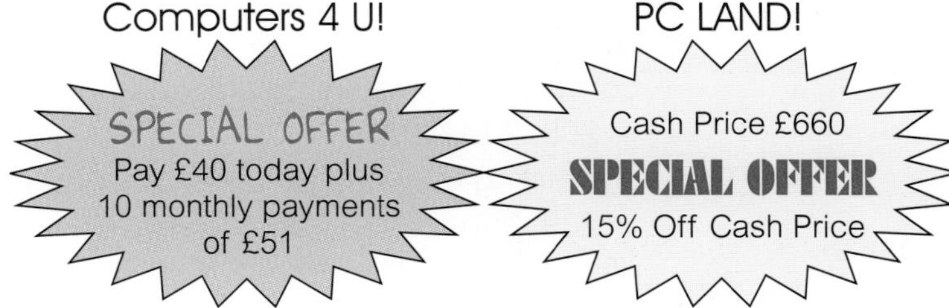

a What is the cost of the computer from Computers 4 U?
b What is the cost of the computer from PC Land?
c How much more does it cost to buy the computer from PC Land?

12 Pink gold is made from 75% gold, 20% copper and 5% silver.
a What fraction of pink gold is made from
i gold ii copper iii silver?
Write each fraction in its simplest form.
b Write the ratio of gold : copper : silver in pink gold in its simplest form.

13 Serena invests £1800 for 5 years at 6.3% simple interest per year.
How much is her investment worth at the end of the 5 years?

Challenge

14 A surfboard in a shop has 20% off in a sale.

For one day only, the shop is advertising an extra 30% off all sale prices.
a Choose an original price for the surfboard. Reduce it by 20%.
Reduce the new price by 30%.
b Is 20% off, then 30% off, the same as 50% off? Explain.
c Explain how you can work out the combined discount of two discounts on the same item.

15 **Reflect** Look back at the tables you completed for Q1 and Q7 in this test.
How did you work out these types of conversions?
a You had a decimal and wanted to find its
i equivalent fraction ii equivalent percentage.
b You had a fraction and wanted to find its
i equivalent decimal ii equivalent percentage.
c You had a percentage and wanted to find its
i equivalent fraction ii equivalent decimal.

3D shapes 32–4

A
adding fractions 187–8, 202
algebra 80
  brackets 83–5
  factorisations 86–7
  powers 80–2
alternate angles 164–6, 178
areas 25–6, 27–8
  units 38
ascending order 135, 136
aspect ratios 146
assumed means 74
axes/axis (graphs) 108

B
back elevations 33
back-to-back stem and leaf diagrams 59
balancing method 93–4, 100
bank balances 4, 141
brackets 8–9, 17
  algebra with brackets 83–5, 98

C
calendar rounds 21
capacity 37, 47
changing scales (graphs) 66
coefficients 216
common factors 86
comparing data 60–2
consecutive numbers/squares 12
consistent results 70
continuous measurement 73
conversion graphs 107–8
converting
  decimals and fractions 192–3, 208, 235–7, 239
  percentages and decimals 239, 250
  percentages and fractions 239, 254
correlation 63, 73
corresponding angles 168, 178
counter examples 7, 195
cube roots 7
cubes (numbers) 7
cubes (shapes)
  surface area 35, 42
  volume 29, 43
cuboids
  surface area 36
  volume 30

D
decimal places (rounding) 136
decimals
  converting between fractions and decimals 192–3, 208, 235–7, 239
  converting between percentages and decimals 239, 250
  dividing 141–3
  multiplying 138–40
  ordering 136–7
  rounding 135–6
decreases (percentages) 242
deposits (banks) 4
descending order 136
diagonals 162, 170
differences between numbers 4
direct proportion 211–13, 220–1, 230
distance–time graphs 109–11
dividing
  decimals 141–3
  fractions 194–6
  negative numbers 5, 16
doubling and halving 1

E
equations 88–90
  balancing method 93–4
  two-step equations 91–2
equivalent fractions/decimals 235
estimating 1, 2
expanding (brackets) 86, 98
exterior angles 171–2, 180

F
factors/factorisations
  algebraic expressions 86–7
  numbers 10–12
financial graphs 66–7
financial problems 245–6
fractions
  adding 187–8, 202
  converting between decimals and fractions 192–3, 208, 235–7, 239

converting between percentages and fractions 239, 254
dividing 194–6
multiplying 189–91
subtracting 187–8, 202
frequency tables 54–5
front elevations 33
function machines 88, 99, 100
functions 88
graphs of functions 116–18

G
gears 147
geometric problems 173–4
GPS trackers 119
gradients (graphs) 110, 214–16, 225, 226, 227, 229
graphs
conversion graphs 107–8
distance–time graphs 109–11
functions in graphs 116–18
line graphs 112–13, 114–15
real-life graphs 119–21
grouped data 56, 72

H
hectare 38
hexagons 170
highest common factor (HCF)
algebraic expressions 87, 99
numbers 10, 11, 18

I
imperial units 38
improper fractions 197, 204
'in terms of' 173
increases (percentages) 242
index notation 10, 11, 80
interior angles 170–2
interpreting graphs 116
inverse functions 88, 89, 100
irregular polygons 171
isosceles trapezia 161

K
kites 161
km/h 212

L
like terms 82, 97
line graphs 112–13, 114–15
line segments 217
linear equations 218
linear graphs 119, 218
lines of best fit 65
lowest common multiple (LCM) 10, 12, 18, 21
lumen (unit) 118

M
mass 37
Mayan calendar 21
means (data) 54, 70, 74
measures 37–8
medians 57, 58
metric units 38, 138
midpoints 217
misleading graphs 66
mixed numbers 197–8, 204, 238
modes (data) 70
multiples 10
multiplying
algebraic expressions 98
decimals 138–40
fractions 189–91
negative numbers 5, 16

N
negative correlation 63, 73
negative numbers 3–5
negative square roots 7
nets (3D shapes) 32
newton (unit) 116
non-linear graphs 121
notation 7
number lines 151, 152

O
open cubes 35
ordering decimals 136–7
origin (graphs) 219
outliers 61
overdrafts 4
overestimates 2

P
parallel lines 164, 167
parallelograms
area 28, 42
properties 161
pentagons 170
percentage decrease 242

percentage increase 242, 253, 256
percentages 67, 238–40, 241–2, 243–4, 250, 254
pie charts 51–3
plans (3D shapes) 33
polygons 170
positive correlation 63, 73
positive square roots 7
power-to-weight ratio 147
powers 6–7, 8–9, 10
  algebra with powers 80–2
prime factor decomposition 11, 12
prime factors 11
products 10, 206
proofs 166
proportions (*see also* direct proportion) 238–40, 250

Q

quadrants 232
quadrilaterals 161–3, 170
quarterly profits 60

R

radius 20, 52
ratios 144–5, 146–8
real-life graphs 119–21
reciprocals 193, 202
rectangles 161
recurring decimals 193, 236
regular polygons 90, 180
revolutions 148
rhombuses 161
root symbol 7
roots 6–7
  brackets with roots 8–9
rounding 1, 135–6

S

sales pitch 240
scales (graphs) 66
scatter graphs 63
sectors (pie charts) 51, 72
simple interest 243
solids (*see* 3D shapes)
solving equations 89
speed 110, 203, 221
square roots 6, 7, 8, 9, 17
squares (numbers) 6, 8, 17
squares (shapes) 161
stem and leaf diagrams 57–9
straight-line graphs 217–19, 224
subtracting fractions 187–8, 202
surface areas 35–6

T

tables (data) 54–6
tablespoons (measure) 231
taking out the common factor 86
Tangram puzzles 163
teaspoons (measure) 231
terminating decimals 236
terminology 237
tessellations 162, 186
three-dimensional shapes (*see* 3D shapes)
time 73
tonne 37
total frequency (data) 53
trapezia
  area 28, 42, 198
  properties 161
trends (data) 115
triangles
  area 26, 41
  interior angles 170
two-step equations 91–2
two-way tables 55–6

U

underestimates 2
unit fractions 207, 208
unit ratios 146
unitary method (percentages) 244
units (measures) 37–8

V

vertically opposite angles 178
volumes 29–31
  units 37

W

withdrawals (banks) 4

Y

y-intercept 218, 225, 227